PEARSON

James D. Morrow

Understanding World Politics

Fifth Custom Edition for University of Michigan

Pearson Learning Solutions, 330 Hudson Street, New York, New York 10013
A Pearson Education Company
www.pearsoned.com

Printed in the United States of America

000200010271998093

AB

ISBN 10: 1-323-24863-3
ISBN 13: 978-1-323-24863-8

Table of Contents

Chapter 1
Six Principles of World Politics

The Syrian Civil War began with demonstrations against the government of President Bashar al-Assad in March of 2011. Assad's government repressed these protests, with troops firing on the demonstrators and the secret police torturing those they captured. Over the next six months, loose bands of rebels arose to fight the government. The Syrian National Congress organized and met outside of Syria in an effort to bring together all the rebel bands under one political umbrella opposed to Assad and his government. The fighting spread across the major cities of Syria over the next two years, Daraa, Idlib, Homs, Hama, and eventually Aleppo and Damascus, the capital. The Syrian government has consistently labelled those who fight against it as "terrorists." Defectors from the Syrian army have joined the rebels, as have volunteers from other countries, including some who identify with Al Qaeda, the international terror network. Amnesty International and Human Rights Watch, two nongovernmental organizations that address the state of human rights in the world, have condemned the repression of Assad's government. Fighters for both sides have committed atrocities against civilians and prisoners of war.

The Arab League, the United States, and European Union condemned the use of violence against protestors, with the Arab League eventually expelling the Syrian government from its ranks and recognizing the Syrian National Congress as the representative of the Syrian people. The Western powers sought a resolution of the UN Security Council to threaten to cut trade with Syria if it did not stop using violence against demonstrators, but Russia and China blocked the resolution, arguing that it was a domestic matter. Other UN efforts to broker a political deal to end the fighting have been unacceptable to the West if they allow Assad to remain in power and opposed by Russia if they included coercion to force Assad to step down.

The rebels have received rocket launchers and small arms from the Arab states on the Persian Gulf with the support of the Central Intelligence Agency of the United States. European governments and the United States have also provided non-lethal military aid to the rebels. Turkey, Syria's northern neighbor, has sheltered rebel groups that cross the border, which has led to some exchanges of fire across the border between the two countries. The Syrian government has received arms from Iran and fighters from Hezbollah, a Lebanese political party with its own army.

Many Syrians have fled the violence, producing an estimated one million refugees in Turkey, Jordan, and Lebanon. Large camps have been set up to house these refugees, although their numbers tax the ability of these countries to care for them. As of May 2013, the UN estimates that 80,000 people have died in the Syrian Civil War.

Why has this destructive conflict occurred? Why are the parties unable to agree on a political settlement to end the fighting? Why have other countries been unable to agree on how to remedy this costly conflict, instead choosing to favor one side over the other? This book teaches you the student how to answer these questions using six principles of world politics, which this chapter introduces and then uses to explain the Syrian Civil War.

Summary Table of the Principles in Action

Principle	How It Applies to the Syrian Civil War
1. Actors have some interests in common and some in conflict.	The international community would like the fighting to end, but they disagree on whether President Assad must leave power.
2. Effective threats and promises hinge on credibility and consequences.	The people of Syria do not think that President Assad's promises of political reform are credible, which is why many continue to fight against his government.
3. People are the foundation of national power.	The people of Syria are divided in their support of President Assad, which has weakened his government.
4. Perceptions matter and are difficult to change.	Many people in Syria do not trust the intentions of the President Assad and so view his statements skeptically.
5. Institutions shape how and when actors cooperate or conflict.	The western powers cannot get a UN Security Council resolution to authorize a no-fly zone over Syria because Russia and China have veto power.
6. National leaders live in two political worlds, one domestic, the other international.	President Obama's reluctance to intervene in the war reflects both the difficulty of prevailing in the war and domestic opposition to another war in the Middle East.

Six Principles of World Politics

This book teaches you how to use six principles to understand the issues of world politics. Each draws out a general observation about world politics that holds across many issues and situations. The principles help you understand how actors pursue their ends in world politics by directing your attention to the critical aspects of a particular issue. If you master these six principles and how they can be applied to specific situations, you will be well on your way to a deep understanding of world politics.

This section states the six principles and briefly describes them. It introduces these six ideas that we will study in greater depth throughout the book. The book develops them as it progresses, adding detail to them and explaining how they apply to the many issues of world politics. The goal is mastery of these principles by the end of the book.

1. Actors have some interests in common and some in conflict.

Actors care about the outcomes of international issues. They rarely know the full consequences of their policies when they act, so they make judgments about what may happen. Their actions may result in good outcomes for the actor or unfavorable ones. Political judgments require weighing the chances of good outcomes against those of bad ones in the eyes of that actor. Additionally, how good or bad each possible outcome is also matters to that actor. We need to understand how an actor sees all the possible outcomes to understand why it does what it does.

More than one actor cares about the outcome of an international issue. On some issues, actors seek the same goals, although they may disagree about how to achieve them. On other issues, they disagree, often sharply. Even when two states see one another as enemies, both would like to avoid war if possible. Actors then have some interests in common and others in conflict. Resolving issues requires them to work together to achieve their common interests. Sometimes, coercion resolves a conflict of interest by forcing one actor to accept an outcome it does not like. The key is that almost all issues in world politics produce some common interests and some in conflict. This combination of shared and opposed interests also means that actors must think about what one another wants when they act. It is rare that one actor alone can secure the outcomes it wants in world politics.

2. Effective threats and promises hinge on credibility and consequences.

Threats and promises are two main tools actors use in world politics. Both seek to get another actor to do as the actor making the threat or promise wants. Both pledge future action based on whether the recipient does as asked. Threats seek to harm the target if it does not do as demanded by the threatening actor. Promises offer benefits to the recipient in return if it does as the actor making the promise requests. Actors make threats and promises because the target is unwilling to do what it wants. Threats and promises differ in that an actor making a threat does not have to carry it out if it works, while the actor making a promise does.

Effective threats and promises get the target to do as the actor making the threat or promise wishes. Efficacy comes from two sources. First, credible threats and promises are more likely to be effective. Both are contingent statements. The actor making the threat or promise states that it will do something in future based on whether the target does as demanded. The target doubts whether the actor issuing the threat or promise will carry it out. This is why credibility is an issue. When the target thinks that it is likely that the actor issuing the threat or promise is likely to carry it out, the more credible the threat or promise. Threats and promises that lack credibility are empty.

Credibility alone does not make a threat or promise effective. The consequences also matter. If the target does not fear the consequences of a threat or does not want the benefits promised, it is unlikely to do as the actor making the threat or promise wants. Actors making threats or promises design the consequences of those pledges to make them more likely to induce the target to do as it wishes. The combination of credibility and consequences lead a target to do as the actor making the threat or promise wants. It complies with the demand because it believes that the threat or promise will be carried out and that the consequences for it are large enough to change what it is doing.

3. **People are the foundation of national power.**

Power provides ways for actors to make their threats and promises more effective, and states create power from their people and what they produce. Used properly, power can increase the consequences of a threat or promise for the target or raise the credibility of either. The most obvious uses of power occur when an actor punishes or rewards another actor or forces the outcome it desires. Successful persuasion raises the credibility of a threat or promise. Actors can also make their threats or promises more credible by limiting their options in the future.

Power takes many forms. Military power, which provides the ability to attack, destroy, and defend, has historically been the key form of power in world politics. It continues to be important because war is still the final arbiter of some disputes. Power can also be economic, through the ability to reward others or harm them economically by limiting their ability to trade freely. Other forms of power arise from the governing institutions of a state, an actor's objectives and purposes, and the creativity and wisdom of its leaders. Power is not an inherent attribute of a state; it is judged relative to other states.

States generate their power from their population and economy. Armies require people to be pulled out of the economy, trained to be soldiers, and then equipped with weapons and supplies. Governments pull these human and material resources from their people through voluntary compliance backed by coercion. Governing institutions can make it easier for a state to extract resources and to make commitments to limit itself domestically and internationally, both of which can increase its power.

4. **Perceptions matter and are difficult to change.**

The world looks different through the eyes of others. We may know our intentions are benign, but the other side may doubt them. We may know we are strong, but they see weakness. Neither of us can see the future clearly and know what will come next. These differences in judgment arise because actors do not know the complete situation they face in full detail. They are uncertain about key elements, such as the motivations and power of others, and so they cannot predict how others will act.

Actors have perceptions of the uncertain elements of their situation. Perceptions reflect chances of multiple possibilities rather than certainties. The other side might hold benign or malign intentions towards us. We would respond differently to each type, so the chance of each influences what we do. If we were confident that the other side was malign, we would see everything they do and what we have to fear from them differently than if we thought they were likely to be friendly. Actors can hold perceptions about any uncertain element of the situation they face. We will often talk about perceptions concerning relative power and others' motivations, but actors may also hold perceptions about other things that could influence what they would like to do. Scientific uncertainty, for example, leads some to see global warming as a looming disaster while others believe it is unlikely to be a serious problem. Perceptions matter because they influence what an actor does.

Persuasion–changing the perceptions of others–a powerful but difficult path to influence them to do as you wish. Perceptions combine what has happened with interpretations of those events. Actors make judgments about the motives of others from their acts, and then use those judgments to interpret future actions. This process of accumulation of evidence and judgments, often over years or decades, makes perceptions resistant to change. Most evidence is consistent with many possibilities.

Persuading another requires something dramatic, something inconsistent with their perceptions. If the other side believes you hold malign intentions, only an act out of type, one that can only arise from a benign type, can change their perception. Acts which some types might take but others would not *separate* the types. These events allows the other side to conclude that it is not facing the latter types, thus persuading them to change their perception. Separation, and so persuasion, is rare because there are few such actions and actors are generally unwilling to take them.

5. Institutions shape how and when actors cooperate or conflict.

Contrary to common wisdom, world politics is not ruled by the "Law of the Jungle." All politics is shaped by rules that explain how some decisions are made, how actors are supposed to act, and define who the actors are. There are formal rules for reaching decisions within international organizations. International law binds a state only when it accepts a treaty through ratification with only rare exceptions. Agreement between actors then is necessary to reach peaceful understandings. Informal understandings of what is proper and allowable in world politics limit what actors can do. Some of these understandings are written down in treaties, such as human rights law, while others are just generally shared across most countries and their people. The key is that these standards of appropriate conduct are shared by many actors in world politics. Other rules define what are actors are and what they may do. The principles of sovereignty define states, their powers, and how they should relate to one another within the sovereign state system. All of these rules are institutions which shape world politics.

Institutions cast a shadow on what actors do. They do not force actors to follow rules, but there are consequences for breaking the rules. Formal voting rules determine how decisions are made within some international organizations. States seeking change in what the organization does must take account of who has voting power and whether they can be convinced to vote for the change. Negotiated settlements have to be acceptable to all parties, which allow one party to block change it does not accept. Actors that violate informal standards of conduct face the reactions of others to those breaches. Other states may be unwilling to work with one which breaks the rules. The citizens of a government which breaks the rules may express their displeasure with that government at the ballot box in their votes or on the streets in demonstrations and protests. Sometimes actors break the rules because they are willing to live with the consequences rather than abandon what they can accomplish by breaking the rules.

Institutions last and are difficult to change. In the short run, they are taken as given. Widespread agreement among actors is required to change the rules. Because institutions influence what actors do, some will gain and some will lose from a change in the rules. Only in rare occasions will a wide range of actors agree to change the rules. At other moments, such as the end of major wars, the victors may have the power to induce others to accept wide changes in institutions. Sometimes institutions change gradually over a long period of time as views on appropriate behavior change. Human rights are now widely asserted as a fundamental value in world politics, even if not all states observe those rights. This was not so a hundred years ago. Because institutions last and are not constantly changed, actors must take account of them.

Actors care about institutions because the rules influence what happens. Institutions then are an object of contention in world politics. Changing the rules allows one to change the outcomes for as long as those rules persist. Disagreement about institutions produces some of the most difficult issues in world politics.

6. **National leaders live in two political worlds: one domestic, the other international.**

National leaders are among the most important actors in world politics because they command the resources of the states they lead. They are also politicians who live in two worlds at once. One is the international arena where countries cooperate sometimes and come into conflict at others. The second world is domestic politics. A leader who fails in this second world cannot succeed in the international arena. She will lack the support of her society, making it more difficult to achieve her international aims. At an extreme, she may be removed by her own people. Retaining office is the first priority of any leader because failure to hold office makes it impossible to accomplish anything else.

Leaders care about foreign policy in part because their supporters care about it. Failure in international politics could lead supporters to withdraw their support from the current leader. Success might compensate for failures in domestic policy. This is not to say that national leaders do not consider the general interests of their nation in their foreign policy, only that those interests depend on what the leader's supporters want and that they judge whether the policy is successful. Foreign policy involves a balance between what domestic supporters want and what is possible internationally.

Different forms of government empower different sets of people in politics. In the United States, most adults have the right to vote and so matter politically. The President must pay some respect to the wishes of the voters, even though he may have great leeway in how he seeks to satisfy their interests. Political rights are limited to smaller groups of people in non-democracies. A traditional aristocracy, military leaders, or a single political party may be the only people whose support the leader requires to hold onto power. The leader of a non-democracy can ignore the wishes of those outside these small groups because they lack the power to throw him out of office. These differences in who matters politically within a country have large effects on their foreign policy. Only the interests of those with a political voice matter in the eyes of their national leader.

Because national leaders live in two political worlds, they can use success in one area to compensate for failures in the other. Domestic policy that pleases supporters may lead them to ignore a failure of foreign policy. Foreign policy may provide access to domestic rewards for supporters. National leaders sit like Janus–the Roman god with two faces, one focused on domestic politics, the other facing the world outside their nations' borders.

Using the Principles to Understand the Syrian Civil War

The principles help us understand events in world politics. This section illustrates how they apply to the Syrian Civil War. These explanations are illustrative rather than comprehensive. The summary table earlier in this chapter lists the six principles and a short statement of how they apply to some facet of the war. A table like this will be provided at the end of most chapters to help you see how the principles have been used in the chapter and the motivating puzzle.

The division in the international community about what to do about the Syrian Civil War reflects the first principle. Most states have said they would like the fighting to end, an interest they share. But they disagree about whether President Assad must leave power. The western powers have argued that he must go as part of any political settlement, while Russia and China contend that whether he stays should be left up to the Syrian people. All want peace, but they disagree about how Syria should be governed after the war.

The second principle explains why the promises of the Assad government have not ended the fighting. Any diplomatic solution needs to hold over time. A settlement today that collapses into renewed fighting tomorrow is no solution. From the point of view of those who supports the rebels, the Assad government has to promise that it will not punish them after such a settlement. But given the record of repression by the Assad government, the supporters of the rebels do not view that promise as credible and so demand that Assad step down before any negotiation begins.

This lack of a credible promise has undermined all efforts to negotiate a settlement to the war. Effective promises rely on their credibility and consequences.

The Assad's government draws its power to fight the rebels from those who support it, an example of the third principle. The supporters of the regime, including those who fight in its army and militias, are predominantly from the Alawite minority in Syria, of which President Assad is a member. The rebels draw their support from the Sunni majority of the population, another sect of Islam. Because Assad's government has lost the support of the Sunni majority, its power both inside and outside the country has been diminished.

The rebels and their supporters do not trust Assad's motivations. They perceive that he will do anything to hold onto power. This perception is based on the record of repression of the government before and during the rebellion. It will be difficult if not impossible for Assad to change this perception and so gain the trust of his opponents. Public promises that he will not retaliate against those who supported the rebellion will not change their perception of his malign intent toward them. Perceptions resist change.

The institutions of the UN Security Council has influenced the response of the international, illustrating how institutions shape world politics. It authorized a no-fly zone during the Libyan Civil War in 2011, where the airforces of the NATO allies patrolled the airspace over Libya to prevent the Libyan airforce from attacking the rebels. The western powers then used the authority to patrol over Libya to carry out a campaign of aerial bombing in support of the rebels. Russia and China have blocked proposals to create and enforce a no-fly zone over Syria in the Security Council. They have the institutional power of the veto as permanent members of the Council, and their acquiescence is required for any resolution. Because the western powers are unwilling to impose a no-fly zone without authorization from the Security Council, Russia and China effectively have a veto over what they do.

The United States could intervene without authorization from the Security Council if it chose, but President Obama must consider the consequences of intervention for both international and domestic politics as in the sixth principle. Despite many statements decrying the fighting and stating that President Assad must go, the Obama administration has not pushed for military intervention by the U.S. in the Syrian Civil War. Such an intervention would be more difficult that the bombing campaign in Libya was and is likely to entangle the U.S. and its allies in another long-term military commitment in the Middle East. The Obama administration has ended U.S. military involvement in Iraq and is winding it down in Afghanistan, in part because these wars have become unpopular with the people of the U.S. This combination of international difficulty and domestic reluctance to engage in another military commitment in the Middle East contribute to the unwillingness of the Obama administration to intervene directly in the Syrian Civil War.

Chapter 2
What is World Politics?

Politics is all the ways that rules for society are set and administered. Within a country, the government does these. For example, in the United States, we have legislatures that write the laws, elections to select top officials with others chosen through appointment by elected officials, agencies to administer the law, and courts to judge disputes about the application of the laws. In other countries, the national leader may not be elected, but the government has the power to write laws, administer them, and judge applications of the law. Not all politics happens within a government; citizens may organize and operate outside the government in an effort to influence what it does. Politics is the keystone of social life because other aspects of social life—business, social relations, and even family life—are regulated by politics.

World politics is the politics of all issues that cross national borders. While some issues concern just the people inside one country, many issues affect people in more than one country, and so become international issues. The location of borders between states, the flow of goods from one country to another, and pollution created in one country that affects another country are all examples of international issues.

World politics differs from politics within a country, also known as **domestic politics**, because there is not a single authoritative world government. Instead, many governments and their people affect what happens in world politics. A **state** is the representation of a country in politics. World politics results from the interplay of what states, their people, and other organizations those people form do to address issues that cross national boundaries. We refer to all the people and organizations that are active in world politics as **actors**.

The Issues of World Politics

The issues of world politics are grouped into three areas: security, political economy, and transnational challenges. This book has three main sections, one devoted to each type of issue.

Security concerns all issues where violence or the threat of violence looms. Because violent conflict can occur on security issues, this group is also referred to as **conflict** by some. War is the most dramatic example of a security concern, and states have fought over a variety of issues including the control of territory and the composition and policies of the governments of other states. Security also includes the steps that states take to prepare themselves for the possibility of violent conflict—building arms and forming alliances. War is a political act, and the politics between and within states at war are also a security concern. States uses diplomacy to ward off the threat of violence, making it a security issue. Violent conflicts within states create international security concerns if other states intervene or if the conflict spills across national borders. Non-state actors sometimes use violence to advance their own ends, making civil wars and transnational terrorism security issues.

Political economy covers the politics of international economic issues. Goods, investment, and people move across national borders in the global economy. All governments impose some controls on these movements, creating international issues over the regulation and restriction of them. Trade, the movement of goods and services across national borders, plays an important role in the development of the world economy. Because countries use different currencies, managing the exchange rates between those currencies has important economic and political effects. Financial flows across national borders can help countries grow more rapidly and allow investors to make more money, but they can also destabilize national economies. Migration, the movement of people across national borders, is the final form of mobility across national borders. Together, the openness of the world economy to these movements is called **globalization**.

Transnational challenges are other issues that cross national borders and require the agreement of multiple countries to be addressed. International environmental issues include trans-border air and water pollution, natural resources shared by multiple countries, and global issues like climate change. While international standards of human rights have been advanced in a series of treaties, not all countries accept these standards or apply them differently. States create international law and organizations to address these transnational challenges as well as concerns in security and political economy. The political organization of the world in the sovereign state system is the deepest question in world politics, where the book will end.

Actors in World Politics

Actors are the basic units of any theory of world politics. An **actor** is an organization or person that attempts to affect world politics through its actions. Actors know what they would like to do, what ends they are trying to accomplish; they have **preferences**. Often, actors disagree about what outcomes are better than others and use their **capabilities**--all the tools they have to induce, cajole, or force other actors--to get what they want. Actors also have **perceptions** of other actors and what they will do. Actors must consider what each other will do when they decide what they will do, so **strategic interaction**—every actor's choices depends on what other actors might do—is central to world politics.

States are often treated as the central actors of world politics and are a distinctive form of political organization to world politics. The **state** is representation of a country in politics. Each country is a state, and we use the term "state" to focus on the apparatus which runs the country and has legal standing with other states. The interaction of states dominates much of world politics. States make war, set rules for goods to enter the country through international trade, and accept and follow international law.

In addition to states, we will consider actors within a state that attempt to affect its international politics. States are political organizations with their own leadership and have their own internal politics. Organized groups, such as political parties, labor unions, and interest groups, either compete for power or seek to influence government policy in their favor. Top political leaders, such as President Obama, are the key actors in some of the arguments we will consider.

There are also non-state actors that operate across or among states. **Intergovernmental organizations** (IGOs), like the United Nations, have states as their members. Their officials and component agencies can be considered to be actors. **Nongovernmental organizations** (NGOs) seek to address key issues of concern to the people who join and support them. Although some NGOs address principled issues, such as Amnesty International's concern for human rights, others like Al Qaeda use violence to advance their political goals.

All of these actors share the ability to determine what they do, and so are actors in world politics. The choice of who the actors are is the starting point for any analysis of world politics. Sometimes, we will treat states as the only actors, other times we will examine the actors inside a country, and yet other times we will focus on IGOs and NGOs that operate across national borders.

Corporate Actors

Many actors in world politics are composed of many people, yet we treat them as if they are individuals. The United States government employs millions of people and answers to an electorate of over 100 million. Even smaller actors, such as interest groups who lobby on trade policy or non-governmental organizations who advance human rights, have many people who work for them. Even though these actors are organizations of many people, we analyze them as if they are individuals who speak, think, and act as an individual. Actors that consist of more than one person are called **corporate actors**. This term does not mean that they are all corporations, such as many businesses are organized as and called corporations. Rather, they incorporate many people who act as one.

A corporate actor has a purpose which limits and defines what it does. The state provides public goods, such as order, within its borders and acts outside its borders to advance the interests of its people. A business corporation seeks to make money for its stockholders, the owners of the company. Nongovernmental organizations, like Human Rights Watch, seek to advance the cause of human rights in the world. The purpose helps all the people in the corporate actor work together towards the goals of that purpose. It also limits what the actor seeks to do. It may be that not all people agree on what the purpose of the actor should be. The role of the state in its own economy varies greatly across states, with some intervening in the economy such as determining who gets what jobs and what goods are produced, while the governments of other states take a "hands off" attitude. It may also be that people within a country disagree about what the purpose of their state should be. The main point here is just that corporate actors have a purpose, which allows us to talk about them acting for that purpose.

Even if everyone agrees about the purpose of a corporate actor, they may disagree about how to accomplish the goals of that purpose. Corporate actors commonly have internal politics to resolve these differences. States have a political purpose to determine how they will act both at home and abroad. Companies also have internal politics to select who will run the firm and aid the boss in critical decisions for the firm. These internal politics are easier to see in some corporate actors than others. In the United States, elections and how legislatures pass laws are open and covered by the press. In a dictatorship, politics to select the dictator and how he or she stays in power are hidden, but they occur nonetheless.

These internal politics of the corporate actor both determine how it will act and seek to control its leader and members so they act to advance its purpose and interests rather than their own. Internal politics seek to fuse their personal interests to the goals of the corporate actors. Firms pay their employees to work for the firm and act in the interest of the shareholders rather than themselves. The internal politics of states seek to induce the leader of the state to act on behalf of some people of the state through limits on the leader's power and the ability to remove him or her from power.

Thinking as a Political Scientist

Political scientists have a distinctive way of thinking about political problems and issues. Our ultimate goal is to teach you how to think about politics the way political scientists do. We try to see the world as others do in order to understand what they do in politics and why. We try to understand what they want, what means they think they have of getting what they want, and how they see others and the situation they face.

This understanding is not about empathizing with others or trying to understand how they feel about their political position. Such empathy could help us understand others' anguish with politics, particularly among those who suffer because of political decisions. However, it would not help us understand why some people take up arms to remedy the wrongs they believe they suffer, while others in similar positions do not. It would not help us see how institutions structure many issues in politics, even when those institutions leads to outcomes we do not like. Instead of empathy, we try to understand what actors want and how they think they can get it. That way, we can understand what happens in world politics.

The core concepts presented in this book answer a set of questions about political situations and how others see them.

1. Who are the relevant actors? What people and groups can influence the issue at hand? Many of the actors in world politics are groups organized to advance a common purpose. Countries have governments to advance the interests of their people, even if only a small set of people in the country have political power. Others organize to advance their economic, social, or political

concerns. Many actors attempt to influence any given issue, both within and across countries. Normally, we consider just a key group of a few actors because it is difficult to understand any process with a large number of moving parts.

2. What do the actors want? What outcomes do they like and which would they like to avoid? Actors commonly disagree about what they want, and often what others want may seem wrong-headed to you. We try to judge what others want from their actions because they act in the effort to achieve their aims. We have to be careful in judging the aims of others from their actions. They may attempt to obscure what they want. Their actions may frustrate what they say they want publicly. Choices often require actors to sacrifice some of their goals to achieve other goals; we do not know which goal is more important to them until they sacrifice one to gain the other. Actors rarely know what will happen when they act, so they must judge what risks of bad outcomes they are willing to run in the effort to achieve others.

3. What tools do they have to influence others? Actors have a range of ways of influencing others in their efforts to achieve what they want. They can offer benefits to others or threaten them if they do not do as they wish. Actors can try and convince others to act as they want. At an extreme, an actor can try and impose the outcomes it wants. Negotiation and bargaining over differences is central to politics. In world politics, these tools of influence provide actors with additional leverage in negotiations. When and how they choose to use these tools is a central concern in the study of politics.

4. What rules exist that might influence how the actors can pursue what they want? Politics is structured by rules, written and unwritten, that affect how actors pursue their interests. Rules exist to help actors achieve shared interests and resolve conflicts of interest. These rules are more obvious in the domestic politics of a country than in world politics. In the United States, there are electoral laws and rules for passing legislation. Beyond these written, formal rules, there are also conventions that limit what is allowable in politics. These rules limit what politicians can do. World politics also has formal rules for international organizations. But the informal rules of conduct play a larger role in world politics. These rules matter because they shape how actors can achieve their ends. Break the rules, and others may not look kindly on those violations. Work within the rules, and you may gain the support of others. Because many of the rules in world politics are unwritten but commonly understood in broad terms, there can be disagreements about them. Because rules matter, actors care about them and argue over them. To understand politics, we have to understand the rules that structure the environment that political actors operate.

The six principles guide us in this analysis. They condense what political scientists know about world politics into a core that will help you analyze issues in world politics. The principles illuminate both specific situations and issues in world politics and general patterns found across many issues. Each war is different and unique, but there are common patterns underlying the explanation of war generally and each war individually.

Political scientists study politics systematically and scientifically. They seek to understand how politics works so that we can explain what happens in politics. They research both general patterns across events and the processes of specific events in the quest to understand politics. They attempt to make their research procedures transparent so that others can judge the quality of their arguments and evidence. This book does not introduce to the process of research in political science; it seeks to help you use the results of that research to understand the world you live in and will in the future.

The analysis of politics–by considering who the actors are, what they want, how they might try to get it, what they think about others, and what rules they operate under–is different from how politics is often discussed. The common focus centers on the choice of the "right" policy. Should the sanctions against Iran for its failure to comply with its obligations under the Non-Proliferation Treaty be stronger or abandoned? What is the right way to move toward a peace settlement between Israel and the Palestinians, put pressure on Israel, support Palestinian factions more willing to negotiate, or some other course of action? These discussions implicitly assume that all the readers agree on what would be a good outcome and disagree only over how to accomplish it. The goal is to persuade those who disagree through argument that shows a "better" way to accomplish a common goal. But many differences in world politics lie deeper than just disagreements about how to accomplish whatever is deemed to be good. Other actors in world politics often act in ways that we may not like, but they are pursuing their own interests in light of their understanding of the world. This is not to say that this form of political analysis neglects the question of what policy we should adopt. It can advance an argument about the proper policy by giving us a clearer understanding of the possible consequences of different policies and an appreciation of the limits of our ability to anticipate all the consequences of any available policy.

The Worldviews of Realism, Liberalism, and Constructivism

The study of world politics has been dominated by three different ways of looking at the world. Each of these focuses our attention on some factors over others and addresses some problems and issues better than others. Although many have found these worldviews helpful in organizing world politics and making it understandable, each is an incomplete understanding. This book develops one view which integrates these three worldviews into one, drawing on the strengths of all of them.

Realism

Realism examines how states survive in an insecure world. In the realist worldview, world politics is **anarchy**–there is no superior power that states must answer to or whom they may turn for their protection. States are forced to rely on self-help to defend themselves against threats, through either their own military capabilities or assistance from other states that also face the same threat. Realists believe a balance of power is the best guarantee of state security, a situation where states will fight to prevent any one state from becoming dominant.

According to the realist view, power and interests determine what states do. When states cooperate, they do so only out of their own interests. Interests can change quickly—today's friend may be tomorrow's enemy—so international cooperation is always tenuous. The pressures of international competition force all states to respond in the same way, and so variation in their nature, such as democracies versus autocracies, are irrelevant to world politics. Realists concentrate on issues of national security over other issues. They believe that national security is paramount and other issues are subordinate to securing the state.

Liberalism

In contrast with realism, liberalism argues that the character of states and international institutions can reduce the insecurity of the international anarchy. According to liberals, although states and their leaders must be concerned about national security, they also have interests in common with other states— interests that can only be realized through international cooperation. Their citizens benefit from international cooperation to address issues which no state can solve alone. Liberalism divides the world into two types of states, liberal ones, where the leader answers to the will of the people who are free, and illiberal ones, run by autocrats who answer only to their own whim and need not take what the people of their country want into policy. Liberal states, according to liberalism can cooperate more readily than other types of states. Democratic leaders must take what their citizens want more seriously than dictators. Democracies are also able to bind themselves to international commitments, removing concerns in other countries that they will break those commitments on a whim. States create international institutions to allow them to resolve problems that obstruct cooperation, and so increase the chance of successful and mutually beneficial cooperation. Domestic and international institutions moderate international anarchy in the liberal view. Liberals focus on economic and environmental issues because institutions are central to cooperation on both, although they also believe that institutions can reduce the security dilemma.

Constructivism

Constructivism argues that shared understandings shape international anarchy in powerful ways. People share ideas of the role of politics in life and what is right and wrong. Norms about proper conduct adhere to the social roles that we fill in life. These conventions mold social life, including world politics. In many cases, they help actors understand what actions are in their interest and understand how others are likely to respond to them. Identities differentiate people and constitute actors; states for example are a particular form of political organization invested with sovereignty. These shared understandings form a backdrop for world politics which actors can draw on to help them cooperate or could propel them into conflict. These ideas are held by many, and they resist change because even actors who abandon these ideas must respect the effect those ideas have on those who still hold them.

Constructivists focus their attention on issues where these shared understandings are easier to identify. Human rights, for example, asserts how states should treat their citizens. These ideas are commonly known, even if they are not always observed. Similarly, support for international cooperation on the environment comes in part from the idea of a shared human fate on the Earth. Non-governmental organizations (NGOs), such as Amnesty International or Greenpeace, often advance these ideals, making NGOs of particular interest to constructivists.

Integrating the Three Views

These three worldviews inform how many think about world politics. Often, they are described as competing views, where only one can be true. Rather, they complement one another. Each is incomplete. Each directs our attention to some factors at the expense of others. Integrating the three into one coherent view improves our understanding of world politics. This book presents a unified view of these three worldviews, a view which is superior to any one of them in isolation.

Review Questions

Each chapter will end with some questions which will help you review the material of that chapter.

1.   Explain the differences between security issues and political economy issues in world politics. Give an example of each.

2.   Explain the difference between positive and normative theory in world politics.

Chapter 3
Actors in World Politics

Actors are the basic units of any theory of world politics. We begin by discussing actors, their properties, and describing some of the many types of actors in world politics. States are often treated as the central actors of world politics and are a distinctive form of political organization to world politics. States are political organizations with their own leadership and politics of many individuals struggling for power and policy within them. Some theories of world politics study the internal politics of states to see how those politics affect what states do internationally. States are members of many intergovernmental organizations (IGOs) which then become important forums for state action. For some issues, these organizations are actors in their own right. There are other actors, such as non-governmental organizations (NGOs), which act across states rather than within or among them. Strategic interaction is central to world politics because there are many actors who must consider what each other will do when they decide what they will do. The choice of who the actors are is critical for every theory of world politics, which is why we begin with them.

What is an Actor?

Actors are able to determine their own actions. States make war, set rules for goods to enter the country through international trade, and accept and follow international law. Leaders, their supporters, and their opponents try to determine their state's policies and actions through the domestic politics of their state. Those outside the government may vote, lobby, or pressure their government to adopt the policies they like. NGOs organize and publicize around issues they are concerned with, such as human rights and the environment. All of these actors share the ability to determine what they do, and so are actors in world politics. They "act" and so we call them actors.

Actors know what they would like to do, what end they are trying to accomplish. Actors have *preferences*. In the next chapter, we discuss preferences, how they are defined, what they mean, and how and they vary across actors. For now, we leave at the recognition that actors understand what they would like to have happen. Otherwise, they could not act.

Actors possess *capabilities* to influence other actors. World politics has many actors that are trying to accomplish what they prefer. Often, they disagree about what outcomes are better than others. Capabilities are one way to resolve such disagreements. Actors' capabilities, which we will also discuss more fully in another chapter, cover all the tools the actors have to induce, cajole, or force other actors in their efforts to produce the outcomes they prefer. Military capability is specific to world politics, and I will discuss such capabilities separately in their own chapter.

Actors have *perceptions* of other actors and what they will do. Actor do not know every aspect of the situation they face. Some of these uncertainties include what all the other actors want or how they intend to influence others to get what they want. An actor might also be uncertain about the capabilities of other actors relative to itself. An actor's perceptions express what it believes about elements of the situation that it does not know. Because it is uncertain, perceptions cover multiple possibilities for each element about which an actor is uncertain.

To summarize, actors have the ability to act. They possess preferences, capabilities, and perceptions. Defining which actors are active in a situation is central to any analysis of world politics. That is why actors are the basic unit of world politics. They are where we start.

Strategic Interaction

Actors do not act in isolation in world politics. In every situation, there are many different actors trying to influence the outcome to what they prefer. Each has to consider what the other actors want in that situation and what they might do in their efforts to accomplish what they want. What does happen is the interplay of what all the actors are doing.

Strategic interaction is central to world politics. The term "strategic interaction" covers two important points. First, actors interact. They have to think about what one another will do in considering what they will do. The decisions of all the relevant actors affect the outcome, so they cannot just do as they please. Second, they strategize. Actors have to think about what others will do and then choose their own actions to get the best possible outcome in their view. Often, they may have to settle for something less than the outcome they think is best because other actors want something else which they are trying to make happen. Actors choose their actions with an eye to what others will do.

Choosing when others also can affect what you get is a harder problem than just choosing for yourself without considering what others might do to influence what you get. Think of shopping in a store. You have to look at all the things you might want to buy and their prices. Then you have to decide what you want to buy, which of those things has the best combination of price and quality for you. This is not a strategic interaction because the store simply displays its goods and their prices and lets you decide what you want to buy. Now think of buying the same things in a market where you can bargain with the merchant over the price of what you buy. Now the price you pay depends on how you bargain with the merchant because you may be able to get him to lower his price. You have to think about how to approach him; do you demand a low price to begin with or ask him about the item which you would like to buy to see if he will cut the price to make a sale? Do you discuss other items with him first to show that you are interested but do not wish to pay the prices he lists? Because the price you pay depends on how well you pay the bargaining game, this purchase, or the failure to buy anything, is a strategic interaction. The choices of both you and the merchant affect whether a sale is made and at what price. Both of you have to think about how the other will react and try to outfox one another.

Negotiation is a very common type of strategic interaction in world politics. Actors negotiate over how to resolve international issues all the time. They disagree about what the outcome of the issue should be. None of them can simply set the issue to the outcome they like. They have to try and influence one another to adopt an outcome favorable to their interests. They might try to persuade one another with arguments or resort to pressure one another to get what they want. That pressure might include threats or promises. They are typically better off if they are able to resolve their differences through bargaining. Sometimes, however, that bargaining will fail, leaving actors with the choice of how to get what they want afterwards.

Anticipations of what other actors will do are important in strategic interaction. What action is best for one actor depends on what other actors will do, so that actor's anticipation of what others will do plays a large role in determining what it will do. Those anticipations may be the result of learning about the other actor and what it wants from past interactions, the result of intelligence work to ascertain what it intends to do, or just speculation in the absence of other information. These anticipations of what other actors will do are *perceptions* because they do not necessarily capture what the other actor will do. They only give what one actors thinks another is likely to do.

Throughout this book, we will examine many different strategic interactions that actors face in various areas of world politics. These areas structure those interactions by specifying which actors can affect the outcome and any rules under which they interact. International institutions may have formal rules for how actors reach joint decisions. Voting rules or rules for recognizing which country speaks next in a formal multilateral negotiation shape how actors pursue their interests in institutions with such rules. In the United Nations (UN), for example, the five permanent powers–the U.S., Great Britain, France, Russia, and China–have the veto in the Security Council. If any one of them casts a veto on a resolution being considered in the Security Council, that resolution fails. Consequently, Security Council resolutions have to be crafted so that none of the five permanent members will veto it. These rules then say who can do what, when, and with what effect. We need to consider the effect of such rules when examining actors' decisions within institutions with such rules. Institutions also set principles of proper behavior that guide strategic interaction on a particular issue. These principles, called *norms*, help actors form anticipations about what one another will do. Norms set rules for what actions are allowed and appropriate for a situation and which are not. They are called norms because they give normative statements of how to behave. International law addresses norms in many different issues of world politics. The World Trade Organization (WTO) has norms of lower barriers to trade and non-discrimination. The former means states that are members of the WTO pledge to remove the policies they have that make imports–goods produced in another country for sale in that country–less competitive with goods produced in that country. Non-discrimination means that members of the WTO must give the same access to its market to all other members of the WTO; it cannot set up a special policy to limit the access of imports from just one country which is in the WTO. A country which breaks these rules of proper conduct may lead other actors to anticipate further bad behavior from that actor, and so act against what it wants. Later, we will discuss the strategic logic of norms more fully. For now, decision procedures and norms are both parts of international institutions that shape strategic interactions.

States as Political Units and Actors

States are the distinctive political unit of world politics. Each country is a state, and we use the term "state" to focus on the apparatus which runs the country and has legal standing with other states. The United States is a state, but not the states such as my state of Michigan that compose those united states because the latter do not have the legal power to act internationally. The interaction of states dominates much of world politics. Almost every inhabited part of the earth is controlled by an international recognized state, which acts on behalf of the people who reside on that territory. Further, states as the unit of political organization are distinctive to the modern world, that is, since roughly 1500 CE.

Ideally, states have internal and external autonomy. *Internal autonomy* means that the state has a monopoly on the legitimate use of force within its borders. Within the United States, the police are authorized to use force against me if I break the laws and resist arrest. I am not allowed to use force against the police; if I do so, it is a crime. Further, other countries are not supposed to send their agents to use force inside the borders of the United States. If I cross the border, commit a crime, and flee back to the U.S., the government of Canada cannot send its police officers into the United States to arrest me without the permission of the government of the U.S. Internal autonomy also means that each state can set its own internal policies as it chooses; its government is sovereign within its borders. Other states do not have the legal right to tell it what it should do within its own borders.

External autonomy means each state has the right to determine its own foreign policy on its own without interference from other states. Other states do not have the legal right to order it to lower its tariffs, submit to their wishes, or surrender criminal suspects. States are legal equals, where none has the right to command others. Legal equality of states is a novel feature of the modern state system. In medieval Europe, rulers often had multiple ties of fealty, where they both had obligations to other actors and held the legal power to command other actors to comply. The King of England, for example, was both an equal of the King of France as a King but also owed obligations to him as the Duke of Aquitaine, a duchy in southwest France. Further, the Pope as the head of the Catholic Church had powers such as that to appoint archbishops and bishops in consultation with the Kings who ruled the territory of the archbishoprics and bishoprics.

States are also supposed to respect the borders and territorial integrity of other states. Within those borders, its rule is law. Borders are often delimited with markers and patrolled by agents of each state on their side of the border. The border crossings between the United States and Canada, one of the most open borders in the world, have customs agents manning posts on both sides of the border. They perform customs and immigration checks of those who seek to cross from one country into the other. Other agents of the state, such as the police, cannot pursue suspects into another country without asking permission to enter and operate in that state. Historically, territorial integrity does not mean that states never disagree about which state should control a piece of territory. Multiple states have had claims over the same territory and have fought wars over its possession. The formal renunciation of claims over territory ends their disagreement about where the border should rightfully be. After the Cold War, Germany formally renounced any claims over the portion of Silesia, a portion of Germany that Josef Stalin took from Germany and gave to Poland after 1945. He did so because he took a piece of eastern Poland and added it to the Soviet Union, the state he led. Germany renounced its claim to Silesia to reassure the Poles that Germany would not seek to change any borders now that Poland could no longer rely on the protection of the Soviet Union to defend it against German claims.

[Map showing territorial changes imposed by Stalin on Poland and Germany with Curzon Line]

In practice, internal and external autonomy of states is often compromised. A weak state may do as a strong state wishes to avoid pressure from it. During the Cold War, Finland was very careful in its foreign policy not to challenge the Soviet Union. Finland had lost two wars to the Soviet Union during the Second World War in 1940 and 1944 and had no interest in fighting a third. As a consequence, Finland did not seek closer ties with the rest of Europe. With the end of the Cold War, the Soviet Union broke up into many states, and the power of Russia, the largest, was greatly reduced. Finland then sought closer ties with Europe, becoming a member of the European Union in 1995. States that have the legal right to exercise internal and external autonomy may choose do as others demand to avoid conflicts with the latter.

States have also fought over territory and borders and continue to do so even today. Territory has historically been the most important issue that states fight wars over. Today, there are territorial disputes that have not been resolved. India and Pakistan still dispute which of them should control the territory of Kashmir. They have divided effective control of Kashmir along the ceasefire line established at the end of Indo-Pakistani War over Kashmir from 1947 to 1948. India also claims the Aksai Chin, a portion of Kashmir controlled by China since it seized it during the Sino-Indian War of 1962. These competing claims mean that these states disagree about which of them should control this territory. Although they are not currently fighting over the territory, Kashmir has been disputed in at least three wars and has a long-running insurgency in Indian-held Kashmir which India blames Pakistan for supporting and sponsoring. Although states are supposed to respect each other's territory, they do not always do so when they have publicly stated that the territory should be theirs.

[Map of Kashmir with claims of all parties and ceasefire lines]

There are also polities that are not states, even though they seem much like states. The Republic of China (ROC) controls the island of Taiwan and some smaller islands close to the coast of the mainland. In 1949, the Kuomintang (KMT) party fled the mainland after losing the Chinese Civil War to the Communists. The KMT had been the government of China since 1920 and called the state the Republic of China. When the Communists established control of the mainland, they created the People's Republic of China (PRC). Both the ROC and the PRC claimed there was only one China, but they disagreed who was the rightful government of China. To this date, each has controlled its own territory and people. The PRC insists that other countries can recognize only one of the two Chinas as the government of China. In 1979, the U.S. shifted its formal recognition from the ROC to the PRC. A small number of countries recognize the ROC as the legitimate government of China, but the vast majority of countries recognize the People's Republic. Other countries deal with the ROC informally because it is not another state in their eyes.

The case of the two governments of China raises the question of the legal definition of a state in world politics. A state possesses the following four properties:

1. A *defined territory*: A state possess some area of land with borders that delimit that territory. Microsoft may be a very powerful corporation which makes more money than some states, but it is not state because it does not control territory with borders. Possession of territory by a state differs from a person or company owning land.

2. A *permanent population*. The territory of a state must be inhabited by people who live there. This permanent population are the citizens of the state, although other people may live within the borders of the state. Antarctica is not a state because no one lives there permanently. The scientists who work at research stations in Antarctica return to their home countries where their research tour is complete.

3. *Effective control of the territory and population by a government*. The territory and its people must have a government that controls both at some level. States are identified with governments because a government is an essential attribute of the state. Cases where the government of a state has lost control of its territory and people are often called *failed states*. There may be a government in the state, but it does not exert any control over the people or territory. A failed state lacks the ability to collect taxes, police the population, or perform services for its people. Typically, a failed state lacks a monopoly of force within its borders as people arm themselves for protection or predation. Somalia is the most-cited example of a failed state.

4. *The ability to enter into relations with other states*. The set of states is like a club in that other states recognize one another as states. Diplomatic recognition by other states creates embassies and the exchange of ambassadors. An ambassador is the formal representatives of a foreign government in a country. The embassy provides a place where you can do business with that government, such as obtain a visa–formal permission to enter the country–if you are not a citizen of that country or seek aid if you are a citizen of that country and you run into trouble in the country where the embassy is located. Diplomatic recognition is the formal tool used by states to accept one another as legitimate political units that control some territory and the population there.

There are political units in the world that are not states because they fail one or more of these provisions. The ROC does not have the ability to enter into relations with other states because most other states do not recognize it as a state. Nevertheless, Taiwan is highly integrated into the world economy and so needs to be able to conduct business both for its people when they are abroad and for citizens of other countries who would like to go to Taiwan. In the U.S., the ROC does not have an embassy or consulates as a state recognized by the U.S. does. Instead, Taiwan has Consultative Committees in major U.S. cities where one can obtain visas to travel there or do other business with its government. The Palestinian Authority has diplomatic recognition of most states in the world as the legitimate government of the Palestinian people. It, however, does not control any territory as the territory where the Palestinian people live is occupied by Israel.

Currently, there are 193 member states in the UN with South Sudan being the most recent member to join. You can find a list of the members of the UN at www.un.org. Beyond those 193 states, there are also microstates that are not members of the UN. Microstates in Europe, such as Monaco and Liechtenstein, are the residue of the medieval order. The smallest state in the world is the Holy See, which controls 110 acres of the Vatican City in Rome. The Vatican holds observer status at the UN as the Holy See rather than membership.

The Nation-State

The state as political unit encompasses the boundaries and people it controls and the government that rules both. The concepts of the state and the state system trace back to Europe around 1500 CE. Modern states like Spain, France, and England began to emerge from the medieval system as distinct political units. Eventually, states would come to control just about every piece of territory inhabited by people on the face of the earth. The state system sets the rules about how states interact with one another, with ideas like internal and external autonomy being the general principles.

The *nation-state* was a key development in the long rise to dominance of the state as political unit. The nation-state fuses a national identity to the state and increases the power of the state both domestically and internationally. People have a *national identity* when they think of themselves as one people or nation and are identified as such by others outside the group. The *nation* is the set of people holding that identity. When the people of a state constitute one nation, so that citizenship in the state corresponds to membership in the nation, the combination is a nation-state. National identities both identify their members and what they hold in common. Such ideas that define a nation include generally a common language, what the people view as distinctive about the history of the nation, and national practices like sports they play, cultural traditions, national holidays, flags and other national symbols. Some countries, like Germany, have defined membership and so citizenship in their state by descent from an earlier member of their nation. Other countries, like the United States, define nationality by loyalty to the state.

One becomes an American either by being born in the country or pledging allegiance to the U.S. through the process of naturalization. National identity answers the question "Who are we?" for the members of a nation.

Although national identities often evoke a long history of the nation and how it came to be, national identities are historical creations. They have not always existed. Several hundred years ago, few people would have thought of themselves as members of any group aligned with the state that ruled them. There were few if any Frenchmen; instead, the residents of France thought of themselves as Bretons, Normans, Gascons, Provincials, Burgundians, and more, that is, members of the smaller medieval regions that were joined together to form France. The people in the South of France used a different dialect of French from those in the North. The idea of one French people was created over the last two to three hundred years by institutions of the state. The common language of French was taught to all in schools, as was a shared understanding of French history and how the country came about. Soldiers inducted into the army were brought together and made into Frenchmen. National rituals like the celebration of the Bastille Day and symbols like the Tricolor flag arose that linked citizens of France to their history. As the people who lived in France began to see themselves as Frenchmen and women, they felt they owed loyalty to the France and the French state.

The nation-state increased the power of the state by identifying the state as the political unit for the nation. People with loyalty to their nation also were loyal to the state. They were willing to fight for their nation-state, particularly against outsiders who invaded their territory. Citizens were also more willing to cooperate with the state's efforts to extract resources from them, such as through taxation. The power of the state increased because people identified with the nation and saw the state as the legitimate political representation of the nation.

Not everyone in a nation-state felt this way, however. Many nation-states contained minority groups that had either been oppressed by the state or identified with a different nation. Different language was often an issue. In Canada, French Canadians, primarily in Quebec, did not identify with the central government and its connection to Great Britain. They considered themselves conquered by Britain since the Seven Years War in the mid-eighteenth century. During the World Wars, Canada sent troops to fight alongside British troops in France, but few French Canadians fought. The Canadian government was careful not to conscript French Canadians to fight, accepting only volunteers of which there were few. In some cases, the minority group identified with a bordering country, which might lead them to detach their region from their current state and join it to that other country. These problems of national loyalty became difficult when more than one national group lived in one area. Romania sought to add Transylvania (yes, the Transylvania from vampire legends like Count Dracula) to its territory to include the ethnic Romanians who lived there. But Austro-Hungary controlled Transylvania where large numbers of Hungarians also lived. As a result, Transylvania passed back-and-forth between the two countries during the twentieth century. Romania gained it after the First World War when the Austro-Hungarian Empire was broken up. Hitler forced Romania to cede, that is formally surrender the territory, it back to Hungary in 1941, with Romania reclaiming Transylvania after the Second World War. After the end of the Cold War, Romania's treatment of ethnic Hungarians raised issues between the governments of Romania and Hungary, which cared about how its nationals in Transylvania were being treated.

The idea of nationalism, that people are members of nations, began to take root with the French revolution and grew through the nineteenth century. By the early twentieth century, the concept of national self-determination arose. *National self-determination* means that each nation should decide for itself what state it should govern it. Large, multiethnic states were seen as unable to hold the loyalty of their citizens because they contained many nations that did not identify with the state. These divided loyalties created international problems when some members of those nations agitated to leave the state and either join another state or form a new state of their own. The Austro-Hungarian Empire was the prime example of the problem of national self-determination. It contained at least ten different ethnicities that considered themselves nations, with the ethnic Germans identifying with the Austrian state, the Hungarians with the Hungarian state, and the rest, particularly the Czechs, wanted their own states. The difficulties of keeping all these nationalities together in one state contributed to the origins of the First World War because Austria felt it had to respond strongly when a Serb assassinated Archduke Franz-Ferdinand, the heir to the throne. Austria-Hungary was one of the losing Central Powers in the war, and it was broken up into many states afterwards. Today, its territory is part of ten different states.

[Map of ethnic groups in Austro-Hungary before the First World War]

[Map of outline of Austria-Hungary overlaid on current borders of states]

National self-determination created as many problems as it solved. On occasion, it has been practiced peacefully, through plebiscites, where the people living in an area vote on which country they should belong. It has also created violent political conflict between and within states as some groups seek to separate from their current country. National self-determination faces the question of what groups qualify as nations. How large or small can such groups be? How cohesive to they have to be? What steps must such a group take to be recognized as a nation by other nation-states? What if their current nation-state does not wish to surrender their territory to them? Nations without states because they may seek to use violence to gain their own state or join another that represents their nationality.

States without nations also pose problems. It is more difficult for a government to command the allegiance of its people when they do not identify themselves as members of the nation whom the state purports to represent. They may identify with smaller groups like a tribe or clan. The boundaries of the state may not correspond to the boundaries of territory occupied by the members of these smaller groups. The state governs many such groups, none of whom feel any allegiance to the state or attachment to those other groups. They may feel stronger identification with other members of their tribe that live across the border in another state. The people owe more loyalty to their ethnic group over the state. Iraq, for example, has three main ethnic groups, the Shiites in the south, the Kurds in the north, and the Sunnis in between. All three groups mix in Baghdad, the capital. All three groups were placed in the state of Iraq when Great Britain and France drew the borders of Iraq when the Ottoman Empire was broken up after the First World War. Both the Sunnis under Saddam Hussein and now the Shiites have used the state to advance the interest of their own ethnic group, and the Kurds have effectively created a state of their own in the north, separate from the central government. All three ethnic groups have staged violent rebellions against the state when another group has controlled it. Although the people may think of themselves as Iraqis, they think of themselves first as Shiites, Kurds, or Sunnis.

The nation-state increases the *legitimacy* of the state–the belief that the state is the legal and proper governing authority within its border. Because the people accept the state as legitimate, they are more likely to follow the law, pay their taxes, and serve in the military if called. A state that lacks legitimacy can still command some power within its borders by coercive force. But it is more likely to suffer rebellions and less able to generate the tools of international power. It is no coincidence that many schools in the United States begin their days with the students reciting the Pledge of Allegiance.

In the extreme, the lack of legitimacy or the power to compel obedience can lead to a *failed state*. The government in a failed state loses its authority to command the people within its territory completely. It is unable to provide order within society, leading ordinary people to arm themselves for protection if possible. Armed groups spring up to take its place. The most famous failed state has been Somalia in the Horn of Africa. The government of Siad Barre collapsed in the face of multiple rebellions in 1991. Many people faced starvation as armed groups extorted money from them and withheld food aid. In December 1992, a UN force led by the United States intervened to ensure that food aid could be delivered in the face of massive starvation. By mid-1993, US forces were fighting one main armed group led by Farah Aideed. They launched a raid to capture Aideed which ended in failure and 19 US Rangers dead. Afterwards, UN forces withdrew from Somalia, and chaos returned. We in the US may take the internal and external autonomy of the state for granted, but it is something which has been created, not something which always must exist.

[Map of Somalia]

Corporate Actors

Many actors in world politics are composed of many people, yet we treat them as if they are individuals. The United States government employs millions of people and answers to an electorate of over 100 million. Even smaller actors, such as interest groups who lobby on trade policy or non-governmental organizations who advance human rights, have many people who work for them. Even though these actors are organizations of many people, we analyze them as if they are individuals who speak, think, and act as an individual. The United States attacked

Iraq, the steel lobby sought protection in higher tariffs, and Human Rights Watch issues reports on violations of human rights. Actors that consist of more than one person are called *corporate actors*. This term does not mean that they are all corporations, such as many business are organized and called corporations. Rather, they incorporate many people who act as one.

A corporate actor has a purpose which limits and defines what it does. The state provides public goods, such as order, within its borders and acts outside its borders to advance the interests of its people. A business corporation seeks to make money for its stockholders, the owners of the company. Nongovernmental organizations, like Human Rights Watch, seeks to advance the cause of human rights in the world. The purpose helps all the people in the corporate actor work together towards the goals of that purpose. It also limits what the actor seeks to do. It may be that not all people agree on what the purpose of the actor should be. The role of the state in its own economy varies greatly across states, with some intervening in the economy such as determining who gets what jobs and what goods are produced, while the governments of other states take a "hands off" attitude. It may also be that people within a country disagree about what the purpose of their state should be. The main point here is just that corporate actors have a purpose, which allows us to talk about them acting for that purpose.

Even if everyone agrees about the purpose of a corporate actor, they may disagree about how to accomplish the goals of that purpose. Corporate actors commonly have internal politics to resolve these differences. States have a political purpose to determine how they will act both at home and abroad. Companies also have internal politics to select who will run the firm and aid the boss in critical decisions for the firm. These internal politics are easier to see in some corporate actors than others. In the United States, elections and how legislatures pass laws are open and covered by the press. In a dictatorship, politics to select the dictator and how he or she stays in power are hidden, but they occur nonetheless.

These internal politics of the corporate actor both determine how it will act and seek to control its leader and members so they act to advance its purpose and interests rather than their own. Internal politics seek to fuse their personal interests to the goals of the corporate actors. Firms pay their employees to work for the firm and act in the interest of the shareholders rather than themselves. The internal politics of states seek to induce the leader of the state to act on behalf of some people of the state through limits on the leader's power and the ability to remove him or her from power.

Domestic Actors: Peering Inside the State

There are many ways to think about the domestic politics of the state as a corporate actor. Much of political science outside world politics analyzes the domestic politics of different countries, including the United States. These political scientists study how elections, legislatures, judiciary, and executive agencies affect the policies of the state. Others study how authoritarian systems, such as dictatorships, make decisions within the top leadership and then enforce those decisions on their population. We can think of the politics of political leadership using the abstract *principal-agent model*. The agent acts for the principal but may have different interests than the principal. The principal doubts whether the agent will act in its own interest or the principal's. The principal has ways to checking what the agent has done and some rewards and punishments to induce the agent to act in its interest. This model has been used in economics to study how a company–the principal–can get its workers–its agents–to do what the company wants, such as working hard and carefully, rather than what they want, such as socializing around the water cooler in the office. We can think of the politics of executive agencies using *organization theory*. Sociologists have studied how organizations work to ensure that all their members work together toward a common goal. The structure and purpose of an organization limits what it can do; we do not ask the Army to process social security claims in the United States, to name a prominent government organization and an important government task. We can think of how firms and workers attempt to influence international economic policies of their country using *interest group theories*. These theories examine how groups, such as firms making similar products like cars or people who work for those firms, form organizations that seek to advance their interests in their government. Both the ease of forming interest groups and how they attempt to induce the government to do as they wish are part of interest group theories. Later in the book, we will discuss all three of these models at greater length. I mention them here just to let you know some of the ways in which we will think about domestic politics of states as corporate actors.

We can think of states as either corporate actors or peer inside them to see how their domestic politics shapes their international policies. The former approach is called the *unitary actor assumption* because it treats the state as one actor, like an individual person. The unitary actor assumption has been common in the historical development of the field of world politics. Diplomatic historians often treat states as unitary actors and talk about what Germany did for example. One does not need to assume that states are unitary actors, and often we will examine the domestic politics of foreign policy of states. Domestic and international politics are inherently intertwined in world politics. Politics within a state influences what it does internationally, and international outcomes influence both states and their domestic politics. The President of the United States considers both the international and domestic consequences when forming foreign policy. The process of globalization, changes in the policies of other states that have increased the flow of goods and services across national borders, has large effects on the everyday lives of many Americans. These are just two examples of the interdependence of domestic and international politics in world politics.

There is no single right way to study world politics; the key question in choosing whether to unpack corporate actors is "what do we learn by doing so?" We gain many important insights into world politics by treating states as unitary actors and ignoring their domestic politics. For other questions, we learn more by examining domestic politics closely. The choice of "who are the actors" is the first step in analyzing world politics, which is why the book begins with this chapter. There is no single, correct answer to this question. Focusing on different actors leads to different insights about the same situation. We learn different, complementary things about trade policy by looking at it first as a state decision to make the country as wealthy as possible and then as the result of competition among interest groups seeking protection from foreign competition. The answer to "who are the actors?" is "what can we learn from thinking about the problem from the view of those actors?"

Other Types of Actors

So far we have concentrated on the state and domestic actors within it. There are actors beyond the state in world politics. Some of them sit above the state, while others work across states. The growth in the types and numbers of these non-state actors was large during the 20th century, particularly beginning after the Second World War. The presence of many non-state actors is one novel feature of the current global system.

Intergovernmental Organizations

Intergovernmental organizations (IGOs) are organizations which have states as members. IGOs typically specialize in an issue where they help states address some common problem. There are political organizations, such as the United Nations (UN) and the European Union (EU). These organization coordinate a wide range of policies and political acts across member states. In the case of the EU, it also deals with non-member states, for example, when it negotiates trade policy with the U.S. There are security organizations which help member countries coordinate their security policies. The North Atlantic Treaty Organization (NATO) is a formal alliance of the United States and Canada with many European states. NATO has an elaborate command structure based in Brussels, Belgium which commands NATO forces, allows NATO members to negotiate joint responses to crises, and coordinates the purchase of military equipment to ensure that all NATO troops can fight with one another. The Organization of American States (OAS) is a looser alliance than NATO which includes almost all states (Cuba is a member but its participation has been suspended since 1962) in the Western Hemisphere. The Organization for Security Cooperation in Europe (OSCE) has almost all European States and some other states near Europe as members. It provides a forum where European states can discuss security issues in the region and has staffed observer missions that keep the peace in troubled areas. The Arab League allies all Arab states; they use the Arab League to consult on common security policies on issues that they face.

Political and security IGOs act separately from their member states when they have parts that can act on their own. The Commission of the EU consists of appointed ministers who are responsible for specific issues handed by the Union, such as employment and the environment. The Commission has power to issue directives to member states that force those states to change to common European policies. Other parts of the EU, such as the Council of Ministers, have representatives from each state who speak for their state on the decisions of the Council. It then does not act separately from the will of the member states. Instead, it provides a place where member states can negotiate their differences on European policies.

Other IGOs address economic issues. The World Bank and International Monetary Fund (IMF) are based in Washington, DC and were created after the Second World War to lend money to states in need. The World Bank makes long-term loans to developing states to help them grow their economies and has a staff of economists and other experts who consult with these countries on what they should do to help their economies grow. The original mission of the IMF was to make short-term loans to countries that were unable to pay for their imports or lacked sufficient reserves to support the value of their currency. Its mission grew to providing loans to countries that could not service their debt, that is, make payments on their loans from other lenders. The IMF began requiring governments to change their policies, such as reducing government spending or raising taxes, as a requirement to receive a needed loan. These *structural adjustment* or *austerity* programs were supposed to force governments to adopt policies that would make it easier for them to pay back all their loans in the future, including those to the IMF. These programs, however, were economically painful as people in the country lost their jobs, government support or paid more in taxes. Consequently, few governments of developing countries borrow money from the IMF now. The World Trade Organization (WTO) encourages international trade, the flow of goods and services across national borders, by reducing barriers to trade in the policies of member states. It holds regular negotiations during which members of the WTO try to reach new reductions in barriers to trade. The current Doha round began in 2001 and continues today with talks about lowering barriers in the developed countries to agricultural imports and those in developing countries to manufactured imports. The *WTO dispute resolution procedure* allows member states to lodge a formal dispute against another member whom it believes has policies that effectively block it from selling its goods in that country. There are also regional trade organizations, such as the North American Free Trade Association (NAFTA) among the U.S., Canada, and Mexico, and Mercosur in South America. Finally, there are also organizations of states that produce primary goods–such as coffee, silver, and oil–that seek to regulate production in their shared interest in raising and sustaining the price. The Organization of Petroleum Exporting States (OPEC) is the most famous of these. It includes many but not all of the largest oil producers and sets production quotas for its members to regulate the price of oil in the world.

Other IGOs address a wide range of environmental issues. The International Institute for Applied Systems Analysis (IIASA) helps European states coordinate their policies to address transnational air pollution. The Intergovernmental Panel on Climate Change (IPCC) was established by the UN to research the status of global warming, its consequences, and policies to prevent or mitigate it. The IPCC shared the Nobel Peace Prize with former Vice President Al Gore in 2007. The North Atlantic Fisheries Organization (NAFO) sets allowable catches of different species of fish in the international waters of the North Atlantic Ocean. It also establishes national quotas for how many fish each member nation can catch.

There are many organizations that conduct and run international sports competitions. The International Olympic Committee (IOC) puts on the Summer and Winter Olympic Games once every four years. It also coordinates the activities of the many sport-specific organizations that conduct those contests in each Olympic Games. The Federation of International Football Associations (FIFA) regulates soccer, the world's most popular sport. It sets rules for player movement from one national league to another as well as providing referees for international competitions. It runs the best sporting event on the planet, the World Cup, once every four years. The final of the 2010 World Cup held in South Africa matched Spain and the Netherlands and was watched live by an estimated 700 million people worldwide. To be careful, most sporting organizations are not officially IGOs because their members are national sports federations rather than governments. The U.S. government is not a member of FIFA; the United States Soccer Federation (USSF) is. Still, given that these sports competition provoke strong national feelings and are organized along national lines, I include them as IGOs.

The United Nations

The United Nations (UN) is the most important IGO in the world. Actually, it is more a collection of related IGOs and decision-making bodies that seek to address global problems of war and peace, economic development, and others as well. 193 states are currently members of the UN, with Palestine and the Holy See as state-like observers. The two main bodies where state representatives discuss issues in the UN are the *Security Council* and the *General Assembly*. All member states have a representative in the General Assembly, which meets annually to consider global issues and passes resolutions that express the sentiments of a majority of countries. Every member state has one vote in the General Assembly, and it takes only a majority of voting countries to pass a resolution. The General Assembly has passed many resolutions that the United States has been opposed. Like the U.S. Congress, the General Assembly has committees that study matters and consider resolutions to recommend for discussion and a vote by the whole membership. The Security Council has five permanent members–the U.S., Great Britain, France, Russia, and China–that were the victorious great powers in World War II and ten temporary members who rotate on the Council for two-year terms. The temporary members are elected with set numbers from the different regions of the world. The Security Council addresses pressing matters of international security and has the right to pass resolutions that place economic sanctions on a state or authorize member states to use military force against a state which is considered a threat to international peace and security. Most Security Council resolutions, however, express the concerns of the Council about the threat to the peace of the world. Each of the permanent members of the Council has a veto; if any of them votes "no" on a resolution, the resolution is defeated. To pass a resolution, it needs nine "yes" votes from all members of the Council and no vetos from the permanent members. The specific wording of Security Council resolution are often negotiated at great length to ensure that they will pass. The power of the veto forces the whole Council to respect the views of each permanent member.

[UN organization chart here]

The *Secretary General* is the head of the United Nations, similar to the President in the United States but with much less power. He (to date all eight Secretary Generals have been men) heads the *Secretariat*, which contains departments that run UN missions authorized by the Security Council, such as peacekeeping and humanitarian missions. The Secretariat consists of UN employees who administer these programs. The UN has a number of Programs and Funds which address international problems. The UN fund you are probably most familiar with is UNICEF, the United Nations Children's Fund, which collects money for child welfare programs in developing countries. UNHCR, the UN High Commissioner for Refugees, administers relief aid to civilians displaced by war. These programs and funds answer to the General Assembly. The *International Court of Justice* (ICJ) is the third main branch of the UN, along with the General Assembly and Security Council as legislature, the Secretariat as executive. It provides a legal mechanism for states to resolve their disputes if they choose to do so.

The UN also has many important specialized agencies. I have already mentioned the IMF, World Bank, and WTO in the economic area. The World Health Organization (WHO) addresses health issues across national borders, such as contagious diseases such as bird flu which could cause an epidemic. The International Telecommunications Union (ITU) administers all forms of telecommunications across state borders and provides an organization where states can negotiate on these issues. There are many other UN agencies; you can find them listed in the organizational chart of the UN.

The UN has a broad mission to advance international peace, development, and well-being. It aids states through its many agencies towards these goals. Nevertheless, the UN is a product of its member states and does not have strong power to determine its own agenda on these goals. The United States has often disagreed with both resolutions and agencies of the UN when they take actions opposed by the U.S. The UN raises the money to cover its budget by contributions by member states, with wealthier states paying more. At times, the U.S. has withheld part of its UN contribution to protest certain actions and to attempt to convince the UN to reform certain agencies. The UN is important in world politics because its agencies touch on so many issues. It also provides a place for states to attempt to resolve their differences peacefully. There are critical limitations on what can be accomplished through the UN, the first and foremost being lack of agreement among member states about what to do.

Non-governmental Organizations

Non-governmental organizations (NGOs) cover wide ranges of organizations that address international issues whose members are not states. They raise money from a variety of sources to support their activities. Some NGOs have large, professional staffs to carry out their activities;

others are small groups of volunteers. Amnesty International (sometimes abbreviated AI) addresses issues of human rights by publishing reports on the state of human rights in different countries and petitioning governments to realize those people that AI considers political prisoners. It is the most famous of many NGOs that now seek to advance the cause of human rights through reporting on their state and lobbying for the negotiation of new treaties and IGOs on the issue. Environmental NGOs work to raise awareness of the state of the global environment and change the environmental policies of states. Greenpeace is the most famous international NGOs, staging dramatic demonstrations to draw attention to situation that they consider threaten the environment. Humanitarian NGOs provide aid to distressed people in many ways. Some like Care distribute food aid to starving people. Medecins sans Frontieres (Doctors without Borders in English) have volunteer doctors who travel to war and disaster zones to provide free medical care to those in need. The most important humanitarian NGO is the International Committee of the Red Cross (ICRC). The ICRC coordinates the activities of the various national Red Cross organizations, provides aid internationally in time of war and disaster, and monitors compliance with the Geneva Conventions that regulate conduct during war. States are supposed to provide ICRC inspectors with access to prisoner of war camps so they can examine whether conditions in the camps meet the standard of the treaty. The inspectors then report privately to the country holding the prisoners about any violations of the treaty that they find. They also have a POW bureau during wartime that collects and sends lists of soldiers held prisoner to their home country and allows people in the home country to send letters and packages to their soldiers held prisoner. Scientific NGOs bring together scientists from many countries for meetings where they report the results of their research to one another and conduct other business in their field. I am a member of the International Studies Association (ISA) which has members from 80 countries who study different aspects of the world. Finally, the oldest, and probably most powerful NGO is the Roman Catholic Church. The Soviet dictator Joseph Stalin may have dismissed the power of the Pope with the comment, "How many [army] divisions does he have?", but his successors found a formidable opponent in Pope John Paul II. He played an important role in the end of Communism and the Cold War in Eastern Europe by serving as a rallying point for Poles in opposition to their Communist system during the 1980s.

The Creation of New Actors

One source of change in world politics is the emergence of new actors. The state and state system as the organization of world politics dates back to 1500 CE at the earliest. New states have been formed by both the conquest of earlier political units and the dissolution of other political arrangements. The forcible unifications of Italy and Germany in the middle of the 19th century from many smaller Italian and German states changed world politics by creating two new major powers in central Europe. The breakup of the European colonial empires created almost all states in Africa and Latin America and many states in Asia. Spain lost most of its empire in

Latin America through the Wars of Independence between 1806 and 1828. The British, French, and Dutch empires were broken up after the Second World War, in some cases by wars fought by the colonized against the colonial power, as was the case in Indochina and Algeria against the French and Indonesia against the Dutch. The Portuguese empire in Africa was the last to free its colonies, again after guerrilla wars against them in Angola and Mozambique. The wave of new states produced by decolonization changed how the UN operated because it introduced a large number of new, economically less developed states. It also created new arenas for political competition between the U.S. and the Soviet Union as they vied for influence in these new states during the Cold War. The end of the Cold War led to the creation of new states through the breakup of multiethnic states. Czechoslovakia peacefully split into the Czech Republic and Slovakia, but the breakup of Yugoslavia into separate states for each of its six constituent republics led to the three large and brutal wars. The breakup of the Soviet Union was mainly accomplished peacefully but has led to tension among the successor states, particularly when Russia exerts its influence on the smaller states.

New types of actors have also emerged over time in world politics. NGOs devoted to the protection of the environment and human rights are a recent phenomenon, with almost all being formed in the last 50 years. Similarly, the number of IGOs has also expanded after first World War I and then again after the Second World War. The expansion of both IGOs and NGOs have changed the character of world politics by introducing new actors representing new interests. These organizations have also created new capabilities to address their issues. NGOs often serve as monitors of what states do on their issues of concern. States create and use IGOs to aid them in cooperating on important issues. Rebel groups now operate openly as political organizations and seek aid from other states in their war against their home government.

[Charts showing growth of NGOs and IGOs during 20th century]

Changes in the nature of states have also altered world politics. Two hundred and fifty years ago, almost all European states were absolute monarchies, where the King, or occasionally the Queen, answered only to the nobility and asserted that he had a divine right to rule. The American and French revolutions created the first democratic republics in modern times, where the legitimacy of the state resided in people and its power in their consent through representative government. Constitutional rule, democracy, and then universal adult suffrage spread during the 19th and early 20th centuries. The aftermath of World War I saw the creation of the totalitarian states, particularly the Soviet Union and Nazi Germany, where a coercive state and an ideology were fused together to create a state that sought to control its citizens' thoughts and actions. Democracy spread across many states in a series of waves, the first after World War I, the second after the Second World War, the third in the 1970s, and the fourth after the end of the Cold War. These changes in the domestic politics of states altered how they act in world politics, making issues like territorial conquest and competition less important and economic growth more important.

[Chart showing spread of democracy over last 250 years]

Changes in actors then have transformed world politics over the centuries. The creation of new actors and changes in their composition bring new issues to the forefront and other to recede. Early modern Europe around 1500 saw the emergence of the state as a political unit which then developed new rules on how states should relate to one another, what we now know as the sovereign state system. At the same time, feudal nobles below the king, such as dukes that were important actors in feudal France and England, lost power to the king and ceased to be international actors. The Reformation introduced the new issue of religion to world politics in Europe. Similar changes have occurred over the last fifty years of world politics. The emergence of NGOs has pushed issues like human rights and the protection of the environment into world politics. Although states are still key actors on these issues, they act in a political setting where these non-state actors are important. The world politics of today differs from that of a hundred years ago because of these new actors.

How to Analyze It
Corporate Actors

Most actors in world politics are corporate actors. The choice of whether to treat them as unitary actors or examine their internal politics is critical to any analysis. We will analyze them both ways in this book. This box describes how to make that choice.

1. What question are you trying to answer? Most situations in world politics pose many different questions. For example, Chapter 1 gave a wide range of questions about the outbreak of the Iraq War. Some of those questions focus our attention on the internal politics of a country, such as the struggle between the Departments of State and Defense within the United States. Other questions focus our attention on the interactions of states, such as why Iraq and the United States could not agree on a peaceful solution. A clear idea of the question you would like to answer often determines whether you should treat corporate actors as unitary or examine their internal politics.

2. Once you have identified your questions, what are the actors trying to accomplish? This is the question of their preferences. Chapter 3 covers preferences and will give you ways to think about the preferences of actors carefully. For now, consider what might happen in the process you are analyzing. What is the range of different outcomes that could result? How does each actor rank all of those possible outcomes?

3. Are the actors trying to accomplish shared interests or do they disagree about what is best? Most situations have elements of both cooperation and conflict between the actors. They have some interests in common while disagreeing about others.

4. How do the choices of the actors produce the outcome of the process? This could be a formal procedure, like voting in the UN. More commonly in world politics, bargaining between the actors produces the outcome of the process. Politics inside a corporate actor are more likely to have formal procedures that shape the bargaining among the key players that shape its decisions.

5. If you are examining politics within a corporate actors, what incentives does it give people inside it to act in its interest? All corporate actors try to get the individuals who compose it to act in its interest. This is why companies pay their workers, to get them to work for the company. Political organizations sometimes use pay but often have other ways of getting the people who compose the organization to work in its interest.

Summary

Actors are the basic unit of world politics. They determine their own actions, have preferences and capabilities, and hold perceptions about what other actors will do. Strategic interaction, when many actors can influence the outcome of an issue, makes choices of what to do complex for both actors and analysts. The state is the distinctive and fundamental, but not sole, unit of world politics. States ideally possess internal and external autonomy, but practically their sovereignty may be compromised. The nation-state increased the power of the state by fusing a national identity to the governmental apparatus of the state. States are one type of corporate actor, actors who we treat as individuals even though they are composed of many people. We can learn more about why corporate actors do what they do if we examine their internal politics; we need not assume that states are unitary actors. There is a wide variety of non-state actors in world politics today. The creation of new actors has changed world politics by bringing new actors and issues into it. Finally, the choice of the actors relevant to a situation is the critical first step in any theory of world politics.

Review Questions

1. Name the characteristics of an actor in world politics. What three things does an actor possess?

2. Define "strategic interaction." How does a strategic interaction differ from other choices you make?

3. Explain what is meant by internal and external autonomy of a state.

4. What four properties compose the legal definition of a state in the sovereignty system?

5. Define a state and a nation, and explain the differences between them. How did the merger of a national identity with the state increase the power of the state?

6. What is a corporate actor? Give two examples of corporate actors, not of the same type.

7. What is the unitary actor assumption?

8. Define an NGO and an IGO, and state how they differ. Give an example of each.

9. Describe two different ways the actors in world politics have changes over the last 250 years.

Chapter 4
Preferences: Specifying What Actors Want

A civil war began in the Darfur region of the Sudan in 2003. Darfur covers a vast area in the western portion of the country. Rebel groups claimed that the central government oppressed the non-Arab residents of Darfur as a justification for their rebellion. In response, the government of Sudan supported Arab militias, called the Janjaweed, which carried out attacks against civilians in Darfur. The Janjaweed are accused of committing murder, plunder, and rape on a massive scale in Darfur. Common estimates are that hundreds of thousands of civilians have been killed with millions have fled their homes in Darfur out of fear of the violence. The government of the United States has called the killings genocide, the recognized crime against humanity of killing people just because they are members of an ethnic or religious group.

[Map of Sudan with Darfur highlighted]

Many around the world have been outraged by the atrocities in Darfur, and there have been many calls for the international community to stop the violence there. Peacekeepers under the auspices of the African Union have been deployed in Darfur since 2004, but the number of troops is small compared to amount of ground they have to cover. Humanitarian aid of food and shelter has been provided in refugee camps set up for those who have fled the violence. Beyond these measures, there has been little agreement about what further measures should be taken. Some have argued that even these measures are too much because they interfere in the internal politics of Sudan. Others prefer the measures already taken and nothing more. Still others argue for a larger and more powerful peacekeeping force, including troops from the United States and its allies. Some think that economic sanctions should be placed on Sudan to block its trade with other countries. Even among those who want to see the killing stop, there is little agreement about what to do.

Part of the disagreement about what to do about Darfur arises from the uncertainty about what will happen if additional measures are employed. Will the government of Sudan respond positively to economic sanctions to preserve its foreign trade or will it withdraw and become isolated? Some of the African Union peacekeepers have been killed; would a larger peacekeeping force get caught in the civil war in Darfur? Might some of the aid to refugees be diverted to support the rebels? Those opposed to intervention often believe that it undermines the principle of internal autonomy that is part of state sovereignty. They worry that further action in Darfur could lead to military intervention in other places where the circumstances are less compelling. The proponents of different responses to the killings disagree about what the consequences of the available policies might be.

They also disagree about how attractive these different consequences would be. Even those who agree that the killing should stop do not agree about what costs they are willing to pay to make that happen. Some are willing to commit their country's troops to combat if necessary. Others do not believe that the situation is important enough to use military force and lose more lives over. Some support the rebels, while others do not. The international disagreement over what to do stems in part from the disagreement about how to view what might happen in Darfur. Any policy to stop the killing will have a range of results from what happens in Darfur to the foreign relations of the Sudan to the politics of the international community. Just being opposed to the killing is not enough to decide what to do about it. One also has to judge these other effects and how attractive or unattractive they are. Preferences are how we think carefully about how actors evaluate all the possible consequences of their policy choices.

Why Do Preferences Matter?

Preferences force us to think carefully about what actors want, what are they trying to accomplish. An actor's capabilities tell us what tools it has to influence other actors, but they do not explain what the actor would like to accomplish by using those tools. An actor's perceptions detail what it thinks other actors will do and how it might influence them, but again they do not say what the actor wants. Principles may explain the situation within which the actor operates, but they do not dictate what players must do. These principles may limit their choices or prescribe proper behavior, but actors may choose to work around those rules or violate those prescriptions.

Preferences matter because of uncertainty. An actor does not know what will necessarily result from its choices. Other factors outside the actor's control also affect the outcome. The choices of other actors are outside the deciding actor's control as are elements outside human control such as the weather. If you go to a store and buy a candy bar, you know what you will get, the candy bar you choose. Decisions in world politics are more like playing a sport where you make decisions about what plays you will try to make, but whether those plays turn out as you planned depends on what the other players do and the breaks of the game. If actors could knew the consequences of their actions, we would only need to know what outcome they wanted to predict their actions. They would always choose the result they liked best. But when other factors affect the outcome, an actor has to think about the possibility of getting an outcome it did not intend and does not like. This uncertainty about what will happen means that actors have to think about all the possible outcomes, not just the one they like best.

As analysts then, we need to know how the actors rank all the possible outcomes. This requirement is more demanding than simply asking what the actor would like to see happen. Decisions involve risks of bad outcomes as well as chances of good outcomes, and we have to know how actors rank both of them.

What is a Preference Order?

Understanding actors' choices relies on identifying what choices they have, what could result from those choices, and the factors outside their control that influence the results of their choices. Each situation where an actor faces a choice then divides into *actions*–the range of options from which the actor chooses, *outcomes*–the possible results of its choices, and *states of the world*–all those things outside its control. We will also refer to actions as *options*, *choices*, or *strategies*. Outcomes are sometimes called *consequences* or *results*. States of the world are often called just states. In a strategic interaction, the states include the choices of other actors because those actions lie outside the control of the actor whose preferences we are examining. The breakdown of the setting of a choice into these three pieces forces us to specify what the actor can control, what the results are that it cares about, and what the actor cannot control and is relevant to its choice.

The actions, outcomes, and states must include all possibilities of each. The actor chooses one and only one action, and one and only one state is the true state of the world. The precise terms for these conditions are that the actions are *mutually exclusive*–choosing one means you cannot choose another–and *exhaustive*–the set of available actions includes all possibilities. Similarly, the states are mutually exclusive and exhaustive. An actor facing a decision has to think about all the possibilities, and so do we when we analyze its decision. Any one of the actions, outcomes, and states could be a small set of possibilities or a very large one. We generally will limit ourselves to small numbers of actions, outcomes, and states to keep our analysis clear and straightforward. Still our analysis assumes that we have all the possible and relevant actions, outcomes, and states. Similarly, a strategic interaction has to include all the relevant actors and their choices. For each of them, the other actors' choices are states from the view of its choice. Generally, we will list the actors and their actions separately for a strategic interaction.

An actor's preference order lists the outcomes from best to worst allowing for ties. The order must be *complete*; every possible outcome must be in the list. If the list is incomplete, we would not know where the actor ranked the omitted outcome. The order must also be *transitive*; if one outcome is better a second and the second is better than a third, then the first must be better than the third. If an order violated this so that the actor thought the third outcome was better than the first, what would the actor choose among the three? It depends on how it compares the three outcomes. Between the first and second, it thinks the first is better. Between the second and third, it thinks the second is better. Between the first and the third, it thinks the third is better. To prevent situations like this where we cannot tell what an actor wants, preference orders are assumed to be transitive. The assumptions of completeness and transitivity ensure that we have a full ranking of the actor's preferences over all possible outcomes.

Preferences are defined over outcomes, but we are more interested in what choices actors make. An actor chooses the action that gives it the most attractive prospects of achieving outcomes it likes best and avoiding the worst, while accounting for the elements outside its control. An example from real life may help clarify this idea. Say you are on a road trip and it is time for lunch. You pull off the highway, and there are two restaurants, a McDonald's and a truck stop. At which one do you choose to eat? You know what you will get if you go to

McDonald's, but the truck stop is unpredictable. Some truck stops serve great food, while others offer only the prospect of indigestion. Is this truck stop one of the good ones? If so, you might prefer it over the McDonald's. If it specializes in bad food, better to play it safe. The trick is that you do not know how good the food is at the truck stop when you choose where to eat. In this example, you have two actions, one for eating at each restaurant. We will exclude the possibility of eating a little at both places or just going into the next exit just to make the choice clearer. There are two states of the world, one where the truck stop serves great food and one where it is awful. The outcomes are a great meal at the truck stop, a terrible meal at the truck stop, and the predictable burger at McDonald's. Notice that you get the same outcome no matter what the quality of the food at the truck stop if you eat at McDonald's. Which restaurant would you choose? Your choice depends on your chances of the truck stop serving good food and how much you value the predictable burger at McDonald's compared to the possibilities of good and bad meals at the truck stop. There are books that rate road food so you can find and eat at the good places and avoid those that specialize in stomach aches. But books are not always correct; the writer's tastes might be different from yours or the truck stop may have changed for the worse after the book was written. Where you eat is your choice based on your judgment. If you think the chances of a good meal are high enough, the truck stop would be your choice. It could also be the case that your preferences are such that you would always choose one over the other. Perhaps you are traveling with small children and want them to play on the playground at the McDonald's. Then you may not care about the relative quality of the food (I know this from personal experience as a parent eating at McDonald's when I would have preferred eating sawdust). You might enjoy the camaraderie of truckers. In both of these cases, your preference over the outcomes, either that eating at McDonald's is the best or worst possible outcome, dictate your choice of restaurant regardless of how good the food at the truck stop is, that is, the true state of the world.

This example may strike you as silly, but it illustrates central issues in making decisions, including those in world politics. Consider a country on the verge of war. The other side has stated the terms it will accept in lieu of war, and now the first country must decide whether to grant those terms or fight. If it fights, it might win or lose the war. Losing the war is worse for it than granting the concessions the other side demands, while winning would be better for it than making the concessions. Whether it fights depends on its chances of winning and the exact consequences of losing, winning, and making concessions. A much stronger country is more likely to fight because it is more likely to win. It still might accept a peaceful settlement before war if that settlement is more attractive than running the risks of war. As one wag once described as the First Law of Social Science, "It Depends".

Important Points about Preferences

When an actor takes an action, it demonstrates a preference for that action over the other actions available to it. This preference over strategies is based on its preferences over outcomes and its judgment about how likely the states are. Preferences over outcomes are fundamental. Preferences over strategies or actions follow from them. Whether the country in the war example goes to war depends on how it rates the possible outcomes and how likely it thinks it is to win a war if fought. Whether or not it goes to war is a preference over strategies; how it views the possible outcomes of a negotiated settlement and war are its preferences over outcomes. The former follows from the latter.

It could change its mind about what it plans to do if it learns something about the situation that causes it to revise its views about the factors outside its control, the states and actions of others. In the where to eat example, you might change your mind about where to eat if you learned something about the quality of the truck stop. Maybe you find one of those books that says that this truck stop is one of the good ones. Now you think it is more likely that you will get a good meal there, and so you are more likely to try it. Because actors can learn about how likely the different states are, they may change their mind about what they plan to do. They can revise their preference over strategies even though their preferences over outcomes remain the same. You still evaluate a good meal at the truck stop as better than McDonald's; you are now try the truck stop because you think it is more likely that you will get a good meal if you eat there.

Now comes a catch. We can see what actors do but not their full preference order over the outcomes. You can tell which action an actor takes and so infer something about its underlying preferences over the outcomes, but that action could be consistent with different preference orders. Say you are thinking about which restaurant to eat at when you see someone else drive past the truck stop and eat at the McDonald's. You can see they think it is a better place to eat. It could be the person is a local and knows the truck stop serves bad food. It could be that they have small children and are going for the playground regardless of the food. You cannot tell which is true, that is, what the other person's preferences over the outcomes are. You can only see what they do and draw some inferences from that act. Preferences over outcomes are *inherently unobservable*. There are several reasons for the unobservability of preferences. First, we only see the actor take an action from those available to it. We do not know how it views the other actions relative to each other if it has more than two. Second, we do not know how likely it thinks each of the states is to occur. We cannot tell what it thinks of the things outside its control. Third, some outcomes may be impossible given the action it took, and so we cannot tell what they think of those outcomes. When the other person walks into the McDonald's, we cannot tell how they view a good meal at the truck stop, only that they were unwilling to take the chance of a bad meal. Life would be much easier if we knew the preferences over outcomes of others. We could anticipate their actions, which would make it easier to avoid conflict and know when and how we could cooperate. Some of the fundamental strategic problems of world politics arise because actors do not know one another's preferences fully. Instead, they must signal their intentions and desires to one another, which is a complicated strategic problem as we will see later.

The unobservable nature of preferences poses a large problem for us as analysts of world politics. How do we know what the actors want? Often, we solve this problem by making simple assumptions about preferences that we think are generally true. In the war example, we had the three outcomes of a peaceful settlement granting the demands of the other side, losing a war, and winning a war. I assumed that the state in question preferred winning a war to the settlement to losing the war. This simple assumption is generally true but might be wrong for some cases. During the Cold War, many people feared the possibility of a strategic nuclear war between the United States and the Soviet Union. In such a war, both sides would have used their nuclear weapons to destroy the cities of the other, killing tens of millions of people on both sides in the process. It is easy to see why many would say that any peaceful settlement would be better than "winning" a strategic nuclear war. The assumed preference order may lead to a misleading analysis in the case of nuclear war, while still being useful for the analysis of decisions for conventional wars. Another simple assumption we will about preferences on issues of political economy is what I call the "Pocketful of Preferences" argument. International economic policies, like creating barriers to imports into your country, affect the economic situation of people in your country. If you work for an auto company, your job depends on how many cars the company sells. You benefit if your government adopts policies such as tariffs or import quotas that limit how many cars made in other countries can be sold in your country. The company you work for can sell more cars at a higher price when foreign competition is blocked. The "Pocketful of Preferences" argument assumes that you prefer those policies that block imported cars over no policy. Your preferences over economic policies is based on what will make you personally wealthier. In this way, we can make simple assumptions about actors' preferences.

The difficulty in knowing actors' preferences fully has important consequences for how we analyze situations in world politics. The simple assumptions about preferences we often make characterize the strategic problems posed in an area generally rather than specifically. It may be very difficult or impossible us to know the preferences of, say, the Japanese government over trade policy fully and completely. But we can assume that their preferences are similar to those in a general model based on the "Pocketful of Preferences" argument. All countries have domestic groups who could benefit economically from trade protection. Whether they can get their government to adopt policies that protect them from foreign competition is a political question we can analyze. Our lack of full knowledge of preferences in specific situations leads us to analyze general strategic problems in world politics. Although we often care about specific situation, like "will Japan open its market for beef to U.S. producers?", we seek to understand the general strategic principles underlying that situation. The lack of knowledge of preferences in specific situations is another reason why this book focuses on the strategic problems of world politics, rather than just discussing specific, current issues.

Clarifications about Preferences

Preferences are a necessary part of an analysis because we need to have some idea what an actor wants to figure out what it will do. Understanding what other actors want is critical to understanding world politics. Ideally, the analyst would like to put him or herself in the position of the actors being analyzed. Being careful about their preferences is one part of "putting yourself in someone else's shoes." Many actors in world politics pursue ends that you and I object to or disagree with. When we try to understand their goals and preferences, we are not endorsing them. For example, a study of the origins of the Second World War in Europe requires understanding why Adolf Hitler, the dictator of Nazi Germany, did what he did. Hitler sought military domination of at least continental Europe if not the world and carried out genocide against the Jews of Europe and other groups in the countries the Nazis occupied. You cannot understand the Second World War without studying Hitler's aims and political program. Doing so does not mean that we endorse his abhorrent aims, merely that we wish to understand the political strategies he adopted in his efforts to achieve them. Hitler is an extreme case, but many times we will study actors whose preferences we find objectionable and morally reprehensible. But understanding what other actors are trying to achieve and what risks they are willing to run to accomplish them is part of any analysis of world politics.

We assume that preferences are fixed over the period of the analysis. Actors then do not change their mind about what outcomes they like and those they dislike. We assume preferences are fixed because they are unobservable. We cannot ascertain when an actor's preferences change because we only observe what they do, not their full evaluation of all the possible outcomes. Further, change in preferences invites circular reasoning. When we see an actor change what it is doing, we could ascribe that change to a change in its preferences. But we would have no way of verifying that the change had occurred. We see its change in behavior, infer that its preferences changed, and then use that change in preferences to explain the behavior we first saw. There is no independent confirmation of the change in preferences, and there is no way we could show that this argument was wrong. Consequently, we assume that preferences are fixed for the duration of an analysis to avoid this circular reasoning.

This is not to say that actors never change what they are doing. One major objective of strategic reasoning is to determine when an actor changes what it is doing. We look for the sources of that change in changes in the options it has, changes in what other actors are doing, changes in its ability to influence the outcome, or changes in its perceptions about other actors and factors outside its control. We explain changes in strategies by looking for changes in the other factors that influence which strategy an actor uses to achieve its preferences, rather than in changes in the preferences themselves.

The period over which preferences are fixed could be very short. It seems difficult to believe that an actor's preferences never change over decades, whereas it is plausible to believe that they are fixed over a shorter period of time. This time period over which preferences can be considered fixed also limits the time periods of our analysis. We do not expect to analyze what actors will do in 2030 because many things will change by then in ways that we cannot anticipate now. Changes in preferences is one of those many things we cannot anticipate.

Even with these qualifications, we will consider changes in preferences in some cases. Changes in leader in a country often lead to new policies by the country. When Ronald Reagan was elected President of the United States in 1980, he changed the foreign policy of the U.S. to end the policy of detente with the Soviet Union and confront it politically and militarily. If we think of the U.S. as an actor, the preferences of the United States changed with Reagan's election. If we think of the President as an actor, we simply have a change in who filled the role. Here we can trace the change in preference to a specific, observable event, the election of a new President. This eliminates the circular logic which we try to avoid by assuming that preferences are fixed. For cases when we can connect the change in preferences to a separate, observable event, we will allow that actor's preferences to change. These cases will be rare to help us avoid the trap of circular reasoning.

Actors make decisions without knowing the full consequences of their actions. They have to judge what could occur and assess which course of action is more likely to produce outcomes they like over those they dislike. We judge their decisions by what they knew at the time they had to choose. Often, decisions do not turn out like the choosing actor hoped they would. This does not mean that the choice was poorly made, only that it turned out poorly. A decision then is evaluated *ex ante*–before the fact–rather than *ex post*–after its consequences are clear. Return again to Adolf Hitler's decisions that led to the Second World War. One has to think that even Hitler realized in April of 1945 that the war did not turn out as he intended. To understand Hitler's decisions for war, we have to examine the conditions of the summer of 1939 when he made the fateful decisions. What was Hitler trying to achieve, how did he perceive the other actors and their intentions, and what means did he think would produce the outcomes he sought? *Ex ante* analysis of decisions is often difficult because many would like to blame one actor for bad outcomes. Many analyses of events then implicitly assume that those who made the choices that turned out poorly must have known what became clear afterwards. Uncertainty, however, is essential to decisions generally, and especially in world politics. Actors do not know whether their policies will succeed when they act. They make judgments about the likely consequences, and for us to understand those judgment, we need to place ourselves in the same situation they were in, before everything was clear.

Variations within Preferences

Full preference orders are complex, and we may not always know the actors' preferences fully. This is a main reason why we make general assumptions about preferences. These assumptions will be clearer if you understand some ways which preferences can vary. These are different elements of outcomes that actors react to in predictable ways. Thinking about these general variations in preferences makes us aware of how preferences could vary across actors. Even in situations where actors have the same overall goals, their preferences could still differ in important ways that would affect their decisions. These variations are one reason why who leads a country is important. Even if all leaders want to do what is best for their country, they may disagree in their evaluations of which policies produce those outcomes.

Many decisions involve trading one good off for another. The outcomes of these choices reflect the levels of both goods produced by the actor's choice. Even if all actors agree that both goods are, well, good–more of each is better, they can disagree how much of one that they would exchange for the other. That is, they would make different *tradeoffs* between competing goods. The classic example is how much a country spends on its military. All else equal, a country that spends more has a larger and more capable military, which increases its ability to win wars and so its security. Everyone in society agrees that more security is better. But the money spent on the military comes from the economy of the society through taxation or deficit spending. More spent on the military means less for other products of the civilian economy. This problem is called the *guns versus butter tradeoff* because one must forego civilian goods–the butter–to buy a better military–more guns. Even though everyone is society agrees that security and civilian production are both good and they would like more of both, they commonly disagree about how much butter they are willing to give up to be a little more secure. Tradeoffs are one important source of variation in preferences that we need to think about for some decisions.

Actors often judge risks of failure and success when making decisions. Each option has chances of producing good and bad outcomes. What risks of the bad ones are you willing to run to have some chance at the good ones? Even if two actors agree on the ranking of the outcomes, that is, which outcomes are good and which are bad, they can still disagree about what risks they are willing to run. War is a risky business, and decisions for war often hinge on a leader's *willingness to take risks*. As in the war example earlier in this chapter, a decision to go to war involves a choice between some negotiated settlement and war with some chance of winning and a complementary chance of losing. All people within a country probably agree that winning is better than the settlement which is better than losing. They can disagree, however, about how big a chance of winning they need before they are willing to choose war over the certain outcome of a negotiated settlement. The Japanese decision to go to war with the United States in 1941 is an extreme example of the willingness to take risks. Diplomatic tension between the U.S. and Japan built up as a consequence of the Japanese war in China and Japanese expansion in East Asia in the late 1930s. Franklin Delano Roosevelt's administration increased the pressure on the Japanese government to end their military involvement in China, culminating in an embargo on oil and steel exports to Japan. In those days, the U.S. was one of the leading oil producers in the world. Japanese leaders had to either end their war in China or launch a wider war to secure new oil supplies in the Dutch East Indies, which are now Indonesia. An invasion of the Dutch East Indies would almost certainly mean war with the United States and Great Britain, which had colonies in Malaya, Burma, and India with its major Asian naval base at Singapore. Japan's choice reduced to ending the war in China in disgrace or war with the U.S. and Britain. Japanese leaders were not optimistic about their chance of winning that war. They recognized the great industrial strength of the U.S. and that they could not win a long war. But they thought they might be able to stage a series of remarkable victories that would convince the U.S. that ending Japanese domination in East Asia would be so costly that the U.S. would agree to what the Japanese called the East Asia Co-Prosperity Sphere, a Japanese empire by any other name. Japanese leaders thought their chances of winning were only about ten percent. Despite their pessimism about their chances of winning, they still chose war because they saw the benefits of victory as so large and the consequences of defeat small compared to the humiliation that the U.S. was offering in place of war. The willingness to take risks comes from the differences between winning and losing compared to the certainty of a settlement in between the two. When an actor sees the benefits of winning as large and the costs of defeat as small, it is willing to fight even when it is unlikely to win. Fortunately, few actors see the consequences of winning and losing this way even though they all prefer winning to a settlement to losing.

[Map of East Asia in 1941]

Many decisions are choices over time. Do you give up something today to get more tomorrow? You are going to college rather than working a regular job now at least partially in the hope that you will earn more after you earn your degree. You are giving up the income you would earn from working now so that you will make more in the future. This is a choice over time, and I think it is a wise one. Economic decisions about investment are choices over time, foregoing more consumption today to have more later. An actor's *discount factor* captures its preference over time. Its discount factor represents how much it reduces future value compared to value now. You can think about a discount factor numerically as a fraction between 0 and 1 which reduces future values by being multiplied by them. A discount factor close to 1, say .95, means that future outcomes are almost as important as outcomes today. A discount factor close to 0, say .2, means that the future plays little or no role in your decisions, as is the case for a small child. Confusingly, the latter is called a high discount factor because it reduces the value of the future greatly. Again, we may all agree that more today is good as is more tomorrow, but we can disagree about how much we would forego today to get some more tomorrow.

An actor's discount factor can vary with its situation. Democratic politicians care a lot about elections because they know they can be voted out of office. The approach of elections can change the discount factor of the leader of a democracy because voters cannot react to what happens after the election. Leaders of democracies may be willing to adopt policies that produce good results in the short run before the election at the cost of bad results afterwards. This change in how they view different policies can be represented by a change in their discount factor.

These variations in preferences remind us that people in the same situation can view the options they have differently. These differences are one reason why decisions about state policy are controversial among the citizens of that state. Even though they all would like their state to have successful policies, they disagree about what is success and how to achieve it. These differences also explain why the leadership of a state matters for its foreign policy. A new leader may evaluate the policy choices differently from his or her predecessor.

Actors' Knowledge of the Preferences of Other Actors

Actors, like us as analysts, do not know the preferences of others fully. If they did, it would easier for them to anticipate what one another would do in advance. Instead, they have to make judgments about the choices others will make and what exactly they are trying to accomplish. This is why we study perceptions in a later chapter, what one actor thinks about what another will do, what the latter is trying to achieve, and what capabilities it has to accomplish those ends. For now, we focus on a simple and clever way to think about the problem of uncertainty about the preferences of other actors.

We assume that actors know their own preferences over outcomes, although they may be unclear about their preferences over strategies, what they will do. Knowing which action will produce the best range of outcomes is a difficult problem. Uncertainty about the others' preferences is part of the problem of determining what course of action is best for you. Actors are not totally in the dark about each other's preferences. They have some idea what each other would like to achieve, but they do not know the full preference order. They cannot fully anticipate what risks one another will take or what tradeoffs they will accept.

We represent this uncertainty about preferences by assuming that each actor is one of several *types*. Its type gives its preferences fully. It knows what type it is, so it knows its own preferences. Other actors only know the full set of types, so they know all the possible sets of preferences it could hold. But they do not know which type the actor in question is. Instead, they have to make judgments about which preferences it has, which type it is. Commonly, we will assume that each player is one of two types to keep our analysis simple.

An example from the logic of threats could make the idea of types clearer. An actor's response to a threat depends heavily on whether it thinks the threatening actor will carry out its threat or not. In the game tree in the chapter on the logic of threats, the threatening actor could carry out the threat or back down. The target's decision of whether to give in or defy the threat depending greatly on whether the threatener would carry it out. The threatener's decision relied in part on how unpleasant carrying out its threat would be relative to the consequences of backing down instead. Its preferences, how it ranks the two outcomes of carrying out the threat and backing down, determine its decision whether to carry out the threat. We can think of two types of threatener, one which prefers carrying out the threat and will do so and another which would rather back down. The target does not know which type of threatener, so it is uncertain about whether the threatener will carry out the threat. Is it the type that is willing to carry the threat or the other type which will back down if forced to choose? If the target knew the preferences of the threatener, if it knew its type, its choice would be easy. But actors generally do not know each other's preferences, and so they must make judgments about what others will do.

We will return to this idea in the chapter on perceptions. For now, we can think of perceptions as beliefs over the types of another player. Is the other actor more likely to be one type than another? Like in the example of a threat, does the target believe that the threatener is the type that will carry out its threat or the other type that will back down? Perceptions influence actions by shaping what each actor thinks others will do.

Think It Through

What to do about Darfur is a difficult issue. There are positions for and against greater involvement in Darfur to stop the killing. Here are some questions to think and discuss about the different policy options for the situation:

1. How would the government of Sudan respond to each policy? Pressure, whether through diplomacy, economic sanctions or military action, could make the government of Sudan willing to restrain the Janjaweed or induce it to move away from the U.S. and its allies. If the latter happens, the U.S. has less influence over Sudan on the Darfur issue and other issues in the future. Even if you think some form of pressure could induce a change in policy by Sudan, you need to consider the possibility that it may have the opposite effect.

2. How might the rebel groups in Darfur respond to each policy? There have been negotiations to end the fighting in Darfur. Some but not all rebel groups have agreed to settlements with the government. Those settlements have failed to hold, and fighting has renewed afterwards. Pressing the government of Sudan to settle with the rebels might produce a final settlement, or it might encourage the rebels to continue fighting in the hope of getting an even better deal with the support of the U.S. and its allies.

3. How might each policy influence Sudan's relations with its neighbors? Chad, its neighbor to the west, contains refugee camps and has rebel groups of its own. Sudan has claimed that rebels use bases in Chad to launch attacks into Darfur and has attacked across the border at times. Will a policy make the local international situation better by ending the fighting or worse by causing the fighting to spread across borders?

4. How will each policy influence Sudan's relations with the rest of the world? Might it turn to states like China that do not make its conduct in Darfur an important issue? Sudan does export some oil, and some countries are accused of turning a blind eye to Sudan's conduct in Darfur to gain access to that oil. Most Arab countries support Sudan. How might each policy affect relations with them?

5. How might each policy affect relations among the great powers? Some think we should pressure China over Darfur because they believe China might have some leverage to get Sudan to stop the killing. But such a policy could alienate China and hurt relations with it on other issues. Is the UN Security Council an appropriate venue for pursuing action on Darfur? How about using the International Criminal Court? What long-run consequences for these institutions might result from using them to address the Darfur issue?

How to Analyze It

Thinking about the preferences of an actor requires careful thought and organization. It is easy to simply say it wants something to happen without thinking about all the possible consequences. The set of consequences may be large or unclear, leading us to ignore some possibilities. The following steps may help you analyze the preferences of an actor.

1. What is the full set of actions available to the actor? Normally, this set is large if you include all the possible variations of a policy. It is often helpful to keep the set manageable by only the major choices. For example, in Darfur, you might describe the actions as Do Nothing, Place Economic Sanctions on Sudan, Send Peacekeepers, and Intervene with Military Forces.

If you write down a game tree of the situation, it has to specify the choices available to each actor at each choice point. Remember that the actions are exhaustive and mutually exclusive; the actor will choose one and only one action.

2. What are the factors outside the control of the actor that produces the final outcome along with its chosen action? These could be the choices of other actors in a game tree, or they could be elements outside the control of any actor, such as the weather. These are the states of the world for the actor's decision. The states are also exhaustive and mutually exclusive; one and only one will happen.

3. What outcome does each combination of action and state produce? Thinking about the possible outcomes may lead you to realize that you have omitted an action or state because there are plausible outcomes that do not result from your sets of actions and states. The outcomes include all the things that happen from that combination of action and state. The political and economic results of a policy, for example, are both part of the same outcome. Again, the outcomes are exhaustive and mutually exclusive; one and only one happens. Different actions and states can produce the same outcome.

4. How does the actor rank the outcomes? Which outcome does it see as best and which as worst? Compare them all to get a complete ranking. Are there outcomes which are about the same in the eyes of the actor?

5. Are you unsure about how the actor ranks some of these outcomes? Consider variations in the preference order. Are there elements of risk, costs, tradeoffs or preferences over time which might be different for the actor than you think they are? These are obvious sources of variation in preferences and types of an actor. End your analysis by considering how the

Chapter Summary

Preferences matter because actors are uncertain about the consequences of their decisions. Outcomes result from actors' choices and states of the world. An actor's preferences rank all the possible outcomes from first to worst allowing for ties. It chooses the action which produces the best overall prospect of producing the outcomes it prefers over those it dislikes. Preferences are unobservable, so we commonly make simple assumptions about them. We also assume preferences are fixed over the period of an analysis to avoid circular reasoning. Actors' preferences often vary over tradeoffs between different goods, willingness to take risks, and time. We represent actors' uncertainty about each other preferences by assuming an actor is one type from a known set. Its type gives it complete preference order.

Review Questions

1. Outcomes, states of the world, and actions are all mutually exclusive and exhaustive. Explain what these two conditions mean for how many outcomes and states occur and actions can be chosen.

2. Preferences over outcomes must be complete and transitive. Explain what each means.

3. Explain the difference between preferences over outcomes and preferences over strategies. Which of the two is fundamental?

4. What does it mean to say that decisions are judged *ex ante* rather than *ex post*?

5. Give three types of common variation in preferences across actors. Explain each briefly.

6. We will often represent actors' uncertainty about one another's preferences using types. What does an actor know about the type of another, and hence its preferences, when we use this representation?

Chapter 5
The Logic of Threats and the Problem of Credibility

The Islamic Republic of Iran has been developing the capability to enrich uranium for several years now. Other countries, particularly the United States, have been concerned about the Iranian nuclear program. Although Iran claims that its program is solely to produce nuclear fuel for reactors to generate power, enriching uranium is also a key step in building nuclear weapons. Uranium normally contains a preponderance of the main isotope, U-238, which is stable. Enrichment increases the concentration of the other main isotope of uranium, U-235, which is unstable. Some enrichment produces a high enough concentration of U-235 to support an ongoing chain reaction, which can be controlled and used in a nuclear reactors to generate heat used to produce electricity. Continue the enrichment process, and the concentration of U-235 can be raised to the point where there is enough U-235 to support an explosive chain reaction, which is the basis of one form of nuclear bomb. Because a large-scale and successful nuclear enrichment program is a major step toward building a nuclear bomb, other countries are concerned that Iran's enrichment program is for that purpose rather than creating fuel for civilian nuclear power reactors. Iran is a member of the Non-Proliferation Treaty (NPT) and so has pledged not to develop nuclear weapons.

Other countries have attempted to convince Iran to stop its enrichment program. The Security Council of the United Nations has threatened Iran with economic sanctions if it does not bring its enrichment program under the supervision of the International Atomic Energy Agency (IAEA). This agency monitors the nuclear power programs of those countries without nuclear weapons to ensure that nuclear materials are not diverted to weapons programs. The efforts of the IAEA to restrain the Iranian nuclear program have not satisfied all countries. The United States, in particular, has discussed publicly a wide range of measures to stop the Iranian program before it can build a nuclear bomb. Most notably, a wide range of U.S. politicians have refused to "take the military option off the table," political code for an implicit threat to attack and destroy Iranian nuclear facilities. U.S. warplanes could be used to bomb the enrichment facilities if all of them can be located with confidence. These threats to use military force by the U.S. government have never been direct, but many observers are deeply concerned that military strikes are both being planned and likely to occur. Will these threats convince Iran to abandon nuclear enrichment?

The Logic of Threats

Threats of many different forms are a common tool that actors use to influence one another. The *game tree* in Figure 1 shows the strategic logic of a threat. Game trees like this provide an easy way to write down a strategic interaction, such as a threat in this case. They strip down the strategic interaction to its essential elements. This simplification allows us to understand how threats work in general, and we can apply that understanding to specific situations like the Iranian nuclear program standoff. A game tree specifies the actors, often called players (it is called a game after all). Here there are two actors, colorfully named A and B. The situation concerns A considering making a threat to B. The first box on the left of the tree denotes A's decision whether or not to threaten B. Each of the two arrows out of the corners of the box represent one of the choices that A has. A could make a threat to B, the top arrow, or it could choose not to make a threat, the bottom arrow. This choice has different consequences for A. If it chooses not to threaten B, we will consider the game over and the situation unchanged. In the Iranian nuclear case, this represents no threat being made and Iran allowed to progress with its enrichment program unhindered. The large bold writing after that arrow shows that the game has ended with the outcome of "No Threat." If A threatens B, then B has a move to decide how to respond. This second choice point is labeled B to show that it is B's choice. If B gets to make a move, it knows about A's threat. A game specifies who the players are, what choices they have, the sequence of those choices, the outcomes of those choices, what the players know when they have to make a choice, and how they evaluate the outcomes.

Figure 1
Game Tree of a Threat

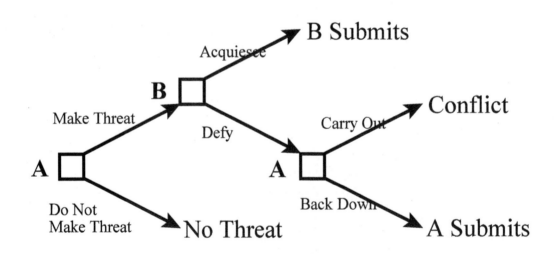

The game in Figure 1 gives the essential elements of a threat. First, A decides whether to threaten B. If it does, its threat is accompanied by some demand that B do as A wants. If A chooses not to make a threat, the situation is over and nothing changes, which is called the "No Threat" outcome in the game. B must respond if A makes a threat. It could either do as A demands, the "Acquiesce" choice in the figure, or it could "Defy" A. If B acquiesces, the game ends with A receiving its demand and the threat is not carried out, the outcome labeled "B

Submits". If B defies A and does not do what A wants, A has a final decision whether to carry out its threat or not. If it does, the outcome is "Conflict" between A and B. If A decides instead not to carry out the threat, the "Back Down" choice, the "A Submits" outcome results. At each choice point, the moving actor knows all previous choices in the game. Because A makes the threat to B, we will often refer to A as the *initiator* of the threat and B as the *target*.

Actors make a wide range of threats in world politics on every possible issue. The strongest type of threat seen is an *ultimatum*, a demand by one state that it will go to war if another state does not do as it wishes. The Iraq War began with an ultimatum from President Bush of the United States to President Saddam Hussein of Iraq that he and his sons had 48 hours to quit their positions in government of Iraq and leave the country for exile. They did not, and so U.S. and British military forces invaded Iraq. Because ultimatums force the target to decide between giving what the threatening state wants and war, they are the strongest threats in world politics. They are also rarely seen because they force a choice where war is likely. Most threats to use military force are not so obvious. The leader of a state may say that the consequences could be unpredictable or grave if the other side does not do as he or she wishes. This sort of threat does not state what those unpredictable or grave consequences will be, leaving that unsaid. Threats are also used on political economy issues. Sometimes a state will threaten another with trade sanctions to induce the target of the threat to change a policy. The demand could be to remove a policy which the threatening state believes is a barrier to trade. These *retaliatory trade sanctions* are used to police agreements to lower trade barriers. The demand could be a policy outside trade. The United States, for example, restricted trade with Myanmar to try to get its military government to step down from power and hold democratic elections to select a new government, a threat that seems to be working. These threats to restrict trade are called *economic sanctions*.

A game requires us to specify the players' preferences over the outcomes. The nature of a threat allows us to make some assumptions about how the players rank the four outcomes. Figure 2 shows B's preferences over the four possible outcomes of the threat game. B prefers not doing what A's wants it to do. After all, A is considering threatening B to get it to change one of its policies. The two best outcomes for B are those where it does not have to do what A wants, No Threat and A Submits. The "A Submits" outcome may be better for B because A's ability to threaten B and other states in the future may be reduced by the failure of this threat, and the figure shows it this way. Having A carry out its threat should be the worst outcome for B. If not, perhaps A needs to find a more effective threat. We will find some specific situations where what A threatens to do to B is not bad enough to get B to do as A wants, but for this generalization of a threat, we will assume for now that the Conflict outcome is the worst outcome for B. Giving A what it wants is better than suffering its threat but worse than not having to do that. The B Submits outcome then is better than Conflict for B but worse than either No Threat or A Submits. Again, these preferences assume that B does not want to do what A wants and that A's threat is effective in the sense that B dislikes it enough that it would rather give A what

Figure 2
B's Preferences in Threat Game

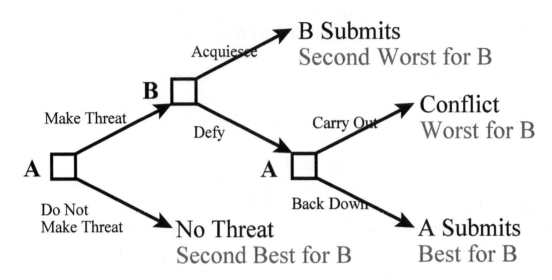

it wants than suffer the threat being carried out. There are times when these assumptions are not true for certain threats, but for now we will assume they are true.

What should B do in response to A's threat? It depends on whether A will carry out its threat if B defies it. If A will carry out its threat–Carry Out, then B prefers to grant A's demand–Acquiesce–because the B Submits outcome is not as bad as the Conflict outcome is for B. If A will not carry out its threat–Back Down, then B would rather not do as A wants–Defy–because the A Submits outcome is better for B than the B Submits outcome. The fact that B's move, whether it does as A wants, depends on A's possible move, whether A carries out its threat, shows the principle of strategic interaction explained in Chapter 2. B's choice depends on what A will do, and so these decisions have to be considered together. To answer the question of whether A will carry out its threat, we need to know A's preferences.

Figure 3 shows what we can conclude about A's preferences from the general situation of a threat. A wants B to fulfill its demands, so B Submits is the best outcome for A. Its threat succeeds in getting B to do as A wishes and A does not have to carry out its threat. The worst outcome arises if B defies A and forces A to choose between carrying out its threat and backing down from it. The situation alone does not allow us to assume that A is willing to carry out its threat. Actors sometimes make threats which they do not carry out later when they are called on them. Others, both B as the target of the threat and us as observers, cannot tell in advance whether A will carry out its threat. This uncertainty lies at the heart of the strategic logic of threats.

Figure 3
A's Preferences in Threat Game

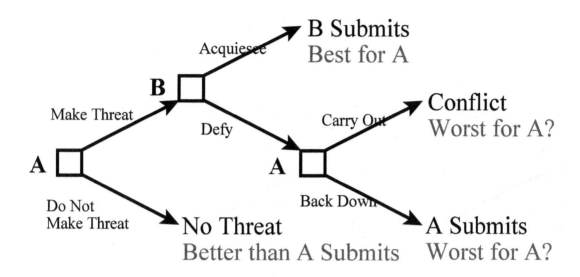

Credibility and Effectiveness of Threats

B does not know whether A will carry out its threat, and so it must judge whether A will do so when it respond to A's threat. How should B's respond to A's threat? If B Acquiesces, it gets the B Submits outcome for sure. If it Defies A, A will either carry out its threat or not, producing either the best or the worst outcome for B. In comparing these two courses of action, B has to judge how likely it is that A will carry out its threat. If A will carry out its threat, B prefers acquiescing to A, as shown in Figure 4. Giving A what it wants is not nice for B, but it is better than having A carry out its threat.

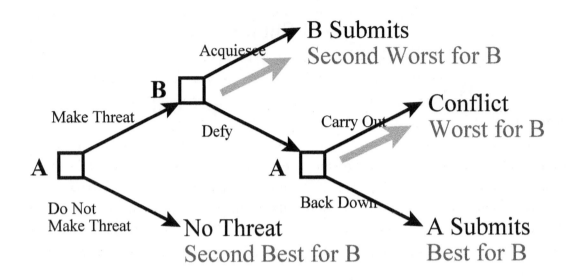

Figure 4
B's Response if A Will Carry Out Threat

If A will not carry out its threat, B would prefer to defy A, as shown in Figure 5. Why do what A wants when the threat is empty?

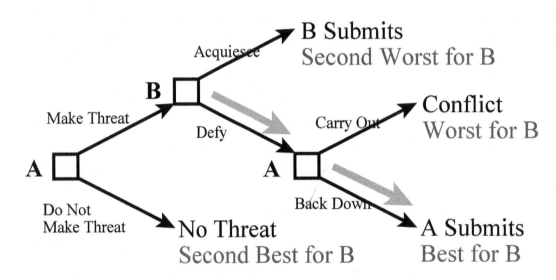

Figure 5
B's Response if A Will Back Down from its Threat

B's problem is that it does not know what A will do. If it did, B's choice would be straightforward. Instead, B has to judge how likely it is that A will carry out its threat when deciding whether to defy A.

The *credibility* of a threat is how likely the threatener is to carry it out. Credibility is measured in degrees because it is rarely the case that others know that the actor making the threat will or will not carry it out. B combines its judgment of the credibility of A's threat with how attractive or unattractive each of these three outcomes are to determine how it should respond. Perhaps suffering the threat is not much worse than doing what A wants. This small difference would incline B towards defying A, particularly if the consequences of A backing down were very attractive to B. A's threat is *effective* when B is sufficiently convinced of the credibility of the threat that it does as A wants. Credibility helps to produce an effective threat, but they are not the same.

The example of trade sanctions may help to clarify the difference between credibility and efficacy of threats. Trade sanctions are a threat to restrict another country's imports if the latter does not change a policy that makes the imports of the former uncompetitive in the market of the latter. The policy in question could be a tariff–a tax placed on those imports that makes imports more expensive–or a quota that restricts how many imports may be sold in a country. The threat to block the imports of the country with the barrier to trade into the former country is credible when the latter believes the former impose that retaliatory sanction. Whether the threat is effective depends on its credibility and whether the former country fears the loss of its trade more than the consequences of allowing free access to its market. It could believe that the threatening state will put the retaliatory sanction in effect but still be unwilling to lower its own barrier to trade. That state values its barrier to trade more than the exports it will lose when the other state carries out its threat. This threat is credible but ineffective.

Threats could also be effective even if they are not very credible. Nuclear weapons are immensely destructive. A single nuclear weapon detonated in a city would devastate it and kill tens or hundreds of thousands of people. Historically, threats to use nuclear weapons have only been made over critical issues such as national survival because of the great destructiveness of these weapons. The United States and Soviet Union, for example, both had second-strike policies of nuclear retaliation. Both promised to attack the other's cities with their strategic nuclear forces–missiles and bombers–if the other attacked them with its nuclear weapons. States with nuclear weapons occasionally make veiled nuclear threats over issues less important than state survival, such as to protect a smaller state allied to it. The target of such a threat might believe that the threat was unlikely to be carried out but still do as the nuclear power demanded. The consequences of the threat would be so great that the target of the threat could not take the chance that it might be carried out. This threat is effective even though it is not very credible.

In general though, higher credibility makes a threat more effective, and so actors try to make their threats credible. We will cover some ways states try to make their threats credible later in this chapter. For now, credibility hinges on whether the actor making the threat wants to carry it out. It will carry out the threat if doing so and producing a conflict between itself and its target is better for it than the consequences of backing down from its threat. Credibility in the eyes of the target matter the most because it influences whether it does as the threatener wants.

Backing Down

Backing down from a threat can have consequences for the actor that made the threat in the first place. It might be forced to make concessions to the target of its threat. Actors other than its target might doubt the credibility of its threats in the future. A state leader might have to answer to his or her supporters who are not happy that the leader made threats that proved to be empty. In threats generally, the actor considering making a threat would be better off not making a threat than making one and then backing down. Even if it does not have to make other concessions to its target, so the issue in question remains as it was before the threat was made, the actor who backed down from a threat is believed to be worse off. Figure 3 shows this assumption by listing the No Threat outcome as better for A than the A Submits outcome.

The consequences of backing down though do not necessarily stop actors from making threats. An actor thinking about making a threat never has a choice between backing down from a threat or not making one in the first place. It has two different choices: one, choosing whether to make a threat in the hope that the target will do as the actor wishes, and two, choosing whether to carry out the threat if the target does not do as it wishes. The actor does not face the second question if the threat proves effective. Once a threat has been made, the actor making it no longer has the option of returning to the No Threat outcome. If it is costly to back down from a threat, actors must think carefully before they make threats.

When to Make a Threat

The decision to make a threat, like the target's response to it, depends on its effectiveness and credibility. The best outcome for A in Figure 3 occurs when B acquiesces and does as A wants. An effective threat does that. Credibility increases the effectiveness of a threat all else equal. The more credible B finds A's threat, the more likely that B will acquiesce. A threat with low credibility is unlikely to induce B to do as A wants, unless A asks for little or threatens to do great damage to B. B's defiance then puts A in the difficult position of choosing between carrying out its threat and backing down. Even if A wants to carry out the threat, it is still better off if B acquiesces, and so A cares about the credibility of its threat when it makes it. The best threats are those that do not have to be carried out because they are effective in getting the target to do what the threatener wants.

The threatener then has to judge how credible the target finds a threat when considering whether to make a threat. Much like the target's problem of judging whether the threatener will carry out the threat, the threatener weighs how likely the target is to do as it wishes. The threatener chooses between the sure thing of No Threat and the chance that the target will Acquiesce or Defy it. In Figure 3, A prefers the B Submits outcome to No Threat but may prefer No Threat to either of Conflict or A Submits. If B is very likely to Acquiesce because it believes the threat is credible, then making a threat will be very attractive to A even if it has no intention of carrying out that threat. Figure 6 shows this comparison along with A's preferences. It does not matter whether A will carry out its threat because it does not have to make that decision if B acquiesces. Figure 6 shows this with question marks about A's final move. A's judgment about whether B will find its threat credible strongly affects whether A even makes a threat.

Figure 6
A Makes a Threat when It Believes that B will Acquiesce

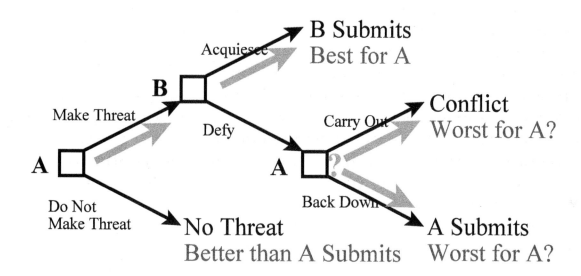

In some unusual cases, A may prefer carrying out the threat to the current situation. This corresponds to the case in Figure 3 where A prefers the Conflict outcome to the No Threat outcome. Figure 7 shows this situation including A's preferences. A will carry out its threat and prefers doing so to not making a threat. The question mark about how B will respond to A's threat indicates that B's response does not matter if A prefers Conflict to No threat. If B acquiesces, A gets its best outcome. If B defies A, A carries out its threat and gets the Conflict outcome which is still better than the No Threat outcome in its eyes. When the Bush Administration made the ultimatum to Saddam Hussein to leave Iraq and go into exile, it clearly preferred war to doing nothing at that time. The threat was credible because most observers judged that President Bush would go to war if Saddam Hussein did not leave power in Iraq. Even if Saddam Hussein did not view Bush's threat as credible or effective, Bush still wanted to make the threat. Defiance would lead to carrying out the threat by invading Iraq, which Bush saw as preferable to the situation before the threat was made. I leave it to history to judge whether President Bush's confidence was wise. When the threatener prefers the Conflict outcome to No Threat, it is always willing to make a threat. It gets an outcome it sees as better than doing nothing, no matter how the target responds.

Figure 7
A Makes a Threat if It Prefers Conflict to No Threat

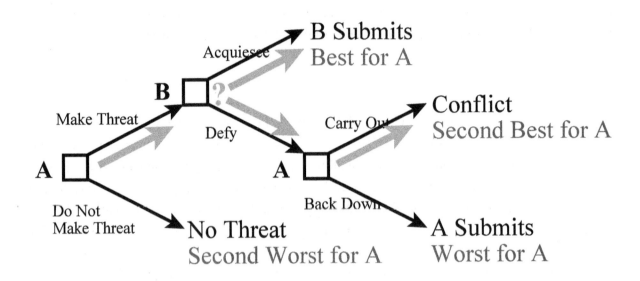

Actors make threats when they believe those threats are effective or are willing to carry them out in any case. They do not make ineffective threats that they are unwilling to carry out. The threats that are actually made then are a selection of all the threats that could have been made. Actors choose threats that are more credible and more effective or where they are willing to carry them out regardless of what the target does. Credible threats are more likely to be made because they are more effective. An example may clarify what sorts of threats are not made. Many in the United States are concerned about the growing concentration of power in the hands of the President of Russia and the restrictions placed on political opposition and the press to criticize the Russian government. The United States could tell Russia that it will launch a nuclear war against Russia if its President does not change their policies and allow opposition parties and the press to operate freely. This is not going to happen, no matter how concerned the U.S. government is about these political developments in Russia. Russia, like the United States, has thousands of nuclear warheads and the ability to retaliate with those weapons against any attack. This hypothetical threat is incredible; no one would believe that any government of the United States would carry it out. Because the threat lacks even a shred of credibility, it will be ineffective. The U.S. can anticipate this, and so will not make the threat to begin with. Ineffective and incredible threats are not made in world politics.

This *selection effect* is very important for understanding threats in world politics. One cannot judge the strategic dynamics of world politics by studying only the threats and events that occur. One must also think about the things that did not happen. You may have read the famous story, "The Hound of the Baskervilles," where Sherlock Holmes deduces what happened because the dog in question did not bark when it should have. When we study world politics, we also must think about the "dogs that did not bark" to understand what happens. Failure to make a threat does not indicate that an actor does not care about the outcome of the issue in question. Instead, it may lack the means to make an effective threat and so remains silent. We will think about selection effects at many different times in this book and try to deduce what the absence of information tells us about what is happening and what policies work in world politics.

Ways to Increase the Effectiveness of a Threat

Actors make threats in the hope that the threat will convince the target to do as the threatening actor wishes. This is true even when the threatener is willing to carry out the threat. The actor making a threat can try to make its threat more effective in two general ways. First, it can try to increase the credibility of its threat. If it can persuade the target actor that it will carry out its threat, then the latter will probably do as it wishes. Second, it can try to manipulate the possible consequences of the situation to induce the target to do as it wishes. It can make doing as it wishes to be more attractive to the target or the consequences of defying it to be worse. Either of these shifts might be enough to get the target to do what the threatener wants.

Increase Credibility

Credibility is central to effective threats. Actors then understandably try to increase the credibility of their threats. Recall that credibility is the target's belief that the threatener will carry out its threat. The threatener would then choose between creating a conflict by carrying out the threat and backing down from that threat. If the threatener can take actions that help to convince the target that carrying out the threat will be better for itself than backing down, those actions will increase the credibility of the threat.

If the target believes that the threatener wants to carry out the threat, that fact alone should make the threat credible. As we just discussed above, some actors make threats that they are happy to carry out because conflict is a desirable outcome for themselves. If an actor making a threat could persuade the target that this is the case, the target will do as the threatening actor wants.

This process of convincing the target that it wants to carry out a threat is trickier than it seems. The threatening actor could just tell the target that it will carry out its threat. Imagine there were magic words that would convince the target that the threatener means business and will carry out the threat if defied. If the target always believed such statements, it would be convinced of the credibility of the threat and so give the threatening actor what it wants. But then any actor, even one unwilling to carry out the threat would want to make that same speech. Actors would always use the magic words, which would remove their magic effect of always persuading the target that the threatener would carry the threat precisely because even those who have no intent to carry out their threat would use the magic words. Persuasion poses a paradox of credibility; it cannot be always effective if it can work at all.

This is not to say that actors in world politics do not try to persuade others that they will carry out their threats. They often try to persuade others that their threats are credible and should not be ignored. The point is just that such persuasion is difficult. We do not have the full set of tools that will allow us to analyze persuasion and credibility carefully yet. We return to the question of how actors might be persuade others that their threats are credible later in the chapter on perceptions when we introduce the tools we need to analyze this difficult question carefully. For now, we will just note that actors making threats often try to persuade their targets of their intention to carry out those threats if pushed to do so.

As this discussion is abstract, an example of persuasion may help you see the issue. Return to the threat that President Bush made to Saddam Hussein and his sons right before the Iraq War. As is obvious now, President Bush did carry out his threat to invade Iraq and overthrow Saddam Hussein when Hussein and his sons did not leave Iraq for exile. Even before the final ultimatum was made, President Bush took a wide range of actions to try and persuade Saddam Hussein that he would carry out his threat to invade Iraq if he did not get what he wanted. The United States did not have a large number of troops in the area, so President Bush ordered a buildup of military forces in the Persian Gulf region, primarily in Kuwait. He and other members of the Bush Administration also made many speeches on the threat posed by Iraq and why that threat needed to be addressed. He tried to enlist the support of other countries in the effort to bring Iraq around to do as he wanted. All of these acts were in part efforts to persuade Saddam Hussein of President Bush's intent to carry out his threat if necessary, that his threats were credible, and so induce Saddam to do as he wanted.

One reason why these efforts to persuade Saddam Hussein failed to make President Bush's threats effective is that Saddam Hussein may also have preferred conflict to doing what President Bush wanted. War may have been a better option for him than the exile offered by President Bush. In such cases, even credible threats will be ineffective in that the target will not do as the threatener demands.

The threatener can also increase the credibility of its threat if it can manipulate the consequences of carrying out that threat and backing down. If it can make carrying out the threat better for itself or backing down worse for itself, others including the target are more likely to conclude that it will carry out its threat if defied. Strategies that do so are called *commitment devices* because they commit the threatener to carry out its threat.

Here again the crisis before the Iraq War has some examples of commitment devices. The movement of troops by the U.S. into the Persian Gulf area raised the chance that it would win a war, making carrying out the threat more attractive for the U.S. Think about the chance of the U.S. winning a war if it simply declared war on Iraq before it built up its forces in the region to what it did. In the former case, it would take months to move U.S. to the Persian Gulf and build up the forces and supplies to launch an attack on Iraq. Some U.S. forces might have to fight very quickly if Iraq seized the initiative to attack U.S. bases and allies in the early before the buildup was complete. The parallel is the Second World War where U.S. ground troops did not begin offensive operations on the Japanese until August of 1942–eight months after Pearl Harbor–and the Germans until November of 1942–eleven months after Pearl Harbor–because it took time to prepare and move them to attack Japanese and German held territory. When states move their military forces during a crisis toward the disputed territory in preparation for war, those moves operate as a commitment device because they make it more likely that the side in question would win a war and so makes them more willing to carry out their threat to go to war. Similarly, states sometimes mobilize their reserves during a crisis to make the threats more credible by preparing for war. Many armies have soldiers who have a commitment to fight in the event of a war but are not in the military full time. In Israel, all Jewish adults have an obligation to serve in the military for three years for men and two for women, although there are some exemptions. After that, they become members of the reserves. Israel calls these reservists back into the army if they need them to fight a war, such as during the 1967 Six-Day War or the 1973 October War. Soldiers in the United States commonly have a reserve obligation after they leave the military and return to civilian life. The U.S. government can also call on the National Guard, which is organized by the states, for military service as it has during the Iraq War. Reserves allow a state to have a much larger army during wartime than it does during peacetime. Military mobilization through the calling up of these reserves into the active ranks then is a commitment device because it makes going to war more attractive by increasing the chance that a side will win.

Other commitment devices work by making backing down less attractive. During the run-up to the Iraq War, many members of the Bush Administration gave public speeches about the threat Iraq posed. President Bush made a speech before the United Nations on September 12, 2002 about the need to address Iraq's weapons of mass destruction and links to Al Qaeda. He also obtained a resolution of Congress authorizing him to use force if necessary in October of 2002. Later in the crisis, Secretary of State Colin Powell outlined the case against Iraq in another speech before the United Nations in February 2003. Additionally, President Bush and other members of his administration made other public speeches and news interviews about the threat they thought Iraq posed during the crisis. Why did they talk publicly? If they simply wanted to tell the leaders of other states of the threat posed by Iraq, they could have met with them privately. Leaders of countries and their representatives meet and discuss issues privately often. But doing so excludes others from that conversation, meaning they do not know what was said. Indeed, leaders discuss sensitive matters privately because they do not want others to know what they are saying. Talking publicly communicates what the speaker is saying to everyone. The potential listeners include the leader of the target of the threat, leaders of other states, interested public actors like journalists and opposition politicians, citizens of the speaker's state, and even citizens of other states. Speaking publicly means all of these people also hear the same speech, although they may understand and interpret it differently. Public threats raise the possibility that actors other than the target of the threat can also respond afterwards. How would Americans respond if President Bush had announced that he had changed his mind and no longer saw Saddam Hussein as a threat after months of speeches stressing the threat he posed? Would they believe anything he said afterwards? Similarly, leaders of other countries may respond later if a leader backs down from threats he has made. Public speeches then could raise the cost of backing down and so commit a leader to carry out a threat.

Commitment devices increase the credibility of a threat by making carrying out the threat more attractive than backing down. These acts are taken publicly because the threatener wants others to see that it is committed to carrying out its threat.

Change Consequences for Target

An actor making a threat could also attempt to get its target to comply by altering the consequences for the target. It could offer rewards to the target if it complies with its demands. These rewards would raise the value of the B Submits outcome in the Threat Game, making B more likely to choose to do as A wants. The threatener could also design the threat to make its consequences worse for the target. Punishment lowers the value of the Conflict outcome to B, making it more likely to do as A wants to avoid that outcome. The threatener could also stress that it will impose its conditions on B if it carries out its threat after B defies it. This change could induce B to comply because A will be able to get what it wants even if it has to carry out the threat.

Rewards make compliance more attractive to the target by giving it something of value back for its compliance. During the Cuban Missile Crisis in October of 1962, President Kennedy of the United States demanded that the Soviet Union remove its medium and intermediate range missiles from Cuba. These missiles were capable of carrying nuclear weapons and had the range to hit most major U.S. cities. The specific threat of what the U.S. would do if the missiles were not removed was left unclear, but President Kennedy considered options such as an air strike on the missiles to destroy them. He did declare and implement a blockade of Cuba that sought to restrict further weapons from reaching Cuba. The crisis was resolved when Premier Khrushchev agreed to remove the missiles from Cuba. In return, President Kennedy made a public pledge not to invade Cuba and a secret agreement to remove U.S. nuclear-armed missiles based in Turkey from where they could attack cities in the Soviet Union. Both of these additional concessions were rewards to Khrushchev that allowed him to claim something back in the crisis and so make it easier for him to agree to remove the missiles from Cuba. The U.S. missiles in Turkey paralleled the Soviet missiles in Cuba. Cuba was led by Fidel Castro, who aligned his country with the Soviet Union after the revolution that brought him to power. The U.S. had already tried once to overthrow Cuba when it sponsored an invasion of Cuba by Cuban exiles in April 1961. The Bay of Pigs invasion was a total failure; indeed, the term is now used to describe any disastrous foreign policy adventure. But it did make Castro very concerned that the U.S. would invade again, possibly with U.S. troops, to overthrow his regime. He pressed Khrushchev to defend Cuba in one form or another. The nuclear missiles would have defended against this possibility through the threat that they could be launched against the United States if it invaded Cuba. Kennedy's public pledge not to invade Cuba then provided some small reassurance to Castro that he would not be overthrown by an invasion and so led him to reduce the pressure he placed on Khrushchev to defend him from that threat. These rewards made the difficult job of removing the missiles from Cuba after a public crisis easier for Premier Khrushchev.

Punishment makes threats more effective by making their consequences more unpleasant for the target. States in trade disputes often threaten to block imports from the other country. Tariffs, quotas or outright bans could reduce or eliminate imports from the target country into the threatening state. This loss of trade would hurt businesses and workers in the target country, and they presumably will communicate their economic loss to their government. But what goods should be targeted? The threatening state can choose which goods it will target, and so can choose those goods that will produce the greatest political pain for the target government. In 2003, President Bush announced that he was placing a 30% tariff on steel imports from Japan and South Korea because he claimed that those countries were dumping steel–selling for less than their price of production–in the U.S. market. Under WTO law, dumping allows a country to place tariffs against the goods being dumped in response to this unfair trade practice. The European Union almost immediately announced that it was filing a dispute against the United States with the WTO because it believed that the steel tariff was not justified and so was an unfair trade practice of its own. The Europeans were concerned that all the Korean and Japanese steel that would have been sold in the U.S. without the tariff would now be sold in Europe, reducing steel prices there and hurting European steel producers. It was widely believed that the Bush Administration adopted the steel tariff to protect jobs in Pennsylvania which would be an important state for Bush to win in the upcoming 2004 Presidential election. The EU chose the goods it would target for retaliation carefully to maximize their political impact on President Bush. A tariff on citrus fruit was selected because that would hurt citrus producers in Florida which was another critical state for Bush to carry for his reelection. In the end, the Bush Administration removed the steel tariff on its own in December 2003 after an judgment by the WTO that the tariff was not justified and before the EU imposed its retaliatory trade sanctions. The threatened punishment in part helped convince the Bush Administration to do as the EU wanted.

Force makes threats more effective when it convinces the target that the threatener can get what it wants if it carries out its threat. The target might as well do what the threatener wants because it cannot stop it from happening and it is likely to suffer other losses if the threat is carried out. Although military force is one way to impose an outcome on a party, the word force is used in the sense of "forcing the outcome you want." Force helped make President Bush's ultimatum to Saddam Hussein just before the start of the Iraq War more credible, even though the threat did not prove effective. The U.S. removed Saddam from power after he refused to leave power and go into exile as demanded. When force is successful, it can intimidate the target into doing as the threatener wishes and so need not be carried out. The Munich crisis concerned Germany's demand that Czechoslovakia cede the Sudentenland–the mountainous border area of Czechoslovakia which was populated with ethnic Germans–to it. In the Munich agreement, France and Great Britain agreed to the cession, while Adolf Hitler of Germany promised that he would not go to war with Czechoslovakia or press it for further demands if he received the Sudetenland. The Czech government was not a party to the agreement and could have refused to cede the territory in question to Germany. However, the Munich agreement made it clear that neither France nor Britain would fight to defend Czechoslovakia if it refused Hitler's demand. Germany had a larger and stronger army that Czechoslovakia and would be able to win a war with it and take the Sudetenland by force if the Czechs refused to surrender it. So they ceded the territory to Germany. The prospective force behind Hitler's threat made that threat both credible and effective.

Force often looms in the background of threat over security issues, but rarely behind threats on other issues in world politics. Actors can threaten force to take territory. On political economy issues, actors generally cannot force others to do as they wish. Instead, they have to secure their agreement to do as the threatener wishes. This fact does not mean that threats are irrelevant to political economy and other issues. Threats are still common on these issues, but actors making threats have to use rewards or punishments if they want to make their threats more effective.

Actors have two ways to make their threats more effective. An actor making a threat can try to make it more credible by persuading the target that it will carry out the threat. It can also try to shift the consequences of conflict and backing down to make the former more attractive for itself, and so convince the target that its threat is credible. Both of these strategies can make a threat more credible, but sometimes the target defies a credible threat because it would rather have the threat carried out than do as the threatener wishes. Altering these values for the target through rewards, punishment, or force is another tactic for making a threat effective. If these tactics shift the target's values for the outcomes of submitting and conflict enough, they could make compliance less painful than defiance for the target.

Although I have discussed threats as if they are made in one single declaration with a sole chance for the target to respond, they often play out over a period of time. The crisis before the Iraq War ran from President Bush's speech before the UN in September 2002 until the invasion in March of 2003. The ultimatum came at the end of this period, but the threat that the U.S. would use force against Iraq and Saddam Hussein was evident from the beginning. This long period provided an opportunity for the Bush Administration to try all of the tools to make its threat more credible and effective. The initial threat was effective in securing the return of UN arms inspectors to Iraq but not in ousting Saddam Hussein from power. The months spent moving troops to the Gulf region both increased the pressure on Saddam's government and prepared for war if necessary. The attempts to rally support from other nations were less successful at raising the credibility of the threat because many countries did not support the movement toward war by the Bush Administration. The opposition of those countries gave Saddam Hussein some hope that the threat of war could be forestalled without fully and publicly revealing his lack of weapons of mass destruction. In the end, the final ultimatum was not effective in getting Saddam Hussein to leave office peacefully, although it is not clear that he could ever have been coerced to do so.

Threats over the Iranian Nuclear Enrichment Program

It is uncertain when Iran began a program to enrich uranium although it admitted it had such a program in 2003. Iran claims its program is solely to create fuel for nuclear power reactors. After the overthrow of Saddam Hussein's regime in April 2003, the Bush Administration began to increase pressure on Iran to abandon that program. It feared that the Iranian enrichment program was the first and most difficult step to Iran building a nuclear bomb. The Bush Administration and the governments of other countries have made a variety of threats towards the government of Iran during the dispute. Threats to use military force to destroy the program have been made implicitly rather than explicitly. Many U.S. politicians, including Democrats, have refused to rule out the military option with statements such as "No option is off the table." These statements do not state that the U.S. will attack Iran's nuclear sites if it does not shut down the program, but they suggest that there are paths the crisis could take in the future that would lead to such an attack. Implicit threats like this try to influence the target by leaving the threat unclear in the hope that it will believe that the threat will be highly damaging. Vague threats like this may also help the threatener to gain domestic and foreign support for its demands by leading these other actors to believe that the threat has not been made or is less likely to be carried. Military strikes on Iran would be unpopular with many American citizens and with many other governments. Iran is a significant trading partner with other states as well as being a major oil exporter. Other governments opposed an attack on Iranian nuclear sites at the time these veiled threats were made. Consequently, the Bush and Obama Administrations have made such threats implicit rather than explicit in the hope of both intimidating Iran in closing their nuclear enrichment program without losing the support of other governments.

Vague, implicit threats also make it easier for leaders to avoid the consequences of backing down. If an actor does not carry through on such a threat, it can claim later that the threat was never made, and so it fulfilled its earlier statements. Yet this ability to slide away from the consequences of backing down from an implicit threat is not an advantage. It weakens the credibility of the implicit threat. The statements alluding to the possible use of force against Iranian nuclear sites have both provoked fear in other states and lacked credibility to the Iranians.

These implicit threats to use military force have proved ineffective; Iran has not stopped its enrichment program. There are good reasons to believe these threats lack credibility. Threats to destroy nuclear enrichment sites through bombing as an example of force as a way to make a threat more credible. In this case, there are serious doubts about whether air strikes could destroy Iran's nuclear enrichment program. Iran is pursuing enrichment through gas diffusion centrifuges, where uranium is turned into uranium hexafloride gas and then spun in centrifuges which slowly separate the lighter, more explosive isotope of uranium from the more common heavier one. Continue the process repeatedly, and you eventually end up with a high enough concentration of U-235 to support an explosive chain reaction. This process requires thousands of centrifuges, each a large and expensive device. Iran's nuclear enrichment facilities are buried under ground, making them more difficult to attack. Even the high-tech weaponry of the U.S. Air Force would find it difficult to hit and penetrate these structures. Locating these plants has been done through a combination of satellite surveillance, reports from Iranian defectors, and inspections by the International Atomic Energy Agency (IAEA). Satellite surveillance can help identify when a building is being built but it cannot look inside that building. Defectors and spies do not always give reliable reports. The IAEA only knows about the nuclear sites than Iran has told it about or that other countries have identified as possible enrichment factories. Even if air strikes could destroy all the known enrichment sites, Iran may have others that are not currently known. Because air strikes will probably not end the Iranian nuclear enrichment program, force is unlikely to make the threat more credible.

Threats to use force to end the Iranian nuclear enrichment program have also foundered on the opposition of other countries. The Bush Administration tried repeatedly to pass strong resolutions through the UN Security Council against the Iranian program. A resolution that imposes sanctions that limit the export of nuclear relevant materials, including centrifuge parts, to Iran was passed. Although many other governments are concerned about that program, they were not willing to make the strong threats that the Bush Administration sought; the Obama Administration has had somewhat more success in securing the support of other countries through the UN Security Council. Security Council resolutions could increase the credibility of threats against Iran in several ways. First, a resolution could help convince the government of Iran that it will not find sympathy from other countries if it continues its program in the face of threats to end it. This would raise the credibility of the threat. Second, economic sanctions are ineffective if important trading partners of Iran refuse to honor them. Iran will simply trade more with those countries. A resolution of the UN Security Council could make the threat of economic sanctions more credible by demonstrating that all the important trading partners of Iran are willing to suffer the loss of trade to end the Iranian nuclear enrichment program. This would be an example of persuasion through public action.

The threatened economic sanctions are primarily punishment designed to make the threat more effective. The sanctions that the UN Security Council has agreed to attempt to reduce

Iran's ability to run its nuclear enrichment program and to expand it further. Those sanctions only limit its ability to buy more equipment and material internationally. General sanctions would try to convince Iran to end its program by imposing economic pain. Iran is a large oil exporter and imports many goods from the rest of the world. Oddly enough, it is the second largest importer of gasoline because it lacks the refinery capacity to turn its crude oil into gasoline. Gas is cheap in Iran because the government heavily subsidizes it. Sanctions aimed at cutting off that trade would hurt the economy of Iran and average Iranians greatly. Other countries have resisted such broader sanctions both because they do not wish to lose access to Iranian oil and because they fear the consequences of pushing too hard on Iran. Hurting average Iranians in the pocketbook may not change what the government of Iran acts, specifically to get it to abandon its nuclear enrichment program.

Other countries have offered Iran rewards if it abandons its enrichment program. Russia in 2006 offered to help build and run jointly an enrichment plant for Iran on its own territory. This move would give Iran access to nuclear fuel while retaining some control by the Russians. Iran nuclear scientists would still learn more about the nuclear fuel cycle which could help a program to produce weapons-grade uranium. The bargain at the heart of the Non-Proliferation system has non-nuclear states pledge not to build nuclear bombs and existing nuclear states agree to provide them with nuclear technology and fuel for power plants. The provision of fuel for nuclear power plants is a reward for those non-nuclear states who follow the system. Some have suggested that the United States should offer a broader political engagement with the government of Iran if it agrees to end its nuclear enrichment program. Since the Iranian Revolution in 1979, relations between the U.S. and Iran have been strained to the point of non-existence. In that year, Iranian students seized the U.S. Embassy in Teheran, the capital of Iran, and held the diplomats there hostage for over a year. Since then, Switzerland has conducted basic diplomatic services, such as issuing visas to enter the U.S., for the U.S. During the Iraq-Iran War in the 1980s, the U.S. Navy accidentally shot down an Iranian civilian jetliner, killing all aboard. Iran has supported various terrorist groups around the world, and the U.S. has labeled it the biggest supporter of terrorism in the world. The U.S. also strictly limits trade with Iran through extensive sanctions. A diplomatic opening to Iran might be valuable to the Iranian government, and so act as a reward for it.

Currently, however, these threats and efforts to make them more effective have failed. Although Iran does not have a nuclear weapons program, it continues to develop the most difficult step in building such a program. Threats do not always work in world politics.

How to Analyze It
The Logic of Threats

The logic of threats is a complex strategic interaction. You need to think carefully about what threats the parties are making to one another. Often, those threats are implicit rather than explicitly stated.

1. Clearly identify the issue and the actors on whom you will focus.

2. Identify the threats that the actors are making to one another. Identify the demand associated with the threat; what does the threatened actor have to do to avoid having the threat carried out? Think about all three possible outcomes of a threat in the game trees in this chapter.

3. Consider the *credibility* of the threat. Does the target believe that the actor making that threat will carry it out? Credibility is rarely a yes-or-no question. It generally a matter of degree. How convinced is the target that the other actor will carry out its threat?

4. Consider the *effectiveness* of the threat. Will it induce the target to do as the actor making it wants? Effectiveness is a yes-or-no question only after we see how the target responds. For most cases, you will have to judge how likely it is that the target will do as the other side wants. Even if the target has responded to the threat, you should think about how close was the target's decision to do as the other side wanted.

5. Think about how the actor making the threat or promise could use *punishment* to make its threat or promise more effective. *Punishment* are actions which raise the cost of noncompliance with the demand in the threat.

6. Think about how the threatening actor could use *force* to make its threat more effective. *Force* allows an actor to secure what it wants unilaterally through conflict with the other actor. Force does not have to be used to make a threat effective; the possibility of force may make the other comply.

7. Think about how the actor making the threat could use *rewards* to make its threat more effective. *Rewards* are actions which make the target more likely to comply by increasing its value for doing so. Do not confuse punishment with rewards; ending a punishment is not a reward. Rewards are received when the target does what the threatening actor wants. Punishment is suffered when the target does not do what the other actor wants.

8. Think about how the actor making the threat could use *persuasion* to make its threat more credible and so more effective. *Persuasion* are actions which seek to change the target's belief that the issuer will carry out its threat.

Chapter Summary

Actors make threats to try and get others to do as they wish. Credibility–the target's belief that the threatening actor will carry out its threat–helps to make a threat effective–to induce the target to do as the threatener wishes. Sometimes credible threats are ineffective, and threats that lack credibility prove effective. Backing down from a threat normally has bad consequences for the actor making the threat, so actors choose carefully when to make threats, creating a selection effect where only threats that have some chance of being effective are made. An actor who makes a threat can try to increase its credibility through persuasion or changing the consequences of the threat to make itself more willing to carry it out if necessary. That actor can also try to make its threat more effective by changing the consequences for the target through rewards, punishment, or force. Threats typically unfold over time, giving the threatening actor time to try these tactics.

Review Questions

1. The decision schematic below depicts a situation where actor A is the target of a threat by actor B. Explain what factors A will consider in weighing its options. When will A acquiesce to B, and when will A defy B?

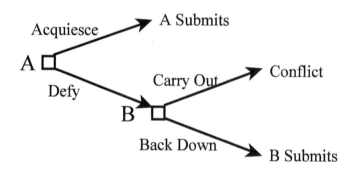

2. What is the difference between credibility and effectiveness of a threat? Define each term. Is high credibility necessary for a threat to be effective?

3. Specify two ways that an actor can make a threat more credible. What comparison of outcomes lies at the heart of credibility?

4. What three ways can capabilities be used to make a threat more effective? Explain how each alters the outcomes for the target of the threat.

5.   Are actors more likely to make promises with little credibility? What does this tell us about the promises that we observe in the world?

Chapter 6
The Logic of Promises and the Problem of Commitment

A promise lies at the heart of economic crisis confronting the Euro, the shared currency of many, but not all, members of the European Union. Sovereign debt is the promise by a government to pay back money that it borrows. By borrowing money from investors, banks, and other governments, a government can spend more than it raises in taxes; that is, it can run a deficit. There are many good reasons why most governments borrow money. They can invest in public works that lead to added economic growth, or they can finance unusual expenditures, such as wars, that cost more than they can raise through taxes. There are also bad reasons for governments to borrow. In either case, the lenders lack the legal protections available for loans to individuals or business. States are sovereign in their own territory, so they can default on loans made to them, either reducing the amount they will pay or refusing to pay any of the debt. The interest rate that states have to pay to get investors to lend them money reflects the risk of default in part. The promise here is that the borrowing government will pay back loans even though the lenders lack the ability to force them to do so.

Shifting economic fortunes can make it difficult for a government to pay its debts, leading a crisis. When a country's economy shrinks, tax receipts decrease while social expenditures increase. A government can borrow to cover this deficit, but then it must pay interest on that debt. If the total amount borrowed grows too large, the cost of this interest can push the deficit upward and make it difficult for the government in question to service its debt. This pressure can lead a government to default, breaking its promise to repay its debt and interest. Further, the approach of such a crisis can lead investors to demand higher interest rates when they lend money to the government, making it harder for the government to pay its debt. The promise then unravels when the investors fear that the government might default in the future.

The failure of the government's promise to repay its sovereign debt hurts both sides. It harms the economy of the state in question and the finances of its government. Investors lose money when a government defaults. Both sides would be better off if the government could make its promise to repay its debt credible. How can they make such promises more credible and more likely to be honored?

The Logic of Promises

Promises are exchanges over time. The game tree in Figure 1 shows the strategic logic of a promise. The actor making the promise, A in the game tree, seeks something from the actor to whom it makes the promise, B in the game tree. The first move is whether A makes the promise at all and what it asks B to do first. B then must choose whether to do as A asks. If it does not–"Defect", A does not have to carry out its promise, and the game ends. If B does as A asks–"Follow", then A must decide whether to carry out what it promised to do. If it carries out its promise–"Carry Out", the promise is fulfilled, and both sides gain the benefits of their deal. But as any six-old knows, adults do not always carry out their promises. If A breaks it promise–"Break", A gains the benefits from whatever it asked B to do without having to carry out its share of the bargain. The sequence of acts is key to a promise. B does not know if A will perform its part of the promise when it must decide whether to do as A asks.

Figure 9
Game Tree of a Promise

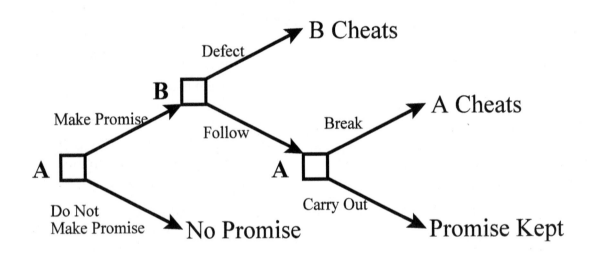

Actors make promises on many issues in world politics. Military alliances often entail a promise by one country to come to the aid of another if the latter is attacked by a third. In the North Atlantic Treaty Organization (NATO) during the Cold War, the United States pledged to fight for the defense of its Western European allies if the Soviet Union invaded them. Here the United States is "A" and its NATO allies "B". The U.S. promised to go to war with the Soviet Union, including the possibility of strategic nuclear war if necessary. The NATO allies were committed to resist Soviet overtures and threats that might separate them from the U.S. If the Soviet Union ever had invaded a NATO ally, then the U.S. would have had to decide whether to carry out its threat and go to war. Because war is costly, some doubted whether the U.S. would carry out that promise. President Charles De Gaulle of France, for one, did not believe that the United States would, in his words, "Trade New York for Paris," that is, being willing to fight a strategic nuclear war with the USSR to defend France. This judgment led France to build its own strategic nuclear forces to provide a nuclear deterrent to the Soviets.

Promises also occur on issues in international political economy. States sometimes turn to the International Monetary Fund (IMF) for short-term funding to refinance their debt on international loans, what is called a *liquidity crisis*. The value of their currency may have fallen recently or their recent revenues may not have been large enough to pay their loans. In either case, the government does not have sufficient funds on hand today to pay their immediate debts. The IMF loans them money to pay those loans but commonly places conditions on the loans, that is, demands that the government change some of its policies to enable it to pay the IMF back in the future. These policies changes commonly include measures to balance the state's budget or raise a small surplus by cutting expenditures or raising revenues. Cutting expenditures could mean firing government workers or cutting social welfare programs. These austerity programs will make people in the country suffer economically. Raising revenues means new or higher taxes, and no one likes paying taxes. These policies are unpopular and so costly for the government. Here the state is "A", making a promise to follow through on these policies if the IMF loans it money. The IMF is "B" which must either make the loans–"Follow" in the game tree, or not, "Defect". If the IMF provides loans, then the government decides whether to carry out the policy reforms it promised. Those policies are effective only if the government carries them out for several years to enable it to repay its loans from the IMF. The government could "Carry Out" its promise even though it is politically painful or it might "Break" its promise.

How does B, the recipient of the promise, rank the outcomes of the Promise game? When A carries out its promise after B does what A wants–Promise Kept–is the best outcome for B. Although it has to do as it is asked by A, A does what it has promised. The IMF is better off if it makes loans that help a country overcome short-term financial problems if the country then carries out the austerity policies the IMF placed as conditions on the loans. The worst outcome for B is if A reneges on its promise after B carries out its part–A Cheats. The IMF will have made loans but not gotten the borrowing state to implement the conditions it insisted on. When B does not carry out its share of the bargain–B Cheats–is much like the situation where A has not even made the promise–No Promise. These outcomes fall between the promise being kept and A breaking its promise after B carried out its part of the bargain. Figure 10 below shows B's preferences over the four outcomes.

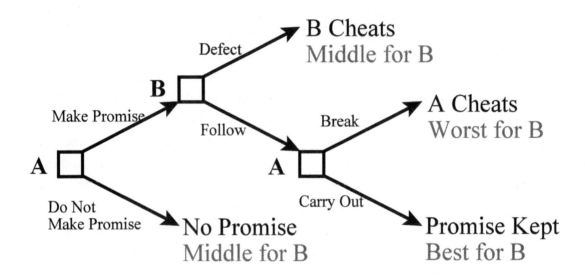

Figure 10
B's Preferences in Promise Game

Should B do what A asks or should it defect? If B does as A asks–Follow, it runs a chance of its best outcome and its worst outcome. If B breaks the deal by defecting–Defect, it receives a result between those two extreme outcomes. What B should do depends on whether A will carry out its promise. To answer that question, we need to know how A sees the outcomes.

For A, the best outcome depends on whether it wants to carry out its promise or not. If it will carry out its promise, then Promise Kept is the best outcome for A. If it is making the promise only to get B to do something it wants and does not intend to carry out its promise, then A Cheats is the best outcome for it. The worst outcome for A occurs when it makes the promise to B but B defects and does not carry out its part of the bargain–B Cheats. If A knew that B will do that, it would be better off not making the promise in the first place–No Promise.

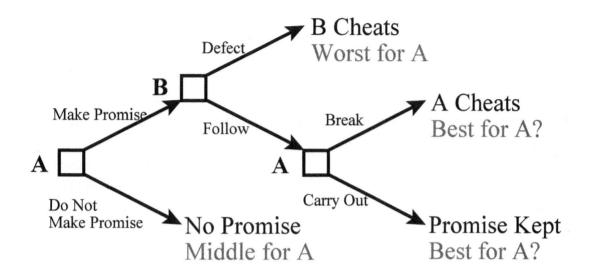

Figure 11
A's Preferences in Promise Game

A has two decisions in the Promise Game. First, it must decide whether to make the promise at all. Second, it will have to decide whether to carry out its promise if B does as A asks after the promise is made. Whether it makes the promise depends on what will happen if it does, so let's begin at the end of the game. For now, assume that A knows whether it will carry out the promise when it makes it. There are situations where A may change its mind about carrying out its promise which we will discuss later in this chapter. A's decision whether to Break or Carry Out its promise follows directly from its preference between the two. A knows its preference between the two but B does not. Earlier, when A has to decide whether to even make the promise, it has to judge whether its promise will get B to do what A wants. If B will Defect and not carry out its share of the bargain, then A is better off not making the promise to begin with. If B will do as A asks–Follow, then A would like to make the promise regardless of whether A intends to carry out that promise.

Consider the alliance example. The bargain was that the U.S. pledged to defend its NATO allies if the Soviet Union ever attacked them. In turn, those allies were to resist Soviet attempts to influence them and pull them away from the U.S. They might do so after threats by the Soviet Union if they feared that the U.S. would not honor its promise to come to their defense if they were attacked. After all, the U.S. benefits as long as they do not succumb to Soviet pressure. For the U.S., making the pledge to defend its NATO allies is preferable only if it induces them to resist Soviet threats. Making the promise to defend them and then having them act against the promise would hurt U.S. interests.

Whether A will carry out its promise is critical to what both sides do in the Promise game. B wonders whether A will carry out its promise when deciding whether to perform what A requests. A wonders whether B will do as it asks when it makes the promise in the first place. A cares about whether B thinks it will carry out its promise because B will not do as A asks if B thinks that A will not. The *credibility* of A's promise–the chance that A will carry out its promise–is critical to the logic of promises. The more credible A's promise, the more likely that B will do as A asks, and the more likely A will make that promise even if A does not intend to carry it out. The credibility of a promise then is like the credibility of a threat.

Let's summarize the logic of promises so far. A is willing to make a promise when it thinks that the promise will convince B to do as it asks. B does as A asks if the promise is credible and attractive enough to B that B would rather take the chance that A breaks its promise than call off the deal. If B does as A asks, then A either carries out its promise or not. Promises are often made because the recipient of the promise doubts the willingness of the actors making the promise to carry it out.

Why Promises Might Not Be Credible

So far, A's decision to carry out its promise has been discussed as a preplanned choice, as if it knows when it makes the promise whether it will carry it out. In this situation, A is deliberately deceiving B with a promise it has no intention of carrying out. Such deliberate deception does occur in world politics, but there are other reasons why A might not want to carry out its promise when it is time to do so are more common.

Promises are exchanges over time. The actor receiving the promise acts before the one making the promise does. Things can change between the time the promise is made and when it has to be carried out. These changes can lead the actor making the promise to change its mind and now be unwilling to follow through on its promise. It made the promise fully intending to carry it out, but now things are different. Three possible changes that could trigger an actor to break a promise are changes in capabilities, change in leaders, and problems of time inconsistency.

Change in Capabilities

If the promise requires the exercise of capabilities, the willingness of the actor making the promise to carry that promise out may change with its capabilities. Capabilities change over time as countries' populations and economies grow and as they convert those elements of potential power into military power. If the actor making the promise has become weaker relative to other states, carrying out the promise may be more costly than when it was made. If it has become stronger relative to others, it may no longer wish to restrain itself as it promised. The possibility of changes in capabilities and how they may change the willingness of the state making the promise to carry it out can create doubts about the credibility of the promise.

In the 1950s, the United States relied on a policy called Massive Retaliation to back up its promise to come to the defense of its NATO allies if the Soviet Union attacked them. The U.S. then had clear superiority in strategic nuclear weapons over the Soviet Union. It could attack the Soviet homeland with its fleet of long-range strategic bombers based both overseas and in the U.S. The USSR had some strategic bombers, but they lacked the range to hit the U.S. from the Soviet Union. U.S. air defenses had a reasonable chance of shooting those bombers that did reach North America. Massive retaliation was the threat that the United States would respond to a Soviet invasion of Western Europe by launching a strategic nuclear war against the Soviet Union. Because of its relative safety from a nuclear counterattack, that threat to the Soviet Union was credible, making the promise to the NATO allies credible.

The advent of intercontinental ballistic missiles (ICBMs) in the late 1950s and their deployment in the 1960s changed the invulnerability of the U.S. to a nuclear counterattack, undermining the credibility of its promise to defend Western Europe. ICBMs could attack any target on the Earth within under an hour, and no defense could stop them. Now the Soviet Union had the ability to respond to a strategic nuclear attack against itself with a strategic nuclear response. This change in capabilities made the U.S. less willing to launch a strategic nuclear war in response to a Soviet invasion of Western Europe, and so led its NATO allies to doubt the credibility of the promise by the United States to come to their defense. France in particular publicly cast doubts on the U.S. strategy, developed its own strategic nuclear forces, and then left the military structures of NATO.

Change in Leadership

Although actors may wish to carry out their promises when they make them, it may be that they are no longer there when it comes time to do so. A new leader of a state may have different preferences than his or her predecessor who made the promise. He or she then breaks the promise of the previous leader because he or she does not wish to carry it out. Changes in leaders can undermine promises by changing state preferences.

The Versailles treaty between Germany and the Allies after World War I sought to guarantee that Germany could never threaten France again with violence. Germany promised in that treaty that it would demilitarize the Rhineland; it could not place troops west of the Rhine River or within a band on the east bank. This demilitarized zone guaranteed that Germany could not build up troops on its borders with France and Belgium and so launch a surprise attack on them to begin a new war. Every German government of the 1920s and 1930s sought changes in the many provisions of Versailles that Germans generally saw as offensive, but all until Hitler honored the promise that they would not place troops in the Rhineland. But Hitler was a different German leader than his predecessors, one that was willing to challenge the provisions of

Versailles directly and militarily rather than through negotiation with Great Britain and France. The German promise not to place troops in the Rhineland was broken by Hitler, which set Europe on the path to World War II.

Changes in leader are more common in democracies. They hold regular elections which the current leader must win to retain power. Most democracies also have ways to remove sitting leaders without an election, such as impeachment in the U.S. and votes of confidence in parliamentary systems. Because new leaders may wish to pursue different policies from their predecessors, democracies face the problem of making their promises credible in the face of alternation of power, that the fact that they are likely to change leader before the promise is carried out. Later in this chapter, I discuss some of the ways democracies can make credible promises despite alternation in power.

Time Inconsistency

Even when the leader of a country remains the same, his or her willingness to carry out a promise may change with conditions. When the promise is made, the actor making it fully intends to carry it out later. After conditions change, though, it no longer wants to carry the promise out because it has lost the incentive to do so. If the party that receives the promise foresees that this change is likely, he or she will not do as the actor making the promise wishes.

The term *time inconsistency* comes from economics where it originated with a commitment problem in monetary policy. To fight inflation–a rise in all prices as the supply of money rises relative to goods, some economists argue that governments should use simple rules to determine their monetary policy. Supplying more money to the economy can, in the short run, create economic growth, making citizens more wealthy and so happy with their government. In the long run, however, supplying more money is counterproductive because it will cause prices to rise and lead to inflation. Inflation occurs because firms demands higher prices for their goods and workers higher wages. Rules to limit the discretion of the government to use monetary policy to gain political support can control inflation by eliminating this possibility. So a government might promise to fight inflation by not using its monetary policy for political gain by announcing that it will follow rules for how much money to supply. If this promise works, firms will not raise prices and workers will not demand higher wages. But if firms and workers anticipate that tomorrow the government will want to break its rules, supply more money, cause its economy to grow, and so raise its popularity, then they will not hesitate to ask for higher prices and wages today. The anticipation that the incentives of the government to follow those rules will change undermines the promise today. The government's rules are inconsistent over time; what it promises today, it will not carry out tomorrow.

The promises of austerity policies made by governments to the IMF often suffer from a time inconsistency problem. During the liquidity crisis, the government may pledge to adopt austerity policies–cutting government expenditures and raising taxes–that it fully intends to carry out. These policies require the confidence of investors in the country that they will be paid back in the future. If they do not believe the promise of the government to follow the austerity package, they may seek to pull their money out of the country immediately, making the liquidity crisis worse for the government. These policies take some time to work and are generally unpopular because they hurt those citizens that see their government benefits cut, lose their jobs, or have to pay higher taxes. Political opposition may coalesce around reversing the austerity policies, promising to stop those policies no matter what the consequences are. If the country has an election, the government will commonly face another party advocating ending the austerity policies. This opposition party may receive enough support from those hurt by the austerity policies that it is likely to win the election. The government then may want to revoke the austerity package before the election in order to win it. Indeed, the IMF might prefer this change in policy because the opposition will end the austerity policies if they win while the government might return to them after the election. This change in policy undermines the credibility of the original promise. If investors suspect that the government will end the austerity policies to win an election, they may demand their loans be paid off well before the election. The government then will not be able to solve its liquidity crisis, and all–government, its citizens, the IMF, and the investors–will be worse off.

Producing Commitment

How can actors make their promises credible in the face of commitment problems? Simply repeating that they intend to do as they promise is not sufficient. Often, actors fully intend to carry out their promises when they make them, but conditions change in ways that undermine their willingness to carry them out as we just discussed. They must take actions that will make them want to carry out their promises even if conditions do change in the future.

Tying Your Hands

If others doubt whether an actor is willing to carry out a promise, it could take actions that make it want to carry out the promise regardless of future conditions. It could create other costs that ensue if it breaks its promise or it could try to make the decision to carry out the promise automatic. These actions effectively "tie the hands" of the actor making them because they remove its ability to act as it chooses in the future.

Return to the promise by the United States to defend its NATO allies against a Soviet invasion during the Cold War. The United States placed troops along the border between West Germany and East Germany. During the mid-1980s, my younger brother was in the U.S. Army and commanded a Bradley fighting vehicle which patrolled that border. His job, and the job of all the other American soldiers along the border and those in West Berlin, was simple. They were there to die in the first hours of any invasion. The Soviets could not invade West Germany or take Berlin without killing some Americans. Once American blood was shed, the United States would then be committed to fight for West Germany, so defending all of Western Europe. No American politician could reasonably resist going to war with the Soviet Union once U.S. troops had already been killed. The Berlin Brigade of U.S., British, and French troops played the same role for West Berlin, which was about 100 miles east of the West German-East German border. NATO could not defend Berlin if the Soviet Union chose to take it by force, but they would have to shed blood to do so. That combat would trigger the NATO countries to go to war with the Soviet Union more generally, and so fulfill their promise to fight for Berlin. The Soviet Union then knew that an attack on Berlin meant a general war.

[Map of West German-East German border showing where US troops posted and Berlin]

States often try to make their promises credible through ploys like this. To work, these commitment devices must be public. The movie "Dr. Strangelove" is a black comedy about nuclear war. The Soviet Union builds a "Doomsday Machine" that will automatically trigger nuclear war if the Soviet Union is attacked. A mad U.S. Air Force general sends his bombers to attack the Soviet Union. The twist of the comedy comes because Premier Kisov (say it aloud) of the Soviet Union has not yet announced the Doomsday Machine to the world, waiting to spring the surprise on his birthday. President Muffley and the rest of the top U.S. leadership then tries to help the Soviet Union shoot down the U.S. bombers because if they attack their targets in the Soviet Union, the Doomsday Machine will be triggered, killing everyone. Now the Doomsday Machine is just a fabrication, but it fails in the movie because it was not public before the attack. Commitment devices are designed to convince the actor receiving the promise that the actor making the promise will carry it out. To do so, such actions must be public.

Second, commitment devices make breaking the promise worse than carrying it out for the actor making it. They typically do so by triggering other consequences if the actor breaks its promise. The Doomsday Machine was triggered by a "gigantic bank of computers" in "Dr. Strangelove", the movie being made in the days when computers were large, rare, and expensive. In the NATO case, politics inside the United States would lead it to war once U.S. soldiers had been killed. Back in the 19th century before the IMF existed, some developing countries would turn over the collection of their customs duties–taxes on imports and exports to the country–to foreigners to secure the country's debt. Because customs were a main source of revenue for governments then, this measure ensured that the government would live up to its promise to paid its debts, making foreigners willing to lend it money.

Tying hands can be dangerous because the actor who does so loses the ability to do as it wishes when the situation arises. No one could turn off the Doomsday Machine in "Dr. Strangelove." Conditions may change between when the actor made the promise and when it has to carry it out to make it regret tying its hands. In the example of the austerity programs imposed by the IMF as a condition for loans to a country in a liquidity crisis, tying the government's hands to make that program last may not be in the interest of either the government or the IMF when the government faces an election. Both are worse off if an opposition party will win the election and then default on the country's debt; the IMF because its loans will not be paid back, and the government because it is now out of power. Both would be better off if the government could then untie its hands.

Ceding Power

Actors can also make their promises credible if they can give some of their control over their decision to carry out the promise to another actor. This actor could be either the recipient of the promise or a third party. This ceding of power then reduces the ability of the actor making the promise to break it, reassuring the actor receiving the promise it will be carried out.

Demilitarized zones (DMZs) are sometimes used in peace settlements to reassure both sides that the peace will hold when neither has won the war clearly. Peace settlements include an implicit promise that neither side will begin a new war with an attack. If an attacker can benefit by making a surprise attack, one or both of the parties may be tempted to resolve the status of territory in contest by launching such an attack. Demilitarized zones are areas along the border where a state may not place its troops. These DMZs can be on one or both sides of the border. The demilitarized zone between North and South Korea was created as part of the armistice–an agreement that ends fighting but is not a peace treaty–in 1953 that ended the active combat in the Korean War. Sometimes the forces of a neutral power, often the UN, are posted in the DMZ to monitor activity there and reassure both sides that the other has not entered that zone. A DMZ was created between the forces of Israel and Syria in 1974 to prevent renewed fighting over the Golan Heights. Israel began the Six-Day War in 1967 with a surprise, as did Syria and Egypt to begin the October War in 1973. UN troops were posted into this zone. They reported troop movements by both sides to the other. That way both Israel and Syria would have advance warning of troops movements of the other that might be the first sign of a surprise attack. This warning reduces the ability to surprise the opponent, makes war less attractive to a party considering a surprise attack, and made their promises to each other not to renew fighting more credible. DMZs work because the party which is demilitarizing the zone in its territory gives up the power to place its troops there.

[Map of DMZs between Koreas and between Israel and Syria]

States sometimes cede some of their power to make decisions to organizations to make credible promises. Some argue that wealthy, developed countries created the World Bank and IMF (known collectively as the IFIs for International Financial Institutions) to allow them to make loans to developing countries tied to development independent of their political interest in those countries. These countries provide the bulk of the funds the IFIs then loan to developing countries. For these loans to spur development, they require promises that the money will be used for development and that they are paid back even if the terms are easier than loans from banks and investors. The latter promise leads the developing country to use the money to invest in activities that support economic growth so it can pay the loan back. The developed countries could make the loans directly themselves, but their political interests in those countries can create a commitment problem around payment of the loans. If a country loans money to a developing countries that is closely aligned with it, it may be unwilling to force the recipient to use the money for development or to force it to pay. If it did so, the developing country might decide to seek a new patron instead. The IFIs are separated from these political interests of the developed countries that provide the money. This means they are more capable of saying no to unproductive projects and to forgiving debts. The promise to make the developing country use the loans for development is more credible because the ultimate source of the money has ceded some of its power over how the loans are administered.

To be careful, not all political scientists who have studied loans by the World Bank and IMF agree that they are immune from political pressure to favor developing states aligned with the United States and its allies. The U.S. has encouraged the IFIs in some situations to be more lenient with developing countries aligned with it, particularly during the Cold War. Ceding power only makes a promise credible when that actor actually loses control.

Reputations

Reputations are one way to create credible commitments. A state could have a reputation for honoring its promises, built up over time by honoring other commitments. The idea is the like reputations, both good and bad, that people have. That reputation could convince others to believe that the state will honor its promises in the future, which will lead them to do as the state wants. A state would then want to keep up its reputation by honoring its promises. If it broke a promise, it would lose its reputation and its ability to get others to do what it wants with promises. If the loss of reputation and the ability to make credible promises in the future was worse than carrying out the promise, then protecting a reputation could be a commitment device.

Former Secretary of State Henry Kissinger argued that the United States had to secure "peace with honor" in the Vietnam War to protect the reputation of the United States. He argued that the U.S. had made many promises to defend other countries around the world, including Western Europe through NATO. Those promises would require the U.S. to go to war if those other countries were attacked. When the United States sought to withdraw its military forces from South Vietnam to end its participation in the war, other states might conclude that the U.S. was not willing to pay the cost in American lives of defending them as it had promised. Kissinger believed that the peace treaty he negotiated with the leaders of North Vietnam would ensure the continued independence of South Vietnam after U.S. left the country. This peace would reassure other countries that the United States would fight for its promises. Protecting the reputation of the United States was not cheap. The U.S. had more men killed in Vietnam during the Nixon Presidency when it was fighting to leave Vietnam "with honor" than it did under the Johnson Administration when it was fighting to win the war. In the end, the United States did not live up to its promises to the government of South Vietnam. In 1975, North Vietnam invaded the South whose armies quickly fell apart. The U.S. Congress refused to allocate more military aid to South Vietnam or allow the U.S. Air Force to bomb North Vietnamese forces in support of the South.

The fall of South Vietnam, as embarrassing as it was for the United States, did not cause U.S. allies to abandon it out of fear that the promises to defend them now meant nothing. Even if the U.S. had lost its reputation for being willing to fight, its promise to defend other allies may still have been credible. South Vietnam was a small country far away from the United States. It was not a major trading partner with the U.S., and no American considered it a central U.S. interest except that it was threatened by Communist North Vietnam. Other U.S. promises were to countries like Japan and those in Western Europe that were core U.S. national security interests and identified as such by politicians of both political parties in the U.S. and a broad spectrum of U.S. public opinion. Promises to defend these countries did not rely on reputation to be credible. U.S. troops were posted in both Asia and Europe to commit the U.S. to fight for those areas.

[Doonesbury cartoon on fall of Saigon?]

Arguments about reputations work best when the parallel from one case to another is clear and strong. South Vietnam varies from other U.S. interests in important ways that reduced the parallel between them. The parallel between cases is stronger on other issues, making reputation a more powerful tool of commitment on them. Countries borrow money from both private lenders like banks and investors and public lenders like the World Bank, IMF, and other governments. All these loans are called sovereign debt because the borrower is a government. The name comes from the time when almost all countries had a king or queen who was the sovereign of the country. The king or queen borrowed the money personally on behalf of their state. Because the king or queen was the absolute ruler in their own country, sovereign debt has the problem of whether the king or queen will live up to his or her promise to repay those loans. A monarch could simply refuse to pay and ask the borrower who intended to force him or her repay the debt with "You and what army?"

Lenders, however, have long memories. Those monarchs who defaulted–refused to pay their debts–who lose their reputation for being faithful borrowers who could be relied on to pay the loans. Lenders then would be reluctant to lend money to them in the future and would demand a higher rate of interest to compensate for the greater risk of default. In an extreme case, like that of Spain in the middle of the 1600s, lenders might refuse to make any further loans to a monarch who had repeatedly defaulted on his or her debts. Losing a reputation for paying one's loans was costly to a monarch, and so he or she could make credible promises to repay loans using reputation as a device to commit him or herself to that promise. A similar logic applies to states now. They have reputations for repaying their national debts which they can lose by failure to pay or changing the terms of the loans on their own, as Argentina did in 2002. The national debt of the United States, commonly issued as Treasury Bills, often called T-Bills, is considered to have a very low risk of default. As a consequence, the U.S. government pays a lower interest rate on that debt than you do on any college loans you may have. When a states loses its reputation as a faithful debtor, it pays a higher rate of interest the next time it borrows money. As most states borrow money to meet some portion of their budget and need to borrow more when they face a financial crisis or a decline in economic growth, they want to maintain their reputations as faithful borrowers.

Arguments about reputations assume several things about the situation. First, there are at least two types of the actor who can acquire a reputation, one which will carry out the promise and one which will not. In the Vietnam example, there would be a type of United States which is willing to pay a high cost in human lives to defend its interests, and another which is not. Second, other actors do not know the type of that player. The other countries in the world, both those whom the United States promised to defend and those who might consider attacking them, do not know if the United States was the high or low cost tolerance type. Three, the actor making the promises has the opportunity to make more than one promise. Reputations are built over many promises and may make other future promises credible. If an actor acquires a reputation for not carrying out its promises, that reputation will last for a long time, leading others to doubt its promises in the future. The United States during the Cold War had many interests to defend around the world. Four, because the type of the actor making a promise influences its willingness to carry out its promises, those other actors can infer it from the player's actions. Breaking promises then hurts the actor who makes them because other actors then think that it will not honor its promises in the future. Those like Kissinger who were concerned that the U.S. withdrawal from the Vietnam War on unfavorable terms would damage the credibility of U.S. promises to defend countries elsewhere worried that the leaders of other countries would conclude that the U.S. was unwilling to pay the costs to defend other countries that it had promised to defend.

Promises can matter even if the cases differ. The parallel, or lack thereof, from case to case can be represented by having the interest of the party trying to build and maintain a reputation vary from case to case. Sometimes that value is small, as it was for the United States in Vietnam, and sometimes it is large, as it would be for the United States defending Western Europe. When a specific promise to defend another country was challenged, the United States then would compare the value of the interest to its willingness to pay costs generally–its type. Critical interests would be defended by either type, while peripheral interests would not be worth the cost for the type with a low-cost tolerance. The leaders of other states would not know the type of the United States and so would have to judge whether the United States was willing to fight for its interests, both critical and peripheral. The low-cost tolerance type of the U.S. then might fight for a peripheral interest, like South Vietnam, to convince other states that it will fight for all its interests. Then its reputation for being willing to fight might deter other countries from challenging U.S. interests afterwards.

Reputations sometimes can create credible commitments. For other issues, the parallel between cases is not strong enough to allow others to draw conclusions about how an actor will act tomorrow from what they do today. The features of each individual event is more important than reputation, and reputation cannot make commitments on those issues credible.

How to Analyze It
The Logic of Promises

The logic of promises is a complex strategic interaction. You need to think carefully about what promises one party makes to another.

1. Clearly identify the issue, the actor making the promise, and the actor to whom it makes the promise.

2. What is the actor making the promise offering to do? Is there a clear time frame for the promise (this is not always the case)? Are there any clear conditions on what the actor receiving the promise must do first?

3. What does the promising actor want the other to do in exchange for its promised action? If you have a positive answer to the last question under point 2, it describes what the actor receiving the promise must do?

3. Why might the actor receiving the promise doubt the willingness of the actor making the promise to carry it out? Consider the following possibilities:
- Change in the capabilities of either actor which could make either incapable or unwilling to carry out its side of the promise.
- Change in leadership or internal politics of the actor which make it unwilling to carry out its side of the promise. Such change might lead the other side to renege on its part of the promise if it opposes the new government.
- Changes in the situation that produce a time inconsistency problem for either side. What might change that would lead an actor away from doing what it promised?
- Perhaps the side making the promise has no intention of carrying out its promise; it is only attempting to get the other side to do as it wishes. These situations are rarer than you (and many observers of world politics) think. They can happen if one or both sides face pressure from third parties to make the promise in a deal.

4. Is the actor making the promise doing anything to make its promise more credible? Look specifically for the following ways of increasing the credibility of the promise:
- Has it adopted any measure that will force it to carry out its promise? These "tying hands" mechanisms make it costly to break the promise.
- Is it ceding any power over the execution of the promise to the other actor? Ceding power can take many forms.
- Has it taken actions to engage its reputation over the promise?

5. Pull the parts together; how does the promise work? Just like a threat, judge the credibility and the effectiveness of the promise. Does the recipient of the promise think that the actor making the promise will carry it out? Is the recipient willing to do as the actor making the

Chapter Summary

Actors make promises to get other actors to do something for them. Promises are exchanges over time; the recipient has carry out its part of the bargain before the actor making the promise does its part. Often the recipient doubts whether the actor making the promise will carry it out, that is, whether the promise is credible. The credibility of a promise measures whether the recipient believes the other side will carry out its promise. Changes in capabilities, leaders, and time inconsistency are three reasons why actors might break their promises. When an actor's promise lacks credibility, it may use a commitment device to convince the recipient that it will carry out its promise. Tying hands, ceding power, and reputations are three commitment devices.

Review Questions

1. Give three reasons why an actor might break its promise even though it intended to carry out its promise when it made it.

2. Explain a time inconsistency problem, and give an example of one.
    Even when the leader remains the same, his or her willingness to carry out a particular promise may change with conditions.

3. Give three ways an actor can make its promise more credible. Give an example of each way.
    Tying your hands, Ceding Power, Reputations
    creates consistent...

1. Change in Capabilities, Change in Leadership, Time Inconsistency

Chapter 7
Military Power: Its Sources and Limits

The United States has the strongest military in the world by a large margin now. Although it is not the largest military, the U.S. spends more on its military than the next six countries combined. It can operate anywhere in the world within a few days after being ordered to do so. The U.S. Navy guarantees the freedom of the seas for navigation of all countries. The U.S. Army has both heavy armored elements that can defeat any other military in a conventional way and special forces that can carry out commando raids and irregular combat. The U.S. Air Force can bomb targets anywhere in the world from bases in the United States using stealth bombers and mid-air refueling. The strategic nuclear forces of the U.S. can devastate any country on Earth. Why does the United States have the strongest military in the world? How do states generate military power and for what purposes?

The Continuing Importance of Military Power

Military power has been and continues to be important in world politics. First, it allows states to control territory. Armies patrol borders to keep out intruders and prevent invasions. The armies of many countries also patrol inside their borders to keep domestic order or fight against rebel groups. Second, states use their militaries to make threats and promises in the effort to get other states to do as they wish. The threats of a state with an effective military are more credible than those of a state without one. Similarly, a promise to come to the aid of another state in the event of an attack on it is more credible when threatening states fear the military of the state making the promise. Third, states sometimes have to carry out their military threats and promises and use their forces. Sometimes, a state uses its military to punish another actor. Turkey, for example, has launched cross-border attacks against rebels of the Kurdistan Workers Party, known as the PKK, which has carried out terrorist attacks inside Turkish territory. Fourth, the most effective military forces do not have to be used to back up their threats because their reputation for fighting effectiveness renders threats to use force effective. Such a reputation for quality is gained through fighting in the past that demonstrates that military's competence and capabilities. Israel won five different wars against its Arab neighbors from 1948 to 1982. Since then, those Arab states have been unwilling to fight Israel directly in a conventional war because of the reputation of the Israeli military. Instead, some Arab states like Egypt and Jordan have made peace with Israel, while others have turned to unconventional war as a way to put pressure on Israel.

Ultimately, military power reduces to the ability to fight and win wars. The features of an army that lead to victory on the battlefield are those that make an army effective and strong. A military at war seeks to win battles and so defeat the enemy. Any given war matches two sides, each of which may be more than one country fighting together. The results of a war then tell us about the military capabilities of one side relative to the other. As we will see, other things also influence the outcome of a war, so side with the best military does not always win a war. Not all wars are the same, so the military capabilities that help a state win one war may not prove victorious in another. The key question then is what type of military a state chooses to build.

The Sources of Military Power

Building a military requires inducting men (and sometimes women), training them how to fight, and providing them with weapons to fight. A state's government generates military power from its population and economy by choosing how many people and resources it will commit to the military. These two dimensions–population and economy–give the potential power of a state. How much of that potential will be mobilized and in what ways are the central decisions for a government in the creation of its military power.

We can assess the potential power of a state from statistical measures of its population and economy. Later in this chapter, I will show you a table of such measures of potential power for the leading states in the world today. These statistical measures are useful because they allow us to quickly judge the power which the state could mobilize. Big differences are meaningful in such measures; small ones are not. It is easy to see that the United States has much greater ability to create military power than Nicaragua. The population of the U.S. is more than fifty times that of Nicaragua, and its economy is over seven hundred times larger. Even if these numbers are somewhat misleading, no one doubts that the U.S. military is stronger than that of Nicaragua. The comparison between Great Britain and France is not so clear. Their populations are about the same size, and their economies produce about the same amount. One could be much stronger than the other if it chose to mobilize more resources from its people and economy than the other. We need to remember then to be careful when using aggregate statistics of a state's potential power.

All states use a mixture of citizen compliance and state compulsion to mobilize resources from their societies for their militaries. Some governments force young men (and occasionally young women) to serve in the military under the threat of imprisonment if they do not report when called. This is called *conscription*, although we in the U.S. refer to it as "the draft." The U.S. government first used the draft during the Civil War and again during the two World Wars. The U.S. had a peacetime draft for the first time after World War II which continued through the Vietnam War. Conscription works most effectively when citizens subject to it report voluntarily, with the state arresting and imprisoning only a few resisters. When a large number of citizens refuse the call up, state power can force some but not all into the ranks. Extraction of resources for the military from the economy is also more effective when citizens comply on their own accord rather than the state have to seize the resources for the military. The U.S. government raises much of the revenue from the income tax on individuals and corporations. My taxes, for example, are withheld from my paycheck, and my employer gives them directly to the government. Once a year by April 15, U.S. citizens and legal residents file an income tax return that documents their income, calculates their income tax liability for the prior year, and reconciles payments with the amount owed. Every country faces some tax evasion, someone who does not pay his or her taxes one way or the other. In some countries such as the U.S., tax evasion occurs but is not rampant. In others, like Brazil and Italy, tax evasion is a way of life. The tax system raises more funds for the government in general and the military specifically when citizens voluntarily comply with the system. The government can then concentrate its tax enforcement on relatively few tax evaders. When few comply fully, the government can catch some and make them pay, but it is difficult and costly to catch them all. For raising both personnel and resources for the military, all governments rely on a combination of coercion and voluntary compliance.

A government can raise resources for the military more easily when the people of the country support how the military is being used. They will comply more readily with the government's demands for their sons for the army and the products of their labor for weapons when they believe their country is under attack and they are threatened. A government's ability to mobilize and use military power varies with the situation and way those forces will be used. An important distinction in how states use their militaries is the difference between limited and total war. The state's existence is at stake in total war, such as the two World Wars. Defeat will have immense consequences for the losing state and its people. States in total war mobilize vast levels of resources from their populations, with the people accepting even the harshest conditions to produce more for the war effort. Workers in Soviet arms factories during World War II worked 12-hour shifts seven days a week to provide the Red Army with the weapons it needed to defeat the Nazi invasion. Total war is fought for total aims and calls forth a total effort by the nation to win. Limited war is fought for lesser ends than the existence of the state. The Vietnam War was a limited war for the United States. It fought to support the government of South Vietnam against the guerrilla movement of the National Liberation Front (NLF, known to Americans as the Viet Cong) and the regular forces of North Vietnam from conquering the country and putting it under Communist rule. Because the U.S. used the draft to raise soldiers for the war in Vietnam, the draft became deeply unpopular as the war continued. Many college students used every available means to avoid being drafted, including the extreme of fleeing the country to avoid prosecution or induction. The U.S. government did not call for a total effort of the American population to fight the war because its aims were limited. How military power will be used affects how willing the population will be to cooperate with the raising of that power and so changes the state's ability to generate that power from its people.

A government can also choose to build its military in different ways, which has implications for how it raises manpower and revenues for the military. As mentioned above, the draft was unpopular in the U.S. by the end of the Vietnam War. President Nixon ended the draft and converted the U.S. military to an all-volunteer force in 1973. The All-Volunteer military allowed the U.S. military, particularly the Army, to rebuild itself after the Vietnam War. By the end of the war, the Army suffered from serious morale problems because many draftees did not wish to serve in Vietnam. Only those who could not find a way to avoid service legally were forced to fight in Vietnam. The All-Volunteer force was composed of those who had agreed to serve, either to make the military a career or for other reasons. Over time, the Army became more selective about the recruits it accepted as it had more volunteers than it needed. Soldiers served for longer periods of time and reenlisted more often, making the Army and other services highly professional. The move to the All-Volunteer Army changed the nature and capabilities of the U.S. military. It was not as large as it could be. The U.S. inducted about 15 million men into the military during the Second World War, about one-tenth of the population of the time. The U.S. military now is about one-and-a-half million people, about one-two-hundredth of the population. By accepting volunteers only, the quality of inductees rose, and their commitment to the armed services increased. The All-Volunteer Army raised the quality of the U.S. military while restricting its size. Other countries also face the choice of what sort of military they build. What people do they induce, how do they train them to fight, and with what weapons do they provide them? All of these choices affect the military capabilities of a state.

The Loss-of-Strength Gradient

Where wars are fought also affect the ability of a military to fight and which side wins. It is difficult for any military to fight far from its bases in the home country. Soldiers and the food, weapons, and ammunition they need to fight must be shipped when they fight away from home. This "tail" of an army takes soldiers and resources to keep those in the front line fighting. It takes fuel to transport the supplies, including the fuel the troops use in their vehicles. Militaries fight at less than full strength when they fight away from home. We call this the *loss-of-strength gradient*. The further from the production centers in the homeland that an army fights, the weaker it is because it must commit more soldiers and equipment to keeping its supply lines open. The U.S. military refers to the "teeth-to-tail" ratio, the numbers of troops fighting–the teeth–to those who work to keep them supplied with everything they need to fight. These supplies include food, ammunition, fuel, repairs for vehicles and weapons, intelligence, and all the other support services in the military. Every military fights less effectively the further it fights from its home base. One of the measures of the immense military capabilities of the United States is its ability to fight anywhere in the world on short notice. The U.S. fought World War II in Europe and the Pacific, the Korean and Vietnam Wars in East Asia, and both Gulf Wars and the war in Afghanistan, all thousands of miles from the American homeland.

Quality versus Quantity

Another central choice in the creation of military power is between quality and quantity. The U.S. military has chosen quality over quantity. The U.S. government has built a highly trained professional military armed with highly sophisticated weapons using the latest technology. Each individual U.S. soldier and airman has the most destructive capacity and combat effectiveness available on Earth today. Because of the choice to build a highly sophisticated and trained military, the U.S. military is not as large as it could be if the U.S. mobilize every possible soldier it could. Other countries have chosen quantity over quality, building a very large army at the expense of training and sophistication of weapons. China under Mao Tse-Tung had a massive army of millions, trained in simple but effective tactics. During the Korean War, the Chinese Army inflicted severe defeats on the UN forces, predominantly American, when they intervened after UN forces approached the Yalu river, the border between Korea and China. Chinese forces moved rapidly on foot across rugged terrain to surround and attack UN columns that were bound to roads by the trucks that carried their equipment and vehicles. The Chinese were also willing to suffer much heavier losses in combat than UN forces were. Later in the Korean War, UN forces used their advantage in material to hold off massive Chinese assaults, inflicting huge casualties on the Chinese.

There are advantages to both quality and quantity, and neither is always superior to the other. We in the U.S. tend to emphasize the advantages of quality because the U.S. has chosen to create a high quality military. A high quality military brings the advantages of greater destructive power per soldier and greater tactical flexibility and initiative allowing its soldiers to adapt to the changing battlefield. A large but less sophisticated military can win through numbers, particularly when the battlefield is large, and when rugged terrain limits the advantages of quantity. A classic match up of quality versus quantity occurred between the Soviet Union and Nazi Germany on the Eastern Front of World War II in Europe. This was the decisive front of World War II in Europe, where the majority of Hitler's army was deployed and then destroyed. The Nazi army and air force were better trained and generally had superior tanks, airplanes, and guns. The Red Army was larger and possessed more of everything. Initially, the Nazis inflicted massive losses on the Red Army, but the Soviet Union rebuilt its army during the war and turned the tide of battle against the Nazis. The immense size of the Russian Front and the high levels of casualties helped the Red Army overcome the Nazis and eventually conquer Berlin, the capital of Nazi Germany. The Red Army did not prevail simply because it was larger; its leaders and soldiers improved their skills through the hard lessons of the battlefield. Although some German tanks, such as the Tiger and Panther, were better than Soviet tanks, the Soviet T-34 was an excellent tank, and the Soviet Union produced more of them than Germany did of all its types of tanks combined. Quantity with enough quality carried the day for the Soviet Union in the war they know as The Great Patriotic War.

The choice between quantity and quality is not obvious then. The U.S. has built a high quality military in part because it has the most productive and technologically sophisticated economy in the world. This makes designing and producing high-tech weapons possible. The U.S. government has also been conscious of casualties during combat and has chosen at least since World War II to use material in place of some of its soldiers' lives. Limiting the size of the U.S. military has other consequences for U.S. foreign policy. For several decades, the U.S. military has been designed to meet the "one-and-a-half war" standard. This standard means the Defense Department planned to develop the capabilities to fight one major war and one minor war at the same time. It would not produce the size of forces required to fight a global war, as the Second World War was for the United States. Recently, the Chinese military has begun to acquire technically sophisticated equipment and raise training levels of its troops. As China has grown economically, it can afford a more sophisticated military with a navy and air force. Sixty years ago at the time of the Korean War, China did not have the choice of building a sophisticated military, but now it does.

Potential Power

States mobilize their military from their population and economy. The size and sophistication of both are primary sources of potential power. Population matters because soldiers are recruited from the population, whether service is mandatory or voluntary. The larger the population, the larger the military that can be built. The pool of skills possessed by the population also matters. Many civilian skills are also needed in a military organization. The United States during World War II gained an advantage because many young American men knew how to drive and how to work on cars. Most recruits could drive a truck or repair a tank that broke down mechanically from their experience in civilian life. Other armies had to train soldiers for these jobs because cars and these skills were not common in their societies. A literate population is easier to train because they can read manuals rather than requiring oral instruction. Officers generally have to be literature to file reports on combat and read orders. Both size and skills of a state's population contribute to its potential power.

A comparison of the Soviet Union and Sweden can make these issues clear. During the Cold War, Sweden was neutral, so it relied on its own military for its defense. Sweden built modern tanks and jet fighters on its own. It could do this because it was an advanced industrial society with the range of industries and skills needed to produce those weapons. The Swedish military relied on conscription, yet it was also highly skilled because the pool of recruits had at least a high-school education. The Soviet Union also produced modern weapons, with some designs such as the AK-47 assault rifle and MiG-21 fighter superior to the comparable American weapons. The Soviet population was not as highly skilled as the Swedish population. The Soviet military used less educated recruits for non-combat tasks like construction that did not call for literacy or need individual initiative. Soviet arms production was also inefficient, wasting resources and labor. Still, the Soviet Union was a superpower during the Cold War, while Sweden could not project power beyond Scandinavia. The population of the Soviet Union (around 250 million during the Cold War) was over 30 times that of Sweden (now about 9 million). No matter how many people Sweden put into its military and how capable their weapons were, Sweden could not be a world power.

We also have to be careful in judging the size and quality of a population to account for the range of skills within that society. Average income in India is still low by global standards, although the Indian economy has grown rapidly in the last two decades. Even though many Indians are poor, India has also had a large highly educated middle class since independence in 1947. India has been the largest military power in South Asia for the last sixty years because it could build a skilled military from ethnic groups like the Gurkhas who have long traditions as soldiers. It bought the most of its weapons from other countries. The size of India's population, estimated at more than 1.1 billion people now, means that the middle class, perhaps around 100 million people, is very large compared to other countries. The sheer size of the Indian middle class means that India has had scientists who had the skills to allow India to build and explode its "peaceful nuclear device" as a demonstration in 1974. Although many Indians are still peasants living on subsistence agriculture (growing the food they eat), the top of Indian society has helped to make India the major power in South Asia.

Size and sophistication of a state's economy also both matter for its potential power. A richer country can spend more on its military because it produces more. High tech industries allow a country to build sophisticated weapons with greater capabilities. Those countries that lack the industries to produce their own weapons must buy them from arms industries in other countries. Even a hundred years ago, countries like Japan and Turkey (then the Ottoman Empire) would contract with British firms to build battleships for them because they could not build their own. Great Britain was the first country in the world to industrialize, beginning around 1750. The great increase in production produced by industrialization helped Britain defeat France in the Napoleonic Wars because Britain had the wealth to finance the anti-French coalition which eventually defeated Napoleon. Britain became the first true global power during the 19th Century because it had the most productive economy in the world. Although Britain relied on a small (for its size) professional military, the British Navy dominated the sea lanes and allowed Britain to exercise power anywhere in the world, from the Opium Wars in China to its control of India to fighting Russia in the Crimean War. British power only declined when the economies of other countries, particularly Germany and the United States, caught up to and then surpassed the size of the British economy when those countries industrialized.

While many countries build some weapons, most have to purchase at least some of their military equipment from other countries. This allows countries to have modern weapons that they could not produce themselves. The Gulf states, the oil producing countries that adjoin the

Persian Gulf, have used the wealth generated by their oil exports to buy sophisticated weapons, such as jet fighters, from countries like the United States. Although these weapons make the militaries of these countries more capable than they would be without them, these states' militaries are still weaker than their more populous neighbors such as Iran. Their economies are heavily based around oil production and other investments of their oil wealth, such as the massive financial and tourist development of Dubai. They have not developed the range of industries needed to produce modern weapons on their own. In contrast, Israel which 40 years ago bought most of its tanks and jet fighters from other countries, now produces a full range of the weapons used by the Israeli military. Unlike the Gulf states, Israel does not depend on other countries for supply and support of its military.

Mobilizing Potential Power

States create their military capabilities by taking people and production from civilian society and then train the people to be soldiers and build them the weapons they need to fight. How do states vary in their ability to mobilize potential power? First, they vary in their *political capacity*, their ability to extract resources from society. Hundreds of years ago, states taxed their citizens irregularly and recruit soldiers through voluntary recruitment and coercion known as the press gang. Most people still lived on the land as peasant farmers. Those who volunteered often had a good reason to leave the village where they grew up, such as being in trouble for having committed a crime. Others volunteered just for the excitement of doing something different. The press gang seized sailors, often drunk at the time, and forced them onto to warships which then left port. Taxation consisted of collecting fees on economic activity that was difficult to hide. Otherwise, people understandably wanted to keep what little they had and would hide their wealth from the King's tax collectors. Tariffs, taxes on goods traded internationally, were easier to collect as the goods were moved through ports. France relied in part on a tax on salt, a necessity that could be collected easily at the point of production, either a salt mine or pens for drying sea water. Put together, armies hundreds of years ago were much smaller than they have been in the last hundred years. Gustavus Adolphus, the warrior King of Sweden who led his country into the Thirty Years War, commanded an army of about 200,000 men at its peak strength. Most of these men were spread around Germany as garrisons for towns and cities he held. The field army under his command was about 30,000 men at its peak. Sweden quickly turned to mercenaries to fill out their armies as the population of Sweden was not large enough to supply new recruits to replace those lost. The Swedish army, like all armies of the time, raised much of their funding from extortion from the local populace. The city fathers would have to raise money to avoid the soldiers taking what they wanted. It was the policy of "making war pay for war."

Now, states have elaborate bureaucracies to recruit soldiers and tax their populations. Those that use conscription keep track of young men (and occasionally young women) so they know everyone available for induction. Once recruits ordered to report for service, their health and abilities are evaluated to see if they will make acceptable soldiers. Those states that rely on a volunteer military, such as the United States, have recruitment offices around the country. The officers there often work with interested prospects as early as high school. The U.S. military advertises the benefits of military service as a career, as you probably know if you have ever watched sports on television. They know what programs young men watch. Modern states also have highly developed tax systems, which both tap a wide range of economic activity and reach almost everyone in society. Modern armies are much larger than those of several hundred years ago. Napoleon mobilized 650,000 soldiers for his invasion of Russia in 1812, with a total French army of about 1,000,000 scattered around Europe. The major European nations raised and lost millions of men during the First World War about a hundred years later and a hundred years before our time. Growth in population is one of the major contributors to the expansion of militaries over time, but growth in political capacity has also increased the size of armies. Similarly, militaries now require many more supplies of many more types, from ammunition, to food, fuel, and spare parts for weapons and vehicles. Napoleon's army still drew heavily on local areas for food, with the threat of starvation present if the army did not move fast enough or if the local area did not produce enough extra food to feed the army as well as the peasants. When the French army invaded Russia in 1812, it lost heavily from lack of food because Russia was more sparsely populated than central and western Europe and so did not raise enough food to support Napoleon's massive army. The advent of the railroad made it possible to feed an army from its home bases, and although soldiers may still steal some local food to make their diet more interesting than army food, they no longer live off the land. Again, the greater ability in the state to extract resources from their own population through taxation has aided its ability to pay for war out of its own pocket.

As mentioned earlier, extraction of resources is easier when the people of a country support the war effort of the state. Voluntary compliance aids both the recruitment of soldiers and the raising of taxes. The more the populace sees the war as necessary to fight, the more readily they will surrender their sons and their wealth for the war effort. The roots of Napoleon's army lay in the French Revolution. Once the French people declared their country a republic, meaning the king no longer reigned over the country, the other monarchs of Europe lined up against France. To defend their republic, the National Assembly of France declared a *levée en masse*, the first draft in modern history. The declaration of the National Assembly described the demands placed on all citizens as,

> From this moment until such time as its enemies shall have been driven from the soil of the Republic, all Frenchmen are in permanent requisition for the services of the armies. The young men shall fight; the married men shall forge arms and transport provisions; the

women shall make tents and clothes and shall serve in the hospitals; the children shall turn linen into lint; the old men shall betake themselves to the public squares in order to arouse the courage of the warriors and preach hatred of kings and the unity of the Republic.

The *levée en masse* allowed France to build what was a massive army for the times, enabling them to fight in Belgium, southern Germany, northern Italy, and Spain against a coalition of Great Britain, Prussia, Austria, Spain, Piedmont (in northern Italy), and the United Provinces (which are now the Netherlands). Furthermore, France was winning more than it was losing in these Revolutionary Wars, expanding its control by establishing republics in the territories it conquered in the Low Countries (now Belgium and the Netherlands) and northern Italy. The French people saw the war as necessary to protect their republic and so were willing to serve and fund the army.

Napoleon then used this mass army as his instrument of conquest. By 1812, Napoleon dominated Europe, having defeated every major power in Europe save Britain at least once and often twice. His former enemies of Prussia and Austria were now reluctant allies, who contributed troops to Napoleon's invasion of Russia. Napoleon took over 450,000 men into Russia with another 200,000 in support; he came back with maybe 60,000. Prussia and then Austria joined forces with Russia to drive Napoleon out of France. He raised and lost another army of 400,000 in 1813 in his efforts to keep control of Germany. In 1814, the allied armies converged on France, and Napoleon made a desperate call for another 936,000 Frenchmen to defend their country. Perhaps 120,000 answered the call. The French people had learned that when their sons marched off with Napoleon, they rarely came home. Recruits took to the hills and forests of France to hide rather than fight. Napoleon's officials sought to position themselves for the aftermath of his demise. Despite fighting some of the most brilliant campaigns of his military career, Napoleon was defeated by the combined might of the coalition and resigned as Emperor of France on April 6, 1814.

Different types of governments vary the combination of coercion and voluntary compliance they use to raise the resources they need to build their military. Democracies tend to rely more on voluntary compliance, while autocracies use more coercion. This difference does not mean that one system is always more effective than the other for building a military. During World War II, war production in the United States and Great Britain was more efficient than it was in Germany or Japan. All of the societies at war called on major efforts from their people to fight the war, with the Soviet Union making the greatest effort. Despite these differences in systems, all political systems rely on the combination of compliance and coercion to get the people and money they need to wage war.

How Wars Are Won

Military power helps win wars, but other factors matter as well. The stronger side, as measured by statistics about their economic production, the size of their population, and the number of men under arms and how much is spent on the military before the war breaks out, wins about 3 out of 5 times, 59% to be precise. This measure combines both potential power and that available at the beginning of the war. One reason why a state which looks stronger on this measure might lose is that the other mobilizes more after the war breaks out, which this measure does not assess. There is also the question of how effectively each side uses the resources they extract to build their military. Even given these qualifications, there are clearly cases where the stronger side loses even with the advantage of a stronger military. As Napoleon said, "God is on the side of the big battalions," but sometimes the weaker side prevails. What factors then affect which side wins a war, particularly those that lie outside statistical measures of how strong each side is?

Wars are won by defeating the enemy on the field of battle, whether on land, on the sea, or in the air. Troops have to be led in battle as well as trained and equipped behind the front line. *Leadership*, the quality of the officers that lead them into battle, matters. Armies with good leaders are more organized and disciplined, take advantage of opportunities on the battlefield, and cope with the losses of combat more effectively. Good officers take time to train, because they need a wide range of skills to lead a small unit. Officers have to read a map, understand tactics so they employ their soldiers effectively, and know the rules and regulations of their military thoroughly. They also need to develop the ability to lead soldiers in mortal combat, preferably from the front. Combat means that some soldiers will die; an army's *morale* is its willingness to continue to fight in spite of those losses. Everyone in combat is afraid of dying, but fighting effectively requires mastering that fear. An army with high morale is willing to fight and take that fight to the enemy. Soldiers in an army with poor morale may refuse to fight or desert. Morale depends on many factors, including how well the army trains and treats the troops, how the war is going, and whether soldiers believe in the war effort. Armies with good leaders and high morale are more likely to win against one with poor leaders and low morale, even if the latter is larger and better equipped. The two factors of leadership and morale are two main reasons why Israel consistently defeated its Arab neighbors in conventional wars in 1948, 1956, and 1967. Israel's citizen soldiers were led by dynamic men who took great risks to gain victory. Arab officers too often led from the rear where they could not react to the changing battlefield even though they were personally safe. Arab generals were chosen for their political reliability rather than their military skill. Poorly led Arab soldiers too often quit the battle rather than fight on.

Where the battles are fought also matters. *Terrain* and geography influence battles by shaping how they can be fought. Open, flat terrain, such as deserts, favor mechanized armies because their vehicles can travel anywhere easily. Long-range weapons can see, fire on, and destroy targets with shorter ranged weapons before the latter can close for combat. Rugged terrain, such as mountains, forces armies to fight on foot and restrict vehicles to roads. Closed terrain, such as forests, provide cover and force the attacker to close with the defender to find out where its defensive positions are. Fighting in cities is probably the most difficult terrain for the attacker. The defenders can hide in any building and lay ambushes for the attacking troops as they move through the city. The deserts of Kuwait and southern Iraq aided the forces of the U.S.-led coalition in the Gulf War of 1991. Mechanized forces moved quickly across the open desert to outflank Iraqi defensive fortification along the border of Kuwait and Saudi Arabia. Coalition air forces could identify and bomb Iraqi target easily because of the lack of cover. By contrast, the jungles, mountains, and rice paddies of Vietnam made it more difficult for U.S. forces that fought there during the Vietnam War. They had to patrol on foot in these areas, which allowed Viet Cong and North Vietnamese forces to fight at a time and place of their choosing. Most combat was at close quarters which reduced the effectiveness of superior American air power and artillery. While the terrain did not dictate the outcome of these two wars, it did shape how they were fought and influence which side won.

Overall battle plans, the *strategy* each side uses, also influence which side wins. Strategy is necessary to coordinate all of the forces of a side to work together to defeat the enemy and its strategy. The clash of battle plans is strategic interaction, what is best for your side depends on what your enemy's plan is. Strategy played a large role in Germany's defeat of France in the 1940 campaign early in World War II. The French and British had about as large an army as Nazi Germany, and they had more tanks. The only area where Germany was clearly superior was in the air, where the Luftwaffe–the Nazi air force–had more and better planes than the French and British. The French and British expected Germany to invade through Belgium as the German army had in the beginning of the First World War. To counter this, and make sure this war was fought on Belgian rather than French soil, the French and British armies raced into Belgium when the Germans invaded on May 10, 1940. But the Germans had a different plan; they attacked with their tank divisions through the Ardennes forest in the south of Belgium. The French had left this sector lightly guarded because they thought that the forested area would be difficult to attack through. The German broke through at Sedan and rolled quickly to the English Channel, cutting off the French and British forces on the Belgian plain. The French had committed all their forces to the battle and so had no reserves to counter the German breakthrough. Although many Allied soldiers were evacuated through Dunkirk to fight again another day, France was defeated and sued for peace six weeks after the German attack. Different war plans for either side would have allowed the French a better chance of stopping the German attack and prolonging the war.

[Map of French and German battle plans in 1940]

Finally, luck matters. It is often better to be lucky than good, and war is no exception to that homily. Many factors outside the control of both sides influence the outcome of fighting, and we think of all those factors as chance. The weather is unpredictable and influences combat. The Russian winter is always long, cold, and snowy, but the winter of 1941-1942 was one of the worst ever. The German military was unprepared for the extreme cold. Motor vehicles had to be kept running because they could not be restarted once turned off. Food served hot turned cold before men could eat it. Many soldiers froze to death from being forced to live in the cold. The chance encounters of the battlefield also produce lucky opportunities for one side or the other. The battle of First Bull Run in the American Civil War turned from a Union defeat into a rout when a lucky Confederate shot hit the bridge on which Union forces were retreating across Bull Run. Luck gives hope to weaker side. It may prevail even if the other side has the big battalions.

War and the Motivation to Win

War kills people, imposes a harsh existence on civilians, and destroys property, even for the victors. No war is costless. Few wars are decided by a single knockout blow, like that the Nazi Germany delivered to France in 1940. Instead, wars drag on until the side that is losing is willing to concede enough to the side winning to end the war. Even if a side is losing, it could extend the war to try and get the winning side to accept less in the final settlement. To do so though, it has to be willing and able to suffer the continued costs of war. The willingness to suffer the costs of war is as important as military power to determining which side prevails in a long contest. If one side can prolong the fighting to the point where its opponent is no longer willing to continue to suffer the costs of more war, it can prevail by forcing its opponent to give it what it wants.

States fight wars to resolve international issues to their satisfaction. Sometimes they fight over the location of a border, other times they fight over political issues. The United States went to war with Afghanistan to force its Taliban government to close Al Qaeda training camps there and surrender the top leadership of Al Qaeda for trial in the U.S. The Taliban refused to do this, leading to U.S. military action in concert with Afghan rebels against the Taliban. The victory in the fall of 2001 drove the Taliban from power and forced Al Qaeda to close its training camps and flee the country. The U.S. did not apprehend many of the top leaders of Al Qaeda, the late Osama Bin Laden in particular. The stakes of a war matter for the motivation of each side because that is what they are fighting for.

States at war may disagree about how important the issues at stake are. One side may see the issues as critically important and worth a total war effort. If the population shares the view of their government that the issue is critical, it is willing to make great sacrifices to prevail. On the other hand, if the issue is not vitally important to either the government or people, that state may be unwilling to make a total effort to win. It may want to get its way on the stakes of the war, but those war aims are not critical.

The Vietnam War is an excellent example of a war where the willingness to suffer costs prevailed over greater military power. The United States was the greatest military power in the world in the 1960s. It had a large and sophisticated military, with the most capable air force in the world, airmobile soldiers carried into battle on helicopters and backed by immense firepower from artillery. When the U.S. was able to use its firepower in a battle, it could inflict heavy losses on North Vietnamese and Viet Cong soldiers. How could North Vietnam, an agrarian country with less than a tenth of the population of the U.S., defeat a superpower? South Vietnam was a "small Asian country far from our shores" as President Lyndon Johnson put it. Although American leaders, including Presidents Johnson and Nixon, did not want to be the first to lose a war, they were unwilling to pay any price to prevail there. The draft was used to raise much of the manpower used to fight the war; the National Guard was not mobilized and nationalized for deployment to Vietnam. President Nixon ended the draft because of its unpopularity as a result of the war and the randomness of who had to serve. President Johnson was reluctant to raise taxes to pay for the war. In contrast, the government of North Vietnam saw the war as an essential struggle to reunify the country. The Viet Minh had fought a guerrilla war to end French colonial control and establish Vietnam. The Geneva Accords in 1954 temporarily split Vietnam into northern and southern halves on the 17th parallel. The United States and France blocked elections originally scheduled to elect a government of a unified Vietnam in 1956. The government of North Vietnam fought the war to restore a unified Vietnam under its own power. Many Vietnamese did not want to live under a Communist government. About one million people fled the northern half for the southern half in the two years after the Geneva Accords were signed. North Vietnam was able to win the war because it sustained its war effort despite very high casualties. The United States suffered 58,217 personnel killed during the Vietnam War, a toll that still weighs on the minds on many U.S. citizens. Estimates of how many people North Vietnam lost in the war range from 440,000 to 1,100,000. These losses were between 2.5% and 5% of the population of North Vietnam. A percentage loss that large for the United States today would mean about 7½ to 15 million American dead. A few other countries, such as Nazi Germany and the Soviet Union during World War II, have suffered losses as large or larger as a percentage of their population, but those countries faced invasion by the enemy. The government of North Vietnam was both willing to accept such losses and sustain the morale of its troops and citizens in the face of such tremendous losses. They are a measure of how important unification of the country was to North Vietnam, and their willingness to suffer them gave North Vietnam an important edge over its enemies in the Vietnam War.

Another way to see how greater commitment to prevail on the issues at stakes can help countries win wars is the advantage that initiators have in wars. The initiator of a war, the side that takes the first military action, wins about two-thirds of the time, 68% of interstate wars since

1815 to be exact. Initiators have many advantages in wars; they choose when and where the fighting begins and generally surprise their opponents at first. Additionally, the side that begins the fighting is willing to fight for what is at stake while the other side may not be that committed. Initiators, however, need to win their wars quickly. The chance that the initiator wins declines the longer the war continues. Targets, the side that is attacked, seek to prolong the war, both to frustrate the initiator and to mobilize their own resources to turn the tide of the war.

Comparisons of the Major Powers

How do the major powers compare in both potential and deployed military power today? Table 6.1 gives indicators of military power for the seven most powerful countries in the world today. The seven countries are, first, the five permanent members of the Security Council, with India and Japan added as the two next most powerful countries in the world. The first column gives the active number of personnel for each country. This is the total of all soldiers, sailors, and airmen in that country's military current. It gives how large the active military is. The second column is reserve personnel. Reserves can be called up for active duty in case of a war. The United States has both troops with reserve commitments and the National Guard, both of which are types of reserves. Reserves have received military training and report to specific units, so they can be mobilized out of civilian society for combat quickly. The United States has one of the largest militaries in the world, although the Chinese military has more soldiers under arms. The number of tanks can be deceiving. Although China and Russia have about as many tanks as the U.S., many of their tanks are older models which are inferior to American tanks. The number of tanks does give us an idea of how mobile each army is because tanks are the main fighting vehicles of a modern military. The U.S. also has a large lead in both quantity and quality of combat aircraft. These numbers include fixed-wing aircraft (that is, excluding helicopters) in the Air Force, Navy, and Marines. U.S. military aircraft are the most sophisticated in the world today, with the ability to operate anywhere in the world from bases, using midair refueling, or based from aircraft carriers. On the sea, the U.S. Navy is dominant. It has almost twice as many naval combatant surface ships as China and more than twice as many aircraft carriers as the rest of the world combined. Aircraft carriers have been the leading ship for command of the seas since early in the Second World War. They also provide the ability to project air power using their complement of naval aircraft. About half of the U.S. Navy's carriers are at sea at any time, with the other half being serviced in port. The U.S. uses its carrier battle groups to rapidly deploy its power anywhere in the world close to water. U.S. Presidents have often used the deployment of a carrier battle group to react to possible military threats around the world quickly. All told, Table 6.1 shows the military dominance of the United States on land, air, and sea. It has created the most powerful and capable military in the world today.

Table 6.1
Comparison of Current Military Forces of Major Powers

	Active Military Personnel	Reserve Personnel	Tanks	Combat Aircraft	Surface Ships (Aircraft Carriers)
United States	1433600	1162250	7620	5871	118(12)
China	2225000	~800,000	7580	~2600	63(0)
Russia	1212700	~2,400,000	7400	2002	27(1)
Great Britain	207630	272550	543	460	34(3)
France	259050	100000	614	536	34(1)
India	1325000	535000	3898	714	25(1)
Japan	239900	87990	980	360	54(0)

All figures taken from *The Military Balance 2004-2005*

Table 6.1 shows what military power these seven major powers have created. Table 6.2 gives five indicators of potential power for these same seven great powers. The first column gives size of population, the first and most important measure of potential power. China, India, and the United States are the three most populous countries in the world. Of the countries excluded from the table, Indonesia, Brazil, Pakistan, and Bangladesh all have populations greater than Russia, and Nigeria and Mexico have populations greater than 100 million. Size of each country's economy is measured by Gross National Product, the total of all goods and services produced by it, measured in Purchasing Power Parity, hence PPP. In an industrial economy, most goods and service are traded for money, so it is easy to evaluate how much each good and service is worth by using its price. In developing economies, such as China and India, there are still substantial numbers of people who produce goods which they consume or are traded locally through barter. It is difficult to put a value on these goods because their prices are often much lower than world prices are and there is rarely a record of the transactions. Economists have developed two ways to do this. One way uses the official exchange rate to value the goods and services that are exchanged. It gives a much lower estimate of the size of the economy of a developing country because it places a lower value on locally produced and traded goods than PPP does. PPP estimates the value of all these goods and services by valuing them at world prices. The differences between these two estimates can be huge. China's GNP is estimated at 3.25 trillion dollars at the official exchange rate and 6.99 trillion dollars at PPP. Further PPP measures of an economy can change greatly with assumptions. Earlier estimates using PPP put the Chinese economy as over 10 trillion dollars. These estimates were revised downward when assumptions about the hidden production were changed. In any case, most observers agree that China has the second largest economy in the world.

Table 6.2

Comparison of Potential Power of Major Powers

	Population (in millions)	GNP-PPP (in billion $)	Military Expenditures (in billion $)	Adult Literacy Rate	% of Populace using Internet
United States	301	13060	534	99%	69%
China	1322	6991	109	91%	10%
Russia	141	1746	30(???)	99%	18%
Great Britain	61	1902	56	99%	55%
France	64	1891	56	99%	49%
India	1130	4164	20	61%	5%
Japan	127	4218	39	99%	69%

All figures taken or calculated from The World Factbook, CIA, https://www.cia.gov/library/publications/the-world-factbook/index.html.

The last three columns give measures of the quality of the population and economy of each country. Military expenditures are measured of resources mobilized for the military, rather than potential power. I include them here to give you an idea of how much each country. Exact levels of military expenditures are often state secrets. Even in the United States, the exact level of money the government spends on the military and related services is difficult to calculate. Much of the budget of the Central Intelligence Agency is secret. The question marks after the military budget of Russia reflect our lack of knowledge about it. The figure is just a guess to be honest. Notice that the U.S. spends more than the other six major powers combined by a wide margin. Literacy rate historically has been a good, simple measure of the quality of a population. Literacy requires primary education, so a high literacy rate means that most of the population has completed primary school. This means a wider range of skills in the population. It is also easier to train soldiers and officers when they are literate. Only India has a substantial portion of its population which is illiterate among these seven states today. Historically, there has been more variation in literacy rates across countries. Percent of the population using the Internet gives a measure of how connected and computer literate the people of a country are. These days it provides another window into the quality of a country's population today.

The figures in these tables also show the rise of China and India to great power status. Both always had immense populations and so were important countries. Both began widespread industrialization and modernization of their economies recently, thirty years ago for China, fifteen for India. The economies of both are growing rapidly, faster than the states like the United States that industrialized over a hundred years ago. Right now, the United States is still the most powerful state in the world because it has the largest and most dynamic economy. The Chinese economy is catching up to the U.S. economy is sheer size, although it lacks the diversity and sophistication of production and the strength of the financial sector that the U.S. has. Should the Chinese economy become as efficient and productive as the U.S. economy, China will be more powerful than the U.S. simply because there are many more Chinese than Americans. If the average Chinese worker was as productive as the average American worker, the Chinese economy would be about four times the size of the U.S. economy. That day has not arrived yet.

How to Analyze It
Relative Power

Judging which side is likely to win a war is difficult. You can find estimates of the size and equipment of both sides' militaries, but many other factors influence which side is likely to win. This box leads you through some steps to think about when judging relative power of two sides in a war.

1. Compare the relative size and equipment of the two sides. Does one side have many more tanks and aircraft than the other? If so, it has a more mobile and powerful military and can do more damage to its opponent. Quality of equipment can be judged from the source. Equipment built by sophisticated economies, such as that built in the U.S., is superior to that built by other countries, such as old equipment from the Soviet Union. Each soldier fights more effectively with better equipment and training.

2. Try to determine how many forces each side has deployed to where the fighting will take place. A larger military will not have an advantage if it only deploys as many troops as the other side. If one side is fighting on its border and the other is a long way from home, the latter will not be able to use all of its forces in the war.

3. Find out what sort of terrain they will be fighting over. Open terrain, such as deserts and plains, favor mechanized, mobile forces with lots of tanks and vehicles. Closed terrain, such as mountains and jungle, force both sides to fight on foot because vehicles will be restricted to the few roads available. The terrain helps to determine how the two sides will fight and can provide advantages to either side. If the two sides will fight a naval war, the size of their navies is more important than their armies.

4. Has either military fought a war recently? If so, how did it perform? A military which has recently lost a war may have demonstrated failings which the other side can exploit. A military which has recently won a war may have experienced soldiers, or it might have suffered heavy losses that reduce morale. Remember that war is a contest of relative strength; defeating a weak country does not mean that a country can now defeat a much stronger opponent.

5. What resources could each side mobilize if the war becomes protracted? Initiators want to fight short wars, but often the target is able to frustrate the initiator's plans. If the war becomes protracted, how capable is each side of raising, training, and deploying new troops to the theater of fighting?

6. What is at stake in the war? How does each side evaluate its ends for the war? If one side is fighting for its existence, it will fight harder and being willing to suffer more losses than its opponent. If one side is fighting for less important goals, it may give in if the fighting does

Chapter Summary

Military power continues to play an important role in world politics. States create military power by training people to be soldiers and building the weapons and equipment they will need to fight. The potential power of a state comes from its population and economy, and the size and quality of each matter. The type of military that a government chooses to build out of its potential is an important decision in world politics. All states rely on a combination of voluntary compliance and coercion to mobilize potential power into the military it chooses to build. An advantage in military power makes a country more likely to win wars, but other factors are also important. One of these factors, the willingness to suffer the costs of war, arises from the importance of the stakes of the war for each country. This willingness has allowed weaker states to prevail over stronger ones in wars where the former cares greatly about the stakes of the war and so is willing to pay a high cost to win.

Review Questions

1. Give four reasons why military power is still important in world politics.
    Allows states to control territory, states use their military to make J+P, states sometimes [illegible] carry out their military threats + promises & use their forces, boost military [illegible] don't need to be used

2. What are the sources of potential power, and what do states need to mobilize military power out of their potential power?
    PP: Population, Economy

3. Why do all countries rely on a combination of coercion and voluntary compliance to raise the people and resources needed to build their military? Do democracies tend to rely more on one than the other compared to autocracies? (?)

4. What does the "loss-of-strength gradient" mean for countries that fight far from their homeland? *The farther away from your homeland that you fight, the more resources are required to fight at the same level.*

5. Are high quality militaries always superior to larger militaries with less sophisticated weapons and less training? If so, give an example where a smaller superior force won. If not, give an example where a larger force prevailed over a more sophisticated military.
    Not always, depends on terrain. Large force can use terrain over [illegible] states high tech equipment.

6. Identify the six factors other than military power and the willingness to suffer costs that affect which side wins a war? Does the side with the greatest military capabilities always win a war? *Leadership, Terrain, Strategy, Luck   And No*

7. Explain why some countries are willing to suffer higher costs to win a war. Give an example of a weaker side that won because it was willing to suffer high costs.

Chapter 8
Perceptions and How They Matter in Decisions

Perceptions and Reality

Perceptions exist and matter because actors are uncertain about relevant factors in their decisions. They do not know the true state of affairs. Instead, they hold beliefs about that factor and try to account for their uncertainty in the policy they adopt. Uncertainty is a key element in decisions in world politics. Actors cannot fully anticipate their consequences of their decisions, which makes them uncertain about what will happen after they make a decision. Perceptions are how we think about these uncertainties.

There are many types of factors that could be uncertain. An actor may not know facts about the situation it faces. Early in the Cold War, the advent of intercontinental ballistic missiles (ICBMs) changed the nuclear arms race. Before the Soviet Union and the United States developed such missiles, long-range bombers were the only way to deliver nuclear weapons to targets in the enemy country. Bombers were slow; it took them many hours to fly to their targets even from the bases that the U.S. had in its allies close to the Soviet Union. The Space Race, the efforts by both superpowers to see who could launch the first satellite, the first man into orbit around the Earth, and finally the first man on the Moon, required missiles that could lift payloads into Earth orbit. Once a missile could do that, it could also carry a nuclear warhead to a target anywhere in the world in about a half-an-hour. The Soviets scored a coup when they launched the first satellite into Earth orbit, Sputnik, in 1957. The United States launched its first satellite in 1958. Both superpowers had demonstrated the ability to build an ICBM then, but how many did each side have? Both sides were secretive about the number of missiles they had and the means of intelligence collection was limited in those days. Senator John F. Kennedy claimed that his Republican opponent, Richard Nixon, had allowed a dangerous missile gap to open up. Nixon was President Eisenhower's Vice President, so Kennedy could use the claim that Eisenhower had ignored this threat to U.S. national security in the presidential campaign. Kennedy claimed that the Soviet Union had many more ICBMs than the U.S. did, but he did not know how many missiles the Soviet Union actually had. This fact was not publicly known because the Soviet Union did not announce how many missiles it had and tried to trick the U.S. into believing it had more missiles than it did. Kennedy won the 1960 election, and when he became President, he found out that there was a missile gap, one that favored the U.S. The Soviet Union deployed few ICBMs while the U.S. had deployed over a hundred. The "Missile Gap" was a fact where perceptions were the opposite of the truth.

[Picture of Kennedy and Nixon from 1960 Presidential debate?]

Even when the facts are known, they have to be interpreted to draw a bigger picture of what other actors are trying to do. Facts alone rarely tell the whole story because actors would like to know what other actors are going to do. Interpretation of facts is difficult because often they are consistent with different motivations, one of the main themes of the next chapter on how actors change their perceptions. The Japanese attack on Pearl Harbor that brought the United States into the Second World War is an example of how difficult it can be to interpret facts to discern the intentions of another actor. The attack was the culmination of a long period of diplomatic pressure by the U.S. government against Japan to stop Japanese expansion in East Asia. Japan had been at war with China since 1937 and had conquered much of the Chinese seaboard. In July of 1941, Japan occupied French Indo-China, now the countries of Vietnam, Laos, and Cambodia. In response, President Franklin Roosevelt froze Japanese assets in the U.S. and blocked oil exports to Japan, later adding steel exports to the ban. The U.S. was one of the world's leading oil producers then, and Japan's war effort would grind to a halt without a source of oil. Rather than back down from their military position in East Asia, the Japanese government resolved to attack southward to capture oil wells in the Dutch East Indies, now Indonesia. They understood that they would also have to attack the British naval base in Singapore as part of that plan. The Japanese leaders believed that these attacks would lead the United States to enter the war and send its Pacific Fleet, based in Pearl Harbor, to intervene in the fighting. Consequently, the Japanese decided to attack the Pacific Fleet at Pearl Harbor on the opening day of the war to prevent it from being sent to fight their attacks in Southeast Asia. The Roosevelt administration was not totally in the dark of Japanese plans. It had clear intelligence reports that Japanese warships including transports carrying invasion troops were steaming southward in order to attack. But attack where? What were Japanese intentions for war? A limited war in Southeast Asia or a broader conflict? The interpretation of what the U.S. government knew on December 6 was the critical issue. The Roosevelt administration had few illusions that war with Japan could be avoided, but it did not know how that war would start. When the Japanese navy attacked Pearl Harbor, President Roosevelt famously labeled it "a date which will live in infamy," and American public opinion rallied in favor of war against Japan.

The interpretation of facts matters because those facts may provide clues into the intentions of other actors. As discussed earlier in the logic of threats, it is often hard to respond to another actor if you do not know what they intend to do. Their preferences, or if you prefer their intentions, are a vital part of understanding what they will do in the future. As discussed earlier in the chapter on preferences, actors rarely know the complete preferences of other actors. Perceptions often focus on the intentions of other actors, which we think of as knowledge of their preferences. Later, we will discuss the perceptual problem faced by Josef Stalin, the leader of the Soviet Union, when he faced Nazi Germany's military buildup on their common border in early 1941. This example shows how difficult it can be to discern other actors' preferences from facts about their behavior. It also illustrates how perceptions enter into decisions.

These perceptions are difficult to form because all countries keep secrets. All countries also have intelligence agencies to collect and assess information about other countries. The

United States created the Central Intelligence Agency (CIA) in 1947 to bring together the collection and evaluation of intelligence in one agency. In addition, the Department of Defense also has a number of intelligence agencies of its own. In 2004, the Director of National Intelligence was created to coordinate intelligence collection and analysis across all parts of the federal government. Put simply, intelligence is the business of spying and then figuring out what the spies have learned. Spies are often called human intelligence because they are people who learn what they can by what ever means, including but not limited to reading local newspapers, talking to people, bribing sources in foreign governments, blackmailing government officials, and stealing state secrets. Technical collection of intelligence has increased immensely over the last 40 years with new technologies for surveillance. The Space Race led to the ability to place spy satellites into orbit around the Earth where they could use high-resolution cameras to take overhead pictures anywhere in the world, including secret sites of other countries. Google Earth, where you can find pictures of anywhere on Earth, is a descendant of this technology. Once all this information is collected, someone has to make sense of it all. Most of the personnel of the CIA are not spies who collect information or "spooks" who engage in covert action but analysts who sort through all the information available and write reports on what they have learned and what they think is going on. Because many of the reports are incomplete or do not tell you what you would like to know, analysis of intelligence is a difficult business. It is, however, a necessary business, and it helps inform state leaders about what is happening in the world and what might happen next to allow them to make decisions about what they should do.

Finally, actors can also be uncertain about the consequences of their policies. They have perceptions about what is likely to happen, but they do not know. Scientific and economic uncertainty both lead to this type of perception. Even though human civilization has made great progress in its understanding of the natural world and economies, there is still much we understand poorly at best. This uncertainty makes policy choices difficult. Policy on global warming is an example of scientific uncertainty and the differences in perceptions it generates. Most scientists who study the global climate have concluded that average global temperatures are rising and that human activity is partially responsible through the emission of global warming gases. But there is still much we do not understand about global warming that is relevant for forming policies to address it. How much will the Earth's climate warm over the next one hundred years? How will patterns of rainfall change? Together, some regions of the world may benefit from global warming while others suffer. Knowing who the winners and losers are is important to designing policies to address global warming. There are also uncertainties about the economic costs of different policies to address global warming. Some experts think that substantial benefits can be gained at little cost; others think that the costs of mitigating the problem are larger than the consequences of continued warming. All of this uncertainty means that different actors hold divergent views about what is likely to happen and what should be done about it. These views are perceptions of the efficacy of the available policies.

Perceptions specify what actors believe about uncertainties that affects their choices. Those uncertainties could be about what other actors will do or about what the likely consequences of their choices are. In all cases, perceptions are related to reality, but they rarely match it. Actors' perceptions capture their understanding of what is going on in the situation they face. Because actors do not fully understand their current situation and cannot fully anticipate what will happen, their perceptions are not always accurate. Perceptions do express the actor's understanding of the situation, whether they hinge on what others want or what is likely to happen from their available options.

Perceptions and Uncertainty

Perceptions give an actor's understanding of reality in the face of uncertainty. Faced with a lack of complete knowledge of their situation, an actor has to make judgments about what course of action is best for it. Its perception of the situation captures its uncertainties about key elements of the situation that matter for its choices. We think of these uncertainties using the idea of types from the chapter on preferences. We represent uncertainty by allowing the uncertain element to be one of several known possibilities, one of which is the reality of the situation. These possibilities, like outcomes in the chapter on preferences, are mutually exclusive and exhaustive, so that one and only one is the true state of affairs. Actors know the full set of possibilities, but they do not which one is the true one. Their perceptions reflect which possibilities they think are more likely to be true and which less likely.

All this seems very abstract, so some concrete examples may help. In the logic of threats, there were two possibilities about whether the threatener would carry out its threat from the eyes of the target of the threat. Figure 1 shows the two possibilities: the threatener will carry out its threat or will back down. The target does not know which is true. The threatener knows whether it will carry out its threat if it has to because it knows its own preferences. The target's perception in this situation concerns how likely it thinks the threatener is to carry out the threat. The target might think the threatener is very likely to carry it out its threat or it might be skeptical of its willingness to do so. The target's perception then gives how likely it thinks the threatener will carry out the threat.

Figure 12
Two Possibilities in a Threat

A Will Carry Out Threat   A Will Back Down

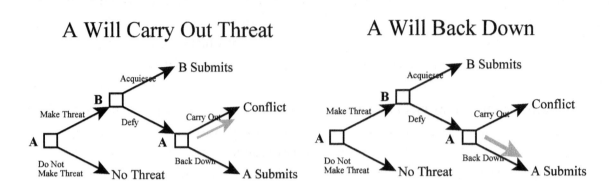

In the example of a threat, the target's perception could concern the preferences of the threatener or its capabilities. If the target knows that the threatener has the ability to carry out its threat but doubts its willingness to bear the costs of a conflict, its perception concerns the preferences of the threatener, that is, how willing it is to suffer the costs of conflict. If the target doubts whether the threatener can carry out its threat, then the target's perception concerns the capabilities of the threatener. In either case, the target's perception concerns the same two possibilities, whether the threatener will carry out its threat if defied. The difference between the two lies in how the target might try to learn more to sharpen its perception and draw it closer to the reality of the threatener's intentions. If the target is uncertain about the willingness of the threatener to carry out its threat, it would try to learn more about the threatener's political costs of carrying out the threat. If the target was uncertain about the threatener's capabilities, it might try to learn more about those capabilities through spying. The uncertainty underlying the perception differ, but they have similar effects on the target's response to the threat.

The uncertainties in the global warming example concern the future effects of such warming. It might be that warming and its effect would be mild or it could be profound with widespread consequences for societies and economies. We have perceptions about these possibilities because we do not know what the consequences of global warming will be if we do not change what we are doing relevant to global warming. There are different views even among climate scientists about how much warming will occur, the effects of such warming, and how likely the different possibilities are. A person's perception of the likely consequences of global warming has a large effect of what that person thinks should be done in response to it. Skeptics who think the effects are likely to be minor rarely advocate policies that might cap or reduce emissions of global warming gases. Those who believe the likely effects are profound advocate dramatic changes in policy now. Research on global warming has informed these perceptions. The belief that global warming is occurring and that human activity is responsible for it is stronger and more widespread now that it was twenty years ago when the idea was first raised publicly. Much scientific research has changed these perceptions over the last two decades. No one knows what the future effects of global warming will be; that is why we hold perceptions about those effects.

Perceptions as Probabilities over the Possibilities

Uncertainty lies at the heart of perceptions, and how we think about perceptions reflects this. An actor has some beliefs about how likely each of the possibilities are concerning whatever it has a perception of. An actor's perception rates how likely it thinks each of the possibilities are. Probabilities are a way to do this. The more convinced an actor is that a particular possibilities is the true one, the higher weight it puts on that possibility in its perception. The less likely it thinks another possibility is, the less weight its perception puts on it. If it was certain that a possibility was true, its perception would place weight 1, all of the weight on it. If an actor was certain that one possibility could not happen, it would place weight 0 on it. The sum of all the weights across all the possibilities is 1. The relative sizes of each weight in an actor's perception gives how likely it thinks that possibility is.

Return to the two possibilities in a threat in Figure 1. The target, B, has a perception about whether the threatener, A, will carry out its threat. This perception could be about A's willingness to suffer the costs of conflict or about its capabilities. For now, let us assume that B is uncertain about whether A is willing to suffer the costs of conflict. There are two possibilities here, either that A will carry out its threat or that it will not. Call the first *A resolute* and the second *A irresolute*. These two possibilities are the same as the types of A that we discussed earlier in the chapter on preferences. B's perceptions rates how likely each of these possibilities are. If A thinks that it is equally likely that B is resolute or irresolute, each has chance ½ in its perception. If B believes that A is likely to carry out its threat, the weight on the A resolute possibility is higher than that on B irresolute, say ¾ on the first possibility and ¼ on the second. The higher the chance that B places on A being resolute, the stronger B's perception is of A's resolve. If B was certain that A was irresolute, its perception would place weight 1 on A resolute and weight 0 on A irresolute.

When perceptions concern the preferences of other actors, as in the threat example above, we will talk about *types* of the other actor as described in the chapter on preferences. The threat example had two types of threatener, resolute and irresolute. Its willingness to carry out the threat gave its type, which the threatener knows but its target does not. That uncertainty is why the target has a perception instead of knowing whether the threat will be carried out. When perceptions cover other elements of choice, we use the same idea although we will not refer to them as types, just different possibilities.

Even though we think about perceptions as probabilities over more than one possibility, it will prove to be the case that one and only one of those possibilities will be true. The threatener is either willing to carry out its threat or not. Unchecked global warming may have profound effects for our world or be a minor inconvenience. But we will not know which is true until that day comes, and if we take steps now that limit global warming, we may never know how bad it would be if we had done nothing. Remember that we have to judge decisions in terms of what actors knew when they took those decisions. We cannot rely on what they would find out later even when we know now what they did not then. Perceptions are central to thinking about uncertainties in world politics and how they influence what actors do.

Perceptions and Actions

Actors consider the likely consequences of their actions when they choose. Perceptions reflect what they think could happen and so help to shape their choices. Consequences–what an actor cares about and has preferences for–result from the chosen action and the unknown factor for which the actor has a perception. The latter includes any actions that other actors take about which the deciding actor is uncertain and so has a perception of it. An actor weights the value of each consequence by the chance it believes it will occur. The most attractive action has the best combination of values of outcomes weighted by the chance that those outcomes will occur if that action is taken.

Return yet again to the threat example. Whether B, the target, defies or acquiesces to A's threat depends on both its perception of whether A will carry out that threat and how attractive B views the three possible outcomes, that is, B's preferences over them. We assumed that A carrying out the threat was worst for B with A backing down from its threat being the best for A and acquiescing to A's demand in between the two. If B perceives that A is very likely to carry out its threat, say with .9 chance, it is very likely to acquiesce and give A what it wants. On the other hand, B is unlikely to do as A wishes if it perceives that A is unlikely to carry out its threat. There is some critical level of belief between the range of perceptions where B is sufficiently convinced about A's resolve that it will acquiesce to A's demand and where B will defy A. This critical belief or perception depends on how bad the threat is in B's eyes and what A is demanding that B do. If the threat is truly awful for B or if A is only asking for small concessions, then even a weak perception that A will carry out its threat can be sufficient to convince B to do as A wishes. Exactly how strongly B has to believe that A is willing to carry out its threat depends on its preferences–how it views the outcomes.

The next chapter examines how and when actors change their perceptions in response to what others do and events in the world. There we will see that current perceptions also influence how evidence moves perceptions and what evidence is persuasive to an actor. Persuasion then entails changing others' perceptions and so leading them to take different actions that they would otherwise.

Stalin and Hitler

A historical example can help illustrate how perceptions affect what an actor does. The example here comes from the early days of the Second World War concerning how Josef Stalin, the leader of the Soviet Union, viewed the intentions of Adolf Hitler, the dictator of Nazi Germany. They signed the Nazi-Soviet Pact in August of 1939. The Pact was a non-aggression treaty in which both sides pledged not to attack one another. This agreement reassured Hitler that the Soviet Union would not intervene in the imminent Nazi invasion of Poland. It also proved to give Nazi Germany a free hand in the subsequent war against France and Great Britain triggered when they declared war on Germany after its invasion of Poland on September 1, 1939. The Pact also contained secret provisions that divided Eastern Europe between the two countries. On September 17, 1939, the Soviet Union invaded Poland and occupied the eastern half of the country. Within a month of the outbreak of war, Stalin forced the Baltic States of Lithuania, Latvia, and Estonia to ally with the Soviet Union. Stalin made territorial demands of Finland and then invaded when the Finns refused those demands. The Soviet invasion of Finland did not go as well as the Nazi invasion of Poland, but after over four months of fighting, Soviet troops broke through and Finland surrendered more territory than Stalin originally demanded. In the summer of 1940, the Soviet Union occupied and annexed the Baltic States after Germany's conquest of France. Finally, the Soviet Union pressured Romania to cede the territories of Bessarabia and Northern Bukovina. All of these territorial additions moved the Soviet frontier substantially westward and added to its strategic depth by forcing an invader to conquer more ground to reach its major cities.

[Map of division of Eastern Europe after Nazi-Soviet Pact]

The Nazi-Soviet Pact also aided Hitler's war effort. Germany and the Soviet Union also concluded an economic agreement at the same time as the Pact. The Soviet Union purchased industrial goods from Germany in exchange for raw materials including oil and food. During the First World War, Great Britain and its allies imposed a blockade on Germany which cut it off from sources of raw materials and foods from overseas and was an important factor in the eventual Allied victory. Access to Soviet raw materials and food reduced the threat of another blockade if war with Britain became prolonged.

The Pact, however, was built on the sand of the distrust between the two dictators. Hitler was a rabid anti-Communist who sent most German Communists to concentration camps after assuming total power. Stalin trusted no one, especially not a powerful Germany. The Soviet Union had been negotiating with France and Britain for an anti-Nazi alliance during the spring and summer of 1939. When they were unwilling to make sufficient reassurances to Soviet diplomats, Stalin turned to Hitler as a way to turn the coming war away from the Soviet Union.

Even after the Pact, both Germany and the Soviet Union had designs on Eastern Europe even in the areas given to the other side. Hitler was particularly alarmed when Stalin pressured Romania to cede territory to it because Romania was Germany's primary source of oil. Although they had pledged not to attack one another, neither believed the other was committed to that pledge.

[Low cartoon of Hitler-Stalin with "scum of the earth"]

Stalin had additional reasons to fear Hitler. Between 1936 and 1938, he had purged the Red Army of almost all its top officers, killing tens of thousands including Marshal Mikhail Tukhachevsky, the best military mind in the Soviet Union. He feared that they were plotting to overthrow him either on their own or in concert with foreign powers. The officer corps of the Red Army needed to be rebuilt after the Purge. Many of the officers who were promoted after the Purge were chosen for their political reliability rather than their military competence. Poor leadership was one reason why Finland was able to hold off the much larger and better armed Red Army for four months in the Winter War of 1939-1940. Officers take time to train, time that Stalin needed to buy with the Pact.

Stalin thought the Pact would buy him time by bogging Germany down in a long destructive war with France and Great Britain. They declared war in response to the German invasion of Poland although they took no major military action to come to aid of the Poles. Most observers expected a war of attrition much like the First World War would result in western Europe, one reason why the British and French were unwilling to take offensive action against Germany. When Hitler's military struck westward on May 10, 1940, it defeated the allied armies and forced France to surrender within six weeks. German losses were hardly crippling. The quick defeat of France put the Soviet Union in a difficult position. The time he expected to rebuild his military was gone. The question was what would Hitler do next?

The Battle of Britain followed the fall of France. This months-long battle in the skies over Britain demonstrated that Germany could not end the war with Britain directly. It lacked the ability to invade the British Isles, and its air force could not force Winston Churchill's government to negotiate a peace settlement. But Churchill was also stymied in that Britain lacked the military power to break Hitler's military domination of the continent. He needed powerful allies, with two obvious candidates, the United States and the Soviet Union. President Franklin Roosevelt of the U.S. slowly and carefully moved the country towards supporting Britain in what ways he could. But isolationist feelings–the idea that the war was a European not American problem–were strong, and the U.S. would not enter the war in Europe until after Hitler declared war on it shortly after Pearl Harbor. The U.S. also needed to build the mass army needed to fight a war against the Nazis. The Soviet Union, on the other hand, had a massive army and a long border with Germany where a second, Eastern front could be opened against Hitler. Churchill was also strongly anti-Communist and saw Stalin as better than Hitler only in that Stalin also was the enemy of Churchill's enemy, Hitler. In one of his most famous lines, Churchill defended military aid to the Soviet Union after Hitler attacked the Soviet Union with the comment that "If Hitler were to invade Hell, I should find occasion to make a favourable reference to the Devil." Stalin then did not trust Churchill because he knew that Britain needed the Soviet Union in the war if Germany was to be defeated.

Stalin's Dilemma

Hitler began a massive military buildup in early 1941 on the frontier between Nazi controlled territory including its allies of Hungary and Romania and the Soviet Union including the territory it acquired after the Pact. A concentration of more than 3 million soldiers cannot be hidden, and Stalin was aware of that military concentration. What was Hitler's intent behind this buildup?

[Map of Nazi buildup on border]

There were two possibilities. The first, which was Hitler's true intention, was that the buildup was preparation for a surprise invasion. The second was that Hitler was planning to renegotiate the Pact to extract further benefits, either territorial or economic, from Stalin. Stalin was not the sort to give up something for nothing, so the buildup would create military pressure to coerce concessions from him. Stalin's problem was that he did not know which of these two possibilities was true. Further, the appropriate response to each of these possibilities was different. If Hitler is planning an attack, vigilance and military preparation was the right response. Prepare yourself for the coming attack. These preparations, however, also raised the risk of military incidents along the border. If Hitler was seeking an opportunity to renegotiate the Pact, he could seize on these incidents as a pretext for opening negotiations. The proper response to the type of Hitler that was seeking to renegotiate the pact would be to prevent provocations by lowering the alertness of Soviet forces on the frontier. "Don't give Hitler an excuse" is the logic of this policy. There was a cost to lowering vigilance; it makes a surprise attack more likely to be successful. During the first six months of 1941, German forces crossed the border on the ground and in the air to learn more about Soviet forces guarding the border. Stalin ordered his troops not to respond to these incidents as most countries do by confronting them militarily. The Soviet Air Force did not routinely send up planes to intercept and follow German planes that violated Soviet airspace. Table 8.1 summarizes the two types of Hitler and the appropriate policy response.

Table 8.1

Two Types in Stalin's Perception of Hitler in 1941

	Hitler's Type	
Hitler's Intent	Attack and Conquer	Intimidate and Negotiate
Reason for Buildup	To invade Soviet Union	Force additional concessions from Stalin
Proper Policy Response	High military readiness	Avoid provocations

Why did Stalin choose the course of action that made Hitler's surprise attack on June 22, 1941 more effective? Stalin's dilemma is that his policy response to the Nazi buildup depended on his perception of Hitler's intention. Stalin did not believe that Hitler would attack and hoped that he could buy enough time to rebuild the Red Army. He hoped at the least to stall any war until 1942. The buildup alone is not sufficient evidence for Stalin to tell which type of Hitler he was facing. Either type would engage in a military buildup on the border because both strategies relied on military superiority, whether it was for an attack or for bargaining leverage. Stalin anticipated a period of negotiations before war broke out. The Red Army could use that period to ready itself for war.

Stalin had extensive intelligence information about the Nazi buildup on his border. This information alone did not reveal Hitler's intentions as argued above. Churchill forwarded to Stalin extensive intelligence that Britain had collected about Hitler's plans to attack the Soviet Union. Stalin did not trust this information because he knew the Churchill would benefit from provoking a war between Germany and the Soviet Union. Ever mindful of Churchill's anti-Communism and the weak position of Britain fighting alone against Germany, Stalin ignored Churchill's warnings. The consequence of Stalin's perception was the devastating surprise attack Hitler launched against the Soviet Union on June 22, 1941. The Red Army was unprepared and suffered immense losses, losing almost its entire prewar strength in the first four months of the war. But the Soviet phoenix rose from the ashes and created a whole new army which eventually turned the tide in front of Moscow in 1941 and in the streets of Stalingrad in 1942, went on to the offensive and blasted its way into Berlin in April of 1945.

It is hard to understand Stalin's perception in this case. Hitler had decided to attack the Soviet Union in December of 1940, and the buildup prepared for a surprise attack. It is easy for us with the knowledge we have now to assume that it must have been easy for Stalin to see what is obvious after the fact. This case is often cited as a classic example of *motivated bias*, which could also be called more plainly as "wishful thinking." The motivated bias argument asserts that Stalin was psychologically blocked from assessing the intelligence information he had that clearly pointed to a coming Nazi invasion. Because he wanted to believe that an attack would not happen, he ignored the evidence of it. Of course, others' intentions are always clearer after they act on them than before. It may be that actors suffer from motivated bias, but actors will still make errors like Stalin's even if they do not suffer from motivated bias. Because other actors' intentions are not clear, an actor cannot fully anticipate others' actions. This uncertainty is why we analyze perceptions in world politics. Perceptions give chances of the possibilities, not definitive predictions of them, and so cannot prove fully correct as events unfold. The uncertainties of which actors hold perceptions are central to understanding world politics and the difficulties of forming foreign policies. The next chapter deals with how actors learn about these uncertainties and change their perceptions. There, we can return to the question of whether actors learn or ignore evidence at their own peril.

How to Analyze It
Perceptions

Perceptions are one of the most difficult topics to analyze in world politics. It is hard enough to think carefully about one's own perceptions–how you think others will act. Thinking carefully about how other actors see your own intentions is even harder. But seeing the world through the eyes of other actors, to understand their perceptions of what you are trying to do, open up deeper understanding of how they might respond to what you do.

1. Perceptions begin with uncertainties over things that affect what happens. The first step in assessing an actor's perceptions describes these uncertainties. What factors could influence the actor's choices about which it does not know the true state of affairs? The most common factors are intentions of other actors. Even when we may think that our own intentions are clear, they rarely are to other actors. About what is it that the actor in question is uncertain?

2. Once you had chosen what the actor has a perception of, the next step is to think of the set of possibilities. This is much easier for events that have not happened yet than for those which have happened. For current issues, there is often speculation in news articles about the possible outcomes. For these possibilities, how would different values of the factor you have determined is uncertain lead to each of those possibilities? For events that have happened, ask what the actor was concerned about. What were alternative paths the event could have taken, and how might the actor in question seen the possibilities of the uncertain factor?

3. Now comes the hardest part. Perceptions are about likely the actor thinks each of the possibilities are. This is very closely guarded and almost always requires some speculation of your part as an analyst. Which of the possibilities does the actor think is most likely? Is it really in the dark about what might happen next? If the latter is true, giving each of the possibilities equal weight is an obvious way to go.

Chapter Summary

Actors are uncertain about key factors in the decisions they face. Perceptions summarize both their uncertainty and what they think about those uncertainties. We think of each uncertain element as one out of a set of possibilities. One of those possibilities will be true, but the deciding actor does not know which is true. Its perception gives how likely it thinks each of the possibilities is to be true. Perceptions affect actions because an actor uses its perception to weight the chance of different outcomes when it thinks about which action is best for it. Actors do not know the preferences of other actors, meaning they hold perceptions of what others want. In this case, we call the set of possibilities the types of the other actor.

Review Questions

1. What elements of a decision can actors be uncertain about, and so make their perceptions of those elements critical to that decision?

2. Explain Stalin's dilemma of perceptions before the Nazi invasion. What were the two types of Hitler, and what was the proper policy response to each type?

Chapter 9
Persuasion and How Perceptions Change

Perceptions and Observations

Perceptions capture an actor's uncertainty about the situation it faces. There is some correspondence between reality and perceptions, even though by definition perceptions do not map reality completely or accurately. The factors over which actors hold perceptions influence events. An actor can learn from events about those factors and change its perception to bring it closer to reality. If the factor in question is outside human control, such as the natural environment, actors can learn through scientific investigation. Fifty years ago, protection of the environment was not an important issue internationally because state leaders did not perceive it to be an issue they had to address. Research on the environment showed that air and water pollution could affect the quality of human life, and so leaders began to pay attention to environmental issues. Large, dramatic events, such as oil spills, demonstrated how industrial processes could harm the environment. Scientific research sought steps that people could take to remedy damage to the environment. There is more to the history of how the environment became an important international issue than just the change in perception, of course. This example just illustrates that perceptions can change in response to events.

The motivations of other actors is the more common case of perceptions changing in world politics. An actor wants to know what other actors intend to do, which is difficult because often those other actors do not want it to be able to anticipate what they will do. Those other actors' preferences are an essential element in their decisions about what they will do. Their actions then reflect their preferences in part. The first actor may be able to learn about the preferences of those other actors by observing what they do. Learning about others' preferences comes from watching what they do and unraveling the judgment behind those actions to infer the underlying preferences from them. Actions do speak louder than words in world politics.

As in the chapter on preferences though, learning about others' preferences is difficult. Often actors obscure their true intentions because they do not want others to know what they intend to do. In some cases, like Hitler's surprise attack on the Soviet Union in the last chapter, it is obvious why an actor conceals his intentions. Even when actors seek to cooperate with one another, they may have good reasons to conceal their complete intentions. Cooperation among multiple actors requires an agreement how they will cooperate. Actors often disagree about how exactly they will cooperate even when all of them wish to work together. An agreement to cooperate then requires concessions by one or more of them. Each would like someone else to make the concessions needed to close the deal. All of them then have a reason to conceal what concessions they are willing to make a deal and how willing they are to make those concessions. Even international cooperation can involve some deception.

Persuasion is the flip side of changing one's perceptions through learning. The question of changing perceptions is "when should I change my beliefs about what someone else will do and how?". The question of persuasion is "what can I do or say to convince another actor to do as I wish?". Persuasion is the art of getting other actors to do as you wish by convincing them that doing so is also in their interest. That typically means changing their perceptions. The same actions, speeches, and events that change perceptions can also persuade.

In the chapter on the logic of a threat, we discussed how the actor making the threat could try to persuade its target that it will carry out its threat if forced to. Whether the target complies with the threatener's demands depends on its perception of the threatener's intent to carry out its threat. The threatener would like to take actions short of carrying out the threat to convince the target that it will carry out the threat and so the target should do as the threatener demands. Changing the perception of the target that the threatening actor might not carry out its threat is necessary for persuasion in this situation.

The cult classic movie "The Princess Bride" ends with an example of persuasion through action. Westley has come to save Princess Buttercup from marrying the evil Prince Humperdink. Alas, his strength has been drained away magically so he can no longer fight Humperdink. The Princess finds Westley lying on a bed as she tries to escape Humperdink's clutches. Humperdink breaks into the room and threatens to kill Westley once and for all. Westley then recites the truly horrible things he will do to Humperdink short of killing him if he has to rise and fight him. But does Humperdink believe that Westley has the strength to fight at all? What could Westley do to convince Humperdink that he can carry out his threat? Is Westley the type that is strong enough to best Humperdink or is he shattered to the point that he cannot move from his bed? I'll tell you later.

Actors could also learn about facts which influence their choices but they do not know. During wartime, actors could also learn about their relative power. War, as mentioned in the chapter on military power, is the ultimate test of power. Battles reveal which side is more likely to win battles in the future, and so the war. Countries hide key aspects of their military capabilities–how many soldiers they have, what weapons they use, and the exact performance of those weapons–as state secrets. Each side of a war has a better idea about many factors that determine which side wins, such as morale and leadership. Because all these factors influence which side wins a battle, combat reveals them and allows both sides to learn about their relative military power. Battles are not deterministic; the winner could be just lucky. So learning about power from battles is not straightforward. The side that wins the first battles is not necessarily the stronger side. How can countries at war sort through these difficulties to learn what the truth is?

More generally, actors could learn from events and others' actions. What sort of actions communicate the most information about what others want? What sort of observation changes perceptions the most?

Learning from Actions and Events

We will discuss learning from the actions of others in detail. The basic characteristics of which events change perceptions the most are the same, but the argument is easier for learning about the preferences of another actor. We represent one actor's uncertainty about another by assuming that the latter is one of several types, where the former knows the set of possible types but not which particular one the other actor is. Its perception of the others' preferences gives how likely it thinks each type is to be the actual preferences of the other side. Because the other side's preferences, and hence type, influence what it does, the former may be able to infer the latter's type from its actions.

Pooling

When the same event happens no matter which possibility is true or if all types take the same action, other actors cannot learn anything about the relative likelihood of the different possibilities. All the possibilities lead to the same observation, providing no new information to the observer. We say that the possibilities or types *pool* when the same event occurs for all or all the types take the same action. The term suggests the idea that all the possibilities stay in one pool together. Observers cannot separate out the possibilities in the "pool" from the event they observed because that event will occur no matter which possibility is true.

Separation

When the various possibilities lead to different events or actions, then observers can learn which is true, or at least more likely, from what happens. If one type would do one thing, while the other types would do something else, you can learn which type you are playing against by what it does. The first event means you are facing the first type, the second event means the second type. We say that the possibilities *separate* in this case because they separate themselves from one another by the events they cause or the actions they take.

The logic of pooling and separation is the same whether we are analyzing unknown causes of events outside of the control of actors or how types of an actor influence what it does. A classic case of separation in scientific knowledge relevant to environmental policy was the "hole in the ozone" found in the 1980s. Before then, some scientists argued that some chemicals rose to the stratosphere where they reacted chemically with ozone, a molecule of oxygen, that helps to block ultraviolet rays from the sun. These scientists worried that if the ozone layer was reduced enough by these chemicals, more ultraviolet rays would reach the surface of the Earth, harming life there. People would suffer more frequent and worse sunburns. These arguments were controversial because the chemicals they suspected have valuable uses in society. Freon, a highly effective refrigerant, was one prime suspect. Using satellite technology, scientists were able to document that the holes in the ozone layer over the poles had grown substantially and were much larger than they had been in the past. This evidence convinced many policymakers that action needed to be taken to reduce the production and emission of these chemicals into the atmosphere. The Montreal Protocol negotiated in 1987 limited and called for the eventual elimination of the production of ozone-depleting chemicals. Political actors found that the evidence separated the reality of damage to the ozone layer through these chemicals from the possibility that changes in the ozone layer observed earlier were just normal fluctuations.

Pure pooling, where all actors take the identical action, or complete separation, where each possibility leads to a different events, are rare. More complete is partial separation, where the different possibilities may lead to similar outcomes with different chances. Actors observing these events can learn something from what happens. Their perceptions change after an event occurs, but they continue to be uncertain about which possibility is true. They become more convinced that causes that are likely to lead to the observed event are more likely to be true than they did before the event occurred. This more common, partial learning from an event, is called *semi-separation* or *semi-pooling* because the types both separate and pool to some extent.

If this seems confusing, return again to the logic of a threat. Whether an actor even makes a threat can provide a clue about whether it will carry out that threat. Imagine that the type that will carry out the threat always makes a threat, while the type that will not carry out the threat makes a threat only one-half of the time. This is semi-separating because there is an event that separates the types–no threat–and another which both types take some of the time–making a threat. What can the prospective target of a threat learn when it expects a threat but none is made. The only type that has a chance of not making a threat is the irresolute type, the one that will not carry out the threat if forced to. The target then learns that the threatener is irresolute and changes its perception to place weight 1 on that type. What does it learn if the threatener does make a threat? If the threatener was the resolute type who will carry out the threat, it always makes a threat. If the threatener was the irresolute type, it might make a threat, with a one-half chance that it does not. A threat then should help convince the target that it is now more likely that it faces the resolute type than it was before the threat was analyzed. Actions then can persuade other actors when they separate types.

How much does an event move perceptions? It depends on how likely the event is to occur for each type and the observer's perception before the event. Using the same types and probabilities of making a threat as above, what is the chance that the threatener is resolute if it makes a threat? If the target's initial perception was that the two types were equally likely, it thought there was a one-half chance of resolute and irresolute types before the threat was made. Say as in the previous paragraph that the resolute type always makes a threat, then the chance that a threat is made and the threatener is resolute is one-half. If, as in the previous paragraph, the irresolute type of threatener makes a threat only one-half of the time, the chance that the threatener is irresolute and makes a threat is one-quarter (one-half chance of being irresolute times one-half chance of making a threat if irresolute). If a threat is made, the chance that the threatener is resolute has moved up from one-half before the threat to two-thirds (one-half chance of resolute and threat divided by the chance of a threat which equals the same one-half plus one-quarter chance of irresolute and threat made). The target changes its perception after the threat because the resolute type is more likely to make a threat than the irresolute type.

The target's initial perception before the threat affects what it learns from the threat. Assume again that a resolute threatener always makes a threat and that an irresolute threatener does only one-half of the time, but now assume that the target thinks it is unlikely that the threatener is resolute. Specifically, let there be only a one-fifth (20%) chance that the target thinks the threatener is resolute before the threat is made. That means there is a four-fifths chance the threatener is irresolute before a threat is made or not. With these assumptions, there is a one-fifth chance that the threatener is resolute and makes a threat (one-fifth chance of resolute times one chance of making threat if resolute). There is a two-fifths chance that the threatener is irresolute and makes a threat (four-fifths chance that the threatener is irresolute times one-half chance of making a threat if resolute). If the threatener makes a threat, afterward there is a one-third chance that the threatener is resolute (one-fifth chance of resolute and makes threat divided by the same plus a two-fifths chance that the threatener is irresolute but makes a threat anyways), up from the one-fifth chance before the threat was made. Compared to the example in the previous paragraph, the target's perception that the threatener is resolute after the threat is made is lower in this case. It takes stronger evidence to overcome a strong existing perception.

To summarize, actions or events change perceptions when they separate the different possibilities. When something happens that should only happen under one possibility and is impossible under the others, you know that first possibility is the real state of affairs. When multiple possibilities lead to the same event, you cannot distinguish among them by observing that event. Complete separation or pooling are rare. It is more common that events or actions partially separate the types. Other actors learn something about the underlying state of affairs, whether it be the type of another player or the true state of something out of the control of any actor. How much they learn and what their new perception is depends on how strong the types separate and their perception prior to the event or action. An actor with strong prior perceptions is difficult to convince. It takes acts that strongly separate the types or the accumulation of much evidence to change the perception of an actor who thinks that one possibility is very likely to be true.

Implications for World Politics

The difficulty of changing strong perceptions affects world politics in many ways. Sometimes countries find themselves in political and military rivalries. They have some conflict of interest, often over bordering territory, which leads to overt conflict between them. In the Cold War, the underlying conflict between the United States and the Soviet Union was ideological. The West led by the U.S. advocated free polities and free economies, both domestically and internationally. The Soviet Bloc adopted communist politics and economics, where the state was led by the Communist Party, other political parties and activities were not allowed, and the government controlled the means of production. In the late 1940s, conflict between the two superpowers began in many areas of the globe. Stalin, then leader of the Soviet Union, used the Red Army's occupation of Eastern Europe to impose Communist regimes on the countries there. The United States and Britain objected to the imposition of these governments but did not act against them. The division of Europe into ideological camps was famously described by Winston Churchill as "an Iron Curtain descending across the face of Europe." Governments of many smaller countries around the world aligned with one of the superpowers. Conflict between these surrogates supported by the superpowers then spread to Asia, the Middle East, and eventually Africa and Latin America. In this rivalry, both sides' developed the perception that the other was hostile to its interests and had to be resisted. These perceptions made the conflict worse because both superpowers believed that they had to contest every area where their interests came into conflict. Although they never fought directly, they did support their proxies with arms, military training, and economic assistance. There were many efforts to defuse the conflicts through peace initiatives. Some were agreed to and reduced tensions, such as the Nuclear Test-Ban Treaty, others were agreed to but had little effect, and others went nowhere. When both parties perceive the other is very likely to be hostile, it is difficult to get them to accept a peace initiative. The side that receives such an initiative may fear that it is simply a ploy by the other side to gain some advantage militarily or politically. Both sides are likely to fear that the other will break any agreement secretly. The side offering the peace initiative may be honest in its desire to reduce the rivalry, but the other is unlikely to see the initiative that way when it has a strong perception that the other side is hostile. Resolving the rivalry requires changing the perceptions of hostile intent, but that is difficult when those perceptions are strongly held as in such a rivalry. It takes actions that only a type with peaceful intentions would take, that is, acts that separate the type that would like to end the rivalry from the type that seeks a short-term advantage through a peace initiative. The Cold War ended when the Soviet Union under Mikhail Gorbachev separated itself from earlier Soviet governments by refusing to stop peaceful revolutions against Communist governments in Eastern Europe. That was something that his predecessors would not have allowed.

Ending long-term rivalries faces the difficulties of changing strong perceptions of hostile intent. Only rarely are dramatic moves that clearly separate out a peaceful type from a hostile one available. Some recommend many small steps to break down these perceptions over time. This is part of the logic of what are called "peace processes." A *peace process* has the parties agree on small cooperative steps that place neither side at substantial risk if they fail. Advocates of peace processes believe that the parties have such strong perceptions of one another's hostile intent that neither believes the other will live with a comprehensive agreement of the issues that divide them. A peace process aims to build trust over time after the parties see that one another can live with these small steps rather than breaking the agreements. These changes are perceptual. They give the parties evidence that the other is not uniformly hostile and is willing to live in peace under some agreement. Sometimes peace processes are successful as in Northern Ireland where a 30-year long civil war was ended through such a process. Others, such as between Israel and the Palestinians, have not been successful yet. One drawback to a peace process is that each small step changes perceptions little. Because the small steps are not costly, any type is willing to take them, which means that the other side learns little about the type of its rival. Slow learning takes many small steps, meaning that peace processes are slow and long. Later we will see that long-term rivalries are also plagued by commitment problems that make them difficult to resolve.

Persuasion in world politics requires separation of types or causes. An actor persuades another when it shows the latter evidence to move its perception enough to change what it does. Sometimes simply making a threat can be persuasive by convincing the target that the chance that the threatener is the type who will carry out the threat is high enough that it is better off giving the threatener what it wants. In the case of the ozone layer, photographs that documented how large the "ozone hole" over the Antarctic had become persuaded many that the issue of ozone depletion was serious. The change in the perception of the problem altered what measures state leaders were willing to take.

Persuasion is often difficult because it is difficult to separate types. If an actor can gain an advantage by persuading another of its type, other types of the same actor may want to mimic the actions of the type that would gain that advantage. Threats are an excellent example of this problem. The willingness of the threatener to carry out its threat, its type, plays a large role in the target's response to the threat. Why make concessions in the face of an empty threat? Even when the threatener does not wish to carry out its threat, it would still like to gain concessions from the target. If the target concedes, then the threatener does not have to carry out its threat, and it does not matter whether it would have or not. An irresolute threatener then would like to imitate a resolute type to gain concessions from the target. If there were some magic word which the threatener could utter, like "Go ahead make my day," that would always convince the target that it was resolute and would carry out the threat and thus convince the target to concede, the irresolute type would always want to say that magic word. But then saying the magic word would not separate the types at all, and so could not convince the target that the threatener was resolute. In short, the magic word of persuasion here poses a paradox. If it works, all types would want to say. But then it would not separate the types, and it could not work.

This *paradox of persuasion* is why actions speak louder than words in world politics. Actors, and states and their leaders particularly, respond more to actions than to statements of intent. State leaders in crises both talk and act in their efforts to make their threats credible. President Bush did not just say that the United States would go to war with Iraq if it did not disarm in the buildup to the Iraq War; he also positioned U.S. troops in the Persian Gulf region so that the U.S. was able to go to war with Iraq. Further, that military buildup was very public. No attempt was made to hide it. Actions often incur costs which only a resolute type is willing to bear. Those costs discourage an irresolute type from imitating the resolute type, which allows the latter to separate itself from the former by its actions and so persuades the target that it will carry out its threat. Later, we will come back to this idea of *costly signals* when discussing bargaining in crises. Words sometimes operate as costly signals when they lead actors other than the threatener or target to change their behavior in the future if the speaker goes back on its word, as we discussed in the chapter on the logic of threats.

The paradox of persuasion arises from the conflict of interest between the two actors. The threatener is trying to get concessions from the target who does not want to do as the threatener wants. Persuasion is more likely and effective when the two actors have important common interests and understand that they do. The scientific evidence in the ozone hole example was persuasive because preserving the ozone layer was in the interest of all. The question was whether something needed to be done and if so, what the international response should be. The scientific evidence answered that question to the satisfaction of most relevant actors in the negotiation. Attempts to persuade that do not involve costly signals are called *cheap talk* (I trust the origin of this term should be obvious to you). Cheap talk can persuade when the actors have significant common interests. Persuasion and cheap talk play a larger role in non-security issues because the common interests of the parties are generally larger on those issues than on security issues. Still, states opposed to one another in a crisis over a territorial issue still have a common interest in avoiding war. Actors on the ozone layer issue had interests in conflict as well as their shared interest in protecting the ozone layer. The hole posed more of a problem for states closer to the poles such as Argentina and Australia. The costs of eliminating the chemicals that reacted with the ozone layer fell differently on various countries. The Montreal Protocol that addressed this issue phased out the production and use of these chemicals in the developed countries like the U.S. but not in developing countries like Mexico. Indeed, there was a period when there was a brisk smuggling trade in Freon, one of the banned chemicals that is also a highly effect refrigerant, from Mexico into southern California for use in air conditioners in cars. Cheap talk is tried often in world politics and works sometimes, while other times it lives up to its name.

How did Westly persuade Prince Humperdink of his ability to carry out his horrible threat? He raised himself up from his bed, stood up, and lowered his sword to face Humperdink. This was something he should not have been able to do if all his strength was gone. Humperdink, being a coward, meekly surrendered and allowed Princess Buttercup to tie him up. Once Humperdink was secured and no longer a threat, Westley revealed his lack of strength by collapsing back on the bed. Humperdink too had revealed his type, a total coward.

Separation of types–getting them to say or do different things–is key to changing perceptions and so persuading other actors. To illustrate this point further, return to the origins of the Second World War and the problem of perceiving Hitler's type.

Perceptions in the Origins of the Second World War in Europe

The Versailles Treaty after World War imposed terms that many Germans found unacceptable. The original German representatives at the Paris Peace Conference in 1919 refused to sign the treaty, and Germany signed only under the threat of a renewal of the blockade on German trade and extension of the Allied occupation of German territory. Versailles took territory away from Germany in the west to France and Belgium, in the east to the new states of Poland, Czechoslovakia and Lithuania, and in the north to Denmark. It demilitarized Germany by limiting the German army to 100,000 soldiers (compared to a wartime high of 5.1 million man army) and denying it tanks, airplanes, and submarines. Further, Germany was not allowed to post troops in the Rhineland, its western border region. This demilitarized zone reassured Belgium and France that Germany could not launch an attack on them without the warning of entering the demilitarized zone first. The territory taken from Germany and given to Poland created the Polish Corridor, a thin neck of land that gave Poland a port city on the Baltic and separated East Prussia from the rest of Germany. Union with ethnic Germans who lived in region adjoining Germany was forbidden, particularly union with Austria, the country of ethnic Germans established out of the breakup of the Austro-Hungarian Empire after the war. Heavy war reparations, payments from Germany to France and Belgium to repair the destruction of their territory, were imposed on Germany. Germans of all ideological persuasions saw the terms of Versailles as burdensome and unfair. The Weimar Republic was created, giving Germany its first fully democratic regime. German politicians saw that they could gain political advantage by pushing for revisions in the treaty.

[Map of territorial adjustments of Germany in Versailles Treaty]

Much of the international politics of the interwar period revolved around revisions of Versailles and the other postwar treaties with the defeated Central Powers. Germany was brought back into the international system through the Locarno Treaty of 1925 with the renegotiation of the reparations and German promises to respect the borders of its neighbors. Despite these changes, revision of the territorial provisions of Versailles continued to be an issue for many Germans. As long as German leaders were unwilling to threaten to use force to change these borders, the demands could be contained. But Adolf Hitler, the leader of the Nazi Party, was appointed Chancellor, the equivalent of Prime Minister in the Weimar Republic, in 1933. Hitler then took apart the Weimar constitution through which he had gained power, established himself as dictator with the self-styled title of Fuhrer (leader in German). Hitler pushed for revision of Versailles more forcefully than any German in the interwar period. He began to rearm Germany openly in 1934. The demands for territorial change would come next.

Great Britain and France would not agree to a substantial change in the territorial terms of Versailles just because Germany asked for one. The demilitarization of the Rhineland gave France warning of a German attack and the ability to attack into Germany so that any new war would be fought on German soil rather than on French soil as World War I had. France also had alliances with eastern European countries, particularly Czechoslovakia, that encircled Germany and force the Germans to fight another two-front war. Any German government seeking to change the territorial settlement would have to back its demands with threats of force. As should be clear now, whether threats succeed depends on the actors' perceptions of their capabilities and the credibility of those threats.

What were the leaders of the three countries uncertain about? For the Western Allies, what were Hitler's objectives? How far reaching were his designs to change the territorial status quo in Europe. If his demands were limited, then they would be better off allowing those changes than denying them through confrontation. The latter course would risk an unnecessary war, one that could be as bad as the First World War. If Hitler's ultimate aims involved redrawing the entire map of Europe, war was in the cards, and Britain and France would be better off fighting sooner rather than later. For Germany, how willing were the Western Allies to fight to resist demands for territorial change? How hard could Hitler push for change without provoking a war when Germany was not fully prepared for one? Finally, for all three countries, what was the military balance? Which side was stronger? The military balance was difficult to judge because all three countries began the decade of the 1930s disarmed. All three began rearmament programs, led by Hitler's Germany with Britain and France trailing afterwards. The military balance then changed over the years of the 1930s. Further, the 1930s was a period of great change in military technology where newer, faster, and more deadly warplanes and tanks were developed. The new models were clearly superior to older models, meaning the side with the newest weapons gained an advantage on the battlefield. It was unclear what was the best way to use these new mechanized killing machines on land and in the air. The uncertainties about the intentions of the other side and the military balance both affected whether the judgments of the leaders of all three countries.

Hitler began to demolish the territorial terms of Versailles in March of 1936. He marched what few troops he had into the Rhineland, remilitarizing it. Britain believed that Germany should have the right to post troops on their own territory and did not see this issue as worth fighting over. France, for who the demilitarized Rhineland was a key guarantee of its security, considered resisting the move militarily. But the French military was convinced that Germany was stronger than it was and counseled caution on the government. Without the support of Britain, France was unwilling to fight and acquiesced in the move. The move was a bluff; the German Army was still weak and could not resist the French alone if they had mobilized their full army. As Hitler himself said in his blustering rhetoric, "If the French had then marched into the Rhineland we would have had to withdraw with our tails between our legs, for the military resources at our disposal would have been wholly inadequate for even a moderate resistance." But Hitler had perceived the sense of weakness and division in the Western Allies which he exploited to his own gain.

[Map of Hitler's territorial gains in 1936-1939]

Hitler's next move was to incorporate Austria into a Greater Germany. The Versailles Treaty banned Anschluss, the union of the two countries. Hitler had tried an earlier attempt in 1934 that was blocked Italy under Benito Mussolini. Since then, Italy's invasion of Ethiopia in 1935 alienated it from Britain and France. Hitler and Mussolini allied after the reoccupation of the Rhineland, and both countries sent troops to fight alongside the Spanish Nationalists of General Francisco Franco during the Spanish Civil War. In February of 1938, Hitler began to pressure the Austrian government to allow the Austrian Nazi Party to operate openly. Chancellor Kurt Schuschnigg was forced to take Nazis into his government. Schuschnigg proposed to hold a referendum, a vote of the Austrian people, on whether Austria should unify with Germany. Hitler threatened to invade Austria. Schuschnigg's government collapsed, and the German Army occupied the country without a struggle. Again, Great Britain and France acquiesced. Unlike the Rhineland Crisis, they had no way to pressure Germany short of threatening war, which neither government was willing to consider.

The Dilemma of Perceptions in the Munich Crisis

The union of Germany and Austria put Czechoslovakia, France's strongest ally in eastern Europe, in danger. Greater Germany now surrounded the Czech heartlands on three sides. There was a substantial German minority living in Czechoslovakia, and Hitler began to agitate during the summer of 1938 that it was oppressed. He demanded the Sudetenland, the mountainous border region, where Czechoslovakia had constructed extensive fortification against a possible German attack. These demands posed major problems for the Western Allies. Czechoslovakia was France's main ally in eastern Europe, its hope of creating a second front in the case of war with Germany. Czechoslovakia also had a sophisticated and substantial army. But Czechoslovakia had a much smaller population than Germany and could not hope to defeat the German Army alone. Great Britain, unlike France, had not accepted Czechoslovakia as a key ally. So the Western Allies were also divided about the importance of Czechoslovakia.

The problem the Western Allies faced had three key elements. First was the military value of Czechoslovakia. Second was the question of whether they thought they could defeat Germany if they fought with the Czechs and Slovaks. Hitler's rearmament program had started sooner and gone much further than those of Britain and France. When asked about France's chances in a war with Germany, the head of the French Air Force replied, "We will be wiped out of the air within two weeks." French and British generals were not confident of victory, and so neither were the politicians in either country. The third, and perhaps most important, factor was their perception of Hitler's ultimate aims. Did they need to fight him now or could war be avoided?

There were two types of Germany consistent with Hitler's actions to the time of the Munich Crisis. The first was what we now know to be Hitler's true type. This type sought domination of Europe and possibly the world through military conquest and intimidation. Even though this type would seek war at some time, it would be happy to grab whatever it could peacefully through the threat of war. Every addition gained peacefully made Germany stronger compared to eventual enemies. This type would then resort to war if its expansion was blocked. The proper response to this expansionist or hegemonic German type was military vigilance and fighting it as soon as possible with as many allies as possible. Germany had more people, a larger economy, and so a larger military than Britain or France alone. They would need all the help they could get to defeat it. They needed Czechoslovakia. The second type of German also sought changes in Versailles but only to bring together ethnic Germans into a Greater Germany. This type was not interested in dominating other ethnic groups but did wish to remove the stain of defeat in the First World War. The Western Allies and its neighbors would not make territorial concessions just for the asking. Military pressure then was a necessary part of this type's strategy to achieve unification of Germans in one country. The proper response for Britain and France to this revisionist, nationalist Germany was to make territorial concessions. Military vigilance could provoke an unnecessary and destructive war. The key to the allied response was how much do you have to give to satisfy this type?

Figure 1
Two Types of Germany and Allied Responses to Each

	Expansionist/Hegemonic	Revisionist/Nationalist
Aims	Continental or global domination	Unify ethnics in Greater Germany
Strategy	Expand peacefully if they let you; otherwise, WAR!	Military pressure as a way to add German regions
Proper Response	Fight as soon as possible with as many allies as you can get	Give them what they want rather than fight a war

This second policy of making concessions to avoid war is *appeasement*, a term which now has a pejorative meaning since its failure in the 1930s. Appeasement means making concessions to a belligerent actor to avoid conflict. As we will see, it failed horribly against Hitler. But against other less belligerent types with lesser aims, concessions may be better than war. Not every type of national leader seeking changes in the status quo is another Hitler.

Whether appeasement is the proper measured response or dangerous folly depends on the ultimate aims of the party you seek to appease. In the face of uncertainty about its motivations, an actor considering making concessions has to judge the ultimate aims of that other party. It can learn and sharpen its perception of the intentions of the other party from the latter's actions. In the case of judging Hitler's ultimate goals at the time was complicated because the two types would have acted the same way. They pooled. The nationalist type and the hegemonic type would both use military pressure to expand Germany's borders to include more Germans within the borders of the Reich. The early expansion of Hitler's Germany did not separate these two types, and so it was not clear whether appeasement was folly or the correct response. The Western Allies made the judgment to appease Hitler by pressing the Czech government to make concessions. In the Munich Conference in September of 1938, the first time that state leaders flew in an airplane to a major conference, Britain and France agreed to the German cession of the Sudetenland. The Czechs, having been left out of the talks completely, chose to give in rather than fight a losing war alone. Prime Minister Neville Chamberlain claimed that the agreement brought "peace in our time," but the length of that peace was less than a year.

Czechoslovakia was also the source of the change in the perception of Hitler by the Western Allies that led to the outbreak of war in Europe. In March of 1939, Hitler stirred up trouble and induced Slovakia to declare its independence from the remainder of the mangled country. He then seized the opportunity to occupy the remainder of Czechoslovakia. This move decisively changed the perception of Hitler among the Western Allies. Not only had he broken promises he made at Munich to preserve the rump of Czechoslovakia, this territorial expansion brought non-Germans into the Reich in large numbers for the first time. This was a move that the nationalist/expansionist type would not make. The scope of Hitler's designs to remake the map of Europe became clear, and both the British and French governments accepted the inevitability of war. Hitler had separated his expansionist/hegemonic type, and neither Great Britain nor France would meekly accept the order he aimed for.

Policy changed with the perception of Hitler's designs. British policy until and through Munich had restrained France by refusing to back it when it considered the possibility of war with Germany. Now the Chamberlain Government guaranteed the security of Poland and Romania, the two countries believed to be next on Hitler's list. Poland bordered Germany, and it had acquired territory at Versailles with large German minorities. Romania was a primary source of oil and so valuable to Hitler's war machine. But were these guarantees credible? Poland and Romania were both in Eastern Europe, and neither Britain nor France could aid them directly. The Western Allies could come to their aid if they declared war on Germany and then invaded the Rhineland in western Germany. Hitler was not overly concerned about these guarantees. How could the British and French made these guarantees an effective restraint on Hitler? They had already shown their reluctance to fight a war with Germany. How could they demonstrate that they were willing to fight now when they had not been in the past? The Soviet Union was one country that could directly aid Poland. But the Poles feared Stalin's Soviet Union as much as Hitler's Germany, and Hitler removed the possibility of Soviet aid to Poland through the Nazi-Soviet Pact. Germany invaded Poland on September 1, 1939; Britain and France declared war on Germany on September 3. They did little to aid the Poles by opening a second front in the west. Germany conquered Poland in less than a month.

How to Analyze It
Persuasion

Separation of types and persuasion is one of the most difficult topics in world politics to analyze because it requires understanding the motivations and perceptions of more than one actors at once. Because you cannot directly observe preferences and perceptions, you have to make reasonable judgments about what they are.

1. The first step is to think about the perceptions of the side that could be persuaded. Follow the steps in the chapter on perceptions to establish what the types of the other actor are and how likely each type is in the eyes of the first actor.

2. Think about what each type of the second actor would do. Are those actions the same or do they differ? This is a judgment about whether they pool or separate through their actions? In the former case, the first actor will not be able to learn about the type of the second from these actions. If so, are there other actions that the second actor could take to persuade the first of its type? The key is whether the types of the second actor want to take different actions.

3. If you find actions that do separate the types of the second actor, how will the first actor respond after it learns of the second actor's type? Does this response advantage one type of the second player over the others? If so, the latter types may want to imitate the first type. It can also be the case that a more motivated type imitates a less motivated type. In the two types of Hitler example, the hegemonic type was imitating the nationalist type because the Western Allies would respond strongly once they knew they were playing against the hegemonic type. Hitler then limited his demands to cover the extent of his ultimate aims. You can think of this as "wolves in sheep's clothing" because Hitler was trying to avoid provoking the Western Allies so far that they took military action. The threat case of an irresolute type acting resolute is like "sheep in wolves' clothing."

4. If one type of the second actor has an incentive to imitate the other type and so deceive the first actor, are there actions which the other type would be willing to take that the first would not? Sometimes in a threat, the resolute type has to find something that only it would be willing to do.

5. Pull the picture together. What does the first actor perceive about the second actor's type? How will that perception change with the actions of the second actor? Do the types of the second actor separate or pool? In the former case, do they separate completely, that is, do completely different things, so that the first case knows what type it is playing with. In the latter case, the first actor cannot learn nor be persuaded.

Summary

Learning about the types of other actors requires that they separate themselves through their actions. These actions could be words as well actions. When the different types of an actor take different actions, others can learn its type by observing its actions. The paradox of persuasion can complicate this process of learning because one type has an incentive to imitate another if the latter gains an advantage by persuading others of its type. Then the types may do the same thing, that is pool their actions, and others learn nothing from their actions. The same logic of persuasion holds for unknown elements of decisions other than the motivations of other actors. Events which distinguish the possible causes or hypotheses about the situation persuade observers of which cause is true. This change in perception can lead actors to change what they are doing now that they understand the situation they face better.

Review Questions

1. Explain how Germany's, France's, and Britain's perceptions about each other's resolve affected the Rhineland crisis.

2. What is the difference between pooling and separation of types? How does each affect perceptions of other actors? What event helped the Western Allies understand that Hitler was the hegemonic type rather than the revisionist type before the Second World War broke out?

Chapter 10
War and the Problem of Bargaining

Between 1998 and 2000, Ethiopia and Eritrea fought a bloody war that you have probably never heard of. They fought over the exact location of their border in a region generally conceded to have little real value. The fighting killed tens of thousands on both sides. After the fighting, they agreed to create an international commission which would set the precise location of the disputed border. Eritrea rejected the judgment of the commission and threatened to reopen the fighting. Why were the two countries unable to resolve the location of their border without fighting?

The Douaumont Ossuary and the Puzzle of War

The one certainty about war is that people die. Countries built monuments of all sorts to commemorate their war dead. The United States has Arlington National Cemetery, war memorials to just about every war in Washington, D.C., and many U. S. cities have had a War Memorial Arena or Stadium at some point. The most somber of these memorials to the dead is the Douaumont Ossuary outside Verdun in France. The Battle of Verdun is the symbol of the pointlessness and inhumanity of the slaughter of the First World War. For ten months in 1916, the French and German armies fought over the hilly countryside north of the city, studded with forts. Both sides fired so many artillery shells into the battlefield that the ground became a moonscape of craters where men fought in mud and filth. Many of the bodies of the dead were never recovered, and even today over ninety years later human remains are found on the battlefield. After the war, the French government constructed the ossuary to hold the bones of all the unidentified remains found on the battlefield. The main floor of the building contains memorial chapel and stones to the French units that fought at Verdun as most of the French army spent some time in the front there during the battle. Below it and visible through windows along the side of the building lies the bones of French and German soldiers together because no one can tell the nationality of these remains. It is a haunting and overwhelming place.

[Picture of the Douaumont Ossuary]

The certainty of death and destruction in war leads to the paradox of war: why do states fight when they know that both will lose people and property in the fighting? Later in this chapter, we will state this paradox more carefully. To do so, we need to understand what states fight over and what role war might play in achieving those ends.

Bargaining over What?

States have conflicts of interest over issues, or perhaps more accurately, we describe what the conflict are over as issues. These issues could be territorial, political, or ideological. Countries have fought over valuable, wealthy territories and trivial changes in their borders. States are fundamentally territorial units where borders define the range and limit of the claim of the government to legally control territory. Military power is the ultimate way to control territory, both to enforce domestic law and prevent violation of the state's territory by outsiders. Because military power can be used to seize territory, war has been a main way that states resolve their conflicts over territory. Sometimes territorial issues concerns members of the national group who live across the border. Territory has receded as an issue that countries fight over, and there are now many borders, such as the U.S.-Canada border, where it is unimaginable that the two countries would go to war over the precise location of the border. We will explore this issue later when we discuss the democratic peace and how domestic politics affects what states fight over.

[Herblock cartoon of Indian soldiers in the Himalayas in 1962]

States have also gone to war to change policies of others that they object to. The United States went to war with Afghanistan after the 9/11 attacks in 2001 when the Taliban refused to close Al Qaeda training camps in the country and hand over Osama Bin Laden and other top members of Al Qaeda for trial in the U.S. Here the issue was the presence of Al Qaeda in Afghanistan with the Taliban's approval. The U.S. did not go to war to conquer Afghanistan. As then Secretary of Defense Donald Rumsfeld said, "The United States covets no one else's territory, especially Afghanistan." U.S. aims in the war in Afghanistan expanded to include the overthrow of the Taliban and its replacement with an Afghan government that would not harbor Al Qaeda. The range of policies over which states have fought is large. Saddam Hussein, the then-President of Iraq, invaded Iran in 1980 in part to stop Iranian fundamentalist agitation across the border; he also sought revisions of the border.

States sometimes fight for ideological grounds. The U.S. fought the Vietnam War to sustain a non-Communist government in South Vietnam. It fought Germany in World War II to overthrow the Nazi government and restore independence to the European countries that Hitler had conquered. The governments of the restored western and southern European states adopted democratic institutions and free and open markets in line with the ideology of the U.S. Of course, states have fought wars over several of these ends together.

The issues in dispute have some current outcome no matter whether they are territorial, political, or ideological. This outcome is called the *status quo*. It continues in force as the outcome of the issues in dispute if unchallenged. In a territorial issue, the status quo is the current border. For policy issues, it is the policies that the states are following when the dispute begins. *Disputes* arise when one side makes a demand for a change in the status quo on some issue or issues. Often this demand is accompanied by explicit or implicit threats of what the state will do if its demands are not granted. The overworked term crisis is often used to describe for the period of international tension that follows a demand for change in the status quo. A conflict of interest between two states can exist for a long time without it generating an open dispute. We will refer to the side that makes the demand for change in the status quo the *initiator* of the dispute, and the party it makes the demand of the *target* of the dispute. Although I will talk of initiators and targets being single parties, they could both be groups of countries with shared interests.

A dispute, once started, ends when either the parties agree to change the status quo in some way or the initiator withdraws its demands or allows it to lapse. Resolving a dispute then requires some settlement that both sides accept. In the former case, the target makes sufficient concessions in the status quo to satisfy the initiator. In the latter cases, the initiator stops pursuing its demand and the target is happy to return to the status quo as the outcome of the issues in dispute. In this sense, both sides accept the settlement of the dispute. The conflict of interest may continue, but it returns to the stage where neither side is threatening to use force to change its resolution. In other cases, the resolution of the issues ends the conflict of interest, creating a situation where both sides view the issues as resolved. No serious politician in Germany or the United States wants to reopen the outcome of World War II by restoring a Nazi government in Germany. In a few cases, the issues may remain open for a long time. The U.S.-led war in Afghanistan removed the Taliban from power, but the fighting did not end because the Taliban and its Al Qaeda allies did not accept this outcome. Instead, a long war fought by irregulars against U.S., NATO, and Afghan government forces has continued in the country.

Once started, disputes and threats to use force have a logic of their own. Settling a dispute requires the agreement of both sides, even if the initiator allows its threats to lapse and the target takes no further action. When a side wants to end a dispute, it has to ask what the other side will accept to do so. Both sides in a dispute commonly make demands of the other. A side which wants to end a dispute can do so by granting all the demands of its opponent. As we will see, the other side may accept less than their complete demands to prevent war. The question of how to end a dispute once started is "what is the *price of peace*?" How much do you have to give the other side to convince them to abandon the use of force to gain all they demand? Peace comes with the price of what you must give up to avoid war.

The Treaty of Brest-Litovsk

World War I did not go well for Russia. It lost millions of soldiers at front, often through the military incompetence of its generals and officers. Behind the lines, it succeeded in raising war production greatly but at the cost of sparking strong inflation. The conversion of factories from civilian to military production meant there were few consumer goods of any sort available. Peasant farmers withheld their produce from the market because the money they received for their food could not buy anything they wanted. The resulting food shortages sparked riots and strikes in the cities. These pressures led to the two Russian revolutions. The first in March of 1917 caused the fall of Tsar Nicholas II, the autocratic dynast who ruled Russia, and his replacement by the Provisional Government of Alexander Kerensky. Kerensky's government was democratic and continued Russia's war effort. The Kerensky offensive in July turned quickly from initial success to disastrous retreat, sparking mutinies at the front and demonstrations for peace in the cities. The Bolsheviks, led by Vladimir Illich Lenin, took advantage of the growing chaos to seize power in the October Revolution which actually took place in November. (Russia still used the old Julian calendar at the time which was about two weeks behind the Gregorian calendar used by the rest of Europe for centuries.)

The Bolsheviks came to power on a platform of bread and peace and sought the latter with Germany quickly. They reached an armistice, a stop in the fighting short of a peace treaty, during which much of what was left of the Russian Army at the front line deserted. Lenin sent Leon Trotsky to negotiate a peace settlement with the Germans and Austrians at Brest-Litovsk. German territorial demands were extensive. Germany wished to keep all the territory they occupied and detach Ukraine from Russia as a separate puppet state of Germany. Ukraine was the breadbasket of Russia, and Germany needed Ukrainian grain to feed its army and people, who were being slowly starved by the Allied naval blockade. The Bolsheviks were divided on how to respond to Germany's demands. Some favored granting them, others to returning to active war, and still others trying to foment revolution inside Germany. Trotsky came up with a novel solution. He declared peace unilaterally with the slogan "no war, no peace" and left the conference to return to Petrograd (later Leningrad, and now St. Petersburg).

[Map of Eastern Front in 1917, showing front line, Ukraine, Brest-Litovsk, and German advance]

Unfortunately for Trotsky, Lenin, and the Bolsheviks, it takes two sides to make peace just as it takes two sides to fight. The Germans responded to Trotsky's unilateral declaration of peace by launching their armies eastward into the Ukraine. The Russian army had disintegrated through desertion after the Bolsheviks came to power. After all, why stay in the army if the government says the war is over? The German Army advanced 150 miles in 5 days. The Bolsheviks realized they needed to yield to German territorial demands to preserve their revolution in Russia. Trotsky and his delegation returned to Brest Litovsk. The Germans wanted more because their military position was stronger than during the first set of talks. They demanded and received additional territory. New states dependent on Germany were carved out of Russian territory in Georgia, Finland, and the Baltic. Trotsky learned that the price of peace can be high indeed.

Proximate versus Ultimate Causes of War

Our focus on the issues in dispute and whether the parties can solve their disagreements over those issues peacefully puts our attention on the *proximate causes of war*. They are the factors that cause the outbreak of war directly. What led the leaders of each country to choose war as a way to resolve their differences instead of negotiation? Relatively few disputes lead to large-scale fighting by both sides. Some end in clear settlements, others peter out, leaving open the possibility that they will flare up again. Attention to the proximate causes can explain the varied responses to conflicts of interest among states.

Other explanations of war attend to why conflicts of interest exist between states and how those conflicts fester with the passage of time. These are the *ultimate causes of war*. Some who seek the ultimate causes of war trace them to factors as basic as the nature of the state and human nature. Others examine how conflicts grow into all-encompassing rivalries where each state in the conflict believes that anything that benefits the other's interest harms its own. Attention to the ultimate causes of war can explain why conflicts of interest exist and how they develop over a long period of time.

The study of the origins of the First World War illustrates the difference between proximate and ultimate causes. International tensions and rivalries built up among the European Great Powers in the decades after the unification of Germany at the end of the Franco-Prussian War. France wanted the return of the two provinces Germany took from it, Alsace and Lorraine. The war demonstrated that France was not strong enough to defeat Germany on its own, so it sought allies against Germany. German policy under Otto von Bismarck sought to deny France such support by tying up Austria-Hungary and Russia in alliances. But those two powers had conflicts over the Balkans. Russia identified with Slavic peoples in the Balkans who sought states of their own that encompassed all their co-ethnics, even those who lived in Austria-Hungary and the Ottoman Empire, which became Turkey after the war. After Bismarck fell from power after Wilhelm II became Emperor, Russia left its alliance with Germany and allied with France. Over time, these alignments hardened. Germany began to build a large navy, which alarmed Great Britain. The latter had historically had stayed out of peacetime alliances with continental powers, but joined with France and Russia to offset growing German power. By 1914, Europe was divided into two armed camps. The countries in both camps expanded their militaries out of fear of the other side. They developed war plans to mobilize and coordinate the millions of soldiers they could raise from their populations that could not be changed and committed them to all-out war. The formation of these two camps are studied as the ultimate causes of the war.

This process, however, does not explain alone why the July Crisis of 1914 precipitated by the assassination of Austrian Archduke Frans Ferdinand by a Serbian extremist led to the outbreak of war. There had been many crises across the two camps in the years before 1914, between Germany and France over Morocco in 1905 and 1911 and Austria-Hungary and Russia in 1908. But these crises had not led to war, while the July Crisis did. Study of how and why state leaders acted in the July Crisis that led to the outbreak of war between Austria-Hungary and

Serbia and then the spread of that war to encompass the two alliances addresses the proximate causes of the war. What choices led to war in the July Crisis?

The example of the origins of the First World War shows why we focus on the proximate causes of war over the ultimate causes in this chapter. The ultimate causes create the conflict of interests between the two sides but do not explain why that conflict flares into war. Often, these conflicts of interest persist for long periods of time, creating international tension but not war. In this chapter, we ask why the parties turn to war as a way to solve their conflict of interest. Later, we will examine some of the processes claimed to be ultimate causes of war, such as rivalries and preparation for war.

Bargaining Theory

Bargaining theory can help us understand the strategic dynamics of why parties sometimes choose to use violence in a negotiation. The ideas here are general to most situations where the parties bargain over some outcome of interest to both of them when multiple deals are possible. They can apply, with some important differences, to two people negotiating over the price in a sale of used car. People, for one, rarely resort to violence to get the price they want. Instead, they may walk away and either seek to buy another car or try and find a buyer willing to pay more. Despite these differences, there are underlying common features of negotiations which we will think about in general terms.

Thinking about Issues in a Dispute

Parties negotiate to agree on one solution to the issues they face. There are many ways they could agree. If there was only one possible solution, they would have nothing to bargain over, having only the choice to adopt that solution or not. As mentioned earlier in this chapter, states have conflicts of interest over many types of issues. What we seek to explain is why states sometimes use force and threat of force to induce another to agree to a change in the current outcome of the issue.

An easy way to think of all the possible settlements arrays them along a line. Each point of the line is a different possible settlement of the issue. If the issue was control of territory, each point would correspond to one way to draw the border. If we were examining bargaining over buying a used car, each point would correspond to a possible sale price. International disputes may have more than one issue dividing the parties, but we can show the essential points about bargaining by treating those issues as if all the possible settlements fall along a line.

The two sides disagree about which settlements they like best. One side, which we will colorfully call state A, prefers outcomes toward the right. The other, state B, prefers those to the left. This is the conflict of interest between the two sides. If we were talking about the sale of a used car, the seller like state A prefers a higher price; the buyer like state B prefers a lower price.

If the issue is the control of territory, settlements towards the right give more of the territory to A, those to the left more to B. But a whole range of settlements is possible, and the parties could place the border between them at any of these places. As Figure 13 shows, the interests of the parties are opposed. Settlements that one side likes better, the other likes less. We focus on the areas of disagreement because the parties can agree to adopt outcomes where both agree on what the resolution of the issue should be.

Figure 13
Possible Settlements on a Line

B gets more of the territory	An even division of the territory	A gets more of the territory

By representing the possible outcomes as all the points along the line, we assume that the parties can divide the issue any way they want in a settlement. With territory, they can draw a border anywhere they want within the disputed territory, giving each less or more. With a negotiation for buying a used car, the two parties can agree to any price. Some issues seem to have only a few possible resolutions, but even these issues can be divided by creative bargainers to provide a more even distribution to both sides. This idea underlies how the plan for a peace settlement between Israel and the Palestinian that President Bill Clinton mediated in 2000 handled the Temple Mount in Jerusalem. The Temple Mount is the remains of the artificial hill built by King Herod two thousand years ago on which the Temple, the center of Judaism, was built. The Romans destroyed the Temple in 70 CE, but the mound remains. Later, Muslims built the Dome of the Rock and al-Aqsa mosques on the top of the Mount. Many Muslims consider this location to be the third-most sacred site in Islam. Jews revere the exposed wall of the Temple Mount as the Wailing Wall, which they captured along with East Jerusalem in the Six-Day War in 1967. Each side would like to have the site under its control. How can both sides control the same place? President Clinton's plan divided control horizontally at the level of the top of the Mount. Israel would control everything below the top, including the Wailing Wall, while the Palestinian state would control everything above the top, including the al-Aqsa mosque. What appeared to be indivisible was divided to give each side what it valued most. Most issues which seem indivisible can be divided by sufficiently creative negotiators. We can use a line then to represent all possible bargains because almost all issues can be divided to give some value to both parties.

[Picture of Temple Mount with al-Aqsa and Dome of the Rock mosques]

The line with the preferences of each side in Figure 1 captures the essence of a bargaining problem. There are many possible settlements, but the parties disagree about which they like best. They bargain to resolve those differences and agree on a settlement. The idea is the same whether it is a buyer and seller haggling over the price of a used car or state leaders attempting to settle a disagreement over an outstanding international issue, such as the location of a border.

Reservation Points and the Zone of Agreement

Each side in a negotiation evaluates all the possible settlements so it can judge what offers it will accept, reject, and make. A side's *reservation point* (sometimes called *reservation level*) is the settlement it views as equivalent to going to war. It will reject any settlement worse than its reservation point and is willing to accept any settlement better than its reservation point if forced to choose between war and that settlement. In this sense, a side's reservation point is its minimally acceptable deal. Figure 14 below shows A's reservation point and the range of settlements that are more attractive to it.

Figure 14
A's Reservation Point and Settlements It Prefers to War

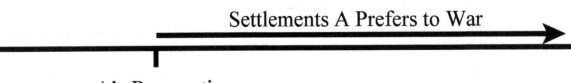

What determines a side's reservation point? Because a reservation point is the settlement an actor views as being as attractive as war, its value for war determines its reservation point. The more attractive war is in the eyes of an actor, the more it will insist on in lieu of war. Three other values to the state's leaders enter into the judgment of how attractive war is. First, how well does the leadership thinks its military will fare in the fighting? The more confident they are of winning on the battlefield, the more they will demand to forestall war. This assessment of what will happen if the bullets start to fly reflects what settlement the side would expect at the end of the war, which depends on how the war goes. Second, what costs of war are they willing to bear? As mentioned earlier, war destroys life and property. The willingness of a state's government to bear those costs of war affects what it would accept to avoid war. In the chapter on military power, the Vietnam War was an example of a state whose leaders were willing to suffer very high costs of war to gain what they wanted. Those leaders then were unwilling to abandon their military efforts to unite Vietnam under their leadership when pressured by the United States. Third, how important are the issues in dispute? Willingness to pay the costs of war depends, as in the Vietnam War case, on how important the issue is to national leaders and their people. Unfortunately, that importance is measured all too often in the currency of human lives. Figure 15 shows how a side's expected outcome of fighting combines with its assessment of the costs of war to produce its reservation level. A's costs of war in the figure drive down its reservation level by moving it further left. This shift means that it prefers war to fewer possible settlements and so is more willing to settle.

Figure 15
Expected Outcome of War minus Costs of War Determine Reservation Point

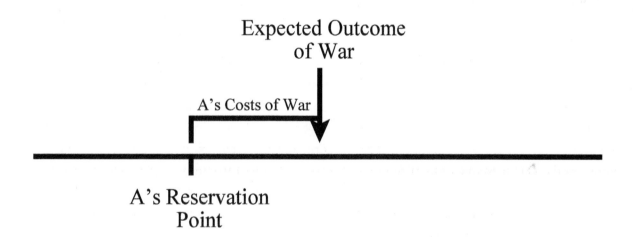

Both sides make parallel judgments about how the possible deals compare to fighting. Figure 16 shows the other side's calculation on the same issue. B's costs of war push its reservation level to the right, making it more deals preferable to war as its costs of war increase.

Figure 16
State B's Reservation Point

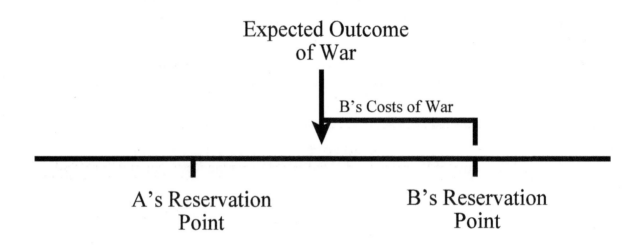

Each side's reservation point shows which settlements it views as preferable to war. Figure 17 shows the ranges of settlements that each side sees as preferable to fighting from their reservation points. A prefers all the points to the right of its reservation level, and B prefers all of them to the left of its reservation point. The costs of war move each side's reservation level away from the expected outcome of fighting, A's to the left and B's to the right. The costs of war then open up a range of settlements that both sides prefer to war. This range is the *zone of agreement*, the range of settlements that both sides prefer to fighting. This range exists because war is costly to both sides. Each side's value for fighting depends on both the outcome they expect and their costs of war. The outcome is largely but not entirely a result of their relative power. If both sides' perception of their relative power are close, they should have similar judgments about which side is likely to win a war and how large the victory will be. The costs of war create a zone of agreement by reducing the value of fighting to both sides and making settlements close to the expected outcome of fighting better for both sides than war.

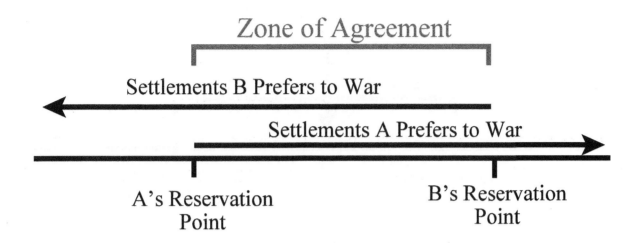

A zone of agreement then should always exist in crisis bargaining. Figure 18 shows how the expected outcome of a war and its costs produce both sides' reservation points and the zone of agreement between them. The existence of a zone of agreement in bargaining in a dispute reflects one of the basic facts about war; afterwards, at least one side regrets having fought the war. The loser, in particular, should always regret having fought. It could have agreed to an outcome at least as good as the result of the war including its attendant costs before fighting began. By 1945 as the forces of the United Nations closed in on Nazi Germany, even Adolf Hitler probably had second thoughts about the wisdom of launching the Second World War. Saddam Mullah Omar, the leader of the Taliban when the war in Afghanistan began in 2001, probably realizes now that he would have been better off to accept President Bush's demands to close Al Qaeda training camps and turn over its leadership for trial in the U.S. Even the winners may often find that they would have been better off accepting something less to secure a peaceful settlement. The U.S. would have been better off accepting less than President Bush's full set of demands on the Taliban, say just the closing of the training camps and the surrender of Osama Bin Laden and a select few top leaders of Al Qaeda. The ongoing fighting in Afghanistan and hunt for Bin Laden would have been avoided. Of course, we cannot be certain about what would have happened if President Bush had accepted less than his full demands of the Taliban. Even with that qualification, often even the victors regret having gone to war in many cases.

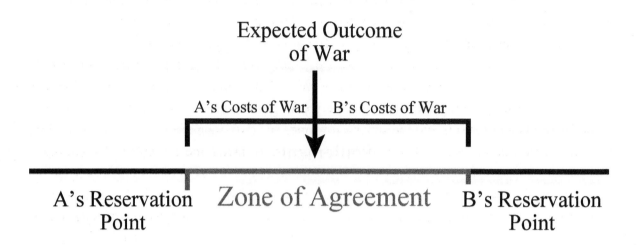

Figure 18
How Costs of War Create a Zone of Agreement

In regular bargaining, there may be not a zone of agreement. This is why I will never drive a Ferrari. Parties bargaining over the purchase of a car negotiate over the price. Seller wants a high price, the buyer a low one. Each side's reservation point is the minimal deal it will accept. This is a lowest price at which the seller will sell, and the highest price the buyer will pay. The seller will reject a price below its reservation level and seek another buyer instead. Similarly, the buyer will look for another car if the seller insists on a price higher than the buyer's reservation level. The zone of agreement, if it exists, is the range of prices between the seller's and buyer's reservation points. It includes all the prices at which both parties are willing to make the sale. I will never drive a Ferrari because no seller would accept the price I am willing to pay to buy one. There is no zone of agreement, and no sale is possible.

Prewar bargaining then differs from bargaining over a sale for at least two reasons. First, there should always be a zone of agreement. Second, the parties do not have the option to walk away and find another party for a deal. In negotiating over the purchase of something, you can always seek someone else to deal with. When you reach the stage of negotiating the price to buy a new car, walking out of the dealership when they do not give you the price you want is a very effective tactics. I know; I have done it. In prewar bargaining, the alternative when the other side will not give you what you want is to increase the coercive pressure on the other side, with war being the ultimate form of coercive pressure. Just as pulling a gun in a car dealership to get a better price is unlikely to work, neither is walking away from a crisis like Trotsky did at Brest Litovsk.

Incentives to Misrepresent

If a zone of agreement always exists over the issues in dispute before war breaks out, why do the parties sometimes fail to reach a settlement and so go to war? This is the puzzle of war. Why do leaders of states commit their countries to destructive warfare when peaceful solutions are available? This chapter and the next will develop two different answers.

The first answer lies in the process of bargaining itself. Even if the parties both want to reach a peaceful settlement and know that there are such that both would accept, each side would like to get the best possible deal it can. The desire for a better deal is like the sale of a car, where the buyer wants a high price and the seller a low one. In crisis bargaining, both sides would like to obtain a resolution of issues that favor their interests. Consider the example of bargaining between the United States government and the Taliban after 9/11 and before the war began. President Bush made extensive demands of the Taliban, which they chose not to make after considering them. As I argued earlier, there were deals that would have made both sides better off than the war has. The Taliban would still be in power in Afghanistan, which is better for them, and the U.S. would have been able to try Osama Bin Laden publicly. The Taliban did not reject President Bush's demands out of hand. They instead asked to see the proof that Osama Bin Laden was behind the 9/11 attacks. The Taliban never made a complete counteroffer in response to President Bush's demands, so neither party explored what peaceful settlements each side would accept. They did not resolve the conflict over which settlement as each side stuck to its negotiating position.

Neither side knows the other's reservation point, and this fact complicates the choice of a peaceful settlement. The factors that determine an actor's reservation point–its judgment of which side is likely to win a war and how willing it is to suffer the costs of war to prevail on the issues in dispute–are known only to that actor. Other observers, including us as analysts, must try to judge what deals the other side might accept. Now if an actor knew the other side's reservation point, it would know exactly the best deal it could obtain, namely the other side's reservation point. The same lack of knowledge of reservation points is present in negotiating over a car. If I list a used car for sale for $2000, you know I will accept that price, but I might also accept less as well. But how much less? You do not know and can only find out by offering less and seeing if I accept a lower price. What price do you offer? $1500? $1800? The Taliban faced the same problem in responding to President Bush's demands after 9/11. They knew his high price for peace. Once they judged that they would not meet those demands, how much less would he accept not to go to war? Because they did not know exactly the minimal deal that President Bush would accept over war, they had to judge what they should offer instead. Their request to see the proof against Osama Bin Laden was not enough to satisfy President Bush.

Each side further has an incentive to exaggerate its negotiating stance to try and induce the other side to offer a better deal. If it acts tough enough, it might convince the other side to offer more, and so secure a better deal for itself. Each side's bargaining stance–the demands it makes, the threats it backs up those demands with, and what actions it takes during the crisis–all depend on its reservation point. The other side then may be able to learn what the first actor's reservation point is from what it does during the crisis. If it learns enough, it may be able to narrow down on a deal that the first side would accept and would favor its own interests. This is the problem of changing a perception by learning from actions that we discussed earlier in the chapter on how perceptions change. A side which believes that war is more attractive will demand more not to go to war in a crisis. If the other side knew that, it would offer that side more. Consequently, those types of the first side which have a lower reservation point would like to imitate the tougher types with a higher reservation level. Again, it is like a bargaining over a used car. As a seller, I can get a higher price than I would settle for if I can convince you that I will not accept less than that higher price and you are willing to pay it to get the car.

Actors in a crisis have an *incentive to misrepresent* their position and act tougher than they actually are. If it convinces the other side to offer more, it gets a better deal than it would if it had simply acted honestly and stated its minimal demands. How should an actor in a crisis respond to the threats and demands of the other side in the face of this incentive to misrepresent? We can think about the problem using the two types of opponents given in Table 10.1. The opponent could be the resolute type whose threats are serious. If so, you are better off making concessions and avoiding war. On the other hand, the opponent might be exaggerating its willingness to carry out its threats in the effort to get you to offer it a better deal. If so, you would be better off rejecting its demands in the hope that it would back down because it is willing to settle for less than those full demands.

Table 10.1
Two Types of Opponents Making Demands in a Dispute

Type of Opponent

	Resolute Type	Irresolute Type
Whether It is Willing to Fight	Willing to Carry Out its Threat	Bluffing to Get Concessions from Receiver
Proper Response for Receiver	Make Concessions to Avoid War	Reject Demands and Prepare to Fight

Incentives to misrepresent produce two effects that contribute to the failure of bargaining and the outbreak of war. The first is the tendency to exaggerate threats and demands in the hope of convincing the other side to make concessions. If a threat works and induces the target to make concessions, the threatener does not have to carry it out. This incentive also influences how the other side responds to those threats. The target of a threat in a crisis knows that the threatener has the incentive to misrepresent and takes account of that incentive in judging the credibility of the threat. The target discounts the credibility of the threats directed at it because it knows the other side has the incentive to make threats that it may not be willing to carry out. It doubts whether the threatener intends to carry out its threat, which reduces the effectiveness of that threat. This second effect of incentives to misrepresent makes it harder even for a resolute type to make effective threats.

Think again about the Taliban's response to President Bush's threats to go to war with it if it did not grant his demands. The internal discussion of the Taliban leadership is not available, so we have to speculate. They probably wondered what the United States could do to them if war occurred. Afghanistan is very far from the U.S. and difficult to reach because it is land-locked and mountainous. There was no easy way to insert U.S. troops into the area for a ground attack. The U.S. had few allies in the region at the time where it could establish bases to launch an attack. Although the Taliban was fighting an ongoing civil war, it was stronger than the local rebel movements known as the Northern Alliance and had control over most of the country. Finally, al-Qaeda provided both money and soldiers who fought for the Taliban. The leaders of the Taliban may have figured that there was little the U.S. could do to them if they ignored President Bush's demands. When war came, the U.S. fought through the Northern Alliance by providing them with arms and air support that shifted the terms of battle in their favor. The U.S. relied on special forces to lead Northern Alliance fighters and direct air strikes from bases in the area from countries that agreed to support the U.S. war effort, aircraft carriers based in the Indian Ocean, and airplanes outside the area that flew very long missions to bomb targets in Afghanistan. It must have been a surprise to the Taliban when their soldiers were routed within two months, and they lost control of the country.

[Map of Afghanistan showing how difficult it is to reach the country]

Costly Signals

How could you tell which type of opponent you face? This is the problem of separation of types from the chapter on how perceptions change. Only actions that separate the types, acts that only the resolute type is willing to carry out, will indicate which type you face. Think about the problem from the position of the other side, the side making the threats. If you were the resolute type, what could you do to convince the other side of your resolve? You have to take actions that an irresolute type in your position would be unwilling to take. Finding such actions is difficult in a crisis because of the paradox of persuasion. If an action necessarily convinced the target that the state threatening war would carry out its threat if its demands were not met, all types of threatener would want to take that action to get what it wanted. Instead, actors trying to demonstrate their resolve in a dispute use actions that an irresolute type might be unwilling to carry out. These actions must have costs which an irresolute type would be unwilling to pay. They are called *costly signals* because the costs they entail enable the actor sending them to signal its resolve.

Some actions in a dispute have costs associated with them. Mobilization of troops and moving them to the region of the dispute costs money to the acting state. When reserves are called into the ranks from civilian life, the people mobilized are taken away from their civilian lives and jobs, which is unpopular and hurts the economy. When President Bush moved U.S. military personnel to the Persian Gulf region before the Iraq War, those troop movements cost the U.S. government the cost of transportation and supporting the troops in the months before the attack. If those military maneuvers require the consent of another nation to place troops in their territory, as was the case of placing U.S. troops in Kuwait before the invasion of Iraq in 2003, obtaining its agreement to their presence can be costly. Turkey, for example, refused a request to base U.S. troops on its soil to launch an attack on Iraq from the north before the Iraq War. Actors can also take limited military action to demonstrate their resolve. These actions do not impose the outcome they like; they try to convince the other side to yield before stronger measures are taken. These actions contribute to the *escalation* of the crisis; they raise the pressure for war. By preparing a side for war, they raise its value for fighting which makes it less willing to settle.

Still, most of the actions that leaders take to demonstrate their resolve are words. They make speeches, declare their positions, and send envoys to meet representatives of the other side. Perhaps the most famous such speech was President John F. Kennedy's television address to the American people on October 22, 1962 that started the Cuban Missile Crisis. He announced that the Soviet Union was placing nuclear-armed missiles in Cuba and that the United States would place a blockade on Cuba in response. During the crisis, both sides used the UN as a public forum to present their positions, and Premier Nikita Khrushchev of the Soviet Union published letters he sent Kennedy on the Soviet position in the crisis. The final bargain was reached privately but then announced publicly.

That words can be effective is part of the puzzle of persuasion. An actor incurs no costs by simply speaking words, leading to the term "cheap talk." But words can persuade when others beyond just their target hears them. As described in the chapter on the logic of threats, other audiences also hear and can respond to what state leaders say during a dispute. When those words escalate the crisis in an effort to convince the other side of its resolve, the other audience also hears the message that the speaking leader believes the issues in dispute are important enough to fight over. One such audience is the people of the country of the speaking leader. Another is leaders of other countries outside the dispute. Both audiences listen to what a state's leader says in a dispute and may hold him or her responsible if the leader goes back on their word. A domestic audience can limit their leader's freedom of action in the future and in the extreme could replace the leader with someone else if they are displeased. Leaders of other countries may be unwilling to deal in the future with a leader who has gone back on his or her word. Words said in the heat of a dispute may then rebound against a leader who acts later against what he said. These audience costs–the consequences of backing down after saying the issues in dispute were worth fighting for–can make speeches in a dispute credible signals of resolve. Although saying the words themselves is not costly to the leader, saying them when you do not mean them could be.

Audience costs can make words and speeches into credible signals of resolve. Irresolute types should be unwilling to make speeches that they have no intention of backing up with force if they are called on them. The other side listening to such a speech can learn that it is more likely to face a resolute type that is willing to carry out its threat. Sometimes these words take the form of an *ultimatum*, a threat to attack if the target does not do exactly as you wish. President Bush made an ultimatum to Saddam Hussein before the Iraq War, a demand that he and his sons quit office and leave Iraq within 48 hours. Ultimata are the strongest threats available in a dispute because they force war if the target does not give in. They are very rare in world politics precisely for that reason. If the target does not give in, the party making the ultimatum almost must go to war. It is clear to everyone, including all audiences, that the leader has not backed up his word if he does not go to war.

Audience costs are conditional; a leader suffers them only if he backs down from his position after stating it publicly and invoking those costs. If the other side gives you most of what you want, you have not backed down from your position publicly. The relevant audience has no reason to hold your actions against you in the future. A leader's word is good as long as he does not go back on it in public. Carrying out the threat by going to war is another way a leader can live up to his word in public. If you say that the issue is important enough to fight over, going to war honors that pledge. Audience costs make a leader more willing to fight than offer concessions because she does not suffer them if she goes to war.

Speeches create audience costs only if they are public. Audiences cannot react to statements of resolve and the importance of an issue that they do not hear. Similarly, states often take actions that escalate a crisis in the open. U.S. Presidents often use aircraft carrier task forces to signal their concern about an issue. Carriers can be sent to the oceans near the location of the crisis within a week. Their complement of aircraft can be used by the President to launch air strikes once they arrive in the area. The U.S. government announces these deployments; it makes no secret when carriers are deployed to a crisis area. In January 2007, the Bush Administration deployed an additional carrier group to the Persian Gulf to increase pressure on the government of Iran on both the nuclear enrichment issue and Iranian efforts to aid insurgents attacking U.S. troops in Iraq. Some observers worried that this deployment was the first step towards a U.S. military strike to destroy nuclear enrichment sites in Iran. The public nature of this escalation is necessary for it to apply coercive pressure to Iran and its leaders.

Public pressure through escalation and invoking audience costs can also have a downside in a crisis. These acts often raise the stakes for the other side as well. The targeted leader may respond in kind creating audience costs for himself if he later makes concessions to end the dispute. Challenging another country publicly can make its leader less willing to make concessions. Often then, states conduct both public and private diplomacy during a crisis. They use their public diplomacy to signal their resolve and convince the other side that they are serious. They can then explore settlements through private diplomacy where other audiences do not know what settlements they discussed. Audiences only learn of these negotiations if both sides agree to a settlement. The Cuban Missile Crisis is an example of the combination of public and private diplomacy. President Kennedy and Premier Khrushchev both made public statements of their resolve and took military steps that escalated the crisis. They explored possible settlements through several private channels where trusted representatives of each country met to discuss options. The eventual settlement had the Soviet Union withdraw its missiles from Cuba in exchange for a public pledge by President Kennedy that the United States would not invade Cuba and a private pledge to withdraw U.S. nuclear missiles from Turkey.

How Might War Occur?

The combination of escalation and audience costs explains how leaders might choose war even when a zone of agreement was present when the dispute broke out. When one leader threatens another to press its demands, the latter does not know how serious that threat is. The threatening leader has to take actions to convince the other that its threat is serious. Escalation of the crisis by mobilizing troops into the region of the crisis prepares a state for war, raising its chance of winning a war. Public speeches signal to domestic and international audiences that the leader speaking places a high value on the issues in dispute. These actions make it more costly for the leader to end the crisis by giving the other side what it wants. For the side that initiated the dispute with the first threat, it gives in by backing off its demands publicly. This period where both sides try to coerce the other into giving them what they want is called a *war of nerves* by some. The risk of war is evident, and it tests the nerves and resolve of the leaders of both sides. After all, both sides would like to get what they want without fighting even if they are willing to raise the specter of war to pressure the other side.

During the war of nerves, each rise in the audience costs that a leader has invoked through her actions make her less willing to make concessions to settle. The increasing audience costs raise her reservation point. At some point in the crisis, a leader can reach a point where its audience costs are high enough that he prefers war to any settlement short of his full public demands. This moment is the point of *lock-in*. After lock-in, the leader may wait to go to war to see if the other side will give him what he has demanded, but he will no longer offer any concessions to settle the dispute peacefully. Audience costs are a dangerous signal of resolve.

They raise the risk of war by making moderate settlements more costly and so less attractive. If both sides become locked-in, then war is inevitable because neither side will back down. The zone of agreement has disappeared. War, which seemed unthinkable before the dispute began, has now become necessary for both sides.

To pull the full picture together, war is a possibility because both sides are uncertain about one another's resolve. The desire to secure the best possible bargain within the zone of agreement gives both sides the reason to act tougher than they are. Because the other side knows the incentive to misrepresent is present, each takes actions which are costly signals, either by invoking audience costs or preparing for war. These acts signal resolve, but they also make a side more willing to fight and less willing to settle. If the war of nerves goes on long enough and the sides escalate the crisis enough, they can become locked in. War now becomes a certainty. Still, few disputes reach this stage. Most are settled peacefully.

Public versus Private Diplomacy

It is not always the best move to escalate a crisis or take strong public stance to create audience costs. These moves signal resolve and make it harder for a leader to end the crisis by making concessions. They also produce pressure on the other side to give into your demands. But if they do not, what do you do next? Choosing between going to war or backing off your demands and suffering the audience costs you have created is not a pleasant choice. Your actions also may make it more difficult for the other side to make concessions. A direct and public challenge to the other state may also engage that leader's relevant audience, making it more difficult for her to make the concessions you demand. Escalation of a crisis poses a *risk-return tradeoff*. It increases the bargaining pressure on the other side, making it more likely that you will get a better deal out of the other side. But it also increases the chance that both sides will end up locked in, leading to war. Escalation is unwise when the issue is not that important. Belligerence is both effective and dangerous in a crisis.

Often state leaders then choose not to go public with their demands. Earlier, I mentioned President Kennedy's use of public diplomacy in the Cuban Missile Crisis to engage the U.S. public about the seriousness of the issue of Soviet missiles in Cuba in his eyes. Much less well known is a second crisis between the U.S. and the Soviet Union over Cuba nine years later. The Soviet Union had not pulled all of its ground troops out of Cuba as called for in the agreement that ended the crisis. When the U.S. discovered this, President Richard Nixon and his National Security Advisor, Henry Kissinger, chose to approach the Soviet leaders privately and request they honor the agreement and remove the remaining troops from Cuba. They could have chosen to start a crisis by making a public revelation like Kennedy did. Private diplomacy sufficed in this case, making a crisis and its heightened risk of war unnecessary for Nixon to get what he wanted. Private diplomacy can allow both sides to explore deals that may be unpopular with some in their country without facing criticism for doing so. The various peace treaties and agreements that attempt to start a peace process between Israel and Arab states all began with private meetings between high-level governmental representatives. The privacy of the peace initiatives insulates those politicians from criticism from those in their country who would oppose any deal not entirely on their terms. At the same time, private negotiations do not produce the same leverage to induce the other side to make concessions as a crisis does. The shadow of initiating a crisis if the talks fail can provide some leverage. Nixon and Kissinger knew that they could go public and start a crisis if their private talks with the Soviets did not produce the results they desired.

The choice of when to go public to advance your country's demands is important then. This chapter has focused on public diplomacy in crises because almost all wars are preceded by such crises. Wars occur when neither private nor public diplomacy succeed in finding a settlement in lieu of war.

Ethiopia and Eritrea Again

The border dispute that led to the war between Ethiopia and Eritrea goes back to the creation of Eritrea in 1991. Before then, Eritrea had been a province of Ethiopia since the brief time when Italy held both countries as colonies that ended after World War II. Eritrea fought a 30-year long war against the central government of Ethiopia to gain its independence. The Eritrean People's Liberation Front joined forces with Ethiopian rebels based in Tigre, the region between Eritrea and the capital of Ethiopia, Addis Ababa. Their joint forces defeated the Marxist regime of Haile Mengistu in 1991, with the rebel movement becoming the new government of Ethiopia. A referendum in 1993 confirmed Eritrean independence.

[Map showing Ethiopia and Eritrea with Addis Ababa and Tigre marked]

Afterwards, both sides claimed several towns and their surrounding areas fell on their side of the border. This disagreement is the heart of the dispute between the two. The border has not been demarcated where physical markers, typically stones, are used at regular spaces to show the exact location of the border. These markers are the physical presence on the ground of the agreement of both parties to the precise location of a border. Both sides claimed the location of the border was set by different colonial era treaties. Both sides' police and military forces clashed violently, killing several in May 1997. In response, Eritrean forces moved into the disputed territory and took positions along where Eritrea claimed the border was. This act was an attempted *fait accompli* (French for "accomplished fact"), an act where one side tries to impose its preferred outcome. The other side must go to war to reverse that act.

War did not immediately follow. There was some fighting, but neither side attacked with their full force. Both sides built up the militaries by inducting people into the army and buying weapons internationally. There were international efforts by the Organization of African Unity (OAU) and by the U.S. and Rwanda to mediate the dispute. When Eritrea rejected the joint U.S.-

Rwandan plan as favoring Ethiopia in February of 1999, Ethiopia launched a massive assault on Eritrean military positions in the disputed territory. The resulting battles killed thousands of soldiers on both sides. Fighting died down after these battles, but mediation efforts again failed to produce an agreement both sides would accept. Ethiopia attacked again in May 2000, and Ethiopian forces advanced far enough into Eritrea that its government accepted the OAU plan and withdrew its forces from any disputed territory they still held. Still, no peace settlement has been accepted by both sides, and the conflict has threatened to trigger renewed fighting several times since the end of the war in 2000.

How to Analyze It

Analyzing the disputes that lead to wars and identifying what bargains are better for both sides than war can be difficult. Both sides make competing claims about the justice of their own position and the falsity of the claims of the other. Neither side states their minimal demands for a settlement publicly out of fear that they will get just that and nothing more.

1. News stories on disputes generally explain the public positions of both sides on the issues in question. They typically provide little detail on those positions. Some news sources, like the major news outlets, provide summaries and time lines for important international disputes. These background articles can help you see the evolution of the dispute. News sources face the problem of being less than complete unless you are willing to go back through the long history of news stories on a crisis.

2. With the advent of the internet, countries use it as a way to communicate their positions in disputes. These websites are statements of a state's position and then to focus on why they are right and the other side wrong. They must be read carefully. Comparing the positions of both sides can be very instructive because it can be like reading about two different events.

3. Judging what concessions each side might be willing to make is difficult. Neither side announces its willingness to make concessions. You can try to think about how each side might view its chances in a war, but many subjective judgments enter into a state's evaluation of its prospects if the shooting starts.

4. The willingness of each side to make concessions can be judged from what actions it takes during the crisis. How strong are its public statements of resolve? You need to be careful here because autocratic leaders often used stronger language than democratic leaders do. Has either side taken military measures to prepare for a war in the region of the dispute?

Trying to analyze the positions of two sides in a dispute can be frustrating. That analysis does give you some insight into how difficult it can be for national leaders to judge what the other side will do in a crisis. It should also illuminate the incentive to misrepresent in a crisis.

Chapter Summary

States fight wars over their conflicts of interest over international issues. These issues are often territorial but sometimes are political or ideological. The question facing state leaders in a dispute is the "price of peace", how much are they willing to concede to the other side to secure an agreement to avoid war. During a crisis, each side has a reservation level, the settlement it views as the same as war. Because war is costly, there should be a zone of agreement, settlements which both sides prefer to war. The position each side states publicly demands more than its reservation level. Each side has an incentive to misrepresent its position, to act tougher than it is, to secure the best possible deal that it can. They also understand that the other has an incentive to act tougher than it is, so they discount the other side's signals of resolve, even when those signals are honest. Resolute types try to separate themselves from the possibility that they are irresolute by sending costly signals. Actions which prepare a state for war make war more attractive to its leaders, and so signal its resolve. Speeches can invoke audience costs which the speaking leader will suffer if he or she backs down after stating how important the issue is to him or her. Escalation and audience costs can lead to a national leader to reach the point of lock-in, where she prefers war to a peaceful settlement. The zone of agreement that was present at the outbreak of the dispute has disappeared, and war will follow.

Review Questions

1. Define a state's reservation point in a crisis. What factors affect a state's reservation point? What is a zone of agreement?

2. Explain why state leaders have an incentive to misrepresent their bargaining position in a crisis. What are the consequences of those incentives for how a state's bargaining position is interpreted by the other side?

3. What role do costly signals play in a crisis, and how can states generate them?

Chapter 11
Commitment Problems and War

The conflict between Israelis and Palestinians is one of the most vexing issues in world politics today, and it has been for decades. Peace efforts have foundered in the 1940s, the 1970s, the 1990s, and in this decade. Although the loss of life from the ongoing violence is not as high as it was in the Arab-Israeli wars of 1947-48, 1956, 1967, 1973, and 1982, the human cost of the conflict is still high for both sides. Average Israelis and Palestinians live in fear of unexpected violent death. During the 1990s, many Palestinians worked inside Israel to provide for their families; they lost their jobs during the Second Intifada in 2000 when the crossings into Israel were closed as a security measure. Estimates of the economic cost of the conflict range from $500 million to $2.4 billion per year.

It is not difficult to imagine peace settlements that would make both sides better off than the ongoing conflict. The territory in dispute was the British Mandate of Palestine between the World Wars. The UN proposed dividing the territory into two states, one Jewish and one Arab, in 1947 when the British were ready to end the Mandate. When the independent state of Israel was declared, its Arab neighbors–Egypt, Syria, Jordan, and Lebanon–all declared war and invaded the Mandate territory. At the end of the Palestine War, the remaining Arab-held territory in the Mandate was administered by Egypt in the Gaza Strip and Jordan in the West Bank. The cease fire line between the two sides became known as the Green Line. During the 1967 Six-Day War in 1967, Israel conquered and occupied the West Bank including East Jerusalem, the Gaza Strip, the Golan Heights in Syria which overlook northern Israel, and the Sinai peninsula. Since 1967, Israelis have moved into and established settlements in these territories, particularly in the West Bank and in and around previously-Arab held Jerusalem. Palestinians routinely refer to the Green Line as the basis for division of the Mandate territory, while Israelis commonly request alterations in that line to account for particular large and important settlements inside the West Bank. In any case, the differences between the two sides are small compared to the cost of the conflict. Many observers envision a peace settlement close to the Green Line with some adjustments for the settlements and some compensating territory inside pre-1967 Israel passing back to a Palestinian state. They differ on the precise location of the lines, but these differences are small. They should not be difficult to negotiate out.

[Insert maps of 1947 UN partition plan, pre-1967, and post-1967 here]

The general populace of both sides wants peace as well. Surveys of both Israelis and Palestinians show clear majorities in favor of a peace settlement roughly similar to the lines described above. Although the desire for peace in both societies is not universal, it is widespread. Why are they unable to reach a peace settlement when the central bargain is obvious and so many on both sides desire it?

Political settlements are not like buying a used car. When you buy or sell a used car, you never need see the other party ever again, and all understand that caveat emptor–let the buyer beware–rules. If the car breaks down a day later, that is the buyer's problem. Political deals instead require exchanges over time. In some cases, one side yields something of value to the other side in exchange for a similar favor later. The Cuban Missile Crisis ended with the Soviet Union withdrawing its nuclear-capable missiles from Cuba in exchange for a public pledge by the United States not to invade Cuba. Once the missiles were gone, what could restrain the U.S. from another invasion of Cuba, similar to the U.S. sponsored invasion of Cuban exiles at the Bay of Pigs in 1961? Only the same measures as Khrushchev's disposal before the crisis and the deal that ended it. In that sense, the Soviet side of the deal always faced the risk that the U.S. would not deliver on its side of the bargain. Was Kennedy selling Khrushchev a used car, and if so, why did Khrushchev not realize it?

Because political deals are made over time as well as issues, they must persist to succeed. Both sides understandably may doubt the willingness of the other side to deliver on their promises in the future. Later in the chapter, we will cover the reasons why actors might not live up to their agreements. For now, we just want to understand the effect of such doubts on whether the parties can reach an agreement. One side may be concerned that the other is not sincere in its pledges during negotiations or that conditions may change, leading the other side to break its promise. Even if the agreement does not entail a promise of future concessions, a party may fear that the other may seek to renegotiate the deal in the future. This problem is called *commitment* because the parties are afraid that one another is not committed to carry out the bargain.

When parties to a negotiation have doubts about whether the deal will hold in the future, each no longer compares the deal to the current situation. Instead, they compare the consequences if they make the deal to the current situation. They consider the chance the other side will break the deal later and the consequences of such reneging. The consequences of the other side reneging could be large if the deal places one side in a vulnerable position. In an extreme case, conflict can be better than a deal. In the extreme, concerns about whether an agreement can be enforced can eliminate a zone of agreement. Deals that both sides would accept if some third party could force them to honor it are not concluded when the parties have to enforce it on one another.

Commitment problems form the second explanation of why negotiations might fail to find an agreement to avoid war. Bargaining explanations center on the logic of threats; how can a party make its threats to use force credible and effective for inducing the other side to make concessions? Commitment explanations center on the logic of promises; inherent in any peaceful deal is a joint promise to honor that deal in the future. The conditions that make promises more credible and effective are also those that might be able to address a commitment problem.

Incentives for Undermining a Deal

Parties generally intend to live up to the terms of the deals they sign. Although there are some cases of parties agreeing to deal which they have no intention of honoring, they are rare. Commitment problems arise because conditions change after the deal is signed. These changes give party incentives to break its promise to honor the deal. When conditions change, so does the willingness of the parties to live by their promises.

Changes in power provide incentives for parties increasing in power to seek to renegotiate a deal. Negotiated settlements should reflect the relative power of the two parties. If one of them becomes more powerful, it gains leverage to reopen the settlement through the threat of force if necessary. One common source of such changes in power is the recovery of the power of a defeated state after a war. Combat kills soldiers and destroys equipment; the forces of the side that loses a war lose both. After the war, the defeated state rebuilds its military forces by recruiting and training new soldiers with new equipment. This growth in military power could give it the ability to secure a better deal than it had to accept to end the war. Alternatively, it could renege on anything it agreed to in the peace settlement.

The aftermath of the Gulf War in 1991 is an example of this incentive to renege in action. The ground phase of the war lasted only 100 hours as the forces of the U.S.-led coalition cut off and decimated Iraqi forces occupying Kuwait. The government of Iraq wanted to end that war as soon as possible and so agreed to strong terms to save its remains of its military, which was also the ultimate guarantor of Saddam Hussein's regime against domestic rivals and rebels. Revolts by the Kurds in the north and Shiites in the south of Iraq were crushed using what was left of the Republican Guard after the war. The government of Iraq and many Iraqis found the terms of the peace settlement burdensome. UN arms inspectors had access to the country to find and verify the destruction of Iraq's programs to produce weapons of mass destruction, nuclear, chemical and biological weapons. The U.S. and Great Britain blocked efforts to remove the economic sanctions imposed on Iraq during the crisis before the war. These sanctions crippled the economy of Iraq, led to widespread smuggling of oil out of Iraq and consumer goods into the country, and impoverished many Iraqis. The U.S. and Great Britain imposed and enforced no-fly zones over the north and south of Iraq. Once the war was over, the crushing military superiority of the coalition forces disappeared as they returned to their home countries. Although Iraq's military was still weak after its defeat, the withdrawal of the bulk of coalition forces reduced the credibility and effectiveness of its threat to enforce the peace settlement. The decade after the Gulf War and before the Iraq War in 2003 saw Iraq attempt many times to renege on the letter and spirit of the peace settlement. It did not fully cooperate with UN arms inspectors and threw them out of the country in 1998. In response, the U.S. and Britain bombed targets in Iraq repeatedly to punish Iraq for its noncompliance. The shift in power from the withdrawal of coalition forces led to this struggle to enforce the peace.

[Map of Iraq showing no-fly zones]

Changes in preferences can also lead to a change in the willingness of a state to live with a peace settlement it previously accepted. Changes in the leadership of a country is a primary source of these shifts in preferences. A new leader may come to power on promises to undo an unpopular agreement. The Versailles peace treaty with the Allies was deeply unpopular in Germany after the First World War. Much of the international politics of the 1920s concerned the revision of Versailles to satisfy German demands for change without undermining France's deterrence of a renewed war. But the territorial changes in the Versailles Treaty remained unchanged until Adolf Hitler took power. His program to overthrow the Versailles system began with rearmament to create the military leverage needed to challenge that system. Although most German politicians of the interwar period advocated changes to Versailles, none of them before Hitler sought to create the military power to forcibly regain former German territory.   The change in leader and Hitler's willingness to use force to obtain what he wanted undermined the territorial provisions of Versailles. The change in regime that Hitler imposed by destroying the democratic institutions of Weimar Germany also aided his program of violent revision by eliminating other possible sources of power in Germany that might have opposed him.

Finally, changes in the situation without a change in power or leader could alter the incentives a national leader has to honor an earlier agreement. A leader whose domestic political position becomes less secure might use revision of an unpopular agreement to restore his popularity and hold on power. Upcoming elections can produce the incentive to break an agreement to secure more votes by appealing to those voters whose interests are hurt by the agreement.

Commitment problems lead to conflict when there are settlements that both sides would prefer to war, but one or both of them doubt that the other will live up to the agreement in the future. As a result of their doubts, they prefer war to agreeing to one of those settlements. If they could solve the commitment problem by making the agreement enforceable, their doubts would disappear and war would be avoided. In this sense, commitment problems can cause war.

Commitment Problems as a Cause of War

Conflict destroys things of value, people and property, for both sides. Both can benefit by avoiding conflict, and as argued in the last chapter, there should always be deals that both sides prefer to conflict. But political bargains must hold over time, and for the three reasons given above, one or both sides may doubt that the other will continue to honor the bargain over time. If at least one side believes that signing that deal will lead to a situation where the other gains an advantage by breaking the deal in the future, it may prefer fighting now to accepting the deal and then facing a much worse situation in the future when the other side breaks that deal. It would accept the deal if a third party could enforce it on both parties, but such third party enforcement is rarely available. War now becomes in the interest of both sides, even though there are deals that both would prefer to fighting *if they knew those deal would hold.*

Commitment Problems and Power Transitions

As mentioned above, shifts in power can produce commitment problems because the side losing power relative to the other fears that the latter may use its increased power in the future to undo the deal and impose terms less favorable to it. Power transition theory examines how long-term shifts in power driven by industrialization has caused major wars in world politics. Briefly as we will cover power transitions in more detail in a later chapter, industrialization causes a major increase in the power of a country as it produces more, its population grows, and its government increases its ability to extract power from its people and economy. These changes happen over decades. This increase in power over decades can produce a long-term shift in power, one that other states cannot stop. The rising state undergoing industrialization will eventually become more powerful than the dominant state, which industrialized earlier and so had the power to dominate the system, leading to a transition in power. Will the rising state use its new-found power to overturn the system established by the dominant state?

There should be bargains that both sides prefer to fighting. The dominant state could make small concessions to the rising state over time, just enough so that the rising state would take them and wait for the next one instead of fighting now for complete control of the system. But is the rising state willing to wait? If the change in power is fast, the concession of the dominant state may not be sufficient to convince the rising state to take it now and wait for more later. If the dominant state is buying peace for a period of time, the bargain has to reflect both their relative power in the future when the rising state is even stronger as well as their relative power today. If the transition is rapid, the dominant state may not be willing to offer enough to satisfy the rising state. Both sides then would rather fight today; the rising state wants concessions that reflect its power in the future, but the dominant state would rather fight now before it loses more power relative to the rising state.

Some argue that a power transition contributed to the outbreak of the First World War. Germany industrialized in the late 19th and early 20th century, making it the most powerful country in Europe. It, however, was not so powerful that it could take on all the other major powers in Europe. France was always hostile to Germany because of the the lost provinces of Alsace-Lorraine, which Germany had taken from France when Germany was unified at the end of the Franco-Prussian War in 1871. But France was weaker than Germany and needed allies to be able to regain its lost provinces. Despite Germany's growing power, it needed an ally to counter any alliance that France might form against Germany. Unfortunately, the two countries that bordered Germany on the east, Austria-Hungary and Russia, were rivals of each other. Germany could not ally with both, and it chose Austria-Hungary. Russia and France formed an alliance in 1893 aimed at Germany and Austria-Hungary. This pairing of rivals was stable for twenty years as German power continued to grow. Russia, the most economically backward of the major powers of Europe, began to industrialize in the early 20th century which threatened this balance. German leaders began to fear rising Russian power because Russia had a larger population than Germany, meaning that once both countries were fully industrialized, Russia would be stronger and could overturn German dominance of central Europe. Their concerns about rising Russian power through industrialization led some German military leaders to argue that the July Crisis in 1914 provided an opportunity to settle scores with Russia and lock in German domination for decades. While this concern was probably not decisive, it contributed to German fears.

The problem is that both sides cannot commit to a changing, flexible bargain over time. If Germany could have committed to making limited concessions to Russia over time, enough to satisfy the Russians, and Russia could have committed to asking for no more than those concessions, no matter how much its power grew, German concerns could have been allayed. But neither side could commit to such a string of concessions, and no other power could force them to live up to such a deal. The commitment problem induced by Russian industrialization could not be solved.

Protracted Conflict

Some conflicts of interest in world politics are protracted. These conflicts remain unresolved in that the parties have not agreed to a settlement of their differences. At the same time, the parties are not using violence against one another at most times. The disagreement of the parties persists, with one of them occasionally turned to violence to advance their position in response to some development between the two. Protracted conflicts remain in a limbo of neither peace through the settlement of their differences nor active war which might end in a resolution. These protracted conflicts can last for decades with the parties cycling through long periods with little violence punctuated with periods of indecisive fighting.

The conflict between India and Pakistan over Kashmir is an example of a protracted conflict. With the division of the subcontinent at the end of British colonial control in 1947, the Maharaja of Kashmir attempted to remain independent rather that acceding to join either Pakistan or India. An irregular militia from Pakistan invaded Kashmir, which was and is majority Muslim. In response, the Maharaja chose to become part of India, and India sent in troops to defend the territory, triggered the Indo-Pakistan War of 1947. These two countries ended the war with a ceasefire agreement that divided the territory on the front line, which became known as the Line of Control. Since then, the two countries have fought three further wars in 1965, 1971, and 1999. Only the last was centered in Kashmir as India and Pakistan also have had other conflicts of interest. There has also been an insurgency in Kashmir since 1989, which India claims that Pakistan provides training and material support, a charge denied by Pakistan. None of these violent conflicts has resolved the status of Kashmir, and now that both countries have nuclear weapons, a clear military victory establishing complete control of Kashmir is unlikely.

When a commitment problem exists between two parties, there effectively is no zone of agreement between them. Any deal that they both would prefer to the ongoing conflict and its periods of violence will be rejected by at least one of them out of fear that the other will renege on that deal in the future, placing the fearful party in a worse position than the protracted conflict. If the parties have a peace agreement, then there is at least one outcome that both sides prefer to fighting, the status quo under that agreement. This is true even if the peace settlement has been imposed by one of the two on the other. As long as the latter sees remaining at peace as better than threatening violence to overturn, there is not a commitment problem. Commitment problems then explain protracted conflict over new violent conflicts.

In a protracted conflict, violence between the parties is rare and short or at a low level below that of active warfare. The question when to use violence is a protracted conflict becomes a question of when and how to do so. It becomes a tactical decision of how much violence to use and for how long. Commitment problems then do not lead directly to violent conflict as the parties may wait for the best time to fight.

War Termination

If war begins when one side turns to violence to advance its bargaining position, war ends when the two sides can agree on a settlement. At an extreme, that settlement may be imposed if the victor has effectively eliminated the defeated's military. Even in these extreme cases, there is still a form of an agreed settlement even if the defeated is willing to sign any agreement to end the fighting. Even Nazi Germany formally surrendered to the United Nations in May of 1945 after Hitler's suicide. War termination often faces a commitment problem, one that can cause war to continue after the point where it is clear which side has won.

States fight wars to accomplish their ends, whether those ends are territorial or political. A peace settlement reflects what is happening on the battlefield. If one side is clearly winning, it will demand concessions from the other side. If the loser fears that its military chances look even worse if it continues to fight, then it may agree to make the concessions demanded. The victor would like what it accomplishes through victory to last so that it does not have to fight another war. Every side winning a war wants to win the peace as well. This requires a settlement that will persist, one that the defeated will not seek to overturn in the future. As with power transitions, shifts in power between the two sides can undermine a possible settlement to end a war. The loser, having made concessions, may seek to undo the settlement if its military power grows relative to the victor after the war is over.

In 1991, the U.S.-led coalition defeated Iraq's army in the first Gulf War. Iraq had overrun and occupied Kuwait in the summer of 1990. The members of the coalition moved an army of 500,000 to Saudi Arabia to prepare for the war. When Iraq refused demands to evacuate

Kuwait and restore its sovereignty, the coalition launched a six-week air campaign, bombing target in Iraq and Kuwait. Then the coalition launched a devastating ground attack which routed Iraq's army in 100 hours. Iraq accepted the terms offered by the coalition to end the war before their army was totally destroyed. The settlement not only restored Kuwait's sovereignty, it also established inspections for Iraq's programs to develop weapons of mass destruction–chemical, biological and nuclear weapons–to ensure that those programs were stopped and that Iraq did not possess any of those weapons. Coalition forces had demonstrated their total superiority during the brief war, a dominance reflected in the peace settlement. But after the war was over, most of the forces of the coalition returned to the home countries and bases outside the Persian Gulf region. Iraq's military power increased relative to the coalition's as these forces withdrew. The government of Iraq began to interfere with the weapons inspections and took advantage of vague provisions in the peace settlement in its efforts to suppress rebellions among the Kurds in the north of the country and Shiites in the south. Although the UN inspections eventually did disarm Iraq of weapons of mass destruction, the success of those efforts were not clear until after the Iraq War of 2003. The shift in power gave Iraq the ability to resist elements of the peace settlement that reflect the military dominance of the coalition during, but not after, the war.

The shift in power after the Gulf War occurred because most of the coalition forces left the region. Often the defeated state recovers its power as it rearms after a war. Because war kills soldiers and destroys equipment, the side that is losing will see its military strength decline relative to the victor. After the war is over, it can train new troops, acquire more equipment, and rebuild its army. If the peace settlement reflects the two sides' relative power during the war, the power of the defeated may rise after the war is over. The victor, anticipating that the defeated may challenger the peace settlement in the future, may continue fighting until it can establish a stable peace afterwards. It could do so by setting the border on defensible terrain, such as mountain range or major river, or by taking territory from the defeated to reduce its potential power. Both require the victor to fight beyond the point where both sides agree that it has won the war, to fight to a point where it can imposes the terms that it believes will hold afterwards.

The First World War imposed a horrible human cost on all sides, but they could find a settlement acceptable to both sides before the collapse of the German army in the fall of 1918. During the winter of 1917/1918, both sides had reasons to be optimistic and pessimistic about their chance for victory in the next year. Germany had knocked out Russia and could shift its troops to the Western Front to face Britain and France, but its population was slowly starving from the British blockade that cut its trade outside Europe. Britain and France could look forward to the deployment of the U.S. Army in the field that would give them a large advantage in manpower, but France had suffered major mutinies in their army in 1917 and British leaders were wary of suffering hundreds of thousands more casualties as they had at the Somme in 1916 and Passchendaele in 1917. Neither side made a serious effort to explore a negotiated settlement, despite the huge casualties they would have to suffer in 1918 even if they won the war that year.

Germany would probably have accepted a peace settlement that restored the prewar borders in the west, provided that settlement recognized German territorial gains and domination of Central and Eastern Europe. The British, and particularly the French, were not willing to do that. Such settlement would give Germany time to integrate those gains into its economy and be much stronger for a renewed war a decade later. So France and Britain endeavored on in the hope of a decisive victory that would allow them to break German power and control of Eastern Europe. It was close in 1918 as the Germans almost defeated the British and French before the United States arrived in force, but when they did, the tide turned, the Allies rolled back the Germans, whose army collapsed and society revolted. The Allies imposed the Versailles Treaty on Germany in 1919 in an effort to ensure that Germany would not rise again to threaten France. It failed.

The commitment problem often posed by war termination explains why wars once started can be so difficult to end. They drag on for years and at a horrible human cost over what appear to be trivial issues as both sides try to ensure that they win the peace as well as the war.

The Arab-Israeli Conflict

As mentioned in the introduction to this chapter, there should be many deals that would make both Israelis and Palestinians better off than the ongoing conflict of decades. The conflict bursted into brief periods of fighting in 2008-2009 and 2012, although low-level violence with Palestinian militants firing from the Gaza Strip into Israel and Israel responding by firing back and targeted bombings. The conflict also imposes a substantial economic cost on both sides. Israel faces substantial costs to secure the lines of control, and Palestine suffers from Israeli restrictions on the movement of goods and people into and out of the Palestinian territories. Given these high ongoing human and economic costs, there are many divisions of the territory that would be better for both sides *if* those divisions led to long-term peace between the two. Two states living in peace with one another would eliminate the threat to people from violent conflict and allow both societies to grow through trade with one another and the world. A number of different plans for the division of the territory have been proposed, most based around the Green Line that was the ceasefire line at the end of the 1947-1948 war with some swaps of territory on both sides of it. Some issues, such as whether East Jerusalem will be the capital of Palestine, are more difficult to resolve; the Palestinians insist that it must be their capital while Israel argues that it must keep the areas in and around Jerusalem where Israelis live now.

Why are they unable to agree on a division of the territory? Both sides worry that any negotiated settlement may lead not to long-term, mutually beneficial peace, but rather renewed violent conflict in the future. There are a variety of commitment problems facing any settlement. The oldest issue concerns the geographical vulnerability of Israel. If the Green Line border separating the two countries, much of Israel is the flat plain along the Mediterranean, which is only eleven miles wide at its narrowest point. Before the Six-Day War, Israelis were always concerned that the combined Arab armies could overrun their country because of its openness and lack of natural barriers to invasion. Israel conquered and then occupied the Gaza Strip, the West Bank, the Sinai peninsula, and the Golan Heights to establish defensible borders against its Arab neighbors. The Sinai peninsula was returned to Egypt in the 1979 Camp David Accords, but Israel's occupation of the Gaza Strip and West Bank, now commonly known as the Occupied Territories, dates back to 1967. If Israel was certain that its Arab neighbors would never again threaten to invade them, then it would not need defensible borders. But to move back to the Green Line would make the country vulnerable again, and there are few certainties about future intentions in world politics.

Both sides have reasons to doubt whether the other will live in peace after a settlement. Both have violated prior interim agreements during peace processes of the last twenty years. Israel has built official settlements on land that Palestinians think is theirs and not consistently stopped illegal Jewish settlements in the West Bank. The Palestinian Authority has not consistently controlled militant factions that conduct attacks on Israelis. Further, both sides have extremist factions that reject settlements that would divide the territory and compromise the most extensive demands of each side. The Charter of Hamas calls for the destruction of Israel by a Palestinian state, and although Hamas leaders have stated a willingness to divide the territory, it would only be for a twenty-year truce at most. Some Israeli political parties have argued for the establishment of "Greater Israel," commonly meant to be all of the Mandated Territory and the Golan Heights (some Israeli politicians change political parties frequently, and the extremists often change parties). Would these factions live in peace with a division of the territory into two sovereign states? Understandably, those on both sides who would like to settle their dispute worry about how these extremists would respond afterwards.

Because Israel is a democracy, we can judge how much support there is for extremism by seeing how many votes parties with extreme position get in elections. The Palestinian Authority and Palestinian political organizations are opaque. It is not easy to tell how strong their support is among the Palestinian public. The extremist factions claim that they speak for the people, but how would we know? Would those factions lose public support after a peace settlement? Can the resulting government on either side control extremists that might wish to subvert a peace settlement with violence? Because a settlement would ease security restrictions, launching violent attacks would be easier after a settlement. On the Palestinian side, Israel will continue to have military dominance over a Palestinian state. Will a future Israeli government use that military advantage to take back territory conceded in a settlement, particularly under the claim to be ensuring its security after attacks by militants?

Arab states are generally autocracies, even now after the Arab Spring. The future policies of autocracies are unpredictable because the autocrat can change policy quickly without a need for broad support. Even for Arab states like Egypt that have started to become democracies by holding elections, will they remain democratic? Might parties with extreme political aims prove popular with Arab publics that hold hostile attitudes towards Israel?

The Arab-Israeli conflict faces large commitment problems that make it difficult to settle the conflict, even though both sides could benefit greatly from such a settlement. Solving those problems requires creating mechanisms of credible commitment that ensure that both sides will observe the peace and that both can trust the other to do so. This is a difficult task.

Summary

Settlements of conflicts in world politics need to hold over time. Commitment problems arise when one or both parties suspect the other will break a settlement and gain an advantage by doing so. If a party sees the result of a such violation in the future as worse than fighting now, it will not accept a settlement, choosing to fight instead. Commitment problems can arise from shifts in power in the future, changes in national preferences, and changes in the situation that alter the incentives of national leader for peace over violence. When you hear about a situation where negotiation is difficult because the two sides "do not trust one another," think of what the commitment problem is. Solving these problems is not just a matter of building trust; it requires taking steps that ensure that both sides will live up to the deal in the future and know that the other side will as well. Because those solutions are difficult to find, commitment problems produce protracted conflicts in world politics.

Review Questions

1. What factors can change over time to create commitment problems after a crisis is resolved?

2. What incentives over time create commitment problems for possible resolutions of conflicts?

3. Explain why commitment issues make the Palestinian-Israeli conflict difficult to resolve.

4. Explain the role of commitment problems in protracted ethnic conflict.

5. Are commitment problems more important in explaining the outbreak of violent conflict or why some conflicts are difficult to end? Briefly explain why.

Chapter 12
Bureaucratic Politics

At times, different branches of the United States government do not know what one another are doing. Before the 9/11 attacks, government policy against Al Qaeda was uncoordinated. The two agencies responsible for counterterrorism, the Federal Bureau of Investigation (FBI) and the Central Intelligence Agency (CIA), failed to catch the hijackers. They did not share the information they had on the hijackers. The CIA, which is responsible for counterterrorist policy outside the United States, had some of the hijackers on a watch list of suspected terrorists. The FBI, responsible for counterterrorism inside the borders of the U.S., could have arrested the hijackers except that they did not know they were suspects. The Department of Homeland Security was formed after 9/11 in part to eliminate this and other failures of federal agencies to coordinate on counterterrorism. More generally, U.S. policy on what actions to take against Al Qaeda was inconsistent. Osama Bin Laden and Al Qaeda were recognized as threats to the United States, its citizens, and interests. They had carried out attacks against U.S. embassies in Kenya and Tanzania in 1998 and the U. S. Destroyer Cole in 2000. President Clinton launched cruise missiles strikes against Al Qaeda training camps in Afghanistan after the attacks on U.S. embassies in East Africa. The CIA had agents in Afghanistan tracking Bin Laden. They asked for authorization to kill Bin Laden if they had the chance. Instead, they were told to try and arrest him for trial in the United States. The Afghans working with the CIA thought the idea that they could walk into a training camp with thousands of Al Qaeda fighters and arrest Bin Laden was ridiculous. At the highest level, the U.S. government did not know how to handle Bin Laden.

Bureaucracies and Foreign Policy

Although we often talk about states as unitary actors, as if they are single individuals, they are not. States are governed by complex organizations with their own political interests inside that government. Some of the important bureaucracies in the United States government for foreign policy are the CIA, the Department of Defense (DoD) including the three branches of the military, the Department of State, and the Department of the Treasury. Each has thousands of workers often scattered around the world, each filling a different role within their organizational structures. These bureaucrats use rules and regulations to carry out their jobs in order that the organization works together as a whole. They also have specific missions in foreign policy; DoD manages military forces including buying weapons and recruiting soldiers while Treasury handles most international economic issues in addition to its responsibility for the finances of the federal government and domestic economic policy. Some organizations have overlapping responsibilities on some issues, as the CIA and FBI do on counterterrorism. Other times multiple organizations duplicate jobs, with both the CIA and DoD collecting and analyzing intelligence about the world. These organizations have their own political interests in maintaining and advancing the organization generally in addition to each seeing the world through the lens of their own position, competence, and mission. All governments use organizations like these to develop and carry out foreign policy.

Political leaders sit atop this pile of organizations. Organizations shape policy in two ways. First, they provide leaders with information. Although Presidents gain some knowledge of the world by traveling and meeting with other leaders, most of the information they act upon is collected by intelligence agencies, such as the CIA. Agents in the field collect information they gather from local newspapers, their contacts in the field, and other sources. They send this collection of facts and rumors back to CIA headquarters through secure cables to prevent unauthorized people, particularly foreign governments and their agents, from reading the information. Analysts then read the cable traffic from a country or given situation and try to determine what is happening now and what is likely to happen soon. Intelligence analysis is as much an art as a science. These reports are passed up the organization where higher-level analysts read and comment on them. Eventually, the President receives an intelligence briefing every morning which covers the entire collection of information about what is happening all over the world. Second, organizations carry out the decisions of national leaders. If the President decides to deploy military force to respond to a situation in the world, one or more branches of the military actually carry out that policy. The military leadership of DoD recommends which units should be deployed, which the President approves. Thousands of soldiers move in response. They act in units with commanders, regular soldiers, and chains of commands so orders can be sent down. In the field, military units have rules of engagement that explain the conditions under which they can fire their weapons. Other agencies carry out other policies of the government. The Treasury and Commerce Departments manage economic sanctions by investigating and blocking companies which trade banned goods with the country under sanction. Government bureaucracies then shape what political leaders know and their menu of choices.

Think of the government as a pyramid. The top political and military leaders, and the President specifically in the United States, sit atop the pyramid. They have ultimate responsibility for policy. Underneath them, organizations with thousands of officials make up the body of the pyramid. The leaders at the top rely on their organizations to feed them information and carry out their policies and decisions. This chapter discusses how the politics of each part of the pyramid influences foreign policy. We will refer to how organizations operate as *organizational process* and how decisions are reached within the political leadership and its immediate advisors as *government politics*. We look at each first separately and then use the results to examine the Cuban Missile Crisis, the closest the world came to a nuclear war during the Cold War.

Organizational Process

The organizations that compose a government exist to serve specific functions for that government. The Department of Defense (DoD) commands the military, buys its weapons, recruits and trains military personnel, and everything else needed to run a modern military. It is responsible for these tasks but not for others relevant to foreign policy such as running the diplomatic corps. Both its power and its responsibilities are limited in this sense. Other foreign policy bureaucracies have different powers and responsibilities, which may overlap in some areas.

Organizations view the world through the lens of their purpose and mission. DoD thinks of issues first and foremost as military problems because the people who work there are trained to do so and the organization has been created to deal with military issues. This parochial view does not mean that DoD always thinks "Bomb first, Do anything else second." After the bombing of the Marine Barracks in 1983, Secretary of Defense Caspar Weinberger announced his "Weinberger Doctrine" concerning when and how the U.S. should use military force. President Reagan had sent Marines into Lebanon in an effort to stabilize it in the wake of Israel's invasion in 1982. A suicide bomber, one of the first in recent history, drove a truck bomb into the barracks. The Weinberger Doctrine argued that military force should only be used as a last resort for clearly defined national interests supported by the public and that overwhelming force should always be used in order to guarantee victory. The mission to Beirut met none of these conditions. Quite simply, Secretary Weinberger did not want to see military personnel placed in harm's way for vague political missions where their hands were tied from using all force available to them. He, as the head of the Department of Defense, saw such missions as counterproductive and an improper way to use the military. Other organizations also view the world parochially through the lens of their own abilities and missions.

The overlap in missions across organizations with different responsibilities and different views has historically led to tensions inside the government. The Departments of State and Defense and the Central Intelligence Agency all have important foreign policy responsibilities, and all three often address the same situation in a given country. All three are present in operations in Afghanistan since the U.S. overthrow of the Taliban in 2001. They see different problems there. DoD sees the military problem of defeating the Taliban; State the political problem of creating and sustaining a government, and the CIA sees the problem of counterterrorist action against Al Qaeda. Now all three see the missions of the other two as important and complementary, but their parochial views change the emphasis across those missions. Much of the history of foreign policy inside the government of the United States since World War II has been the struggle for power among these competing organization, particularly State and Defense. The National Security Council (NSC) was created in 1947 to coordinate foreign policy across these organization, a mission it has carried out with varying success depending on who was the National Security Advisor. It was strongest during the first term of the Nixon Presidency (1969-1973) when Henry Kissinger filled that job.

Organizations consist of many people with different jobs who should work together to fulfill its missions. Organizations rely on *standard operating procedures (SOPs)* to coordinate these people in their tasks. The military uses rules of engagement whenever it deploys units in the field, whether in active combat or in peacekeeping operations. These rules explain when soldiers can fire their weapons, including any steps they must take before shooting at a target. Rules of engagements are a standard operating procedure for that deployment as all personnel are supposed to follow them. They ensure that deadly force is used in a way consistent with the mission at hand. SOPs are like the plays a football team runs. It has to coordinate eleven different players with individual abilities to work together to achieve the goal of the team, winning. Each play explains what each player is supposed to do, allowing for some freedom and initiative within the structure of the play. Teams use plays because even the eleven best players in the world will lose if they do not work together. SOPs allow the personnel of an organization to work together to achieve what it sets out to do. SOPs give organizations capabilities beyond those of its people acting individually.

There is an important downside to the SOPs that allow an organization to work as one. SOPs also limit what it can do. A football team with only running plays will not have passing plays it needs to catch up in a game. The SOPs of an organization form a menu of what it can do in response to a problem. Problems are fit to solutions, rather than the other way around. Leaders ask which SOP is appropriate to address the situation they face instead of crafting an ideal solution to it. The U.S. Navy has 11 aircraft carrier battle groups, groups of ships that support and protect a carrier with a full complement of 85 aircraft. Because these carrier groups can sail anywhere on the oceans quickly, U.S. Presidents have often relied on them to deploy military force in response to crises. The choices are limited to sending one, two, or more carriers because you cannot send a half-a-carrier. Also you cannot have a carrier sail across land, so their effectiveness is limited to places within range of their aircraft from their station at sea.

SOPs also make it difficult to coordinate different organizations. Each has its own procedures and rules for action, which may not match those of another organization. Operation Eagle Claw in 1980, the failed attempt to rescue U.S. embassy personnel held hostage in Iran, is an example of this problem. The plan called for Navy helicopters to meet Air Force transport planes at a desert air base to be established inside Iran. Army Rangers were supposed to board the helicopters piloted by Marine pilots after refueling and then fly onto Teheran where the hostages were held. The team and the plan were all ad hoc and pulled together in a few months. Despite training together, the teams from the different services did not work well together. The chain of command on the ground in Iran was not clear to all personnel. Afterward, DoD created a command for special operations to bring together Special Forces from all branches of the military to avoid such problems in future missions.

SOPs also limit how rapidly organizations can change in response to their environment. It takes time to develop procedures and then train people in them. SOPs represent the accumulated wisdom and experience of the organization in dealing with its common problems. Starting over from scratch is a large task, requiring time when the organization will not be able to act. Organizations change their SOPs slightly and slowly over time, adjusting them from their experiences. Organizational change is *incremental*; it occurs in small increments over time. Organizations then cannot adopt quickly to large changes in environment. The larger the organization, the more detailed the SOPs are, and the more difficult change is.

Finally, organizations require people and funding to carry out their tasks. An organization's budget is the simplest measure of its success. An organization whose budget is growing can hire more people to increase its capabilities; one whose budget is shrinking is in trouble. Heads of organization care about their budgets because that money determines the ability of the organization to carry out its tasks and take on new ones. Organizations then also guard their budgets carefully and often try to create excess capacity or funding as insurance against a budget cut in the future. DoD, often referred to as the Pentagon, is famous for retaining weapons development programs which many believe to be unnecessary or too expensive for their mission. The careers of program development officers depend on their ability to carry their programs from design to deployment. Additionally, conditions might change, and a weapons system which looks redundant today become necessary tomorrow.

Organizations have a parochial view of problems, driven by their mission and purpose. They use SOPs to help their members work together, but these procedures limit their flexibility, forcing choices among a few possible solutions rather than a best response to the issue at hand. SOPs also limit their ability to change rapidly. An organization's budget is the clearest sign of its health.

Government Politics

Life at the top of the U.S. government looks very different than it does in the bureaucracies below. The bureaucracies are full of career government employees who have been or will be there for decades. The top leadership is almost all political appointees who serve as the whim of the President. Some of them at the top may be at the end of a long career in and out of government depending on whether their political party holds the Presidency. Others are seeking to build such a career, leading to a top job some day. In George W. Bush's administration, Secretary of Defense Donald Rumsfeld was an example of the former, National Security Advisor and then Secretary of State Condoleeza Rice was closer to the latter. Rumsfeld had been a member of the House of Representatives from Illinois before beginning a progression of appointed jobs including White House Chief of Staff and Secretary of Defense under President Ford. He then led several business corporations, while keeping a finger in the political world by serving on appointed boards and commissions. His return to run DoD a second time allowed him to finish his career by advocating what he called the "Military Revolution" emphasizing high-tech weaponry to increase the rapidity and firepower of the U.S. military. Rice, on the other hand, entered government service as the Director of Soviet and Eastern European Affairs on the National Security Council for the first President Bush. Her term included the extraordinary period of the end of the Cold War. She then returned to Stanford University where she had been a professor of political science, being appointed to Provost, the second highest job in the university in 1993. She then left that position to become a foreign policy expert in George W. Bush's successful campaign for the Presidency, which led to her two jobs in his administration. When the Republican party next wins the Presidency, her name is likely to be mentioned for one of the top foreign policy jobs. This is how political careers are built from the bottom to the top. There are always many people in both parties interesting in climbing that ladder.

Policy is the outcome of a political struggle among these appointees. They have different views about what is right to do on a given issue, so the contest is over both principle and power. It is a contest of persuasion and influence, where the President is the ultimate arbiter of what the country will do. Issues are studied among the relevant cabinet secretaries, their subordinates, and others the President wishes to include in the process. Reports present options, which are then discussed in competition with one another. A decision on an issue is rarely made in one meeting, even for the most pressing issues. There is time then in between meetings for the advocates for different options to work on their arguments. The core set of players for foreign and national security policy in the United States now is the Secretaries of Defense and State, the National Security Advisor, and the Director of National Intelligence. Others are added based on the issue and whether the President wants them at the table. Vice President Cheney, for example, was always an important player in George W. Bush's administration, but other Presidents have excluded their Vice Presidents from policy discussions. It is also quite common now for the top political advisor of the President, such as David Axelrod for President Obama, to be present in policy discussions to consider the ramifications of a decision for domestic politics.

The stream of decisions to be made is constant and fast. Some problems, such as crises, force their way onto the policy agenda; others are there because someone in the Administration wants to advance that issue. The flow of decisions means that options must be considered quickly, even though most decisions require multiple meetings over days or weeks. There is not the luxury of mulling all imaginable options over long periods of time. Decisions have to be made and often they have to be made soon. The stream of decisions mean that top officials play many policy contests with one another during their time in office. Gaining an upper hand may lead to greater credibility and success in getting decisions in the future to come out as you like. There are also always options to recover and win tomorrow's decision if you lose today's.

Who plays on an issue is one critical way to control the decision. Excluding strong advocates of positions you oppose and including proponents of your own position can carry a policy discussion. The progress an issue takes through the decision process is its *action channel*.

Who is present at the main discussion and which lower level personnel get to write the reports that describe the options and their possible consequences influence which policy is chosen. In the Bush Administration, both Vice President Cheney and Secretary of Defense Rumsfeld were known as strong, experienced bureaucratic players who knew how to manipulate the policy process to get the policies and decisions they wanted. They knew who to include and who to exclude from the relevant committees, how to wrest control back when the decision seemed to be going against them, and never gave up on an issue they cared about. They also advanced the careers of their proteges, younger appointed officials who worked for them and thought like them.

The President is the "500-pound gorilla" of the process. If the President wants something, he (or she someday) gets it. At the same time, the President's plate is very full; he has ultimate responsibility for every decision his office faces. Of course, the President cannot make every decision. That is why he has advisors, staffs, and agencies to work for him. The President's day is filled with policy meetings, ceremonial occasions, and political events. There are so many issues that a President could work on but lacks the time to do so that he must choose which issues he will work on and which he will delegate–turn them over to others he trusts. But he still has the last work, which is why face time with the President is the ultimate measure of power in Washington.

Players' positions on issues are driven in part by the jobs they hold in the government, as is the case for the organizations they head. The phrase "where you stand depends on where you sit" summarizes this observation nicely. Political appointees see issues from the perspective of the agencies they lead for at least two reasons. First, they are chosen to lead those agencies because they have policy expertise in the issues the agency addresses. Second, the bureaucracy they lead provides them with information and expertise, shaping their views. Casper Weinberger was Director of the Office of Management and Budget and Secretary of Health, Education and Welfare under Presidents Nixon and Ford in the 1970s where he acquired the nickname "Cap the Knife" for his zeal in cutting budgets. When President Reagan took office, he appointed Weinberger Secretary of Defense. At first blush, this appointment seemed brilliant. Reagan planned a large military buildup, and who better than "Cap the Knife" to watch the budget to ensure that the country got all the bang for its buck. Alas, Weinberger proved to be "Cap the Rubber Stamp" as Secretary of Defense, supporting every weapons program DoD wanted. Where he stood depended on where he sat.

Some top bureaucrats participate in policy discussions, although their position in the process differs from that of the political appointees who dominate the discussion. These officials have risen to the top of their organizations through long and successful careers in them. The Chairman of the Joint Chiefs of Staff, the highest ranking military officer in the country and the principal military advisor to the President, is present for discussions which touch on military affairs. Although he and the other Joint Chiefs of the services are appointed by the President, they all have long and successful careers in their services, which is why they rise to the level to be considered for these important jobs. Top bureaucrats tend to have a longer view of issues than many political appointees. They have worked for the government for decades and will work there until they retire. Political appointees, on the other hand, typically hold any one job for a few years and then move back to a job outside government in business, academia, or the policy world of lobbying, consulting, and think tanks. They have to make their mark on policy quickly because they may be out of government soon.

Political appointees also differ among themselves based on where they are in the political career; chiefs at the top have a different view than staffers below them. Secretary Rumsfeld was at the end of his career of public service during the Bush Administration. He sought to leave his mark on U.S. defense policy and the U.S. military. He played in every foreign and defense issue and won many of them until he retired after the 2006 off-year election. The under secretaries and assistant secretaries of the various executive agencies are often younger than the secretaries who head them. They aspire to those higher-level jobs and hope to build a record in government to be appointed at a higher level in the future. Because of their lower level in the government, they are included only on issues in their area of responsibility. The Under Secretary of State for Economic, Business and Agricultural Affairs covers economic issues in U.S. foreign policy but is unlikely to be involved in security affairs. Lower-level appointees then have to make their name and be noticed when they have an opportunity to participate on issues in their area. Condoleezza Rice took advantage of her opportunity in the George H. W. Bush administration to make a name as a bright and capable foreign policy expert, which led to her appointment when the younger President Bush was elected.

Government politics is a struggle among the political appointees of the President to get their views adopted as policy. Policy decisions are political because they can advance the careers of these officials as well as their views concerning the proper policy. The position of each player influences their views of the proper policy. The constant stream of decisions leads to a perpetual contest for influence over policy and power within the administration. Who plays on an issue is always an important concern because it is one way to produce the policy a player would like. This is how the game at the top of the pyramid of the government works.

An Example: The Cuban Missile Crisis

The Cuban Missile Crisis is the closest the world has come to a nuclear war to date. The Space Age dawned in 1957 when the Soviet Union launched Sputnik I, the first artificial satellite. Missile which could launch satellites into orbit could also carry nuclear weapons to target anywhere on the Earth in less than an hour. Ballistic missiles led to an arms race between the United States and the Soviet Union over the deployment of missile carrying nuclear weapons, known as ICBMs, short for InterContinental Ballistic Missiles. The U.S. took an early lead in this arms race, deploying more missiles than the Soviet Union.

After the Cuban Revolution in 1959, Fidel Castro, the new leader of Cuba, aligned his country with the Soviet Union during the following years. The decisive break with the U.S. came with the ill-fated Bay of Pigs invasion in April of 1961. The CIA created a small army of Cuban exiles who invaded Cuba at the Bay of Pigs in the hope of overthrowing Castro. The invasion failed in a matter of days, and the exile soldiers fell into Cuban hands. U.S. pressure, through diplomatic means and covert action–on Cuba continued, leading Castro to seek further protection from the Soviet Union. The Soviet leadership, headed by Premier Nikita Khrushchev, decided to deploy shorter-ranged missiles capable of carrying nuclear warheads to Cuba. The deployment of both IRBMs (Intermediate Range Ballistic Missiles) and MRBMs (Medium Range Ballistic Missiles) began in September, 1962. The MRBMs could hit targets as far away as Houston and Washington, DC, while the longer-ranged IRBMs could hit targets almost anywhere in the continental United States. If theses missiles became active, it would close the gap in strategic nuclear forces that the Soviet Union faced. They would also provide the ultimate defense, nuclear retaliation, against a U.S. invasion of Cuba.

[Maps of missile bases in Cuba and ranges of MRBMs and IRBMs from Cuba]

The U.S. continued surveillance of Cuba through overflights of U-2 spy planes which took pictures from very high altitudes. It took time for the film to be developed and analyzed after each flight. In mid-October 1962, the U.S. government discovered the deployment of the missiles through these spy flights. President John F. Kennedy was informed of the existence of the nuclear-capable missiles in Cuba on October 15. He created an ad-hoc committee, known as ExCom for Executive Committee, to discuss the appropriate response to the missile deployment. As it was campaign season for the off-year Congressional election, President Kennedy continued his normal campaign schedule and joined ExCom sessions over the next week only when he was in Washington.

Time Line of Cuban Missile Crisis

9/8 and 9/16: Soviet missiles arrive in Cuba; deployment begins
10/15: US discovers missiles through U-2.
10/16: ExCom formed to meet in secret. Decision to blockade Cuba
10/22: JFK goes public with US knowledge.
10/23: First Khrushchev letter; blockade moved closer to Cuba.
10/24: Blockade begins.
10/25: Marcula intercepted.
10/26: U-2 shot down over Cuba; Khrushchev hand-written letter
10/27: Soviet broadcast proposing missile swap
10/28: The public deal: US pledge not to invade Cuba
     The secret deal: missiles in Turkey for missiles in Cuba

The ExCom considered three main options for dealing with the missiles: 1. Diplomatic action; 2. A military strike to destroy the missiles; and 3. A blockade to put pressure on the Soviets to remove the missiles. The ExCom consisted of the top military, foreign and defense leaders of the government. The Attorney General, the top lawyer and head of the Department of Justice, also took part because he was Bobby Kennedy, the President's brother, someone he could trust to represent him when he was on the campaign trail. President Kennedy addressed the nation on television on the evening of October 22 to announce the existence of the missile and the decision to place a blockade on the delivery of offensive weapons to Cuba to force their withdrawal, effective October 24. Kennedy called the blockade a "quarantine" because a blockade is an act of war under international law.

Premier Khrushchev responded with a stern telegram to the President the next day, resisting Kennedy's demand to remove the missiles. Kennedy ordered the blockade to move closer to Cuba to delay the first confrontation between Soviet ships and the U.S. Navy. The Soviets stopped most of their ships, allowing the Marcula to be the first ship to test the blockade on October 25. Its cargo contained no weapons, and the Navy allowed it to continue to Cuba. Negotiations between the two government continued, publicly in UN Security Council, through formal letters between the two leaders, and through various back channels including one between the Soviet Ambassador to the U.S. and Attorney General Kennedy. On the evening of Octover 26, Khrushchev transmitted a long, hand-written letter to President Kennedy, proposing what would be the deal–Soviet removal of the missiles in exchange for a U.S. pledge not to invade Cuba. The crisis came to a head on October 27 when the Soviet government broadcast a message proposing a trade of Soviet missiles in Cuba for the removal of U.S. missiles based in Turkey. A public deal to remove U.S. missiles in Turkey would weaken the NATO alliance. Kennedy chose to ignore this statement, and a deal was announced on the basis of Khrushchev's letter on October 28. The Soviet Union agreed to remove the missiles in coming months, and the United States pledged publicly not to invade Cuba. The U.S. also pledged privately to remove similar short-range nuclear missiles which it had deployed in Turkey, a U.S. ally on the southern border of the Soviet Union. This agreement ended the public phase of the crisis although tension continued through the following weeks.

This was the signal crisis of the Cold War, the closest that the world came to nuclear annihilation. Bobby Kennedy later claimed that his brother the President thought there was a one-third chance of nuclear war during the crisis. The Cuban Missile Crisis has been studied extensively for the crisis bargaining between the two governments. How did bureaucratic politics affect the crisis?

Organizational Issues in the Crisis

The drama and resolution of the Cuban Missile Crisis happened at the highest level of both governments. How did organizations the leaders depend on influence what they knew and the options they had?

American intelligence analysts were surprised how easy it was to find the missile sites once they had aerial photographs of them. Their layout was identical to those they had found earlier in the Soviet Union. No effort was made to camouflage the missiles or lay out the various facilities–launching pads for the missiles, bunkers for nuclear warheads, anti-aircraft defenses, and barracks for the crews–differently. When Soviet leaders decided to deploy missiles to Cuba, three military units, which the Soviet would have called "strategic rocket forces," were ordered to deploy to Cuba. Once there, those units followed the given rules for building and operating a missile base. Two launching pads for three missiles were built, the bunkers holding the warheads had to be placed a set distance away from the fuel for safety, the anti-aircraft defenses deployed around the edge of the base, and the troops housed in barracks. Although someone thought enough to clothe the troops in civilian clothing, they revealed their military organization by marching in formation when they traveled as a unit. Clearly, the unit followed the "book" for building a missile base, even when breaking the rules might have obscured what they were doing and bought more time before the U.S. detected the missiles. The standard way Soviet strategic rocket units built bases was the SOP here. It was a fixed choice which the Soviet leaders had; the solution was not customized to the problem at hand.

The U.S. was not immune to the SOPs of military units. The Kennedy Administration was very concerned about the conduct of the blockade once it began. The interception and boarding of a ship by blockading vessels is a dangerous moment. The two crews do not speak the same language, creating the possibility of a misunderstanding. The blockading vessel follows a protocol to intercept a ship in violation, beginning with approaching it and hailing it over a loudspeaker, and progressing to firing a warning shot across the bow if it does not stop, and then a shot into the rudder to disable the vessel running the blockade. President Kennedy and

Secretary of Defense McNamara were both afraid that a shooting incident on the high seas could escalate the crisis. Despite their numerous efforts to manage individual interceptions, the Navy resisted their intrusions. After all, the U.S. Naval Regulations, a massive book, had existed for almost 200 years and gave explicit instruction how to conduct a blockade. As Secretary McNamara said in exasperation to one admiral, "I don't care how John Paul Jones [a famous naval hero from the Revolution] would have conducted the blockade, I want to know how you are going to!" The Naval Regulations are, of course, an SOP.

Organizations also follow routines in order to coordinate their members. The routines of the collection and analysis of intelligence information delayed the detection of the missiles by the U.S. government. This was not a time when one could find satellite photographs of any part of the Earth's surface on Google Earth (some of which are edited to obscure secure features). U-2 spy planes would fly regular patterns taking aerial photographs. These photographs would be developed and then delivered to intelligence analysts who would go through the immense collection to look for suspicious sites. Rapid identification of sites was a valuable skill for analysts because there was so much material to go through. Still, the routine took over a month to photograph and inspect all of Cuba. This lengthy routine delayed the identification and location of the missiles. Once the sites had been detected, they could be monitored daily for changes to see if the missiles were active yet.

Organizations and their interests limit the options from which national leaders choose. Early discussions in the ExCom favored the air strike option. It did not require agreement from the Soviet Union, and it was a decisive act to match the deep concern and outrage by many ExCom members had about the missiles. The blockade would impose only indirect military pressure as it could do nothing about the missiles already in Cuba. President Kennedy favored a surgical strike, one that would only hit the missiles, to limit the chance that the strike would provoke Soviet retaliation elsewhere. The precision munitions which can be guided to the target by either a remote operator or computer guidance had not been invented yet, so "dumb" bombs would have to be used. The military proposed a larger strike that would hit the anti-aircraft sites, the weapons bunkers, and troops in the vicinity of the missile bases. They were concerned that one strike would not destroy the missiles, so a second might be necessary. Kennedy eventually turned against the air strike option because the military was unwilling to consider limiting the strike. The option he might have liked best was not available.

Internal Politics in the Crisis

The internal politics of both sides influenced the stances they took in the crisis. The policy positions of different members of ExCom matched their positions in the government closely. Military leaders favored the air strike option. Adlai Stevenson, the ambassador to the UN, was the prime proponent of a diplomatic approach. He traveled down to Washington to make the case for diplomacy over military coercion. His appeal failed quickly as other members of ExCom argued that diplomacy without military pressure was inadequate to address the severe threat posed by the Soviet missiles. He returned back to New York where he had the great moment of his diplomatic career in a confrontation during a Security Council meeting. Stevenson displayed pictures of the missile bases and directly asked Soviet ambassador Zorin whether the Soviet Union was installing offensive missiles in Cuba. As Zorin stalled answering the question, Stevenson shot back, "Don't wait for the translation, answer 'yes' or 'no'!" Where people sat did not perfectly fit where they stood during the crisis. Secretary of Defense McNamara was dubious of the most aggressive options despite his position. The Chiefs of Staff of the military thought the missile deployment had a profound affect on the strategic nuclear balance between the U.S. and the Soviet Union, a belief which McNamara dismissed.

Given the importance of the crisis, the ExCom was limited to the main security and foreign policy players in the Kennedy Administration. Unlike issues that develop over time, lower-level staffers were not brought into the process for their expertise. The only players outside the national security leadership in State, Defense, and the CIA were close personal advisors of the President, such as his brother Bobby and Ted Sorenson, his long-time friend.

The primary motivation for the Soviet decision was defense of the Castro regime in Cuba. Closing the missile gap was a secondary reason. We do not have complete evidence on the considerations weighed by the Politburo before and during the crisis, as we do for the ExCom. But the proposal to base missiles in Cuba should have been attractive even to those Politburo members who did not have positions responsible for military or foreign affairs. Ministers in charge of the economy may have welcomed the missile deployment because it was an inexpensive way to deal with Cuba and the missile gap. Although each would have seen the decision from the perspective of their own position, they could all agree on the missile deployment.

Limits of Bureaucratic Politics Arguments

It is no accident that this chapter has illustrated bureaucratic politics with the Cuban Missile Crisis, the best documented crisis of the Cold War. Not only do we have accounts from the major players on the ExCom, their discussions were secretly recorded on tape, which are now publicly available. U.S. Presidents no longer record their policy discussions, having learning from the experiences of the Johnson and Nixon Administrations. Both organizational process and government politics are easier to trace after the fact when the policy and its outcome are known. It is not clear what these arguments predict. It is useful to know that top deciders will view issues through the eyes of the position they hold in the government, but it is how the group resolves these differences that matters. In the period before the Iraq War, Secretary of State Powell preferred using the UN Security Council to advance the U.S. position, while Secretary of Defense Rumsfeld opposed such action. But the key to the decision is how this disagreement was resolved. It is useful to know that organizations will tend to do what they have done in the past, but often change in what they do is more consequential. Organizations tend to change their standard operating procedures dramatically after a crisis or failure. Again, these arguments do not provide us with a guide to how or when they will change until after it happens.

National leaders also try to control what the bureaucracies that compose their government do. Despite the organizational issues described above, Khrushchev and Kennedy were able to reach a resolution of the Cuban Missile Crisis short of war. U.S. presidents since the crisis have tried to exert direct control over the details of military missions. President Lyndon Johnson asked at times to review lists of targets in North Vietnam in advance of air strikes during the Vietnam War. President Bill Clinton and Secretary of State Madeline Albright approved targets to be hit during the bombing of Serbia and Kosovo in 1999. In both cases, the President was concerned about the political consequences of what targets were bombed and were unwilling to leave those political consequences to a purely military judgment. Johnson feared escalation with China and the Soviet Union, while Clinton and Albright sought to restrict civilian deaths and losses as the bombing sought to coerce Slobodan Milosevic's government to stop its abuses against civilians in Kosovo. These political restraints from the President create friction with military leaders. They prefer that they control military operations within the political mission set by the political leadership. The military leadership is responsible for their own casualties and the success of the military mission. Successful civil-military relations–how the civilian and military authorities relate to one another–depend on both military leaders staying out of civilian politics and civilian leaders respecting the authority and professional judgment of the military.

Bureaucratic politics arguments focus our attention on how decisions are made and carried out within a government. They do not explain how states relate to one another. The Cuban Missile Crisis ended because the leaders of both countries in the face of the pressure of the crisis crafted a deal which both could live with. Bureaucratic politics have much in common with the study of domestic policy, such as health policy, where the government does not face another government that can influence the outcome. But world politics is the result of what many governments do, and while we can learn things by examining how each operates alone, we also must attend to the interaction of their policies.

Later in this book, we will examine other ways that domestic politics influence the international policies that governments adopt. While political leaders sit atop of a mass of organizations that shape the information and options they have, they also answer to others for the decisions they make. In a democracy, the leader answers to the electorate through regular elections. Leaders in non-democracies also answer to others, although many citizens are excluded from that process. When we examine election and selection pressures, we will return to examine the political consequences of the Cuban Missile Crisis for President Kennedy and Premier Khrushchev.

U.S. Counterterrorism Policy before 9/11

The FBI and the CIA were the two main agencies of the U.S. government responsible for counterterrorism policy before 9/11. Afterwards, responsibility for countering terrorists was concentrated in the Department of Homeland Security (DHS). The FBI had responsibility inside the U.S., the CIA outside its borders. The two agencies did not cooperate with one another. Legal walls existed between the two agencies that prevented the CIA from operating within the U.S. because of earlier CIA spying on U.S. citizens. The two organizations have different ways of operating from their organizational missions. The FBI exists to catch criminals and put them behind bars. Agents advance their careers with successful prosecutions, making them very careful to pursue only those cases where they can get sufficient evidence to get a conviction. They are also very scrupulous about following legal rules. CIA agents, on the other hand, live in the shadowy world of intelligence. They are concerned with collecting intelligence to identify security threats before they happen. Intelligence sources rarely meet the standards of evidence for a criminal case. Additionally, information is power in organizations. Agents of the two bureaucracies would not share information in case the other used that information to gain the credit for dealing with the threat. After 9/11, steps were taken to produce greater cooperation between the two agencies while preserving the separation of their areas of responsibility, the FBI within the U.S., the CIA outside.

When it became clear that Al Qaeda posed a threat to the U.S., a special unit was establish to trace Osama Bin Laden and his associates. Richard Clarke was the head of the unit, and he became famous after 9/11 as the government official who pointed to the inconsistency of U.S. policy toward Al Qaeda before the attacks. The Bin Laden unit was known for its relentless focus on him, a focus not shared by others with wider responsibility. As is true for all organizations, they saw every issue from the perspective of their own particular mission. They even referred to themselves as "the Manson family" after the followers of the notorious murderer Charles Manson as a comment on their obsession. This focus was easier to justify after 9/11 than before when the magnitude of the threat was not clear.

[Picture of Richard Clarke]

At the highest level, policy towards Al Qaeda before 9/11 was inconsistent. For President Clinton, the issue was how to handle Pakistan. Once Bin Laden declared "war" on the United States in 1997 on CNN, he became a target. Going after his bases in Taliban-controlled Afghanistan was a thorny mission though. The key question was "how to handle Pakistan"? Some parts of the intelligence agency in Pakistan had close ties to the Taliban and might provide them and Al Qaeda with information about U.S. actions. Clinton could not push Pakistan too hard because this was also the period when Pakistan tested its first nuclear weapon. Which issue was more important, going after Al Qaeda or stopping the Pakistani nuclear program? Different people in the government put either issue first. U.S. policy became inconsistent in part because of this conflict. At one time, permission to kill Bin Laden if necessary was denied, while cruise missile strikes were launched against Al Qaeda's training camps in Afghanistan after the bombings of the U.S. embassies in East Africa. When President Bush took office, he sought a complete review of U.S. policy. This review was just getting finished by 9/11. President Bush did not want to "swat flies", wasting time and effort on minor and immediate threats while leaving the main threat alone. He wanted a comprehensive policy, but it takes time to develop and implement such a policy.

Summary

Internal politics under national leaders matters. Governments are composed of organizations with their own interests and missions. They have standard operating procedures which limit what they can do. They see the world through the eyes of their parochial interests. At the top, political officials contend over the control of policy. They, too, see the world through the eyes of their own position. Because the President faces many decisions every day, other officials, such as cabinet secretaries and political appointees, carry much of the burden of making policy. Winning those policy battles is the measure of success for them. Controlling who is "in" on a decision can determine what decision is made. Policy then is the result of a political struggle at the top, which is then implemented by organizations below them.

This view has an important implication for studying world politics, even though it is rarely predictive. Much of what states do is the result of their bureaucracies and not necessarily a deliberate act of policy. You should not read too much into the details of what another states does. Some analysts focus on every little detail as evidence of the intentions of a foreign government. But some of these actions do not reflect those intentions, and reading them as such is a mistake. In June of 2004 and March of 2007, Iran seized British marines operating in the Shatt al Arab waterway that forms part of the border between Iraq and Iran. Were these seizures evidence of the hostility of the government of Iran or the act of the Revolutionary Guards acting without authorization? It is hard to tell. Indeed, the seizures may have been provocations against Iranian national policy to provoke a reaction. What you see depends on where you sit. The difficulty of discerning intentions from many things a government does leads us to focus our attention instead on the deliberate acts of a government. Formal diplomatic actions are a better guide to what another government wants than the details of its policies.

Review Questions

1. What is an SOP, and what are its consequences for state action in a crisis?

2. How do standard operating procedures shape leaders' choices and information in a crisis? Give two examples of how an SOP affected the Cuban Missile Crisis.

3. What affect did SOPs have on how the Cuban Missile Crisis transpired?

4. Explain the difference in actors and their role in the formation of policy between the two sides of bureaucratic politics theory: organizational process and governmental politics.

Chapter 13
Arms and Alliances: The Elements of Security Policy

The North Atlantic Treaty Organization (NATO) was formed in 1949 to provide for the common defense of the West. That alliance committed its members–the U.S., Canada, Great Britain, France, the Netherlands, Belgium, Luxembourg, Italy, Greece, Turkey, Iceland, Denmark, and Norway–to come to the defense of one another in the event of an attack on any of them. Its purpose was, in a memorable phrase, "To keep the Russians out, the Americans in, and the Germans down." The mutual defense commitment was supposed to deter an attack by the Red Army by ensuring that such an attack would lead to war with all the members of the alliance, including the United States with its nuclear weapons. That same commitment would ensure that the U.S. would continue committed to the defense of Western Europe. Finally, the alliance would reassure states that had been overrun by Germany during the Second World War that a renewed German military would not threaten them again. NATO built a common command structure to coordinate military policy among the many member states so that their forces would fight as one during wartime. In 1955, West Germany joined NATO as a new member and a new German army, the Bundeswehr, was created and integrated into NATO forces. Eventually, Spain and Portugal joined NATO, although France reduced its participation in the alliance from full status to joint maneuvers and consultation. By the 1980s, NATO fielded a large, multinational army and air force in West Germany, Italy, and Norway, with supporting naval forces on its flanks in the Mediterranean, Baltic, North, and Norwegian Seas. Turkey and Greece defended their own countries with air and naval support from the U.S.

In 1991, the Soviet military threat to Western Europe disappeared along with the Soviet Union itself. The disappearance of the Soviet threat led many to speculate that NATO too would disappear soon thereafter. Instead, NATO expanded eastward, adding former Communist states in Eastern Europe as new members. NATO forces fought their first combat when it conducted bombing missions in the wars in the former Yugoslavia in 1995 and 1999. The 9/11 attacks triggered the first use of the mutual defense clause as the European allies rallied to the defense of the United States. NATO since 9/11 has played a large role in Afghanistan where a multinational NATO force fights with American and Afghan troops against armed resistance to the government there. The puzzle NATO presents is "why has the alliance expanded when many thought it would disappear?" To answer this puzzle, we need to know more about what states do in advance of war to prepare for it.

Security Policy

States take many different measures to prepare for war in advance of it. These policies are called "security policies" because they seek to make the state more secure against threats linked to the possibility of war. *Deterrence* of threats and war is the first goal of security policy. Those policies are most successful when they convince other states that the chance of winning a war against the state in question is small. Specifically, that chance is small enough that another state does not believe that its chance of winning a war is large enough to justify taking the risks of war and paying the costs of fighting. That other state would also be unwilling to make threats to go to war in the effort to coerce concessions from the state in question. Successful deterrence prevents both war and threats of war, keeping the peace and the status quo for the country with the security policy.

There are two ways a state can improve its ability to deter other states. First, it can increase its ability to win a war by building a stronger military or by seeking new allies or strengthening the reliability of the allies it has. A stronger, better prepared military is more likely to win if a war is fought, lowering the other side's chance of winning and so its willingness to go to war. Alliances raise the chance that the country will not fight alone if it is attacked, again raising the chance it wins a war. Alliances, however, are promises by other governments, and like all promises, others including the state in question may doubt the promise of the ally to fight for the state in question. A state could also increase its deterrent ability by making the promises of its allies more credible; later in the chapter, we discuss some commitment mechanisms that could make the promises of aid in an alliance more credible.

Second, a state could improve its deterrence by changing the perception of other states that it poses a threat to them. Security policies are measures to increase a state's ability to fight and win a war. The country which the first is trying to deter may see those steps as increasing the threat posed to itself. The state in question is now more likely to win a war, making threats and war more attractive. The other country that sees a higher threat from the state in question may respond with stronger security policies themselves. It may increase its own military or seek new allies in response. The net effect of both countries' security policy may be that neither is more secure but both are more suspicious of the other. Both will have spent more money or forced more young men to join the military but not be any safer for that preparation for war. This problem is called the *security dilemma*. Measures which make one country more secure may make others less secure, leading them to respond and leaving both worse off.

A state could increase its security by reassuring others that it does not threaten them. If it can change the perceptions of other states that it poses a threat to them, they might relax their vigilance against that state. They could redeploy their military, shrink it in size, or end alliances which are now unnecessary. These policies of reassurance are very difficult to carry out because a state might also try to deceive others that its intentions are benign in the effort to get the latter to lower their guard. Changing perceptions requires separating types, and there are two types of states that take actions to reassure other states of their benign intent. One has truly benign intent, the other is trying to gain an advantage over its rival. If you are the former type, how do you demonstrate that you are not the latter type whom others fear?

The long rivalry between the United States and the Soviet Union during the Cold War saw a number of attempts by both sides to reassure the other that it did not pose an existential threat to the other. During the 1970s, Presidents Nixon, Ford, and Carter followed a policy of detente which engaged the Soviet Union through arms control negotiations, economic deals, and cultural exchanges in the effort to reassure the Soviet Union that the U.S. accepted it and so both sides could stop expanding and improving their military forces. Detente foundered in the late 1970s on the perception of many American politicians that the Soviet Union was taking advantage of the policy both to improve its own military and to expand its influence in the developing world. The steps taken by the Soviet Union did not reassure Americans of benign intent; instead, they provoked concerns about the threat posed to the U.S. by the Soviet Union. When President Reagan was elected, he reversed detente and renewed the rivalry of the Cold War by building up the U.S. military and criticizing the Soviet Union, its policies and intentions in blunt words. Most memorably, Reagan referred to the Soviet Union as the "Evil Empire." When Mikael Gorbachev came to power in the Soviet Union, he wished to reassure those in the West that his Soviet Union would be different. His rhetoric talked about a "common European home". Gorbachev engaged in arms control negotiations with President Reagan and launched his policies of Perestroika and Glasnost to change the Soviet Union. But many in the West were unconvinced by these measures, they were not reassured that the Soviet Union was now benign. What convinced most in the West that the Cold War was over was the collapse of Soviet hegemony in Eastern Europe in 1989. When Gorbachev made it clear that the Red Army would no longer keep Communist regimes in power in the face of popular unrest, this was too high a cost for a malicious Soviet Union to carry out to deceive the West of its intentions. A Soviet Union that would allow its Eastern European client governments to fall did not pose a threat to Western Europe. Although there are times that a state could increase its security by reassuring rivals and defusing the security dilemma, it is difficult to do and rarely tried.

States generally rely on security policy to strengthen their deterrence of other states by expanding their own military or securing aid from other states. Deterrent policies do not always succeed, and the second goal of security policy is *defense* of the state. Defense here means the ability to defeat the enemy during a war and so prevail and protect the state. Security policy is preparation for war. Successful policies of arming and alliances increase a state's ability to fight and win. A state's *security* is its ability to deter and defeat if necessary threats to use violence from other states. A state with a high level of security has the ability to refuse demands made of it to change the status quo backed by the threat of war.

Security policies can also increase a state's ability to change the status quo, the third possible goal of security policy. Arms and allies raise a state's chance of winning a war, and so make its threat to go to war more effective. The threat of war is the strongest tool a state has to try to coerce others to accepting changes on issues that the state desires. The fact that security policy can increase the ability of a state to compel change means that other states often believe that the security policies of their rivals often pose a threat to themselves, the origin of the security dilemma. There are ways states can try to shape security policies that increase their own security without threatening other states, but many security policies do not have these features. Even though states may not be seeking to acquire a capability to change the status quo through their security policies, other states rarely perceive such policies are purely defensive and benign.

The three goals of security policy are deterrence, defense, and increasing the ability to change the status quo. The two main tools of security policy are *arming* and *alliances*. As mentioned earlier arming strategies increase the strength of a state's military, and alliances seek commitments of aid from other states. All states use combinations of these two tools. Arming and alliance strategies have different strategic effects on a state's security. States can arm themselves for war by increasing the size of their military, by building new and improved military equipment, or by training their military more effectively. Arming takes time to build a state's ability to win a war, a disadvantage. New recruits troops take months to train to be ordinary soldiers, and capable officers take years to train. New weapons requires time for factories to build them. New military doctrine–how soldiers are trained to fight together–can take years to develop and then retrain soldiers in those new ways to fight. The advantage of arming strategies is their increase in security is reliable. The state in question can rely on its larger, more capable military to fight for it if war occurs and other states know that. They may doubt that the changes have improved the state's ability to win a war, but they do know that the changes will affect the outcome of a war. Alliances, on the other hand, produce an immediate increase in security but are unreliable. Your ally can fight to help defend you tomorrow if you sign an alliance today. But alliances are promises at their heart, and as we have seen earlier, others often doubt promises. War is costly in human lives and property and requires crushing amounts of money to pay for an army, navy, and air force, money that cannot be spent on other things. State leaders are understandably reluctant to fight in order to avoid these costs. The costs of fighting then make carrying the promise to defend another state costly for an ally and leads both a state with allies and its rivals to doubt whether the ally will fight on its behalf if the latter attack it. These strategic effects–between the reliability of arming and the immediacy of alliance–are an important element in the choice of security policies.

How Much is Enough?

Security policy involves judging risks and weighing them against the costs of taking measures to lower them. Deterrence is the threat of going to war to defend your interests. Like all threats, other states may doubt the credibility and effectiveness of that threat. Those doubts may lead them to threaten force to get what they want from the deterring state. Furthermore, the state with the deterrent policy does not know the intentions of the other side. How important are those issues to them? Are they willing to fight to press their demands? States have to judge these risks when they determine how strong a military to build and whether to form a new alliance. Is the risk that another state will attack large or small?

During the Cold War, the United States and the Soviet Union used threats of nuclear deterrence to defend themselves against each other. Both sides invested large amounts of money and scientific research in developing strategic nuclear forces, from long-range bombers and tens of nuclear bombs in the 1950s to sophisticated missiles based both on land and on submarines at sea carrying thousands of nuclear warheads. Each of these missiles could hit many different targets in the other country. They had large command facilities built to withstand nuclear attacks to ensure that they could command their strategic forces even after receiving a nuclear attack. Most famously, the U.S. dug out the inside of Cheyenne Mountain in Wyoming to provide a secure location for the command of its Strategic Air Command (SAC). All of these provisions failed to make either side perfectly secure against nuclear attack. Many on both sides worried that the other might consider a nuclear attack if it thought the issue in dispute was important enough. The Cuban Missile Crisis was one such dispute. The Nixon Administration raised the alert status of SAC to threaten the use of its nuclear weapons to dissuade the Soviet Union from sending troops to the Middle East at the end of the 1973 October War to save the Egyptian Army from total defeat. The Nixon Administration ended the crisis by pressing Israel to accept a ceasefire. Other times the superpowers' strategic nuclear forces seemed irrelevant to stopping the other from using force. The looming threat of nuclear war did not stop the United States from intervening in the Vietnam War nor the Soviet Union from invading Afghanistan. In both cases, neither side thought the issue was important enough to threaten using nuclear weapons. By the end of the Cold War in 1989, both sides' policy of deterrence succeeded in preventing nuclear war and deterring war against their core interests in Europe but not in stopping all challenges to the status quo. Those other interests rarely rose to the level where either side was willing to risk nuclear war. The policy of building strategic nuclear forces required judgments by both sides of how important their interests were and how large the risks were to them.

These policies are costly to a government because they require it to take actions that may be unpopular with the people in their state. Building a stronger, more capable military involves raising the money to pay for new weapons and inducting more people into the military. The money can come from higher taxes, printing money, or cutting other government expenditures. No one likes to pay taxes, printing money risks inflation of the currency, and someone in the state benefits from the government expenditures to be cut. Inducting more people into the military either requires raising volunteers by paying more or drafting people. Both measures hurt a country's economy by taking people out of the civilian economy and putting them in the military. Conscription, known in the U.S. as the draft, forces young people into the military with the threat of jail. It has been unpopular in almost every country and every time it has been used. You may have heard of "draft dodgers" during the Vietnam War, young American men who fled to Canada when they received the summons to the Army. When President Lincoln imposed the draft during the Civil War, New York City burned with three days of violent anti-draft riots in July of 1863 after the battle of Gettysburg. Building up the military is often unpopular because it takes away money from citizens and pulls young people away from the family and friends and puts them in the military.

Alliances are promises as so often may lack credibility. The steps that states need to take to raise the credibility of their promises to defend one another can be unpopular. Commitment devices that induce a state to go to war when its ally goes to war may also encourage that ally to take risks that it would not if it could not count on the assistance of the first state. Allies are more likely to fight together if their interests are close. If two allies have many divergent interests, others may doubt their willingness to fight together on issues where they disagree. One way to strengthen an alliance is for the allies to compromise on their divergent interests. The Triple Alliance brought together Germany, Austria-Hungary, and Italy before World War I. It pledged them to come to the defense of each other in the event of an attack on one of them. But Italy and Austria-Hungary were also rivals as Italy had been unified in the 1860s at the expense of Austria and Italy still sought to add parts of Austria populated by ethnic Italians, particularly the Trentino and city of Trieste. Other European powers understood that Italy could be separated from the Triple Alliance because of their territorial ambitions in Austria-Hungary. When World War I broke out, Italy remained neutral because Austria-Hungary declared war on Serbia and Germany declared war on Russia and France. It claimed that it was not obligated to go to war because they were not attacked, they had started the war. Italy joined the Allies, the enemies of its former allies, in 1915 after Great Britain and France promised that Italy would gain territory from Austria-Hungary after the war. Italy's promise in the Triple Alliance was limited because of its differences with its Austrian ally. The Triple Alliance could have been strengthened if Italy had agreed to abandon any territorial ambitions in Austria or if Austria had ceded the territory to Italy, but neither government was willing to pay that price. Italians wanted to unify all of their nation in one state. Austria-Hungary feared further demands from other non-German and Hungarian minorities within the Empire, particularly from the Czechs and Serbs. Credible alliances come with a price.

[Map of Italian-Austrian border areas before WWI]

Security policy is costly for states because it requires the government of a state to impose on its citizens. A government has to weigh the benefits of added security against the costs of political opposition that new arming programs or a new alliance may provoke. These domestic political costs are a major reason why states do not pursue all possible measures to defend their security. France in the years just before World War I felt very threatened by Germany. Germany had seized the provinces of Alsace and Lorraine in the peace treaty that ended the Franco-Prussian War in 1871. France considered those provinces as French and wanted them back. This issue made Germany and France rivals and drove much of the international politics of Europe from 1871 to 1914. Unified Germany was more powerful than France because it had more people and became one of the world's leading industrial powers during these decades. The Kaiser's government turns these advantages in potential power into a larger and better armed army than France had. Both countries formed alliances and built up their military. The last step that France took before World War I was the Three-Year Law in 1913. Countries at that time required all adult males to serve in the army for several years. These men served as the active army, the units that were always complete and ready to fight. Once trained as soldiers and released at the end of their service, men were obligated to serve in the reserves for another five to ten years. The reserves would be called back into the army to make it much larger if war broke out. The Three-Year Law sought to extend the period of active service from two to three years in France. Once complete, the Three Year Law would have increased the size of France's active army by one-half, closing much of the gap between the French and German armies. The law was strongly opposed in the National Assembly, the legislature of France. French citizens did not want to serve three years in the military, even if their country would be somewhat safer if they did so. Political parties on the left feared that the new larger army would be used as a tool to indoctrinate young men with right-wing ideology and could be used against the French people if they raised in revolution as they had in 1789, 1830, 1848, and 1871. After a difficult legislative battle, the Three-Year Law did pass, but World War I broke out before the full effect of the law could be felt.

Because security policy is politically costly, the question at the heart of security policy is "How much is enough?" Threats to a state wax and wane over time, and each government must decide how much security it wishes to create through its policies. No state is or ever has been perfectly secure. Security policy requires judging the threats the country faces, the added security that different measures could produce against those threats, and the costs of those measures. How much security a measure adds depends on the strategic situation, how it changes the military capabilities of the country in question, the credibility of any alliance promise, and the reactions of other states.

The final factor that influences the judgment of "How much is enough?" is the reactions of other states. As noted earlier, other states may see another state's security measures as threatening them. The increased threat they see may lead them to pursue a new ally or increase their own military forces. The net result could be to make both sides less secure with domestically unpopular policies. The reactions of other states might restrain a state from strengthening its own security policy.

Rearmament before the Second World War

During the 1930s, security policy of the European states depended largely on arming strategies rather than alliances. Germany, the Soviet Union, Great Britain, and France rebuilt their militaries that shrank in size after World War I. All built new planes and tanks that were much better than earlier models. All three expanded the size of the military. Although several attempts were tried to form an alliance against Nazi Germany, these efforts did not produce an alliance strong enough and credible enough to deter Hitler's designs for territorial expansion. Why did security policy before the Second World War focus on arming over allies?

The 1930s were a period of great change in military technology. Much improved gas combustion engines made it possible to make faster vehicles and airplanes powered by these new engines. The slow, undergunned tanks of the First World War were replaced by faster, heavier models mounting a powerful, high velocity gun. Fighting other tanks became one of the main jobs of armored fighting vehicles. The monoplane–planes with one wing–replaced the biplane with its two wings as the warplane of choice. Biplanes were more maneuverable than monoplanes, but the latter were much faster, allowing them to shoot at another plane and fly off. The multi-engine heavy bomber came of age, making the strategic bombing of cities first tried during World War I a practical strategy. Heavy bombers had longer range and higher payloads. Air transport, and so the innovation of paratroopers, because a reality. There were also many other smaller innovations in weaponry before and during World War II.

New forms of military organization for fighting were also introduced. We often think of changes in military technology driving greater capabilities, but often the changes in organization and how troops fight together are more important. The British, German, and Soviet militaries experimented with concentrating tanks in single formations to make war move at the speed of the motorized vehicle rather than the infantry soldier marching on foot. Germany arrived at the proper combination of tanks, infantry carried on vehicles, self-propelled artillery, and aircraft flying close support to bomb and strafe targets holding up the advance, which would be known as *blitzkrieg*–German for lightning warfare–when the war broke out. The U.S. and Britain created strategic air forces of heavy bombers to target military industry in enemy cities. The invention of radar by Great Britain made a coordinated air defense possible by allowing the defense to detect aerial raids before they reached Britain. Japan and the U.S. built aircraft carriers that could carry up to 100 airplanes as a way to bring airpower anywhere close to an ocean where these movable air bases could operate. Using the new weapons effectively required new ways to teaching troops to fight together, including coordination across the services. Amphibious warfare, where ships and airplanes supported invasions by Marines and soldiers, requires both specialized landing equipment and a high degree of inter-service coordination and training. Troops in the Second World War fought differently than those in the First.

These changes in weaponry and doctrine made arming strategies unusually attractive. Newly built forces had better tanks, airplanes, and other weapons and were organized in a way to take advantage of those weapons. Existing forces were quickly made obsolete by these changes. All the major powers launched rearmament program which developed and then produced these new weapons in mass. Disarmament in reverse you might say.

The disarmed state of the world also meant that countries could increase the security rapidly through arming. The Versailles Treaty limited the size of the German military to 100,000 soldiers with no tanks, airplanes, or submarines. The victorious allies reduced the sizes of their armies after the war as well. All of them, save the Soviet Union, had small militaries at the beginning of the 1930s. When Hitler came to power, he sought to rearm Germany and ignore the provisions of Versailles. The German military quickly became stronger than the French or British. In turn, they also began to build new weapons for a larger military out of the fear of what the *Wehrmacht* and *Luftwaffe*–the German army and air force–could do. It took new weapons to defeat the new weapons of the Germans.

The pace of rearmament–who rearmed with which weapons when–influenced the politics of the Nazi challenge to the status quo in Europe in the late 1930s. The French were reluctant to stand up for its ally Czechoslovakia during the Munich crisis because French military leaders believed they would lose a war with Germany quickly. The head of the French air force told political leaders in the French government that the Germans would wipe his planes from the sky within two weeks of outbreak of war. The British were developing new fighter aircraft and an air defense, but it was not ready and they felt vulnerable to attack from the air by Germany. A year later, both countries' rearmament programs had gone further, and they were willing to fight for Poland.

Why were alliances difficult to form in response to the threat the Nazis posed to all? Germany was vulnerable to a two-front war, having to fight on its eastern and western borders. France created a series of alliances after World War I with some of the new Eastern European states formed in the breakup of the Austro-Hungarian Empire. These states, however, were small relative to Germany; the real power to deter Germany through an alliance with France and Britain was the Soviet Union. The fall of Czechoslovakia made it clear to the Western Allies that only force could stop Hitler's push for domination of Europe. Great Britain and France quickly offered pledges to defend Poland and Romania if the Nazis attacked them. They opened talks with the Soviet Union during the summer of 1939 to conclude an anti-Nazi pact. The military representatives of both countries distrusted the Soviet Union, viewing the Communists as being as large a threat as the Nazis. Soviet Foreign Minister Molotov pushed for specific promises that Soviet troops could enter the Eastern European states to fight the German army. Great Britain and France refused to agree to any specific provision to allow such passage. The Eastern European allies of Britain and France feared the Soviet Union as much as Nazi Germany. As the Estonian foreign minister put it, "Once the Red Army [of the Soviet Union] gets into your country, it never gets out." Britain and France would not abandon these Eastern European states to Soviet domination. The talks foundered, and the Soviet Union turned to cut the Nazi-Soviet Pact with Hitler.

[Map showing situation in Eastern Europe in 1939]

Arming dominated security policy of the 1930s because countries could easily build up their military strength by making new weapons and expanding their small military establishments. Alliances were difficult to form because important political groups in the Western Allies feared the Soviet Union as much as Nazi Germany. Further, it took the Fall of Czechoslovakia in March of 1939 for Great Britain and France to realize that Hitler would only be stopped by war or the threat of war. By then, Britain and France preferred to trust their rebuilt militaries rather than pay the price the Soviet Union demanded for an alliance against the Nazis.

Alliances

Alliances are military agreements between states. They are written down like a contract between the parties and generally, but not always, made public. Many alliances, like NATO, commit the parties to come to one another's defense in the event of an attack on one of them. These alliances are called *defense pacts*. *Ententes*, like that between Great Britain on one hand and France and Russia on the other before World War I, only bind the parties to consult in the event of war. That consultation may lead to them to fight together during the war, as Britain did fight with its allies during the First World War. *Non-aggression pacts* are promises by the countries not to attack one another. They could be used to defuse the security dilemma between two countries, or to allow the allies to focus on attacking other countries free from fear that its alliance partner will attack it. They are also other variations on these types. Some alliances are one-way pledges. The United States and Japan, for example, concluded an alliance in 1952 that commits the U.S. to defend Japan but does not commit Japan to defend the U.S. The Constitution of Japan, which the U.S. imposed on the country during its occupation after the war, limits the use and character of the Japanese military. Indeed, the Japanese military is called the "Self-Defense Forces" to reflect its mission of just defending the Japanese islands.

Alliances can be formed by just two countries or by many. The former are *bilateral alliances*; the latter *multilateral alliances*. Bilateral alliances have been more common historically, although some of the most important alliances, such as NATO, have been multilateral. Occasionally, two countries will be members of both a bilateral alliance and a multilateral alliance. The Soviet Union and most of the Communist Eastern European states had both bilateral defense pacts and were members of the Warsaw Pact, a multilateral alliance that bound all of them together in imitation of NATO. For most purposes, the bilateral alliance was more important. Those bilateral pacts allowed the Soviet Union to station troops in their Eastern European allies.

The promises made in alliances are often limited by conditional clauses. They are not blanket promises of coming to an ally's aid no matter what happens; they are contracts which bind only under specific conditions. As already mentioned, Italy did not join with its fellow members of the Triple Alliance when World War I broke out because it claimed that they had not been attacked. The triggers in alliances can be very specific. The Little Entente bound together Czechoslovakia, Romania, and Yugoslavia against their common threat of Hungary during the interwar period. All three countries feared that Hungary had territorial designs on them because each of them had a Hungarian ethnic minority within their borders. The alliance only bound them to come to one another aid against an attack by Hungary. It did not bind them to fight for one another against other countries. Each of the three also faced a serious threat from a neighboring major power. Czechoslovakia bordered on Germany, Romania on the Soviet Union, and Yugoslavia on Italy, and all three had good reason to fear those major powers. The Little Entente did not address these threats because they were not common to the three countries. Because the other two did not share common borders with the other threatening major powers, it would be difficult for them to help one another during a war. Further, all of them together were still weaker than any one of these major powers as you can see in the Table of the capabilities of these states in 1922. The Little Entente focused on the threat of Hungary because the members could defend one another against that threat.

[Map showing Little Entente, Hungary, and major powers]
[Table comparing capabilities of these states with major powers in 1922]

States generally form alliances to increase their security by joining together against a common threat. The allies all gain security to the extent that their alliance pledges are credible to the threatening power and they possess the military strength to defeat it in a war. Each contributes its own military capabilities to a joint war. Strong countries then are more attractive alliance partners than weak ones because they have more capabilities to contribute to the joint effort. But there are many alliances between strong countries, like the United States in NATO, and weak countries, such as the smaller European states like Belgium and the Netherlands in NATO. What do the strong countries get in those alliances? One, they may want to protect the smaller country. These alliances often grant basing rights to the stronger country, which increases the alliance's ability to defend them. Second, the stronger state may receive other concessions over other policies of the smaller state, in essence paying for the protection of the stronger. During the Boer War in 1899-1902, Great Britain and Portugal concluded an alliance whereby Britain would protect Portugal and its colonies in Africa from other major powers interested in expanding their African colonies at Portugal's expense. In exchange, Portugal agreed to close the ports in one of its colonies, Mozambique, through which the Boers were smuggling arms to support their war against the British in what is now South Africa. Military bases could be such a concession if they allow the major power to project its power into parts of the globe it could not otherwise. The U.S. used bases in Thailand, Okinawa (a large island which is part of Japan and lies south of it), and the Philippines during the Vietnam War, basing aircraft used in bombing missions and staging troops into and out of Vietnam through those places. Alliances where both parties gain security are *symmetric*; those where one parties gains security and the other something else are *asymmetric*. The symmetry or asymmetry of interests is often matched by equality or inequality of capabilities. Symmetric alliances require both parties to be strong enough to defend one another, while asymmetric alliances have unequal partners where the stronger protects the weaker in exchange for other concessions.

[Map of Boer War and Mozambique showing ports]

There are also alliances which do not increase the security of the parties, instead helping them coordinate their efforts to change the status quo. Nazi Germany, Fascist Italy, and Imperial Japan formed the Axis before World War II. This alliance advanced their shared interest in overturning the interwar status quo. Their goals were complementary and did not directly conflict. Germany sought territorial expansion in Central and Eastern Europe, Italy in the countries around the Mediterranean, and Japan in East Asia. If they all sought the same territory, they would have had to decide how they wished to divide that territory to make their alliance credible because otherwise they would have fought over who got how much of the spoils. Still, the Axis powers did not coordinate their efforts during World War II as effectively as the Allies did. Italy entered the war once it became clear that France was defeated in June of 1940. Italian entry opened up the Mediterranean as a theater of war, one which the Germans wished was not open. When Germany attacked the Soviet Union with some Italian aid in the summer of 1941, Japan remained neutral and did not attack Soviet East Asia. The Japanese also allowed the United States to send military aid to the Soviet Union across the Pacific to the port of Vladivostok even after Japan was at war with the U.S., out of fear of war with the Soviet Union. *Offensive* alliances, like the Axis, may founder because the parties share only their interest in changing the status quo. Once one of them achieves its ends, it is rarely willing to continue fighting. Offensive alliances are also formed for immediate gains, making them short-lived.

The Reliability of Alliances and Creating Credible Commitments

How often do allies fight together when one goes to war? It depends on how you do the counting. If we simply count how often allies fight on the same side when one of them goes to war, only 27% of allies fight together. Alliances then appear unreliable. But this calculation includes all possible conditions for war, so it includes many cases where the allies have not pledged to come to one another's aid. If we ask how often specific alliance pledges are honored, 75% of the time a state comes to its ally's aid when the specific provision of the alliance are triggered. The interventions of the United States into the Korean and Vietnam Wars illustrates this pattern. The NATO alliance was not triggered in either case because no member of the alliance was attacked. Many NATO allies of the U.S. did send troops to fight in Korea, with the British and Turks sending substantial numbers of troops, because the U.S. succeeded in getting a resolution through the UN Security Council calling on member states to come to the defense of South Korea. The Soviet Union could not veto the resolution because its UN Ambassador was staging a boycott because Communist China had not been admitted as a member in the place of the Nationalist government which it had defeated in the Chinese Civil War a year before. No

NATO ally fought in Vietnam. The defense provisions of the alliance had not been triggered, and the U.S. could not get a resolution through the Security Council because the Soviet Union would have vetoed one. Allies of the U.S. in East Asia and the Pacific, notably South Korea and Australia, did send troops to fight in Vietnam with the Americans. Alliances are generally unreliable but specifically reliable. The specific pledges in an alliance matter.

Still, one-quarter of these specific pledges are not honored in wartime. Why? There is a selection effect where unreliable alliances are more likely to be tested that those where the allies are likely to fight together. When an alliance is credible and the allies are likely to come to one another's aid, states that threaten either of the allies anticipate that war with one of them means war with both. Few states feel strong enough to fight two other states at the same time. When other states doubt the credibility of the allies' pledges to defend one another, the alliance will not stop them from pressing their demands with the threat of war. The alliances that are challenged are generally those where parties outside the alliance doubt the credibility of the alliance.

How can possible predator states identify which alliances are unreliable before they test them? Alliance pledges are most credible when they are first made because the allies can strike a bargain that makes those pledges credible. They can tailor the specific conditions of the alliance to fit their current circumstance. The fact that both are willing to sign the alliance indicates that both are willing to live up to their promises in that alliance. When conditions remain the same, alliance promises are almost always honored, at an estimated rate of 96%. Conditions, however, change over time. Large shifts in capabilities can undermine a state's commitment to an alliance. If it becomes stronger, it may no longer need its ally for deterrence and defense against threats to itself. If it becomes much weaker, its may feel that its contribution is not large enough to save its ally. A change of 10% in a state's capabilities, either upward or downward, increases the chance of a state failing to honor its commitment when its ally is attacked rises to 41%. When the political system of a state changes, it is less likely to honor the alliance commitments of the earlier government. A change in political institutions raises the risk of breaking an alliance commitment when challenged from 6% to 30%. The new government often does not feel bound to the pledges of its predecessor. The characteristics of the state called on to honor an alliance promise also matter. Major powers are more likely to fail to honor their alliance pledges to minor powers, that is when they are in an asymmetric alliance. Democracies are more likely to honor their pledges. Indeed, no democratic major power has failed to honor an alliance commitment. This result is consistent with the argument that democracies generate higher audience costs than non-democracies. Higher audience costs for breaking a public promise could be sufficient to convince a democratic leader to honor its country's pledge to go to war on behalf of another.

What can allies do to make their commitments to one another credible to other parties? Commitment devices can make promises more credible as we discussed in the chapter on the logic of promises. These measures create incentives for the party to honor its promise because the consequences of backing down from it are worse than carrying it out. Breaking a public pledge can trigger audience costs that punish a leader for breaking that promise. As with threats, the audience could be domestic supporters who could restrict the power of the leader breaking the promise at home or even remove him or her from power. The audience could also be leaders of the other states who might diminish the reputation of the leader for living up to his or her word. With this public promise broken, other leaders would doubt other, less important promises of the leader. Alliance are often made publicly both to communicate the pledge to fight together to other states and to bind the parties to one another by creating these audience costs. But publicity alone does not make all alliances credible. When a war is likely to be long and bloody, all state leaders may doubt the credibility of a pledge to go to war to save an ally. In the years before the First World War, Great Britain abandoned her historical policy of having only interests not allies on the European continent and aligned herself with France and Russia against the Triple Alliance. British policy was directed against the threat posed by Germany. Britain and France held military talks to coordinate how the small British army would land and fight in France alongside the French army against the Germans. When General Wilson of Britain asked Marshal Joffre how many British troops he wanted sent to France, Joffre replied, "One, and we will make sure he dies." Everyone understood that the British government was divided over the commitment to fight on the continent. Shedding British blood to defend France would rally British public opinion to support a war, making even the doubters within the government willing to fight. When war came, the British promise to come to France's aid was not sufficient to deter Germany. The Kaiser's Government did not believe that Britain would fight with France or that its small army would make a difference if they did. The alliance here was not credible in the eyes of the Germans. The specific public pledge by Great Britain was only to consult with France and Russia in the event of war. The military talks over how to deploy the British army in France were secret. The divisions within Prime Minister Asquith's government over whether Britain should commit itself to a land war on the continent were profound. Several ministers resigned from the government when Britain did go to war in 1914. Only public commitments to deploy British troops to the continent might have convinced German leaders that Britain would fight on the ground in France if Germany attacked France, and so deterred World War I. One reason why a state may allow its ally to deploy troops within its territory is to commit that ally to coming to its defense by literally making an attack on one an attack on both.

The Disadvantage of Commitment

If commitment devices are necessary to make alliances credible, why do states, like Britain in this example, sometimes refuse to bind themselves to their allies through such devices? Strong commitment devices make the promise to come to the defense of an ally more credible, but they also bind that state to the policies of the ally no matter what. One can become too committed to the ally, where the commitment devices in place force you to go to their aid no matter how the war is precipitated. If your ally knows that you will fight with for it no matter what, it may feel that it can take greater chances in its foreign policy than it would on its own. It might challenge a stronger state, hoping that you are committed to its defense if it provokes a war. You would then find yourself fighting a war you did not want. *Entrapment* occurs when a state's commitment to an alliance is so strong that its ally leads it into a war it did not want. The stronger ally often fears entrapment by a weaker ally. Because it is stronger, the support of its capabilities had a larger effect on the ability of its weaker ally to fight and win a war.

The opposite risk in an alliance is *abandonment*, the fear of the weaker party that the stronger will not live up to its pledge to defend it in its hour of need. Alliances between states with unequal capabilities have to balance these two risks when they set the level of their commitment to one another. The stronger ally fears entrapment, and so wants looser ties that will preserve its freedom of action if the weaker ally provokes a crisis. The weaker ally fears abandonment, and so wants stronger ties that will ensure that its stronger ally will fight with it if necessary.

Great Britain's entry into the Second World War shows the problem of entrapment and how domestic politics can induce a government to live up to its promise to defend an ally. After Nazi Germany occupied the rump of Czechoslovakia in March of 1939, Britain and France offered security guarantees to Poland and Romania. They feared that these two important Eastern European countries would align with Germany because they were intimidated by Nazi power and also afraid of the Soviet Union. The security guarantees reassured them that Britain and France would fight with them if they resisted Hitler. During the Summer of 1939, a crisis occurred as Hitler demanded concessions in the Polish Corridor, a portion of Poland taken from Germany in the Versailles Treaty after World War I that split East Prussia off from Germany and was populated by ethnic Germans as well as Poles. Hitler also put pressure on the free city of Danzig to force it to unify with Germany. The Western Powers wanted to thwart Hitler's designs, but many also feared war with Germany. The skeptics states their opposition to war with the rhetorical question, "Die for Danzig?" The security guarantee from Britain and France helped convince the Polish government that it should resist Hitler's demand for concessions in the Polish Corridor. Although Germany had a stronger and more modern military than Poland, it thought it could resist the Nazis if the British and French opened a second front against Germany on its western border.

[Map of Polish Corridor and Danzig]
[Cover of Newsweek with "Poland's Biggest Army Wants No Appeasement"]

Poland resisted Hitler's threat and refused to concede an inch on the Polish Corridor. On September 1, 1939, Hitler launched a surprise attack on Poland. Neither the British nor French government, haunted by the memory of the immense losses of the First World War, was enthusiastic about a war with Germany. Both governments spent the two days after the invasion trying to find a way to undo the German invasion through all possible channels, most notably through Germany's Italian ally, Mussolini. These efforts failed. On the evening of September 2, 1939, Prime Minister Chamberlain and Foreign Minister Halifax of Britain reported their efforts to avoid war to the House of Commons, the main chamber of the British legislature. Chamberlain described how his efforts to forestall war had not succeeded. He said nothing about whether Britain would fulfill its pledge to Poland by declaring war on Germany. The members of Commons were livid that Chamberlain was trying to get out of the security guarantee to Poland. As is the custom in the House of Commons, Leo Amery, the leader of the opposition, rose to respond, opening with the line "Speaking for the Labor Party..." An unknown backbencher (a low-level member of Parliament) shouted out "Speak for England!" Amery then made it clear that Britain must go to war to fight for Poland, that the government would fall in a vote of no confidence if it did not. The next day Chamberlain's government declared war on Germany at noon, followed by the French government that evening. The public commitment to defend Poland both encouraged the Poles to resist Hitler's demands and produced the domestic consensus to force Chamberlain and Halifax to go to war when they would have rather not done so.

How can allies control these problems? Ceding power is one way to make promises more credible and reassure a party that its ally will not take undue risks of war. The weaker party can grant some control over its own policy to its stronger ally in order to secure a pledge to defend it against attack. The United States and South Korea agreed that U.S. forces would continue to be deployed in Korea after the end of the Korean War to help defend against a renewed attack from North Korea. The two countries concluded a formal defense pact in 1954, and U.S. Army troops were deployed close to the demilitarized zone (DMZ) along the routes that North Korean troops would have to take to attack Seoul, South Korea's capital and largest city. This deployment of U.S. troops was a commitment device that reassured the South Korean government that the U.S. would honor its commitment to defend South Korea. American troops would be on the front line from the first moments of a new war. But the certainty of U.S. involvement raised the problem of entrapment for the U.S. Might the South Korean government take actions that could provoke a North Korean invasion, counting on the U.S. military to win the resulting war for them? To address this problem of entrapment, the South Korean military was placed under a joint command headed by an American general. South Korea could not redeploy its troops close to the DMZ without explicit permission from that general. Joint military exercises, where U.S. and South Korean troops would practice maneuvers in the field, were held away from the DMZ to avoid any chance that North Korea might interpret those troop movements as preparation for an invasion. Ceding control over their military was costly for the government of South Korea. Many Koreans found the command structure humiliating. Many also objected to the free rein which U.S. soldiers posted to Korea were often given. These measures, however, controlled the dual fears of abandonment and entrapment and helped make the U.S. promise to defend South Korea credible.

[Map showing Korean DMZ, Seoul, and position of U.S. forces]

Do alliances make states more secure against demands backed by the use of force? Yes, a defensive alliance reduces the chance that another state will press demands against it backing by the threat of force by one-quarter to one-third. The specific pledges in the alliance matter because only defensive alliances convey this benefit. Offensive alliances and non-aggression pacts can be used by states that wish to change the status quo to enhance their ability to do so. When a state has an offensive alliance, the chance that it makes a demand backed by force of a state other than its ally rises by one-half. An offensive alliance aids a state seeking change by increasing the force behind its threats. If it has a non-aggression pact, the chance that it makes a demand on some third state rises by close to three-fifths. The non-aggression pact acts as a confirmation that the ally will not interfere if it uses force to secure its demands; it guarantees that the other party in the non-aggression pact will remain neutral in a war. Alliances generally reduce the risk of demands, but sometimes they are used to make it easier for the allies to advance their demands.

Arming in Preparation for War

Arming is the other primary form of security policy. By improving its military, a state increases its chance of deterring threats and winning wars if necessary. Arming strategies cover the wide range of ways that a state can improve its military. Expanding it by adding more soldiers is one way, but so is improving its equipment by buying new weapons. Technological change can make existing weapons obsolete, leading states to build newer, better weapons and war machines. A state can also improve its military in some cases by reorganizing it or adopting new ways of fighting together. All the branches of the U.S. military–Army, Navy, Air Force, Marines–devote substantial effort to studying how to fight and training their troops in new methods of combat. Most states prepare some fortifications which they can use to defend their country from attack. All of these ways of improving a state's ability to fight and win wars are arming strategies.

As mentioned earlier in this chapter, arming takes longer to increase a state's security than alliances do. It takes time to train troops or to design and build new weapons. Armies rely on their officers, both commissioned and non-commissioned, to command and lead soldiers in combat. Good officers take years to train. Modern armies are highly specialized with many troops in support roles for the combat troops. In the U.S. Army, the ratio of fighting troops to support troops–cooks, supply officers, command personnel, maintenance men for vehicles, medical personnel, and more--is known as the "Teeth-to-Tail" ratio, and that ratio is roughly 3 support troops for every combat infantry soldier. Of course, the support troops may have to fight themselves if they come under attack. The development of new combat aircraft takes years; the new F-22 fighter jet has taken 17 years from the initial request for designs for a new fighter aircraft through the competition among the different designs submitted to acceptance of one of those design to production and testing of the aircraft until finally it is deployed with active air units. The delay between the decision to expand the military and the increase in capabilities may affect states' security policy.

The Role of the Military

The military of a state has two uses, domestic security and international power. Throughout history, the first mission, protecting the state and its leaders from rebels domestically, has been the primary mission of the military. Napoleon Bonaparte came to power in France in part because he was willing to turn his cannon on the Paris mob to defend the Directory, the revolutionary government at that time. For many states even today, defense against domestic threats is the preeminent mission of the military. Saddam Hussein divided his army into a large regular army and the elite Republican Guard. The Republican Guard received extra pay and special privileges to serve as the military force which Hussein used to violently suppress revolts by the Kurds in the North and Shiites in the South of Iraq in 1991 after the first Gulf War. The Chinese government used army units to clear Tiananmen Square in 1989 of pro-democracy protestors, killing hundreds of them in the process. In the United States, we do not think of the military as the last line of defense of the government against its own people, but this it unusual in history and internationally.

Civil-military relations cover the relationship between the military and civilian authorities. In the United States and most advanced industrial democracies, the military is fully professional and under the control of the civilian authorities. The professional military has authority to make decisions over its own internal matters, such as the promotion of officers and setting military policy. In autocracies, the military is politicized or may be the government itself. Military leaders are chosen not for their ability but for their loyalty to the leader of the state. Disloyal officers might use their troops to seize power for themselves and so must be removed by whatever means is necessary. The military is almost always plays an important role in the government of an autocracy because it both poses a threat to the government and is the last line of defense of the government. In some systems, like the Soviet Union, the military has a privileged but subservient position to the government, which was the Communist Party in the Soviet Union.

The political role of the military means that its composition is often a major issue in the politics of a country. The broad boulevards of Paris are evidence of the struggle over the character of the French Army in the 19th century. France underwent a series of popular revolutions, in 1789, 1830, 1848, and finally in 1871. The citizens of Paris rose up in these revolutions, blocking the narrow, old streets of Paris with barricades created out of whatever they could find. They would use these barricades as protection from which they fought the police and the army. The type of army that France would have was an issue throughout the 19th century and up to the First World War. The Right wanted a small, professional army where soldiers would serve long terms under the colors. Soldiers could be indoctrinated in conservative values and would have primary loyalties to the Army. Such troops could be relied upon to clear the streets of Paris if necessary. The Left wanted a large, popular army with short terms of service. An army of the people would not kill its fellow citizens if they rose up against the State. The choice between a small, professional army and a mass army based on conscription became even more politically controversial when France's defeat in the Franco-Prussian War made it clear that the Army needed to expand to meet the threat of a unified Germany. Napoleon III tried to resolve some of this dilemma by having his architect Baron Haussmann carve wide boulevards through the old neighborhoods of Paris to prevent the Paris mob from ever again blocking the streets with barricades. These broad boulevards, such as the Champs-Elysees, remain a distinctive feature of Paris. Now these broad boulevards are now a way for the French to demonstrate their discontent with their government through marches and demonstrations.

[Picture of the Champs-Elysees]

The other main job of militaries, and the one that is relevant to this chapter, is deterring threats from other states or fighting their forces should deterrence fail. The domestic role of the military may complicate choices of what military to build to counter external threats. Other factors also enter into the decision of whether and how much to strengthen a state's military. First, the threat posed by other states plays a large role. Does the state have conflicts of interest with other states where military force could be used to resolve them? How strong are the militaries of those other states? Assessment of external threat combines perceptions of the intentions of other states and their capabilities. Some states pose no threat whatsoever, while others may be deadly rivals. Germany and France viewed one another as enemies after the Franco-Prussian War because of the provinces of Alsace and Lorraine that Germany took from France at the end of that war. France wanted them back. Other states do not view each other as threats even when one of them is much stronger than the other. Canada does not feel threatened by the power of the United States, despite the history that the U.S. invaded Canada in 1775 and 1812 when it was a British colony. Judgment of which states are threatening and how large is the conflict of interests is the first element of deciding whether to arm. Second, the size of the military threat posed by other states that the country has conflict with matters. The U.S. does not feel threatened by Cuba because it is militarily weak compared to the U.S. More powerful states are larger threats because they are larger, more capable militaries. Third, how the country could expand its military and how those improvements might counter the threats posed by other countries matters. Before World War I, Germany began building a navy designed to match the British Navy. Britain's response was to expand its Navy, not its Army, even though its Army would play a more important role in the defeat of Germany during the war. The German threat before the war was naval and provoked a naval response. The British only created a mass army after they were already in the war and fighting on the ground in France and Belgium. The judgment of how large and strong the military must be to defend against external threats is a political decision. The political leadership of a state judges how significant external threats are and what the appropriate response is.

The two roles of the military shape the militaries that states build. In those states where the military is first and foremost the guardian of the state, political loyalty and the ability to fight rebels are the main requirements of the military. In states where the military is under civilian authority, its role is to defend the state against external threats.

Arms Races

As mentioned earlier in this chapter, the expansion of one state's military can threaten other states. A rival may conclude that the increase in the first state's military now poses a larger threat to its own interests and so must be countered with arming policies of its own. As I mentioned above, Great Britain felt threatened by the German program to build a large, powerful navy before the First World War. Historically, Britain depended on its command of the seas to protect its trade carried by ships. It had been the dominant naval power since replacing the Dutch as such around 1670. If another power gained control of the seas, it could starve Britain into submission because Britain relied on imported food to feed its people. When Admiral Tirpitz of Germany declared the German naval program, Britain responded by building more ships of its own. When the first state then feels threatened by the response of its rival and builds more weapons in response, the parties begin racing to see which side can build a bigger, better military. An *arms race* occurs when both sides expand their military rapidly in competition with one another.

Changes in technology can make arms races worse. When new weapons are superior to existing stockpiles, each side in the race may think that it can gain a decisive edge by building those new weapons. These better weapons are more threatening to the other side, and so provoke a stronger response in turn. When Germany began its naval challenge to Great Britain, battleships had both turrets with large guns and others with small guns and were slower than smaller warships. Britain built the Dreadnought in 1906 to respond to the German naval threat. It had a revolutionary design, carrying more big guns and better engines that made it much faster and allowed it to carry thicker, heavier armor. The design changed the way every country built battleships, to the point where new battleships were called dreadnoughts and ships of the earlier design became known as pre-dreadnoughts. The introduction of the Dreadnought made all the pre-dreadnoughts obsolete. The change made the naval arms race between Britain and Germany worse because both sides realized that only the number of Dreadnoughts mattered. Britain's advantage of more pre-dreadnoughts would not help her win a naval war against Germany. Both sides began building many dreadnoughts and improving their design to pack more guns on faster ships. When World War I broke out, Germany had 15 dreadnoughts, 22 pre-dreadnoughts, and 5 battlecruisers, a faster, less armored variant on the dreadnought design. Britain had 22 dreadnoughts, 40 predreadnoughts, and 9 battlecruisers at the outbreak of the war. Even though the Royal Navy had more of all three classes of ships, its advantage was smaller in modern ships than pre-dreadnoughts. The change in naval design and technology sped up the naval arms race and, ironically, reduced Britain's advantage over Germany on the high seas.

[Picture of line of dreadnoughts before World War I]

Military strength is a relative comparison between countries. It is more important to have more weapons than your rival than to have more weapons. An arms race can cost both countries and make neither more secure. One side's increase in its military is matched by the other's increase. Both would be better off if they could agree not to build up their militaries; they would be as secure without the additional expense of building more weapons or inducting more people into their military. This idea lies behind *arms control*, agreements between rivals to limit the growth of their militaries. If both follow the agreement, they would benefit over unconstrained military competition. Left to their own devices, however, each country is better off building no matter what the other side does. If the rival is restrained in its defense efforts, your country is more secure because it is now stronger compared to the rival. If the rival does not restrain itself, your country protects itself by building up its own military. Arms control seeks to break this competition through mutual agreement. Even after such an agreement, both sides may fear that the other may violate the agreement to get a military advantage. Arms control then faces the problem of enforcement of agreements, which we discuss later in the book. For now, I just note that arms control agreements are often plagued by fears of cheating by the other side.

The Cold War saw military competition as well as political competition between the superpowers. The nuclear arms race between the United States and Soviet Union was a major feature of their competition. Only the U.S. had nuclear weapons at the end of World War II, but the Soviet Union tested its first atomic bomb in 1949. Both sides built tens, then hundreds, and finally thousands of nuclear warheads and the means to deliver them to the homeland of the other. Intercontinental ballistic missiles (ICBMs) replaced bomber aircraft as the primary means of delivering nuclear bombs to their targets, with the missiles then being placed either in hardened silos dug into the ground or on submarines hidden in the vastness of the sea. These latter measures sought to make it impossible for the other side to destroy those missiles in a surprise attack. In the 1960s, the U.S. and Soviet Union began discussing arms control measures to reduce the burden of the nuclear arms race. In 1972, they agreed to the first Strategic Arms Limitation Treaty (SALT I) which limited how many missiles each side would deploy and restricted the deployment of anti-ballistic missiles (ABMs). Some in both countries worried that the other side was not keeping its side of the bargain. In some cases, it was difficult to tell if specific measures violated the treaty or not. The Soviet built a radar installation at Krasnoyarsk that some in the U.S. believed to violate the ABM provisions of SALT I. The SALT II treaty was negotiated but never ratified because of strong opposition in the U.S. Senate, partly because of fears that the Soviet Union was not restrained in its behavior. The end of the Cold War stopped the nuclear arms race by ending the political rivalry between the U.S. and the Soviet Union. Once the two countries no longer saw one another as rivals, the need for large nuclear arsenals disappeared, and both countries reduced their stockpiles of nuclear weapons.

As we discussed earlier, states often have domestic motivations rather than international ones for their military. This can be true even in countries where the military's primary responsibility is protection of the country from external threats. The production of weapons and war material is a big business in countries with sophisticated high technology militaries. Many businesses have contracts with their own government and other governments to build weapons. President Eisenhower famously warned the American people of the *military-industrial complex*, the connections between firms that received military contracts and the portions of the government that oversaw military production. He was concerned that their interests in expanding business would drive the U.S. into buying more and more expensive weapons that it needed for its defense. Some argue that defense contracts provide jobs in the places where the factories and design shops are located. In the U.S., members of Congress care very much about the defense contracts and military bases in their districts and work hard to see that those jobs stay in their district. Others worry about the arms trade, where firms sell almost all types of military hardware–small arms, artillery, helicopters, tanks and jet aircraft to name some–to almost every government. The critics of the arms trade are concerned that the buying countries are wasting their money on weapons they do not need. They also fear that the arms trade increases international tensions by making it easier for developing countries to equip their military with modern weapons. The weapons could be used by an oppressive government to repress their own people as well.

Determining whether an arms race is occurring is complicated by these domestic motivations. If countries acquire sophisticated weapons for domestic reasons, we might find that their militaries appear to grow at the same time, like in an arms race. But this situation is not an arms race because neither side is responding to the other's increases in their military; both are building more weapons only in response to domestic demands. The arms expenditures of the United States and Canada have increased together over time, but they are not arming in response to one another. They are NATO allies. Their military expenditures have grown over time as both countries have become richer.

[Graph showing how U.S. and Canadian military expenditures grow together over time]

The Cost of Defense

How much can a country spend on defense? As I discussed earlier, spending on the military faces significant political costs because the resources could be used elsewhere in society to produce other goods. How much states spend on defense during peacetime is not a good indicator of how much they can spend. When a country is faced with an threat to its existence, almost everyone in that country will agree that everything possible should be done to win the wars. What is the point of having more butter if the enemy's guns will just take it away? The Second World War was fought to the bitter end with the combatants committing all the resources they could to their war effort. From the table, we can see that countries generally spent about one-half on the military during the peak of the war. Germany spent noticeably more at the end of the war, and the U.S. spent a little less. As a rule of thumb, I use the one-half figure because it is easier to remember and close to the historical record. The other half of domestic production has to support the civilian population with food and other necessities of life so they can produce for the war effort. All countries in World War II limited civilian access to many goods including food to save them for the war effort. The United States rationed items like car tires and nylon stockings to save their material for army trucks and parachutes.

[Table of military expenditures as percent of GNP during WWII]

During peacetime, states, even those in arms races, spend a much lower proportion of the GNP (Gross National Product–a measure of the size of the economy) on the military. The ratio of GNP spent on military expenditures is called the *defense burden*. The graph below gives U.S. military expenditures as a proportion of its GNP before, during, and after the Cold War. U.S. defense spending ranged from 5% to 10% of GNP during the Cold War, reaching its high point during the Kennedy Administration. The wars in Korea and Vietnam increased defense spending because fighting wars requires much equipment and material. The first part of the graph shows that U.S. military expenditures were a much larger proportion of GNP during World War II, reflecting the fact that countries spend much more on the military during war than during peacetime. After the end of the Cold War, the U.S. defense burden dropped in what was called the "peace dividend." The wars in Afghanistan and Iraq after 9/11 caused military expenditures to rise again, but as a fraction of GDP they are smaller than during the Cold War. The amount of money spent on defense controlling for inflation is larger now, but the burden is less because the U.S. economy has grown substantially since the end of the Cold War in 1991.

[Graph of US military expenditures as percent of GNP from 1935 on; show Cold War years on it]

The defense burden of the Soviet Union is more difficult to calculate. The Soviet Union kept both the amount spent on weaponry and even how much the country produced–its GNP–as state secrets. The CIA estimated these quantities regularly from what information they had. The common figures cited for the Soviet defense burden is 15-25% of its GNP. This figure underestimates the economic cost because the Soviet Union drafted soldiers to fill its massive army. The loss of the labor of these young men to the Soviet economy is difficult to calculate. Even with these adjustments, the Soviet military effort during the Cold War was much less than its titanic efforts when it fought the Nazis during World War II.

The defense burden of other countries are typically less than 5%. The table gives the defense burden of a selection of states around the world. Those countries in long-term military rivalries do spend more, as you can see from the defense burdens of Israel and the Arab states. Defense burdens this high are unusual, though. Even India and Pakistan who have clashed repeatedly over Kashmir have defense burdens under 5%. Countries in peaceful parts of the globe spend even less on their defense. Costa Rica is the extreme case here; it abolished its army in 1948 and has just a small paramilitary constabulary now.

[Table showing defense burden for selected states, including major powers, Arab states, Israel, Pakistan, and some South American and African states]

What is the big picture these figures paint? Countries spend much less on their military during peacetime than they do when they are in a war for their existence. Even countries in arms races spend less than they would if they fought. This is a choice. It reflects the economic cost of arming. That cost is paid in the production lost to the civilian economy when it is devoted to producing weapons or training people to be soldiers rather than fill productive jobs in the economy. This is not to say that military expenditures are wasted; citizens of a state value the security produced by their military forces. Because the people of a country pay the cost of their military, arming decisions reflect this cost and weigh it against the benefit of added security. The key question is "How much is enough?"

NATO after the Cold War

Return to the puzzle of NATO expansion. The alliance was created early in the Cold War to counter the threat of Soviet expansion and subversion of Europe. It extended the protection of American power over most, but not all, of Western Europe. In turn, it committed most of the countries of Western Europe to one another's defense and created multinational forces in West Germany and on the naval flanks of Europe in the Mediterranean and Norwegian Seas. Those countries that were shielded behind NATO forces, such as France, Belgium, and the Netherlands, were induced to join and participate in the alliance's military structures. NATO also solved internal conflicts among the alliance's members. When West Germany rearmed in the 1950s, its military forces were under NATO command, reassuring its traditional enemy, France, that this new German army would not invade France as earlier German armies had done three times in the previous hundred years. The alliance could have unraveled if it had not controlled internal divisions. It welded together the militaries of many nations into one coherent fighting force, which was not tested in battle during the Cold War. NATO integrated the member armies through formal command and decision making structures. Political decisions focused on interoperability–the use of compatible military equipment and joint maneuvers to train the many armies to work together in the field. This integration increased the ability of the NATO armies to fight together and win wars, increasing their ability to deter a Soviet attack westward. The history of working together for decades created a joint sense of purpose among the allies and developed security institutions that made the many armies into one.

Many thought the alliance would disappear when the Soviet threat did. Instead, it expanded eastward to include many of the former communist states of Eastern Europe. The alliance offered security guarantees to these new members to face two threats to the peace of Europe. The first threat was the resurgence of a Russia seeking to reestablish its control over Eastern Europe. That threat seemed remote at best in the 1990s when NATO began to consider adding new members to the East. The staunchly anti-Communist governments in Eastern Europe, however, wished to be included before that threat became real. The second threat was territorial wars among the Eastern European states themselves. The borders in Eastern Europe were redrawn several times during the 20th century. Most Eastern European countries have ethnic minorities with a neighboring nation-state for that minority. Bulgaria has a Turkish minority, Romania a Hungarian minority, and Poland contains ethnic Germans. The possibility of cross-borders over the treatment of these minorities was a real possibility that became a real horror when Yugoslavia broke up into its constituent republics. NATO could enforce a peace among its new members. NATO first and foremost solved these two security threats to the benefit of new members and the older NATO allies.

The new members faced important demands before they would be allowed to enter the alliance. These demands helped establish the credibility of the alliance to solve both of the security problems. The new members had to rebuild their militaries to allow them to operate with NATO forces. These countries had Soviet military equipment from their years as members of the Warsaw Pact, the alliance that the Soviet Union forced on them to counter NATO. They needed to buy new equipment and develop military bases where NATO forces could operate. Again, the credibility of the alliance hinged on whether the many national armies of NATO could fight as one. Eastern European countries that wished to join NATO first had to join the Partnership for Peace. This arrangement for military cooperation was extended to many countries after the end of the Cold War. It provided regular military talks and joint military exercises between NATO and these countries outside the alliance. When countries wished to apply for NATO membership, their qualifications were reviewed, and not all countries were allowed to join the alliance as quickly as they desired. These states also had to show that they had stable democratic governments that guaranteed minority rights. These demands helped to remove the threat of conflict among NATO members by only allowing in countries which were unlikely to reopen the status of their co-nationals in neighboring countries. These measures helped the alliance solve the two security threats posed by expansion.

NATO has also expanded its focus as it has added new members. The alliance fought for the first time in 1999 when NATO air forces, primarily the U.S. Air Force, bombed Serbian targets in Kosovo and Serbia proper. The allies sought to force Serbia to end oppression of ethnic Albanians, referred to as Kosovars, inside Kosovo. Eventually Slobodan Milosevic's government yielded to end the bombing, and a NATO force was deployed in Kosovo to keep the peace between Serbs and Kosovars there. NATO also leads the mission to Afghanistan. The invasion and overthrow of the Taliban in Afghanistan by the U.S. led to the need to deploy troops to help the new Afghan government control the countryside. This deployment was NATO's first outside Europe, although the force there is still heavily American. It is also the first time that NATO has suffered casualties from combat. The expansion of NATO's area of interest to security issues outside of Europe, known as "out of area," is new for the alliance. This expansion in coverage has produced friction among the allies. The U.S. has strongly favored this expansion in geographic focus, while some European members have opposed that expansion and contributed little to the mission in Afghanistan.

During the Cold War, NATO focused solely on European security. The U.S. often saw NATO as part of its global strategy, but many Europeans were concerned to restrict the alliance to the defense of Europe. When many members of NATO fought during the Korean War, they did so under a UN flag, not the command of NATO. No NATO ally sent troops to support the U.S. in the Vietnam War. Many Europeans strongly objected when President Reagan deployed short-range nuclear missiles in Western Europe to counter similar Soviet missiles aimed at Europe in the early 1980s. There were mass demonstrations in Britain, the Netherlands, and Germany against the missile deployment. The protestors feared that the missiles would make their countries more of a target by allowing the U.S. to wage nuclear war without using weapons based in the U.S. The change in focus is new for the alliance in the post-Cold War period. That change has created political tension within the alliance because not all members agree about what out-of-area issues the alliance should address. Some NATO allies of the U.S. sent troops to Iraq to support the military occupation after the war, but others actively opposed the war and did not.

How to handle Russia is the other main issue confronting NATO's expansion eastward. Many Russians view NATO as a threat pointed directly at them. They remember NATO as the enemy alliance during the Cold War and see it now gobbling up their former Warsaw Pact allies in Eastern Europe. NATO has tried to reassure Russia that its intentions are solely defensive. Reassurance, however, is a difficult business. NATO also wants to guarantee the security of its new members who fear a resurgence of Russian power. How can NATO both guarantee small countries like the Baltic states of Estonia, Latvia, and Lithuania and reassure Russia that NATO military power based in those countries is not aimed at it? Verbal statements of peaceful intent rarely reassure because they are not costly for the speaker. NATO has included Russia in the Partnership for Peace to build ties between the Russian and NATO militaries. It is clear, however, that Russia will not be invited to join NATO. The offer of the Partnership for Peace does not provide Russia with an incentive to do as the NATO allies would like. NATO had leverage to get Eastern European countries to change their policies before joining the alliance. Without the prospect of eventual admission, why would Russia do as NATO wants?

NATO has expanded eastward and broadened its mission to advance the common interests of the democracies in Europe and North America. It has continued even after the Soviet threat disappeared because the allies still saw they had common security interests. The alliance with its strong institutions continued to be a valuable way for the allies to advance those interests, both within Europe and out of the area.

Chapter Summary

States build arms and form alliances to prepare war, forestall the threat of it, and advance their interests. Security policies seek to deter threats, defend against them, or enable a state to advance demands to change the status quo. The choice between arms and allies depends on the speed and reliability of each and the domestic political costs of each. Because security is costly, national leaders must ask "How much is enough?" when forming security policy. The security dilemma can make rival states worse off when they match one another's security policies, such as in an arms race. Alliances face problems of credibility, which states can address through the specific promises they make, commitment devices, and institutional restraints on their freedom of action. States during peacetime do not spend as much on defense as they do during wartime because of the costs of committing more resources to the military at the expense of the civilian economy.

Review Questions

1. What two ways can states use to increase their security? What factors drive the choice between those two tools of security policy?

2. What tools of security policy are available to states, and what factors drive the choice between them?

3. What two risks do states face when allied to another state? Illustrate your argument using the U.S. and Taiwan.

4. Alliance commitments are promises to come to another state's aid if it is attacked. Give two specific actions a state can take to make its alliance commitments credible before a potential attacker threatens its ally.

5. What percentage of GNP do states commonly commit to their militaries during peacetime; what is the upper limit of how much they can commit during total war? What do these two numbers tell us about states' choices of how much arming to do during peacetime?

Chapter 14:
Structural Theories of War:
Balance of Power and Power Transition

In 1978, Deng Xiaoping began to open the Chinese economy to the world. The Communist government had established state-owned enterprises which dominated the industrial portion of the Chinese economy at that time. Agricultural production was collective at the village level. The government controlled prices and production of all goods and services. Deng's reforms allowed peasants to sell additional produce on the market for whatever price they could get. Special economic zones were created where business could be established to produce for export to other countries. As is the case commonly for developing countries, these new firms produced cheap manufactured goods using unskilled labor, which China has in abundance.

The combination of these two triggered the amazing growth of the Chinese economy over the last thirty years. Peasants began to accumulate wealth from the sale of their produce on the market. Manufacturing firms began producing simple goods and then moved to more sophisticated production as their workers and managers gain experience and foreign markets. China's economic growth has averaged 8% a year over the last thirty years, meaning the economy has grown over eightfold in that period. China has also become central to international trade with a 6% share of total world trade. Its economy is now linked into the world economy, both exporting goods of high and low sophistication and importing raw materials and high-end manufactures. The living standards of most Chinese have risen dramatically over these three decades, particularly in the coastal cities which are heavily involved in trade. It is one of the amazing stories of world politics over the last thirty years.

[Graph showing growth of Chinese economy over this time]

Chinese power has grown with its economy. Its government has accumulated vast currency reserves and invests heavily in U.S. Treasury Bills which fund the U.S. government. The goods it exports fill the shelves of shops in the developed world, particularly here in the United States. Greater wealth means the Chinese military can buy and build more sophisticated weapons. China has begun to build a navy which can show its flag around the world. China has always had a very large army, drawing on its massive population. It now has a more technologically sophisticated military, although it is not as capable as the U.S. military.

What are the consequences of the growth of China for world politics? Some fear that China will use its new-found power to change East Asia and the world in ways that others may not like. In 1996, China conducted ballistic missile tests into the waters around Taiwan during a presidential election there. Acts like this lead the critics of China's growth to argue that China will one day challenge the territorial status quo in East Asia or perhaps even the current international system. At other times, China has been responsible in its use of power, participating in joint naval actions against Somali pirates in the Gulf of Aden. Others see China becoming a responsible and important member of the international system. Some go so far to call the interrelationship of China and the U.S. as "Chimerica". How will China use its new-found power, and how will the rest of the world respond to it?

Structural Theories

The growth of China is a dramatic change in the structure of world politics. Structural theories of world politics seek to explain how the characteristics of the system explain what states do and when wars happen. Proponents of such theories argue that how the system is set up limits what state leaders can do because they must operate within that system. They often use the "burning house" analogy; everyone does the same thing when they are in a house on fire, they try to escape. The situation overrides any individual differences and compels everyone to act the same way. These theorists contend that the demands of the international system are so great that state leaders who act contrary to those demands suffer and may be removed or their states eliminated. They focus on the structure of the system because they believe that individual variation in states are irrelevant in the face of the incentives of the system. For instance, they believe that whether a country is a democracy or not does not change its foreign policy.

This chapter presents and analyzes two structural theories of world politics. Balance of power theory emphasizes the distribution of power among the major powers. Concentration of power in the hands of one state threatens others. They may work together to counter that threat, "balancing" against the threat. Because threats may change over time, states must be vigilant and willing to band together with any other state. Today's enemy may be tomorrow's ally. China's rise to power leads to the question of whether other Asian states will band together with the United States to contain that threat, from the perspective of balance of power theory. The distribution of power explains the occurrence of war and the stability of the international system.

Power transition theory, in contrast, examines how long-term shifts in power lead to major wars and changes in the international system. Industrialization increases the power of a state in many ways. States have industrialized at different times, leading to the rise and fall of the major powers over the 250 years since the Industrial Revolution began in Great Britain. The rise of a newly industrial state raises the possibility that it will seek to change the international system in its favor. The state which established the international order, having industrialized earlier than this challenger, may feel threatened by the challenger's rise. In some cases, war will break out between the two, and because that war will resolve the rules of the international system, it will drag in other states as well. China's rise, from the view of power transition theory, poses the question of whether China will seek to overturn the system created by the United States after World War II and whether that challenge can be resolved only by war.

Both of these structural theories emphasize the distribution of power as the prime element of the structure of the international system. Both also assume that the requirements of countering power are so important that they override particular interests and characteristics of states. Both treat all states as driven by the same fundamental systemic process. But they disagree sharply with the character of competition over international power and its consequences for the system. In this sense, they make a nice comparison.

Balance of Power Theory

Assumptions

Balance of power theory begins with the assumption that the international system is an anarchy. As mentioned earlier, the assumption of anarchy does not mean that there is no regularity to competition in the international system, only that there is no overarching authority in the international system which states can appeal to for protection. Balance of power theorists contrast this international anarchy with domestic hierarchy where the government does have authority over its citizens. The international system is a "self-help" system; a state can only rely on its own resources and whatever help other states are willing to provide. If others provide aid, they are purely self-interested, not motivated by a desire to maintain the system or the state under threat. States are sovereign, with no other actor having the ability to tell a state what to do. States then are the central actors of world politics in balance of power theory. There is no superior authority over them, and they do not have to answer to any other actor, including non-state actors, for what they do.

The primary threats to any state are other states then. States seek to maximize their security–that is, their continued existence–in balance of power theory. Once a state is eliminated, it is gone forever, so states are very protective of their existence. States would also like more power, in part to ensure their security in the future, but will seek more power only when that pursuit does not threaten their existence. Security is a dynamic judgment in balance of power theory. States consider their position in the future as well as today in the efforts to remain secure. More power today is not worthwhile if you are conquered tomorrow.

States in balance of power theory do not care about other preferences because the demands of security in the international system are pressing. They do not care about the ideology of other states; Churchill stated this position during World War II, "If Hitler invaded hell, I would make at least a favorable reference to the devil in the House of Commons." Similarly, different types of states all act the same in balance of power theory. The pressure of international competition overrule different preferences and perceptions. Those who do not adjust to the imperatives of the system are eliminated by it.

What is a "Balance of Power"?

To get ahead of the argument, balances of power are what will maintain the peace and secure the continued existence of states. It is easy to think of a balance of power when there are only two states. They must be roughly equal in power. If one is much stronger, it can expect to conquer the other in a war, which would eliminate any threat to itself now and in the future. What is a balance among three or more states? Balance of power theorists begin by counting the number of major powers in the system. *Major powers* are countries that are sufficiently powerful that they play an important role in the system. They are much more powerful that other states termed minor powers; we will be more precise later. The major powers wrote the history of European politics from the 17th through the 19th centuries. They fought one another in wars large and small and, at the end of some of those wars, met together to organize the international system. A system with two major power is *bipolar*, meaning that there are two poles or centers of power in the system. Think of poles of magnets rather than psychological conditions. The minor power line up around these two poles. The Cold War is the prime example of a bipolar system, with the two superpowers each arranging a coalition of allies and clients around themselves. Each was much stronger than even the other nuclear powers in the system. Systems with more than two major powers are *multipolar*. The key distinction is between two and more than two. Some will talk about a *unipolar* system, particularly describing the dominance of the United States after the end of the Cold War. Systems with three major powers are called, surprise, surprise, *tripolar*. Some described the late Cold War system as tripolar, arguing that China had become important enough and independent enough of the Soviet Union that it could play the Soviet Union and the United States off one another.

To think about balance in a multipolar systems, begin with a tripolar system. At first blush, one might think of three equal states as being the only balanced system. But two of the states can gang up on the third, making them likely to win the resulting war. How could the third state ensure its security in this "balanced" system? If it could convince the second state that the first would threaten its existence after they eliminated the third, the second state might join with the third to save itself from the first. This is an example of how security concerns are dynamic in balance of power theory. Each state has to think not only of its security today but also of the consequences of today's decisions on its security tomorrow. States in a tripolar world create a balance by always joining together to counter any one of them that threatens to become dominant. As long as each is less powerful than the other two together, any pair of states, including the weaker two, have the ability to match the power of the third if they work together. Further, they have the incentive to work together against the third when it approaches dominance if only to save their own skin.

With more than three major powers, the idea of a balance is the same. The countries do not need to be equal in strength, but none can be more powerful than the others put together. If one state approaches that strength, the others should join together to prevent it from achieving that level. If it does, it can eliminate all of them. Each state's concern for its own security binds them together to defend one another.

The "balance" in balance of power theory is not the distribution of power. It is the tendency of states to join together against threats to dominate the system. Balance of power theorists speak of *balancing behavior* as necessary for the system to maintain itself. The distribution of power matters only to the extent that no member state is powerful enough to defeat all the others if they balance against it.

States do not have to form alliances to balance against a threat. During the Cold War, the U.S. and the Soviet Union were both nuclear superpowers. No other state was strong enough to shift the balance between them, no matter which side it joined. The superpowers balanced one another through their arms race, where they competed over the number and quality of their nuclear and conventional forces. Each had to rely on the resources they could generate from their societies to prevent the other from achieving dominance. Balance of power theorist call this competition *internal balancing* because each state depends on capabilities internal to itself to balance the threat it faces. When states join together in a multipolar system against a common threat, they call this *external balancing* because each relies on the capabilities of others.

Balancing of either form does not require that wars be fought to maintain the balance. If all states balance carefully, threats to the system can be deterred. Any state threatening the system knows it cannot win the resulting war if others balance against it successfully, so it will not start a war that can only end in defeat. Balancing leads to deterrence when it is most successful, such as during the Cold War when balance of power theorists belief that the nuclear arms race helped keep the peace between the superpowers.

Conclusions

Balance of power has four main conclusions:

1. Balances of power form in response to threats to the system. Each state's concern for its own security leads them to join together against any one who threatens the entire system. In a multipolar system, balancing leads to large coalitions against a state approaching dominance. In a bipolar system, the two powers balance one another internally through an arms race. Internal balancing through arms races can also occur in a multipolar world if the powers have formed two opposing alliances.

2. Balances of power protect the existence of key states. Balancing does not guarantee peace as sometimes states must fight one of them that threatens the system. Balances do produce *stability*, the continued existence of states. After all, security is the overriding goal of states in balance of power theory. A state is *essential* in balance of power theory if it can turn the balance, that is, turn a losing coalition of states into a winning one. If this is true, other states will fight to save it because they might need it later to counter some other threat. If this is not the case, their own security does not depend on its continued independence, and they may choose to let it be conquered.

3. <u>Bipolarity is more stable than multipolarity</u>. External balancing is less reliable than internal balancing, according to balance of power theorists. States may have to fight costly wars to defeat a near-dominant state. Each would prefer that others fight those wars. If the others defeat the threat while it remains at peace, its security is ensured at no cost. For this reason, balance of powers theorists worry about the maintenance of the balance in a multipolar world. In contrast, the two superpowers of a bipolar world can only rely on themselves to balance one another. Their concern for their own security leads to a more stable balance because arming is a more reliable way to gain security than alliances are.

4. <u>Essential states should never be eliminated</u>. Because other states may have to rely on an essential state, they will fight to preserve its existence. The only states that should be eliminated are those which are not essential to the balance.

Historical Examples

The history of modern Europe, that is since 1500, is punctuated by large wars fought to prevent the dominance of a single state. In the first half of the 16th century, Charles V became the joint ruler of all the Hapsburg domains around Europe, including Spain, Austria, the Netherlands and Belgium, Southern Italy, and other scattered territories as well. His empire was also funded by the great wealth Spain was extracting from the Americas at this time. Others, including France, the Ottoman Empire (what eventually became Turkey), and the Protestant states of Germany, feared the possibility of Hapsburg dominance. All fought him at the same time. Although his empire was mighty, it could not fight everywhere in Europe at once. Charles' bid for dominance in Europe failed, and he eventually retired to a monastery outside Madrid to live out his last years.

[Map of Charles V's empire in Europe]

Louis XIV of France posed the next threat to gain dominance in Europe in the end of the 17th century. France had the largest population and the most wealth in Europe after the Thirty Years War. Once Louis established his control over France about 1650, he began to expand eastward in a long series of wars. This growth in French power concerned other states such as Austria, the Netherlands, and England. Louis' bid for dominance peaked in the War of Spanish Successions from 1701-1714. The King of Spain died with no clear heir and left Spain and its colonies to Louis' heir, his grandson. This meant that France and Spain would be joined under one king when Louis died. The other major powers of Europe, particularly the three mentioned above, joined together against France in the greatest war Europe had seen to that time. The French were defeated, and Louis' grandson chose to be King of Spain and not that of France.

[Map of Europe before the War of Spanish Succession]

France under Napoleon was the next threat to gain dominance in Europe, and he came closer than the earlier attempts. The French Revolution sparked the French revolutionary wars where a coalition of European monarchs attempted to reverse the French revolution. But France was winning those wars, and Napoleon was the greatest French general. He seized power in what we now call a coup d'etat (blow to the state) in 1799. He then fought a series of wars against all the major powers in Europe–Great Britain, Austria, Russia, and Prussia–sometimes together and other times separately. He defeated all the continental powers by 1807 and remade the map of Europe, placing family members as kings and queens of new states he created in Italy and Germany. In 1812, Napoleon invaded Russia in an effort to get the Tsar to work with him against Britain, the one country Napoleon could not invade because the British Navy rules the seas. He lost almost all of his army of 600,000. The other major powers of Europe rose up against Napoleon and fought together against him. By April of 1814, the combined powers had taken Paris and deposed Napoleon and sent him to exile. He returned briefly in 1815 only to lose to the British and Prussians at Waterloo. The British then exiled him to St. Helena, an island in the South Atlantic that he could not escape from, and he died there six years later.

[Map of Europe at height of Napoleon's power in 1812]

Adolf Hitler posed the last great attempt to dominate Europe militarily. World War II broke out in 1939 after Hitler's Germany invaded Poland, triggering intervention by Britain and France. In the next few years, Germany defeated and conquered Poland, Denmark, Norway, France, Belgium, the Netherlands, Greece, and Yugoslavia and induced Romania, Hungary, and Bulgaria to join with it and Italy. In 1941, Hitler invaded the Soviet Union and almost took the capital of Moscow before winter. The United Nations, the alliance led by the United States, the Soviet Union, and Great Britain, but also joined by tens of other countries around the world, fought back against Hitler and crushed Germany in 1945.

[Map of Hitler's control in Europe in 1945]

As mentioned earlier, balance of power theorists see the Cold War as a period of internal balancing and competition between the two superpowers. Although they contended for advantages, seeking new allies and clients around the world, the nuclear arms races maintained the balance, preventing either from dominating the other.

Balance of power theorists believe that balancing has preserved the existence of most states throughout the history of modern Europe. Although the small states of Germany and Italy were consolidated into those two countries and borders have changed over the preceding centuries, the major powers of European history have continued in one form or another. Even small states like Belgium have continued, in part because the major powers were willing to fight to prevent them falling into the hands of others. Britain fought France to keep Belgium separate in the 18th and 19th centuries and then Germany in the world wars in the 20th. Other minor powers have not been so fortunate. Poland was divided among Russia, Prussia, and Austria in the last 18th century and did not reappear as an independent state until after World War I. It would be an example of how a state which is not essential may be eliminated.

Changes in Power Over the Last Two Centuries

Balance of power theory examines how states respond to the distribution of power; it treats that distribution as fixed by the amount of territory that a state controls. States can arm to raise their capabilities to match what other states are doing, and they could raise their capabilities by conquering additional territory. Power transition theory, in contrast, begins with the observation that industrialization has produced large shifts in power over time, independent of arming, alliances, and the conquest of territory. Different countries industrialized at different times, leading to rises and fall in relative power. How has industrialization shifted power between the major powers?

Industrialization produces three large changes in a country's power. First, the society becomes more productive as machine power replaces muscle power in the manufacture of goods. Workers become more productive when they use machines. Additionally, new types of goods can be produced as manufacturing processes improve. Mass production is now possible, leading to huge increases in the wealth of the nation and its members. As the size of a country's economy is a key element of national capabilities, the economic power of a country increases through industrialization.

Second, industrialization leads to a growth of the country's population and also their range of skills. Before industrialization, most people live on farms and grow the food they eat. The death rate, particularly of children, is high. Farmers have many children to ensure that some of them survive to adulthood to provide for them in old age. As industrialization proceeds, people move to the new industries in cities where they can improve their standard of living. Although growing cities produce their own problems, health generally improves along with growing wealth and knowledge. The death rate falls while the birth rate remains high. This change leads to a large increase in population. At the same time, the skills of the population rise as they learn new skills for their jobs in industry and as education spreads to more people. Literacy rises because literate employees can learn new skills more easily through reading. Eventually, the birth rate begins to fall as people become wealthier and understand that most children will survive to adulthood. Industrialization leads to a growth in the size and capability of the population of a country.

Third, the political institutions of the state expand their capability and roles in respond to the increasing complexity of production in an industrial economy. Government expands its role to cover some form of social security for industrial workers and its ability to raise taxes from society. Mass conscription becomes easier as people move to cities and become literate. Mass literacy also raises the ability of the government to communicate with the people. Government acquires a larger role in the economy as production centralizes in large industrial firms. The complexity of production also expands government's role in regulating the economy through agencies and law. All of these changes aid the government of a state undergoing industrialization in raising a larger share of the resources of their growing economy and population.

Industrialization then raises the power of a country by increasing the size, productivity, and diversity of its economy, the size and quality of its population, and the government's ability to mobilize those resources. Because states underwent, and some are still undergoing, industrialization at different times, the process led to changes in power as one country after another increased its capabilities. Because power is relative, it matters how countries compare to one another, the rise of the later industrializing nations reduced the relative power of those who industrialized earlier. The figure below tracks the rises and falls of the great powers over the last two hundred years. The data the figure uses changes from year explaining some of the peaks.

Figure 19
The Major Powers since 1815

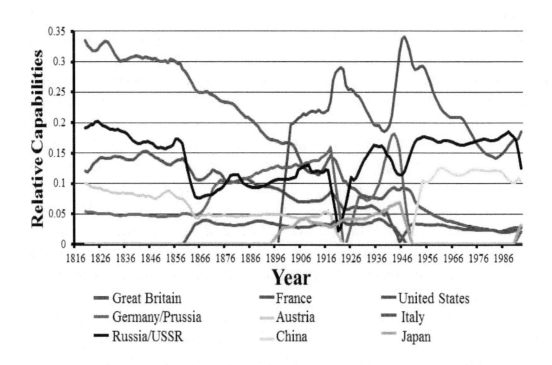

Source: National Material Capabilities Data, Correlates of War Project,
http://www.correlatesofwar.org/

Great Britain emerged from the Napoleonic Wars in 1815 as the only industrial power, albeit one in the early stages of industrialization. It used its economic and financial advantages to provide subsidies to the countries that fought Napoleon on land. The British Navy dominated the oceans, although its army was small by European standards. Britain also controlled an extensive colonial empire from Canada and the Caribbean to India. Russia had the largest population and army, making it the second strongest country in the world. France fell to third place followed by Austria. Both countries had large populations and armies. After the fall of Napoleon and the Bourbon Restoration, the French army abandoned conscription in favor of a smaller, professional army similar to other European armies. Prussia was the least great power in Europe, but still powerful within Germany.

Great Britain maintained its predominant position in Europe and the world throughout much of the 19th century. Britain dominated the industries of the early Industrial Revolution, textiles and railroads. British manufactured goods were traded widely around the world in exchange for raw materials like cotton which British factories made into finished cloth. Britain used its dominant position to push for the removal of trade barriers to its manufactured goods. Italy and Germany unified between 1860 and 1870, altering power through the introduction of Italy as a major power and the increase in Prussia's power when it controlled Germany. The long-run change came from new technologies, such as steel and chemicals, and the spread of the industrial revolution to other countries, particularly Germany and the United States. These emerging industrial powers dominated the new industries, allowing them to surpass Britain around the beginning of the 20th century. Both countries had larger populations than Britain, meaning that they would be more powerful once their economies caught up to the British economy. France industrialized slowly, and, unusually, its population did not grow greatly as it industrialized. The emergence of the U.S. and Japan as great powers at the end of the 19th century was the final change. Although the U.S. was clearly capable of generating power from its large population and growing industries after the Civil War (the spike in the figure for the U.S. around 1920 reflects U.S. power when it mobilized a large army during World War I), it only emerged on the world stage in the aftermath of the Spanish-American War in 1898. Similarly, great power status for Japan is dated to its victory over China in the Sino-Japanese War in 1895. Japan had closed itself off from foreign trade and influences until Commodore Matthew Perry forced Japan to open up in 1853. Its leaders moved to modernize the country quickly after the shock of Perry's forcible opening of the country.

The 20th century opened with Great Britain yielding its leading position among the great powers as Germany, the United States, and Russia all passed it or were catching up as they industrialized. The German challenge to British dominance ended in the two World Wars.

Germany was divided, the other defeated Axis powers of Italy and Japan fell from the ranks of the great powers, and Britain and France became important allies of the United States. The two superpowers, the U.S. and the Soviet Union, emerged as rival for global domination after World War II. The U.S. slowly came to take on a position of global power, retreating to isolationism after World War I, and only fully exercising its power during and after World War II. The U.S. dominated the new industrial technologies of the 20th century, automobiles and airplanes. At the end of World War II, the United States stood astride the world as a colossus, commanding close to one-half of world production as the other industrial economies lie in ruins from the war. The U.S. instigated the creation of a range of international organizations and institutions for politics and economic affairs, including the UN, the World Bank, the IMF, and the GATT. The Soviet Union began to industrialize under the Tsars, but the Soviet government accelerated industrialization in part out of fear that they needed to be powerful to defend their revolution. Stalin's crash industrialization caused immense suffering in the Soviet people, but it produced the steel plants and machinery that built the planes, tanks, and guns that defeated Nazi Germany. Both countries had much larger populations than any European country, giving a larger base on which to build their power. The two became rivals in the Cold War, each a pole of power surrounded by states that shared their political and economic systems.

The Cold War covered much of the second half of the 20th century. Slowly, U.S. economic superiority began to tell against the Soviet Union. The U.S. led the next wave of industrial technologies in electronics and computers. The Soviet economy, in contrast, slowed beginning in the 1960s. China emerged as a great power after the Communists won the Chinese Civil War in 1949. It had the largest population in the world but had no industries to speak of. Its army fought the U.S.-led UN forces to a draw in the Korean War, preventing the unification of Korea under the South Korean government. Mao Zedong tried to industrialize China quickly, but his efforts caused great hardship and did not succeed generally, most notably in the "Great Leap Forward". China split with the Soviet Union in the 1960s, fighting two brief border wars in the late 1960s. The split allowed China to act independently, and it shifted toward the United States and against the Soviet Union in 1972. This split is why some refer to this period as tripolar. China's rise to power began after Mao's death when his successor Deng Xiaoping slowly opened up the Chinese economy, triggering its rapid growth. The end of the Cold War in 1991 saw the dissolution of the Soviet Union, greatly reducing Russian power, and the re-emergence of Japan and reunified Germany as great powers. Still, the United States stood above and ahead of all other countries, leading to the period some call unipolar.

Power Transition Theory

Power Transition theory examines how these long-run shifts in power have influenced the character of the world system and the occurrence of major wars over it.

Assumptions

Power transition theory assumes that the dominant state orders the international system. Hierarchy, rather than anarchy, is the central concept of international politics according to power transition theorist. This does not mean that the dominant state can control everything, only that it establishes the "rules of the game" in order to advance its own interests. The dominant state is the most powerful state in the system, generally because it has industrialized and won the most recent major war. The dominant state leads the international system.

Other states fall into two groups based on whether they accept the international order of the dominant state. The *satisfied coalition* consists of all the states that accept that order. Those states which reject it are the *dissatisfied*. Unlike the satisfied coalition which are unified in their acceptance of the international order, the dissatisfied do not form a single group. They are divided by their own visions of how the world should be run. For example, the United States was the dominant state during the Cold War. The countries that aligned with the U.S.–most of Western Europe, Japan, South Korea, South Vietnam, Thailand, Taiwan and the Phillipines in East Asia, Israel in the Mideast, most of Latin America–constituted the satisfied coalition. The dissatisfied were the Soviet Union, its allies and client, Communist China, and many non-aligned states. They disagreed not only with the capitalist system of the U.S. but also with one another's vision for the international system. The figure below shows the satisfied coalition and the dissatisfied arranged in a pyramid with the dominant state on top and other states ranked by their power. Although the satisfied coalition may be fewer states than the dissatisfied, their unity and the leadership of the dominant state maintains its system. Satisfaction and dissatisfaction are state preferences about how the international system should be organized.

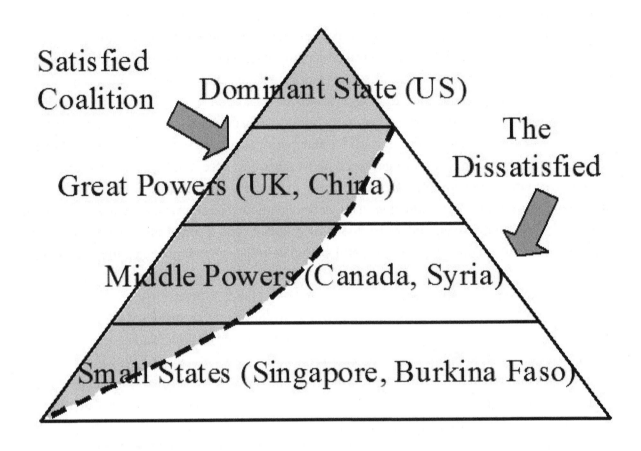

Figure 20
The Hierarchy of Power in Power Transition

Industrialization drives long-term shifts in power according to the power transition theory. It gives lesser states the chance of overturning the system of the dominant state. Because industrialization drives these shifts, foreign policy cannot alter them. Economic growth through industrialization, while it can be aided by other countries when they favor it, cannot be stopped when they oppose. No country could stop Stalin from industrializing the Soviet Union in the 1920s and 30s. Similarly, the dominant state cannot stop its relative decline as other states undergo industrialization. Often, the states which industrialize later, dominate the new technologies which drive further growth. The dominant state does not become poorer, rather states entering industrialization grow more rapidly, allowing them to overtake the dominant state. Even though the satisfied coalition supports the dominant state, alliances are irrelevant to whether other states catch and surpass the dominant state through industrialization. Unlike balance of power theory where alliances form against growing concentrations of power, power transition theory centers on how industrialization drives challenges to the order of the system.

Commitment Problems at the Transition Point

Differences in industrialization can lead a state to catch up to the dominant state in power and then exceed it. This state is the *challenger*. The *transition point* comes when the challenger surpasses the dominant state in power, making it the most powerful country in the system. This is the moment power transition theory focuses on. It is the first time that the challenger has the ability to overturn the system of the dominant state. The figure below shows the changing power between the dominant state and the challenger along with the transition point. Again, the decline of the dominant state is only relative; the challenger catches up because its economy is growing

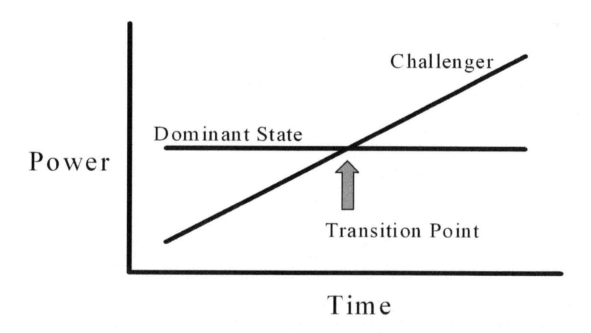

Figure 21
The Transition Point during a Power Transition

faster than that of the dominant state.

Power transitions pose a pair of related commitment problem. The rising power of the challenger will lead to changes in the international system in its favor. Will the demand for such changes lead to war, or can the parties resolve their differences peacefully? The change in power occurs over decades, so the series of small concessions by the dominant state to the challenger

-231-

might be acceptable to both sides. For the dominant state, the alternative to such concessions is a preventive war to crush the challenger before it catches up in power. A deal over time requires the challenger to promise to limit its demands in the future, to commit itself not to use its growing power in the future. The inability of the challenger to make a binding commitment not to use its power in the future when it is stronger is the source of the first commitment problem. A possible deal would have the challenger accept the system of the dominant state when it is weak with the dominant state making concessions to the challenger after the transition point. If the loss from the concessions in the future are greater than the costs of war early, the dominant state is better off launching a preventive war early in the transition.

Power transition theorists focus on the second commitment problem, the inability of the dominant state to commit itself to defend its system as it grows weaker. The challenger could undermine the system of the dominant state by asking for a series of small concessions over time. No single demand would be worth fighting over, but their full effect would transform the system. The dominant state could threaten to fight over any concession, but that promise is not credible.

Conclusions

Power transition theory has three main conclusions:

1. <u>The challenger attacks the dominant state before the transition point</u>. The challenger's rise in power is a heady event for its leaders. If they overrate their rise, they may deem the concessions offered by the dominant state to be insufficient. Eager to overturn a system they judge to be unacceptable, they go to war when they think they have sufficient power to win. Because they overrate their power, the challenger attacks before the transition point.

2. <u>Alliances are irrelevant to the resolution of the challenge</u>. Industrialization is the key source of the economic, demographic, and political capabilities that determine which side wins a power transition war. Even though the satisfied coalition supports the dominant state, a power transition war is a struggle matching the dominant state and the challenger. The challenger might be able to win even if its allies are weak.

3. <u>A peaceful challenge is possible if the challenger comes from the satisfied coalition</u>. A challenger from the satisfied coalition accepts many of the features of the system of the dominant state. The range of concessions it demands are less than those demanded from a dissatisfied state. It should be easier for the dominant state to grant the demands of a member of the satisfied coalition.

Two Views of the World Wars

The two world wars in the first half of the 20th century look different from the perspective of these two systemic theories. Both address the threat posed by the rise of Germany. From the view of balance of power theory, other nations joined together against that threat, although it was difficult to form each anti-German coalition. Before World War I, Great Britain abandoned its historical position of isolation during peacetime out of fear of the rise of German power. It aligned with France and Russia and committed to send its small, professional army to fight alongside the French if Germany attacked. It then built a mass army during the war, which carried the brunt of the fight beginning in 1916. The entry of the United States shifted the weight of the armies fighting against Germany, but it took a coalition of France, Britain, the U.S., and Italy to defeat Germany. The rebirth of German military power under Hitler posed a second threat to establish German hegemony in Europe. Although all faced the same threat from the Nazis, it was difficult to pull together a coalition to stop Hitler. Each country wanted others to bear the costs of fighting Hitler. Stalin's deal with Hitler in the Nazi-Soviet Pact of 1939 was the most dramatic example of trying to avoid the costs of fighting Hitler, as it turned Hitler's ambitions westward against France and Britain. But others were also reluctant to balance against Hitler; the U.S. stayed out of the war until Hitler declared war on it in the days after Pearl Harbor. That declaration and Hitler's invasion of the Soviet Union in June 1941 led to the formation of the United Nations, the coalition that defeated the Axis powers. It grew to encompass almost all countries of the world not allied to Germany and established the organization of the same name at the end of the war in 1945.

These events look very different through the lens of power transition theory. German industrialization drove its rise to power and threat to the system Great Britain had established in the 19th century. Germany demanded a "place in the sun," colonial and trade concessions that would recognize its new status as a world power. These demands led to the rivalry between Britain and Germany and two world wars to resolve it. Britain bore the weight of the fight against Germany in World War I, but the outcome of that war did not end the threat of German hegemony. Because its power was based on its industrial might, German power revived after the war and rocketed upward when Hitler remilitarized the country. The renewed threat led to World War II. The massive industrial power of the United States decided that war, and the U.S. emerged as the new dominant state at the end of the war. It created international institutions including the UN, the World Bank, GATT, and the IMF to run the system it created. Because it had been a member of the satisfied coalition under the British system, the transition from British to American dominance was resolved without a war between the two. But that transition was not costless for Great Britain. The U.S. forced the end of the colonial empires of its British and French allies. The American century had arrived.

Doubts about These Systemic Theories

Systemic theories focus on the properties of the system as a whole and contend that the incentives produced by those properties override different national preferences and perceptions.

Doubts about these systemic theories center on these national variations. Balancing–states joining together against a common threat–is central to balance of power theory. What distributions of power can support balancing? Under bipolarity, the two powers must be roughly equal; under tripolarity, none of them can have more than half of all capabilities; under multipolarity, many distributions can support balancing, provided that no state is dominant. How can we explain failures to balance then? No state has been dominant in Europe in the last 500 years. Balance of power theorists claim that this fact explains why no state has been able to dominate Europe during this period; balances have always formed, in their view, against any state that came close to doing so. The closest any state has come to dominance is the United States at the end of World War II when it possessed close to half of world industrial production. Yet no balance formed against the U.S. The Soviet Union broke with it in the Cold War, but the other major powers aligned with the U.S. until the Communists won the Chinese Civil War in 1949.

If balances of power stop challenges to achieve dominance and prevent wars, then a near-dominant state must be deterred by a coalition slightly stronger than it. Deterrence requires that the near-dominant state is risk-averse; it must be unwilling to fight when it has only a 50-50 chance of winning. But some states, like Hitler's Germany and Imperial Japan, have accepted such risks of defeat in an attempt to impose an international system to their own liking. Balancing then assumes that states are not willing to run risks, but states with preferences that lead them to take great risks have occurred historically and cannot be excluded.

Balancing also requires that the balancing states share the same perception of the threat they face. If they disagree about the nature or size of the threat, they might not work together to stop it. Such disagreements about the nature of the threat posed by Hitler complicated efforts to form a coalition to stop him. Many in Britain and France thought Stalin's Soviet Union was as large a threat as Hitler's Germany. Joining with Stalin might end one threat while strengthening another. Understandably, these British and French elites opposed an alliance with the Soviet Union against Hitler. In the U.S., many did not see how a threat in Europe was their problem. Isolationism, the belief that the U.S. should stay out of the problems of Europe, was strong in the country. President Franklin Roosevelt had to judge what steps he could take against Hitler in the face of the isolationist opposition. It took the Japanese attack on Pearl Harbor to convince the U.S. public to join the coalition against the Axis.

The historical evidence does not match the conclusions of balance of power theory. Bipolarity did not appear to be more stable or peaceful than multipolarity. The bipolar era of the Cold War was peaceful for 46 years from its start in 1945 to its end with the demise of the Soviet Union in 1991. The earlier multipolar world had comparable long periods of peace. There was no major war in Europe for the 38 years from the end of the Napoleonic Wars in 1815 and the outbreak of the Crimean War in 1853. There was no major war in Europe from the end of the Franco-Prussian War in 1871 until the outbreak of World War in 1914, another 43 year period of peace. Given these periods of peace under multipolarity, it is not clear that the 46 years of peace under bipolarity are more stable. The Cold War did not see a war between the superpowers, but it did see many destructive wars in the developing world. The Korean and Vietnam Wars killed hundreds of thousands if not millions as did the Iraq-Iran War from 1980 to 1988. Repeated wars were fought in the Middle East and between India and Pakistan. Bipolarity contributed to these wars as the superpowers competed for client states in the developing world.

Balancing is also supposed to ensure the existence of essential states, those which can shift the balance between some grouping of states. Poland, for example, was not an essential state in the late 18th century when it was divided among Austria, Prussia, and Russia. The breakup of Austria-Hungary and its loss of great power status after World War I contradicts this prediction of balance of power theory. It should have been able to balance off different coalitions to preserve itself, but it clung to Germany as an ally before and during World War I. Its preference for Germany as an ally led it not to balance.

The historical record also differs from the conclusions of power transition theory. It contends that alliances are irrelevant to the outcome of power transition wars. But Britain did not defeat Germany alone in the two World Wars; the aid of its allies, particularly the United States, was critical for its victories. Similarly, Germany was stronger than Britain when those wars broke out. In Figure 19 showing the relative power of the major powers, Germany passes Britain around 1900. It falls behind it after it was demilitarized by the Versailles Treaty. Once Hitler remilitarizes Germany, it again leaps ahead of Great Britain in power. The course of fighting, the ultimate test of military power, showed that Germany was stronger than Britain. In both World Wars, Germany fought Britain and its allies for years on its own with little appreciable support.

Power transition theory assumes a single challenger rises up against the dominant state, but that has not always been the case. Around 1880, three possible challengers to British dominance could be identified: Germany, Russia, and the United States. Each of the three had started to industrialize, although Russia was behind the other two. Each posed different threats to the British Empire. The U.S. bordered Canada and could build a navy that could challenge the British Navy for command of the seas. Russia was extending its control in Central Asia which threatened India, the "Jewel in the Crown" of the British Empire. Of the three, Germany seemed to pose the least threat, yet it was the power that Britain fought in the World Wars. The German threat grew as it began to build a large navy. Britain was able to resolve its differences with the U.S. and Russia to focus its attention on Germany. Those differences in preference could be bridged, while Britain perceived that those with Germany could not. That outcome was not obvious around 1880.

Finally, one of the commitment problems posed by power transitions leads to the conclusion that the dominant state should crush challengers militarily before they become strong. But preventative war does not happen. There were some in the U.S. who argue in the 1940s and

1950s that the Soviet Union should be attacked before it could develop a robust nuclear capability, but few in government took that position. Similarly, Britain allowed Germany to unify under Prussian leadership in the 1860s. In the latter case, British leaders did not see Germany as an eventual threat, leading them to stand on the sidelines during the Wars of German Unification.

Systemic theories argue that the incentives of the system are so great that they override what state leaders want and how they perceive the situation. These variations in preference and perception matter, however, in explaining when states balance and how they respond to long-term shifts in power. The flaw in systemic theories lies in their assumption that the incentives produced by the system are strong enough to override all other considerations. Consider the "burning house" analogy again. While it is true that everyone would act the same if they were in a burning house, how many people do you know who have been in a house on fire? States have balanced against powers like Hitler's Germany or Napoleon's France, but those systemic threats are the exception, not the rule, in world politics.

Even with these flaws, we study systemic theories because they contain grains of truth. States have balanced against a single power threatening to gain dominance. Long-term shifts in power caused by industrialization have shaped world politics over the last 250 years. Power transition theory is explicitly a theory of world politics since the industrial revolution. It is time-bound by definition. Balance of power theory may also be more appropriate for the world politics of the pre-industrial era. Before industrialization, taking territory was the only way to increase a state's power by adding the people who lived there and whatever they produced to the state's pool of potential power. Shifting coalitions were common and necessary because seeking allies was the main way to counter a threatening state. The industrial revolution changes that and, along with the political changes wrought by the French Revolution, altered world politics after from balance of power. The time-bound nature of both of these theories also shows that the character of world politics changes over time, adjusting to changes in power, preferences, and perceptions and giving rise to new principles.

The Rise of China

China's economy has been growing faster than the U.S. economy for several decades, closing some of the gap in production between the two countries. Although the average Chinese is still much poorer than the average American, the gap will continue to close if China grows more rapidly than the U.S. It is difficult to say when the Chinese economy will overtake the U.S. economy in total size. The figure below shows projections based on two ways to assess the size of an economy, using market exchange rates or purchasing power. The gap could close as soon as 2020 or much later depending on how fast both countries grow. Additionally, Chinese power is not closing on U.S. power as quickly as the economies are. Even when Chinese production equals that of the U.S., the U.S. economy will still be more sophisticated and the average American much wealthier. In any case, the gap is closing, and many experts expect that China will surpass the U.S. in power, economic, military, and political, some time in the coming decades.

[Graph projecting economies of US and China to 2030]

What will be the consequences of this long-term shift in power from the U.S. to China? Already, China is taking on a larger role in world politics. Regardless of when the transition point occurs, the rise of China will continue to change world politics. How will other countries respond? The two theories covered in this chapter give different answers.

According to balance of power theory, other countries will band together against China if it poses a threat to the system. The "system" could be just East Asia or the entire world. Some Chinese believe their country has a claim to other territories that were once under Chinese rule. If China presses demands for territorial change, this could induce its neighbors to join together against it. The countries around China might also turn to the United States for support in their efforts to deter China. Some argue that an arms race has already begun in East Asia as other states seek to balance greater Chinese power. Balance of power theorists would worry that some states might try to defuse the threat by siding with China. These defections could undermine the coalition needed to prevent Chinese dominance. Of course, China might not press demands that would alarm other states and so lead to a balancing coalition. The type and size of the military it builds would also affect these balancing judgments. The key is how China handles its rise to power and how other states respond to that rise.

Power transition theory sees a bleaker world. China is the challenger; the United States the dominant state. China's rise challenges the U.S.-led system and is already changing the "rules of the game" of that system. But will Chinese demands for change fundamentally threaten the U.S.-led system? It depends in part on whether China is a member of the satisfied coalition in that system. China has benefitted greatly from entry to the world economy as much of its economic growth has been driven by production for export. But does, or more importantly, will China continue to accept the rules of the system? The response may depend on the issue. On economic issues, it may be content to continue the system; on political issues, it may have a very different view of how the system should be organized. Human rights, for example, is a central principle of the post-World War II U.S.-led system, whereas China places greater weight on state sovereignty over the rights of individuals. In either case, the American Century will end according to power transition theory.

There are other theories that speak to the rise of China. Those who believe economic interdependence leads to peaceful relations see China's rise as less threatening as long as the global economic system remains open. Others who points to domestic systems as critical wonder whether China will democratize as it grows wealthy.

Think It Through
The Rise of China

Many think that Yogi Berra said, "It's tough to make predictions, especially about the future." Long-run predictions in world politics are difficult because we know little about what future conditions will be. What factors could play a significant role in how China's rise to power will play out in the future? Rather than focus on how China is growing and when it might overtake the United States, here we examine factors that are important to how the transition works out but are unclear at this time.

1.   What are the issues that China will attempt to change as its power grows? If it focuses on territorial change in East Asia, those demands are likely to alarm neighboring countries. That common alarm would make forming a balancing coalition easier. If China instead focuses on broader political and economic issues, it would be harder to form a balancing coalition because other states would not feel as threatened by China. These latter changes might be objectionable to other countries and undesirable in the eyes of many, such as watering down human rights at the international level.

2.   What sort of capabilities will China build? Will they be primarily local for defense of the Chinese mainland and control of the adjoining seas, or will they seek the global presence that the U.S. military now has? A Chinese military with global reach might not be a bad thing if it is used to support international order, such as policing piracy on the high seas and supporting humanitarian military intervention.

3.   What political role will China advance? The system advanced by the U.S. has values of open economies with free polities as central values, even if those values are not always observed in practice. Will China advocate for greater state sovereignty at the expense of the advocacy of free politics?

4.   What position will China adopt on economic issues? It has benefitted greatly from its ability to export the goods it produces on international markets. Will it continue to advocate for free trade, or will it shift to managed trade favoring its own economic benefit?

5.   Will the domestic system of China change from the dominance of the Communist Party to a more open system? China's position on the issues above might change if it adopted political competition in some form of democracy. Such a system would not necessarily be the same as a Western democracy.

6.   How will the United States respond to its relative decline?

Chapter Summary

Systemic theories contend that the imperatives of the international system and how it is organized determine what states do. Balance of power examines how states balance against threats to the system in the effort to preserve themselves. Balancing is the strategy of joining against such threats to the system, rather than the distribution of power necessary to support a balance of power. Balances of power are supposed to preserve the stability of the system–the continued existence of the major powers–rather than peace. Balance of power theorists argue that bipolarity–a system with two major powers–is more than multipolarity–one with more than two powers.

Power transition theory argues, in contrast, that the system is hierarchical because the dominant state–the strongest country in the system–organizes the system in its own interest. Some states accept this system as members of the satisfied coalition, while others reject it and are dissatisfied. Differences in when states industrialize drive long-term shifts in power. Such shifts give rise to the challenger, a state which will pass the dominant state in power. The challenge can lead to a cataclysmic war for dominance in the system or see dominance pass peacefully if the challenger is from the satisfied coalition.

Although both theories contain elements of truth, evidence contradicts both of them. Systemic incentives do not override variations in preferences and perceptions.

Review Questions

1.   Explain the "burning house" analogy underlying systemic theories.

2.   What is a balance of power according to balance of power theorists? What do they believe are the consequences of a balance of power?

3.   Do balance of power theorists think that bipolarity or multipolarity is more stable? Provide the reason they give.

4.   How does industrialization cause the power of a state to rise? What three elements of national power does industrialization change?

5.   Explain the power hierarchy in power transition theory (a.k.a. The Pyramid of Power).

6.   According to power transition theory, when should war break out during a transition? Which state should start that war?

7. Explain the two commitment problems created by long-term shifts in power, one for the declining state, the other for the rising state.

Chapter 15
The Fate of Leaders:
The Domestic Consequences of International Conflict

During the Gulf War in 1991, a coalition led by the United States defeated Iraq by evicting its army from its occupation of Kuwait. It was one of the great routs of history. The war began with an extended aerial bombing campaign that lasted six weeks and attacked military and infrastructure targets in Iraq and Kuwait. The ground campaign that followed lasted just 100 hours and ended with a quick settlement ending the occupation. The coalition suffered 379 dead, half killed by Iraqi forces and the other half by friendly fire and accidents. Iraqi dead is not known precisely with a common rough estimate of 30,000 soldiers and civilians killed.

[Map of Iraq, Kuwait, and Northern Persian Gulf showing Gulf War]

The domestic political consequences of the war are striking because they do not match the outcome of the war. President George H. W. Bush of the U.S. lost the 1992 election to Bill Clinton despite the great victory of the Gulf War. Meanwhile, President Saddam Hussein of Iraq continued in power despite the two disastrous wars into which he led Iraq. The Iraq-Iran War from 1980 to 1988 killed hundreds of thousands on both sides and ended in a draw. The aftermath of the Gulf War was another disaster for Iraq and its people. Kurds in the north of the country and Shiites in the south rebelled against Hussein's rule after the Gulf War. His Republican Guard violently suppressed these rebellions, killing thousands if not hundreds of thousands of Iraqis. After the war, the U.S. and Great Britain refused efforts to end economic sanctions placed on Iraq by the UN Security Council during the crisis before the war. These sanctions cut off Iraq from the world economy. It could not sell oil internationally nor import goods like medicines or spare parts to repair the damage of the bombing campaign. The Iraqi economy collapsed from the combination of war damage and the sanctions during the 1990s. Saddam Hussein, however, continued to build vast and lavish palaces for his own use. He was overthrown in the Iraq War of 2003, captured in December of 2003, and executed by the new government of Iraq in 2006 after a trial. How can a leader who does so poorly for his country continue in power so long?

War and the Fate of Leaders

All state leaders answer to some group of people who help to keep them in office. As the political philosopher David Hume put it,

> The soldan [Sultan] of EGYPT, or the emperor of ROME, might drive his harmless subjects, like brute beasts, against their sentiments and inclination: But he must, at least, have led his *mamalukes*, or *prætorian bands*, like men, by their opinion. (Hume, "Of the

First Principles of Government.")

Even the worst dictator requires the loyalty of those who carry out the oppression he uses to stay in power.

Those people who keep the leader in power care about the results of the policies that the leader carries out. But that concern is often personal rather than public. The Praetorian Guard of the Roman Empire made and broke emperors because they were the personal guard of the emperor. If he displeased them, they could kill him and elevate someone else to the imperial purple. Not surprisingly, the first act of many Roman emperors was a large gift of money to every member of the Praetorian Guard. Not all systems are as brutal as the Roman one, but the necessary supporters of the leader do care about the consequences of what he or she does in office. In other systems, those supporters care about the well-being of their state as well as the well-being of their own pocketbook. The results they care about cover the range of all the things the state does, from economic to social to security policies.

War is the most dramatic result of all the things that a state does. It touches many in a society and forces some to pay the ultimate price, their lives. The consequences of war are also diverse. The costs of war are the lost lives, the destroyed property, and the loss of production diverted to the war effort. There can also be benefits for those who fight. Historically, soldiers have looted and plundered on campaign. In the Middle Ages, enemy noblemen taken prisoner were held for ransom, enabling a common soldier to become wealthy. In more recent times, veterans often take pride in their wartime service afterwards. Wars also have political consequences which can benefit or hurt the population of a state. World War II ended the threat of the Nazis for U.S. citizens and ensured freedom of government, trade, and movement of people in Western Europe. Countries have added territory through conquest. States sometimes fight for ideals, such as the U.S.-led bombing campaign in Kosovo and Serbia in 1999, waged to end Serbian oppression of Kosovo. The population of a state weighs many different things in assessing whether a war was worth fighting. The costs and benefits are not shared equally nor generally. But the populace does assess them, and some of them are in a position to act on their assessment.

Because war is the most dramatic result of state policy, the fate of the warring state's leaders hangs on how the war goes. Those in the losing state may wish to punish their leader for taking them into a disastrous conflict. Those in the winning state might reward their leader. Even the threat of conflict affects the popularity of leaders. When the United States uses force, even force short of war, public support for the President as measured in public opinion polls often rises. This rise in support for the President is known as the *"Rally 'Round the Flag" effect*. These rallies are generally short-lived as support drops back if the crisis ends quickly or if the conflict drags on and kills U.S. soldiers. The graph below shows presidential approval ratings for President Bush through his two terms. He entered office with a little more than a half of the U.S. public approving of his performance as President. The first rally in his support came after the 9/11 attacks, but this rally faded over the next year-and-a-half. The Iraq War produced a second rally of about 20 points which also faded over time. As the war dragged on and more U.S. soldiers were killed in Iraq, his approval ratings dropped to record lows in the history of such polls. However, President Bush's support was high enough that he was reelected in 2004 despite the growing unpopularity of the war.

[Graph of support for President Bush over time]

Other results of state policy than war affect the retention of leaders. Good economic performance is often important for leaders to be reelected in democracies. As the sign in President Clinton's campaign strategy office said, "It's the economy, stupid." The range of policies which leaders can be evaluated on cover anything the state can do and sometimes those it has no control over but could remedy the effects of. President Bush also lost support in the wake of Hurricane Katrina which devastated New Orleans and the Gulf Coast in 2005. No one blamed Bush for the hurricane, but many did for the weak government response to shelter and provide for its victims during and after the hurricane.

Because the outcomes of war are so important to state leaders' continuing hold on power, they think carefully before going to war and choose their wars carefully. If a loss can cost you your job, you only want to fight winning wars. But the course of any war is unpredictable; the stronger side does not always win. Even if a winning war has its setbacks as well as its successes. The public judges a war through all of its impacts, although they may pay more attention to some over others. Still, every war has a losing side, forcing us to explain why some leaders choose wars they end up losing.

This argument does not mean that leaders go to war to raise their public support, although such charges are often made. It means only that war has consequences for support of the leader of a state at war and that leaders take those consequences into account when deciding whether to go to war and how to fight it. They often fight for the international reasons, such as security of their state and its people. But they view these considerations through a lens of domestic politics, which makes some consequences loom larger than others.

War and Removal from Office

What are the general patterns of the domestic political consequences of war for state leaders? Starting an international crisis reduces the risk of removal by about half. Being the target of demands raises the chance of removal by about half. Winning a war reduces the risk of removal by about one-quarter, although suffering higher casualties during war raises the risk of removal. The table below summarizes these results. They are statistical estimates of the average effects drawn across many cases. Each individual case differs, so the risk of removal a leader faces from international conflict depends on his or her own political situation. In the case of the Gulf War, President Bush was removed from office even though he won the war, while Saddam

Hussein was able to hold onto power despite his defeat. The general pattern here is that domestic audiences prefer winning to losing internationally, and so punish leaders who lose and reward those who win. They also rally around the government at lower levels of conflict.

Table 15.1
Summary of How International Conflict Changes Risk of Removal for Leaders

Result of International Conflict	Risk of Removal as Percentage of Risk without Conflict
Initiate Crisis	50%
Be Target of Crisis	150%
Win War	75%
Suffer Higher Casualties	Raises risk of removal

The Cuban Missile Crisis is an example of how a crisis can affect the political futures of both leaders. Premier Khrushchev of the Soviet Union ordered the deployment of nuclear-capable missiles to Cuba. When the U.S. government discovered the missile bases, President Kennedy announced a blockade of Cuba to force the withdrawal of the missiles. After a week of high tension, Khrushchev agreed to remove the missiles in exchange for a public pledge by the U.S. not to invade Cuba. Kennedy's political standing rose dramatically. His approval ratings rose to 75%, a very high level historically. The Democratic Party did well during the midterm Congressional election in November 1962. All the members of the House of Representatives were up for election as were one-third of the seats in the Senate. The midterm election allows the voters to respond to how the President is performing in office by voting against members of Congress of his party. On average, the party of the President loses 28 seats in the House and 4 in the Senate. In the 1962 midterm election, Kennedy's party, the Democratic Party, lost only 4 seats in the House and gained 3 senators. This is one of the best results for the party of the sitting President in the last 70 years of midterm elections, only surpassed by President Clinton in 1998 and President Bush in 2002. The public expressed its disapproval of the pending impeachment of Clinton in 1998 led by the Republican majority in the House and its support of Bush and his policies after 9/11 and before the Iraq War.

The result of the Cuban Missile Crisis was not so happy for Khrushchev. Two years later, a group in the Politburo removed him from the Premiership and forced him to retire to his dacha, a vacation cottage, outside Moscow. He lived the rest of his life in obscurity until he died in 1971.

Selectorate Theory

The question left open up to now is "who is the relevant audience?" Not everyone in a country has a say in politics. In the U.S., we do not allow children to vote until they are 18, unlike in Iran where the voting age was 15 until it was recently raised to 18. In the early years of the U.S., only propertied white males were allowed to vote, a small proportion of the total population. Restriction requiring the ownership of land to vote were replaced by the poll tax in the first half of the 19th century. Freedmen, that is ex-male slaves, gained the vote in the 15th Amendment after the Civil War, although their ability to cast their votes was restricted through a wide range of measures in southern state. Women gained the vote with the 19th Amendment in 1920. The last barriers to voting were removed with the Voting Rights Act of 1965, although there continue to be cases where some voters feel their ability to cast their votes are blocked. Effectively, the relevant audience for the President of the United States now is the adult population of the country.

The relevant audience in non-democratic systems is much smaller. The political class in a traditional monarchy or oligarchy was the aristocracy. In Louis XIV's France, the nobility is estimated at 2-5% of the total population. Not all nobles were equally important politically , but non-nobles certainly were not. The Communist Party in the Soviet Union was the largest group with any influence over politics. Many joined the Party as a requirement for high-level jobs in science and business even if they had no interest in politics. Party membership was necessary to hold political offices. Its membership varied from 2% of the population after the Great Purge under Stalin to 10% in the early 1980s. Candidates for Party membership were vetted carefully. Most Party members had little influence politically as the Politburo–a small committee, at most 15 men, of the top leaders of the party–set policy. The Politburo was formally selected by the Central Committee of several hundred which was selected by Party Congresses which met every five years. In practice, these elections were not competitive, and the lower bodies simply approved the lists of candidates for the higher bodies. The political relevant audience of the Politburo then was somewhere between several hundred and tens of thousands of party members.

The leader of a country does not need to keep the loyalty of everyone within the politically-relevant audience. No leader is universally loved, not even the autocratic leaders who stage mass demonstrations of support. But those who hold personal doubts about the leader and would like to see a change may not matter. They may lack the power to remove the leader from power or to help select his or her replacement. Even if they are in the politically relevant audience, others who approve of the leader may be able to keep him in office despite the opposition of others. The critical group of supporters can be very small.

All political systems have ways to remove their leaders and select their replacements. Elections are how modern democracies select their leaders. In ancient Athens, leaders were selected at random by drawing lots to fill key offices. Some systems have smaller bodies which select their leaders, as the Soviet Union did under communism. Other systems have no regular procedure to remove leaders, using violence, intrigue, and displays of power to remove leaders whose support has failed. Assassination and civil war were the main ways that Roman emperors were removed and replaced. The internal politics of these systems are often difficult to study because usurpations of an autocrat must be done secretly. These autocrats worry constantly about their supporters because they know any of them could be plotting against them at any time. Who participates in these processes determines who is politically relevant in a society.

Concepts of Selectorate Theory

Some simple concepts can help us think about how different societies remove and replace their leaders. Every leader has her *support coalition*, the set of people who currently support her continued hold on power. (For convenience, I call the leader "she" to avoid saying "he or she" repeatedly.) We will consider only those people who are politically relevant as members of a leader's support coalition; others outside that group are irrelevant to whether the leader retains power. A leader's support coalition changes over time as some supporters become disillusioned with the leader while others become convinced that she should remain in power.

The size of the *winning coalition*, or W, is the minimal size the support coalition must be for the leader to hold onto power. As long as the leader's support coalition has at least W people, she remains in power. If her support coalition falls below W, she could be replaced by a challenger. Many leaders build support coalitions larger than the size of the winning coalition. That way, the leader can afford to lose the loyalty of a few supporters without threatening her hold on power.

A *challenger* to the leader seeks to replace her by one, reducing the leader's support coalition below W by encouraging supporters to defect from the leader, and two, creating a support coalition of his own of at least W people. (I refer to the challenger as *he* to make it easy to tell him apart from the leader.) The first requirement undermines the current leader and the second makes it possible for the challenger to become the new leader. Politics according to selectorate theory revolve around the efforts of the leader to hold the loyalty of her supporters and those of the challenger to undermine her support coalition and create one of his own.

The *selectorate* is all the people from which a support coalition can be constructed. It is the politically relevant class. The term parallels the electorate because the electorate is the selectorate in a democracy. In other systems, the selectorate may be a small group of people, such as the Communist Party in the Soviet Union. Their key property is that they could be members of a support coalition.

The size of the selectorate is referred to S. We can then compare the sizes of the winning coalition and the selectorate as the ratio of W/S. In a democracy, this ratio lies between one-quarter and one-half depending on the electoral rules. In the United States, for example, the Electoral College selects the President, and they vote on a state-by-state basis. A Presidential candidate need only win just over half the votes in half the states to win the Electoral College. Of course, Presidential candidates do not run in only one-half the states, although their campaigns rarely put much effort into states where the preelection polls show that one of them is very likely to win. The dispersion of effort across more states than is needed for election reflects the tendency to build support coalitions larger than W. Other systems have much smaller ratios of W/S, so the leader needs to hold the support of few people. Most selectors in this system could be politically relevant, but the leader does not need their support to continue in power.

S and W together define the *selection institutions* of a political system. Any system can be characterized by these two quantities. Of course, every political system also has other institutions that matter. Selectorate theory abstracts away from these other institutions and focuses on how the sizes of these two groups influence the policies of the leader.

Different Political Systems according to Selectorate Theory

The selectorate of a modern mass democracy is the electorate, which is all adults in most democracies today. As mentioned earlier, universal suffrage was not typically even a century ago. The electorate is the selectorate in a democracy because elections ultimately determine who is the leader. Even when a leader is removed through other ways, the shadow cast by a future election drives that removal. Former Prime Minister Tony Blair of Great Britain was removed by his colleagues in the Labor Party in 2007 and replaced by his Chancellor and long-term political ally, Gordon Brown. The leaders of the Labor Party saw that Prime Minister Blair was very unpopular with the British people and feared they would lose the next election if Blair continued in office. They gave Brown the chance to rebuild the popularity of the party before the next election had to be called. Although party politics removed Blair from office, it was his loss in popularity in the electorate that drove the process. Even though Blair had won three elections in a row, a feat no other Labor leader had done, he was removed when he lost support in the electorate. As mentioned in the previous paragraph, W lies between one-quarter and one-half of S in a modern mass democracies. Ultimately, a democratic leader needs the support of a large portion of her population to hold onto power.

The selectorate of a monarchy or military dictatorship, in contrast, is a small segment of society. Monarchs often rely on the aristocracy for their support, while military dictators answer to the army, navy, and air force and whatever security services they use to control the population. W is typically very small in these systems. A military dictator need only hold the loyalty of the key officers to keep the support of the military. Monarchs in medieval Europe were often elected by a group of a few hundred at most of the leading nobles. Autocrats often create multiple security services to play them off one another. That way a challenge from one does not necessarily lead to the overthrow of the leader because she can rely on the loyalty of the other security agencies. This is an example of the leader oversizing her support coalition to make it difficult for a challenger to pull off enough supporters to reduce it below W. The choice of which officers fill which positions in a military dictatorship also shows how the ability to be part of a support coalition is the key property of a member of the selectorate. A military dictator needs the support of the leaders of each of the branches of the military: army, navy, air force, and often a paramilitary police or militia. The leader of any one of these organizations could conduct a coup d'etat to seize power if he was disloyal. Many officers could be promoted into one of these positions, so a new leader does not need to hold the loyalty of the old heads of the services or even a majority of the officers in the military. Instead, a new leader promotes his own supporters to the key positions. W remains small even compared to the small set of the selectorate in these systems.

The Soviet Union was another type of autocracy, a one-party state. The Communist Party ran the government, and key members of the regime often held positions in both the party and the government. One had to join the Party if one wished to be involved in politics. All politics was internal to the Party. The size of the winning coalition was a majority of the Central Committee or a Party Congress as these bodies approved the members of the Politburo was policy was set. The membership of the Party can be considered the selectorate as party members could be promoted into the higher bodies if those at the top chose to do so. Mikhail Gorbachev became a Party member when he was 21 and was promoted to the Central Committee at the young age of 40 because of his patron Mikhail Suslov, a Politburo member. Many others could have been put on the fast track to the top of the political system. One-party systems have larger W than military dictatorships or traditional monarchies, although their sizes are still small compared to mass democracies. Their selectorates are much larger than those of other types of autocracies, although again they are much smaller than the mass electorate of a democracy.

The table below summarizes these three types of systems in the sizes of their selectorates and winning coalitions. The comparison is rough as each system has its unique political rules and properties that determine the precise values of these quantities.

Table 15.2
Size of the Selectorate and Winning Coalition for Three Political Systems

Type of System	Size of Selectorate (S)	Size of Winning Coalition (W)
Modern Mass Democracy	Large: all adults	Large: roughly ¼ to ½ of S
Monarchy, or Military Dictatorship	Small: Aristocracy or Military	Very Small: Fraction of S
One-party Autocracy	Medium: Party Members	Small: Leadership of Party

How Selection Institutions Affect the Policies of Leaders

The leader needs to hold the loyalty of her support coalition and prevent it from falling below W in number to retain her position. Leaders use the resources of the state to reward their supporters and hold their loyalty. They provide a combination of public goods and private benefits through their policies. *Public goods* benefit all members of society, even those outside the selectorate. Some examples of public goods provided by different political systems are the rule of law and domestic order, free road systems, national defense against external threats, and cleaner air and water. Not all members of society benefit equally from these public goods, but no one can be excluded from their benefits. *Private benefits* are targeted to specific individuals who receive them alone. Political systems through history have rewarded individuals with state monopolies over key industries, personal pensions, grants of land, and many other types of private benefits.

These two types of benefits a government can provide to its people are extreme cases. Most government policies provide a combination of public goods and private benefits. Consider the Social Security system in the United States. It provides cash payments to individuals who have retired or been disabled and have paid social security taxes into the system when they were working. The cash payments are targeted to individuals, matching the exclusion of private benefits. But the system also provides a base level of retirement income and insurance against disability, which many would consider public goods. Even some policies which provide private benefits can also provide some public goods. Patents allow their holders to collect money by selling the right to use that idea, producing a private benefit for the holder. Others cannot copy the invention without the permission of the patent holder, who licenses or sells the right to do so. The patent system as a whole increases innovation by rewarding inventors with patent rights. The increase in innovation benefits everyone in society. This combination of private benefits and public goods is common to most government policies.

The central insight of selectorate theory is that the sizes of the winning coalition and the selectorate influence the mix of public goods and private benefits a leader produces through state policy. From the leader's point of view, private benefits are an attractive way to reward supporters because she can target them on just her supporters. Nothing is committed to those who do not support the leader. Public goods, in contrast, also reward non-supporters, even those outside the selectorate. The question for a leader is which creates greater rewards for her supporters. The sizes of the winning coalition and the selectorate determine the mix of private benefits and public goods that a leader produces in her policies.

The bigger the winning coalition, the more the leader shifts her effort away from the provision of private benefits and more toward public goods. The size of the winning coalition acts like a price to provide private benefits; the more people you have to reward, the more expensive it is to reward them with private benefits. When a good becomes more expensive, people buy less of it and look for substitutes. The population of a state sets cost of providing public goods. It does not change if the winning coalition expands. Consequently, a leader's policies shift effort and resources from the provision of private benefits toward the production of public goods as the size of the winning coalition increases. This statement assumes all else is held equal, the wealth of the country, the size of the population, the type and character of the private benefits and public goods that could be provided.

A simple numerical example shows the logic. Imagine there are 1000 people in a country, and the leader has $1000 of resources to use. She could provide a public good which everyone in society values at $20 if she uses all of the money. Instead, she could simply divide up the $1000 among her supporters. If W is 10, she can give each of them $100, which they prefer to the benefits of the public good. If W is 100 people, she can only give each of them $10 in private benefits. Now the public good is a better way to reward her supporters, even though the 900 non-supporters benefit from it. Her efforts shift away from private benefits and toward public goods as the size of the winning coalition increases. This is the primary insight of selectorate theory.

The size of the selectorate affects the loyalty of supporters increasing the pool of people who could be members of a support coalition. Holding all else equal again, the larger the selectorate the more loyal supporters will be. Imagine that you are a supporter of the current leader and the challenger tries to entice you to defect to him. He may offer a lot today and promise you much in the future when and if he comes to power, but should you believe his promises? After all, he could rely on anyone in the selectorate for his support coalition once he comes to power. Perhaps he just wants to use you to remove the current leader and then discard you afterwards. It is common in autocracies that close supporters of a new leader are cast aside once she attains power. The challenger faces a commitment problem in his promises to supporters of the current leader. They doubt whether they will continue to be members of his support coalition if he comes to power, costing them the private benefits they now receive from the current leader. This doubt is the *risk of exclusion* from the new support coalition.

A larger selectorate means more people who could be members of a support coalition, which increases the risk of exclusion for supporters of the current leader. The ratio of the winning coalition to the selectorate, W/S, reflects the risk of exclusion. Again, a simple calculation shows the logic. Imagine W is 10, S is 20, and the challenger will choose the members of his support coalition from the selectorate at random. Every selector has a ½ (= 10/20) chance of being in his new support coalition, and the risk of exclusion–not being in the support coalition is also ½ (= 1 - ½). If S is 100 while W remains 10, the chance of being in his new support coalition has dropped to 1/10 (= 10/100), and the risk of exclusion rises to 9/10 (= 1 - 1/10). Now leaders do not choose their supporters at random, but these simple calculations reflect the reality that a larger selectorate means more candidates for a new support coalition, and so the greater chance that a challenger's promises to a supporter of the current leader will not come true if he comes to power.

The risk of exclusion, and the importance of the size of the selectorate, is greater in systems with small winning coalitions. Leaders who answer to a large winning coalition rely more on public goods to hold the loyalty of their supporters. A challenger will also have to provide public goods, which a defector will continue to receive if he comes to power. With more public goods provided, the risk of exclusion becomes less important. In a system with a small winning coalition, supporters receive substantial private benefits, and their possible loss makes the risk of exclusion loom larger in supporters' minds. This risk makes them more loyal to the current leader in order to preserve their access to private benefits. Because supporters are more loyal, the leader can provide them fewer private benefits and still retain power. For the leader, a system with a small winning coalition and a large selectorate is best; she has the greatest chance of holding power and needs to provide less private benefits to do so. Generally though, systems with very small winning coalitions—monarchies and military dictatorships—also have small selectorates.

Another way to think about how selection institutions affect policy is through political competition. Every political system has ways to replace leaders which produce competition among those who would like to be leader. In some traditional monarchies, the competition happens behind closed doors among the sons (typically) and their mothers when the king dies. In democracies, elections are the main forum of political competition. In dictatorships, competition lies in the plots of those who seek to overthrow the leader and the efforts of the secret police to ferret them out before they can launch their plots. Political competition in systems with small winning coalitions is about the distribution of private benefits and the deterrence of plots against the ruler. Opponents are either bought off or repressed. Consequently, opposition to the leader, even among her closest supporters, is secret. Political opposition in democracies, in contrast, is open. It is a competition in competence as each party attempts to convince voters that it will produce the most public goods for them.

All political systems produce a mix of public goods and private benefits. Democracies, as mentioned earlier, often have policies that produce both public goods and private benefits. Social welfare policies both put money in the pockets of particular citizens and provide insurance against the risk of unemployment and disability for all citizens. Even the worst dictatorship provides some public goods. The chaos after the U.S.-led invasion of Iraq in 2003 showed that Saddam Hussein's government at least provided domestic order that reduced crime to the benefit of most Iraqis. The mix of public goods and private benefits varies with selection institutions, but all systems provide some of both.

The mix of the two goods also produces one of the essential tensions of politics. Is a specific policy in the public interest or does it serve only the interests of a few? Because even the most democratic system produces some private benefits, politicians try to convince the public that those policies are actually in the public interest. With many policies producing some of both, it is often unclear who benefits from them. A common argument in democratic politics then addresses whether a given policy produces a public good or only a private benefit. Rarely is the answer to that question clear.

Simplifying Assumptions in Selectorate Theory

Selectorate theory is a simple but powerful argument that can be applied to any political system at any time in history and anywhere in the world. This is why it is useful for studying how domestic politics of countries affects their international policies. It gains this simple elegance by making assumptions about how political competition and the formation of policy work in political systems. Understanding these simplifying assumptions helps us understand the limits of the theory.

First, selectorate theory treats all selectors as equal. Even in a democracy, some citizens have a greater effect on politics than others. Some voters are alienated from politics and do not vote. Democratic politicians are primarily concerned with attracting the support of voters rather than citizens. Some citizens have greater effect on politics because they have other means than their votes to influence political leaders. Lobbying–talking to politicians to convince which policies are right for the country–occurs in every political system. Not everyone can have access to a politician's ear. Often the policies that lobbyists argue for are those which benefit them personally. When the government has the power to make and break business and the economic fortunes of people, it is hardly surprising that some seek to use the government to their own advantage. In autocracies, some supporters of the leader are more important than others. It is more important to hold the loyalty of a general than a captain in a military dictatorship. The theory treats all selectors as identical and equal. We could assume they have different weights, as if some people had more than one vote. Those who carried greater weight would receive more private benefits than others. But the essential character of the argument would not change, just the distribution of private benefits. For simplicity then, we assume all selectors are equal.

Second, we assume that the leader alone holds the power to set policy to produce public goods and private benefits. There are systems where the leader holds this absolute power, but they are rare today. In the United States, power over policy is spread across many institutions and the people who comprise them. The President proposes legislation, has power to administer the laws after they are passed, and is given wide discretion as Commander in Chief of the military. Bureaucrats in executive agencies write and carry out regulations on a wide range of issues. Congress passes laws and oversees what the executive agencies do. The courts rule on how laws should be applied in specific cases and whether those laws are constitutional. State governments have responsibility and power over many areas of policy. Even some autocracies spread the power for policy over more than one leader. The Politburo of the Soviet Union had ultimate authority over policy which was shared among its 10-15 members, even if one of them was recognized as the first among them. Distribution of responsibility and power over policy create another form of political competition. Selectorate theory assumes away this competition and assumes policy is set by a single leader.

Third, selectorate theory assumes all citizens agree on what policies produce public goods. There are many policies where people disagree about what the public good is. Abortion is one of the most controversial issues in U.S. politics over the last decades. Pro-life advocates believe that abortion is murder, and the public good would be banning it. Pro-choice partisans believe that women have the right to control their reproductive processes and want abortion to be legal and available openly. The two sides disagree about which policy on abortion produces a public good. Selectorate theory assumes away this element which is central to political competition, particularly in democracies. Part of electoral competition is an argument over which candidate will do a better job as leader, but also part of that competition is also about which policies are right for the country.

Selectorate theory gains its power from these simplifying assumptions. They reduce the complexity of politics in many very different systems to the efforts of a single leader to hold the loyalty of her supporter by producing public goods and private benefits. We need to understand what has been assumed away in the argument to grasp its limits. Selectorate theory is a powerful and useful theory, but it is not an exact mirror of domestic politics.

Autocracies versus Democracies in Foreign Policy

The selection institutions of a state affect a wide range of its public policies. Many policies from social welfare through economic regulation produce mixtures of public goods and private benefits. Leaders can design these policies to favor their supporters over others. Later in the book, we use selectorate theory to evaluate international economic policies. In this chapter, we are concerned with the outcomes of war and peace as such policies, specifically how supporters in different systems view winning and losing in wars and the consequences of war for the warring leaders' hold on power. In the next chapter, we will consider the public good and private benefits produced by foreign policy in greater detail.

No matter what the specific goal of foreign policy, success is better than failure. Failure in war brings both the costs of war on the populace and the frustration of the ends the state went to war to achieve. Victory has a thousand fathers and mothers, while defeat is an orphan. As mentioned earlier in this chapter, losing a war or crisis increases the risk of removal to a leader. The end of a war often leads to a political crisis in the losing state. It is a prime opportunity for challengers to aim to take power because the current leader has publicly failed. Further, if success is a public good, a democratic leader may be at greater risk for her failure to provide it.

How can a leader sustain her hold on power in the wake of defeat? The leader of a non-democracy can seek to increase the private benefits received by her supporters. They may be willing to overlook her error in going to war and then how she fought it if the other rewards of their position are attractive enough. A democratic leader, on the other hand, relies on her ability to provide public goods. The defeat denies the public good of success in the war and opens her to challenges from those who criticize her effort in the war. Autocrats can compensate for their failure in war by providing private benefits to their supporters, while democratic leaders rely on a large winning coalition, making such compensation difficult to impossible. Autocrats may also be able to fight wars to shelter their supporters from the worst consequences of the fighting. In all, autocrats should be less prone to losing office as a consequence of war.

The consequences of crises are profound for the leaders of democracies. Again, statistical averages across many cases can help us see patterns not evident from individual cases. Winning a crisis reduces the risk of removal by about three-quarters (77%) in the year afterwards. Using violence in a crisis hurts a democratic leader's hold on power. It raises the risk in a range from one-quarter (25%) to more than tripling it (213%). The specific increase depends on why she must resort to violence to advance her ends in the dispute and whether she won or lost. Using violence to defend the status quo is worse for her because it shows that deterrence has failed. The use of violence here includes cases of low-level use of violence, such as the sending of troops that does not lead to full-scale war. For democratic leaders who lose a crisis, the risk of removal almost doubles (increases 90%). Comparing the risks, it is better for a democratic leader to use force to prevail in a crisis than to lose that crisis. Some crises end without a clear winner and loser, so not winning is not the same as losing. These are averages across many cases and their pattern is more important than the specific numbers. Winning is better than losing, using force is bad, but better than losing if necessary to avoid a defeat.

The picture of autocrats is different. The risk of removal if an autocratic leader loses a crisis is two-fifths (38%) lower than that of a democratic leader. Losing is bad for an autocrat's hold on power, but she is more likely to be able to hold onto power than a democratic leader who loses. Use force or the threat of force to gain territory increases an autocrat's hold on power, reducing the risk of removal by over one-half (56-65% depending on the exact conditions). We return to the question of how specific war aims and domestic politics affect one another in the next chapter. Although winning is good and losing is bad for autocrats as with democratic leaders, the risks of removal are not as large.

The Fates of Presidents Bush and Hussein

How did the Gulf War, one of the great routs of military history, affect the political fortunes of the leader that took the main combatants to war? President George H W. Bush's popularity soared in the immediate aftermath of the war. Months later, concerns rose that although the war had been won, Saddam Hussein had not been removed from office, putting the ultimate aims of the war at risk. Some U.S. citizens saw it as an empty victory. President Bush's popularity dropped as the U.S. economy went into recession after the war. He lost the 1992 election to Bill Clinton when Clinton focused on the economic pain that many voters felt. The victory had passed, and the U.S. electorate decided to replace the victorious leader for his failure to provide the public good of a healthy economy.

Saddam Hussein had dubbed the Gulf War "The Mother of All Battles," but the performance of the Iraqi military was poor during the war. He was able to preserve a large portion of the Republican Guard, elite troops who protected the regime and him. Hussein unleashed the Republican Guard to put down the postwar revolts of the Kurds in the north of Iraq and the Shiites in the south with extreme violence. Estimates range up to more than 100,000 Iraqis killed in the suppression of the revolts. The Iraqi economy did not recover for most Iraqis after the war. The aerial bombing of the country had damaged its infrastructure–bridges, power plants, and communications, and the economic sanctions kept in place by the United States and Great Britain prevented the import of spare parts and foreign experts needed to rebuild it completely. The sanctions also limited the import of food and medicine, raising their prices for average Iraqis. Saddam Hussein failed the Iraqi people both in war and in peace. Yet he did not bear the cost of that failure in his hold on power. Oil was smuggled out of the country to raise revenue, money that was spent on those who kept him in power and palaces for his own use. Despite his many failures as the leader of the people of Iraq, he held power until the U.S.-led invasion of Iraq in 2003, which we return to in the next chapter.

Chapter Summary

War has profound consequences for leaders' hold on power. In the short run, the people rally to the support their leader during a conflict. In the long run, they judge their leader by whether their country prevailed and at what cost. Domestic audiences prefer winning to losing. Losing wars and crises raises the risk of removal substantially. The relevant domestic audience varies with the political system of the country. The winning coalition (W) measures the minimal number of supporters the leader must keep loyal to remain in power. For autocracies of all sorts, W is small; for democracies, W is a substantial fraction of the total population. The selectorate (S) is the politically relevant portion of the population, those who could be members of the leader's support coalition. Leaders produce public goods and private benefits through their policies to retain the loyalty of their supporters. Leaders shift their efforts away from private benefits and toward public goods as the size of the winning coalition increases. The risks of conflict are greater for democratic leaders than autocratic ones. Autocrats can insulate themselves from the consequences of an international defeat by providing private benefits to their supporters.

These selection pressures do not determine what a state's leader does internationally, but leaders do act with one eye on the domestic repercussions of their actions. State leaders view foreign policy through a lens of domestic politics, which shapes in part how they respond to international forces and challenges. The international effects of policies also matter because the supporters of the leader care about the results of those policies. State leaders sit across two political arenas, the international and the domestic. Successful leaders are those who can craft policies that succeed in both.

Review Questions

1. Define winning coalition and selectorate for a leader. How does the size of each affect the leader's relative emphasis on private and public goods?

2. How do the outcomes of a war affect the probability of a leader losing office?

3. Is an autocratic or democratic leader more likely to survive a defeat in war? Explain briefly why.

4. What is the rally-round-the-flag effect during an international crisis? Is the effect temporary or permanent?

Chapter 16
The Enemy Outside:
External Changes in Leaders and Regimes

The 1991 Gulf War restored the independence and sovereignty of Kuwait, but it did not resolve other outstanding issues between the United States and Iraq. Iraq agreed to destroy its weapons of mass destruction (WMD for short)–chemical and biological weapons–and dismantle its programs in pursuit of nuclear weapons as part of the peace treaty ending the war. It also agreed to destroy its ballistic missiles, which it had fired during the war at Israel and Saudi Arabia. UN inspectors had the mission to track down Iraq's weapons programs and verify that they were dismantled. Although we now know that these programs were successful, Iraq made their job as difficult as possible. Iraqi agents attempted to assassinate former President George H W. Bush while he was visiting Kuwait in 1993. President Clinton retaliated by bombing the headquarters of Iraqi intelligence in Baghdad once sufficient evidence was public to link its agents to the attempt. The U.S. and Great Britain maintained no-fly zones over the north and south of Iraq. They flew air missions to monitor and shoot down any Iraqi aircraft entering these zones without permission. These missions also led to a shadow war between the aircraft and Iraqi anti-aircraft defenses, where the aircraft would occasionally bomb anti-aircraft sites that activated their radar to lock onto planes in the air. The United States and Britain also blocked the removal of economic sanctions put in place during the crisis before the war. These sanctions hurt the Iraqi economy greatly. France and Russia sought to have the economic sanctions lifted. The UN established the "oil-for-food" plan in 1995 to alleviate the hardship caused by the sanctions. Iraq was allowed to sell oil it produced and use the proceeds to buy food and medicine from other countries. The program proved to be corrupt and allowed Iraq to skim off some of the proceeds and use them to purchase banned items. Finally, Saddam Hussein expelled the UN weapons inspectors in 1998, which led President Clinton to conduct a four-day bombing campaign in Iraq along with the Royal Air Force of Britain. Clearly, there were many issues between the U.S. and Iraq even after the Gulf War.

On March 21, 2003, the United States and Great Britain invaded Iraq. They overthrew Saddam Hussein's government in less than a month and began the period of military occupation with the support of other countries. What was the underlying strategic problem that the Iraq War sought to solve? To answer this question, we need to examine the war aims of states and how their selection institutions influence them.

Regimes and War Aims

Selectorate theory explains how the selection institutions of a state shape the policies of its leader. The larger the winning coalition–the minimal number of supporters whose loyalty the leader must hold to retain office, the more the leader shifts to producing public goods over private benefits. When the winning coalition is small, as in an autocracy, the leader primarily relies on private benefits to hold the loyalty of her supporters. In that case, the larger the selectorate, the greater the risk of removal for each supporter, and so the more loyal they will be. The last chapter present selectorate theory more fully and argued that successful foreign policy acts like a public good. This result could explain why the consequences of crises and wars were larger for democratic leaders than autocrats.

War aims could be primarily public goods or private benefits. Security of the members of society is the central public good of foreign and defense policy. States are responsible for protecting their citizens from attack by those outside the country. In this sense, the terrorist attacks of 9/11 inside the United States were a failure by the U.S. government to keep its citizens safe. We take the public good of personal security almost for granted these days. Through history, however, the threat of invasion or cross-border raid and the threat they pose to personal safety and property have loomed large. When a government successfully deters or thwarts such attacks, all in society benefit from that protection. Security is a public good which can be produced by arming, forming alliances, other foreign policies to stop such threats, and ultimately war if necessary.

War could produce other public goods as well. The key to judging whether a war aim is a public good or private benefit is whether no one can be excluded from the benefits of it. Ideological goals are public goods then. An example is the bombing campaign the U.S. and its NATO allies undertook in 1999 to force Serbia to stop committing atrocities against the Kosovars. The aim there was ideological in that the protection of human rights is an idea rather than a material benefit, particularly for defending the human rights of others. The aim of protecting human rights is a public good for the citizens of the United States because they all would enjoy the benefits of that policy if successful. Of course, an individual may not care about the protection of human rights of people in other countries, but he or she could not be excluded from that good when the bombing coerced Serbia into ending its campaign of atrocities in Kosovo. Other ideological goals, such as the promotion of democracy or open and free market economies, are public goods.

Private benefits, on the other hand, can be targeted to particular members of a society, with others not receiving them. Loot is a classic private benefit of war. Soldiers historically have seen seizing the goods of others as the right of the victors or even just any soldier on campaign. Wars were fought in part to gain the right to make one self wealthy at the expenses of others, including civilians with nothing at stake in the war. Although looting has declined over time, it has not disappeared. Iraq stripped Kuwait of cars, medical equipment, and art from its museums, all to the benefit of the leaders and soldiers of Iraq. Soldiers from the U.S. 101st Airborne Division who had occupied Hitler's alpine retreat in the last days of World War II celebrated the surrender of the Nazis by breaking into Herrmann Goering's private wine cellar and getting drunk on champagne. Goering had accumulated that wine cellar by looting French wineries of their best bottles after the fall of France to the Nazis in 1940. Historically, there were often rules within armies for the division of the loot among soldiers after a town was taken, with officers receiving larger shares than common soldiers. Although loot could be used for the benefit of the society of the conquering army, it almost always remains as the personal property of the soldiers of that army.

War can create other private benefits for the leader of the state to distribute. If land is conquered, it can be redistributed to supporters. During the Middle Ages, the Teutonic Knights extended their control eastward by conquering territory which then became the personal domains of individual knights. In the feudal system, knights claim a proportion of all produced in their territory, so control of territory was how they supported themselves. More territory meant more wealth. This process carried over in the early modern Europe where the territory of the state was effectively the King's property, and taxes were how the King extracted wealth for his own purposes from that territory. That wealth could be used to reward key supporters by the King. Again, private benefits are targetable, so the leader can give them only to her supporters.

Territory as a War Aim

States have long fought over territory. Whether territory produces public goods or private benefits depends on why the territory is being acquired. If the territory is parceled out to supporters as land they own or rule over, added territory produces private benefits for the supporters who receive control over it. The material value of a piece of territory comes from the people who live on it and the resources produced by them. Some pieces of territory, like the arctic regions through much of history, have little material value because few people live there and it does not produce valuable goods. The United States purchased Alaska from Russia in 1867. At the time, the purchase was called "Seward's Folly" because few could understand why Secretary of State Seward was willing to spend $7.2 million to purchase the vast, remote, and desolate land. The value of the Arctic changed when the ability to extract resources found there were developed. Alaska became more valuable after gold was discovered in the late 19th century. Now most Americans see the acquisition of Alaska as a bargain at only 2¢ an acre. Most territory that has changed hands between countries over time has material value from the people who live there. The government of a state can extract some of that production through taxes. Whether added territory produces public goods or private benefits depends on how the leader uses the taxes she collects from the people there. In 1740, Frederick the Great of Prussia triggered the War of Austrian Succession by invading the Austrian province of Silesia. He hoped to take advantage of the new Queen of Austria, Maria Theresa, who ascended to the throne at the age of 23 when her father died without a male heir. Frederick made Silesia his target because it was a wealthy and productive province of the Austrian Empire. Although he grabbed it quickly, he had underestimated Maria Theresa, and the War of Austrian Succession spread into a general war in Europe involving Great Britain and France as well. She was willing to fight on to regain Silesia because it produced one-quarter of her tax revenue in the years before the war. But Frederick was able to retain Silesia at the end of the war and then again after the Seven Years War, fought by Austria to regain it from Prussia. Frederick used some of that new revenue to build grander palaces for himself in Potsdam, his seat of government just outside Berlin. This territorial acquisition produced greater opulence for Frederick and private benefits for his supporters among the nobles and his army.

[Map of Prussia and Austria showing Silesia]

Territory has other properties than just the people who live there and what is produced there. Some pieces of territory have strategic value. Some are located in critical places in world geography that make them militarily important. Great Britain seized Gibraltar from Spain in 1704 during the War of Spanish Succession and has kept it as a British territory since. Gibraltar is a small peninsula which juts into the Strait of Gibraltar between the Atlantic Ocean and the Mediterranean Sea. It is dominated by the Rock of Gibraltar, a mountain more than 1000 feet high. Because of its location and the Rock, Gibraltar commands sea traffic between the Atlantic and the Mediterranean. Britain fortified it and has used it to command the Strait over the centuries. Because Britain has historically relied on its Navy for the security of the British Isles and its commerce overseas, control of Gibraltar produces a public good for the British people. Other pieces of territory have strategic value as well. Panama was the easiest place to build a canal between the Atlantic and Pacific Oceans that would reduce sailing times between the East and West Coasts of the U.S. greatly. The U.S. tried to acquire Panama from Colombia by negotiation. When the Senate of Colombia balked at ratifying the treaty, the U.S. fomented a revolt which led to the independence of Panama. The U.S. then built the Panama Canal and purchased the Canal Zone from Panama to control it. The U.S. agreed to return the Zone with the canal to Panama in 1977 and sovereignty passed over on December 31, 1999. The U.S., and Britain to a lesser extent, have kept strategic territories around the world as military bases. These territorial acquisitions help these governments produce the public good of national security.

[Picture of Gibraltar showing the Rock from ground level]

Territorial gain could also add strategic depth to a country. There would then be more country which an invader would have to conquer to reach the capital and other key cities in the country. After the Nazi-Soviet Pact in 1939, the Soviet Union under Stalin coerced territory out of the countries between Nazi Germany and it. It seized the eastern half of Poland, annexed the Baltic States, fought a war with Finland to add territory near Leningrad (now St. Petersburg), and forced Romania to cede Bessarabia and Northern Bukovina. When Hitler did attack in 1941, this added territory forced the Nazi armies to cross more territory in their invasion. These gains may have provided the margin of safety for Moscow and Leningrad, the two largest and most important cities in the Soviet Union, in 1941.

[Map showing Stalin's post-Pact acquisitions]

Territorial gain could also produce greater national security by shifting the balance of capabilities between two states. Germany has a larger population and larger economy than France, allowing it to build a larger and more capable army. Before World War I, France's alliance with Russia helped to balance Germany's greater power by forcing Germany to fight a two-front war, one in the east with Russia and one in the west with France. Russia left the war after the Bolshevik Revolution, and Germany concentrated her army in the west against France and its British and American allies. After the war, France might not be able to rely on its allies to counter Germany. Instead, France sought territory, specifically the provinces of Alsace and Lorraine lost to Germany at the end of the Franco-Prussian War in 1871. Lorraine contained mines and steel mills that increased French industry. This territorial gain did not make France more powerful than Germany, but it did reduce the gap.

Territory can also produce a public good if many people in a country consider the territory an essential part of their nation. Many French citizens felt that way about Alsace-Lorraine when it was part of Germany; it was a vital part of France that had been ripped from the country. Some of the intractable conflicts of our time arise from territories which more than one state believes are part of its nation. During the process of Great Britain leaving the Raj and the creation of India and Pakistan from it, the Maharaja of Kashmir chose to join his territory to India. A wide majority of the population, however, was Muslim and preferred joining the Muslim state of Pakistan. Irregular fighters crossed the border from Pakistan into Kashmir and began fighting Indian troops occupying the province, starting the first Indo-Pakistani War. The Pakistani army eventually entered the war in support of the irregulars. Kashmir was divided along the cease-fire line at the end of the war and has remained divided since. Both India and Pakistan continue to claim the territory as their own, and the conflict remains open to this day. It has contributed to three other wars between the two countries as well as terrorist attacks inside India.

Territory as a war aim can produce either public goods or private benefits, depending on the territory and how the victor uses it. The conquest and control of territory is one of the major roles of the military in any state. Military force can be used to settle territorial disputes unilaterally, although such attempts rarely succeed. Even after a territorial grab succeeds, the state losing the territory may continue the conflict over which state should control the territory, as France did with Alsace-Lorraine after the Franco-Prussian War. It may threaten to use force to reverse the earlier conquest. But the territory will remain in the hands of the conqueror until something is done to reverse that conquest.

Policy as a War Aim

States also fight over the policies of others. These aims generally produce public goods for the selectors of that state. The disarmament of Iraq's WMD programs was a policy aim of the United States during and after the Gulf War. The elimination of those programs would make

U.S. soldiers and citizens safer. During World War II, the United States fought Nazi Germany to restore the independence of European countries conquered by the Nazis, such as France and Belgium. The U.S. had no intention of annexing these countries to its territory, simply that it did not want them under Nazi control. This war aim was a public good for the American people because it reduced the Nazi threat to the U.S. homeland and allowed free trade with the people of the conquered countries.

Autocracies also pursue policy aims in war. The Iran-Iraq War began when Iraq attacked Iran in 1980. There was a territorial issue over the exact location of the border between the two countries in the Shatt al Arab waterway. It linked Basra, Iraq's second largest city and its main port, to the Persian Gulf. There had been several disputes over the waterway, and Iran had won concessions from Iraq, moving the border to the center of the waterway in the prior dispute in 1975. This concession gave Iran the ability to block naval traffic to and from Basra. The Iranian Revolution in 1979 created the Islamic Republic of Iran. Islam has two main sects, Sunni and Shia. Most of the Arab world is Sunni, while almost all Iranians are Shiites. There are important Shia minorities in the countries around the Persian Gulf, and Shiites are the majority in Iraq, even though Saddam Hussein and his government were Sunni. His government of Iraq understandably feared the possibility of a revolution by the Shiites. After the Iranian Revolution, the new government began to promote the idea of Shia revolution in other countries through propaganda broadcast. Saddam Hussein's government wanted this to stop. This dispute escalated in low-level fighting across the border during 1980. Iraq's war aim was an end to Iranian agitation for Shiite revolution, which threatened its government. This demand was for a change in the policy of the revolutionary government in Iran.

There are some policies aims which produce private benefits, such as the protection of specific firms doing business in other countries. Iraq's demand for an end to Iranian agitation aimed to produce both the public good of domestic stability and the continuation of private benefits received by the supporters of Saddam Hussein's government. Generally, however, policy aims produce public goods.

Policy aims generally require the agreement of the defeated state to be realized. Military force by Iraq could not stop Iran from broadcasting revolutionary propaganda to Iraqi Shiites. Force might be able to convince the government of Iran to stop those broadcasts to end the war. Later, the disarmament of Iraq's WMDs and their programs would be more effective if the government of Iraq agreed to do so. During World War II, the United States could evict Nazi forces from other Western European countries, but the Nazis could re-invade them later after U.S. forces returned home. A government in Germany that was willing to live in peace with its neighbors was the best guarantee of the U.S. aim to ensure free countries in Western Europe. In all these cases, those governments making the concessions could change their minds about continuing those changes in policy after the settlement, and this change would threaten the policy aims of the other side.

Policy aims then create a commitment problem for the victor in a war. It worries whether the defeated state will continue to cooperate and sustain the changes in policy for which the victor fought. The war will have been fought and won in vain. What the victor fought to gain will have been lost because the losing state stopped cooperating with it. Disarmament of Iraq would have been much easier and more certain had Saddam Hussein's government cooperated with the UN weapons inspectors. In the end, those inspection programs did disarm Iraq, but doubt about their effectiveness continued until and after the Iraq War in 2003.

The commitment problem is heightened because often the government of the defeated state can gain in domestic politics by refusing to cooperate with the victor. Often, the policy changes demanded by the victor are unpopular with the population of the defeated state. They may be seen as an imposition of the sovereignty of the defeated state. The changes may be unpopular with the people of the defeated state. A government of the defeated state which seeks to live up to its obligations in the peace settlement may find itself facing political opponents using that issue against it. This political pressure could convince that government to end its cooperation with the victorious state or it could bring a government hostile to those concession to power.

The Versailles Treaty which the Allies forced on Germany after World War required measures designed to reassure France of its security against Germany. Territorial concessions moved the border to the east and gave France a more defensible border on the Rhine River. It also disarmed Germany, limiting it to 100,000 soldiers and no tanks, airplanes, or submarines. Germany was not allowed to post troops in the Rhineland adjoining France and Belgium. This measure would make it difficult for Germany to launch a quick attack against either country because they could see German troops moving into the Rhineland in advance of an attack. Many Germans saw these provisions as offensive and excessive given the long, hard war where Germany had almost beaten the Allies on its own. The German delegates initially refused to sign the treaty until the Allies threatened to restore the blockade that cut off Germany from imports of food and other necessities. Eventually, two politicians agreed to go to Paris to sign the treaty even though they knew that act would end their political careers in Germany. Popular political opposition to Versailles was common across the political spectrum from left to right in Germany. The Allies did make some concessions to bring Germany back into world politics during the 1920s. Germany secretly violated the disarmament provisions by cooperating with the Soviet Union on military development and training using the banned equipment. It circulated men through the military after training, allowing it to build up more than 100,000 trained soldiers. Versailles was politically unpopular in Germany, making it easy for German politicians to act against it. This lack of cooperation increased French concerns for its own security, thwarting the object of Versailles.

Winning the Peace

Any victor in war has to worry about winning the peace as well as winning the war. Its losses during the war are for nought if the peace afterwards is lost. The loser may gain politically at home by challenging the postwar settlement. Challenging a territorial settlement requires the threat of force, a direct challenge to the new status quo. Territorial change requires either the agreement of the victor or renewed use of force to take it back. The army of the victor prevents the defeated from simply grabbing the territory back. The cooperation of the defeated after the war is needed to realize the policy aims of the victor. The loser may try to thwart those goals of the victor by withholding its cooperation after the war is over. Further, domestic politics in the losing state may push any leader of that state to work against the victor after the war is over. Now the victor carries the burden of threatening force if the defeated refused to cooperate. All war aims face the possibility of a challenger by the defeated later, but policy aims pose a larger commitment problem than territorial aims.

One solution to the commitment problem posed by war aims is to remove the leader of the enemy state and put someone in power who will do as the victor wants. Leaders put into power by another state and kept there to do its bidding are called *"puppets,"* and sometimes such states are called *puppet states*. Those leaders answer not to their own people but to the other government that sustains them in power. Such an arrangement can solve the commitment problem of the victor by ensuring continued cooperation in the issues for which the victor fought. This is a major reason why countries declare that the overthrow or destruction of the regime of the enemy state is their war aim. Those states believe that they cannot achieve their war aims as long as the enemy leader remains in power.

Installing a puppet is more difficult than simply winning the war. The leader of the defeated state is unlikely to go peacefully. If one side declares that it seeks to remove the leader of its opponent, there is nothing worse that it can threaten the leader of the latter with to induce him or her to surrender and leave peacefully. That leader is likely to fight the war to the last, expending every last hope to stave off his removal from power. The first disadvantage of seeking to remove the enemy leader through war is that the war will be as long and costly as possible. During the Iran-Iraq War, Ayatollah Khomenei, the leader of Iran, announced that the fall of Saddam Hussein was one of the goals of Iran in the war. He stated that peace would not be possible until Hussein was gone from Iraq. Although Iranian forces reversed the course of the war and advanced into Iraqi territory, they were not able to completely defeat the Iraqi army, even with losses of hundreds of thousands of dead on both sides. Eventually, Iraq's army turned the tide of battle and evicted the Iranian army from its territory. Khomenei was then willing to settle for a border very close to the prewar one and Saddam Hussein still in power.

President Franklin Roosevelt of the U.S. and Prime Minister Winston Churchill declared unconditional surrender of Germany and Japan as their joint war aim shortly after the U.S. entered the war. They did not believe that any peace deal would hold as long as Hitler or the

Nazi Party was in power in Germany, and so both had to go to have peace. Unconditional surrender meant that there would be no terms agreed to with Germany; it would have to surrender without any conditions and at the mercy of the Allied powers. Because Germany was powerful, the war would be long and costly. It ended only when the Soviet Army entered and conquered Berlin, the capital of Nazi Germany, block by block. Hitler killed himself in his bunker on April 30, 1945 rather than be captured by the Soviets. Germany surrendered unconditionally a week later with its once-proud military and the country in ruins. Japan, on the other hand, did secure one concession from the United States when it agreed to surrender on August 15, 1945; the Emperor was allowed to remain as the head of state in Japan, although he lost his influence and ultimate responsibility for policy. The military clique that led Japan into the war was removed from power, and several of the top leaders were tried for war crimes afterwards and then executed. Fighting to overthrow the enemy leader prolongs the war, forcing you to fight to the complete destruction of the other side's forces, making such wars costly.

Fighting to put a puppet in power also faces the problem that the puppet may have a mind of his own later on. The puppet leader may decide to try and untie his strings. He might do so to head off political opposition or because he thinks that defying the power that installed him is in the interest of his country. During the Vietnam War, the Communists referred to the leaders of South Vietnam as puppets of the United States. The U.S. had approved the coup that overthrew Ngo Dinh Diem in 1963, but it did not choose his successors in any of the wave of coups and political instability that followed. Any leader of South Vietnam was dependent on the U.S. for the military power that fought off the collapse of the Army of the Republic of Vietnam (ARVN) and the regime from the Communist forces of the National Liberation Front (NLF, commonly known as the Viet Cong) and North Vietnamese Army (NVA). The leaders of South Vietnam had to follow U.S. policy after it intervened on a large-scale beginning in 1965. Elections were held, but they were not considered free or fair. The final withdrawal of U.S. troops from South Vietnam was negotiated by President Nixon and his National Security Advisor Henry Kissinger in 1972. President Thieu of South Vietnam balked at signing the four-party agreement at the end, even though he had depended on the U.S. for his position. He thought that the deal meant the eventual fall of South Vietnam because it allowed North Vietnam to keep substantial forces inside South Vietnam. Nixon and Kissinger coerced Thieu into signing by threatening him that the U.S. would sign and complete its withdrawal even if Thieu did not sign. Puppets sometimes have minds of their own, a second drawback to the strategy of placing a puppet in power.

Territory versus Policy as War Aims

Policy aims in war generally lead to public goods for the people of the victorious state, while territorial aims can produce public goods or private benefits depending on the material and strategic value of the territory and what the leader of the state gaining the territory does with it. Consequently, leaders who answer to a small winning coalition are more likely to pursue territorial gain than policy aims in a war. They aim to expand the private benefits they can provide to their supporters. They could do this through looting the territory, taxing it to increase state revenues which then produce private benefits for supporters, or by granting control over parts of the territory to supporters. Again, all leaders provide some public goods and some private benefits, so leaders who answer to small winning coalitions do fight for policy aims and strategic territory at times. The need to produce private benefits for supporters pushes them toward favoring fighting for valuable territory.

In contrast, leaders who answer to a large winning coalition seek policy aims over territorial gain in order to produce public goods, generally the security of their citizens. When they fight for territory, it tends to be strategically valuable territory that aids their ability to defend their own people. These leaders may also fight for territorial gain if that territory is seen as part of the nation, as France saw Alsace-Lorraine. Their policy aims often face the commitment problem of getting the defeated state to cooperate after the war is over. The emphasis on policy aims makes it more likely that leaders who answer to a large winning coalition will attempt to overthrow enemy leaders to solve that commitment problem. Because doing so means the war must be fought to the complete defeat of the other side, they are more willing to seek to overthrow the enemy leader of a small, weaker country. It is difficult to completely defeat a country as powerful as their own.

Territorial and policy aims are not exclusive to one another. Some countries both take territory and install a favorable regime after the complete defeat of another. The size of the winning coalition still shapes their war aims. During World War II, the Western Allies–the United States, Great Britain, and France, all democracies with large winning coalitions–did not take territory from the defeated Axis powers. Nazi Germany and the Soviet Union–two totalitarian states whose leaders answered to smaller winning coalitions–both annexed territory into their homelands after conquest and installed or supported favorable authoritarian regimes in countries they conquered. After Germany defeated France in 1940, it took back Alsace-Lorraine and began drafting young Alsatian men. It occupied the northern and western coast of France. In the southern portion, Marshall Henri Petain, a French hero from World War I, installed an authoritarian government that cooperated with the Nazis, including deporting French Jews to concentration camps in Germany. Germany annexed parts of Poland, Belgium, the Soviet Union, and Yugoslavia and all of Luxembourg during the war. Reichsmarschall Hermann Goering, one of the Nazi leaders, assembled a personal economic empire from the conquered countries by seizing businesses he wanted in them. After the war, Stalin pushed the border of the Soviet Union westward, regaining much of the territory he had taken in 1940 and more. To this day, the city of Kaliningrad, the former German city of Königsburg, remains part of Russia, even though it is now not connected to Russia by land. Stalin seized the territory from Germany and repopulated the destroyed city with Russians.

[Map showing the Kaliningrad Oblast and frontier of Russia to show separation]

Imposing a New Regime

When the victor installs a new leader, it can also change the regime of the defeated state. Stalin encouraged or imposed Communist regimes on the Eastern European countries the Red Army occupied at the end of World War II. The occupation forces of the United States wrote the Japanese constitution in 1946. These changes in regimes sought to change the political incentives of the leaders of those countries. What sort of selection institutions should the victor install to ensure that future leaders of the defeated state will cooperate?

Leaders who answer to a large winning coalition have to respect the interests of their selectorate. If they adopt policies that are unpopular, their voters may replace them with someone else willing to do what they want. When cooperation with the victor is unpopular, the leader of the defeated state will have political incentives to end that cooperation if she answers to a large winning coalition. When cooperation is popular, a democratic system–meaning a large winning coalition–will push future leaders of the defeated state to cooperate with the victor.

Such cooperation, however, is often unpopular with the people of the defeated state. The victor then should install an autocracy–a system with a small winning coalition. The new leader can carry out the unpopular policies that the victor wants. He can insulate himself from the popular opposition to those policies by appeasing his supporters with private benefits. They may not like those policies any more than the population, but opposing their puppet leader will lead to the end of their private benefits. In short, the puppet can buy off the opposition to cooperating with the victor. Stalin followed this policy with the communist systems he imposed on Eastern European countries. The Communist leaders cooperated with the Soviet Union during the Cold War, but that cooperation was often unpopular. These countries underwent regular rounds of unrest, notably in East Germany in 1953, Hungary in 1956, Czechoslovakia in 1968, and Poland in 1980. In all of those cases, Soviet military intervention was used or threatened to ensure that the government of those countries continued to follow the Soviet line. This was the Brezhnev Doctrine: the Soviet Union would use force to support Communist governments. When Gorbachev decided to end that doctrine, the Communist systems of Eastern Europe all fell quickly in 1989. They had no real popular support. The new governments in Eastern Europe all aligned with the West.

Installing a democracy in a defeated state can lead to its refusal to cooperate with the victors later. Although the Allies in World War I did not impose a democratic system on Germany, they did insist on the fall of the Kaiser as one of their terms. Weimar Germany–the short-lived democracy established by Germans after the war–led to German demands for revision of the harsh terms of the Versailles Peace Treaty. Many German political parties sought revisions to Versailles because many Germans thought it treated Germany unfairly. It also allowed Hitler to come to power through democratic means. Although the Nazis never won a majority of the seats in the Reichstag–the German legislature, President Paul von Hindenburg invited Hitler to form a government and become Chancellor in January of 1933. Hitler then used his power to destroy the restraints on his power in the Weimar Constitution and set Germany and the world on the path to World War II.

When the population supports cooperation with the victors after the war, a democratic system can give the new leader of the defeated state the political incentive to cooperate with the victor. The most notable successes in installing democracy in defeated states are Germany and Japan after World War II. Before the war, both countries had short-lived and unsuccessful times as democracies. The United States installed democratic politics in both countries, which led to both becoming the stable and successful democracies that they are today. Further, both countries have been close allies of the United States after they became democracies. In both cases, cooperation with the United States protected them from Communism during the Cold War and provided them with access to the world economy and long period of economic growth. The democratic systems of both countries help support this cooperation with the United States because the people of both countries see it as in their interest. Breaking completely with the United States would be unpopular with the voters of both countries.

Installing new regimes is not an easy job even when the victor occupies the defeated state. The United States occupation of Japan lasted seven years from 1945 to 1952. West Germany only regained its full sovereignty in 1955, ten years after the war. Most democracies take many years before they are consolidated, meaning that there is no longer a real threat of a revision to autocracy. Autocratic governments face threats of a coup from within and revolution from outside the regime. Many in the country may oppose the new government because it is a puppet of the state that defeated them completely in war. The victor may have to continue to use force to ensure that its puppet remains in power, as the Soviet Union did in its Eastern European satellites. Imposing a regime on a defeated state is tried more often than it succeeds.

The First British Invasion of Iraq

Later in the chapter, we return to the U.S. and British invasion of Iraq in 2003 and examine it in light of the argument above. But it was not the first invasion of Iraq that overthrew its government in favor of one more friendly to Western interests. The territory that now comprises Iraq was part of the Ottoman Empire before World War I. After the war, Great Britain and France broke up Ottoman territory outside of Turkey proper into separate territories they controlled as mandates under the League of Nations. This division established the borders of Syria, Lebanon, Jordan, and Iraq as well as the British Mandate of Palestine. The Kingdom of Iraq gained its independence in 1932, although Britain had a treaty with it from 1930 that gave Britain the right to base troops in the country and move them freely throughout it.

The Second World War was not going well for Britain in early 1941. It had no powerful allies, with France being knocked out of the war the previous year and neither the Soviet Union nor the United States in the war yet. It faced Germany alone, aided only by the Commonwealth countries, notably Canada, Australia, and New Zealand, and its imperial domains in India. It faced new defeats when its forces met German forces around the Mediterranean. Britain sent troops to aid Greece after Italy invaded in 1940. The German invasion of the Balkans in April of 1941 pushed out these troops quickly. In North Africa, a small contingent of German troops and tanks led by General Erwin Rommel drove back British forces from their advances the previous year against the Italians. It looked like Nazi Germany would sweep right through to the Middle East and take control there.

The final development triggering the invasion took place inside Iraq. Rashid Ali, a former prime minister with pro-Axis leanings, seized the government in coup on April 3, 1941 with the Regent (person heading the country while the King was still a minor) fleeing the country. He had contacts with Germany and Italy, and the British government began to fear that his government would invite German troops directly into Iraq, by air if necessary. Such a move would threaten oil supplied from the Persian Gulf region. Although oil production there was not as important as it is now, it was still an important source of oil. As Germany had limited supplies of oil from the parts of Europe it controlled, the oil could provide substantial advantages to Germany's capacity to fight the war.

Even though Britain was stretched militarily, it acted quickly. It accumulated what troops it could during April of 1941 and prepared its bases inside Iraq for a military confrontation. Britain used its rights under the treaty to land troops in Iraq. This led to a confrontation with Rashid Ali's government and an Iraqi siege of a British base outside Baghdad. The siege led to military escalation where British forces pushed back the Iraqi forces. Other British forces then invaded Iraq from the west through Jordan and pushed up from the port of Basra in the south of the country. Within a month, the fighting was over, Rashid Ali fled Iraq, and the British installed a favorable government in place of his. British forces remained in Iraq throughout the war and did not leave until 1947.

Some Evidence on the External Removal of Leaders and Regimes

What changes do leaders impose on the defeated when they win a war? According to the argument in this chapter, democratic leaders should be more likely to remove the enemy leader if they win than autocrats are. Autocratic leaders are more likely to take territory than democratic leaders are. The argument does not say whether democratic leaders remove enemy leaders more often than they take territory because we cannot control for the cost of fighting the war to the complete defeat of the other side. The claim is just that selection institutions lean autocrats toward taking territory and democrats toward removing enemy leaders.

Both of these patterns exist in the history of wars over the last two centuries. Leaders who answer to a small coalition takes territory over two-fifths (42%) of the time when they win a war, while those who answer to a large winning coalition do so only one-quarter (25%) of the time.

Autocratic leaders remove the enemy leader rarely, only one-twentieth (5%) of the time after their victories, while democratic leaders do so one-sixth of the time (17%). These patterns are consistent with the argument. When the enemy leader is removed, the victor should prefer installing a regime that answers to a small winning coalition. Victors are more likely to shrink the size of the winning coalition in the defeated state from large to small, doing so three-quarters (75%) of the time than expand a small winning coalition to large one, doing so less than one-sixth (15%) of the time. This last piece of evidence is weak. States with large winning coalitions rarely lose wars, so there are only four cases where the victor removed a defeated leader who answered to a large winning coalition. There are more cases of defeated leaders who answer to small winning coalition losing, and the victor rarely imposes a democratic system on the defeated state in those cases.

Further Implications

Territorial conflict has receded over time, along with the long-term decline in the occurrence of war. States fought almost constantly over territory in the 17th and 18th centuries. Since World War II, territorial conflicts have been limited to places where borders are not accepted by all parties, such as Kashmir and the Middle East. The expansion of democracy and suffrage in democracies are one reason for the decline of territorial conflict. Democratic leaders answer to a large winning coalition, compared to other systems. The winning coalition of a democracy grows further when it adopts universal adult suffrage as has become common in the last hundred years. Because democratic leaders are less likely to seek territorial gain through war, territory has become less important as a source of conflict and been replaced by other issues. The spread of democracy is not the entire story of the decline of territorial conflict, as the growing destruction of war and the spread of the norm of territorial integrity–the idea that borders should not be changed by force, only by mutual agreement–have also played an important role.

State leaders face the threat of external removal when they go to war. Although leaders have been overthrown by the armies of other states, internal removal is far more common. Because the leader's supporters care about how their state fares in wartime, they may remove their leader if he or she fares poorly during a war. For leaders, the enemy within–those who might seek to remove him for poor performance–are more dangerous than the enemy outside–leaders of other countries that might seek to oust them.

Back to Iraq

At the end of the first Gulf War in 1991, the U.S.-led coalition imposed terms on Iraq that required its cooperation to achieve. Weapons inspections to verify the destruction of Iraq's programs of weapons of mass destruction would be more effective if Iraqi officials led the inspectors to the relevant sites and provided documents on the program. Other states at the time, South Africa and Ukraine, cooperated with inspectors from the International Atomic Energy Agency (IAEA) to demonstrate clearly and credibly that they were eliminating their nuclear capabilities and any ability to build bombs in the future. Iraq did not; they opposed and obstructed the UNSCOM inspectors in every way imaginable. The government of Iraq viewed the inspectors as spies for its enemies, particularly the United States, a charge that was not groundless. More broadly, Iraq continued to take actions to defy the coalition. The primary aim of the coalition to liberate Kuwait from Iraqi occupation and restore its sovereignty was achieved. The U.S. and Great Britain also sought wider goals to rein in Iraq's power and behavior in the Middle East. Both countries kept up coercive policies–economic sanctions, no-fly zones, and aerial bombings–to hem in Iraq and change its behavior. These actions were opposed by other major powers, notably France and Russia, that wished to return Iraq to the community of nations by ending the sanctions and other extraordinary measures. The wider aims of the U.S. required the cooperation of Iraq, cooperation that was not forthcoming.

The decade-long period of U.S. frustration with Iraq reflected the commitment problem of winning the peace when the victor seeks to change the policies of the defeated state. Removal of Saddam Hussein was a way to solve that commitment problem. In 1998, the removal of Saddam Hussein became stated U.S. policy through an act of Congress under President Clinton. This act did not say how his removal was to be accomplished. The rebellions in the Shiite south and Kurdish north of the country had been put down brutally after the war in 1991. Attempts to organize an Iraqi opposition outside the country made little concrete progress, and a covert action inside the country collapsed in 1996.

The 9/11 terrorist attacks raise the importance of the commitment problem. Al Qaeda had demonstrated both the desire and ability to kill large number of the U.S. citizens through terror attacks. The ultimate fear is that such groups will obtain and use WMDs, particularly nuclear weapons, in an attack. Concern in the Bush Administration focused on the three countries President Bush labeled "the Axis of Evil": North Korea, Iran, and Iraq. Each of them had a nuclear program at one time and a reason why they might share nuclear weapons with terrorist groups if they build them. There was no hard evidence that Iraq armed terrorist groups directly, although the world of intelligence is shady and few facts can be established absolutely. In retrospect, the inspection programs in the 1990s had ended Iraq's WMD programs, but its lack of cooperation with the inspectors obscured this fact and led many to suspect that Iraq still had a program in hiding. Iraq continued to refuse to cooperate fully with the new inspection teams sent by the UN in 2002, a lack of cooperation that some saw as justifying the war that followed. Removal of Saddam Hussein was one way to achieve the long-term policy aims of the United States concerning Iraq. 9/11 was not the reason for the 2003 invasion of Iraq, but it did heighten the concerns of the Bush Administration about achieving its aim of an Iraq that would not disrupt the Middle East or support terrorists. This is not to say that the resulting invasion was justified or wise; it is only an attempt to understand why some saw it as necessary.

Reconstructing the government of Iraq after the war proved a major challenge. U.S. forces along with the "coalition of the willing"–a group of 39 countries which sent troops to Iraq after the war–occupied the country. The U.S. ran Iraq through the Coalition Provisional Authority (CPA), a group of U.S. officials appointed from Washington. They appointed the Iraqi Governing Council, a group of Iraqis who worked with the CPA and chosen to represent different communities and groups in Iraq. Iraq regained its sovereignty and a government of Iraqis, the Iraqi Interim Government, on June 28, 2004, more than a year after the occupation began. The officials of the interim government were selected by the United States again, with an election held only in January of 2005 to elect the Iraqi Transitional Government that wrote the new constitution for Iraq. A fully elected government under the new constitution was elected in December of 2005 and took office in May of 2006. The country was still occupied, and U.S. forces had authority to conduct military operations as they saw fit. Even the elected government could act only after consultation with U.S. officials and with their agreement. Only within the last few years has the government of Iraq developed the power and authority to disagree with U.S. officials and act as they see fit. The effort to create a democratic government for Iraq has been long and is not complete yet as Iraq cannot be considered a consolidated democracy even nine years after the overthrow of Saddam Hussein.

Throughout this period, violent resistance to the occupation grew. Many groups, some small, some large, most difficult to trace, formed the insurgency. Foreign fighters traveled to Iraq to fight the U.S. occupation, although Iraqis made up the bulk of the insurgents. Opinion polls of Iraqis registered strong and wide opposition to the occupation. It is one of the few things about which Iraqis agree.

Has the overthrow of Saddam Hussein led to a government favorable to U.S. interests? There is no doubt that the WMD programs have ended, and the new Iraq is unlikely to try and restart them. Given the loss of life during the insurgency and Al Qaeda's role in it, any Iraqi government is unlikely to tolerate Al Qaeda, much less support it. The government of a democratic Iraq will respond to the wishes of its people. The unpopularity of the occupation with the people of Iraq leads Iraqi politicians to push for an end to it. Two other issues are likely to separate Iraq and the United States. Iraq has the second largest proven reserves of oil in the world, while the U.S. consumes more oil than any other country in the world. Iraq as a producer would like a high price for oil; the U.S. as a consumer a low price. The U.S. is the major supporter of Israel, while Iraqis sympathize with the Palestinians. As of now, it seems unlikely that a democratic Iraq will be a great friend of the United States. It will in any case be less of a thorn in the side of the U.S. and less disruptive of the Middle East than Saddam Hussein's Iraq was.

How to Analyze It
War Aims

States fight wars for many reasons. Sometimes they seek a range of goals through fighting. Here is how to analyze what they are fighting for and whether those aims will produce public goods or private benefits.

1. War aims are often declared publicly, although such statements are often for public consumption rather than full statements of what the leadership is trying to accomplish in the war. Has the government in question made a public statement of why it is fighting and what it is fighting for?

2. Has the government in question made a claim on territory outside its borders? Often a territorial dispute between countries can exist for years without either side resorting to the use of force to resolve it. Each side commonly has a public position on where they think the bordr should be. Public claims can often be difficult to abandon precisely because they are public and the people of the country will react negatively if concessions are made.

3. What are the characteristics of the territory in dispute? Many characteristics could matter.
- Do people live there? Is the local population wealthy or have something in common, such as ethnicity, with the people in the country in question?
- Are there valuable resources that could be extracted? Often there are claims that the territory in question might contain oil, for example. How significant are those resources? Is their existence proven or speculation?
- Does the territory have strategic value? Is it located such that it would be a good position for military bases that might allow the country in question to project military power? Does it command the area or seas around it?

Private benefits can be generated with the proceeds from valuable territory, while strategic territory can increase security.

4. Has the government of the country in question described what policies it wants its enemy to change? How do these policy aims map into public goods or private benefits? Security is the most common public good pursued. Some regimes are more concerned with their own security, including threats to overthrow the regime from inside the country, than the security of the people of their country.

5. Has the country called for the overthrow of the enemy leader? If so, have they said why they believe he or she must go? Do they appear to have intentions of fighting the war out to complete the conquest of the other side and the overthrow of the enemy leader? Often, countries at war may attack or demonize the enemy leader. It is important to determine whether the critical comments are empty propaganda or a serious intention to fight the war to a total victory.

Chapter Summary

The selection institutions of a state influence its aims during war. Leaders who answer to a small winning coalition are more likely to seek territorial gain, particularly valuable territory. Leaders who answer to a large winning coalition favor policy aims in war, most often the security of their citizens, although they may seek to add strategically important territory in their quest to secure their citizens. These policy aims often lead to a commitment problem because the defeated state may be unwilling to cooperate with the victor after the war is over. Removal of the enemy leader and replacing him with someone who will do as the victor wants is one solution of this commitment problem. Overthrow of the enemy leader requires fighting the war to the last, making it attractive only when the enemy is weak relative to the other side or the policy issue is important enough to justify a long and costly war.

Review Questions

1. Leaders who answer to a small winning coalition more likely to seek territory through war than leaders who answer to a large winning coalition. Explain. When a leader who answers to a large winning coalition seeks territory, how do their territorial goals differ from those of a leader answering to a small winning coalition?

2. Explain the commitment problem involved in winning the peace after a war. How do the winning coalition and selectorate of the losing state affect the magnitude of this commitment problem?

Chapter 17
The Democratic Peace

Democracies almost never fight wars with one another, even though they fight about as often as other states do. This pair of regularities is known as *the democratic peace*. This chapter seeks to explain this pattern and its significance for world politics. We do so by examining a series of different explanations for why this pattern has occurred. We explain the logic of each argument and examine evidence for and against each. This examination also shows how political scientists try to think though a puzzle about politics by proposing possible explanations, thinking through how each explains the puzzle, and comparing further explanations from each to evidence.

The democratic peace is one result from the scientific study of world politics which has penetrated the real world of international politics. Both Presidents Clinton and Bush cited the democratic peace in speeches that sought to promote democracy through the foreign policies of the United States. If democracy causes states not to fight one another, a world of democracies would be a peaceful world. But the explanation of the pattern matters for this projection. If the pattern has occurred for some other reason, then a world of democracies would not be peaceful. The promotion of democracy would not lead to peace in this case. This is why the explanation of the pattern matters. It influences how we understand whether the pattern will continue to hold in the future with states that are not yet, but could become, democracies.

The Spread of Democracy

Democracy as a form of government is recent in world history. Although ancient Athens was a democracy of sorts and the source of the word is Greek meaning "rule of the people," with *demos* meaning people and *cracy* for who rules (as in aristocracy, another word we get from ancient Greece), modern democracy traces its roots back two to three hundred years. Great Britain developed from aristocratic institutions into its modern system of democratic representation with the adoption of competitive elections and as Parliament slowly gained control over policy from the monarch. The United States Constitution adopted in 1787 created a federal system where both national and state officials were elected by the voters, with suffrage restricted to adult white males who owned property. Switzerland has also allowed voters, again adult males only, to elect those who govern them in some cantons (the parallel to states in the U.S.) since the Middle Ages.

Democracy means many things to many people. For our purposes, the people elect those who govern them in regular, competitive elections in a democracy. The suffrage–those who can vote legally–is widespread although it need not be universal to all adults. As mentioned in the earlier discussion of selectorate theory, the expansion of suffrage to all adults has expanded the size of the winning coalition within democracies. Elections are regularly held, not at the whim of the leader. One election does not a democracy makes; the anticipation of future elections is essential to democracy. Elections are competitive with more than one candidate with some real change of winning running for most offices. Those elected have control over the policies of the country. The people must have the ability to remove their political leaders through free and fair elections. Political parties, like the Democrats and the Republicans, commonly organize nationally to contest elections with each party having some political program for the country. The legislative power–the ability to make laws–and the executive power–the ability to administer the laws–are separated, although both may be held by the same political party at once as in Great Britain. The government faces a political opposition which can openly state its positions and criticize the government. Citizens have civil rights so they can organize openly and freely for politics. Courts are not controlled by the government to make political decisions in its favor, and citizens charged with crimes have rights to fair trial. There is not agreement on which rights are fundamental, just that democracies allow free and open politics. Competitive elections for office are at the heart of democracy, even though democracies may require a range of other institutions to tie those elections to the formation and execution of policy.

There are different types of democracy. The United States has a presidential form of democracy with a strong executive (the President) elected separately from the legislature. Parliamentary systems, which are common in Western Europe and other states which trace their heritage to Great Britain, elect the legislature and form the government among the parties which won the most seats there. If a single party has a majority of the seats, it forms a government by itself, and the leader of that party becomes the Prime Minister, the executive of the country. Some elect the legislature by majority vote within fixed districts, as in the United States and Britain, while others use proportional representation, where seats are allocated in proportion to the votes won by each party. Single-member districts commonly lead to two parties (at least within each district), while proportional representation leads to more than two parties. In some cases, these parties appeal to very few voters in the country. In all democracies, though, leaders are selected and removed through elections. Democratic leaders may not always be running for office, but they do have an eye on the next election when they govern.

Successful democracy requires a range of political institutions including but not restricted to how elections are conducted, how the legislature makes laws, who carries out the laws with what limits, and how courts function. It takes time to establish these institutions: time to develop the rules and see how they work in practice, time to train people into the specific roles of the institutions, and time for everyone in the society to accept elections and representative legislatures as the way politics in conducted even when they lose. As in the case of Weimar Germany, a new democracy may falter, slipping back into non-democratic governance. We will speak of *consolidated democracies* (also referred to as *stable democracies*), those where democracy is widely accepted across the spectrum of political views and will continue to govern the country in the future as far as we can tell. There may be doubt about whether *new democracies* will become consolidated.

A hundred years ago, there were relatively few democracies in the world, almost entirely in North America and Western Europe. Other states had some elements of democracy but were not because elections did not lead to control over national policy. In Germany before World War I, the Reichstag–the legislature–was elected by all adult males, but the Kaiser could run important areas of policy, particularly military and foreign policy, without the support of the Reichstag. These hybrid systems which combined some elements of democracy but not all existed then and now. The end of World War I led to new states in eastern Europe, many of which experimented with democracy, although only Czechoslovakia consolidated before World War II. The end of World War II brought democracy to Japan and most of western Europe including countries like Germany and Italy where it had failed before. The breakup of the European colonial empires created many new states, but few of them became stable democracies with the notable exception of India. The democratic transitions of Spain and Portugal in the mid-1970s triggered a wave of democratizations first among some but not all autocracies aligned with the United States in the Cold War. The end of the Cold War spread democracy to the former Communist regimes of Eastern Europe and then more generally to regions like Africa and Asia. Democracy has spread more widely now than ever in history, but some states revert to authoritarian rule while others adopt some, but not all, democratic institutions, leaving them as hybrid states as Wilhelmine Germany was.

[Graph showing growth in number of democracies
and percent of states which are democracies since 1900]

Democracies and War

Political scientists began to study the democratic peace intensively beginning in the mid-1980s when the pattern was first reported. One line of research concerned whether the pattern was actually present in the historical record. There has been disagreement about what states are democracies, in part because there is disagreement about what democracy is, means, and requires. Similarly, there is disagreement about what acts constitute "war." Depending on the precise definitions of democracy and war, there are events that could be considered wars between democracies. Finland, a democracy, fought with the Axis powers during the Second World War, but it fought only the Soviet Union, which most certainly was not a democracy. Spain during the time of the Spanish-American War in 1898 had an elected legislature as did Germany at the outbreak of World War I. In both countries, the monarch held effective political power; the power of the legislature was limited. There are also smaller uses of violence between democracies that do not commonly reach the level of warfare. The United States used covert action several times during the Cold War to remove democratically elected leaders in countries aligned with it, such as Iran in 1953 and the Dominican Republic in 1963. While there are cases of conflict between democracies in the grey area of whether they are war or whether the states were truly democracies, we can say that democracies are much less likely to fight one another than other pairs of states.

A second line of research has examined the other half of the pattern: do democracies fight wars about as often as other states? Here the claim is that democracies are less likely to fight overall. This question is complicated because other factors than just the system of a country influence whether it fights. Major powers, the most powerful countries in the world, fight more often than other states, often called minor powers. Historically, democracies have often major powers, such as the U.S., Britain, and France. If they fight wars as often as other states, might we say that their major power status leads them to fight more often which obscures their tendencies as democracies to fight less often. The general, but not universal, view among scholars is that if democracies fight less often than other states, the difference is not large. The democratic peace then is the peaceful tendency of democracies when they deal with one another, not with non-democracies. This is the puzzle then, why have democracies been able to resolve their differences without war almost all the time even though they have resorted to war about as other types of states?

We turn now to lay out three different plausible explanations of the democratic peace.

Explanation 1: Historical Coincidence

As noted earlier, democracies were uncommon before World War II. The democracies after the war were primarily in Western Europe and North America. During the Cold War, most of them aligned with the United States. Those that did not, like Sweden and Austria, remained steadfastly neutral between the two blocs. The number of democracies expanded greatly when the Cold War ended. The first explanation is that the democratic peace is a historical fluke, devoid of any special meaning or significance. The pattern occurred by chance when there were few democracies before World War II and then alignment with the United States kept the peace among the democracies during the Cold War.

War between states has been rare over the last two hundred years, even if it has been devastating when it did occur. Because there were few democracies before World War II, there are not many pairs of democracies. When an event happens only rarely, as war does, and there are few cases that could go to war, it may just be a matter of luck that there were no wars between democracies before World War II. Political scientists use statistics to check whether patterns we find in the historical record could have occurred by chance. These tests cannot rule out the possibility that the absence of war between democracies before World War II simply occurred by chance.

During the Cold War, the world was divided between armed camps headed by the United States in the west and the Soviet Union in the east. Both camps had a distinctive ideology and form of government. The West was generally democracies that believed in capitalism and free markets; the East had Communist governments which controlled the means of production and the economy generally. As the European colonial empires ended and new states were formed in Africa and Asia, some of these new states aligned with one side or the other, but many chose to remain neutral in what was called the Non-Aligned Movement. The common interests within each bloc and the demands of political competition between the two blocs held the West together and at peace. Democracies did not fight during the Cold War then because they needed to stick together.

These two points together are the first candidate explanation for the democratic peace. There is nothing to explain according to this view. Because of luck, democracies did not fight when they were not bound together by the common interests of the Cold War. Most of the cases for the pattern come from the Cold War when only the common interests of the democracies stopped them from fighting. There is further evidence for this view; democracies engaged in disputes with one another about as often as other states did before World War II. Disputes occur more often than wars do. While all wars begin with a dispute, many disputes are resolved before war breaks out. This lesser form of international conflict is easier to find than wars, and pairs of democracies had disputes with one another about as often as other pairs of countries before World War II. Democracies were not reluctant to threaten one another with force to resolve their differences during that time.

The historical record contradicts other implications of this explanation though. If common interests produced through the bipolar competition of the Cold War prevented war among the democracies, it also should have prevented conflict within the Communist bloc. It did not. The Soviet Union invoked the Brezhnev Doctrine to intervene with military force in the Communist states of Eastern Europe. It invaded Hungary after the Communist government there fell and the new government considered taking Hungary out of the Warsaw Pact. The resulting brief war killed about 10,000, mainly Hungarians fighting Soviet tanks. Soviet forces intervened in Czechoslovakia in 1968 to put an end to a liberalizing government there, although the fighting did not rise to the level of a full-fledged war. The United States also used military force against some non-democracies aligned with it, notably the Dominican Republic in 1965. It also used covert action to influence the internal politics of even some of its democratic allies, particularly supporting conservative parties in France and Italy against Communist parties in the late 1940s. These acts did not rise to the level of wars, of course, but bipolar competition drove these conflicts rather than discouraged them. Later, when democracies in the western bloc found themselves in disputes with one another, they managed to resolve them without fighting. At the same time as the Soviet invasion of Hungary, Britain, France, and Israel went to war with Egypt so that the British and French could regain control of the Suez Canal which Egypt had nationalized. President Eisenhower disapproved of the invasion and used economic threats to force the British and French to withdraw from Egypt. Democracies in the Western bloc ended their disputes without fighting, something which the non-democratic Eastern bloc could not.

This explanation also hinged on the observation that pairs of democracies did not act differently from other types of states before World War II. This is only partially correct. The escalation rate–how often disputes ended in war–for pairs of democracies is noticeably lower than it is for other pairs of countries during this period. This pattern matters for the democratic peace. The difference in escalation rates shows that pairs of democracies are able to resolve their differences without fighting. It does not claim that democracies never have serious disagreements with one another. The other two explanations we examine focus on how democracies are able to resolve their differences without resorting to war.

Explanation 2: Signaling

Signaling of resolve is critical to resolving disputes short of war. One state's resolve is its private information, meaning that the other side must judge it from its actions. The other side doubts the credibility of claims of resolve because each side has an incentive to misrepresent their resolve to gain what they want. These doubts can lead a side to remain firm when it needs to make concessions to avoid war. The ability of a government to communicate credibly that the issues in dispute are important enough to it to use force provides an advantage in crises. It gives that government the ability to extract concessions from the other side. It also helps avoid war by sending credible signals that aid in reaching a resolution of the dispute.

Open political opposition to the government is essential to democracy. Although individual citizens can speak out against their government, the political parties not in the government form the opposition. Currently in the United States, the Republicans are the opposition to the Democratic government of Barack Obama. The political opposition seeks to get into power in the next election. They criticize the government in part to draw a contrast with it, pull support away from the government, and attract voters to their party for the next election. The opposition must judge when and how to criticize the government carefully. If the policy or act of government they criticize is popular, they will lose support rather than gain it. The most effective criticisms of the government point out policies that have clearly failed. All political parties try to portray their own actions and statements in the best light and those of their opponents in the worst. These explanations are now called "spin" from President Clinton's campaign for President in 1992. Although all parties spin their own line, the electorate can judge clearly successful policies from those that have obviously failed. You can fool some of the people all of the time, but you cannot fool all of the people all of the time.

International crises pose a problem for opposition parties. They often lead to clear outcomes of success or failure for a state and its government. If the government has been foolish and pushed an issue where the other side is unlikely to give in, the opposition can gain ground politically by challenging that stance and doing so early. But if the issue in dispute is vital to the country and the government is willing to fight over it, the opposition will lose politically if it does not support the government. Because the outcome of a crisis is often clear and public, the voters will be able to cut through the spin and draw their own conclusions about it.

The opposition in a democracy works like a second signal of the government's resolve in a crisis. The opposition understands the resolve of its government better than the government of the other state in the crisis. The opposition deals with the government every day. Additionally, it has a better understanding of what is important to its country and what the country's military capabilities are. Because the opposition has a more accurate view of what its government will do in a crisis, its actions and responses to what the government are another source of information about the resolve of the government. An autocracy lacks this second signal because political opponents are afraid to speak out against the government out of fear that they will be punished if they do so. Two signals are better than one.

When will the opposition speak out against the government in a crisis, and what effect does it have? The figure below shows the resolve of the government along a line. The resolve of the government increases toward the right end of the line. The figure also shows what actions the government will take in a crisis without considering the consequences of political opposition. It shows then both what a democratic government would do if it had no opposition and how an

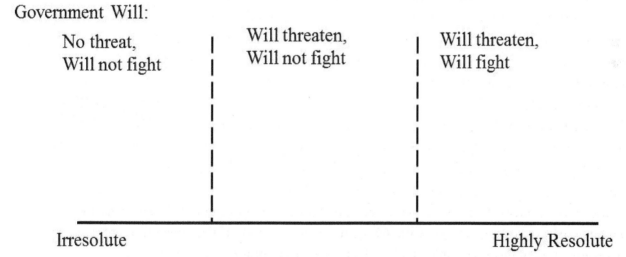

Figure 22
Action of the Government in a Crisis based on its Resolve

autocratic government acts. The most resolute governments are both willing to make threats and to use force to achieve their aims if the threats do not succeed. The least resolute governments do not make a threat at all, and no dispute occurs. Those in the middle range are willing to make a threat. They consider the issue important enough to demand concessions, but they are not confident enough in their ability to prevail militarily to use force to get what they want.

Given what the government would like to do acting on its own, how should the opposition react during the dispute? When the government is highly resolute, the opposition is likely to know this and that the government will probably prevail. That outcome will be popular with the electorate. The opposition will lose politically if it opposes the government in this case, and so it should support the government in the crisis. It will not gain politically, but at least it will not lose ground politically to the government. The area on the right of the figure below shows the range of resolve where the opposition will support the government. When the government is not highly resolved, it is unlikely to prevail in a dispute. Knowing this, the opposition sees this as an opportunity to criticize the government and gain politically if it does falter publicly in the crisis.

Figure 23
How the Opposition Responds based on the Government's Resolve

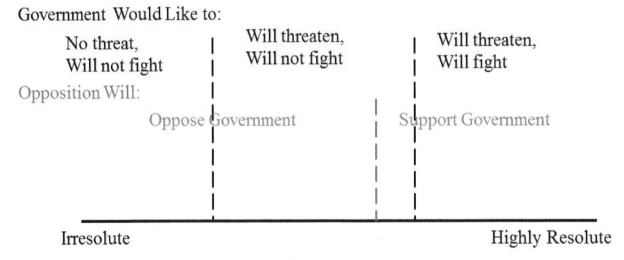

What effect with the reaction of the opposition have on what the government does during the dispute? It can anticipate how the opposition will respond. If the opposition will support the government, then the government can do as it likes. Even if it has to back down in the crisis, the opposition will not gain a political advantage because it supported what the government did. When the opposition will criticize the government during the crisis, there is an additional cost to the opposition beyond the international consequences of what it does. The opposition will gain politically if the government fails to prevail in the crisis. In some of the cases where it would like to make a threat, the government will not out of concern for the domestic political consequences of doing so and then losing the crisis. The prospect of opposition and the political costs it could have discipline the government. It does not make some threats that it would like to on its own. Further, these threats are likely to be speculative; cases where the government does not think its position is strong but is willing to make a threat in the hope that the other side will give it what it wants without fighting.

Figure 24
How the Government Acts considering the Reaction of the Opposition

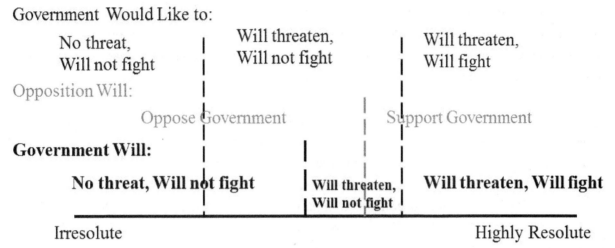

Resolve of Government

The prospect of open political opposition has two effects on how a democratic government acts during a crisis. First, when the opposition supports the government in a crisis, it makes the signal of resolve stronger. As you can see in Figure 3 above, the government is likely to be resolute enough that it will fight when the opposition supports it. The other government can see the public support of the opposition, will understand that it must either concede the stakes or fight. Second, the possibility of the opposition exploiting the crisis for political gain disciplines the government from making some threats. In Figure 3, this is the region between the thicker, dashed black line on the left and the thinner dashed line in the middle. These are cases of weak, speculative threats, cases where the government is seeing whether it can gain concessions from the other side easily. Although the government would like to test the resolve of the other state here, it declines to do so because the opposition will speak out against it and failure internationally has consequences in domestic politics as well.

This argument leads to two patterns we can find in the data. One, threats by democracies should be more effective than those by other types of states. They should cause the other side to make concessions more often. This is true in historical data sets, although the effect is not strong. Further, threats by some types of non-democracies are about as effective in extracting concessions from their targets. Second, the opposition should support the government almost all the time when a democratic government makes a threat. The cases where the opposition publicly criticizes its government during a crisis should be rare. The government tries to find another way than a public dispute to address its concerns if it believes the opposition will not support it.

The reaction of Democrats in Congress to the two wars the United States has fought against Iraq in the Middle East exemplify how a political opposition responds to its government during a crisis before war breaks out. Before the Gulf War in 1991, President George H. W. Bush sought a Congressional resolution allowing him to make the decision whether to use force to expel Iraq from its occupation of Kuwait. There were public concerns that the war would be costly and difficult. Iraq built a massive army, the fourth largest in the world, by inducting most of the young men in the country. It constructed extensive fortifications in Kuwait. Most believed that the United States would have to fight a hard war to force the Iraqi Army out of Kuwait and suffers thousands, perhaps tens of thousands, of casualties doing so. The vote in the Senate was very close, 52-47. Few Democratic Senators voted to give President Bush the authority to go to war on his own, but they were also unwilling to block him from acting. One of the few Democratic Senators who voted to give that authority was then-Senator Al Gore, who had run for the Democratic nomination to be President in 1988 and would run for the Presidency again in 1992 and 2000. He was concerned in part about the effects of a "no" vote on his viability as a political candidate. The war proved to be short and much less costly than most feared. In 2003, President George W. Bush sought Congressional authorization to use force against Iraq earlier in the crisis, in October 2002, five months before the war. It was generally believed that the United States could invade Iraq and win quickly at a low cost from the experience of the Gulf War 12 years earlier. Congressional Democrats split on the resolution, with 29 of the 50 Democratic Senators voting in favor of authorizing President Bush to use force. Prominent Democratic Senators considering the possibility of running for President later, such as Senator Hillary Clinton of New York (now Secretary of State) voted for the resolution. Although the invasion and overthrow of Saddam Hussein was accomplished easily and at a low cost, an insurgency against the occupation broke out, leading to the long, military involvement of the United States in Iraq. Interestingly in both cases, the Democrats who were then next elected to the Presidency, Bill Clinton and Barack Obama, were not in Congress at the time of those votes, and so did not have to take public votes for or against those wars. President Obama did speak out against the war beforehand, but as an Illinois State Senator, his opposition was obscure and had no effect on whether the U.S. went to war. That opposition did help him greatly during the campaign for the Democratic nomination for the Presidency in 2008.

The Fashoda Crisis

Crises between democracies are relatively rare. The Fashoda Crisis in 1898 was the last political and military confrontation between France and Great Britain. They had been great rivals for centuries, going back to the Middle Ages. They fought massive wars, some of which determined that Britain would dominate North America and India. After Fashoda, Britain and France became allies and worked and fought together throughout the 20th century, although not always harmoniously.

The "Scramble for Africa" began in the 1880s. The European powers began establishing formal colonial control over large regions of Africa, before this time, they had limited their colonial control to coastal regions of the continent. France made most of West Africa its colony, while Britain established a protectorate over Egypt with putative control over the Sudan south of Egypt up the Nile River. In 1885, a large rebellion led by the Mahdi ended effective British control over the Sudan. In 1897, the Foreign Minister of France, Gabriel Hanotaux, came up with a plan to try and establish a French claim to at least part of the Sudan. He ordered a military expedition led by Major Jean-Baptiste Marchand to set out from French West Africa, cross the continent, and establish a French base on the Nile at Fashoda. Given the state of rebellion, Britain had no effective control over Sudan, and France could then claim that it deserved part of the Sudan through its effective control. On May 1, 1897, Major Marchand's small force set off. It arrived at Fashoda on July 10, 1898, triggering the crisis.

[Map of Central Africa showing Sudan and routes of Marchand's expedition across Africa and Kitchener's force up the Nile]

Britain at the same time organized a much larger Anglo-Egyptian military force under Sir (later Lord) Herbert Kitchener to travel up the Nile and reestablish control over the Sudan. The expeditionary force crushed the Sudanese at the Battle of Omdurman on September 2, 1898. Kitchener led a force of gunboats up the Nile, arriving at Fashoda on September 18. The meeting of the forces was amiable at Fashoda but brought the crisis to a head. Both countries mobilized their navies in anticipation of the possibility of war. The new French Foreign Minister, Theophile Delcassé, gave into British demands and withdrew Marchand's force on November 3. Several months later, Britain and France agreed to a dividing line between their colonial empires in Africa, a division that gave all of the Sudan to Britain. This is another example where the final resolution of the issue comes after the end of the crisis. Delcassé's decision to withdraw Marchand's expedition made it clear that France would make concessions to satisfy Britain.

Why did Britain hold firm and France back down? The British Navy was superior to the French Navy, but a war would have been costly to both countries. Delcassé was more focused on Germany and saw Britain as a prospective ally, an alliance eventually formed in 1904. Although these factors favored Britain in the crisis, they do not answer important questions. Was Britain willing to fight for Fashoda? Was Britain willing to make concessions over this remote area of the Sudan to avoid war? If Britain was willing to fight, how could it communicate that resolve to the French government? Would the French understand those signals? The peaceful resolution showed that the French government, and particularly Foreign Minister Delcassé, were convinced that Fashoda was not worth risking war over.

Both Britain and France were democracies of different sorts. There were two parties in

British politics at the time, the Conservatives and the Liberals. Lord Salisbury of the Conservative Party was Prime Minister at the time of the crisis. During the crisis, the Liberal Party publicly supported the government, arguing that British interests in Sudan were vital and worth fighting for. France, on the other hand, was a multiparty democracy. The opposition parties owned newspapers which they used to advance their views to the French public. The criticism of the government in these papers was fierce. This opposition led the British government to conclude that the French government would give in, strengthening their resolution to insist on the withdrawal of Marchand.

The Fashoda Crisis is an example of how democracies can signal their resolve more credibly than other types of states. This observation by itself does not explain the democratic peace however. What happens if two highly resolute democracies face one another in a crisis? Both would signal their resolve, but neither would be willing to back down. To answer this puzzle, we need the third explanation.

Explanation 3: Leader Incentives

As discussed in the two previous chapters, the threat of removal from office enters into the judgments of political leaders in a crisis. Leaders of democracies answer to a large winning coalition and so tend to produce public goods to reward the large number of supporters they need to retain power. Success in a crisis or war acts like a public good. Further, democratic leaders pursue public goods such as security through their foreign policy. Autocratic leaders, on the other hand, can remain in power by continuing to provide their small group of supporters with private benefits. Those supporters will be unhappy if their leader fails in a crisis but may be unwilling to remove him out of fear of losing their substantial benefits under him. All told, it is easier to remove a democratic leader from office than an authoritarian. Very few democratic leaders hold office for ten years in one stretch, but many authoritarians held power for multiple decades. This list includes many of the worst dictators of the 20th century, including Josef Stalin and Mao Zedong.

Democratic leaders face a greater risk of removal from office if they lose a dispute than autocrats do. This greater risk leads them to choose their crises carefully. They are reluctant to engage in public crises if there is a substantial risk they will need to back down to prevent war. This caution means democratic leaders will only threaten to use force when they are confident that they can prevail with or without war. A democratic leader enters or starts a crisis only when his country is in a strong position. The most common advantage is having much greater military capabilities than the opponent. War if necessary is likely to be short and successful when your country is much stronger than its opponent. Democratic leaders choose their wars carefully.

It is unlikely that both sides enter a crisis thinking they are very likely to win if war breaks out. Their relative military capabilities are generally public, even if the specifics of the military comparison depend on elements of private information. Put another way, if the United States and Panama fight a war, all in both countries expect that the U.S. will win and relatively easily. It may be the Panamanians will fight very hard because the issue at stake for them is vital and that the U.S. may not be willing to pay a high cost for those stakes. But the general picture of how the war will unfold is seen by all. Indeed, the United States did invade Panama in 1989 with the objective of overthrowing the leader of Panama, Manuel Noreiga, who had defied the U.S. government concerning the Panama Canal, was involved in smuggling illegal drugs into the United States, and then fixed the results of an election to the Presidency of Panama which he lost. Noreiga and his supporters had every reason to fight for, and the issues were not vital to the U.S. But the cost was low and the war but a few days because U.S. military power was overwhelming. Noreiga cannot have had much hope of victory, but fighting was no worse than giving in for him. When power is more even between the two sides, both sides may hold some credible hope for victory. War is likely to be long and costly in these cases. Comparing these different situations, it is unlikely that both sides in a crisis think they are likely to win easily. There are unequal cases when both sides recognize which side is stronger and likely to win. There are equal cases where neither side thinks it can win a war easily. But there are not cases where both sides think they will win a war easily.

These expectations combine with the caution of democratic leaders to explain the democratic peace. Democratic leaders are willing to fight only when they are very likely to win, but both sides cannot enter a crisis with that optimism. When democracies face one another in a crisis, either one is much stronger than the other or they are roughly equal. In the former case, the weaker side will seek out a peaceful resolution rather than fight. In the latter case, neither democracy will want to fight, making it easier for both of them to reach a peaceful settlement.

Autocrats, being able to sustain their hold on power despite failure, may be willing to take greater risks in international conflicts. Failure may be an option for them. This is not to say that autocrats wish to lose war, only that they are willing to run greater risks of losing a war than democratic leaders are. Because they can insulate their political fortunes from the consequences of their bad decisions, they are willing to take actions with a substantial risk of failure. War against a stronger state is one such risk. Put another way, autocrats can indulge their "taste for war" because they avoid the domestic political consequences of such decisions. This observation does not mean that autocratic leaders always seek war or are universally belligerent, only that in some cases they are willing to fight in circumstances when a democratic leader would seek peaceful settlement.

Selection institutions influence how national leaders judge the risks in a crisis and what settlements they are willing to accept to avoid war. Judging the risk of war compares the consequences of war–winning and losing with all their consequences–to reaching a settlement somewhere between the two. What concessions is a leader will to grant to reach a moderate settlement that avoids the lottery between winning and losing that war presents? For democratic leaders, losing a war is much worse than a settlement while winning is not much better than such a settlement. This is why democratic leaders need to have confidence that they will win before they venture war. For autocratic leaders, winning is much better than a moderate settlement while losing is not much worse than a settlement. Democratic leaders are willing to offer more in a settlement to avoid war, while autocrats need not do so.

This difference in willingness to fight and to make concessions to avoid war explains why democracies and autocracies fight one another. Autocrats are willing to run the risks of war even when they are unlikely to win. They recognize that democratic leaders are willing to make concessions in general to avoid war. Threatening democratic states with war may compel concessions without war. They are more reluctant to threaten other autocrats with war because they are more likely to fight back. Autocrats adopt belligerent tactics with democracies to intimidate them into concessions. In some cases, these tactics work, such as they did for Hitler in the Munich Crisis in 1938. In other cases, the democratic leader judge that she is in a strong position to win a war and so fights back. She judges the issues are important enough to fight for and her chance of winning high enough to merit the risks and costs of war. Autocracies go looking for trouble, and sometimes they find it.

Together, these arguments explain both parts of the democratic peace. Democracies do not go to war with one another because their leaders are willing to fight only when they believe they are likely to win and it is unlikely that both leaders will believe. Democracies fight wars as often as other types of states because autocracies and democracies are more likely to fight than pairs of autocracies. The autocrats think democracies can be intimidated and so are willing to threaten them with force. Sometimes the democracy fights back because it believes it is likely to win.

Other Implications

If the third explanation is correct, it implies other patterns in when and how democracies fight. If democratic leaders choose their wars carefully and are willing to fight only when they are likely to win, democracies should win the wars they fight. Over the last 200 years, democracies have won four-fifths (80%) of the wars they have fought. Although there are notable defeats by democracies, such as the Vietnam War was for the United States, democracies overwhelmingly win the wars they fight. Choosing to fight only when they are likely to win is not the only explanation of this pattern, but it is an important part of the explanation.

Second, democracies should be more likely to attack autocracies than the other way around when they fight. War between autocracies and democracies occur because the autocracy believes the democracy will not fight. War occurs in these cases when the democracy demonstrates its willingness to fight by initiating the fighting.

Third, democracies should fight wars which are shorter and less costly than those fought by autocracies. Because they choose to win only when they are much stronger, they should overwhelm their opponents quickly and at a low cost. Democracies do generally fight shorter war with fewer casualties. Selection is part of the explanation here, although again there are other reasons. If the initial expectations of a short war are proven false, democracies are more willing to end these wars with moderate settlements instead of fighting on for a complete victory.

Open Questions

For each of the three explanations, we looked for their further implications. If this explanation was true, what else should be true beyond just the basic pattern of the democratic peace? If these additional implications are true, we have more confidence that the explanation is true. We also learn more patterns about world politics, such as the strong tendency for democracies to win the wars they fight. This is one way that political scientists sort through different explanations of a pattern or an event. The first explanation that the democratic peace was a historical coincidence implies that the Communist bloc also should have been peaceful during the Cold War, but that was not true. The signaling explanation implies that threats by democracies should be more effective, which has been the pattern in the historical record. The leader incentives explanation implied that democracies were more likely to win the wars they fight, which has also been true so far.

Both the second and the third explanations could be true together. Neither of them asserts that the other is false. The democratic peace could be the result of both more credible signals of resolve from democracies induced by open political opposition and the reluctance of democratic leaders to wage war when the odds are not greatly in their favor. Neither of these explanations is complete. Both leave some questions open for further research. The signaling explanation does not account for why democracies win the wars they fight nor why democracies and autocracies are more likely to fight than pairs of autocracies. The autocratic peace, the observation that pairs of autocracies are less likely to fight than the mixed pairs of a democracy and an autocracy, is weaker than the democratic peace. Neither explanation accounts fully for that pattern.

Finally, neither signaling nor leader incentives account for why some democratic borders become so peaceful that war is unimaginable across them. No one in the United States or Canada seriously believes that war is possible between their two countries. Their long shared border is open and easily crossed, although border security has been tightened since 9/11. Borders in Western Europe have acquired the same quality of certainty that neither side seeks to challenge them through force and so they become open to the movement of people and goods over the last 50 years. This certainty that neither side will revert to war also produces a contrary effect, the willingness to use force to emphasize the importance of a given issue. Canada seized a Spanish fishing boat just outside Canadian territorial waters in the North Atlantic in 1996 to focus attention on Spanish, and more generally European, violations of restrictions on the number and type of fish caught. No one thought the seizure would escalate to war, although it did produce a small crisis between Canada and the European Union. Of course, few borders in the world have this "taken-for-granted" acceptance and openness. But it is a characteristic that these explanations do not account for.

Democracies and Foreign Policy

The democratic peace also points to important insights about the foreign policies of democracies. First and foremost, democracies are not peace-loving states. They are willing to use force against other states to get what they want. They are more likely to do so when they are much stronger than their opponent. The United States has used force many times since it engaged with the world after World War II, typically against smaller countries where there is little chance of clear military defeat. Democracies have also been willing to use covert action—violence conducted by agents in ways to make it difficult to trace the responsible party. They turn to covert action when the open use of force would be politically embarrassing or the risk of failure is significant. Covert action allows the acting government to publicly deny what it has done. Democracies then are willing to engage in violence to advance their own ends. The difference is that when democracies face off against one another, they almost always find a way to resolve the issue without resort to war.

Democracies use force cautiously because of the domestic political consequences of failure. This caution means that democracies make fewer and smaller blunders in foreign policy compared to other types of systems. They do make mistakes, some of them costly. Many Americans consider both the Vietnam and Iraq Wars as major disasters for U.S. foreign policy and the country more generally. But neither of these wars matches the blunders of launching the Second World War carried out by Nazi Germany and Imperial Japan. Both societies were devastated by these wars, and both governments removed through conquest by the victors they had attacked. Democracies also reverse their policies more readily than other types of states. The ability to change leaders more easily aids such change in policy. Because a leader in power is the strongest advocate for his policies, the easiest way to change such policies is to change leaders. Democracies do this as a matter of course through regular elections. Leader change in autocracies happens through violence or behind closed doors.

Should We Create a World of Democracies?

The democratic peace, if real, holds out the hope for a peaceful world. If democracies do not fight with one another because of their democratic nature, war would disappear in a world of democracies. This promise was one reason why both Presidents Clinton and Bush appealed to the democratic peace in speeches that acknowledged the spread of democracy as goal of U.S. foreign policy. But should democracy be spread, by force if necessary?

First, increasing the number of democracies may increase, rather than decrease, the chance of war in the short run. Recall that the mixed pairs, a democracy and an autocracy, pose the highest risk of war among the possible pairs of systems. A world of half democracies and half autocracies would have the maximum of these mixed pairs and so the highest overall risk of war. The number of democracies in the world is less than one-half of all states. Converting more autocracies to democracies would increase the number of mixed pairs and raise the risk of war in the world as a whole. In the long run, increasing the number of democracies would bring down the number of these mixed pairs, leading to a more peaceful world. Nevertheless, the question of whether the long-run decrease in war outweighs the short-run increases is open and unresolved.

Second, democracy is difficult to establish and consolidate in a state. It is more than simply holding an election for high office. As noted earlier in the chapter, it often takes decades for democracy to consolidate in a country, until it reaches the stage where democracy is taken for granted. Groups that benefitted from the previous autocratic system often work against the new democratic system, sometimes through violence. In Iraq, members of the Baath Party formed one key element of the insurgency that fought against the occupation and the Iraqi government. They intimidated many voters in the 2006 elections, and few Sunnis voted. Even when there are no organized groups fighting against democracy, the establishment of democratic institutions, such as political parties and an independent judiciary, takes time. Iraq may be on the road to becoming a stable democracy but that will not be clear for a decade at least.

Third, partial moves to democratization may raise the risk of war, rather than lower it. Few systems jump from autocracy to democracy. Instead, they add some elements of democracy, such as national elections, but not the full range of democratic institutions. In some cases, the need to attract voters to gain power leads politicians to make ethnic appeals or target external enemies. Slobodan Milosevic rose to power in Serbia during the breakup of Yugoslavia by appealing to Serbian nationalism and encouraging the use of violence to protect the privileges of Serbs. He is held largely responsible for the breakup of the Yugoslav Federation and the resulting wars among and within the successor states, although he was not alone in his appeals to ethnic solidarity and the use of violence in those states. Political scientists disagree about whether moves toward democratization are dangerous by themselves, or whether moves to restore autocracy are the primary danger.

In summary, spreading democracy by force is unlikely to lead to a peaceful world. Establishing democracy by force when there are organized groups opposed to it is difficult at best. The process of opening up a closed system may release demands that raise the risk of violent conflict. This is not to say that democratic states should not seek to encourage democracy around the world. Rather, the proper role is supporting those countries that are attempting to democratize. The economic appeal of joining the EU has been a powerful tool in encouraging European states to commit to becoming democracies. First, Spain and Portugal did so in the

1970s in part so they could join and gain access to its common market. The EU has waited until these new democracies have consolidated before allowing them to join. Spain and Portugal, for example, were not admitted as members until 1986. The appeal of joining was also used to encourage the post-Communist states of Eastern Europe to commit themselves to democracy. The promotion of democracy is easiest when the people of a country want to become a democracy.

Chapter Summary

Democracies are very unlikely to fight one another, even though they fight wars about as often as other types of states do. Several explanations have been proposed for this pattern. Explaining the pattern as a historical coincidence has some plausibility but the evidence is inconsistent with the full implications of this view. The political opposition serves as a second signal of the resolve of a democratic government. The prospect of open opposition enhances the credibility of signals of the government's resolve when the opposition supports the government during a crisis. It also discourages the government from making threats when its resolve is weak. The ease of removing political leaders in a democracy shapes their incentives in conflicts. The greater risk of removal leads democratic leaders to choose their wars carefully.

Review Questions

1.   What pair of regularities define the puzzle of the democratic peace?

2.   Give the three possible explanations of the democratic peace. Explain each in one sentence.

3.   Are democracies or autocracies more likely to win the wars they fight? Briefly explain why.

Chapter 18
Diplomacy: Foreign Aid, Economic Sanctions, and the Termination of Rivalries

Although crises provide dramatic moments when the status quo can be changed, diplomacy provides a way to change issues without a crisis. States have a variety of tools they can use in their efforts to influence other states to agree to changes on international issues without having to threaten to use force. Security policy examined the steps that states took to prepare for the possibility of war; diplomacy examines the steps they can take to avoid the need to threaten others with war to get what they want.

This chapter examines three different tools of diplomacy. Foreign aid covers the provision of monetary aid from one country to another. Economic sanctions restrict trade from one country to another. Sometimes aid and sanctions are referred to as the carrot and the stick of economic diplomacy. Persuasion seeks to convince another state to change its position by altering its perceptions; this chapter will examine diplomatic efforts to end international rivalries through persuasion.

Foreign Aid

Foreign aid is the provision of economic aid through grants or loans, commonly from an economically developed state to a developing state. States give foreign aid for a variety of reasons. Some foreign aid is given for humanitarian reasons, such as disaster or famine relief. Other times, states give foreign aid to advance the economic and political development of the recipient state. States do not always have high-minded motives when they grant foreign aid to another. Foreign aid can be tied—a requirement that the funds be used to buy goods and services from firms based in the donor country. Tied aid then helps to subsidize those firms by giving them additional business from the recipient country.

Countries that receive aid are supposed to use it for development. They can build infrastructure—like roads, ports, power plants, and dams—that make it easier for enterprises in their countries to make their goods and get them to market. They can also use aid to build schools and health facilities that provide public goods that improve the lives of their citizens. Some aid provides goods and services directly to the recipient country. Disaster relief and food aid is often given as the things people need in the face of disasters and famines. Military aid is used to buy equipment and train soldiers.

Some aid is given directly to the recipient government; other is funneled through NGOs that carry out the work in the recipient country. The World Bank loans money to developing countries for projects, often at reduced rates of interest, including interest-free loans to the poorest countries. As developed countries provide the Bank's budget, this is foreign aid sent through and managed by an IGO. The Bank's professional staff also selects projects and monitors their progress.

Of course, not all recipient governments use all of the aid for development. Construction projects open room for kickbacks and other forms of corruption. Some governments have directed food aid only to their supporters instead of the population at need. Infrastructure projects may be chosen more for the political consequences than their economic impact.

Some Facts about Foreign Aid

The United States is the largest donor of foreign aid. Even though it gives more money than any other state, other countries give a larger share of their Gross National Product (GNP)—the common measure of how much the country has produced in a given year. The U.S. typically gives around 0.25% of its GNP in foreign aid each year. As a percent of GNP, the Scandinavian countries—Sweden, Norway, and Denmark—are the most generous, giving about 0.75% of their GNPs in a typical year. The Netherlands is similarly generous. Few other developed countries give the amount that the UN recommends, 0.5% of GNP.

The United States sends a disproportionate amount of its foreign aid to countries aligned with it. Egypt and Israel have received over a billion dollars of aid in constant dollars each year since they signed the Camp David Accords in 1979, which included a peace treaty between the two countries and has been a cornerstone of Israeli security policy since then. Iraq and Afghanistan are also major recipients of U.S. foreign aid during the time that U.S. forces were fighting wars in those countries. Pakistan is also a major recipient of U.S. aid despite the complex and often tense relationship between the two countries. In all these cases, the U.S. gives large amounts of economic aid in support of its security interests in their countries. Similarly, the Soviet Union directed economic aid to its allies around the world. The collapse of the Soviet Union and the resulting cut-off of aid hurt these countries greatly, particularly Cuba and North Korea.

Other developed countries direct their aid more to countries with economic need than the U.S. does. The former colonial powers, Great Britain and France, tend to favor their former colonies. The European Union (EU) also gives aid to less developed regions of Europe, predominantly in Eastern and Southern Europe.

The Puzzle of Foreign Aid

The Marshall Plan was the most successful foreign aid program in history. Named after its designer, U.S. Secretary of State George C. Marshall, the Marshall Plan offered a broad plan of foreign aid to help Europe rebuild after the devastation of the Second World War. Most of the aid was tied to purchases from the United States, which helped U.S. firms as well as the European countries that accepted the aid. It was offered to all European countries affected by the war, including the Soviet Union and Eastern European countries under its influence. The aid also required recipient countries to open up their economies and advance European integration.

Stalin rejected Marshall Plan assistance, and the Eastern European states followed in step. He feared that accepting the aid would force the Soviet Union to accept an inferior position in a U.S.-led system. The Soviet Union and its allies then moved to separate their economies from those of the West.

The economies of the European states that accepted the Marshall Plan grew rapidly during the four years the Plan was in effect. Total economic output exceeded their prewar heights, meaning that Europe had recovered from the damage of the war. Growth had been underway before the Plan, but it accelerated under it. This improved economic performance stabilized Western European states against the threat of Communism. Before the Plan, the Communist parties of Italy and France were powerful and could have come to power through elections. After the Plan, they remained important political parties in both countries but were no longer considered contenders to take power. The Soviet rejection of the Marshall Plan also increased the tension and suspicion of the Cold War. The push to remove barriers to trade began the process of European economic integration that eventually created the European Union (EU). Most foreign aid programs do not have this record of success. Statistical studies show that foreign aid generally does not lead to a noticeable increase in economic growth in the recipient country. The puzzle of foreign aid is why most foreign aid fails to produce economic growth in contrast to the success of the Marshall Plan.

In some cases, the donor's objective in granting the aid is not to produce economic growth in the recipient country but rather to gain favor with its government. During the Cold War, much of the aid granted by the superpowers sought to reward and reinforce friendly regimes in the developing world. If the aid helped to grow their economies, that was a secondary benefit. In contrast, the United States wanted to strengthen European economies through the Marshall Plan in order to make it less likely that those countries would fall to the Communists through elections. Strong economies would undercut the claim of the Communists that only their system could provide for everyone.

Some of the leaders of countries receiving foreign aid are more interested in using the aid for other purposes than economic growth. Leaders who answer to a small winning coalition hold power through the provision of private benefits to their supporters rather than public goods for all. Broad based economic growth acts like a public good; some leaders who answer to a small winning coalition either divert aid through corruption into payoffs to their supporters or choose projects which benefit only a few. In contrast, most of the European countries that received Marshall Plan aid were democracies, whose leaders' hold on power was strengthened by the provision of broad based economic growth.

The donor may not care if the recipient does not use the aid for economic growth. Combining the two points above, the donor may go along with the recipient government diverting the aid. The donor's objective may be to strengthen the leader of the recipient government, in which case it will not object if the aid is used for other purposes than economic growth. The United States continued to provide former Egyptian President Mubarak's government with immense amounts of aid in part because that aid helped to keep him in power, and thereby keep the peace with Israel.

Combining all three points above, the donor country may have no leverage to get the recipient to use its foreign aid to produce economic growth. If it ends the aid, it may destabilize a friendly government. Put another way, a promise lies at the heart of whether foreign aid produces economic growth. The recipient government promises to use the aid in a way that will help its economy develop. But if it does not, the donor government is unwilling to stop providing aid. The Marshall Plan differed because the U.S. wanted to produce growth in Europe, the European government saw economic growth as in their political interest, and the aid was designed to be a short-term program rather than an indefinite commitment to provide money. These problems have led to a move to tie foreign aid to performance by the recipient government. Targets to improve governance, how the recipient government manages its money and its economy, are set, and the continuation of aid depends on meeting those targets. By linking future aid to performance, the recipient government should use the aid to produce growth. But are donor governments willing to cut aid to the poorest countries in the world, those where foreign aid is a substantial proportion of their government's budget and many survive through foreign aid even if they never develop economically?

Economic Sanctions

On January 1, 1959, Fidel Castro led the soldiers of his 26th of July movement into Havana, the capital of Cuba, and overthrew President Fulgencio Batista. Despite the historical close economic ties between the United States and Cuba, relations between the U.S. and Castro's new regime deteriorated. The Cuban government nationalized some businesses owned by Americans, and in response, the United States government began to restrict trade with Cuba. As the relationship deteriorated, both sides continued to take economic measures against each other. Eventually, President John Kennedy extended U.S. measures to prevent all trade and travel between the two and freeze Cuban assets in the United States. Given Cuba's close proximity to the U.S., its economy suffered, and it turned increasingly to the Soviet Union, the rival of the U.S., for trade and economic aid. Although these measures aimed at ending Castro's regime and democratizing Cuba, Fidel Castro continued to hold power until he stepped down in 2008 in favor of his younger brother, Raul. Over 50 years of stringent economic sanctions have not dented the hold of the Castros on power in Cuba. Even today, you cannot buy a Cuban cigar, widely believed to the best in the world, in the United States, and U.S. Customs agents will confiscate any they find when people try to enter the country.

Economic sanctions cover all measures that one or more states, which we will call the sanctioning state or states, take to restrict economic exchange with another state, which we will call the target state. Sanctioning states can limit exports—goods and services produced in their country and sold in the target—or imports—goods and services produced in the target country and sold in the sanctioning state—in part by banning particular goods and services or in whole. They can also forbid investment or freeze assets that the target government holds in the sanctioning state. In some cases, government officials are not allowed to enter the sanctioning country. Sanctions seek to punish the target in order to get it to change its behavior on some issue of importance to the sanctioning state. These demands could be specific and narrow or very broad and sweeping, like the U.S. demand that Cuba democratize in order to lift its sanctions on the Cuban economy. The target may change those policies to stop the damage to its economy from the limits on exchange. This is the logic of a threat once again, backed by a promise to lift the sanctions if the target state complies with the demand.

Why Don't Sanctions Work?

Economic sanctions rarely work in the sense that the target does all that the sanctioning state demands, just as U.S. sanctions on Cuba have not convinced it to democratize. Statistical studies across all instances of sanctions in the 20th century find that sanctions produce substantial concessions from the target between 20-30% of the time. These substantial concessions are not full concessions where the target does all that the sanctioning state demands, but they are more than minor concessions. Targeted sanctions connected to a limited demand are more likely to work than broad sanctions tied to demands for major concessions.

The most successful example of economic sanctions leading to a major concession is the ending of apartheid in South Africa in 1993. The apartheid system of racial discrimination denied black South Africans political, economic, and social rights in favor of the white minority and mixed race groups. Opposition to apartheid grew in Western countries throughout the 1970s and 1980s, leading to calls to cut economic ties with South Africa. The United States adopted limits on further investment and sanctions on certain products in 1986. Divestment, which would have forced U.S. companies to end all operations in South Africa and remove any investment they had there, did not pass. This period also saw an example of a limited, successful sanction. The U.S. government wanted South African Airways (SAA) to integrate their flight crews and threatened to deny SAA landing rights at U.S. airports. Faced with a threat that would end their ability to connect to the U.S. market, SAA quickly changed their policy. The more general sanctions on South Africa contributed to capital flight as companies and wealthy South Africans moved money out of the country to keep it secure. In 1990, the South African government opened negotiations with the African National Congress and released its jailed leader, Nelson Mandela. Apartheid ended in 1993 with a negotiated transition to full adult suffrage for all South Africans.

States that use economic sanctions have other, more forceful, options as well. They choose to use economic sanctions because they are unwilling to use force to produce the outcome they desire. Before the U.S. placed its comprehensive sanctions on Cuba, it had sponsored Cuban exiles who wished to invade the island to overthrow Cuba. Their effort was the fiasco of the Bay of Pigs in April of 1961. The Central Intelligence Agency (CIA) recruited, sponsored, and trained Cuban exiles into military units to invade Cuba and overthrow Castro. Their invasion floundered within days afterwards, with all of the surviving exile fighters captured by Cuba. At the end of the Cuban Missile Crisis in 1962, the U.S. pledged not to invade Cuba. The option of sanctions became more attractive once force had failed. States that choose sanctions over force send the signal that they do not consider the issue at hand to be important enough to fight over. Sanctions often mean that force is off the table.

How should the target respond after the sanctioning state sends the message that the issue is not important enough to go to war over? If it can wait out the sanctions, that is, suffer the economic costs until it can convince the sanctioning state that it will not concede on the issues in dispute, the sanctioning state may eventually lift them. The signal of sanctions then can reinforce the target in its willingness to hold firm and not make the concessions demanded.

The target's response to the threat of sanctions depends on whether it thinks it can weather the economic costs of them. If it thinks that the costs of the sanctions are so great that it must yield, then it may yield upon the threat, that is, before they come into force. If it thinks that the cost is not too great to bear, it may wait them out, suffering in the knowledge that the sanctioning state is unwilling to use force to get what it wants. Put another way, sanctions that work never get put into place because the target yields before they come into force. Sanctions that cannot force the target to yield are those that do get put into force, with the result that both sides suffer with them over time. Sanctions that work do not happen; those that do happen cannot work, which explains why the sanctions we see rarely compel the target to do as the sanctioning state wishes.

As the fifth and sixth principles imply, the domestic institutions of the target state affect whether sanctions happen and whether they induce compliance. If the sanctions are costly by hurting the economy of the target state, leaders who answer to a small winning coalition, like Fidel Castro in Cuba, may be able to wait them out and retain power by rewarding supporters with private benefits. Those who answer to a large winning coalition may concede before the sanctions are in force to avoid their economic damage. Further, sanctions can strengthen the hold on power of a leader who answers to a small winning coalition. Sanctions make smuggling of contraband goods more valuable, which creates a private benefit for supporters.

In summary, sanctions that would work do not happen; those that happen are unable to coerce the target into making concessions. Economic sanctions suffer from a selection effect; the only ones that are selected to happen are those that will not work. This selection effect explains in part why economic sanctions rarely succeed. Neither the carrot nor the stick of economic diplomacy prove effective off in practice.

Ending Rivalries

International rivalries center on the shared perception that the other side poses a threat. Changing these perceptions, as the fourth principle tells us, is difficult because they are based on a history of actions deemed to be hostile. Further, these perceptions of mutual hostility are sunk deeply into the domestic politics of both sides, where those who are relevant in politics see the rival as a threat. How can they break these perceptions and end their rivalry?

The complete defeat of one side ends a rivalry. The long rivalry between Germany and France began with the Franco-Prussian War in 1870-71 and ended after the Second World War when Germany renounced any claim to the disputed provinces of Alsace and Lorraine. The U.S.-Soviet rivalry ended with the collapse of the Soviet Union at the end of the Cold War in 1991. In both cases, the state that lost no longer pressed its claims against the other, which eliminated the perception of mutual threat.

Few rivalries end with a clear victor when the other side abandons its claims. Negotiation of a settlement of the issues underlying the dispute is the other way to end a rivalry. These negotiations are difficult because the parties are suspicious of one another's motives. Is the rival offering concessions honestly or is it simply a trick to get our side to lower its guard? How can a party that wants to end the rivalry and is willing to make concessions to do so reassure the other that its motives are sincere?

The problem is how to change the other side's perception that it holds hostile intent. From Principle 4, separation of type from other types is key to changing perceptions through persuasion. The type that wishes to end the rivalry must find some action that types that simply wish to trick their rival are unwilling to take. That action will separate its type from the insincere ones.

Egypt and Israel were rivals since the creation of Israel in 1948. They fought five wars—in 1948, 1956, 1967, 1969-70, and 1973. Although Israel did not lose a single war to Egypt, it was still Israel's primary threat because Egypt is the one Arab state powerful enough to pose a substantial military threat to Israel. After Nasser died in 1970, Anwar Sadat succeeded to the Presidency of Egypt. He wished to negotiate with Israel because Israel occupied the Sinai Peninsula, and Egypt wanted its territory back; an initial effort in 1971 failed. Because Israel did not take Egyptian overtures to negotiate seriously—a sign that they were skeptical of Sadat's motives, President Sadat launched the October War of 1973 with simultaneous surprise attacks by Egypt in the Sinai and Syria on the Golan Heights. Although Israel suffered setbacks early in the war, it turned the tide of battle and gained the upper hand before the superpowers stopped the war. An interim agreement separated the forces of all sides and established demilitarized zones patrolled by peacekeeping forces, but talks to conclude a peace treaty remained stymied. What could Sadat do to convince Israel of his interest in peace?

In November, 1977, Sadat announced that he would go to Jerusalem and offer peace at the Knesset, the Israeli parliament. Sadat was the first Arab leader to take a state visit to Israel. Speaking in Jerusalem was particularly controversial because Israel annexed East Jerusalem after the Six-Day War in 1967, which no Arab state recognized out of respect of the desire of the Palestinians to make East Jerusalem the capital of an eventual Palestine. This step carried major political risks for Sadat as it was widely condemned across the Arab world. The visit moved the negotiations for peace ahead. The Camp David Accords mediated by U.S. President Jimmy Carter in 1978 then led to a peace treaty between Egypt and Israel on March 26, 1979 which returned the Sinai Peninsula to Egypt and limited how many troops Egypt could station there. Since then, peace has held even though relations between the two countries are not close. They are no longer rivals.

Sadat's trip to Israel and the peace treaty provoked widespread anger in the Arab world. The Arab League suspended Egypt's membership in the organization after the peace treaty. Plots against Sadat sprung up inside Egypt, with an attempted coup failing in June 1981. He cracked down on those he suspected of plotting against his regime, but he did not get them all. On October 6, 1981, the eighth anniversary of the October War, Sadat was assassinated by a lieutenant in the Egyptian army while reviewing a military parade.

The anger that Sadat's trip to Jerusalem provoked is the cost that allowed Sadat to persuade Israel that he was serious about making peace and ending their rivalry. A type that merely wished to exploit a peace overture for political gain and held no interest in ending the rivalry would not have taken the risk of going to Jerusalem. This added costs separated the type that really wanted peace—Sadat—from any type that was not serious about peace.

Taking a dramatic step to convince a rival that you are serious about ending the rivalry faces the risk of a commitment problem. Perhaps the rival will accept your concessions and push you for more, thinking that you are the type that will do anything for peace. Ending rivalries is doubly difficult then; you have to convince your rival that you are serious about seeking peace but also resolute enough that you will not do anything to realize that peace. Hawks—leaders that both sides recognize as willing to defend their own interests—are more able to this than doves—leaders recognized for their commitment to seek peace no matter what. Sadat, for example, demonstrated his willingness to use force against Israel when he launched the October War in 1973. The Israelis could see both his desire for peace and his commitment to defend Egyptian interests.

Nixon's opening to China in 1972 is another example of how a hawkish leader is less likely to be exploited in a peace overture. Relations between the United States and the People's Republic of China were non-existent since the Communists took control of the mainland in 1949. The U.S. continued to recognize the Republic of China as the legitimate government of China even though it only controlled Taiwan and few other islands. Nixon was well-known as a staunch anti-Communist from his time as a Senator and Vice President during the 1950s. When he sent Henry Kissinger, his National Security Advisor and later Secretary of State, to negotiate secretly with the Chinese, they knew Nixon would not abandon U.S. interests, such as in Vietnam, to secure an opening to China against their common rival of the Soviet Union. Nixon and Kissinger began the process of opening up relations with the People's Republic, first acquiescing in the shift of China's Permanent Membership on the UN Security Council from the Republic of China to the People's Republic in 1971, then shifting diplomatic recognition from Taiwan to the mainland in 1979. Now the two countries are the largest trading partners in the world and have a complex, intertwined relationship.

Summary

Foreign aid rarely leads to higher levels of economic growth in the recipient state. It may induce compliance by the recipient to the wishes of the donor state. The donor's aims, however, may be something other than producing economic growth in the recipient state, including stabilizing a friendly regime in the recipient state. If the recipient state knows that the donor is likely to continue aid no matter how it uses the aid, the donor lacks the leverage to induce the recipient state to use the aid to increase economic growth.

Economic sanctions do not occur when they work; when they occur, they do not work. Consequently, the record of economic sanctions in producing change in the target state is poor. Neither the carrot nor the stick of economic diplomacy are powerful tools of diplomacy, even if they are used often.

Ending rivalries requires a dramatic step to change perceptions of hostility. This dramatic step needs to be an act that a type that seeks to trap its rival would be unwilling to do. Negotiations to end rivalries also face a commitment problem where the side seeking to end the rivalry worries that its rival may push it to make greater concessions than it is willing to. Hawkish leaders are less likely to be taken advantage of this way, and so are more likely to be able to act to end a rivalry.

Review Questions

1. What three reasons do developed states have for providing economic aid to less developed states? Define each in one sentence.

2. Give two reasons why foreign aid might not produce economic growth in the recipient state.

3. Economic sanctions are effective only about 20-30% of the time in producing compliance with demands. Give two reasons why sanctions are rarely effective.

4. How does the regime of the target of the threat of economic sanctions affect its willingness to make concessions before sanctions are put into effect? If sanctions are applied, how does the regime of the target affect whether they will succeed in changing the policies of the target state?

5. Explain why rivalries are difficult to end through diplomacy. What type of leaders can credibly make the concessions needed to end a rivalry

Chapter 19
The Problem of Civil War

Afghanistan has suffered through a series of civil wars over the last thirty-five years. On April 27, 1978, the People's Democratic Party of Afghanistan (PDPA) overthrew the government in a military coup. The combination of their policies to end many traditional practices and their repression of any one who might oppose them triggered a widespread revolt. On December 25, 1979, Soviet forces crossed the border into Afghanistan and overthrew Hafizullah Amin's government two days later. The Soviet invasion and participation in the civil war led to military support for the rebels from the United States and Saudi Arabia, funneled through Pakistan. Arab men traveled to fight with the mujahideen, as the rebels were known, including Osama bin Laden. In 1987, the Soviet Union decided to wind down its involvement in the war, and it withdrew its last troops from Afghanistan on February 15, 1989.

The civil war did not end. The mujahideen were composed of different factions, often organized from the various ethnic groups in the country. President Najibullah's Communist government held on for another three years until Kabul, the capital, fell to the rebels on April 17, 1992. The rebel factions began to fight among themselves for control of Kabul, destroying much of the city in the process. Although ceasefires and peace settlements were negotiated, none held for long. The factions aligned, realigned, and fought one another in confusing succession. This period of the civil war ended when the Taliban, a new faction organized around Islamist students drawn from the majority Pashtun ethnic group, took control of Kabul on September 27, 1996. Factions organized from the other ethnic groups retreated from Kabul to the areas populated by their ethnic group and formed the Northern Alliance against the Taliban. Osama bin Laden left Sudan and moved to Afghanistan in 1996 and established training camps for Al Qaeda there.

After the 9/11 attacks, the United States presented the Taliban government of Afghanistan with an ultimatum. On October 7, 2001, the United States intervened in the Afghan civil war in support of the Northern Alliance against the Taliban, as it judged that the Taliban had not met the conditions of the ultimatum. Over the next three months, the support of the United States allowed the Northern Alliance to defeat the Taliban and end their rule over Afghanistan. After that initial success, an insurgency against the new Afghan government supported by international forces grew. The Afghan Civil War continued.

This chapter analyzes the problem of civil war. What are civil wars, and how do they differ from interstate wars? Civil wars typically last longer than interstate wars; why are civil wars difficult to end? How can the international community help to end civil wars?

What is Civil War?

In interstate wars, the states at war recognize one another as legal equals, even if they are doing everything in their power to crush the other. In civil wars, the legitimacy of the state is in question. The rebels do not accept either that the government of their state is legitimate or that the claim of that state to rule their territory is legitimate. Civil wars are fought over legitimacy of the state to rule the territory it claims. The government in turn views the rebels not as legal equals, but as traitors to the state because they challenge the legitimacy of the state.

Most civil wars are fought over the control of the state. The rebels seek to replace the government and install their own government in its place. The civil wars in Afghanistan are an example of such civil wars as the warring parties have attempted to seize control of the state of Afghanistan. Wars of secession, in contrast, are fought over the legitimacy of the integrity of the state's territory. The rebels claim that some portion of the state's territory should be a separate, independent state from that of the government. The American Civil War was a war of secession as the Confederacy did not wish to control the Northern States; it only claimed to establish a second country based on the slaveholding states of the South.

Rebels hold some grievances against the government, which is why they deem its rule illegitimate. These grievances range from the inability of the government to provide public goods to the people to claims that the government has no right to govern the population from which the rebels recruit to ambition to overthrow the leader and rule in his or her place. Grievances underlying civil war can be ideological, personal ambition, or ethnic. They matter because rebel groups attract supporters to fight for their cause, which is why civil wars are political, even if many produce a great deal of chaotic violence in a country as well.

All sides in a civil war use violence to advance their aims. Control of territory and the population that lives on it is a primary goal for both sides. Government forces use violence in an effort to hunt down and destroy the rebels and suppress their supporters in the civilian population. Rebel groups use violence to establish their control over an area by attacking government officials and symbols of the government's authority. The use of violence by both sides often includes attacks on civilians who each side suspects of sympathizing with the other. Lack of personal security for civilians is common in civil wars. As personal security is a primary public good that every government provides, rebel groups may carry out attacks that undermine the sense of personal security of civilians in their efforts to demonstrate the illegitimacy of the government.

The legitimacy of a government is the degree to which its rule is accepted as binding, correct, and proper by people and groups. People believe they should comply with a legitimate government. Few may enjoy paying their taxes, but they recognize that they have an obligation to pay them if the government is legitimate. The monopoly on the legitimate use of force within its borders is a key characteristic of the state as an institution. The state is allowed to use force against those who violate its laws, while citizens are not allowed to use force against the government. Civil war attacks this idea by encouraging people to take up arms to resist their government and break its monopoly on the legitimate use of force. One can accept the legitimacy of a government even if one disagrees with some of its policies or laws provided that the person in question accepts the government's rule generally.

The legitimacy of a state is difficult to judge because it resides within views of the people of the state but we can only observe what they do, not what they believe. Most U.S. citizens accept the legitimacy of their government, even though many disagree with many of the things it does. The citizens of the United States as a democracy have the ability to express their opposition to government policies and law through their representatives, political parties, and public protest. In an autocracy, those forms of open opposition to the government are illegal and repressed with violence. Many people who live in an autocracy may oppose their government and view it as illegitimate, but because they do not act on their views, we cannot judge whether the government is legitimate in the eyes of its citizens. The term for this is preference falsification, where people do not act on their belief that the government is illegitimate out of a fear of the consequences to them personally if they do. Revolutions are unexpected events because of preference falsification. An autocratic government can exercise power for decades because few citizens are willing to run the risks of opposing it publicly. When enough people come onto the streets to do so, however, the risks go down because the government cannot repress them all, which encourages even more opponents of the government to participate. The legitimacy of a state is key to its power inside and outside the country, but it is one of the most difficult things to judge in politics.

There are also ideas of international legitimacy that matter in world politics. States have reasons for what they do in world politics. Ideas about what values should be advanced in world politics are one basis for international legitimacy. When and how force can be used is a key element of international legitimacy because others may oppose illegitimate uses of force. Many around the world viewed the invasion of Iraq by the United States and Great Britain in 2003 as illegitimate and not justified, which is why they did not support the invasion or occupation afterwards. International law embodies many of these ideas about international legitimacy, and we will return to the concept of international legitimacy when we consider international law.

Civil wars are struggles over the legitimacy of a government. This nature has important implications for how civil wars are fought that make them different in character from interstate wars. As mentioned above, rebels attack the legitimacy of the government and state, attacking its agents such as the police and government officials in addition to the armed forces of the government. The government in turn does not view the rebels as their legal equals; it views them as traitors and criminals and often punishes them as such if they capture them. In interstate wars, soldiers are more likely to be treated humanely if they are taken prisoner because their taking up arms and using them violently is recognized as legal. This is not true for rebels. Rebels in turn may use violence in ways that are seen as illegitimate in interstate wars, such as directly killing civilians and targeting government officials who are not combatants. Civil wars lack reciprocity–the idea that you should treat the other side as they treat you–between the two sides because they do not accept one another as legitimate and equal. In interstate wars, reciprocity helps to support some restrictions on the use of force.

Civil wars also have international consequences. Outside countries may provide aid to the government and the rebels, prolonging the fighting. This aid could be arms, munitions and military equipment or a third party country could provide soldiers to train and fight with the soldiers of either the government or rebels. As with the Soviet intervention in the Afghan civil wars from 1979 to 1989, a foreign government may send in troops to fight on behalf of one side. This external involvement could be open, like the Soviet intervention, or it could be covert so that others inside and outside the country are not certain of the involvement of the third party. Sometimes third parties enter into civil wars to separate the combatants and end the violence. This external intervention can be done in support of a peace agreement between the two or against their will. Civil wars can also spill over national borders into neighboring countries. Rebels often cross into foreign countries to escape from government soldiers, particularly into regions where the neighboring government has little control or presence. They may also recruit in neighboring states or receive military aid through them. Some civil wars spread over time as rebels operate in neighboring countries. They may trigger a response from the government of the neighboring country and begin fighting it as well. Some ethnic groups extend across national borders, making co-ethnics a population from which the rebels can recruit and raise support. These international spillovers explain why civil wars have become a significant concern in world politics in addition to the concern to limit violence and its destruction; civil wars are not just internal to a country.

Insurgency

Some civil wars are fought as conventional wars with large set-piece battles as the American Civil War was or with a clear front line separating the two armies as was the case in the Spanish Civil War. Many civil wars are fought as insurgencies, a different kind of war, also called guerrilla war or irregular warfare. Insurgents operate in small units among the population, often doing so covertly, such as not wearing uniforms that would separate them from the local populations. Insurgent bands roam in a local area, drawing support such as food from the local population. That support is sometimes given freely because the population identifies with the rebels or coerced at other times, where the population supports the guerrillas because they fear they will be attacked if they do not. The small units of the insurgents decide when and where to attack government forces and officials. This allows them to fight only when they have local superiority and so are likely to win that small-scale battle. Afterwards, the insurgents melt back into the population and countryside to hide from counterattack by government forces. In this way, they can sustain their presence in the field in the face of more numerous government forces that have more firepower. In doing so, they contest the control of their local territory and prevent the government from controlling it. Mao Zedong was the primary theorist who explained how an insurgency works, how it should relate to the local population, and how it can eventually grow in strength to the point where it can defeat the government and win the civil war. Mao successfully created an insurgency that fought the Nationalist government of China and the Japanese forces that invaded and occupied much of northern China and eventually won the Chinese Civil War and took control of the country from the Nationalists in 1949.

Fighting an insurgency poses large problems for the government. Because the insurgents hide among the population and cannot be easily identified, the government's army cannot bring them to battle when it wants so that it can use its superior firepower and numbers. Instead, government forces often sweep through areas with guerrillas, searching for them. They question the local population who may know where the insurgents are hiding. But informing is a dangerous business because the rebels or their sympathizers may take revenge on those who cooperate with the government forces. Civil wars fought as insurgencies often lead to killings of civilians by both sides.

Insurgencies spread fighting widely through the countryside. Guerrillas operate in small bands primarily in rural areas to control or contest territory. When government forces search for them, combat is spread around the countryside. Civilians are pressed for information about where the other side is and what their plans are. The insurgents want this information so they can avoid battle with superior government forces and only fight when they have a local advantage. The government forces want this information so they can find the rebels, bring them to battle, and destroy them. Civilians then become victims of both sides as both sides press them for information and try to root out or intimidate supporters of the other side. At the same time, civilians may use both sides for their own ends, providing incorrect information to use either the rebels or the government soldiers to settle their own feuds or grievances. Rebel groups and government forces also both try to operate like a government, administering justice by resolving disputes. Civilians can use those efforts to exert authority to get what they want.

Sweeping for the guerrillas to bring them to battle is one strategy to fight an insurgency; counterinsurgency is the other. Sweeping focuses on destroying the guerrillas in battle, while counterinsurgency aims at separating the insurgents from the people. The counterinsurgents provide security for the people by denying the guerrillas the access they need to intimidate civilians into supporting them. This security reassures government supporters that they will be protected if they cooperate with their forces. The added security also allows the government to provide other public goods that reinforces the claim to be a legitimate government that works on behalf of their people. Counterinsurgency spreads government troops throughout contested regions, so they will be present in local communities to counter the insurgents when they attempt to patrol to contest government control.

The surge in 2007-2008 during the civil war in Iraq during the occupation by the United States was a successful campaign of counterinsurgency. After the invasion in 2003, an insurgency against the occupying forces and the new government of Iraq grew. In 2006, attacks by extremist Sunnis Muslims affliated with Al Qaeda triggered a civil war primarily between the majority Shiite Muslims and Sunni groups, although armed groups of both sides also fought the occupying and government forces. Many civilians of both ethnic groups were killed on the suspicion of being militants; Sunnis often turned to the Al Qaeda affliated groups for protection against Shiite militants. Before the surge, the occupying and government forces used a variety of strategies against the growing insurgency, including large assaults on Fallujah, a city where Sunni insurgents took control and operated openly. In 2007, President Bush changed strategy. He installed General David Petraeus as commander in Iraq and increased U.S. soldiers in Iraq. Petraeus, who had developed an Army training manual for counterinsurgency, used the additional troops to improve security in Baghdad, the capital and largest city in Iraq where much of the killing of civilians had taken place. At the same time, contacts with local Sunni leaders convinced many of them to change sides and turn on Al Qaeda groups. The surge was criticized in U.S. politics as many wished to see the U.S. occupation end and the troops come home. Although the surge increased U.S. casualties in 2007, it eventually created a sense of security and reduced civilian killings in Iraq. The increased security and lower level of fighting led to the withdrawal of U.S. troops by President Obama in 2001.

The Size of the Problem

Civil war has been a primary security concern of the post-Cold-War world. Interstate conflict has become more rare over time, and the threat of superpower conflict and competition receded with the dissolution of the Soviet Union. Civil wars in contrast have become more common. Internationalized civil wars, those where other countries send troops to fight with one side or the other, account for the largest interstate conflicts of the post-Cold-War period. The number of ongoing civil wars is declining over the last twenty years, but the decline of interstate conflict has led to civil wars being the overwhelming majority of war in the world.

[Graph of numbers of interstate and civil wars by year since 1945]

Civil wars last longer than interstate wars. The longest interstate wars are about a decade long; the longest war the United States has fought is its involvement in Afghanistan, which is now over twelve years. U.S. involvement in the Vietnam War was about eight years from 1964 to 1972. Both of those long interstate wars were internationalized civil wars, where the U.S. fought on behalf of a government facing an insurgency. The two world wars were shorter than these wars; World War I lasted four years, World War II less than six, although Japan's war with China went on for eight years (1937-1945). In contrast, it is not difficult to find civil war that last decades. The Afghan civil wars have stretched on for thirty-five years as of writing. Sudan suffered through a pair of civil wars between the north and the south of the country with the first running from 1955 to 1972 and the second from 1983 to 2005. The issues were similar, making the Second Sudanese Civil War a continuation of the first. The civil wars only ended with an agreement that led to the independence of South Sudan in 2011.

[Graph comparing durations of interstate and civil wars].

The predominance of civil wars in the post-Cold-War results from an accumulation of long-running civil wars rather than an increased risk of civil war. The fundamental problem is that civil wars are difficult to end once they begin. While some civil wars are brief, lasting only a few weeks or even days, others linger for decades.

What factors make a civil war more likely in a state? Poorer societies are more likely to suffer from civil war. Some comment on the "African peace," the observation that there have been very few interstate wars in sub-Saharan Africa. Instead, Africa has suffered from many long and destructive civil wars. Scholars disagree about why poorer societies are more likely to undergo civil war. The state and its security institutions are weaker in poorer societies, making it harder to suppress rebellions at the their early stage when there are few rebels. This allows rebel groups to grow to the size where the conflict is considered a civil war. Richer societies are more likely to be democracies, which may be more able to deal with the grievances of groups that could motivate armed rebellion if not dealt with. India, however, a poor democracy suffers from a number of civil wars, most notably in Kashmir and by the Naxalites. Richer societies are also have the state resources to deal with group grievances. Countries with rough terrain, such as mountains or heavy forests and jungles, are more likely to suffer from civil war. Rough terrain provides places for insurgents to hide, making insurgencies easier to start, grow, and sustain. Rough terrain is not necessary for an insurgency, as the example of Iraq shows.

How Do Civil Wars End?

If the problem of civil wars is the accumulation of long-running wars, how they end is the critical question to addressing the problem. Some civil wars end with a complete victory of the government, ending the rebellion. The American Civil War, a civil war fought primarily conventionally, is a case of this. Insurgencies, however, are difficult to defeat militarily and so rarely end with a clear government victory. An insurgency can be sustained by smaller groups of fighters than a conventional war, sometimes requiring as few as several hundred active guerrillas continue attacks on government forces and officials at a high enough level to be an active civil war. The ability of insurgencies to sustain themselves with little support contributes to the greater length of civil wars compared to interstate wars.

Civil wars also end sometimes with a complete victory by the rebels. In 1991, the Marxist government of Ethiopia fell to a coalition of rebel groups called the Ethiopian People's Revolutionary Democratic Front (EPRDF) based in the northern provinces of Tigre and Eritrea. The EPRDF established a new government in Addas Ababa, and the Eritrean People's Liberation Front took power in an independent Eritrea after a referendum split it off of Ethiopia. The rebel groups had accomplished their aims by victory, the overthrow of the Ethiopian government and the independence of Eritrea. Rebel victories, however, are rare and difficult to achieve in civil wars. Rebel groups are typically weaker than government forces and so are unlikely to win a war. Insurgency as a strategy seek to prolong war to give the insurgents a chance to grow their forces slowly, exhaust the government militarily and morally, and extend their control over more territory. It is a long-term strategy, not one for quick victory. Because many civil wars are fought as insurgencies, it is unlikely that the rebels will win decisively or quickly. Even when they win and take control of the government, remnants of the government forces may continue fighting against the new government, either by crossing international borders or establishing an insurgency of their own.

Most civil war then end in some form of negotiated settlement. The Second Sudanese Civil War ended with the agreement that led to the referendum that made South Sudan an independent and sovereign state. Such a settlement was possible because the aims of the South Sudanese rebels did not include overthrowing the central government of Sudan in Khartoum, the capital. When the aims of the rebels include overthrowing the central government, then a negotiated settlement has to focus on power sharing, creating a government that includes both the current government and the leadership of the rebels. Power sharing agreements are tricky to negotiate. They have to divide power in the new government in accord with the military power of the two sides. If not, the side that receives less political power than it has military power will not agree to the deal. Power sharing deals also have to manage a transition period where the sides will stand down while the new government is being created and extends its authority over the country. Cease-fire agreements and power sharing deals are often negotiated during civil wars, particularly when both sides recognize that they cannot win on the battlefield. Still, many of these deals fail, and fighting resumes, often quickly after the deal is struck.

Power sharing agreements have to create stable political bargains in the future for the parties to commit to them over time. Otherwise, one side may return to violence to get what it cannot get through politics. Peace agreements to end civil wars face large commitment problems. First, the legacy of fighting can poison the trust needed to sustain an agreement. Some on both sides may believe that continuing to fight is preferable to sharing power. Second, the two armies, one government and one rebel, need to be reduced to one. The rebels needs to be disarmed, although many may be incorporated in a new national army. If rebel fighters are not incorporated into the army, they need to be reintegrated into society. If they cannot find jobs, returning to the bush to fight and engage in crime may be their best option. Third, power sharing over time requires political institutions that will allow all sides to protect their interests in the political process. But those institutions are untested when the agreement is signed, and if they fail to give a party enough power to protect their own interests, that party may see renewed fighting as better than losing political power peacefully. Fourth, there is often more than one rebel group fighting, and more than two parties complicates any negotiation. The different rebel groups may have been fighting each other in addition to fighting the government and not want to enter into a government with one another. Fifth, the leaders of both sides may believe they are personally better off continuing to fight than ending the conflict. A rebel leader may prefer running the territory he controls as unquestioned leader to accepting second place in a national government. Sixth, both sides may contain spoilers, factions who disagree with their leaders about the need to settle to end the fighting. After a peace settlement, these spoilers may use violence to try and undermine it. Renewed violence by spoilers may convince parties that wish to live with the deal that the other side is reneging and so they too should return to fighting. Rebel groups are particularly likely to generate spoilers as they often are composed of loose factions with a common cause.

Creating Credible Commitments

How can these commitment problems be solved to end a civil war? Political institutions can help actors create credible commitments to one another to allay the concerns that create commitment problems. Constitutions limit the power of actors and can provide legal protections for members of minority groups, which can reduce their concerns of being at the mercy of the majority after a peace deal. They can also create checks and balances on actors, so that those with more popular support cannot take advantage of those with less. Creating a true national army that owes its loyalty to the state and all its people instead of the supporters of one faction in the country can reassure those of other factions that the army will not be used to repress them in the future. An impartial judiciary can deter spoilers by prosecuting those who turn to violence while reassuring former rebels who do not that they will not be arrested for their former acts. Processes of national reconciliation can allow victims to voice their suffering and perhaps receive justice for it. But political institutions are not a panacea. New institutions are not established and may not work as they are designed. Parties may subvert them to expand their own power and threaten their former enemies. Often all actors have doubts about living under institutions that limit their power and work against their consolidation.

International intervention could also address a commitment problem through external enforcement of a peace settlement. Third party enforcement could reassure both sides that a deal will hold and that should either side break it, they will not gain an advantage by doing so. But outside states rarely intervene in civil war solely to uphold the peace; they do so to help the side they would like better. The United States' military intervention in the Vietnam War beginning in 1964 and 1965 did not aim to establish and enforce peace; it was an effort to prop up the government of South Vietnam in the face of imminent collapse. Intervening states may also lack the willingness to commit to the intervention over a long period of time to enforce a peace settlement, like the United States eventually tired of the high costs of its intervention in the Vietnam War, negotiated a settlement with North Vietnam and the National Liberation Front, as the rebels called themselves, and left. Unilateral intervention by outside states generally prolongs civil wars rather than shorten them.

Multilateral peacekeeping missions is another form of international intervention that could help the parties keep the peace after a settlement. Peacekeeping missions draw on the military forces of more than one country to create a multinational force operating under an international organization to help keep the peace. In Afghanistan, forces operate as the International Security Assistance Force (ISAF) under NATO. Forty-nine countries have sent troops to participate in ISAF with a total of 97,920 in Afghanistan as of this summer, although the precise composition and size of the force varies over time. The UN runs a number of peacekeeping operations around the world as do some regional IGOs.

There are different types of peacekeeping missions with different mandates for their operations in country. At the lowest level, peacekeepers can just monitor the peace by separating the combatants and investigating violent incidents. This limited peacekeeping tries to prevent spoilers from instigating a renewed civil war by attacking the other side. If they can convince both sides not to retaliate against spoiling attacks, they can help keep the peace. Some peacekeeping missions take a more aggressive role and enforce the peace by actively enforcing the peace against violators. Those missions use their military capabilities to fight those who seek to renew the civil war. Peacekeepers can also be useful in disarming the rebels, called decommissioning. If the end of a civil war means that one army must be created from two or more, then disarming the rebels is a critical and difficult step in establishing the peace. Some rebels may not want to give up their arms as they are the ultimate guarantee of their political power. But the government wants to be sure that all the rebels will live in peace in the future, so they need to be disarmed. If government forces disarm the rebels themselves, the latter may be reluctant to surrender their arms. Having peacekeepers decommission the rebels reassures both sides that it will be done in accord with the agreement. Peacekeepers can also help weak governments by increasing their capabilities to run the country effectively; the UN refers to these missions as peacebuilding because of their greater involvement in creating the conditions for peace to hold. They can provide experts who will train new police officers and government officials, advise on running government ministries, and provide services to address the human costs of the war. Peacebuilding missions are used when the civil war has heavily damaged the country's ability to govern itself.

Peacekeeping and peacebuilding have had mixed records of success. Some missions have succeeded, peace has held and the country has created a stable government. Other missions have been unable to put a halt on fighting. In some cases, peacekeeping soldiers have committed crimes in the countries where they are deployed. One recurrent problem is that these missions may be too small for the job or not receive sufficient funding. Peacekeeping and peacebuilding are not a panacea for the commitment problems faced in ending civil wars.

Return to Afghanistan

The civil wars in Afghanistan illustrate many of the issues that make civil wars difficult to end. The international interventions into the civil war, first the Soviets in the 1980s, then Pakistan's support for different armed factions during the 1990s, and finally the United States and NATO in the last decade have favored one side over the others and prolonged the conflict. These parties intervened because they wanted one side to win or at least not to lose. Their interest in peace came only after their side won. The government of Afghanistan has been very weak through this period so that it cannot fight rebels on its own nor deliver public services that might convince supporters of the rebel to switch their loyalties. It has not been able to commit to peace agreements nor deliver afterwards. From the point of view of leaders of Afghan armed groups, control of the government has been a tool to advance their own political agendas rather than bring order and justice to the country. The terrain of Afghanistan is mountainous and large, providing cover for insurgent groups. The countryside is ideal for insurgency. These rebel groups have repeatedly spoiled peace settlements, particularly during the period of fighting after the Najibullah government fell in 1992. The Taliban takeover in 1996 was a relief to make Afghans if only to bring peace and some order to most of the country. Finally, international efforts to build and keep peace have been insufficient. Given the devastation of the civil wars, the amount required to rebuild the country is immense. Even the billions of dollars spent by the United States in aid since 2001 has been insufficient.

Summary

Civil wars last longer than interstate wars and can be very destructive of government and society. Victory is difficult to achieve, in part because many civil wars are fought as insurgencies. Negotiated settlements to civil wars face commitment problems, and all sides are often reluctant to live up to such deals once they are in place. Many civil wars then have a pattern of more intense periods of fighting followed by respites. Under the right conditions and with sufficient effort, peacekeeping missions can help address these commitment problems, end civil wars, and ensure they do not start again.

Review Questions

1. Define the concept of legitimacy (of a state). Explain why legitimacy is always an issue in a civil war.

2. Do interstate wars last longer on average than civil wars? Give a reason for the difference in the duration of the two types of wars.

3. Explain the commitment problem involved in reaching a peace settlement to end a civil war. Give two of the four ways that peacekeeping can help resolve the commitment problem.

Chapter 20
Terrorism

The attacks of September 11, 2001, often referred to simply as 9/11, killed more people than any other terrorist act in modern history. Terrorist attacks are not novel to recent history. The Anarchists of the late 19th and early 20th centuries killed political leaders and officials by shooting and bombings. President William McKinley was assassinated by Leon Czolgosz, an anarchist, in 1901. The term "assassin" traces back to the medieval cult of the Hashshashins who trained members to infiltrate and kill leaders they opposed. Contrary to popular belief, they did not use hashish to drug themselves before their attacks; the name came from the religious devotion or the name of the founder of the cult. Insurgent movements of the 20th century often attacked civilian targets, particularly in anti-colonial struggles. International terrorist attacks began in the late 1960s, primarily through hijackings of airplanes. These attacks differed from earlier terrorist attacks by being the main form of violence of these groups and by targeting victims internationally rather than locally. Al Qaeda, the organization responsible for the 9/11 attacks, extends the trends of relying on terror attacks alone against transnational targets with a transnational organization. Terrorism is now a major international concern. This chapter answers the following questions about terrorism:

- What is terrorism?
- How and why do non-state actors use terror?
- What are the effects of different responses to terrorism?

The table below shows the deadliest terror attacks of the last four decades of transnational terror. The 9/11 attacks which brought down the two towers of the World Trade Center in New York killed more people than any other attack by a factor of almost ten. Several of the events include multiple bombings if they were coordinated at the same target population at the same time. Some of these attacks are isolated incidents, such as the bombing of the Federal Building in Oklahoma City carried out by American extremists. Terrorism is most deadly when the responsible groups carry out campaigns of many attacks over time. Although each individual attack may not reach the table below, the cumulative effect of many attacks kills more people. To cite three infamous terrorist campaigns, the Irish Republican Army killed about 1,800 people, 650 of whom were civilians, during the period from 1969 to 1998 known as "The Time of Troubles." The others killed were generally British soldiers and government officials. Terror attacks during the Second Intifada from 2000 to 2005 killed 649 Israeli civilians. Israeli responses killed over 3000 Palestinians, some of which were civilians. The death toll from terrorist attacks and response killings in Iraq is difficult to know precisely. It is almost certainly in the tens of thousands and maybe in the hundreds of thousands. The big attacks in the table catch the attention of the world, but the cumulative effect of many smaller attacks over a long period of time is larger.

Table 20.1
Deadliest Terror Attacks of the Last 30 Years

Event	Death Toll
WTC/Pentagon: September 2001	2982
Bombings targeting Yazidis, Iraq: August 2007	796
Air India bombing, Irish Sea: June 1985	329
Pan Am bombing, Lockerbie: December 1988	270
Bombings, Mumbai, March 1993	270
US embassy bombings, Kenya/Tanzania: August 1998	224
Bombings, Sadr City, Iraq: November 2006	215
Bali bombings: October 2002	202
Madrid train bombings: March 2004	191
Mumbai train bombings: July 2006	183
Bombings, Baghdad and Karbala, Iraq: March 2004	181
UTA bombing, Chad: September 1989	170
Oklahoma City: April 1995	168

Not Included: Marine barracks bombing, Beirut: October 1983–299 dead; Beslan school siege: September 2004–334 dead.

What is Terrorism?

There is no internationally accepted definition of terrorism, despite efforts over the last several decades to negotiate an official definition of the term in international law. Further, the term is difficult to define because of the political nature of the attacks and the pejorative sense of the word. Terrorism is taken to be bad, and so describing the use of violence by those opposed to you politically as terrorism casts their political goals as well as their acts in the worst light. You have probably heard the line "one man's terrorist is another man's freedom fighter." Acts which the victims' side sees as terror, the attacker's side often sees as justifiable to gain their political goals.

Our object in this chapter is to understand why some groups use terror attacks, not to judge their goals. For our purposes, terrorism is

Violence by a non-state actor directed at non-military targets for political purposes.

All three parts of the definition are important and essential. All three of them also reflect the illegal nature of terrorism. Other acts of violence could be justified under international law or simply be violations of domestic law. The illegality of terror attacks strikes as the legal basis of the international system in addition to those who are killed and maimed. It is a political rejection of the principles of the system.

First, we will consider violence by non-state actors. States have often killed civilians in pursuit of their goals. The United States and its allies carried out aerial bombing campaigns against Germany and Japan in World War II which killed hundreds of thousands of civilians in both countries. Both bombing campaigns were justified as military actions and legal under existing international law. Other states have killed thousands of their own civilians during civil wars. Some speak of "state terrorism" where a government kills its own civilians to suppress opposition and intimidate the general population from openly opposing the government. We focus on violence by non-state actors not because these government acts are not appalling in their own right, but direct the analysis at non-state violence. States have the legitimate right to use violence when it is constrained by domestic and international law, while non-state actors do not. Often states engage in violence that is unlawful, although there is disagreement about the legal status of some uses of violence by states. The point is just that non-state actors do not possess a legal right to use violence to advance their political goals.

Second, the violent acts target civilians in terrorism. Often, terrorist tactics–bombings and assassinations for example–are often used against military targets. These attacks could be justified as military actions. Deliberate attacks on civilians are not allowed under international law, even though they do occur. The bombing of the Marine Barracks in Beirut, Lebanon in 1983 is not included in Table 1 because it killed U.S. and French military personnel. This attack both led the U.S. to withdraw its troops who were present in Beirut to stabilize the situation after the Israeli invasion of Lebanon and the resulting siege of Beirut in 1982. It was also the first suicide bombing, innovating that tactic which has now become unfortunately familiar. Because attacks on military targets could be considered legitimate military actions, they are excluded from this definition of terrorism. As we will see later in the chapter, it is common that groups that conduct terror attacks also attack military targets as well.

Third, the attacks must have a political motivation. After many attacks, a group claims responsibility. Such groups have known political goals, even if those goals are very broad and general. Iraqi insurgent groups often claim they seek an end to the occupation of their country with no clear idea of what type of government would follow afterwards. Terrorist groups often commit the same violations that criminal gangs do: kidnapings, bank robberies, and bombings for extortion to cite three examples. Criminal gangs do not have political motivations; they seek to gain wealth and control through violence. Terrorist groups use criminal acts to raise money through ransom, robbery, and extortion. In a few cases, terrorist groups change into criminal gangs, where ill-gotten gains takes the place of their political program. In the other direction, criminal gangs seek political influence to protect their criminal enterprises. Criminal behavior violates the laws of the country where it occurs, making it a matter of domestic law rather than international concern. There are transnational criminal gangs, particularly those which smuggle illegal drugs or people across national borders. But their acts are crimes in all the countries involved, and they do not seek political ends.

Terrorism covers a wide range of violent acts. Kidnapings of prominent people raise ransoms and demonstrate the inability of a government to protect its own people. Bombings of public places inflict indiscriminate death; other bombings target government buildings and officials. Assassinations allow terrorists to attack just government officials. Hijackings target national airlines or provide a way for group members to flee to a country that will provide them with shelter. All of these acts can lead to the extortion of protection payoffs to prevent future attacks. Bombings produce the greatest number killed compared to more selective terrorist attacks. There are some groups, such as ETA (Euskadi Ta Askatasuna), the Basque separatist group in Spain, that plan their bombings to minimize casualties. Not all terrorists want to kill as many as they can.

Strategies of Opposition

Political goals motivate terrorism. Those goals commonly oppose some feature of the status quo. The IRA sought to end British control of the six counties of Northern Ireland and join them to the Irish Republic. Palestinian terrorist groups seek at a minimum to end the Israeli occupation of the West Bank and Gaza and allow those who fled or were driven off during the formation of Israel to return; Hamas calls for the destruction of Israel in its 1988 charter. These goals are supported by a population larger than just the members of a terrorist group. They share the desire to change the status quo, even if they do not agree fully with the program of the terrorist group that purports to represent their desire.

The question is how to advance that shared desire to change the status quo. Groups that oppose the status quo have a range of different strategies they can use to advance their position. At one extreme, there are non-violent strategies; terrorism lies at the other. In between the two is irregular or guerrilla warfare. The strategies vary first in their violence and then also in the number of active people needed to make them effective. Violence and the number of active participants are related. Fewer people are willing to engage in violence, making it harder to recruit people in engage in guerrilla war or terrorism. At the same time, the more violent strategies require fewer active participants to have an effect. There is a range of levels of violence and participation within each of these three broad strategies of opposition. There are also a range of different acts of opposition within each, as we have seen with the range of attacks that terrorist groups conduct. Even though these strategies are presented as three distinct types of strategies, they form a line with combinations between the pure type of each. Further, opposition movements often use multiple strategies, particularly when more than one group purports to represent the desire for change. Terrorist groups often have links to open political parties, such as the IRA had with Sinn Fein. Sinn Fein ran candidates in Northern Ireland for Parliamentary elections during the Time of the Troubles, winning seats in Commons. Fatah, the main Palestinian political organization, has ties to the Al Aqsa Martyrs Brigade, a group which has carried out suicide bombings inside Israel in addition to other attacks on military targets.

Figure 25
Range of Strategies of Opposition

Less Violent		More Violent
Many People Required for Effect		Few People Required for Effect

---

| Non-Violent Action | Guerrilla War | Terrorism |

Non-violent strategies of opposition cover all forms of open political opposition, from forming political parties to contest elections or lobby the government to protest demonstrations. All of these activities take many different forms in action. There are political parties that run candidates to protest government policy with no intention of entering government, while others seek to replace the government to enact the changes they desire. There are large protest marches which operate under rules set for them by government officials and other protests which confront the government and its police. All of these strategies require a large number of active participants to be effective. Most university towns have small, regular protests on the street which are commonly ignored. Political parties need to recruit candidates and win the votes of many citizens to win office or attract attention to their cause. There can be risks attached to this political participation. Nondemocracies typically repress opposition political activities, whether they are political parties or public protests. Even in democracies, some protesters seek confrontation with the police, leading to the possibility of arrest and some violence. Still, the risks of non-violent opposition are less than in other strategies of opposition. Successful non-violent action requires hundreds of thousands or millions of participants.

Guerrilla movements seek to engage government forces and officials militarily. They form military units with commanders and training for the regular combatants. Generally, these units are small, around ten to fifteen combatants, which then form larger units for some attacks. Both police stations and military bases are common targets because guerrillas fight government forces typically at the time and place of their choosing. They spend the rest of their time moving to avoid government forces. They also move around to establish a presence in the territory they seek to control. They get supplies, particularly food, and information from the areas they move through, using a combination of sympathy with their cause and intimidation to extract what they need. Guerrilla movements are smaller than protest movement, typically numbering in the hundreds to thousands of combatants. They are often outnumbered by government military forces seeking to bring them to battle. They also seek to justify their use of violence as being the same as going to war against an unjust government. The risk to participants is much greater than for protest movements because they will have to fight in combat with government forces. Understandably, it is more difficult to recruit people to join guerrilla units than it is to recruit them for protest demonstrations.

Terrorist movements are the smallest and most violent opposition movements. They are commonly organized into small cells of only a few people. This cellular organization makes it difficult to break the organization as each member knows only a few other members. Terrorist organizations are typically small, numbering in the tens to the low thousands of members. It is more difficult to recruit people into a terror organization because the individual risk is great and few people are willing to engage in indiscriminate violence even when they support the cause behind it. Governments view terrorist acts are crimes, and many governments use all available means to break terrorist groups. The government of Saudi Arabia cracked down on Islamic extremists in the Kingdom after a campaign of attacks on foreigners and government officials in 2004 and 2005. The small size and secretive nature of terrorist groups makes it easier for them to avoid government detection. Even small groups can wreak serious damage. The Red Brigades, which numbers in the tens of members, carried out assassinations and kidnapings in Italy in the 1970s which prompted a strong reaction from the Italian government.

Terrorists and Resources

Any of these opposition groups requires resources–people and money–to create and support an organization. Although the mass demonstrations after the Iranian election this summer appear to have been organized spontaneously through Twitter and other forms of internet communications, movements that continue over a long period of time require some structure. All movements require leaders to decide how and when to act, they require ways to communicate with their supporters about the cause and how they are advancing it, and violent movements require weapons and supplies for those who carry out the violence. Sometimes, guerrilla and terrorist movements steal the weapons they use, but it is more common that they buy them from smugglers or obtain them from friendly foreign governments. These movements also need active members–demonstrators or party activists for a non-violent movement, soldiers for a guerrilla army, and operatives for a terrorist group. These members are recruited from the larger population sympathetic with their goals.

This sympathetic population could be within the country itself or external to it. If the movement advances the interest of an ethnic group, it can draw support from others of that ethnicity within the country and from those who live in other countries. The diaspora population was an import source of monetary support for the Kosovo Liberation Army (KLA) which built a guerrilla army that fought against the Serbian government in the late 1990s. The IRA raised money from Irish-Americans to support the cause broadly. These appeals claimed that the money would only support IRA widows and families whose husbands were in British jails for their IRA activities. Some of the money was skimmed off to buy weapons and support IRA men. The governments of other states all too often support guerrilla or terrorist movements as a way to get at states they oppose. Arab governments have provided monetary and military aid and safe places to live for the leaders to Palestinian groups of all sorts as a way to support the Palestinian cause against Israel. These *state sponsors* of terrorism were more common during the Cold War. Now some governments arm and encourage rebel movements in neighboring countries to use against those neighboring governments. As noted above, guerrilla bands and terrorist groups often commit criminal acts, including bank robbery, kidnaping for ransom, and drug smuggling, to raise money. All these groups also recruit new activists, soldiers, or terrorists from the sympathetic population.

Communicating how the group advances the grievance shared by the sympathetic population is important for this recruiting. People and governments give money to groups that act to advance causes with which they agree. The political goals of the terrorist groups are an important part of their appeal. A group also needs to show how providing it with support will advance the shared grievance. This is one reason why terrorist launch public attacks and claim credit for them. It demonstrates to their supporters that the group is doing something. Fund raising may be done through charitable appeals as well as directly. Transnational fund-raising and recruiting is one of the hallmarks of Al Qaeda, but other groups raise support from sympathetic populations in other countries.

Terrorism needs some perceived grievance with the status quo. This grievance may not be justified, but it is felt by the members of the group and the sympathetic population from which it draws support. Even if many in the sympathetic population do not favor the use of violence to advance their cause, the group can still draw support from that population as long as enough people are willing to give money or join the group. Understanding the grievance underlying a group is important to understanding why they use terrorism to advance it. Again, we are not judging such ends as justified by studying them. We are only trying to understand why some turn to attack civilians to advance their causes.

These grievances can motivate groups that use all three strategies of opposition. Although political parties generally do not use violence to advance their political agenda (although it does happen more often than we in the U.S. think), they may find links to those who are willing to use violence useful. These links are often kept secret to the advantage of both. The open political party can claim they know nothing about the terrorist group, and the terrorists can claim they are the vanguard of those seeking to address the grievance. The party can provide aid to the terrorist group while being able to deny publicly that it is involved in terrorism. The links between the IRA and Sinn Fein were a clear example of such links. As an IRA document puts the matter,

> "Both Sinn Féin and the IRA play different but converging roles in the war of national liberation. The Irish Republican Army wages an armed campaign... Sinn Féin maintains the propaganda war and is the public and political voice of the movement".

Whether a political party controls terrorist groups linked to it is rarely clear. It serves the interests of both to deny such control. It is also common for guerrilla movements to be associated with a political party and terrorist groups. They can advance their cause using all three strategies of opposition.

Choosing among Strategies of Opposition

The strategy a group chooses to advance its concerns depends on the likely costs and benefits of the available strategies. The chosen strategy and the response of the government being challenged affect how many people join the group in its efforts. Governments which allow open political participation and do not threaten or punish those who oppose them publicly make such open political opposition more attractive to opposition groups. People sharing the goals of the group are more willing to join public demonstrations or support political parties if they will not pay a personal cost for such actions. This makes it easier for the leaders of a group to attract the large support needed to make non-violent opposition effective as a way to realize their goals. Joining a demonstration is a dangerous act in a society where the government uses the police to break demonstrations up violently. Oppression discourages open, non-violent opposition to advance complaints against that government.

This cost for open political opposition does not mean that groups with grievances always turn to violence. Violent opposition has costs as well, and the choice of strategy depends on relative costs and benefits. All governments react against violent opposition with the force of government, although how they do so varies. Democracies commonly use law enforcement against violent opposition. They arrest and prosecute those responsible for the violence. The limits of fair trials means that not all those who use violence will end up behind bars. Autocracies use secret police and oppression against violent opponents. They aim both to make sure that all responsible pay a personal cost for their actions and to intimidate others considering joining that opposition. They proceed against anyone under even the slightest suspicion. The difference between law enforcement in a democracy and oppression by the secret police in an autocracy implies that violent opposition is more attractive in a democracy than an autocracy. Together with the greater ease of non-violent opposition in a democracy, the costs of these strategies suggest only that democracies should have more opposition of both types. The ease of open, non-violent opposition in a democracy may lead those with grievances toward that option. Those in autocracies may be inclined toward violent opposition only because non-violent opposition is unlikely to work. The choice of strategies then may depends as much on the circumstances of individual groups themselves: how easily they can recruit supporters and what strategies they can use more effectively.

One group is particularly likely to find non-violent opposition ineffective and so unattractive: foreigners. The United States government has done many things that people in other countries dislike. Those people have demonstrated against the U.S. government and what they consider its evil actions. Such demonstrations rarely seem to change U.S. policy. Their greatest effect is on the government where the demonstrations take place, discouraging that government from working with the U.S. The Reagan Administration sought to deploy nuclear-armed, short-ranged missiles in some of its NATO allies in the early 1980s. These deployments were very unpopular with many in those countries because they feared that those missiles made their countries targets for similar Soviet nuclear-armed missiles. Anti-nuclear groups organized mass demonstrations against the missile deployments. The U.S. deployed those missiles despite the demonstration, although it produced great political tension within the NATO alliance. People outside the U.S. may then turn to terrorism against symbols of the U.S. because they lack the ability to change either U.S. policy or the stance of their own government through other means.

Specific terrorist tactics and targets are chosen for the ease of carrying them out and the value of the target attacked. Ease of attack depends on both the capabilities of the terrorist group and what targets the government defends and how it defends them. Some terrorist groups acquire special skills in bomb construction and delivery, while others focus on armed attacks. Governments seek to harden some targets against bombings, as the United States has done for all of its embassies by placing barriers at a distance from each embassy to make it impossible to drive a car bomb next to the building. Terror groups and government respond to what one another does with each trying to gain an advantage. As mentioned earlier, hijackings of international flights were a common terror tactics in the late 1960s and early 1970s. It was easy to smuggle some guns or a bomb aboard and commandeer the plane. There was even a verb for such attacks (which I doubt you have heard before): "skyjacking." Skyjackings were stopped by a combination of metal detectors at airports, which made it likely that attempts to smuggle guns or bombs on planes would be detected before boarding, and armed sky marshals who could deter attempts to hijack planes once in flight. Terror groups changed their tactics in response. Attacks on U.S. diplomats rose in the 1970s following the adoption of these measures to stop skyjackings. The type of attack and its target depend on what the group can do and how easy it is to attack different targets.

The value of the target attacked varies with the publicity for the attack and how it strikes at where the government feels vulnerable. During the 1972 Summer Olympics in Munich, Germany, Black September, a Palestinian terrorist group, entered the Olympic Village and seized 11 Israeli athletes and coaches as hostages. They negotiated free passage out of the resulting siege, but the German police attempted to rescue the hostage at the airport. Eleven of the hostages died in the attempt to save them. The attack dominates the memories of that Olympics; the whole world was watching. The cameras of the world's news organization were more important than the number of the dead. Over time, terrorist groups have sought to kill more victims and launched bigger attacks, in part to gain attention for their attacks. Terrorist groups also seek to provoke governments into overreacting to their attacks. The Red Brigades kidnaped Italian politicians and industrialists to provoke the Italian government. They hoped to show the repressive nature of that government to people who might have sympathized with their cause but were unwilling to adopt their violent methods. The Italian government did increase police powers in response to the attacks, but these measures were broadly popular among Italians and gave the government the power to break the Red Brigades over several years. When provocation works, it leads the government to adopt repressive measures that create more active supporters of the terrorists. Some Palestinian groups carry out attacks to provoke harsh responses from the government of Israel, responses that will convince some Palestinians that terror is the only way they will achieve their national ambitions for a state of their own.

Terror groups divide into two types based on their goals and why they use violence. Moderate groups use violence to achieve possible political aims. Violence for them is a strategy. It is not unusual for former terrorists to become legitimate politicians later. Prime Minister Menachem Begin of Israel was a central figure in the Irgun, which carried out terror attacks against British forces and officials before the end of the British Mandate of Palestine. After the creation of Israel, he became a legitimate politician and the first Likud Prime Minister in 1977. He then reached a peace treaty with President Anwar Sadat of Egypt under the assistance of U.S. President Jimmy Carter at the Camp David Peace Accords of 1978. Begin and Sadat shared the Nobel Peace Prize as a result of that peace settlement. Moderates use terror to advance their political goals, understanding that they may eventually have to cut a deal with those they attack today. Extreme terror groups have wide-reaching ends, goals which their targets are unlikely to ever accept. These groups are willing to use greater violence to draw support to their extreme aims. The hard liners gain by provoking a strong response from their target government. That response convinces those members of the sympathetic population who are sitting on the fence that the most violent actions are necessary to advance their common cause. A government facing such threats cannot tell whether their terrorist attackers are moderates with whom a deal can be struck or extremists with whom no realistic deal is possible.

Government Responses

Governments can respond to a terrorist threat in many different ways. Counterterrorist measures fall into two broad groups: active and passive measures. Passive measures attempt to make it difficult for terrorists to launch attacks. We are all familiar with airport security measures, passing through the metal detector, having our luggage screened, and taking off our shoes. All of these passive measures were adopted in response to specific types of terrorist tactics. Metal detectors responded to skyjackers who used guns. When the 9/11 skyjackers used box cutters as weapons to commandeer the planes used in the attacks, metal detection was strengthened and the list of items you could not carry on a plane was expanded. Removing checked luggage if a passenger checked in but did not board the plane responded to earlier attacks where a bomb was loaded into the luggage compartment that way. Scanning shoes responded to Richard Reid, the "Shoebomber," who attempted to blow up a trans-Atlantic flight with bombs built into his shoes. Passive measures also include hardening targets against bombings and posting guards and checkpoints around buildings. Passive measures only catch terrorists if they try to carry out an attack.

Active measures seek out terrorists to capture, kill, or arrest them before they carry out an attack. Police work to round up a network of terrorists before they carry out an attack is an active measure. Intelligence work which seeks to uncover terrorist organization and dismantle them is a broader active measure. In the extreme, the U.S. and Israeli governments have used their militaries to attack suspected terrorists in places where their police forces and intelligence services have difficulty penetrating. The U.S. military uses unmanned aircraft to launch missile strikes in places U.S. soldiers and intelligence operatives dare not go, such as the back country of Pakistan and Yemen. Active measures try to eliminate the ability of terrorists to carry out attacks before they occur.

Both types of measures have limitations. Terrorists can avoid passive measures by changing which targets they attack and how. Attacks on U.S. diplomats substituted for skyjackings when metal detectors and sky marshals made those attacks less likely to succeed in the 1970s. The "shoe bomb" was a novel way to avoid the screening for planes at that time. Bombings of public places are the most common terror attack in Iraq because it is extremely difficult to prevent such attacks with passive measures. Checkpoints screen cars and people for bombs, but some guards can be bribed to look the other way. More generally, you cannot defend all possible targets with passive measures. Active measures face the problem that terrorist work in secret, only revealing their intent to attack when they do. Terrorist organizations are difficult to infiltrate agents into or convince members to inform on. Even when a government can place agents in a network or recruit informants, the cellular nature of terrorist organizations makes it difficult to identify and then arrest a large number of their members. Because it is difficult to identify terrorists, active measures which seek to kill or arrest terrorists before they strike may target innocent people instead. Missile strikes often kill innocent passers-by in addition to their targets. Active measures that hurt innocents can increase the grievances that the sympathetic population has with the government carrying them out. This makes it easier for those groups to raise support and recruit new members from that population. They may end up creating more terrorists than they eliminate. Active and passive measures have different drawbacks then.

Counterterrorist measures can also be observable or unobservable to those they seek to protect and defend. Airport security is observable. Everyone getting on a plane knows that they are protected by airport screening because they all passed through it. Hardening of buildings is often easily observable, such as the concrete barriers that prevent vehicles from approaching building too closely. Intelligence and police detective work is unobservable to most citizens. Vice President Dick Cheney frequently defended a number of counterterror provisions adopted by the Bush Administration by claiming that those measures stopped many attacks before they happened. It is impossible for an average U.S. citizen to verify his claims. Some people were tried and convicted as a result of these investigations, which provides public verification of those plots. But many of these investigations and their results are kept secret in part for security purposes. Revealing means of surveillance used in intelligence operations allows terrorists to change to other more secure locations and ways to communicate. After Al Qaeda bombed U.S. embassies in Kenya and Tanzania in 1998, President Clinton later authorized cruise missile strikes on Al Qaeda training camps in Afghanistan in an effort to kill Bin Laden and disrupt those camps. The U.S. government used intercepted cell phone traffic to locate Bin Laden at one of the camps to be struck. Afterwards, Bin Laden learned that cell phones were not a secure form of communication, and Al Qaeda shifted to other forms that were more difficult to trace. These missile strikes were observable because they were reported in the news. How effective they were against Al Qaeda was not observable to most Americans, however.

Politicians favor observable counterterror measures over unobservable one because they can claim credit for the former with voters. When terror attacks become a concern for a country, there will be a general demand that the government stop or at least limit those attacks. In a democracy, counterterror becomes an issue in elections. The opposition often charges that the government has not done enough. The government wants to demonstrate publicly what it has done to protect its public. Voters judge such claims in part through what they can see and observe. Politicians can claim anything they want during a campaign, but claims backed up by facts are more convincing to voters. Voters cannot verify the effectiveness of unobservable measures, as was the case with Vice President Cheney's claim that such measures stopped many attacks before they happened. Political leaders should favor observable measures over unobservable ones because voters can see that something is being done to protect them. This political incentive leads democratic governments to provide more observable measures and less unobservable measures than they would if they were only concerned with stopping future attacks. The level of airport security we have now does prevent attacks by imposing substantial delays on travelers. Making everyone take their shoes off at a screening point prevents a second shoe bombing, but at what cost? Observable measures could be active or passive, so this pattern does not determine which will be used. It only contends that democratic politicians will provide more observable measures than they should.

Negotiating with Terrorists

It is often said that "you should never negotiate with terrorists," and many governments and political leaders have loudly proclaimed this commitment to never give in. Yet, many governments, including the United States and Israel, have negotiated with terror groups. Sometimes these negotiations are tactical, such as securing the release of hostages. Other times, they attempt to find a political settlement to address the grievance underlying the terrorist movement. The most successful and famous example of the latter is the Good Friday Agreement that ended the Time of Troubles in Northern Ireland. It created a local legislature for Northern Ireland with authority to run many affairs in the six counties and included both Protestant and Catholic representatives. It set up commissions on human rights and equality where citizens could bring complaints. It eventually disarmed the IRA, what is called "decommissioning," and reformed the police services which had been dominated by the Protestants. The agreement was signed in 1998, and while peace did not immediately follow, the agreement has ended "The Time of Troubles."

Negotiation is a third way that governments can respond to terrorism. Active and passive measures do not attempt to deal with the underlying concerns motivating terrorism; they only attempt to prevent further attacks. Negotiated settlements on the grievances underlying the movement aim at convincing the sympathetic population that their concerns have been addressed, and so there is no need to continue to support terrorist groups. They aim to separate the terrorists from those who support them with resources and recruits. Commonly, negotiations are held with political parties which also advance the grievance which the terrorist group draws on. A settlement also hopes to pull these political parties away from the terror groups and draw them into regular politics. Sinn Fein had elected members to the British Parliament before the Good Friday Agreement. That agreement brought them into local government of Northern Ireland as a main, legitimate political party representing Catholics. Negotiations seek to separate the moderates away from the extremists by addressing their grievance.

Negotiations, however, often fail to end all terrorist activity. First, negotiations do not reach an agreement which both sides accept. Open negotiations between Israel and the Palestine Liberation Organization (PLO) began with the Oslo Accord of 1993. This agreement created a framework for a process that would create an independent Palestinian authority (the PA) which would run Palestinian territory. Although progress toward a final settlement was made, the PA was created and it gained autonomy to rule some areas of the West Bank and Gaza, both sides charged the other with not living up to the terms of the process. Israel charged that the PA did not do enough on its commitments to enforce security, while the PA charged that Israel did not withdraw quickly enough and continued to build settlements for Israel citizens on land that the PA would eventually control. The Oslo Accord ended with the failure of negotiations to reach a final settlement in 2000, leading to the break out of the Second Intifada. Subsequent attempts to restart such "peace processes" such as the Arab initiative at the Beirut Summit in 2002 or President Bush's "road map for peace," have foundered. Second, even when settlements are concluded, one or more parties violate them afterwards, leading to renewed violence. Why is it so difficult to negotiate with terrorists successfully?

Negotiations to address the issues underlying terrorism face two, matched commitment problems. Such deals call for the government to address the underlying concerns while the opposition groups renounce terrorist tactics to advance their cause. Often those associated with terror become open politicians. In cases like Northern Ireland, they become legitimate politicians in the country making the concessions. The first commitment problem arises from doubts of former terrorists that the government will continue to honor their concessions and allow the now-former terrorists to operate as an open political party. Once the terrorists disarm, what leverage do they have against the government if it reneges? Most governments have overwhelming power within their borders. Once former terrorists live openly, they could be arrested and tried for their earlier crimes. The concessions may be unpopular with many citizens in the country, providing a political motive for government leaders to renege. All of these possibilities can raise doubts in the minds of groups associated with terrorism during and after the period of negotiation.

One way these groups can hedge against those risks is to keep some capability to restart terror attacks if the government reneges. If terrorism was the source of leverage that induced the government to make concessions, keeping a potential to attack again provides leverage against the government. The second commitment problem comes from the government's doubts about whether the groups they are negotiating with have renounced terrorism and disarmed for good. After all, ending terror attacks is what the government seeks. Why make concessions if they do not produce what you want? Terrorist groups operate in secret, making it difficult to find and arrest their operatives. This secret nature heightens government concerns that terrorists may simply remain armed and underground, waiting for the appropriate moment to renew attacks. Such attacks could be used to extract further concessions beyond the original peace deal.

The Good Friday Agreement faced both of these commitment problems. "Decommissioning"–disarming the IRA–was a key element of the agreement. The IRA did not fully comply with this at first, turning over some but not all of their weapons. When links between the leaders of Sinn Fein and these holdouts became public in 2002, the entire process almost ended. Complete disarmament of the IRA was not final and verified by clergymen from both sides until 2005. Even then, a faction of the IRA broke off, called itself "the Real IRA," and refused to give up their weapons. Loyalists, Protestants who opposed the IRA, and their paramilitary groups were also reluctant to give up their arms. The Real IRA is an example of how the secret and diffuse nature of terrorist movements create commitment problems. Few people in a terrorist organization know much about the full organization; they mainly know the people they work with locally. This loose structure makes it easy for small groups to splinter off into a new armed faction. Even if the moderates in a group wish to make peace, others may not and instead create their own splinter group to continue the armed struggle. This is particularly likely when the members of the splinter group hold extreme views of the goals of the group. The Real IRA sought to have the six counties of Northern Ireland incorporated into Ireland, rather than remaining within Great Britain. The combination of dispersion and splintering accentuate the commitment problem posed by terrorist disarming.

One possible solution to these commitment problems uses the moderates from the terrorist factions and parties against the extremists. The government takes measures to reassure that the moderates can operate as an open political party. In turn, the moderates either disarm or identify the extremists so the government can crack down on them. Various efforts in the peace process between Israel and the Palestinians use this idea. Even with networks of Israeli informers, the PA has better knowledge of where members of Palestinian terror cells are. Many of the interim agreements call on the PA to arrest or control these extremists to prevent renewed violence. This experience has not been entirely successful. The PA often claims that it lacks the ability to find and control those who still wish to carry out attacks; Israel often charges that the PA could do more. Whether lack of will or lack of capabilities explains why many Palestinian terrorists remain free is not clear. Their continued freedom raises Israeli concerns that a final settlement will lead to renewed attacks rather than their end. On the other hand, Israeli security measures and overwhelming military power raise Palestinian concerns that Israel will renege on a deal, and so some capability for further terrorist attacks should be retained. These fears show that the strategy of using the moderates against the extremists faces problems of its own, not that it is doomed from the outset.

If a settlement is reached with moderates, extremists will want to show their displeasure with it. They may engage in terror attacks in an attempt to provoke the government into breaking off the agreement. If they can demonstrate that they still possess the ability to carry out attacks, that may be sufficient to convince the government to renege to protect its citizens. Settlements then may increase violence in the short run, while reducing violence in the long run. The extremists launch attacks in the hope of undermining the agreement.

Chapter Summary

Terror is the weapon of the weak and the extreme. Non-state actors use terrorism to attack non-military targets to advance their political ends. They choose to use terror because other strategies of opposition are less attractive for advancing their ends. Terror is difficult to defeat because terrorists can change their tactics in response to passive government defenses, terrorist groups operate secretly making it difficult to find and stop their members before attacks, and active measures may harm innocents, creating more support for the terrorists. Under the right circumstances, governments should negotiate with terrorists to address the grievances underlying it. Successful settlements could pull off the moderates, weakening support for extremists who use violence. Any settlement faces a pair of commitment problems as both sides fear that the other will not live up to the terms of the deal of remedy of the grievance for an end to violence.

Review Questions

1. Identify three different strategies open to non-state groups with grievances against their government or the international order, and explain what factors influence a group's decision to use each of them.

2. Explain the difference between active and passive measures that governments can use to reduce the threat of terrorist attacks. Specify the disadvantages of each. Give an example of a passive measure and an active measure.

3. Two commitment problems complicate the resolution of issues that generate terrorist movements. What type of reneging does the government fear after a negotiated settlement? What does the former terrorist group fear if it transforms into an open political party?

Chapter 21
International Cooperation and the Problem of Enforcement

The Organization of Petroleum Exporting States (OPEC) has influenced the price of crude oil since the early 1970s by restricting the production of its members. Its members include many of the major oil producing countries in the developing world, including Saudi Arabia, Kuwait, Iraq, Iran, Nigeria, and Venezuela. Several important oil producers in the developing world, particularly Russia, Mexico, and China, are not members of OPEC. Major producers of oil among the developed world, namely the United States, Canada, Norway and Great Britain, are not members of OPEC either. OPEC's leverage on the oil markets comes from its control of about 40% of world oil production and a majority of the world's proven oil reserves, that is, oil which has been discovered but has not yet been pumped out of the ground. OPEC members also dominate the international trade in oil, producing more than half of all oil traded internationally.

[Table of top oil producing countries, their reserves, and whether they are members of OPEC]

OPEC holds meetings of the oil ministers of its members regularly twice a year and occasionally holds special sessions in response to unusual conditions in the oil market. The representatives of the member states agree on production quotas for member states in the near future. They consider market conditions for the international sale, such as how the demand for oil rises and falls with the state of the international economy. They also respond to other factors influencing the production and sale of oil, such as the Gulf War in 1991. Oil available to the world market was restricted during the Gulf Crisis and War by the occupation of Kuwait by Iraq and economic sanctions placed on Iraq by the UN Security Council that prevented Iraq from selling its oil production on the world market. OPEC member states generally produce less than their maximum possible oil production, so the production quotas typically restrict how much each member state produces. At times, OPEC has asked its members to increase their production to prevent the price of oil from rising too high too quickly. Generally though, OPEC acts to limit production which raises the price of crude oil above what it would be if all oil producers pumped as much oil as they could.

OPEC has the incentives of an economic cartel, an agreement by producers to limit their production to raise prices. Because OPEC members produce a predominant share of the oil traded internationally, they have influence over the price of oil through their production. As producers, all benefit through a higher price because they receive more money for their oil. Limiting their production restricts the supply of oil, which causes the price of oil to rise. OPEC does not set the price of oil because there is substantial production outside of its members and it cannot control how much oil is used, the demand for oil. A cartel organizes producers of a good, oil in the case of OPEC, to restrict their production to raise the price of what they supply and so make more money for all members.

Cartels commonly face a problem that their members often have incentives to cheat on any agreement to restrict production and so raise the price of the goods they supply. They try to set quotas for production by each member to set their overall production at a lower level than they would if each determined its production on its own. Each individual producer can make more money if it produces more than its quota. It pockets all the extra revenue from its production above quota. This additional production has little effect on the price of the good the cartel produces if all the other members honor their production quotas. The amount of additional oil on the market is small, so it has little effect on the price. The state producing over its quota gains all the revenue from that overproduction while all members suffer from the small decrease in price. But if all members produce over their quotas, the effect of the cartel is diminished because it is not restricting the supply of oil. This incentive to overproduce and pocket the extra revenue produces a problem of *enforcement*. The members of OPEC share an interest in raising the price of oil, but they individually have an incentive to break any deal that seeks to raise the price by restricting output through national quotas.

Any agreement to restrict production also faces the problem that it can be hard to tell if any OPEC member is producing above its quota. Oil is traded on the open market, commonly called the "spot market," for delivery in the near future measured in months. Crude oil is classified by type because the different types vary in their composition of hydrocarbons and level of sulfur; my personal favorite is "Mars Blend." But the different grades of crude oil do not vary so much that their type tells you where the oil was produced. Countries can sell their production on the spot market without the traders knowing about the precise source. Oil is a commodity in the sense that any barrel of oil in a particular grade is the same as far as refiners care. The spot market provides a way for OPEC member states to sell production above quota without the organization or other members knowing that they have broken their production quota. Nevertheless, OPEC has been able to influence the price of oil since the first oil shock in 1973. The Arab states in OPEC pushed for an embargo on oil exports to the United States and the Netherlands in response to their support of Israel in the October War. This restriction in supply caused the price of oil to rise about 300 percent. The embargoes were removed in March 1974, but the price of oil remained at its new, higher level. Since then, OPEC has been able to influence the price of oil both up and down. The price depends on demand and other suppliers, so OPEC cannot set the price where it wants. For example, Russia is the second largest producer of oil now and it did not trade oil on the international market during the Cold War. How has OPEC been able to get its members to produce close enough to their quotas to influence the price of oil?

The Problem of Cooperation

There are many issues in world politics where states share some common interest but disagree about exactly how to pursue those interests. In international trade, states can increase their national incomes by lowering trade barriers. Free trade produces the common interest of a wealthier world. However, all states also place some barriers to the movement of goods, so completely free trade has never occurred. Each country thinks its own barriers to trade are fine while those of other countries which prevent its exports from being sold there are wrong and must be removed. For states to gain the shared interest in lower barriers to trade, they have to agree which barriers are acceptable. They wish to cooperate on freer trade but have to agree how. In the global economy, national economies are interdependent. What happens in one country affects the economy of its trading partners and those who invest in it. An economic slowdown such as that produced by the credit crisis in the United States in 2007 and 2008 affects other countries' economies because the U.S. buys less from them. An economic contraction produces personal hardship because people lose their jobs, firms go bankrupt, and investors lose money. The bland inoffensive term for this economic pain is the "price of adjustment." This personal hardship often leads to demands for politicians to remedy it through government action. The government of a country could try to ease the economic pain by blocking imports or driving down the value of its currency. Both of these measures reduce its imports–goods produced by other countries and bought in the country–and increase its exports and so help workers, firms, and investors in the country. But those same measures hurt the economies of its trading partners. They in turn might take similar measures to block the exports of the first country. The end result would be that all would be worse off economically. States with interdependent economies need to agree on how to handle the costs of adjustment. Left to their own devices, all may pursue policies that hurt them all. Some environmental issues cross national borders, and so are international. States have a shared interest in cleaning and preserving the environment, but such action is not free. Each would like others to pay those costs or at least they disagree about how the costs should be divided. They need to agree on who pays for the cleanup. On all three of these issues, states have a common interest, in freer trade, in controlling the international economy, and in cleaning up the environment, while also disagree about how exactly to achieve each of these common aims. These are problems of cooperation.

Cooperation can be difficult because states disagree about how to pursue their common interest. It is not enough to just say that all share some interest. They also have to agree on how they will pursue that common benefit. An agreement to realize that benefit could involve active coordination of their policies, require the creation of an international organization to support those policies, or simply have states refrain from policies that hurt other states. These disagreements are part of the explanation why states do not always reach agreements to realize apparent common interests. A second reason why states might fail to cooperate lies in whether the parties will follow through on an agreement. This chapter explores this second reason why cooperation fails and the next tackles the first reason. Together they address the general issue of why states so often fail to act in their common interest.

Although we are taught to cooperate with others as early as preschool, international cooperation is not always a good thing. Sometimes a few states cooperate in an interest they share that hurts other countries outside their group. OPEC is an example of cooperation that does not benefit all. Oil exporting countries benefit from a higher price, while oil importing countries lose from it. Economists commonly attribute much of the global economic difficulties of the 1970s to the sharp rise in the price of oil in the first oil shock of 1973 produced by OPEC. OPEC maintains that it acts in the interest of all by producing a stable oil market through its regulation of production in national quotas. But I think few in the developed world feel those benefits when they fill their gas tank. It is important to remember that international cooperation is not always a good thing. Even when it is not good, states that benefit from it still face the difficulties of cooperating for their specific, shared interest.

Issues where cooperation occurs differ from those we studied in conflict. Issues of conflict, particularly territory, raise the possibility that one side could impose the outcome it wants. Force, in the sense of an actor imposing its preferred outcome, is present on issues of conflict but not on issues of cooperation. On economic issues, countries cannot force other states to lower their trade barriers, to revalue their currency, or take policy steps that contract their economy. On environmental issues, one state cannot make another lower its emissions of pollutants. On human rights, the conscience of the world cannot compel a dictator to respect those rights for his people. This is not to say that actors do not try to influence one another on issues of cooperation. They attempt to persuade others to do as they wish, they apply pressure by threatening to impose costs on others if they do not agree to cooperate as they like, and they offer rewards to others who accept how they would like to cooperate. In all these cases, cooperation requires the active consent and often the active participation of other governments and actors. Effective solutions of these issues require the cooperation of many states, unlike on issues of conflict.

Enforcement and Agreement: The Two Stages of Cooperation

Successful cooperation requires two things:
1. An agreement on how to cooperate, and
2. Each side then does what it is supposed to do in that agreement.

There are many ways that states could cooperate on a given issue. If we think of cooperation as solving some joint problem that states face, they have to choose one of the possible solutions to that problem. To cooperate, they have to agree on one of them so they know what one another will do. For OPEC, the members have to set quotas about how much oil each member is supposed to produce. The total of these quotas give the target production for the organization's members. They cannot control how much oil other producers will pump nor how much oil the world market will demand. But they can negotiate how much oil they will produce. The next chapter analyzes this stage of international cooperation, which we will call *agreement*.

Once an agreement on how to cooperate has been reached, then the parties have to live up to the agreement. If not, they will not be cooperating with one another. Their policies will not be coordinated to their mutual benefit, although presumably each will be trying to realize some individual benefit. OPEC members must limit their production to make the price of oil rise or at least not fall. As mentioned earlier, each member acting on its own has an incentive to produce over quota to increases its national revenues from oil. Parties to a cooperative agreement may still realize some benefits from it if any cheating on the agreement is minor. Agreements to lower trade barriers can still produce some of the benefits of freer trade even though all states keep barriers to the move of some goods and services. Because self-interest often leads parties to violate agreements to cooperate, I refer to the strategic problem at the second stage of cooperation as *enforcement*. How might the parties enforce the agreement on one another given individual incentives to cheat on that agreement?

Inability to enforce an agreement can undermine any reason to reach a cooperative agreement. If the parties believe that one another will not live up to the terms of agreement, an agreement to cooperate is empty because it will not produce its benefits. Occasionally, states will sign such empty agreements just to claim credit for "doing something" on the issue. These agreements are often just vague statements that action should be taken on the issue with no detail or plan about what steps each state will take. Such agreements can be the first step toward cooperation without actually leading states to cooperate. The first major international agreement on global climate change was the UN Framework Convention on Climate Change (abbreviated like almost everything associated with the UN by its initials, UNFCCC; don't ask me how you say it). States finalized this treaty for the 1992 Rio Conference on global climate change. The treaty sets no binding national limits on emissions of global warming gases nor does it contain any enforcement proceedings. It is not binding on state parties to the treaty in those senses. It does call on member states to negotiate such limits in follow-on agreements, of which the Kyoto Protocol in 1997 was the first major such agreement. UNFCCC is the first step toward international cooperation on this issue even though it did not require states to adopt policies to address climate change. Most observers consider the later protocols as the first real cooperative agreements on the issue.

Compliance versus Effectiveness

States do not have to fully live up to all the terms of an agreement for them to cooperate. International cooperation is often partial. No state carries out all of its obligations but they realize some benefits from the partial steps they take. Members of OPEC often pump above their quotas, but they can still realize a higher price of oil if they still limit themselves to producing less than their full capacity. The logic of partial cooperation matches that of speed limits on roads. It is well-known that the police will not pull a car over for speeding if it is going just a few miles per hour above the limit. The ways of measuring how fast a car is going are imprecise, so the citation may not hold up in court if the driver chooses to defend him or herself against it. Instead, the police focus their attention on cars driving much faster than the speed limit or those driving dangerously, like weaving through traffic. Casual observation of highways shows that many drivers routinely exceed the speed limit. This does not mean that speed limits have no effect on how fast people drive. The threat of a ticket does cause many drivers to drive more slowly (or more accurately, less fast) than they would in the absence of any limit. You can see this when a speed limit is changed on a highway. Similarly, states can realize some benefits from international cooperation even though they do not fully meet their obligations.

There is a difference then between compliance and effectiveness on agreements to cooperate. *Compliance* is whether the states do what they agreed to do. *Effectiveness* is the degree to which the benefits of cooperation are realized. Both matter for cooperation, and enforcement can increase both. States could comply with an agreement that had little effectiveness because it asks them to do little to change their behavior. The Kyoto Protocol is an example of such an agreement. As we will see in the chapter on international environmental issues, many states that have ratified Kyoto do not need to take steps to reduce their emissions. They are already in compliance with the agreement. But the agreement has little effect on the emission of global warming gases because emissions from the states that have ratified have gone down a little and the biggest emitters, particularly the United States, have not ratified the treaty and so are not bound by it. On the other hand, an agreement could be effective even if states often fail to comply with it. The WTO system on trade has aided the growth in international trade even though disputes–formal complaints by one member state about another member state's policies–are common. The target of these disputes is not complying with the treaty on the policy in question. At the same time, they have lowered their barriers to trade for many other goods and services, making the WTO effective.

So far, I have described cooperation as having a fixed sequence where first states agree on how to cooperate and then try to enforce it on one another. In reality, agreement and enforcement are often mixed up together. States generally must make multiple agreements over time how to cooperate, with the acts that produce cooperation changing with circumstances in the world. OPEC ministers meet every six months to set new production quotas in response to changes in the oil market on both the producing and consuming side. Sometimes, a member's new quota is changed based on how it has acted in the recent past. This change is a form of enforcement. Because conditions addressed by international cooperation change, the cooperative policies that states adopt must change with them. Cooperation among states is an ongoing relationship. There are examples of issues where the parties reach a single agreement which then persists unchanged in the future, but these issues are rare. The metric system is an internationally accepted standard for measurement in every country except the United States, Liberia, and Myanmar (also known as Burma). A standard measure means that parts manufactured in one country will match the specifications in another, which would be difficult if the two used different measurement systems. Countries do not meet to renegotiate metric system although the standards for the various measurements have changed as technology has provided more precise ways to measure distances, weights, and time. Even though agreement and enforcement are mixed up together as states cooperate, we will treat them as separate stages of cooperation in that order for analytic purposes. It is easiest to think about international cooperation happening in these two stages even when both occur after one another and often together in the real world.

Why is Enforcement a Problem?

It might appear at first thought that enforcement of cooperative agreements should not be a problem. After all, the agreement produces a benefit that all will share, even if some like that agreement better than others. Enforcement matters because states do not always live up to their cooperative agreements. Further, they have no recourse to outside parties to enforce their deal. They must enforce it on themselves to the extent they are capable. This is the assumption of *anarchy* in the international system. If two people in a country draw up a contract to pursue a common interest, say opening a business venture, they have recourse to the court system if one of them should break the contract. The aggrieved party bringing the lawsuit can use the power of the government to aid in the collection of any damages the court rules against the other party. Although there is the International Court of Justice, it rarely resolves disputes between countries. Even when it does make a ruling, the parties still have to enforce it among themselves. Anarchy does not mean that international politics is ruled by the law of the jungle. States often cooperate and are able to enforce many agreements among themselves. If they did not and could not, there would be no international cooperation to study.

Why then is enforcement a problem? Some cooperative agreements are self-enforcing and require no enforcement. There is no reason for a state to cheat on the metric system. The benefits of a common standard of measurement are realized only when many follow it, but those who cheat on it suffer the loss of that standard. The fact that the U.S. does not use the metric system for everyday membership hurts the U.S. and does not prevent other countries from gaining the benefits of standardization in the trade amongst themselves. Treaties that define international standards are often self-enforcing in this way, and enforcement is not a problem for them. The choice of standard may be controversial and divide states, but it is self-enforcing once agreed.

Getting states to live up to cooperative agreements can be a problem on issues other than standards for several reasons. First, a state may lack the capability of doing what is asked of it. Developing states often do not report publicly required information on government activity and performance. They claim that they lack the trained government personnel to collect the information. Second, their incentives to live up to the agreement may change over time. There could a problem of time-inconsistency where the situation changes the incentives of the political leadership. Or the leader could change, bringing in a new leader who is not committed to the agreements of his predecessor. Third, the agreement could be unclear about what the state is supposed to do. It might think it has cooperated when its partner does not. Fourth, a state could fail to cooperate to gain an advantage. Although we often think of the last possibility of self-interested defection as the major reason why states do not comply with their agreements to cooperate, we should remain alert to the other possibilities. Notice that these reasons are similar to those why an actor might not live up to a promise given in the chapter on the logic of promises. Agreements to cooperate are mutual promises.

The Prisoners' Dilemma

Figure 1 gives the payoffs of a game that captures the problem of self-interested defection from cooperation. In this game, both players choose either to "Cooperate" or "Defect" at the same time without knowing the other's choice. Each pair of entries in a cell of the table gives how much each player receives if each plays the corresponding moves, with the payoff to the player choosing the row given first and the player choosing the column second. For example, if the row player plays "Defect" and the column player "Cooperate," the row player receives 10 and the column player -10.

Figure 26
The Prisoners' Dilemma Game

	Cooperate	Defect
Cooperate	(5,5)	(-10,10)
Defect	(10,-10)	(-5,-5)

This game acquired the name of Prisoners' Dilemma from the story used to motivate it. The police arrest two suspects who they believe have robbed a store. They lack the evidence to convict either of them of the robbery, however. The District Attorney separates the two of them in different interrogation rooms and offers each of them separately with the following offer:

If you agree to confess to the crime and your partner does not, I will let you go free after you testify against him (the 10 payoff). On the other hand, if you do not confess and your partner does, you will do hard time based on his testimony (the -10 payoff). If both of you confess, I will have the evidence to convict both of you but will not seek as long a prison sentence as I will if you do not confess when your partner does (the -5 payoff). Finally, if neither of you talk, I can only get the two of you on minor gun possession charges (the 5 payoff). Do you want to talk?

In the story, "Cooperate" and "Defect" are in the eyes of the suspects, not the District Attorney or society generally. It is the *Prisoners'* Dilemma after all.

The strategic logic of Prisoners' Dilemma is straightforward. No matter what the other player does, you are better off playing "Defect". If the other player plays "Cooperate," you raise your payoff from 5 to 10 by shifting from "Cooperate" to "Defect". You can see this for the row player by comparing the first numbers down the first column. If the other player plays "Defect," you are also better off playing "Defect" and receiving -5 than playing "Cooperate" and getting -10. Compare the first numbers in the second column to see this. Both players should play "Defect" then, meaning both will receive -5 in the lower cell in the second column. But this result makes both players worse off than if they both played "Cooperate" in which case each would receive 5 in the upper cell in the first column. This is the dilemma. Both are worse off when they pursue their own self-interest.

Prisoners' Dilemma also represents the problem of enforcing international cooperation in the face of opportunistic violations. The strategic logic is the same. Now the players begin with an agreement to cooperate. The "Cooperate" move now means living up to the terms of that agreement, and the "Defect" move means breaking it for a short-term gain. Both players have an incentive to break the agreement for their own gain if the other follows through on the deal, and they both have the incentive not to live up to the agreement if the other breaks it if only to protect themselves. These incentives lead to the joint failure of the agreement, which makes both worse off than if they had followed through on their agreement. How can the players enforce their agreement on one another to their mutual benefit?

The suspects play Prisoners' Dilemma only once, but international cooperation generally requires new agreements and an ongoing relationship. Repetition opens up the possibility of enforcing an agreement to play "Cooperate" by responding in kind after one of the parties violates that agreement. Because both players lose when they both play "Defect," that outcome can be used to punish a player who cheats on an agreement. Imagine that the players will play Prisoners' Dilemma repeatedly. They agree to play "Cooperate" on every round and to enforce that agreement by both playing "Defect" for one round if either of them violates the agreement by playing "Defect" while the other is playing "Cooperate". Consider the consequences of cheating under this agreement. If you follow the agreement and play "Cooperate," you will receive 5 every round. If you cheat on the agreement, you will receive 10 in this round but -5 in the next.

Across the two rounds, you will receive more by following the agreement than breaking it. The threat of retaliation in kind enforces the agreement.

Reciprocity is the principle of responding to others in kind. Meet good acts with good acts and hurts with retaliation. It is the "Golden Rule" of world politics; "Do unto Others as They Have Done unto You".

Under the right circumstances, reciprocity can enforce agreements to cooperate. But it requires that the parties place some value on the future of their relationship. The calculation in the paragraph above fails if an actor does not care about what happens in the next round. Grabbing 10 today by defecting is more attractive than cooperating when you do not care about the punishment of -5 in the next round. Every parent of small children learns that all punishments must be immediate because small children have no sense of the future. They do not make the connection between their misbehavior today and a punishment tomorrow. Political leaders facing the end of their term in office sometimes act like small children and take actions they would not have dared earlier when they looked forward to more time in office. President Clinton ended his two terms in office by issuing a number of criminal pardons to controversial figures, and he is not the only U.S. President to have done so. When a cooperative relationship is going to end, reciprocity is ineffective to enforce cooperation. So actors have to care enough about the future for reciprocity to be an effective form of enforcement of agreements.

Reciprocity as Enforcement

Reciprocity–responding in kind–provides a way to enforce international agreements. It is central to many areas of agreement in world politics. International law often assumes that reciprocity will be used to enforce the agreement. Those who violate those agreements will suffer in kind in turn. States may refuse to sign treaties with a state that ignores or violates its treaty obligations. The recognition and status of diplomats is subject to reciprocal treatment. Occasionally, one country may accuse the diplomat of another of spying; the United States and Soviet Union made such accusations almost regularly during the Cold War probably because both of them used diplomatic cover for spies in the other country. The first country cannot prosecute the diplomat because he or she is protected by diplomatic immunity. Instead, they expel the diplomat/spy from the country, sending him or her back to the homeland. The other country then commonly retaliated by expelling a similar number of the first country's diplomats. The number reflected whether the second country thought the original expulsion was justified, expelling fewer if it was justified and more if it was not.

Reciprocity enforces agreements to lower trade barriers. Back even into medieval Europe, countries have fought trade wars where each in turn blocks the import of goods from the other in a cycle of retaliation. Today, the international trade regime run by the World Trade Organization (WTO) has rules for when member states can take actions that reduce imports from another member. There are specific legal categories which can be used to justify barriers to trade, such as tariffs (taxes on imports that make them more expensive) and quotas which limit the volume of imports. Countries abuse these rules, and their trading partners and fellow members of the WTO use the dispute resolution procedure to bring complaints against the policies that they consider abuses. Reciprocity enters at the end of the dispute resolution procedure. If a country wins its case in the WTO that the policy it has questions is indeed an illegal barrier to trade, the losing country must change that policy. If it does not do so, the WTO panel determines the value of the trade that the harmed party can block from the country that lost the dispute. This value is supposed to be set to be of the magnitude of the harm caused by the violating policy to the country that brought the dispute. These actions are known as *reciprocal trade sanctions*.

Noise and Monitoring

Reciprocity also requires actors to know when one another have broken their agreement to cooperate. You cannot respond in kind when you cannot tell if the other side has broken the agreement. In the Prisoners' Dilemma game, both sides announced their moves publicly. This openness of action is not always present in international cooperation. First, it might be unclear whether a particular act violates a cooperative agreement. During the Cold War, the U.S. and the Soviet Union signed arms control agreements to regulate their nuclear arsenal. The Anti-Ballistic Missile (ABM) treaty restricted both countries' deployment of missile systems designed to intercept and destroy incoming ballistic missiles. Nuclear deterrence depended on the ability of both sides to launch retaliatory strikes that would devastate the other's cities if the other side started a nuclear war. The fear was that effective ABMs might lead a side to think that it could shoot down enough missiles in that second strike to preserve most of the cities and people. That side might be tempted to start a nuclear war then. By sharply limiting ABMs, both sides remained vulnerable to retaliatory strikes and so deterred. The Soviet Union deployed a radar complex that many in the United States thought violated the ABM treaty. The Soviets claimed that it was for air defense, a radar system that could track incoming airplanes and coordinate fighter jets to shoot them down. U.S. arms experts thought it could be used for missile defense as well. The question was whether the radar complex violated the treaty, and the answer was unclear. Those American experts who did not trust the Soviets saw it as a violation, those who believed in arms control did not. How should the U.S. have responded to this possible violation? If the U.S. responded reciprocally and began building its own radar that probably violated the ABM treaty, the Soviet Union might perceive this "retaliation" as a violation of the treaty on its own and respond reciprocally in turn. Arms control as a cooperative venture might collapse if the sides continued to violate their agreements in the belief that the other was breaking them.

[Picture of ABM site and radar]

What exactly the other party to a cooperative agreement is doing might also be unclear.

In the OPEC example, oil producing states could pump extra production and sell it into the spot market without the other members of OPEC knowing where the oil came from. Members can and do cheat and overproduce on their quotas in ways that cannot be tracked easily. All that the members of OPEC can tell is that the resulting price ends up lower than they expected. A lower price is consistent with more supply of oil from someone producing over their quota. It is also consistent with lower demand than forecast. A lower price for oil may mean that someone is overproducing or that circumstances are not as OPEC expected. Should the members respond reciprocally when the price is lower than they expected?

Third, the other party may simply hide what it is doing. The Nuclear Non-Proliferation Treaty (NPT) regulates the use of nuclear materials in nuclear power plants. States are supposed to fully account for all the nuclear fuel that they use to prevent a non-nuclear power from diverting some of that fuel and using it to build nuclear bombs. The International Atomic Energy Agency (IAEA), a UN agency based in Vienna, exists to account for nuclear materials. Countries that have tried to build nuclear weapons in violation of the treaty, like North Korea, have built secret facilities and then deny IAEA inspectors access to those facilities. Other countries then cannot tell whether those programs violate the NPT

The inability to observe fully whether other parties are complying with a cooperative agreement is called *noise*. The term comes from the static one hears on a radio when it is not tuned properly to a single station. You can hear some of what the station is broadcasting but you have to separate the signal from the noise. The problem of judging whether other countries are complying with an agreement when you cannot tell exactly what they are doing is similar. You have to judge what they are doing by separating away other effects. The problem of determining whether other states are complying with an agreement is *monitoring*. The IAEA monitors compliance with the NPT by accounting for nuclear materials and inspecting nuclear facilities to ensure that they are not used to build nuclear weapons by a state that does not have them.

How does reciprocity work in the face of noise? How do you respond in kind when you are not sure what the other side has done? First, reciprocal responses become irregular. Reciprocal enforcement in Prisoners' Dilemma was regular. Every time one side broke the agreement, there was a reciprocal response. When neither side is certain whether the other side has done but can only react to the state of cooperation, some violations will be ignored. Similarly, both sides will mistakenly respond with a reciprocal response even when the other side has not intended to violate their agreement to cooperate. Second, the threshold to trigger a reciprocal response will rise to reduce the number of mistaken reciprocal responses. Under noise, you have to judge whether the other side has cooperated from the state of the cooperative relationship because you do not know whether they have committed an intentional violation. Maybe that Soviet radar complex was only for anti-aircraft defense. Small violations will be ignored, while large ones draw a response. Third, reciprocal responses will be disproportionate to the perceived violation. In Prisoners' Dilemma, the punishment was proportionate to the violation. It had to be large enough to take away any short-run gains from cheating on the agreement. Noise means that not all violations will be punished. To retain the same deterrent effect, the size of punishment must rise when it does occur. If I respond with a reciprocal punishment to only one-half of times I think you are violating the agreement, my punishments have to be twice as big to have the same effect. For issues where it is harder to tell whether your partners in cooperation have comply with your agreement, reciprocity becomes erratic and disproportionate.

What Makes Cooperation More Likely?

The efficacy of reciprocity as a tool of enforcement depends on the conditions of cooperation and the available reciprocal responses. Reciprocity enforces a cooperative agreement by hurting prospective violators tomorrow for their failure to cooperate today. It deters attempts to gain in the short-run by cheating on the agreement by breaking off the benefits of that agreement for a period later. First, reciprocal enforcement becomes more effective as the parties care more about the future. If you do not care about what you will receive tomorrow, a punishment then will not deter you from grabbing a gain today. Concern for the future is called the *shadow of the future*. The greater it is, the more effective reciprocal enforcement will be.

Second, cooperation is more likely as the temptation to cheat becomes smaller. The less to be gained by breaking the agreement today, the more likely the reciprocal response will deter such violations.

Third, larger reciprocal punishments have greater deterrent effect. Reciprocity deters by punishing your violations later. A bigger stick hurts more.

Fourth, cooperation is more likely and stronger as noise is lower. When it is difficult to determine whether your partner has complied with your cooperative agreement, reciprocity is less effective at enforcing the agreement because it becomes erratic. Additionally, noise leads to mistaken punishments, and the side suffering such a punishment may respond to it. Good monitoring is central to effective international cooperation.

Fifth, reciprocal enforcement is more effective when clear standards of behavior and appropriate reciprocal responses exist. Reciprocity deters violations when the parties anticipate that any attempt to cheat on the agreement will be met with a response. A clear standard of what each side is supposed to do allows them to know when they have crossed the line and will be considered in violation of the agreement. Explicit reciprocal responses allows them to know what the response will be. Knowing when a punishment should occur and how large it will be enhances deterrent of violations.

Institutions and Enforcement

The last point is one way international institutions aid cooperation by making enforcement more effective. Political institutions are like the "rules of the game". They shape how actors interact but do not determine what they do. Clear standards of conduct do not prevent actors from breaking cooperative agreements, but they do make is clear when an agreement has been broken. Violations become commonly known. This both helps other parties know when they should respond. It also helps restrain tit-for-tat feuds by making it clear that those reciprocal responses are not violations themselves. Reciprocity means that the punishments are acts that would be violations if not in response to another's violations. Reciprocal trade sanctions are barriers to trade that would be against WTO law if a state adopted them on its own. WTO law helps to clarify which policies are illegal trade barriers. When a panel rules that a policy is a violation of WTO law, it also allows the damaged state to respond with reciprocal trade sanctions if the policy is not changed. WTO law does not make states reduce their trade barriers, but it makes it easier for them to enforce deals to do so.

Monitoring is a second way institutions can support cooperation. Organizations can be established to collect and disseminate information on state compliance with cooperative agreements. As mentioned earlier, the IAEA conducts inspections of nuclear programs to verify that the programs of non-nuclear weapons states are purely peaceful. These inspections are useful for those non-nuclear states who wish to demonstrate that they do not have nuclear weapons programs. Because states with such programs can and do try to hide them from the IAEA, the real evidence of compliance is a state's cooperation with IAEA inspections. Both South Africa and Ukraine after the end of the Cold War wished to demonstrate that they no longer had nuclear weapons. Ukraine inherited nuclear weapons from the Soviet Union when its separate republics became independent states. The apartheid-era government of South Africa had a nuclear weapons program, which Nelson Mandela's government dismantled when it came to power. Both countries actively assisted the IAEA inspection teams, revealing all information they had, taking inspectors to former nuclear sites, and allowing them to witness the destruction of nuclear materials. In contrast, those states who have been suspected of having hidden nuclear weapons programs, such as Iraq under Saddam Hussein, Iran, and North Korea, have not cooperated with IAEA inspectors and denied them access to certain sites. Here the institution is the program of inspections–the rules for the accounting for nuclear materials and providing access to nuclear sites. The IAEA supports these institutions. They make cooperation on nuclear non-proliferation easier by allowing most states to reveal their compliance with the treaty and focusing attention on those who may not be in compliance. Without these rules and the IAEA, knowing which states were building nuclear weapons would be more difficult.

Even with explicit rules, actors can disagree about what acts are violations. It is impossible to write a set of rules to cover all possible cases that might arise. A third way institutions can aid international cooperation is to resolve disputes over what the agreement and rules mean when they arise. Chapter Seven of the UN Charter gives the UN Security Council the power to "determine the existence of any threat to the peace, breach of the peace, or act of aggression" and what to do about such threats including the use of military force. In some situations, such as Iraq's invasion of Kuwait in 1990, there has been general agreement on the threat and what should be done about it. In other cases, there is no consensus, such as one concerning Iraq before the Iraq War in 2003. The Security Council votes to resolve these disagreements about whether a situation constitute a threat and what should be done about that threat. The veto power of the five permanent members means that they must agree on the threat, or at least be unwilling to block action, for the Security Council to act. The veto power then limits the power of the Security Council. Without such limits, the major powers who hold the veto would not have agreed to give the organization the power to order the use of force. Because states can act on their own against threats, voting on the Security Council does not stop the major power from acting even in the face of a veto, as the United States and Great Britain did in 2003 against Iraq. The voting does clarify which countries support action and which are opposed.

Fourth, institutions can also help coordinate reciprocal responses by many states against a violator. The UN Security Council imposed economic sanctions on Serbia in 1992 in response to its wars with Croatia and in Bosnia-Herzegovina. These sanctions then were a collective punishment against Serbia for its actions in these wars. They blocked trade with Serbia which hurt the Serbian economy, but they did not end the war in Bosnia. Without a Security Council resolution, some states would have continued trade with Serbia.

Finally, institutions can aid reciprocal enforcement by clarifying what the response will be to a violation. Findings of the WTO dispute resolution procedure that the policy in question is a violation also determine the loss of trade it caused. The country who lost the dispute has a period of time to change its policies to bring them into compliance. If it does not do so, the damaged state which brought the dispute has the right to adopt measures that will shift trade between the two in its favor by an amount equal to the damage as judged by the panel. Before this procedure, states did retaliate against their trade partners to try to get them to lower their barriers to imports. But they chose when they chose to respond and in what way. Sometimes, the country suffering the "retaliation" thought it was excessive and responded against imports from the first. This could and did produce "trade wars" where two countries raised barriers against goods from one another. Neither side won these wars. The WTO procedure clarifies when states can retaliate and how large that response will be. Both make reciprocal enforcement more effective.

OPEC Again

How does OPEC use reciprocal enforcement to maintain its agreements to regulate the oil production of its members? OPEC seeks to influence the price of oil by setting quotas for how much oil each member will produce. Members can gain by overproducing on their quotas because they keep the additional revenue while all suffer the loss from a lower price than the

OPEC target. Additionally, members cheating on their quota can avoid detection by selling their overproduction on the spot market. Despite these issues, OPEC has been able to influence the price of oil for 35 years now since the first oil shock.

Saudi Arabia takes the position of the enforcer of OPEC agreements. It has the largest proven reserves in the world, and its production costs are low. It has produced less oil than it is capable of it during most of the period of OPEC's influence on oil prices. This surplus production allows Saudi Arabia to enforce quota agreements by threatening to flood the oil market by producing a full capacity. It has done so occasionally to punish members who have cheated on their quotas too often. This reciprocal response drives down the price of oil, hurting all OPEC members and reminding them of the benefits they receive from following their national quotas. Saudi Arabia has also used its position as the dominant producer to take a leading position in OPEC. It has a longer view of the oil market than other OPEC members because it can produce for an estimated 100 more years at the current rate from its proven reserves. The Saudis have always been concerned that high oil prices will drive the industrialized world to find substitutes for oil. This would hurt all members. Other countries with smaller reserves relative to their production are not as concerned about how a high price today might hurt the oil market in the future. At times since the first oil shock in 1973, Saudi Arabia has used the leverage of its ability to produce to get higher levels of production and lower the price of oil.

OPEC also uses the setting of national quotas to reduce the incentive to cheat on agreements. Countries often suspected of overproducing, notably Iran and Nigeria, often receive quotas which are a larger proportion of the ability to produce than other members. If we think of OPEC quotas as agreements to limit production, they are not asked to limit their production as much as other members. Their higher production limits reduce both countries' interest and ability to overproduce. In turn, future quotas can also be used to enforce national production quotas. OPEC can lower a country's production target if the other members feel that it has exceeded its quota too often by too much. This is an example of how the two stages of cooperation, negotiation on how to cooperate and then enforcement of the agreement, are intertwined in practice. Setting national quotas every six months allows OPEC members to negotiate over how they will cooperate, with the ability to use those changes in quotas to punish members who have cheated in the recent past.

These reciprocal punishments are erratic as we should expect when noise is present. Because members can sell excess production on the spot market, it is difficult to know when a member has exceeded its quota. OPEC then ignores low levels of overproduction, responding only when members think the problem has become significant. When they do respond, the Saudi can turn on the taps and increase their own production greatly. This drives down the price of oil. Because these reciprocal punishments hurt all members, they are reluctant to use them. Occasional large retaliation helps to control overproduction.

OPEC is losing its influence over the recent rises in the price of oil, but in a way that is good for its members. Demand as well as supply influences the price of oil. Most observers of the market believe that increases in the demand for oil drives the large recent increases in its price. As developing countries have industrialized, their demand for oil has increased. Both China and India have developed to the point where many people in those countries can buy cars where oil is the dominant fuel. Demand in the developed world has not gone down with increases in the efficiency of use of petroleum products. OPEC members are now producing at close to full capacity, although they have tried to restrain their production from these high levels when the price slumps. High oil prices will stay with us as long as demands continues to be strong and no new major production capability is created by finding new oil fields.

Think It Through
Reciprocal Enforcement

Reciprocal enforcement is sometimes explicit, sometimes implicit in world politics. This box gives you some guidance in how to study how international agreements to cooperate are enforced.

1. What is the cooperative agreement between the actors? What is each supposed to do to produce the common benefit? The next chapter will analyze how these agreements are reached, so now we only ask what the agreement is.

2. Is that agreement self-enforcing? Some agreements in world politics do not pose an enforcement problem because the actors want to live up to their agreement. Self-enforcing agreements do not need enforcement as compliance is not a problem.

3. For agreements that are not self-enforcing, what acts constitute a violation of the agreement? Put another way, what acts constitute compliance? Often, whether a specific act violates an agreement is unclear. It is easier in such cases to begin by asking what acts clearly violate the agreement.

4. Does the agreement contain specific provisions for how the parties should respond if one of them violates it? Some agreements spell out appropriate responses to violations.

5. If the agreement does not contain specific provisions for enforcement, could reciprocity be used to enforce? Are responses-in-kind acceptable to use after a violation?

6. Is there a problem of noise in determining whether a party has complied? Is it easy to tell when a party has violated the agreement, or are such cases commonly in dispute? If noise is present, is there an institution that exists to collect and spread information on compliance?

7. Pull the picture together. What acts are violations, and what response if any do they provoke? Does the threat of a response seem credible and effective in preventing violations?

Chapter Summary

States can benefit from international cooperation on many issues. Successful cooperation requires an agreement on how to cooperate and then compliance with that agreement. Compliance can be a problem because states often have incentives not to do so. Compliance with an agreement–doing what the agreement says–is not the same as an effective agreement–one that changes state behavior for the better. Reciprocity–responses in kind to violations–can enforce agreements in some cases where compliance is a problem. Reciprocal sanctions are more effective when actors care more about the future, the temptation to cheat is smaller, the punishment larger, and when it is clear to all when an agreement has been violated. Noise can make enforcement difficult by making it hard to determine when an agreement has been violated. Institutions can support enforcement of cooperative agreements by setting clear standards, monitoring compliance, resolving disputes, coordinating multilateral responses, and setting punishments.

Review Questions

1. How has OPEC (the Organization of Petroleum Exporting States) been able to enforce agreements to limit production among its members?

2. Explain the relationship between enforcement and bargaining in international cooperation.

3. What three reasons exist for why states might opportunistically defect from an agreement to cooperate?

4. Write down a Prisoners' Dilemma game. Explain the logic of enforcement using your game.

5. What problems make reciprocal enforcement of agreements difficult? Give an example.

6. Give two ways international institutions can alleviate enforcement problems by making reciprocity more effective.

Chapter 22
The Problems of Cooperation: Distribution and Information

The world has a marvelous system of telecommunications. One can call from almost anywhere people live to anywhere else people live. It is amazingly cheap, particularly in the developed world. This entire system has been created in the last 150 years. The most important developments have been technological from the introduction of the telegraph to its replacement by the telephone to the introduction of wireless service. The growth of mass telecommunication also required international cooperation. States have to agree on a wide range of issues, such as standards for international messages, which technology to adopt, how to divide the costs and charges of messages, to create a system where one can communicate across national borders. The International Telecommunications Union (ITU) is the intergovernmental organization which exists to aid member governments with issues in telecommunications. It was formed in 1865 as the International Telegraphic Union to help states coordinate the transmission of telegraphs across their borders. Its name changed with the technology, and today the ITU is located in Geneva, Switzerland across the street from where my office was when I worked there. I ate lunch occasionally at the cafeteria there; do not go there for the food.

States find the ITU a useful organization because it helps them solve important problems of cooperation in the area of telecommunications. In its early days, it helped states coordinate the rates from cross-border messages and how they would divide the payment for each message among the national telegraphic agencies that carry it part of the way from sender to receiver. It followed developments in the technology of telegraphy to provide member states with independent expert advice on issues when they negotiated. It organized regular international conferences where state delegates met to discuss and negotiate changes in the way international telegraphy was handled.

Intergovernmental organizations like the ITU are plentiful these days. Most of them operate as part of the UN. These organizations exist because states find them helpful in addressing problems of cooperation. The last chapter discussed the problem of enforcement–how can actors enforce deals to cooperate? You need a deal on how to cooperate before you enforce any deal. The negotiation stage, when the actors decide what policies they will follow to cooperate, precedes the enforcement stage. This chapter focuses on two related problems–distribution and information–that occur at the negotiation stage.

Cooperation as Agreeing on a Solution

International cooperation occurs when states and other actors coordinate some set of policies to their mutual benefit. These agreements evolve over time and change with circumstances. Some types of international cooperation, such as the agreement to use the metric system for measurement as just about everyone outside the United States does, require one unchanging agreement. These cases of one permanent agreement are rare though. More common are situations such as coordination of macroeconomic policy among the G-8 countries, which are the leading industrial economies of the world: U.S., Canada, Japan, Great Britain, Germany, France, Italy, and Russia. Their leaders meet on a regular basis to discuss economic issues and what policies they should undertake to ensure that their economies continue to grow and prosper. These policies change as their economies go through cycles of growth and contraction. Most issues of international cooperation require actors to decide on how they will cooperate–what measures will they take for their mutual benefit. Such problems have the following four properties:

1. There are always multiple ways to cooperate. Deciding how to cooperate is as important as whether the resulting deal can be enforced. Problems have multiple possible solutions with different consequences. International cooperation requires the parties to agree on which solution they will adopt. A solution does not require that they all do the same thing, only that they coordinate on a common response.

2. Everyone is better off when they adopt one of these solutions compared to no agreement. Cooperation produces mutual benefits, so actors are better off if they can agree on a common approach to a problem. If one of the actors loses from cooperation, it could choose to "sit this one out.

3. They often disagree which solution is best even though they are not fully certain of the consequences of each solution. Some actors will believe one solution is better than another, while others will favor the latter solution over the former. These differences arise because different solutions pose different costs and benefits on the actors. All may win from cooperation, but some win more than others in particular solutions.

4. The precise value of solution is generally not known when the actors have to decide how to cooperate. Actors have some idea about the consequences of the policies they may adopt, but they are uncertain about their full consequences. This uncertainty leaves room for them to persuade one another about whether one solution is better than another.

An example from the early days of the ITU may clarify these four properties of choosing how to cooperate. A system for managing cross-border messages has to deal with how the charges the sender pays will be calculated and then distributed among the PTT agencies (which stands for Post, Telephone, and Telegraph–government agencies that offer these services in most European countries at the time) of countries which carry the message. If you wanted to send a telegraph from Paris to St. Petersburg in those days, you would go to a French PTT office in Paris, place the order to have the telegraph sent, and pay for it. The telegraph operator would send your message to a Russian PTT office in St. Petersburg, where an operator would decode the message and have someone deliver it to the person to whom you were sending the message. Additionally, the message would have to cross Germany on telegraph cables owned by the German PTT. There are many ways the revenue could be split up among these three countries. The sending country could keep the entire cost of your message, which France would like. The receiving country could get all the money, which Russia would like. Germany should also get some part of the payment too. Obviously, they would not negotiate over each individual payment, but they needed a system to account for how much each national PTT agency would receive. The ITU then provided a way for member states to reconcile all these payments at the end of a year. A country could receive more money than its share of all the messages that were sent from it, to it, and across it if more messages were sent from it than to it because the senders paid. It would pay the difference between the money it collected and what it earned to another country which did not collect as much as it earned. The key point here is that there are many possible ways to divide up how much money international telegraphs generated. All states agreed that senders, receivers, and transit countries should all receive some revenue, but often disagreed on how exactly to split that money.

Unit size was another issue that had to be resolved to create a system for international telegraphy. Messages were billed by units, with the customer paying for the number of units in their message. European countries commonly used a twenty-word unit. You paid for every 20 words you sent rounded upwards. It cost you as much to send a one-word message as a twenty-word message. Governments outside Europe preferred a one-word unit where you paid a smaller amount for each word. European governments created their PTT agencies to carry government messages and saw commercial and private traffic as a way to subsidize those agencies. They were concerned that too much private traffic would crowd out important government messages, so they wanted to restrict private traffic by setting the price high. They were also worried that they would lose revenue if they shifted to the one-word unit. Just like with text messages, private customers sending messages under a one-unit billing system used short cuts to reduce the word count while still communicating the message. Each message would generate less revenue with a one-word unit. Governments outside Europe thought that the one-word unit would generate more revenue by increasing traffic greatly. They wanted to generate more revenue to help pay the cost of laying the telegraph cables of their systems. Would more but shorter messages produce as much revenue as the twenty-word unit did? The only way to find out if the increase in traffic would generate as much revenue was to try it.

The billing unit size has all four properties of a cooperation problem. First, there were multiple solutions. Countries could agree to use a one-word unit, a twenty-word unit, or anything in between. Second, they needed to agree on a common solution. When an operator sent a message from one country to another, he or she had to know how to bill the customer. Third, they did not know what the precise consequences of each billing system. No one knew whether revenue would fall if they shifted to a one-word unit, although everyone had some ideas about what would happen. Similarly, European governments did not know if the additional private traffic generated by a one-word unit would overwhelm their systems. Fourth, they disagreed about which solution was best. The Europeans preferred the twenty-word unit, those outside Europe the one-word unit.

As you might have guessed, they settled the issue by splitting the difference. Messages sent inside Europe were billed with a twenty-word unit. Messages that went or came from outside Europe were billed with a one-word unit. Traffic inside Europe was much higher than traffic outside, so the Europeans were willing to live with a one-word unit on the smaller volume of private messages. Experience quickly showed that the one-word unit was superior. It generated many more messages and produced more revenue than a twenty-word unit. The technology of telegraphy improved so that European systems could easily handle the higher volume of private messages without compromising their ability to carry government traffic. After ten years, European governments adopted the one-word unit for all messages, and the era of short, dramatic telegraphs like you see in movies from the 1930s and 1940s had arrived worldwide.

Problems of Cooperation: Distribution versus Information

Two important and related problems are distribution and information. Cooperation requires states to coordinate their policies to produce a mutual benefit as we saw in the last chapter on enforcement and monitoring. Many such solutions are possible. Two issues captured in the four properties above complicate the selection of how to cooperate:
- *Distribution*: The actors disagree about which solution is best.
- *Information*: The actors are uncertain about the exact consequences of each solution.
Negotiations on how to cooperate address these problems, but they cannot solve both at the same time. As in the billing unit example from the history of the ITU, countries have to work through their differences to cooperate.

Distribution and information occur on many issues of international cooperation. In trade, national incomes of countries rise when barriers to trade, such as tariffs, are lowered. At the same time, all governments try to protect some domestic industries with those barriers. Any system to produce freer trade, a benefit for all countries, in the face of the desire to keep some barriers requires judging which barriers to trade are tolerable and which are not. Each country would like its own barriers high and its trading partners' barriers low in order to favor its domestic producers. The information problem in managing trade barriers arises because national governments do not know how important those industries are in their trading partners. A state does not know which barriers their trading partners see as politically necessary and so do not know which their trading partners are willing to eliminate in return for it lowering some of its own barriers to trade.

On environmental issues, people generally benefit from a reduction in pollution, but who pays? Water pollution can be a significant problem on rivers that flow through multiple countries. A paper mill upstream can ruin the water quality for a city that relies on the river for water downstream. Either one of cleaning up the effluent from the paper mill or building a water-treatment plant at the city solves the problem, but each would rather the other pays for the problem. Cooperation here requires determining who pays, a distribution problem. The information problem is the cost of the two solutions. The city might be willing to pay for treatment of waste water at the plant if it is cheaper than a water treatment plant at the city.

On human rights, there are many different ideas about what rights citizens should have with respect to their states. Western countries believe in a wide range of political rights for the individual such as free speech, protection from arbitrary arrest and prosecution, and the right to vote. They disagree about the range of social rights, such as a right to basic sustenance, to which individuals are entitled. Other countries believe that social order and the state take precedence over individual rights. These societies have restrictions on the individual that many in the West consider oppressive. Setting a universal standard of human rights faces a distributional problem because people disagree about which rights are fundamental. Existing human rights treaties tend to adopt a Western view of rights because Western states were central to the negotiation of those treaties beginning in the late 1940s. The information problem in human rights comes from the uncertainty about the consequences of different systems of rights for social order and individual happiness. People disagree about what rights are essential in part because they foresee different consequences from different systems of rights.

Figure 1 shows a game that represents a distributional problem. Like the Prisoners' Dilemma game that represents an enforcement problem, the Battle of the Sexes game has the players choose one of their two strategies at the same time without knowing which strategy the other is playing. The game was first analyzed during the 1950s, and the name comes from a story to explain the game. A man and a woman would like to go on a date together but disagree about where they should go. The man wishes to attend a prize fight (that is a boxing match) while the woman would like to go to the ballet. We now of course live in a time free from these gender stereotypes, so I have given the choices in the game in Figure 1 as taking a joint vacation at the beach or in the mountains. Like the Prisoners' Dilemma games discussed in the chapter on enforcement of cooperative agreements, the players make their choices at the same time in Battle of the Sexes. The strategic problem here is that both would like to do the same thing, spending their vacation together, but they disagree where they would most like to take that vacation. It is a simple representation of a distributional problem.

Figure 27
The Battle of the Sexes Game

	Beach	Mountains
Beach	(2,1)	(0,0)
Mountains	(0,0)	(1,2)

The decision how to cooperate often poses distributional problems captured in the Battle of the Sexes game. In the ITU case, states disagreed about unit size for billing. The one-word unit and the twenty-word unit were two different solutions they could adopt. The Europeans favored the latter, while those outside Europe favored the former. Both could benefit from an agreement on how to bill telegraphs because such an agreement was necessary for international messages. As we saw, this distributional problem was solved at first by dividing the difference, using a twenty-word unit within Europe and a one-word unit outside. Often, distributional problems can be solved by finding a compromise solution that splits the difference. Other distributional problems cannot be solved so easily. Coordination on a common system of measurement poses a distributional issue. Almost all of the world outside the United States uses the metric system to measure distances, while the U.S. clings to the English system of inches, feet, and miles. Although the U.S. considered adopting the metric system in the 1960s, there was strong resistance and the effort was abandoned. A common system of measurement simplifies international trade because parts then are all made on the same scale. Go to a hardware store and compare metric screws with those measured in fractions of an inch. You cannot replace one with the other. The resistance to adopting the metric system came because many in the U.S. had extensive investments in the English systems. American understand driving distances in miles, not kilometers. Everyone would have to relearn common measurements. Road signs would have to be replaced to change the scale of the distances, and machines would have to be retooled. These costs of transition are substantial. Some countries, notably Great Britain and Canada did "go metric" around that time. They needed to adopt the metric system to keep their trade with other countries that used it. The U.S., however, still only uses the metric system for scientific purposes and athletic competitions. Its economy is large enough that producers will make parts in the English system just for the U.S. market.

How should one play the Battle of the Sexes game? There are three stable configurations of play. The players can agree to coordinate on either strategy, going to either the mountains or the beach for sure. These solutions guarantee that the players cooperate, although to the advantage of one at the expense of the other. Each would like them to coordinate on the choice it prefers. If they cannot agree, each would have to guess what the other will play. This uncertainty raises the possibility that they will fail to coordinate their choices, making both worse off. Both are better off if they can coordinate their choices, but they will have to negotiate over how to coordinate. The Battle of the Sexes game illustrates a problem of distribution because both players cannot receive their best outcome at the same time.

If the players play the game more than once, they can agree to alternate between the two ways to cooperate. This arrangement ensures cooperation and does not advantage one player over the other. It is like the decision in the ITU to use a twenty-word unit within Europe and one-word unit outside. Neither player gets its best outcome, but each gets it some of the time. Splitting the difference in this way is one way to solve a distributional problem.

Informational problems arise when the actors are uncertain about the exact values of the available solutions. Figure 2 gives another coordination game, which is easier to resolve than Battle of the Sexes because both players prefer a vacation at the beach to one in the mountains. If they know that they are playing this game, it should be simple for them to agree that they should play Beach over Mountains. At the same time, each would play Mountains if it believed that the other would as well. That unhappy outcome is stable because it is self-enforcing. But if the players can communicate on how they should cooperate, they would presumably quickly agree to play the moves they both prefer. A game like that in Figure 2 is called a game of pure coordination because the players agree the value of the available ways to coordinate. There is no distributional issue here.

Figure 28
Both Prefer the Beach Game

	Beach	Mountains
Beach	(2,2)	(0,0)
Mountains	(0,0)	(1,1)

What if the players do not know which game they are playing? Figure 3 gives three different games of coordination, Battle of the Sexes and two other games of pure coordination. I have now called the available ways to coordinate in each game with my usual colorful names of A and B. If you like the ITU example, you can call A "twenty-word unit" and B "one-word unit". If you are sick of the ITU example, you can use two possible solutions of some other issue where countries try to cooperate. The actors can probably figure out how to cooperate if they know which game they are playing. An agreement should be easy to reach in each of the two Both Prefer games because the players agree on which solution is best. Cooperation in the Battle of the Sexes is more difficult but there are ways that the players could cooperate here as well. We can represent an informational problem by having the players not know which game they are playing. They only know that they are playing one of these three games. Now choosing how to cooperate is more difficult. Even if the players knew that they were playing a Both Prefer game, what do you agree to if you do not know which game you are playing? You would like to choose the solution, A or B, that will be best for both of you, but neither of you knows which that is. You might always agree to just play A and hope for the best.

Figure 29
Three Coordination Games with an Informational Problem

Battle of the Sexes	Both Prefer A	Both Prefer B

	A	B			A	B			A	B
A	(2,1)	(0,0)		A	(2,2)	(0,0)		A	(1,1)	(0,0)
B	(0,0)	(1,2)		B	(0,0)	(1,1)		B	(0,0)	(2,2)

How can players cooperate in the face of an informational problem? For now, let's assume that the players know they are playing one of the two Both Prefer games but do not know which one. This is a situation where they know they want to coordinate on the same policy and have identical interests, but they do not know which is the best way to coordinate. Each actor has some information about which game they are playing, so they have some ideas about which solution is best for them. In the unit size issue in the ITU, governments had some ideas about what the consequences would be of each unit size for the amount of private telegrams sent and the revenues that would be produced. They did not know what those consequences would be exactly, which was part of the disagreement during the negotiations. If the players face only an informational problem, they should share all the information they have about the values of the solutions freely. They know that their interests are identical and that they all face the same issue of deciding which available solution is the best way to cooperate. Sharing their information freely is in their common and self interest.

This hybrid game where the players do not know which game of the three games in Figure 3 that they are playing has both a distributional problem and an informational problem, however. The distribution problem lies in the possibility that they are playing Battle of the Sexes, even though they do not know that. The information problem lies in their lack of knowledge of which game they are playing. This uncertainty means they do not know what is best for them, even if they recognize they have the identical interests. They have some idea about which game they are playing, but neither of them knows for sure. Each has a perception about how likely it is that they are playing each game. These perceptions capture what they know about the consequences of the solution, and so how they value them. They might think it is likely that one solution is better for them than the other for example. Both problems are present in this hybrid game.

The hybrid game also shows the problems of choosing how to cooperate that we discussed earlier in this chapter. There are two ways they could cooperate, A and B. All would like to adopt one of those solutions by playing the same strategy in the game. They may disagree about the values of the ways they could cooperate. They do not know fully the consequences of the two solutions when they have to decide which to adopt. The hybrid game in Figure 3 illustrates the combination of a distribution and information problem found in deciding how to cooperate.

Solving the combination of problems is much more difficult than solving either a distributional or informational problem alone. Distribution problems could be solved by trying to split the difference between the parties. Neither got its best outcome nor its worst outcome. Information problems could be addressed by revealing information honestly so the actors could evaluate and adopt what appeared to be the best solution. When both are present, each interferes with the way to address the other.

Consider a situation where you are the first player and you know that you are not playing Both Prefer B. You can conclude that A is the better solution of the two for you, but you are not certain that the same is true for the other player. You will get 2 if both players play A after discussing how to cooperate. You want to try and convince the other player that it is in her interest to also play A. You are most likely to succeed if you can persuade her that the two of you are playing Both Prefer A because then she will think it is in her interest to coordinate on A instead of B. How you act in this case is straightforward.

Now consider a situation where as the first player, you know that you are playing either Battle of the Sexes or Both Prefer B. You know that you are not playing Both Prefer A. You are uncertain about which solution is better for you because coordinating on B gives you 1 in Battle of the Sexes and 2 in Both Prefer B. Should you reveal your uncertainty to the other player in the hope that her information will help you decide which is better for you? Let's say that you think it is likely that you are playing Battle of the Sexes but there is a small chance that the game really is Both Prefer B. You think it is likely that the two of you disagree about which solution is best, and that A is best for you, even though you are not certain of it. Maybe you should not admit your uncertainty about which solution is best for you and push for a solution that splits the difference between the two of you or even push for the adoption of solution A.

In the same situation, the other player is likely to know that B is the best solution for her. She is going to try and convince you to play B, arguing that the game is really Both Prefer B and that you will be better off coordinating on B, just like you would have in the parallel situation in the earlier paragraph. Do you believe her? She might also think that it is likely that you are playing Battle of the Sexes and wants to convince you to play the solution in that game that is better for her at your expense.

The combination of the problems of distribution and information creates similar incentives in bargaining to those present in crises. Actors have incentives to argue for solutions they prefer in their own self interest. These incentives impede efforts to reveal information about the values of solutions fully to aid all in determining the value of those solutions. Actors have both the incentive to misrepresent what they know and to discount the claims of others because of the possibility of a disagreement about which solution is best.

This argument is all very abstract, so another example from the ITU may help clarify it. Another issue faced in the early days of the ITU was the division of the fee among the nation a message was sent from, the nation where it was received, and any nations whose wires the message had to transit on to reach its destination nation. State representatives recognized that each had a claim to charge some for its contribution to the transmission of a telegram. The sender nation provided the station where it was sent from and the agents to code the message and send it. The recipient state provided the station where it was received, agents to decode the message, and delivery of the message to the final recipient. The transit country provides wires linking the sender and recipient state networks. The billing arrangements had to be coordinated so that the sending office could calculate how much to charge the customer by adding up the charges of the sender and recipient PTTs and any transit charges. States disagreed the most about how large the transit charges should be compared to sending and receiving charges. States in the center of Europe, particularly Germany, argued for larger transit fees. Their systems would carry more transit traffic, that is, telegrams from senders outside their country to recipients also outside. Countries on the periphery of Europe disagreed. Clearly, the German PTT would benefit from higher transit fees, while customers in the peripheral countries would lose in the form of higher charges. This is an issue of distribution. Part of the negotiation concerned an informational issue. How costly was the creation and use of the wires of a national network for transit traffic? If the transit fees were too low, Germany and other central European countries might refuse to carry transit traffic. At the same time, peripheral countries suspected that Germany was inflating its estimates of the cost of transit traffic in an effort to negotiate higher transit fees. The distribution issue that the central European countries gained from high transit fees while peripheral European countries lost interfered with the information issue of setting transit fees at an appropriate level to cover the costs of handling transit traffic.

The combination of distribution and information problems lead to inefficiencies in negotiations over how to cooperate. These inefficiencies can take two forms. At the extreme, the parties may fail to reach an agreement which all would prefer to the absence of any agreement. More commonly though, they reach bargains that are not as good as they could be. In the word-unit case, everyone would have been better off with one-word unit, including the European states that opposed it during the negotiations. Their shift to adopt the one-word unit as the international standard for billing demonstrated their recognition that it was a superior solution to the mixed unit size originally adopted. Agreements to advance international cooperation then are often the best that the parties can negotiate at that time, rather than the best possible deal.

Institutions as an Aid to Negotiations

International institutions are the "rules of the game" for international bargaining on issues of cooperation. They can aid in reaching agreements that benefit member states. Institutions shape bargaining by setting rules for how the parties bargain and for agreement and disagreement. The ITU is an international organization; the institutions connected to it concern the role it plays in hosting and supporting international negotiations on telecommunications issues. Institutions and organizations are not the same. Organizations consist of a professional staff commonly housed in office buildings who perform tasks to advance the mission of the organization. Institutions shape how actors interact. Many institutions have organizations that support them. The ITU supports negotiations on telecommunication issues by providing impartial technical advice. It also did the work of reconciling the accounts of national PTTs in the days of telegrams.

Institutions provide settings for states to hold negotiations. The United Nations holds international negotiations across the wide range of issues that its member organizations address. Although some of the negotiations receive much press coverage, most do not. When I lived in Geneva, the International Labor Organization (ILO) held an international conference for a two-week period at the Palais de Nations, the main UN compound there. I doubt the meeting was covered by any major U.S. newspaper. When an institution is a forum for negotiations, it not only brings state delegates together to negotiate, it also sets the rules for discussions: who gets to speak when, the agenda of topics for discussion, and any division of the representatives into smaller committees to work on specific issues. It also typically allows for regular negotiating sessions over the course of years. Then states can anticipate that any issues that cannot be resolved in a given meeting can be raised again in the future. All of these institutional features affect how states negotiate over these issues of cooperation.

As I mentioned with the ITU, institutions often have bodies that strive to produce expert information about the issues being negotiated. They collect data about the current state of affairs in the issue-area and provide analyses of the likely consequences of possible options for international cooperation. The UN produces a huge number of such technical reports from its agencies, some of which are quite valuable. Because these agencies are not controlled by any single state, it is hoped that states will view their reports as providing accurate and impartial information. Needless to say, this is not always the case. Still, institutions that collect and disseminate information attempt to deal with the informational problem present in issues of cooperation.

Institutions as rules also define the consequences of no agreement. They limit the time for negotiations. Time limits can produce political pressure to make concessions to reach a settlement. Most major international conferences to negotiate a major new treaty have a strict limit on how long they will run. There are typically many years of background work in committees negotiating drafts of portions of the treaty. A major international conference is held to complete the draft and allow state representatives to sign the final treaty. In 1998, the Rome Conference produced the statute to create the International Criminal Court. Negotiations on this treaty had been held under UN auspices for four years before the international conference in Rome. It lasted a month of public and private sessions where the treaty was finalized. Even though most nations signed the treaty, the negotiations were not entirely successful. The United States pushed for important limitations on the Court that were not adopted in the final text, despite last minute negotiations into the night after the conference was scheduled to end. The United States and other important countries, such as China and India, voted against adopting the treaty and did not sign it at the end of the conference. President Clinton did sign the treaty on December 31, 2000 after President Bush's election, but the United States has not ratified the treaty and is not bound by it legally.

The separation between signing and ratification is another important institutional rule in the law of treaties. The representative for a state at a negotiation can sign a treaty for his or her state, but signing alone does not commit his or her state to honor the treaty. Ratification is the term for formal acceptance of a treaty obligation by a state government. Governments ratify treaties in different ways. The United States requires a two-thirds vote of the Senate to ratify a treaty, making treaty ratification difficult. This supermajority—requiring more than the usual one-half-of-the-votes plus one needed to pass laws–makes it difficult for the U.S. to ratify any treaty without support from members of both political parties. Notably, the U.S. Senate refused to ratify the League of Nations treaty in 1920 and the SALT II (Strategic Arms Limitation Treaty) in 1979-80 that Presidents Wilson and Carter respectively negotiated and pushed for ratification. For some international agreements, the President chooses to make them executive agreements, which are less binding but do not require Senate ratification. Other countries use other procedures to ratify treaties. Some simply affirm their ratification of the treaty, some pass a law ratifying the treaty in their legislature, and others ratify treaties with a referendum, an election of all eligible votes in the country on whether their state should ratify the treaty. The Treaty Establishing a Constitution for Europe (TCE) sought to advance the depth of cooperation in the European Union. It was rejected by French and Dutch voters in referenda in 2005. These rejections killed that treaty and forcing European politicians to negotiate a new treaty to deal with the issues of organization that the TCE would have. The institution of ratification prevents the representative of a state from committing the state to a deal that its government will not accept.

International institutions in different issue-areas tend to focus on either distribution or information problems at the expense of the other. The institutions in international trade have large multilateral negotiations with enforcement and negotiations at the bilateral level as well. The large multilateral round of first the GATT (General Agreement on Tariffs and Trade) and now the WTO (World Trade Organization) negotiate the general structure of the political regulation of international trade. They seek to strike bargains that will lower trade barriers on many goods by many countries at the same time. These negotiating rounds now take years, which led some to claim that GATT stood for "The General Agreement to Talk and Talk." Much of the regular action on international trade occurs between pairs of countries, that is, bilaterally. Even though states have negotiated to reduce trade barriers in the major GATT and WTO rounds, they are still allowed some leeway to protect some goods against foreign competition. In addition, there are many policies of states, such as some environmental protection laws, health regulations, and produce quality laws, that are illegal under WTO law if they favor foreign produced goods to the benefit of domestically produced ones. Many of these laws are legal under WTO law because they have equal effect against goods no matter what they are made, and so do not discriminate against imports to the country. WTO law allows member governments to lodge formal complaints about each others policies that may constitute illegal barriers to trade through its dispute resolution procedure. One country, say Japan, brings a specific complaint against a policy of another WTO member, say the United States, that it believes is a barrier to its imports into the latter country. Disputes are bilateral because one country brings a complaint against another. The system for handling trade emphasizes the distribution problem–ensuring fair treatment for all goods by lowering illegal barriers to trade–over the information problem. The information problem in trade concerns the political value of barriers to trade. All governments protect some goods in many different ways. They do so to gain political support from producer groups, both labor unions and trade associations. Other governments do not know how important these policies are politically to the government which has them. We will discuss trade more fully in a later chapter, but for now, the bilateral structure of the dispute resolution mechanism focuses on distribution over information.

Environmental agreements, on the other hand, focus on information over distribution. These issues require extensive scientific knowledge, first to identify the problem and then to diagnose the problem and the consequences of possible solutions. Environmental issues have stages of progress where they first begin with agreements to collect and analyze information through international organizations addressed to the specific issue. Later, states conclude more specific agreements that lay out coordinated policies for that issue. Regulation of fisheries on international waters, for example, requires scientific study of the types of fish, the number of each, and a determination of what the allowable catch is. Then an international body allocates portions of the allowable catch to member states. Distributional issues are still thorny problems on environmental issues, even when international bodies exist to collect and analyze the state of problems.

The UN Security Council has the best-known institutional rule in world politics, the veto held by the five permanent members of the U.S., China, Russia, Great Britain, and France. A single veto cast by one of these five countries stops any resolution of the Security Council. This institutional rule was designed to make it impossible for the Security Council to act if one of the most powerful countries in the world was opposed. It ensures that these countries will not work against any action of the Security Council. It prevents issues where distributional concerns are significant from being matters of the Security Council. Action is only possible with a consensus, when all five members agree that something must be done. The five countries were the main victorious powers at the end of World War II and were given the veto power when the UN was formed in 1945. Over time, other countries have become as or more powerful than the weaker members of the five permanent members. Some of them, like Germany, Japan, and India, have sought permanent status along with veto power on the Council. To date, all measures proposed to change the permanent members of the Council and their veto powers have failed. As is the case with many issues of international cooperation, institutions may help states make agreements, but do not ensure that beneficial agreements are always reached.

Enforcement and Bargaining

We have discussed the two stages of cooperation as if they were totally separate. First, states bargain over how to cooperate, and then, they enforce that agreement against one another. In practice, the two stages are interrelated. New agreements on how to cooperate are needed because conditions change over time. If states want to coordinate their macroeconomic policies, the policies must change as their economies grow and then contract. Regulating fisheries in international waters requires yearly calculations of the allowable catch and then division of that catch into national shares. In practice, changes in what states will do to cooperate with one another can be used to enforce earlier agreements that a member state has violated. OPEC sometimes reduces the quota of oil exporting states which have sold more oil than they were allowed to under their previous quota.

States anticipate the need for enforcement when they are negotiating over how to cooperate. If an agreement is unenforceable, then why negotiate one in the first place? Human rights agreements are a special case which we will discuss in a later chapter. The design of measures of enforcement are part of the negotiation of how to cooperate.

This link between the design of enforcement and choice of policy poses an important puzzle. A longer shadow of the future makes it easier to enforce agreements. Reciprocity as an enforcement strategy punishes you tomorrow to prevent you from cheating today. When your concern for tomorrow rises relative to your concern for today, reciprocal enforcement is more likely to work. A longer shadow of the future, however, also makes distributional problems more difficult to solve. I call this the *pizza problem*. Imagine that you and a friend are negotiating over what to put on a pizza you are ordering to share. Your friend loves anchovies which you despise. You could ask the pizzeria to put anchovies on one half of the pizza, splitting the difference, but even the sight and smell of anchovies makes you sick. You have to argue it out while both of you are getting more hungry every minute. This is not an easy distributional problem to solve, but your hunger might lead you to give in and allow your friend to get the horrid fish on your pizza. Now imagine you are negotiating an agreement to place a standing order with the pizzeria where you will receive the same pizza every night for the next month, perhaps to get a discount that could save both of you money. Stomaching the sight and smell of anchovies for one night when you are very hungry could be done, but anchovies for a month? No way. Negotiating a long-term agreement, here placing an order for the same pizza every night for a month, raises the shadow of the future for all parties. It makes enforcement easier but makes distributional problems more difficult to solve.

How to Analyze It
Problems of Distribution and Information

The problems of distribution and information in international cooperation occur because there are many ways actors could cooperate. Analyzing them requires close attention to all the possible solutions, particularly those that were not chosen.

1. Clearly identify the issue and the actors on whom you will focus. It is easiest to focus on a single pair of actors, rather than just a single actor or all the actors involved on the issue. Of course, many issues involve many actors, which can make this difficult.

2. Think about how your chosen actors could cooperate on this issue. In what ways might they cooperate? Make a list of some different possible agreements to cooperate on this issue. Begin with ideas that your actors have proposed or are discussing. Phrase your answer in terms of differing levels or values of a characteristic of a settlement. Avoid "yes/no" answers; solutions such as "agreement with high standards vs. one with low standards" is more helpful than "cooperate vs. don't cooperate".

3. Make a table with your actors from step 1 on one side and the possible solutions from step 2 on the other. For each actor, list how that actor sees the possible solutions from the one it thinks is best to the one it thinks is worst; this is its preference order over the possible ways to cooperate. Remember that preference orders list all solutions in order from best to worst. Do the actors agree or disagree about the order of the attractiveness of the solutions? If they disagree, this is a problem of *distribution*.

4. Returning to your table from step 3, how certain are the actors about the value of the outcomes associated with each possible solution? Are the future consequences of each option clear for the actors, so that they are certain about their preference order? Or are they uncertain about how closely the consequences will match their intentions and so uncertain about which solutions they prefer? The less certain the actors are about the consequences of the solutions, the larger the *information* problem is.

5. Pull the parts together; which of these two problems looms larger on your issue?

Chapter Summary

International cooperation happens in two states, the first when the parties decide how they will cooperate, and the second when the parties must carry out and enforce the deal. International institutions are the "rules of the game." They can aid states negotiating how to cooperate by setting rules for the negotiations and defining the alternative to an agreement. Negotiations cannot solve the problems of distribution and information at the same time. Consequently, international institutions that support the first stage of international cooperation tend to focus on one of those two problems over the other. The interaction of the two problems also means that international cooperation is inefficient. Sometimes, negotiations over how to cooperate fail or reach less than the best possible agreement. The two stages of international cooperation interact and are often intertwined. A longer shadow of the future makes agreements more enforceable but harder to reach.

Review Questions

1. Define a coordination problem, a distribution problem, and an informational problem in terms of selecting one solution from a set of possible ways that states could cooperate.

2. What are the two types of inefficiency that can occur in bargaining over international cooperation? Give an example.

3. How does the shadow of the future affect enforcement and bargaining in international cooperation? Does a larger shadow of the future make cooperation more or less likely for each of these problems?

Chapter 23
Economic Development

Countries differ greatly in their level of economic development. The table below gives the Gross Domestic Product per person (GDP per capita), a commonly used measure of economic development, for a range of countries. The average person in the United States has roughly 100 times the income of the average person in the Democratic Republic of Congo. Widening out these figures, the advanced industrial democracies in North America, Europe, and around the rim of the Pacific Rim among the wealthiest countries, along with oil-producing states with small populations, such as Qatar. The developing world varies greatly in its wealth, with Latin America better off than most and Africa worse off than most. Why are some countries wealthy and others not?

Table 23.1
Per Capita Income for Different Countries

Country	Per Capita Income (PPP)
United States	49,000
Russia	17,000
Mexico	14,800
World	12,000
China	8,500
India	3,700
Congo	400

Data from CIA World Handbook 2011

Economic product per person, like GDP per capita, is one way to assess economic development. More developed countries produce more per person. These statistics are also correlated with other measures of development. For example, countries with higher GDP per capita tend to have longer life expectancy than those with lower GDP per capita. Still, GDP per capita is a crude but easily available measure of economic development. There are also questions around how exactly to measure the GDP of a country. For the U.S., it is easier to measure because almost all goods are bought and sold, which places a price on their value; in a developing country, many people may grow their own food, so we cannot price how much that product is worth. Some countries with high GDP per capita have very unequal distributions of income, where some are very wealthy while most of the population is poor. Development covers a wide range of things that improve peoples' lives, such as education. We can also talk about political development, where a country has an effective government that improves the lives of its citizens, and social development, where the quality of life is high. Economic development generally improves all of these, which is why we use measures of it, like GDP per capita, as an easy way to assess the development of a country. The UN and other organizations have tried to create more complex indicators of development and quality of life, which show there is variation in these indicators around GDP per capita. For our purposes, we will treat GDP per capita as a measure of development, although it is important to remember that there is more to development than just more money.

Economic development has occurred over the breadth of human civilization as living standards and quality of life have improved. The Industrial Revolution accelerated economic development by replacing muscle power of people and animals with machine power. This change greatly increased the productivity of workers, meaning they could produce more in the same time. New products were also introduced that improved life. Innovations gave us electric lights to use at night and steel that allowed the manufacture of many new products, like skyscraper buildings and automobiles. The Post-Industrial Age continued this trend of economic development. Manufacturing and agriculture became so productive that a small proportion of workers could produce vast amounts of food and industrial goods that many people moved into producing services. Computer technology is transforming our lives in many complicated ways. The period since the advent of the Industrial Revolution around 1750 has transformed peoples' lives in many ways, leading to an immensely high standard of living that in the past. What drives these great changes?

What Causes Economic Growth?

Societies gain in wealth as their people are able to produce more. Some of this increase comes from new ways to produce old products, such as food, more efficiently. Some comes from new products, like cellphones, or improved versions of products that make them much cheaper to buy. Three processes drive economic growth.

Specialization occurs when people apply themselves to specific tasks rather than trying to produce all the goods they need for life. Even a hundred years ago, most people lived in the countryside where they grew their own food, make their own clothes, and took care of all their own needs with their own labor. Now, most of us buy food from the store, which is produced by farmers who are experts in agriculture and animal husbandry. Specialization takes many forms, from the skills and expertise workers acquire in their job to the coordination of many workers doing different tasks that allow them together to create products of daunting complexity. Specialization increase productivity of workers and allows for teams that work together to complete projects no single worker could do.

Exchange allows the benefits of specialization by giving people access to all the things they do not make. People can specialize in what they do well because they can get everything else they need through exchange. Barter, where the two parties have to find others who want what they make, is the simplest form of exchange. Money aids exchange by creating a common store of value that all will accept in exchange. Money also allows for prices, which reduce the value of a good or service to a single number, making it easier to determine if one wants to buy or sell the good or service. Exchange and specialization work together to increase what society can produce and ensure the distribution of that produce to its members.

Accumulation results when people do not consume all that society produces immediately, putting aside some products for future use or to increase future production. Many things can be accumulated. Goods can be put aside to provide for insurance against future losses, such as food stocks. Money can be accumulated in financial instruments, like bank deposits, stocks, and bonds, that can then provide resources for new investments. Knowledge accumulates, giving new ways to produce more.

Economists talk about **factors** of production, what can be used to produce goods and services. Land, labor, and capital are the simplest system of factors, although there are other systems that break each of these three into smaller groups, such as if we separate skilled from unskilled labor. Land covers all the ways that production needs land; so the plot that a factory is built on and the mineral deposits of a mine are both types of land. Labor is the value contributed by people in production, both in terms of work and management. Capital is all the other elements that make land and labor more productive; factories are one example as is livestock that farmers use to produce food. Capital is commonly produced through other work, and the accumulation of capital is a sign of economic development. People own factors, including their own labor, and we refer to the land, labor, and capital one owns as the person's factor endowment.

These three drivers of economic growth—specialization, exchange, and accumulation—lead to economic development. Growth results from five different processes. First, the accumulation of capital makes people more productive by increasing their ability to produce. Physical capital, such as factories and improvements to land, is the most obvious form of capital accumulation. Human capital—education and all skills that workers learn that make them more productive in their jobs—also accumulates in individuals and across society. One reason why modern industrial society is highly productive is the accumulation of knowledge of how to produce goods and services.

Second, increases in productivity—the efficient use of factors—contributes to economic growth by allowing more to be produced by the available factors. Alternatively, if the same levels of production can be sustained with less land, labor, or capital, those factors are freed up to be used to produce something else. The ancient Egyptians could build the Pyramids through the application of a mass of labor. The accumulation of knowledge about construction and the use of modern building equipment and materials allow industrial society to build structures unimaginable to the ancient Egyptians. Productivity can be difficult to measures because even inefficient ways of production can produce large amounts of goods.

Third, innovation and the creation of new knowledge give people better ways to produce. Technology provides new products and new processes of production. For example, the technology to produce steel on an industrial scale was developed during the 19th century, revolutionizing transportation, construction, and production generally. Since then, the technology of steel production has improved greatly, making modern steel mills vastly more productive than those of 150 years ago. New forms of organization are another form of organization that makes people more productive. Henry Ford did not invent the idea of a production line, where manufactured goods proceed from worker to worker with each worker performing just few tasks in the production process, but he did raise that form of organization of production to heights unimagined before him.

Fourth, trade and the exchange of products and knowledge spread the benefits of economic development. Trade gives us access to goods not produced in our country. Trade also advances specialization, allowing all to produce more. Innovations can spread from country to country through trade, making workers more productive.

Fifth, political, economic, and social institutions aid the process of economic growth by setting the conditions for economic growth. Governments establish property rights, which clarify who owns what and specifies their rights to use and dispose of their property. These rights aid investment and protect accumulation. Governments also seek to ensure the security of persons and property. This security allows people to accumulate goods and capital without fear that someone else will take away the benefits of their work. A lack of security discourages investment and forces people to invest in protecting their own security, resources that could be used for production. Finance as an economic institution helps move resources from those who own them to those who have productive opportunities to use those resources to create new and more productive operations. Governments create and administer legal systems to resolve disputes between parties involved in economic exchange and joint production and to increase security by deterring crime through punishment. Finally, government can foster political stability and stable policy which makes it easier for investors to judge whether an enterprise will succeed, and thereby be worth investing in. Good government sets the rules that create fertile growth for economic growth, and there are many ways that it can obstruct economic growth.

How Does World Politics Influence Economic Growth?

Politics within and between states influences economic growth. As described above, governments within states set the rules under which economic activity occurs. This is a large and important topic, but it lies in the realm of domestic politics rather than world politics. World politics influences economic development primarily through international exchange, the movement of goods, services, capital, ideas, and people across national borders.

International exchange has contributed to economic growth in five ways. First, trade increases the productivity of countries involved in it. It provides them with access to goods, services, and innovations they do not produce. International competition can induce businesses to improve their efficiency, increasing economic growth. International markets can allow domestic firms to produce more than they can sell in their home country; depending on the industry in question, it can be more efficient per unit to produce more.

Second, international exchange aids the diffusion of innovations from country to country. Firms in our country may have to imitate more efficient foreign firms to be able to compete. Investors may take new ideas and production processes to other countries to establish new businesses. The free exchange of scientific ideas and technology make it possible for more people to work on advancing science and improving technology.

Third, cross-border financial flows direct investment to countries and businesses where capital is needed. Developed countries, those with the highest per capita incomes, are capital rich because economic development requires the accumulation of capital. Developing countries, on the other hand, are short in capital and can use additional capital to aid their development. Cross-border capital flows can take the form of foreign aid for development from government or international financial institutions, foreign direct investment (FDI) where a company builds or buys assets in a country, portfolio capital where private investors buy bonds or shares in a company, and remittances where migrants working in other countries send money home. All of these flows increase the ability of a developing country to increase its capital stock.

Fourth, international exchange can spread institutions that foster growth. International institutions can provide advice to countries about what institutions are likely to increase their economic development. Countries may have to compete for international investment, making them more likely to create conditions attractive to investors.

Finally, migration of people spreads skills and ideas. Students from developing countries can receive education in developed countries that may not be available in their home country; when they return to their home country, they increase its human capital. Managers from developed countries may work in developing countries as expatriates, increasing the pool of skills of the labor used in the developing country. Migrant workers also remit some of their earnings home as mentioned above.

International exchange is the primary contribution of world politics to economic development for these five reasons. Governments influence international exchange by the policies they set that manage access to their country for people, goods, and capital and by the international institutions they have created to manage the challenges of international exchange. These lead us to focus on the politics of trade, money, and finance and how politics shapes them. Trade concerns the movement of goods and services across national borders. Finance centers on cross-border investment. Money and how countries manage exchange rates among their currencies affect both trade and finance.

Summary

Countries differ greatly in their economic development. Specialization, exchange, and accumulation are the three drivers of economic growth. International exchange has increased economic development through trade, the diffusion of innovations, cross-border financial flows, the spread of institutions that favor growth, and migration. World politics affects economic growth by influencing the movement of goods, money, people, and ideas.

Review Questions

1. What are the three drivers of economic growth throughout the history of civilization? Explain each in one sentence.

2. Specify two of the five ways that international exchange contributes to economic growth.

Chapter 24
The Politics of Trade

The global economy has grown greatly in the period beginning in 1945, and trade has been one of the major engines of that growth. Regions of the globe, such as East Asia, have industrialized because of their ability to sell the goods they produce in other industrialized countries. The world economy now is more integrated than it ever has been. Advances in transportation and telecommunications have greatly aided the growth of trade. The introduction of the container ship, some of which are now capable of carrying up to 15,000 standard containers, made the movement of manufactured goods much cheaper and easier. The shipper fills the container which is a large, long steel box. The container is loaded on a truck or train which carries it to a port for loading on a ship by a crane. The container ship is stacked up with containers and sails for another port where the containers are unloaded onto trucks and trains for overland shipping to their destination. The entire system makes the movement of goods across water much cheaper and easier. Similarly, the introduction of the internet has made outsourcing, the movement of some business services from industrialized countries to developing ones, much easier. This movement of jobs has made businesses more efficient, increased economic growth in countries like India, but cost some workers in developed countries their jobs.

[Picture of container ship]

Politics has also played a large role in the growth of trade. Trade traditionally has been taxed when it leaves the country of production and enters the country of purchase or consumption. States did this because it was economic activity that could be taxed easily at a port or border crossing. Taxes on trade, known as tariffs when placed on imports, make trade less efficient by making imported goods more expensive relative to domestically-produced competing goods. The General Agreement on Tariffs and Trade (GATT) entered into force in 1948. This treaty sought to reduce tariffs and so increase trade among its members. In a series of seven negotiating rounds, GATT reduced tariffs on manufactured goods greatly. The tariff reductions under GATT were reciprocal, all members agreed to similar reductions, and non-discriminatory, a reduction granted on the goods of one member had to apply to all members. The eighth and final rounds of GATT talks, the Uruguay Round, produced the treaties that formed the World Trade Organization (WTO). The WTO is an organization, unlike GATT which was simply an agreement to negotiate reduction of trade barriers.

The postwar period has also seen a great growth in intrafirm trade. Trade is often thought of as goods produced by a company in one country and then sold to consumers in another. Intrafirm trade occurs when one company moves goods or parts to be assembled in one country to another part of itself in another for final assembly or use. Companies use intrafirm trade to internationalize their supply chain, to create a production process located in many countries at once to take advantage of production possibilities in each country. The Coca-Cola Company, for example, produces the syrup used by bottling companies, some but not all owned by Coca-Cola, to make the drink which they then sell in their region or country. These bottlers can add sweeteners to Coca-Cola to local tastes, so the product is not the same everywhere. Coke's low-calorie version, which I drink too much of, tastes different in Europe, where it is known as Coca-Cola Light, than the United States, where it is Diet Coke, because different sweeteners are added. Intrafirm trade then has contributed to the industrialization of developing countries as firms from the developed world have built factories or struck production deals with manufacturing firms in developing countries. You may have heard the Nike produces its shoes primarily in Southeast Asian countries. It signs contracts with local producers to make the parts and stitch them together rather than owning the factories that make its shoes.

GATT was very successful in reducing tariffs as barriers to trade. Today, average tariffs among WTO members are very low, so imported goods are competitive with domestically produced goods. Beginning with the Tokyo Round of GATT negotiations, attention shifted to non-tariff barriers (NTBs). These barriers to the free movement of goods and services include any policy which discriminates against imports and in favor of domestic goods. Quotas on imports prevent foreign producers from selling above the quota in a country. Subsidies to domestic firms for their production also favor their goods over imports by making it cheaper to produce them. More controversially, product quality laws and environmental regulation of products are seen as barriers to trade if they favor domestic producers over foreign competitors. The reduction of non-tariff barriers is a primary objective of the WTO.

The GATT system exempted two major types of goods, agriculture and textiles. The Multi-Fiber Arrangement (MFA) regulated international trade in textiles from 1974 until 2005. The production of textiles uses a lot of labor and does not require special skills. Developing countries can produce textiles more cheaply than developed countries because the labor cost is lower. The MFA imposed a quota on textiles and garments made in the developing world which could be sold in developed countries. Most developed countries have agricultural subsidies to farmers and other producers. These subsidies make it more difficult for farmers in the developing world to compete to sell their produce on world markets. Farmers in developed countries use machinery, fertilizer, and pesticides to make each farmer far more productive than those in developing world who rely on their own labor to grow crops. These subsidies then lead to overproduction and stockpiles of many agricultural products. Both agriculture and textiles have been protected because both are politically sensitive in many countries.

Politics has contributed to the expansion in trade by removing barriers to free movement of goods and services from country to country. Although trade moves more freely now that it did after the Second World War, there are still important barriers to trade. Every country protects some goods with tariffs. Further, there is not agreement on whether some policies are legal under WTO law or are NTBs, and hence must be changed. How does politics shape trade?

The Logic of Comparative Advantage

States set their trade policy because of its economic effects. These policies makes some people richer, others poorer. People will advocate for policies that put money in their pockets and against those that take money out of them. This is the *"pocketful of preferences"* assumption: people judge their country's economic policies based how those policies affect their own economic welfare. We make this simple assumption about people's policy preferences to study which policy a country adopts. Whether the winners or the losers from a policy prevail depends on which interests are organized for political action and whether and how the government of that state listens to those competing interests. In either case, the economics of trade are central to understanding the politics of trade. This means we will review important results about the economic effects of trade for countries, firms, and individuals.

The law of comparative advantage is the basic insight about trade in economics. It was identified almost 200 years ago. Comparative advantage begins with the observation that countries differ in their abilities to produce goods. How much it costs to produce each good varies relative to other goods across countries. These differences create *comparative advantage*, the ability of each country to produce something more efficiently relative to other goods it can produce. The logic of comparative advantage is simple:

> If every country specializes in producing goods where it has a comparative advantage and they then trade those goods, every country consumes more goods than they would if each produced the full range of goods for itself and did not trade.

When each country produces the goods it makes more efficiently, total production across all countries goes up. Trade then allows each to exchange the goods it produces for the full basket of goods that can be produced. For example, growing grapes for wine requires a warm climate and lots of sun. Coal is produced most easily when it is abundant and close to the surface of the Earth. Historically, it has made sense for France to produce wine from its grapes and trade them for English coal. Both countries are better off because France is better at making wine than digging up coal and the opposite is true for Britain. Each state produces goods where it has a comparative advantage and then trades.

Comparative advantage does not require a country to have an absolute advantage at producing anything. Developed countries, like the United States, produce a wide range of goods more cheaply than developing countries. Even though it is cheaper to produce many things in industrialized countries, both they and developing countries can benefit from the logic of comparative advantage. The developed country focuses on the goods it produces much more efficiently than a developing country can, like computers and financial services, and the developing country does the same, focusing on some types of agricultural products and goods that can be manufactured by unskilled labor. By focusing on what they make most efficiently, each country produces more than if it spread its productive resources to make the full range of goods. Trade is necessary for the logic of comparative advantage to work by providing people in all countries with the full range of goods produced around the world. If trade was blocked, each country would produce everything that it consumed. It would have to devote resources to produce goods that are relatively expensive to make there. The U.S., for example, would have to grow coffee beans for its citizens to be able to drink coffee if it could no longer import coffee beans from the tropical states that grow them, like Colombia and Brazil. Some coffee is grown in Hawaii, but it is very expensive. If U.S. consumers could only drink coffee from beans grown in the country, coffee would be a luxury, and few of us would drink it daily. Similarly, the countries that grow coffee can trade it for other goods that are harder to produce in their own countries.

Trade causes the national incomes of both countries to rise. Each is able to consume more goods and services than it would if it relied entirely on its own to produce everything. National income measures the total of goods and services consumed in a country. It does not tell us that everyone in the country is better off, only that the total of what everyone consumes goes up.

Advantages of Free Trade

The logic of comparative advantage is one reason why almost all economists favor free trade. The free movement of goods allows each country to specialize in the goods it produces most efficiently. When countries trade what they produce efficiently for the goods they do not, national income and global production rises. Free trade also has two other beneficial effects for a state's economy.

First, competition from foreign goods forces domestic firms to produce more efficiently. Forty years ago, the Big Three automakers–General Motors, Ford, and Chrysler–dominated the U.S. car market. Japanese car producers like Toyota did not sell many cars in the U.S. and were limited to selling small, cheap, economy cars. But those firms had more efficient production processes than the Big Three did. They relied on "just-in-time" production to manage their supply chain of auto parts for final assembly. Modern auto firms separate the production of cars across many factories. Most specialize in producing some parts of cars, like the body or drive train. These parts are then shipped to an assembly plant where cars are built from them and finished with paint and trim. The Japanese car makers kept the supply of parts used in automobile assembly restricted to the small amount needed to complete cars in the next day or two. The Big Three in contrast kept large stocks of parts at their assembly plants. These stockpiles are expensive because the company has money tied up in all those parts before they are made into cars and sold. "Just-in-time" production though requires careful management of the production process from manufacturing the parts through final assembly. Missing even one part shuts down the final production line. As Japanese firms gained market share in the United States, the Big Three had to make their production processes more efficient to compete with the

Japanese firms. Now "just-in-time" production is common in most car firms. The Big Three now also produce cars more efficiently than they did forty years ago. They use less raw materials and labor to build one car. Foreign competition has reduced the share of the U.S. that the Big Three control, but it has forced them to become better car manufacturers.

Second, free trade provides a country with greater access to innovations from foreign countries. Innovation–changes in production processes and the goods produced–is a major engine of economic growth. Economies become more productive when they make better goods and do so more efficiently. Technological innovation helps economic growth by providing new ways to make things. The introduction of the tractor revolutionized agriculture by replacing animal and manpower with machine power. The assembly line increased the efficiency of production by having each worker specialize in one task which they then mastered. The transistor and integrated circuit made modern computers possible, although the computers we have now required many other innovations as well. Countries that do not trade are limited to the innovations of their own people and those they can imitate from other countries. It is more efficient to trade with another country to buy novel ways to make new products. Trade then increases economic growth in a country by aiding its adoption of new technology from other countries.

Most economists argue for free trade based on these three reasons. The logic of comparative advantage raises national income. Foreign competition forces domestic producers to become more efficient. Trade increases economic growth by providing access to innovations from other countries. Despite these advantages, no country has completely free trade. All countries place some barriers to trade. The rest of this chapter examines why by considering different reasons why governments seek to restrict the import of foreign goods into their country.

Tools for Protection

Governments have many tools to restrict competition from foreign goods in their own markets. All of these measures make imports–goods produced in another country and sold in its domestic markets–more expensive, and so less attractive to purchasers than domestically produced goods. Tariffs are taxes on imports, typically levied when the goods enter the country at a port or border crossing. Tariffs make imports less competitive with domestically produced goods by raising their price. The importer can pass on some or all of the tariff to those who purchase the goods. Tariffs are commonly placed as a fraction of the value of the goods; a 10% tariff imposes a tax of 10% on imports based on their value. An imported good priced at $100 would have to pay $10 tariff. There are other ways to levy tariffs on imported goods. In the 1600s, the British government placed a tariff on wine imports from France. British people generally drank cheap wine from France. Because Britain often fought wars with France, the British government wanted to deny the French government the revenue from the wine trade. The tariff was based on the volume of wine imported, not its value. The wine trade from France to Britain consisted of cheap wine imported in bulk and sold to the lower classes and vintage (read expensive) wine imported in bottles and consumed by the upper classes. A tariff based on value would have raised the price of both by the same percentage, but a tariff based on volume raised the price of cheap wine greatly but that of vintage wine only a little. At the same time, the British government subsidized beer production in Britain and port (a fortified wine) production in Portugal. The combination of the tariff and cheap beer shifted the consumption of the British lower classes from wine to beer and cost the French money. At the same time, the upper classes who were important politically were still able to afford and enjoy vintage wine from France.

Non-tariff barriers cover any policy of a government that makes imports less competitive that is not a tariff. Quotas are a simple form of NTB. By limiting how much of an imported good can be sold in a country raises its price if the quota is set below the consumption of the good without the quota. The Reagan Administration negotiated a voluntary export restraint (VER) on Japanese imports of cars into the U.S. market in the early 1980s. The Japanese government agreed to restrict how many cars their auto firms would sell in the U.S., making the quota "voluntary". The Reagan Administration wished to help domestic car manufacturers who had lost market share to the Japanese producers. Dealers of Japanese cars could set their sale price above the list price for most cars because more Americans wished to buy Japanese cars than could under the quota. Those dealers would add mysterious lines to the sticker price with titles like "ADP," which stood for "Additional Dealer Profit". Economists estimated that the VER added $1000 to price of the average car during the time it was in force. The VER also had the unexpected effect of leading the Japanese invasion of the larger, higher-value car market. Before then, Japanese imported cars tended to be small, economy cars. The Big Three still dominated the family and luxury car markets, which produce higher profit per vehicle sold. The Japanese firms, now limited in how many cars they could sell, focused on adding options and luxury features to the cars they built for the U.S. market. The VER then triggered the Japanese firms' invasion of the high-end, high-profit part of the car market, leading to the introduction of their luxury marks of Lexis (Toyota), Infiniti (Nissan), and Acura (Honda).

Product safety laws and health and environmental regulations can also operate as NTBs under some conditions. The effect of such laws on trade is not clear; governments can disagree whether a particular policy is a barrier to trade or not, unlike a tariff which openly favors domestic goods over imports. A famous case before the WTO determined that U.S. rules that required fishermen to limit how many dolphins they killed when fishing for tuna were an illegal barrier to tuna produced in other countries (see http://american.edu/TED/TUNA.HTM for a description of the case). The U.S. adopted these rules in the 1972 Marine Mammal Protection Act when U.S. fishermen dominated the tuna catch in the Eastern Pacific Ocean for the U.S. market. Over time, fishers from Mexico and other countries entered the U.S. canned-tuna market but did not follow the same rules. The U.S. government adopted rules to prevent canned tuna from these markets being sold in the U.S. but did not enforce this embargo until forced to do so by a lawsuit brought by the Earth Institute, an environmental protection group. Mexico appealed that this embargo was illegal under GATT law. The GATT panel found the U.S. embargo on Mexican tuna was a violation of GATT law, although other laws that required dolphin-safe labeling were not. The difference is key to GATT and WTO law. A policy is an NTB only if it discriminates against imports and in favor of domestic-produced goods. The embargo was a violation because it simply blocked imports of tuna from Mexico regardless of how they were caught. The labeling law did not because Mexican producers could adopt the fishing practices, obtain dolphin-safe labels, and then sell their tuna in the United States. It treated tuna produced in any country the same provided it met the standard.

Finally, other trade practices that favor exports are also against GATT and WTO law. Some countries provide subsidies to their exports. This is against trade law because it favors exports over imports in the countries where those goods are sold. Again, provisions which favor one country's goods over competing goods from its trading partner are against trade law. It seeks to create national markets where all goods and services compete on price and quality rather than where they are made.

Optimal Tariffs and Reciprocity

Why then might governments choose to protect domestically produced goods over imports? A state can capture the gains from trade for itself using an *optimal tariff*. Such a tariff can increase the *terms of trade*–the price of its exports relative to its imports. A tariff raises the price of imports, meaning people in the country imposing the tariff will buy less of it. At the same time, the country that makes the imports collects less of revenue from sales of the goods because of the tariff. Done properly, an optimal tariff shifts the terms of trade in its favor so that the country using it captures the added value from the logic of comparative advantage. At the same time, an optimal tariff makes its trading partners worse off than free trade. They realize none of the gains from specialization from the logic of comparative advantage. Countries with large economies are in the best position to use an optimal tariff. A large domestic market buys more imports than a small one, and a country with a large economy produces more goods for itself and export. Its size gives it the leverage to shift prices in favor of goods produced within its borders. A country with a small economy, on the other hand, lacks the power to shift the terms of trade in its favor. It has to import many goods and does not export many. Optimal tariffs then favor large economies, like the United States, over small ones.

An optimal tariff only works, however, if a country's trading partners do not retaliate with a tariff of their own. In the face of an optimal tariff, other countries may place tariffs of their own on the exports of the country using an optimal tariff. This retaliation makes both sides worse off. It shifts the terms of trade against the country that placed the original optimal tariff in favor of its retaliating trade partner. Now the tariffs of both countries are higher, which makes both worse off. They lose the gains from comparative advantage, and national income decreases in both.

Optimal tariff policy then has the structure of a Prisoners' Dilemma as we discussed in the chapter on enforcement. Figure 1 shows a game of setting and responding to optimal tariffs. Each state is better adopting an optimal tariff regardless of what the other side does. If its trading partner does not adopt such a tariff, it shifts the terms of trade and gains the surplus produced by specialization from the logic of comparative advantage. If its trading partner uses an optimal tariff, the country's own optimal tariff prevents it from being exploited by its partner. Both sides are worse off when both use an optimal tariff compared to when neither uses one. How can states enforce agreements to trade freely in the face of incentives to use optimal tariffs?

Figure 30
Optimal Tariffs as a Prisoners' Dilemma

	Free Trade	Optimal Tariff
Free Trade	(5,5)	(-10,10)
Optimal Tariff	(10,-10)	(-5,-5)

Free trade agreements can be enforced through reciprocal sanctions as discussed in the chapter on enforcement. The states agree to lower trade barriers and to respond in kind if any of them uses an optimal tariff. If all the states care enough about the value of their trade in the future, the threat of retaliation can enforce the deal, and member states will not use optimal tariffs.

The fundamental structure of GATT and the WTO systems reflects reciprocal enforcement. These agreements are *multilateral in nature* and *bilateral in enforcement*. Members of either system agree that any trade concession given to one member must be given to all members. This principle is called *nondiscrimination* and operates through *most favored nation* (MFN) status. Once one state grants MFN status to another, which GATT or WTO members can do for non-members, it can no longer discriminate against imports from the latter. Further, GATT negotiating rounds focused on tariff reduction among all members. The broad agreements in the GATT system were multilateral. Sometimes members would violate these agreements, triggering retaliation by other members. Individual members carried out retaliation against another member judged to be in violation of GATT agreements. A country would propose a retaliatory tariff on the offending country's exports to it. It could seek a decision by a GATT panel, although both states had to agree to the formation of a panel to handle the dispute. Often, the two would negotiate a solution to the dispute before the retaliatory trade sanction was put into force. The country whose policies were declared in violation of GATT law could also ignore the panel's decision. Other countries were not called upon to participate in the retaliatory sanctions, making enforcement bilateral–between two countries rather than many. Bilateral sanctions were also effective because the states that had to carry them out benefitted directly from their enforcement actions. Sometimes a reciprocal trade sanction would lead to retaliation by the country being sanctioned, creating a mini-trade war. GATT was very successful, both in expanding its membership as the world economy grew and in reducing tariffs as barriers to most manufactured goods. Agriculture and textiles remained where GATT did not reduce barriers to trade.

[Political cartoon on trade war between US and Europe during Kennedy Administration]

The Domestic Politics of Protection

The GATT did not eliminate all barriers to trade. The system lowered tariffs across the board. Still, states found other ways to protect their domestic industries from foreign competition. Free trade raises national income, but this does not mean that all people within a country gain when it lowers its barriers to trade. Trade creates winners and losers. Some gain business by gaining access to new markets for their products in other countries. Others lose when imports replace the goods they were producing. The losers from trade may try to get their government to adopt measures that will protect them from foreign competition. Their government in turn may adopt such measures to gain the favor of those who lose from trade in their country. Trade protection then is often a tool for governments to gain support. Those who benefit from protection against foreign competition provide political support because of that protection. Protection from trade can target particular goods, making it attractive for politicians seeking support from those who work or own an industry. Some industries are concentrated in a few localities in a country. Protection for that industry can have a large economic effect in those areas, which means politicians who represent that area can gain greatly by securing protection for that industry. The automobile industry, for instance, has historically been concentrated in southeastern Michigan, within a hundred miles of where I live. Members of Congress from Michigan have been among those who have argued for protection for the car industry from competition from foreign cars.

The U.S. steel industry has undergone a long, slow decline since its heyday in the first half of the 20th century. Steel produced in other countries, particularly Japan and South Korea, has taken much of the market away from American steel producers in the U.S. and in other countries. Both the unions that represent steel workers and steel manufacturers have sought protection from the U.S. government against this foreign competition. On March 5, 2002, President Bush announced that the U.S. government was putting a tariff on imports of steel into the United States, ranging from 8-30% for a period of three years. He claimed that these tariffs were consistent with WTO law under its anti-dumping provisions. Anti-dumping law allows a country to impose a short-term tariff to counter a sudden surge of imports into the country. Many believed that these steel tariffs were enacted for political purposes. The steel industry plays an important role in the economy of the state of Pennsylvania, a state which was recognized to be a key state for President Bush to carry in his re-election campaign for President in 2004. While the steel tariff may have helped steel workers and those who own stock in steel firms, it hurt other U.S. firms which use steel and American consumers who had to pay higher prices for products made with steel, such as cars.

Trade protection then can be good for the leader of a country and some people in it, while hurting others by raising the price of the protected good. Those who produce the protected good are small in number, while consumers are a much larger group. One might think then that politicians would favor consumers over producers and not protect their markets from foreign competition. But the gains from protection for each individual workers and owner of the industry being protected are larger than the loss to each consumer from paying more for one of the many goods they consume. Further, workers and producers are often organized into unions and trade associations. This organization makes them more effective in domestic politics. This pattern has *concentrated benefits, dispersed costs*. Political leaders are more likely to respond to the concentrated and organized interests which benefit from protection than the dispersed and unorganized larger number of consumers.

For the leader of a state, more protection of domestic producers can be good politically. For its trading partners, increased trade protection is bad. Producers who import their goods into the country adopting protection sell less of the good in that country, losing business. Their government in turn may take action to get the government protecting its market to change those policies. Reciprocal trade sanctions are one way to do so. By hurting other producers of the country protecting some products, the government of its trading partner hopes to convince the leader to remove its protection. Those sanctions should be designed for their political effect, sanctions that will hurt the targeted leader politically rather than those that change trade between the two countries the most.

President Bush's steel tariffs provoked a quick response from other countries. The EU announced that it would file a dispute with the WTO claiming that the tariffs were illegal. EU representatives argued that the tariffs were not allowed under anti-dumping law because there had been no surge of steel imports into the U.S. market before Bush enacted them. The EU placed this case even though the tariffs targeted primarily imports of Japanese and South Korean steel into the U.S. They feared that Japanese and Korean steel firms would then ship the steel they could no longer sell in the U.S. onto the European market. This diversion of trade would hurt European steel firms and workers. But the WTO dispute resolution does not operate swiftly. It ruled in autumn of 2003 that the U.S. steel tariff violated WTO law. The EU announced retaliatory trade sanctions that focused on goods produced in swing states that President Bush needed to carry in the 2004 election. In particular, they planned to place a high tariff on imports of citrus fruit and products from the U.S., citrus grown heavily in Florida, a state everyone knew would be close and vital to Bush's re-election effort. They understood that the most effective sanction was one with the greatest political effect.

States manage this system of limited protection for political advantage by negotiating over policies of one another that they consider to be barriers. Uncertainty about the importance of the support of the protected group complicates these negotiations. European governments did not know exactly how important the support of steel workers would be to President Bush. They had to make judgments about how easily they could convince the Bush Administration to remove the tariff. In some cases, governments refuse to change their policies that protect domestic producers. They would rather accept the retaliation of their trading partners than eliminate the protection of the favored group. Some barriers to trade protect sufficiently important economic groups that their state's leader will defend them, while others are simply politically convenient. For the system of limited protection to work, states have to be able to sort out which barriers are politically crucial and which just convenient. This is a problem of information because each government can judge its own domestic politics better than its trading partners can. Would President Bush accept retaliation rather than remove the steel tariff? A system of freer trade requires states to determine which barriers are too important politically to expect states to remove them.

Trade: Who Wins? Who Loses?

Producers can lose business to foreign competition as barriers to imports into their country fail. Other producers could gain if they get greater access to export their goods to other countries who have lowered their barriers to the goods they produce. Two ideas from economics are useful to describe who loses and who wins from freer trade. *Factors* are the basic elements of any production process. The simplest set of factors are *land*, *labor*, and *capital*. Land is used to grow crops for agricultural producers, mine raw materials, or for the location of manufacturing plants, offices, and places to sell goods. Location as well as quality of land affects its value. Labor is the product of people working with their hands or minds to produce goods. In some cases, we will distinguish *skilled labor* from *unskilled labor,* where the former possess some special skills that make them produce certain goods more efficiently. One main reason why you are in college is to improve your skilled labor in the hope of earning more than if you did not go to college. Capital covers machinery and other aids to production that people own. All these factors can be shifted from one industry to another, although they may not be as useful in the production process of the latter. People own factors. Some own land and capital, while all of us own our own labor.

Sectors are areas of specific goods produced in the economy, particular industries if you like. Automobiles, types of agricultural products, and day care are all different sectors of the economy, although day care is not traded internationally as the first two are. The U.S. Department of Commerce You can find trade data for the United States broken down by sectors and states for any country the U.S. trades with at http://tse.export.gov/. Everyone works in some sector of the economy, or as an economist would put, employs their factors in that sector. People shift their factors from one sector to another if they change jobs (although they do not if they move from one company to another in the same industry).

When a country opens up to trade, both making imports into the country and its exports to other countries more competitive, its businesses face greater international competition. Whether owners of the different factors benefit or lose from the competition and opportunities of international trade depends on how much foreign competition they face. Factors are either *scarce* or *plentiful* within a country relative to the global economy. A factor is scarce if the country has less of it than is typical around the world; it is plentiful if it is more common in the country than in the world. The United States is plentiful in land, skilled labor, and capital and scarce in unskilled labor. This is not to say that there a few unskilled laborers in the U.S., just that unskilled labor is easier to find in other countries than in the U.S. Again, the supply of factors within a country is always measured relative to the world economy.

Plentiful factors win from greater openness to trade because they can now sell their goods in foreign markets. Scarce factors lose because they face greater international competition in their domestic market. Wages for labor and returns to capital and land are prices for those factors. Supply and demand set prices with the price rising as supply is lower or demand higher. When a factor is scarce in a country which is closed to trade, its price is higher than on the world market because the supply of it is less within that country. When the country's economy opens up to international competition through trade, that factor now faces competition from the products of owners of that factor in other countries. The price the scarce factor commands decreases. Plentiful factors in a country benefit because they can now sell their products abroad. There is a simple way to remember this pattern: scarce factors suffer, plentiful factors prosper.

What should the owners of a scarce factor do as their country opens up to trade? The products of some of the industries they work in will suffer from foreign competition. This will cost jobs and profits and, in the extreme, may bankrupt companies. Their sector has become less successful because of competition introduced by trade. They may be able to shift to a different sector by changing jobs or redeploying their capital. If they can find another sector where they command as great a return, they will do so. But other times owners of the scarce factor will not be able to command as high a return as they did before their country opened to trade. The ability of factors to move across sectors–its ability to produce different products at a similar return–is called the *mobility* of factors. Mobile factors can be used to make many different products with a similar return; that is, wages for labor and return on investment through profits for capital and land. A factor is immobile when it loses much of its value when it is used in a different sector. As a college professor, I own a lot of highly skilled labor which is immobile. It takes years of study beyond college to earn a Ph.D. degree in an academic field and then years more doing research in that field. Because of the skills I have developed through my education and experience, The University of Michigan pays me and other professors well compared to many others in the U.S. Professors could not earn as much if they changed fields. No one would pay me as much to teach chemistry classes as they do to teach political science, not to mention what I would earn in totally different sectors. Fortunately for me, skilled academic labor is plentiful in the U.S. which means people like me benefit because the U.S. is open to foreign students. When they come to the U.S. to study, it is a form of international trade. The owners of immobile, scarce factors seek protection from trade because they lose when their country opens up to international competition and they do not have the option of changing sectors and making as much money.

The automobile industry in the U.S. is an excellent example. Fifty years ago, the Big Three automakers–General Motors, Ford, and Chrysler–dominated both the U.S. and world markets for cars. GM always returned a healthy dividend to those who owned shares of the company, and auto workers were paid well. Over time, producers from other countries, particularly Japan and Europe, entered both markets. At first, they were restricted to selling only in a part of the car market. Japanese firms produced fuel efficient, small cars, while European firms aimed at the luxury market. By the late 1970s though, foreign competition was taking market share away from the Big Three. Because auto workers were paid well and profits in the Big Three had been high, these factors were immobile. Retooling a car factory to build something was costly and what it would produce was not as profitable as making cars had been. Auto workers could not find jobs that paid as much. The Big Three and the United Auto Workers (UAW) turned to the U.S. government for protection. The Reagan Administration gave them temporary protection by negotiating the VER discussed earlier in the chapter. It limited Japanese imports into the U.S. for three years to give the Big Three a chance to make their businesses more efficient and competitive with the Japanese. The Reagan Administration protected the auto industry for these years even though it was ideologically conservative and believed in free markets and free trade. Over the last twenty years, the Big Three have continued to lose ground to competition from foreign automakers in U.S. and international markets, and the owners of the companies and auto workers have suffered for it. The U.S. government, however, has not provided them with protection from that foreign competition despite the pleas of both management and the UAW for protection. Organized interests do not always get their government to protect them from international trade.

The Institutions of International Trade: The GATT and WTO

The World Trade Organization (WTO), like the GATT (General Agreement on Tariffs and Trade) before it, exists to support the international politics of freer trade. At the end of the Second World War, the victorious Western Powers led by the United States sought to establish global economic institutions to prevent another economic catastrophe like the Great Depression. The Bretton Woods conference planned for the International Trade Organization (ITO) to manage international trade and lower barriers to trade. The U.S. Senate, however, did not ratify the treaty creating that organization, and it died before it was established. Meanwhile, the first negotiation round of GATT in 1947, the Geneva Round, lowered tariffs. GATT replaced the ITO as the institution which addressed international trade.

GATT held seven rounds of multilateral negotiations on the reduction of barriers to trade. These rounds primarily focused on tariffs, taxes on imports. Tariffs are easier to observe that other barriers to trade, namely NTBs, making it easier for members to verify that one another was living up to the agreements. The primary role of GATT was organizing and holding these negotiations that cut tariffs through reciprocal concessions.

GATT relied on norms of nondiscrimination and multilateralism. If a member cut a tariff on an imported good of another member, it had to offer the same cut to every other member on that good. Members could not discriminate against the goods of another member. Nondiscrimination lowered tariffs overall within the members of GATT and encouraged states to join GATT to gain this benefit. Multilateralism meant that tariff reductions were negotiated among all the members participating in a given round. This made it easier for all members to realize some benefit from the negotiation. Each received some lower barrier on its exports to some other member in return for lowering its own tariffs. Multilateral negotiations were also more efficient than having each pair of countries negotiate tariffs between themselves separately. Before GATT, states negotiated trade treaties in pairs, that is, bilaterally, or occasionally small groups. Each would lower some barriers to the goods of each other in a trade of concessions. 23 countries participating in the first Geneva round of GATT in 1947. It took them seven months to agree to cut their tariffs on over 45,000 items. If all these reductions had been negotiated in bilateral deals, each country would have had to agree to 22 different treaties, and 263 treaties would have been required in the place of the first GATT agreement.

Each round negotiated new cuts, allowing for exceptions for particular goods. Each round also took longer to complete with the Tokyo Round in the 1970s taking over six years to reach a final agreement. These lengthy negotiations led some to say that GATT stood for "General Agreement to Talk and Talk". More countries joined the negotiations over time, and the topics became more contentious as tariffs were negotiated down to very low levels historically. The Tokyo Round attempted to address some non-tariff barriers. GATT did not address tariffs and other barriers to trade in agriculture and textiles. Both types of goods were seen as too important to governments politically to address through GATT. Many industrialized governments subsidize farmers, which can make the products of farmers from the developing world uncompetitive on world markets. Clothes and the cloth they are made from is commonly produced by unskilled labor, making developing countries an attractive place to produce them. The governments of developed countries wished to produce their domestic producers of textiles from this competition from cheaper labor, leading to the exclusion of textiles from GATT via the Multi-Fiber Agreement. The Communist world did not join GATT because they had a system of managed trade, where their government would negotiate specific deals for the international movement of goods. In the West, import-export businesses chose what goods to trade across countries based on when they thought they could make money. Communist governments did not allow such competition and managed trade instead.

Signing a treaty, of course, does not mean that states automatically follow the deal. Under GATT, a state could lodge a dispute if another did not live up to its obligations to lower tariffs as agreed. The dispute procedure in GATT was voluntary. No state was forced to submit to that procedure nor obey the ruling of one. Instead, the GATT system relied on voluntary compliance and bilateral negotiations. Instead of lodging a dispute with GATT, a state which believed one of its trading partners was in violation would negotiate with the latter. This voluntary system of enforcement worked as long as GATT addressed tariffs as barriers to trade. Tariffs are easy to observe because they are levied when imports enter a country. All countries understand that tariffs are barriers to trade. As tariffs became very low through GATT, governments became more concerned about the other policies of their trading partners that favor domestically produced goods over imports, that is, their NTBs.

The Uruguay Round of GATT from 1986 to 1994 centered on areas outside GATT and created the WTO to address those concerns. NTBs became more important as tariffs were lowered. States may disagree about whether a particular policy is a non-tariff barrier and so illegal or an acceptable provision. GATT focused on manufactured goods and some states wished to cover services and goods previously left out, such as textiles and agriculture. Some developed states, particularly the United States, were concerned about the lack of protection for intellectual property, that is, the ideas and processes which provide much of the value of the resulting products. Some examples of such goods are prescription medicines, computer software, and movies. Copyrights and patents protect intellectual property domestically so that those who create new ideas benefit from them. These countries were afraid that firms in other countries would copy inventions by their firms to produce competing but cheaper goods if those inventions were not protected internationally as they are domestically. Some object to the protection of intellectual property because it makes the resulting products more expensive, in some case so expensive that people in developing countries cannot afford them.

The WTO introduced the dispute resolution procedure, trade policy reviews, established conditions under which states could legally put up barriers to trade, and extended coverage to services, intellectual property, textiles, and agriculture, although not over all products in these areas. Even with these expansions in coverage, the WTO, like GATT before it, is primarily a forum for states to negotiate over freer trade. The WTO reviews the trade policies of its members every two to six years depending on the importance of the country in world trade, with nations involved in more trade being reviewed more frequently. These reviews help make those policies clearer to companies engaged in trade with the country. Members are allowed to put up barriers to trade on their own but only under specific conditions. *Anti-dumping* allows a country to place a tariff on imports which are "dumped"–sold at a lower price in its market than they are in the country where they are produced. President Bush justified the steel tariffs as an anti-dumping measure, although a WTO panel rules that this was incorrect. *Countervailing duties* can be levied in response to another country subsidizing its exports. Subsidies–payments to producers for exporting goods–are against WTO law if they favor exports over domestically produced goods. *Safeguards* can be put in place to prevent serious damage to a domestic industry from a surge in imports. They are temporary barriers to those imports which can only be used if the country can demonstrate the potential for damage. Countries employing safeguards also have to negotiate compensation with the countries whose exports to it are blocked by the safeguard.

Each of these three types of legal barriers to trade involves judgments about market conditions. Is the target country actually dumping the good in question? Is there a surge in imports which will damage the domestic industry? The dispute resolution procedure provides a way to resolve disagreements about specific measures that members take under WTO law. A process takes about two years to run its full course, but members are encouraged to negotiate their disagreements when it emerges and as the process runs its course. The WTO establishes a panel of trade experts who judge the merits of each side's case. They render a ruling on the specific claims relevant to WTO law. If the side bringing the complaint wins the judgment, the other state has several months to eliminate the policy which is illegal under WTO law. If it does not, the panel then recommends a retaliatory act which the winning state can place on the trade of the loser. The panel gives a specific amount of trade which can be blocked, and the winning state is allowed to choose which goods to retaliate against. President Bush's steel tariff is an excellent example of the dispute resolution procedure. The U.S. government justified the tariff on steel imports from Japan and South Korea as anti-dumping. Most trade experts did not believe that was the case at the time the tariff was imposed. The European Union (EU) quickly lodged a dispute against the tariff with the WTO. Negotiations between the U.S. and the EU began while both sides assembled and presented their cases for and against the tariff with the panel. The panel ruled against the U.S., which ended the tariff before the EU retaliated.

The WTO system reflects the shared interest in freer trade in the face of political advantages from protecting specific industries. Enforcement of the general agreement to lower trade requires all members to make their trade policies transparent. The trade policy reviews help to do this. The need to justify particular measures which restrict trade as either anti-dumping, countervailing duties, or safeguards limits when those measures can be used. Many criticized the Bush Administration's steel tariff because it seemed to be unjustifiable under the anti-dumping provision of WTO law. At the same time, these measures allow governments to protect politically important producers when they are threatened by trade. Governments might act to protect those producers under those market conditions if trade law banned any response. These unilateral actions could undermine the general agreement in favor of freer trade. Allowing these legal exceptions helps to sustain the general agreement for freer trade. Additionally, these measures must be temporary. No member can use them to erect permanent barriers to its market. The time limit on these actions limits how much they can affect exporting industries in the country's trading partners. The legal conditions and limits on these measures also provide political leaders with a reason they can give to those within their country seeking protection from foreign competition about why they cannot do more for them. Protecting an industry in a country helps those who work in it or own companies that produce the good, but it hurts everyone else by raising the price they pay for the good in question. A political leader who answers to all the people in a country then would like to protect only the most politically important producers from foreign competition. WTO law gives leaders an additional reason to restrict their own use of protection. Finally, WTO law links specific acts of protection to possible retaliation by a country's trading partners. Those inside a country who export to other countries will be hurt by that retaliation. They will argue inside their country against protecting that other industry. The WTO then indirectly encourages exporters within a country to argue for lower barriers to goods and services imported into their own country. The end result is freer movement of goods and services across borders while allowing some temporary protection of politically important groups.

Chapter Summary

International trade increases the production and wealth of countries through the logic of comparative advantage. States benefit from lowering barriers to trade through the resulting increase in national income. Despite these gains, all states have some barriers to trade, whether they are tariffs on particular goods or non-tariff barriers. States with large economies could employ an optimal tariff to gain the benefits from specialization created by comparative advantage. Governments protect specific industries for the support of those who own and work in those industries. Owners of scarce and immobile factors seek protection to prevent losses from foreign competition. The GATT/WTO system uses reciprocal trade sanctions to enforce the general agreement to lower trade barriers. When one member state thinks one of its trading partners has a policy which is an illegal barrier to trade, it can take action under WTO law in two ways. It can levy a retaliatory tariff if the illegal policy falls under anti-dumping, countervailing duties, or safeguards. It can bring a dispute to the WTO if it believes that the policy in question discriminates in favor of domestically produced goods. The ruling of the panel determines whether that policy is against WTO law. Trade faces the mixture of enforcement of lower trade barriers with the information problem of determining which policies are illegal barriers to trade.

Review Questions

1. What is the logic of comparative advantage for international trade? Give three reasons why international trade makes countries wealthier.

2. Why might a state use an optimal tariff against its trading partners? What effect does an optimal tariff have on the distribution of benefits of international trade? Explain how states can enforce an agreement not to use optimal tariffs.

3. Explain the effects of free trade on national income and the incomes of individuals in terms of the factors they possess.

4. What does the acronym NTB stand for? Give an example. What special problems do NTBs–as opposed to tariffs– pose for cooperation on trade?

5. Explain the difference between the multilateral principles and bilateral enforcement in the GATT and WTO systems that regulate international trade.

6. In what two ways did the formation of the WTO strengthen the GATT system? What two types of products did the GATT exclude which are brought into the WTO system, although not fully successfully?

Chapter 25
The Politics of Monetary Affairs

The movement of goods and people across national borders requires the ability to exchange national currencies for one another. If you travel to Europe, for example, you will need to pay your expenses there in the local currency, probably the Euro, rather than U.S. dollars. How many Euros each of your dollars buys is the exchange rate between the two currencies. Exchange rates play a large role in international trade. Firms engaged in trade make their goods in one country and sell them in another. Their expenses are in the currency of the first country, but their revenue is in that of the latter. The exchange rate then affects trade by changing the relative prices of goods across national borders. This chapter focuses on how exchange rates are set internationally and how politics affects them.

There have been different systems to handle exchange rates over the last one hundred and fifty years. The Gold Standard existed until the Great Depression. The value of paper money is set to a fixed weight of gold, hence the name "Gold Standard." Governments agreed to exchange their money for that fixed amount of gold upon demand. The fixed value of each currency in gold created fixed exchange rates relative to the British pound. London was the financial center of the world at the time, and the British Pound was the reserve currency. Anyone involved in an international transaction would know how much of their own currency they would receive from that fixed exchange rate. Most international transactions were conducted in pounds. Governments held pounds and gold to back up their currency. The Great Depression ended the Gold Standard because many governments sought to devalue their currencies–reduce their value–and the British Government felt it could no longer defend the value of the pound.

The Bretton Woods system returned the world to a monetary system similar to the Gold Standard. The U.S. dollar replaced the pound as the reserve currency, so governments held dollars to defend the value of their currency. Exchange rates were fixed, but devaluations were allowed. The U.S. dollar was backed by gold at the rate of $35 for 1 ounce of gold. The International Monetary Fund (IMF) was established to aid countries in their efforts to support the value of their currencies. This system was successful in restoring stable exchange rates which helped the world economy recover from the physical devastation of the Second World War in Europe and Asia. The system faltered in the 1960s as those economies began to accumulate large amounts of dollars from the goods they produced and sold in the United States. Speculators believed that the value of the dollar must fall and so exchanged their dollars for gold, draining the gold reserves of the U.S. Treasury.

In 1971, President Richard Nixon ended the convertibility of U.S. dollars into gold and allowed the value of the dollar to "float". The market for dollars determined its value with respect to gold and other currencies. The price of gold rose sharply. This began the current system of floating exchange rates. By 1973, floating exchange rates were the norm for countries.

Relative demand for currencies determines their value. Some governments "peg" the value of their currency to another, typically the dollar. Those governments then intervene in the market to support that fixed exchange rate. Other governments try to keep the value of their currency within "bands" of value, allowing its value to rise or fall within that band. Still other governments allow market forces alone to determine the value of their currency, so they "float freely".

The period of floating exchange rates saw two other major events. The Asian Financial Crisis in 1997 saw the values of several East Asian countries–Thailand, Malaysia, South Korea, and Indonesia–drop dramatically in a short period of time. Investors pulled their money out of these countries, and many businesses in them failed. A sharp economic contraction followed, costing these countries some of the economic growth in the decade before the crisis. Governments fell during the crisis, including the 30-year rule of Suharto in Indonesia. Eventually, they recovered from the crisis. The second major development of recent years in the European Monetary Union (EMU) leading to the creation of the Euro, the European currency. Before EMU, each European country had its own currency: the French franc, the German mark, the Dutch guilder, the Italian lira and so on. The Euro has replaced many but not all national currencies of the countries in the European Union. Before EMU, you had to change money if you traveled from one country to another. As you typically pay a fee to exchange money, the separate currencies made cross-border business more expensive in the EU than it is across state lines in the United States. The creation of the European Central Bank accompanied the advent of the Euro to manage financial policies within the Euro zone. Countries that wish to replace their national currency with the Euro must meet a series of rigorous conditions in their use of national debt before joining. While some new members of the EU have adopted the Euro, others cannot meet the conditions yet. Other EU countries, notably Great Britain, have chosen to retain their national currencies rather than use the Euro. Since its introduction in 2002, the value of the Euro has risen sharply against the U.S. dollar, raising the possibility that it could replace the dollar as the world's reserve currency.

Why Do Exchange Rates Matter?

An exchange rate is the relative price of two currencies. How much of one do you need to buy a set amount of the other? For example, the British pound (£) is worth about $1.75 when I wrote this. This means that you need $1.75 to buy 1£, and vice versa. This value has changed greatly in this decade. Early in the decade, the value of the pound was lower, with the exchange rate around $1.40 to 1£. It rose over time to a high level of about $2.05 to 1£ about a year ago. This is a large swing in value. If I bought 10£ at the lower rate, it would cost me about $14. If I held them and sold at the higher rate for the pound, I would have about doubled my money to $20.50, a very profitable investment. Of course, I would have had to bought and sold at the right time to make this profit. If I waited and sold my 10£ now, I would only get $17.50 back.

Exchange rates matter for international politics because they affect the prices of exports and imports. When the value of a currency rises against those of its trading partners, as the British pound did earlier in this decade, it makes imports into the country cheaper and its exports to the latter more expensive. On the import side, a good made in America which cost $14 there would have cost £10 at the initial lower exchange rate. After the pound appreciated, it would cost less than £7 (= $14/2.05). British people could afford to buy more of this import from the U.S. At the same time, a price of a good which cost £10 in Britain would have risen from $14 to $20.50. Now these simple calculations ignore other factors like the cost of moving the goods from one country to the other, but they illustrate the effect of exchange rates on the prices of imports and exports.

Devaluation then helps a struggling economy by making imports more expensive and exports cheaper. When a country's economy begins to shrink, businesses and consumers have less ability to buy goods and services. Lowering the value of the currency makes the country's products more competitive with imports in the country and against goods produced in other countries in those countries. Businesses in the country lose less business when the currency is devalued, and so do not need to cut jobs as much as they would without the devaluation. A tariff helps domestically produced goods by making imports more expensive, and an export subsidy helps those goods when they are exported by making them cheaper than the goods they compete with which are produced in other countries. Devaluation like these two tools of trade policy helps domestic producers against their competitors in other countries. There are three important differences. One, devaluation helps all goods and services produced by a country which face international competition at home and abroad. A tariff has to cover many goods to have the same broad effect on a slumping economy. Two, devaluation typically has a smaller effect on prices. A tariff can be set high enough to block imports by making them too expensive for anyone to buy. Currencies generally lose at most 10-20% of their value in a devaluation. Three, it is more difficult to use devaluation to aid particular industries because it affects all goods that face international competition. Tariffs and subsidies, on the other hand, can cover just a single industry and sometimes can be crafted to favor a particular firm.

The movement of exchange rates created an additional risk for those engaged in international trade. If you sell products made in one country in another, you get paid in the latter currency but your costs are in the currency of the former. If the exchange rate of the country of sale with respect to the country of production drops, the business makes less money in the currency of production than anticipated. For example, both General Motors and Ford build successful fuel-efficient cars in Europe which are sold there profitably. They do not export these cars to the North American market where they have lost sales because they lack a small car which U.S. and Canadian buyers will buy in great numbers. The value of the U.S. dollar relative to the Euro and British pound is so low that these small cars would be too expensive to compete effectively in the U.S. car market. Car manufacturers have spread their auto plants around the world in part to counter exchange rate risk between the U.S., Europe, and Japan. If they made all their cars in only one region for sale in the others, they would lose money if that currency appreciated relative to the other two.

What Moves Exchange Rates?

Exchange rates are prices for a state's currency in the currencies of other countries. Like all prices, they respond to demand and supply. Trade and investment across borders affect the demand and supply of a currency. As more of a country's goods get sold in other countries, its business will collect more foreign currency which they will want to convert back into their own currency to pay their workers and shareholders. This higher demand for their home currency will drive up its value against that of the other currencies. The exchange rate of a country growing faster than its trading partners should rise. International investors seek the highest rates of return on their investments. Countries with higher interest rates should attract more international investment. This also increases the demand for its currency, which should push up the value of the country's currency. Similarly, the value of a currency declines as economic activity slows or the country becomes a less attractive place to invest. *Inflation*–the general rise in prices over time–and the anticipation of inflation relative to other currencies drives down the value of a currency. Inflation of a currency means that a given amount of that currency will buy fewer goods in the future. Savers and investors can preserve more of the value of their money by moving it into another currency with a lower rate of inflation. The value of a currency depends on the economic activity and conditions within that country.

The exchange rate, however, does not always reflect the underlying value of the currency. Under fixed rates, governments take action to maintain their exchange rate as the value of their currency changes. The central bank of the country does this by selling or buying its currency. The Federal Reserve is the central bank of the United States, while the Bank of England is for Great Britain. When the value of a currency rises, demand is greater than supply. The central bank needs to provide a greater supply of the currency, so it sells its currency. When the value of a currency declines, it buys its own currency to decrease supply. Central banks can buy or sell their country's currency in either gold or the currencies of other countries. Countries hold reserves of gold and the currencies of other countries so they can intervene to support or reduce their exchange rate. The reserve currency in the world, which was the British pound under the Gold Standard and the dollar since World War II, is generally held in reserve because it is widely accepted and so can be used to buy or sell currency. When a country has a fixed rate, it buys and sells its currency to keep the exchange rate fixed as the value of the currency changes with economic activity in the country.

Under floating rates, a country's central bank allows market forces to determine its exchange rate. When economic conditions in a country improve, its exchange rate will rise. This movement makes imports into the country cheaper and its exports more expensive. When economic conditions in the country deteriorate, its exchange rate falls, which makes imports more expensive and its exports cheaper in foreign markets. A floating exchange rate then helps to moderate economic conditions in a country. It boosts the economy when times are bad by making the country's products cheaper in home and foreign markets. It slows the growth of the economy when times are good. Few countries allow the exchange rate of their currency to float completely freely. Their central banks intervene in the foreign exchange market by buying and selling to influence the exchange rate without fixing it.

Currency Speculation

As you may have realized, one can make a lot of money by speculating in exchange rates of currencies. Sell currencies that will drop in value, buy those that will appreciate, and you make money. Return to the example of the shift in the value of the dollar in this decade. If you had $1400, you could have exchanged it for £1000 when the dollar was strong. Holding the money until the value of the dollar relative to the pound dropped and then exchanging your money back into dollars would have given you $2050, close to a 50% gain in your money. This movement in the exchange rate happened over about five years, but speculators can make large amounts of money quickly if they time when an exchange rate changes sharply.

Currency speculation makes defending the value of a currency more difficult for central banks and governments. They defend the exchange rate of their currency against depreciation by buying their currency. If speculators believe that the exchange rate will drop soon, they will sell that currency to buy those that will appreciate against it. These trades mean the central bank of that country must buy up even more of its own currency to maintain the current exchange rate. Private investors typically have access to more funds for speculation than central banks have reserves. They often borrow money to sell more of the currency under attack. If the exchange rate drops, they can pay back the loans and still make a profit. Central banks then cannot defend the exchange rate of their currency if speculators move aggressively against it.

Speculation can lead to runs on a currency, creating a crisis. A currency crisis often ends in the devaluation of that currency, although not always. Many disparage currency speculators then. During the 1960s, Prime Minister Harold Wilson of Great Britain referred to speculators who attacked the value of the pound as "the Gnomes of Zurich." Eventually, the Gnomes won, and the pound was devalued. George Soros made billions in currency speculation against the European Monetary System, the first attempt to create a single currency for the European Union. Currency speculators only make money if the exchange rate of the currency they attack drops. If not, they may lose money to the central bank.

Whether a currency depreciates in a crisis depends on whether it is overvalued. If it is not, other traders will buy up the currency sold by speculators. This action by the market defends the exchange rate. The difference between the exchange rate and the value of the currency determines whether a run on a currency can succeed. In this sense, exchange rates reflect the economic fundamentals of countries' economies. It is often difficult to tell what the true value of a currency should be, making the job of central bankers and currency speculators more difficult. But speculators can only make money if the value of a currency is much higher than its value in the market. An attack on a currency only changes into a run when investors who are not speculating become convinced that the exchange rate will drop soon and so wish to sell their investments in that currency to avoid the loss.

Financial flows, movements of money and investments in stocks and bonds, across borders have grown greatly in the last few decades. Stock markets have been created in developing countries which allow international investors to buy shares in companies in those countries. These financial flows are now much greater than the reserves on any central bank. They make runs on a currency easier to carry out if the currency is overvalued. Some countries limit people from moving their money into and out of the country easily. These *capital controls* require investors to get the approval of the government to make investments in the country or to move their money out if they fear that the exchange rate will drop. Capital controls can sustain an exchange rate which does not match the value of the currency. Speculators cannot easily sell or buy the currency, making a run difficult to execute. The removal of capital controls by many countries in the last twenty-five years have contributed to the greater financial flows in world markets. Free-moving capital provides countries with greater access to funds for investments from the world market, but that money also makes it easier to attack the value of a currency. The absence of capital control is called *capital mobility* because money for investments can enter and leave the country freely.

At an extreme, some developing countries do not allow their currency to trade outside its borders. You have to buy its currency when you arrive in the country at an official fixed rate. When you leave the country, you have to sell what local currency you have left. The governments with such a system restrict which of their citizens have access to foreign currency at the official rate. Only these people can import goods into the country because you need a foreign currency to buy the goods to import from another country. People in the country without official access to foreign currency will often pay much more to buy foreign currency on the black market inside the country. The difference between the official exchange rate and the prevailing rate on the streets of the country is called the *black market premium*. The local currency often suffers from inflation, and the black market premium is large. Foreign currency is known as *hard currency* in such cases, and people in the country want it because it holds its value and can buy scarce foreign goods while the local currency does neither. Those with access to hard currency can use the privilege to make money for themselves by buying hard currency at the official rate and exchanging it on the black market for much more local currency. Official access to hard currency in such countries then is a valuable private benefit, which those governments provide only to their supporters, not the general population.

Tools of Economic Adjustment

People suffer when the growth of a country's economy slows, stops, or shrinks. Workers lose their jobs, businesses lose money, and some businesses go bankrupt. Bad economic times lead people in a country to call for economic action. What policies can a government use to revive the growth of its economy? Who pays the *costs of adjustment* when an economy stops growing?

There are international tools. It can raise barriers to imports. It can devalue the currency if its exchange rate is fixed or fail to support it if its exchange rate floats. Either of these measures makes imports more expensive, leading people in the country to buy less of them as their finances suffer. The costs of adjustment are then exported as foreign companies lose business, profits, and jobs.

Governments use two types of tools in domestic policy to respond to an economic slowdown. First, they can use *fiscal policy*, how much the government spends and collects in taxes to try and encourage economic activity. Earlier this year, the U.S. government passed a stimulus package where each taxpayer was sent a check for $600 to $1800 based on family size and how much taxes they had paid. The idea was that people would spend this extra money they received. When they bought goods or services, they would stimulate the economy with their "found" money. Other forms of fiscal policy include spending on infrastructure, which provides jobs to construction workers, and tax cuts, which like the stimulus package, puts more money into the pockets of those who spend. When a government spends more than it receives in taxes, it engages in *deficit spending*. It borrows money to cover the difference between spending and tax revenues. The Treasury Department of the U.S. government sells Treasury Bills and Bonds, known as T-Bills, to pay for the deficits the federal government usually runs. It then has to pay back those loans over time, presumably when the economy is stronger. In practice, almost all governments run deficits, and none pay off all of their national debt.

Second, government can use *monetary policy*, increasing the money supply to produce more economic activity. Monetary policy is usually falls into the hands of the central bank. Central banks have a variety of ways to increase the supply of money in an economy. They can influence the interest rate that banks charge one another to borrow money, the *interbank rate*. Banks are often reluctant to loan money to businesses during a recession out of fear that the company may lose business and be unable to repay the loam fully in a timely fashion. Similarly, businesses may be reluctant to borrow money out of the fear that they will not be able to sell what they make. A low interest rate on loans makes credit cheaper which encourages companies to borrow to expand. This increases jobs and economic activity. The central bank also lends money to banks, which then lend that money to businesses for investment and to expand their business. The central bank charges the banks receiving the money interest, as is common on all loans. By lowering the interest rate the central bank charges banks to borrow from it, called the *discount rate*, banks will borrow more money, charge less to the businesses and people that borrow from them, and together the businesses and people buy more and the economy begins to grow again. In the extreme, the central bank can simply give money to banks to recapitalize them, as has happened this year in the financial crisis. Bad economic times mean more people and companies cannot pay back their loans, and the banks which lent them the money lose money themselves on the bad loans. An extreme case, like this year's crisis, can mean that banks stop lending money from the combination of their own losses and the fear that the borrower will not pay it back. Many businesses depend on short-term loans to finance operations because their sales are not consistent over time. When this short-term lending stops, these businesses may have to shut down some production. Making credit available through monetary policy can address this problem.

Either fiscal or monetary policy can stimulate a faltering economy, but there are risks to these policies as well. Deficit spending and growth in the money supply risk inflation in the future. Either policy means more money in circulation, and more money chasing fewer goods and services is one source of inflation. Either policy also pushes down the value of the currency compared to other currencies, creating a risk of currency depreciation. In the short run, neither effect may be that great. If, however, a country consistently uses these policies to stimulate its economy, it may induce substantial inflation or currency depreciation. Neither is good for an economy.

Fiscal versus Monetary Policy: The Mundell-Fleming Trilemma

Governments are not completely free in their choice between fiscal and monetary policy as tools to manage their economy. Two economists, Robert Mundell and Marcus Fleming, showed that the exchange rate regime, an open economy, and effective monetary policy are related. A country cannot have all three of the following:
• Fixed exchange rate
• Monetary policy autonomy, and
• Capital mobility
It can only have two of them.

This trilemma holds because capital mobility means that a country cannot control both its exchange rate and its interest rate at the same time. When a country's economy is open to capital, it will flow in and out of the country based on the interest rate in the country. If that rate is higher than the rate in other countries, investment capital will flow in because investors make more money at a higher rate. If the interest rate is lower than in other countries, then capital will leave the country to make more money elsewhere. This movement of capital puts pressure on the exchange rate to move up or down respectively. If the exchange rate floats, the flow of capital into the country raises the exchange rate when capital flows into a country. Demand for that currency is higher than for other currencies. The new, higher exchange rate reduces the value of the higher interest rate for foreign investors because now they can buy less of their own currency from the proceeds of their investment in the country. If the interest rate is lower than the world rate, capital leaves the country, which forces down its exchange rate. The country can use monetary policy to push up or down the interest rate in its country with a floating exchange rate, but this leads to changes in its exchange rate when its interest rate differs from the world rate. If the exchange rate is fixed, the country's central bank has to intervene to defend that exchange rate when capital enters or leaves the country. It loses its ability to manipulate the interest rate, which makes monetary policy ineffective.

The Mundell-Fleming trilemma then forces governments into a choice between two alternatives. They can fix their exchange rate and use only fiscal policy to influence their economy or they can allow their exchange rate to float, making monetary policy an effective tool for managing their economy in addition to fiscal policy. A few governments take the third choice; use capital controls to prevent the free flow of international capital in and out of the country. Capital controls are difficult to implement when a country's economy is highly integrated with the global economy. Multinational businesses can shift money in and out of the country by changing how much they produce in the country. Canada, for example, was one of the countries to have mobile capital because its economy was integrated with the U.S. economy by the 1960s. This integration meant that Canada allowed the Canadian dollar to float when most other countries still had fixed rates under the Bretton Woods system. For most governments now, capital controls are not a practical choice.

When to Fix, When to Float

Fixed and floating exchange rates have different effects on an economy which influence which choice a government makes in response to the trilemma. A fixed rate reduces exchange rate for trade in and out of the country. This stability encourages trade. Small countries tend to have a large proportion of their economy involved in trade. The figure below gives trade into and out of a country, that is, the sum of all its imports and exports, divided by gross domestic product, the total value of what the country produced. Smaller countries, such as Ireland and the Netherlands, have more of their economy involved in trade because they must import many goods. To do so, they must produce goods to be exported to pay for those imports. Singapore is an extreme case because they transship many goods, that is, import and export them without adding value to them. Large countries, such as the United States and Japan, produce and consume many goods produced in their own country and so are not greatly exposed to trade. Small countries, such as Ireland and the Netherlands, prefer a fixed exchange rate to encourage the trade they rely on by reducing exchange rate risk. Both of those countries use the Euro which fixes their exchange rate with all other countries that use the Euro because it is the same currency.

[Graph of trade as share of national economy for 20 countries]

Governments may also prefer a fixed exchange rate when instability in the value of the currency is feared. A fixed exchange rate reassures investors that the currency risk of holding money in that economy is low. This increases their willingness to keep their money in that currency and country. Countries with a history of high inflation sometimes try to fix their currency to the dollar to reduce fears of continued inflation. Defending that fixed exchange rate forces the government to take steps to reduce inflation. If it does not, the value of the currency against the dollar will go down, and eventually the exchange rate will drop. Argentina linked the value of its currency, the Argentine peso, to the U.S. dollar in 1991 as a step to end its history of inflation. The policy worked at first, and inflation dropped to low levels compared to what it had been in Argentina. The fixed exchange acts like a commitment device to ensure a stable currency.

Floating rates make monetary policy an effective tool to manage the domestic economy. A floating rate also changes with the economic fortunes of the country, rising as the economy grows strongly and falling when it slows or shrinks. The change in the exchange rate then helps the country's economy adjust to changes in economic growth relative to its trading partners. The falling exchange rate in a weak economy helps domestic producers relative to their international competitors. This consequence of a floating exchange rate is most attractive for a country with a large and diverse economy. Trade is typically a smaller portion of a large national economy, so changes in the economy move the exchange some but not a lot. Exchange rate risk for trade is then small because the shifts in the exchange rate are small. Argentina's link to the dollar eventually collapsed in the face of a recession in its own economy and those of its trade partners in South America. The government lost the ability to defend the exchange rate and had to allow the currency to float. The peso dropped relative to the dollar. With many international debts pegged to the value of the dollar, the liabilities of these loans rose dramatically, and Argentina was unable to service its debt. This large movement in the exchange rate helped make the recession in Argentina into a depression and political crisis as Argentina went through four Presidents in one year.

Winners and Losers from Exchange Rate Policy

The arguments above center on the general interest of an entire country concerning exchange rate policy. What about individuals and firms in a country? Who are the winners and loser in a country from its exchange rate policy? There are two dimensions to a country's exchange rate that affect people in the country: one, whether the exchange rate is fixed or floating, and two, whether the currency is overvalued or undervalued relative to economic fundamentals. Again, we use the "pocketful of preferences" argument to ask how each dimension affects the economic situation of different people in a country. We then assume that they prefer policies that put money in their pockets A fixed versus floating rate changes the stability of the currency which also affects the ability of the country's economy to use the exchange rate to respond to ups and downs in the economy. A fixed rate favors those involved in international business: exporters and international investors. A fixed rate eliminates exchange rate risk which reduces the risks and costs that these businesses face. A fixed rate hurts those solely involved in the domestic economy. These people include import competitors–those who produce goods in the country for domestic sale but who compete with imports. Import competitors lose from a fixed rate because exchange rate risk has been eliminated for their foreign competitors. Producers of nontradables also lose from a fixed rate because a fixed exchange rate cannot be used to moderate the swings in the country's economy. Every economy produces a wide range of goods and services which are sold in the country and do not face competition from imports. No one goes to a foreign country to get a haircut. Construction of houses and most office buildings are nontradables. Everyone who works in these sectors or owns a business in them is a producer of a nontradable good. A floating exchange rate has the opposite effects from a fixed rate. Exporters and international investors lose, while import competitors and producers of nontradables benefit from a floating rate.

The value of a currency can also be held above or below its value by intervention in the currency markets by the central bank. A high rate, that is, a currency that is overvalued, benefits domestic investors and producers of nontradables. A high exchange rate means that people in country can buy more goods produced in other countries because the high exchange rate makes them cheaper. Everyone in a country is both a producer and a consumer. The consumer side benefits from a high exchange rate because imports are cheaper. Everyone can buy more which raises the amount of goods and services consumed in the country. But by making imports cheaper, a high exchange rate hurts those who compete internationally. This includes both those who produce domestic goods that compete against imports and those who export their goods to other countries. The latter are hurt by a high exchange rate because their products are now more expensive for people in other countries to buy. A low exchange rate has the reverse effects. It benefits those who produce goods and services with international competition and hurts those who are only involved in the domestic economy.

The exchange rate then has important political effects in a country by putting money in some people's pockets and taking it out of others. China has held its exchange rate with the dollar low for some time. The low exchange rate makes it easier to sell Chinese goods in the U.S. and reduces imports from the U.S. into China by making them more expensive. U.S. government officials have tried to convince the Chinese government to allow the exchange rate of the yuan against the dollar to move upward. They have had some success, but many still believe the yuan is undervalued relative to the dollar.

A high exchange rate makes the people of a country "wealthier" in the sense that they can buy more imports than they could if the exchange rate were lower. Some governments use a high exchange rate to allow people in the country to buy more imports and so raise their standard of living. Some politicians use this effect to increase their popularity at key times. Mexico used to run a regular currency cycle around their Presidential elections. The President of Mexico is elected for one six-year term and cannot run for re-election. The Presidency of Mexico was held for decades by the Institutional Revolutionary Party or Partido Revolucionario Institucional in Spanish and known by its acronym of PRI. The outgoing President would push up the value of the Mexican peso against the dollar before an election. Mexican consumers would then buy many American-made goods, like refrigerators, that were suddenly cheaper. The PRI hoped that this rise in consumption would make voters feel better about the outgoing PRI President and so vote for his hand-picked candidate to succeed him. After the election, the new government would let the value of the peso fall, often quickly and dramatically. The last great Mexican currency crisis in December of 1994 led to a bailout by the U.S. government and an end to this regular policy of overvaluing the peso before Mexican elections.

Whether a country has a fixed or floating rate in the current system comes down to a political judgment of its government. First, there are economic factors like the size of the country's economy, what it produces, and how connected it is to international trade. Second, how organized, and so how important politically, are the groups of people and firms that prefer a fixed or a floating rate. If one side is organized and effective in domestic politics while the other is not, the former is likely to get its way. Third, does the government itself have reasons for adopting a fixed or floating rate for its own purposes? Those countries that prevent their currency from circulating outside the country and sustain an official rate very different from the market rate would be an example of the latter.

Monetary Systems

The world's monetary system now allows states to choose between fixed and floating exchange rates. Neither the Gold Standard and the Bretton Woods system allowed this choice generally, with a few notable exceptions. What are the requirements of a system of fixed exchanges such as those two systems? First, they require a central currency which becomes the primary source of state currency reserves. Defending a fixed exchange requires reserves which are widely accepted so that the central bank can intervene to support the exchange rate when it is under pressure. Gold and the British pound was the reserve currency during the Gold Standard, while the U.S. dollar played this role during Bretton Woods. Currently, central banks often hold Euros and Japanese yen as part of their reserves as both currencies are accepted as sound and strong. Second, a system of fixed exchange rates requires member governments to defend the values of their currencies. They have to be willing to spend their reserves to support their exchange rate. This pressure can become large when the country's economy goes into decline. The value of the currency falls, requiring the central bank to spend its reserves to defend the exchange rate. Allowing the exchange rate to depreciate is attractive because it would help the domestic economy by raising the price of imports and cutting the price of the country's exports in foreign markets. Devaluation then becomes politically attractive as a way to counter the economic downturn. Governments in a fixed rate system have to be willing to avoid devaluation to maintain that system.

When an economic downturn spreads to many countries that trade with one another, devaluation poses a problem like a Prisoners' Dilemma. Each country acting on its own benefits from a devaluation of its currency. Imports into the country become more expensive, its exports cheaper, and the economic pain of lost jobs and business is sent to the country's trading partners. But if every country devalues its currency, the prices of imports and exports remain the same, and no country's economy benefits. Further, the uncertainty of shifting exchange rate creates exchange rate risk for those involved in international business. This hurts trade and lowers overall economic activity across all countries. Devaluation during a widespread economic downturn is called a *"beggar-thy-neighbor" policy*, an attempt to avoid the political pain of the loss of economic activity by sending it to the country's trading partners. Raising trade barriers during periods of international economic decline is another "beggar-thy-neighbor" policy. Fixed rate systems falter when too many states adopt "beggar-thy-neighbor" devaluations.

Fixed rate systems fail when the country of the reserve currency can no longer defend its value. The Bank of England ended the gold standard when it devalued the pound and ended the convertibility of the pound into gold in 1931. Other countries followed suit. The Bretton Woods system ended in 1971 when President Nixon ended the convertibility of the U.S. dollar into gold at the fixed price of $35 an ounce. In both cases, the reserve currency came under pressure to convert it into gold because the widespread perception that each was overvalued compared to gold. After Nixon closed the "gold window," the price of gold in dollars rose sharply, showing the overvaluation of the dollar at the end of the Bretton Woods system.

Floating rate systems, such as the one that emerged after the Bretton Woods system collapsed, give states the option of fixed or floating exchange rates. As mentioned earlier, a government's choice whether to fix its exchange rate and whether to defend a particular exchange rate even if the currency floats depends on both its domestic politics and its international economic position. Some government allows their currency to move in response to economic pressure while trying to keep the exchange rate around a fixed value. A "peg" attempts to keep the exchange rate near the "pegged" value by intervening when the exchange rate moves too far away from that value. A "band" tries to keep the exchange rate within a fixed range with no preference of its value within that range. These mixed systems try to discourage speculation against the currency without committing the central bank to fight small movements in the value of the currency. They can face a credibility problem if the central bank proves unable to defend the "peg" or the "band" against strong movements in currency markets. The other choice is capital controls as a way to avoid the choice between a fixed exchange and effective monetary policy through a floating rate. Capital controls, though, limit the country's access to investment capital from other countries. They also can restrict access to technology from other countries that could be introduced when foreign companies invest in new production plants in the country.

The International Politics of the Great Depression

The Great Depression saw the collapse of economic activity on a broad scale around the world. The GDP of the United States dropped by over a quarter in the four years from 1929 to 1933. Unemployment in the U.S. rose to 25% of the work force. The Great Depression also struck other countries around the world that were tied into the world economy. International trade collapsed, falling in 1933 to one-third of its level in 1929. How did international politics contribute to the international nature of the Great Depression?

First, many countries raised high barriers to trade. The most famous of these was the Smoot-Hawley Tariff in the U.S. Passed in 1930, this act of Congress doubled tariffs on a wide range of manufactured imports. Imports to the U.S. dropped dramatically afterwards. Other countries, notably Canada, responded with tariffs of their own on U.S. exports to their countries. Other countries devalued their currencies in an effort to shift the costs of the depression to their trading partners. These "beggar-thy-neighbor" devaluations added exchange rate risk to trade, reducing as did the new tariff barriers. The devaluations also made it difficult for the Bank of England to defend the value of the pound, because it used up much of its supply of gold doing so. Britain abandoned the gold standard, and other European countries followed over the following years. Exchange rates began to float freely until the establishment of the Bretton Woods system after World War II with the U.S. dollar as the new reserve currency.

Why did some countries respond with trade barriers, while others devalued their currency? First of all, leaders whose domestic political position was weak were more likely to take either action. The pressure of an election that a sitting leader is likely to lose concentrates his mind on trying to restore growth to the economy. Second, countries with small economies devalued their currency, while those with large currencies raised tariffs. Trade is a small portion of a large economy. A tariff protects those producers who face international competition without affecting most of the economy. If the country's trading partner responds with a tariff of its own on the country's exports to it, that tariff will not hurt many in the country. The resulting reduction in trade hurts a small economy more than a large one. Small countries instead devalued their currency to try and shift the cost of the depression onto other countries. Devaluation does not reduce trade as tariffs do unless many countries devalue. Devaluation also makes a country's exports more competitive in other countries unlike a tariff which just makes imports more expensive. The jobs of many people in a small economy rely on trade and their ability to sell their products to consumers in other countries. Devaluation helps the companies they work for maintain their exports. Third, the ideological composition of governments also matters because different governments have different bases of supporters. Governments of right-wing parties favored their supporters in business and owners of capital. They raised tariffs to reward the owners of firms who supported their parties. Governments of the left devalued their currency to keep the employment of the workers who voted for them up.

The experience of the Great Depression and the collapse in world trade had a profound effect on political leaders in Western countries. The economic turmoil made it easier for dictators like Hitler to come to power and contributed to the political problems of that difficult decade. After World War II, international institutions like the GATT were created to help governments manage trade and exchange rates. GATT helped to lower tariffs, which advanced freer trade among its members. The Bretton Woods monetary system restored stability to exchange rates, even though it eventually collapsed in 1971. The world launched into the greatest period of economic growth it had ever seen, and the growth of trade promoted by the lower barriers and predictable exchange rate contributed greatly to that growth.

Chapter Summary

Exchange rates have important effects on the prices of goods and services which are traded across national borders. Exchange rates are now a main tool of economic policy, and so are a political issue in most countries. Different monetary systems influence the range of freedom that governments and central banks have to influence their exchange rate. The current system allows for both fixed and floating exchange rates. The Mundell-Fleming trilemma forces governments to decide between fixed rates which make monetary policy ineffective as a tool to manage the economy or floating rates which allow for the use of monetary policy. A government could also control the flow of capital into and out of the country, but this limits its access to international investment. Those involved in international trade and investment prefer a fixed exchange rate to reduce exchange rate risk; others prefer floating rates. Those who compete with foreign producers either in domestic or foreign markets prefer a low value of their currency to make their products easier to sell everywhere. Those who produce nontradables prefer a high exchange rate for their currency because they can buy more imports and so are wealthier. Finally, the Great Depression saw the collapse of trade driven by "beggar-thy-neighbor" policies of high tariffs and competitive devaluations.

Review Questions

1. Define fiscal and monetary policy. Assuming mobile capital, when can monetary policy be used for managing economic growth, inflation, and unemployment?

2. Describe the basic features of the international monetary system in the following periods:

before the 1930s, after World War II to 1971, and now.

3.   According to the Mundell-Fleming trilemma, what three financial policies cannot be realized at the same time, so that states are forced to choose two out of the three? Assuming mobile capital, when is fiscal policy effective for managing national economies as opposed to monetary policy?

4.   Who in a country benefits from fixed exchange rates instead of floating rates? Who benefits from an overvalued currency?

5.   Does a country with a small economy prefer devaluation or trade barriers as a way to respond to a downturn in its economy? Explain why.

Chapter 26
Globalization:
The Politics of Trade, Money, and Finance in the Global Economy

The world economy has become more interconnected as it has grown over the last sixty years. Trade has risen from 7% of the global economy in 1950 to 31% in 2007. Finance also moves across national borders more now than ever. International financial flows, that is, the purchase of stocks and bonds, have grown four times since 1980. Foreign direct investment (FDI) has increased six times since 1980. This increased interdependence of the world economy is called globalization. It is the uniting of national economy into one global economy.

Globalization also refers to the more general process of growing interconnectedness of the world. Improvements in transportation and telecommunications move people and ideas as well as goods around the world more rapidly than ever before. Multinational corporations have built supply processes–how they manufacture and then distribute goods–that are global. These companies move their executives around the world for tours of service in different countries where their business is located. You can fly from any major city in the world to another in forty-eight hours or less. Vacations in exotic places are easy for those who can pay for the travel. Telecommunications make it possible to speak to most other countries in the world for pennies a minute. The internet serves as a global repository of information and comment and allows other forms of communication possible. Culture–movies, music, and even news services–attracts global audiences. The movement of people, goods, and ideas across national borders is greater than it ever has been, all through the increasing ease of moving them long distances cheaply.

This chapter focuses on economic globalization. Although the cultural and social dimension of globalization are a unique feature of our world, political science has said little about them to date. It has more to say about the effects of the increasing movement of goods, services, and finance across national borders and how politics shapes and responds to those movements.

Is Globalization Good?

Globalization has many consequences, some good and some bad. It is great that we can move easily and quickly around the world and talk to most anyone cheaply and clearly. The array of goods and services available to us as consumers is astounding, much of them at lower prices than before. International financial flows help provide investment capital to developing countries that needs the funds to develop their economies and societies. At the same time, the easy movement around the world makes illegal immigration from one country to another feasible. Cheap and anonymous communications allow terrorists to operate international networks that can strike far from their bases. International trade produces competitive pressures that can drive some firms out of business, costing workers their jobs and investors their money. Financial flows can destabilize exchange rates and lead to attacks on the value of a country's currency, harming that country's economy.

Specifically, three charges are commonly laid at the door of globalization. First, the freer movement of goods and services leads to the exploitation of labor in developing countries. Labor conditions are worse and wages lower in developing countries than in developed ones. This is one reason why firms have relocated some of their production to developing countries. They can produce goods more cheaply there, which they can then sell for less. This relocation of production has reduced employment in the developed world in sectors such as textiles and some electronic goods. The first concern address how the free flow of goods could hurt workers in both the developed and developing countries.

Second, free financial flows could make financial crisis more likely and more severe. Financial flows are often much larger than the movement of goods and services across national borders. As money has flown into countries, it can also flow out. When investors wish to pull their money out of a country, it can produce a run on its currency. When many attempt to exchange a country's currency for a recognized "hard currency," such as the U.S. dollar or the Euro, the value of the country's currency will drop. The run by investors hurt the companies they have invested in and the run on the country's currency can bankrupt its firms involved in international trade. Similarly, the global movement of investment allows financial crises to spread from country to country.

Third, the free movement of capital allows investors to choose the countries that are most favorable for investment. Some worry that mobile capital will seek those countries with the lowest labor and environmental standards and the lowest taxes on capital in an effort to make the most money. This pursuit of profit could produce a "race to the bottom" on standards and tax rates. Those countries that lower their standards and taxes would attract more investment. Other governments would have to match their low standards to attract the capital they need to develop their economies. The net result could be that all would be worse off as standards raced to the bottom.

As we will see, there is some merit in these points, but the full picture of globalization is more complicated. These issues allow us to review the political effects of the free movement of trade and capital in the global economy. They also show how politics moderates economic forces and shapes how globalization works out on the ground.

Who Benefits from Free Trade?

The free movement of goods and services increases national incomes. Countries specialize in the goods where they have a comparative advantage. More goods overall are produced which raises how much is consumed across everyone. Opening to trade, however, also produces winners and losers within a country. Some firms lose business to international competitors, while others gain new markets in other countries. Who are these winners and losers from trade?

According to trade theory in economics, plentiful factors prosper and scarce factors suffer. Factors–land, labor, and capital–can be used in many different sectors–types of goods produced. The value each factor commands depends on how scarce it is and how it can be used to produce goods and services. When a country is closed to international trade, the scarce factors will command a high price, while the plentiful ones command a lower one. Scarcity of a factor within a country is judged relative to how much of the factor is available globally. So is whether the price it commands is high or low. When a country opens up to trade, a scarce factor in the country now must compete against owners of that factor in other countries. At the same time, the plentiful factor can sell its output in foreign countries, raising what it can command for its products.

Developed countries are plentiful in capital and skilled labor and scarce in unskilled labor. We separate skilled labor from unskilled labor as different factors for this argument. Skilled labor covered both highly educated people and those who have acquired specialized skills for their job, such as machinists, that require years of training. Capital and skilled labor are plentiful in developed countries because they have accumulated capital through development and their average level of education is higher than in other societies. As trade has expanded between developed and developing countries, capital and skilled labor in developed countries has gained. Capital has more places where it can be invested. Skilled laborers can sell the goods and services they produce in more countries. Unskilled labor loses as trade grows between their developed country and developing countries. The large number of unskilled laborers in developing countries can produce goods which compete against their products. Industries like textiles and shoes have almost entirely moved from developed countries to developing ones through this process. It is one reason, but not the only reason, why the gap in incomes between high-income and low-income people has grown in the U.S. over the last thirty years. It is also a reason why the costs of the products produced with unskilled labor, such as clothing, have dropped over time.

Unskilled labor is plentiful in developing countries. These countries have large numbers of laborers with only a basic education and a willingness to work. As trade has grown between developed and developing countries, unskilled labor in the developing countries should benefit. Capital can be imported to build factories where they can build the products that require only unskilled labor. These new industries allow skilled labor to move from agriculture to the jobs there. This process has happened in many developing countries that produce goods for international trade. In Mexico, factories known as maquiladoras have opened up along the U.S.-Mexico border which exist solely to carry out part of the manufacturing process on a wide range of goods. These factories take advantage of the fact that unskilled labor in Mexico is much cheaper than in the U.S. In contrast, local capital and skilled labor in the developing countries should lose as their economies open to international competition. They now must compete with global capital and the pool of skilled laborers.

Wait a minute. This is the opposite of the charge commonly leveled at this process: industrialization of the developing countries for export to the developed world leads to the exploitation of workers there. The following quote summarizes many of the concerns in this charge:

> Factory workers, often children, forced to work fourteen-hour days. Forced to work overtime without pay. Exposed to dangerous chemicals. Physical punishment. Emotional abuse. And still earning only pennies a day, not nearly enough to be a "living wage." (http://www.suite101.com/article.cfm/politics_east_asia/12111/1)

How can workers in developing countries gain when they work at jobs under such conditions?

First, their gain is relative to their situation before those factories were built. In many developing countries, unskilled labor comes from the countryside where they worked in subsistence agriculture. Working long hours in a factory may not be appealing to Americans, but it looks better to those whose alternative is working in the fields.

Second, many who work in such factories make more money and can afford more than they could before. Incomes of workers have risen substantially in developing countries with factories that produce goods for export to developed countries. Trade has allowed some countries, like South Korea and Taiwan, to move from the ranks of developing countries into those of the developed world. Still, many in developing countries still live on less than a dollar a day. They have not moved out of a traditional life, tied to the land.

The real puzzle lies in the distribution of the wealth created by the move of industries that employ unskilled labor to developing countries. Owners of capital and skilled laborers should lose through the process of opening developing economies to international trade. But in many developing countries, the owners of capital and managers of businesses, who are skilled labor, have grown wealthy at a faster rate than unskilled laborers. China now has the second-most billionaires in the world after the United States. These tycoons have built successful businesses and profited greatly from them. What accounts for their growing wealth; why have they been able to command a substantial proportion of the wealth generated by the employment of unskilled labor in their countries?

Here the criticism of labor practices in developing countries plays a role. Managers often have ties to government officials in these countries. They can use those ties to shape laws and how they are enforced. This allows them to gain a larger share of the gain in production from the employment of unskilled labor. Local managers also hold advantages over competitors from developed countries. They can use laws that require a local partner for foreign investments. They have local knowledge, connections, and language skills that foreigners do not. All of these advantages are greater in countries with a small winning coalition. The leader relies on the distribution of private benefits, which they can do through law and its enforcement as well as simply handing out benefits. Because these leaders do not answer to most of the population, they care more about the economic fate of their supporters. More open politics could lead to changes in law that would increase the ability of unskilled labor to earn a larger share of what it produces.

In developed countries, unskilled labor suffers as their countries open to goods produced by unskilled labor in developing countries. Organized labor often opposes liberalization of trade and favors new barriers to these goods. At the same time, though, developed states have benefitted greatly from expanded trade. Even in unskilled labor is hurt by this trade, others in society benefit from cheaper prices. These consequences pose the issue of how developed countries can remain open to trade given that some lose from it.

Trade increase national income even when some lose from it. Because countries can gain from freer trade, they need a way to compensate the losers. Otherwise, the loser may organize politically against trade. This idea of compensating the losers from trade is *embedded liberalism.* The free movement of goods is embedded in a system of compensation for those hurt by trade. Social programs such as welfare and unemployment insurance are one form of such compensation. Small, industrialized countries rely heavily on trade compared to the United States, and they also typically have much larger social welfare programs than the U.S. The U.S. has programs of trade adjustment assistance which offer training to workers who lose their jobs to foreign competition through trade. These programs are designed to increase the mobility of labor, that is, make it easier for workers who lose their jobs because of trade to move into other jobs. The losers from trade are most likely to organize against it when they cannot easily move to comparable jobs in other sectors. These programs seek to make freer trade sustainable by reducing the incentive to organize against it. Embedded liberalism does not stop demands to raise barriers to trade in developed countries, but it does limit them.

Who organizes against trade in developed countries? Those who have the most to lose from foreign competition. In France, farmers often demonstrate against freer trade in agricultural products. The European Union subsidizes agricultural producers and places tariffs on many agricultural imports. In the United States, some labor unions have argued for greater restrictions on international trade to protect the jobs of their members. Those who lose from trade demonstrate against it.

[Picture of Wheat field on Champs d'Elysees]

The WTO

The World Trade Organization was created in 1995 as a result of the Uruguay Round of GATT talks. It strengthened the GATT process of lowering barriers to trade. Like GATT, the WTO provides a forum for the negotiation of multilateral treaties to lower trade barriers. The current Doha Round began in 2001 and has been close to collapsing in failure several times since then. The WTO covers trade in services and the protection of intellectual property in addition to the trade of goods covered under GATT. It allows states to petition to raise temporary barriers to trade under certain conditions. To do so, they must show specific damage which can be remedied by a temporary tariff. The Bush Administration justified its tariff on steel imports from Japan and South Korea in 2003 using this provision.

The WTO created a new dispute resolution procedure. A member state can bring a complaint about policies of another member which it believes discriminates against the goods and services it exports to that other member. For example, the EU filed such a case against the steel tariff of the U.S. as soon as the tariff was imposed. The procedure resembles a lawsuit. Each case makes its case under WTO law before a panel of trade experts. They reach a judgment about the legality of the policy in question. If they decide against the policy in question, that country has to change the policy. If it does not, the panel will rule on the size of the damages to the country bringing the complaint, and it is allowed to impose trade sanctions on the other country of the size of those damages. The dispute resolution procedure legalizes trade disputes and the use of reciprocity to enforce them.

Under GATT, there was a similar procedure, but it was not binding. It only worked when both sides agreed to use it and follow its judgment. The WTO procedure is binding on both states; targets of complaints cannot ignore the rulings. Still, negotiations solve most trade disputes. The dispute resolution procedure shapes those negotiations by clarifying the alternative to a deal. The parties can judge the strength of their cases and the likely result before they negotiate. The procedure also limits the size of reciprocal sanctions and prevents trade wars. It sets how large reciprocal sanctions are, although the party winning the case can choose the goods to target. States could use reciprocity before the WTO to induce one another to lower trade barriers, but the target state might respond with sanctions of its own. A trade war happened when both sides continued to respond with further trade sanctions of their own. Both sides lost as both raised their barriers in the trade war. The WTO dispute resolution procedure stops this by limiting reciprocal trade sanctions.

The dispute resolution procedure is opposed by some. It covers any policy that might discriminate against imports, including health, safety, and environmental regulations. The critics believe that such rules should not be subject to challenge under trade law. Economics should not override concerns for the other values advanced by these laws, according to the critics of the WTO. WTO law only judges a policy to be illegal if it favors domestically produced goods and services over imports. Regulations for health and environmental reasons are permissible as long as they do not discriminate against foreign products. The requirement of the United States for dolphin-safe tuna was originally ruled to be illegal because it targeted canned tuna produced in Mexico. The law was rewritten to treat all canned tuna the same, which was allowable under WTO law. The critics also argue that the WTO favors the large and powerful developed countries over the developing countries. The developed countries bring the most disputes to the WTO. The provisions also reflect their interests in protecting intellectual property, such as movies, recorded music, and computer programs. But would their dominance of world trade be less if there was no WTO? Trade negotiations would be bilateral where the economic advantages of a developed state negotiating with a developing state would be greater. Some developing states, like Brazil, bring disputes to the WTO. Their size allows their governments to hire the trade lawyers needed to make a successful case.

Free trade is a critical element in globalization. The free movement of goods and services has raised incomes in all sorts of countries, particularly in developing countries heavily engaged in trade. It has hurt some, who sometimes organize against trade. The WTO is a common target of such protests, although the protestors may misunderstand its role in trade.

Finance and Globalization

Finance covers a range of investments in assets. International finance is when these investment cross national borders, where someone or some organization invests some money in another country. Foreign direct investment (FDI) is the purchase or construction of assets in another country. A company building a factory in another country to produce goods for sale either in that country or export to others is an example of FDI. The investment is direct in the sense that it creates fixed assets in that country. Portfolio investment covers the purchase of financial instruments rather than real assets. Stocks and bonds are the two main forms of portfolio investments. Stocks give the purchaser part ownership of the firm, with a claim on a share of the profits and the right to vote on management. Bonds are loans to a company or government, where the party issuing the bonds promises to pay the holder back with interest over some period of time. Governments issue bonds to cover deficit spending, companies use debt to finance their operations or invest in new facilities.

There are important differences between FDI and portfolio investments. Portfolio investment is more *liquid*, that is, it is easier to sell, than FDI. Firms do sell factories and other local assets, but there are few buyers for these assets. They have to look for a buyer and then negotiate a price with that buyer. Stocks and bonds are commonly sold on markets, such as stock exchanges, where there are many buyers and sellers and the prices of trades are public. An investor can sell stock or bonds on such markets when he or she chooses rather than having to search for an interested buyer. Markets do differ in their liquidity; those in the United States and other developed countries have a large number of buyers and sellers, making it easy to find someone who will buy or sell assets. Some markets in developing countries have fewer active buyers and sellers, making it more difficult to buy or sell the assets listed there. The values of all assets ultimately rely on the price they would fetch at sale. Those prices are easy to see at any given moment for portfolio investments, but those values change with market prices. The value of FDI is harder to determine because there are no public markets for these investments. Both types of assets have some underlying value. Stocks and bonds provide a claim on future revenue of a firm, although they lose their value if the firm goes broke. FDI has the value of the assets themselves, what a factory can produce or the usefulness of a center for the distribution of goods.

Any investment, such as bonds, where one party provides the money which the other uses to poses several risks for both parties. These deals are promises where the borrower gets money today in exchange for a promise by the lender to pay back with interest later. The party lending the money worries that the borrower might be unable to pay it back. The venture could fail, the borrower could use the money for other purposes, or its other activities might use up all its future revenue. Collateral is one way that lenders can reassure borrowers that the borrower can recover something if the lender cannot pay. Mortgages are long-term loans secured by the property which is financed by that loan. If you cannot pay your mortgage, the lender can legally take the property and sell it to recover some of the value of the loan. The borrower can call the loan back early if it needs the money. The lender has to raise the money to pay back the loan or else surrender the collateral. The lender fears that the borrower might demand its money back because that call will disrupt the activity in which the lender has invested. Bonds deal with these issues through being trading on markets. The holder of the bond is the lender, and it can recover its money by selling the bond on the bond market. It still faces the risk that the borrower, whoever issued the bond, might be unable to pay, leading it to default on the bonds. Then the bonds can be sold only at pennies on the dollar if at all. The borrowing company benefits by issuing bonds to borrow money because it draws on a larger pool of lenders. It is unlikely that all the bond holders will want to sell their bonds at the same time. Companies rate the quality of bonds in an attempt to let buyers in the bond market judge the risks they are taking by owning particular bonds. As in the current economic crisis, these ratings do not always prove accurate.

Financial institutions help to match those with money to lend to those who would like to borrow. Banks take deposits and lend the money out to others. All three parties gain. The depositor makes interest on his or her money without having to take on the job of judging whether the lender will pay the money back. The borrower deals with an institution with some stability, meaning it is unlikely to call its loan because it needs the money. The bank gains because it takes in more interest on the money it loans out than it pays out in interest on the deposits. It lends out most of the money it receives on deposit, retaining some as reserves in case a depositor asks for his or her money back. The essential job of a bank is judging risk when it makes loans. Every bank makes some bad loans, ones where the borrower ends up unable to pay the loan back. Too many bad loans and the bank will not be able to pay depositors back. Banks have the advantage of developing the capability to judging the creditworthiness of prospective borrowers.

Capital mobility–the ability for investors to move their money into and out of a country–is a central feature of our globalized world. Some governments restrict foreign investment in their economies. Some ban these investments, others require local partners, while others allow foreigners to buy and sell assets freely. Even the most liberal countries sometimes block some investments. The United States Congress objected to Dubai Ports World, a government-owned firm from the United Arab Emirates, buying the business of managing 22 ports in the United States in 2006. Dubai Ports World withdrew its offer to buy the contracts to run the ports in the face of this opposition. Restrictions on the movement of capital are low by historical standards. Mobile international capital gives countries greater access to investment than if they had to rely on their own pool of capital alone. Developing countries in particular gained access to finance they could not raise domestically. These investments, both FDI and purchases of stocks and bonds, helped their economies grow. Investors also benefit from the wider range of types and places of investments. They make more money when they can choose to invest their money where it will make the greatest return.

Financial Crises

Normally, finance works fine and helps an economy grow. Borrowers get money to conduct worthwhile projects which they could not afford if they had to rely on their own funds. Firms can increase production, and individuals can buy houses and cars without having to save for years to do so. Lenders get to share in the benefits of these projects without having to manage those projects themselves. Financial institutions make money match lenders and borrowers and reassuring the lenders that the borrowers will pay back loans. Companies that sell shares raise money to invest in their businesses. The shareholders gain a claim on the future profits of the firm, a vote over who runs the firm, and the ability to sell their shares on a market. Shares commonly rise in value as a company is successful as others would like to buy them.

Unfortunately, things do not always go well. A borrower may run into troubles and be unable to pay back the money it borrowed. A lender may demand the money back early. A bank might make too many bad loans. A company's investment might not generate the sales and profit it thought it would. In isolation, such events are part of normal business. When they become widespread, a financial crisis can result.

Financial crises can take several forms. A bank run occurs when depositors fear that the bank where they have deposited money may fail. Each tries to withdraw his or her money as soon as they can. Because banks loan out most of the money they receive in deposits, no bank can pay all of its depositors from its reserves. It may be able to borrow money to pay some depositors, but if everyone wants their money, it will fail. Bank runs become a crisis when they spread from one bank to another within or across countries. When one bank fails, those with money in another fear that it too might fail before they can get their money out, triggering runs at other banks. Central banks–a national bank with responsibility for financial matters in a country, such as the Federal Reserve (known as "the Fed") in the United States–support banks facing a run to prevent such a crisis. Financial crises in markets occur when parties become unable to honor promises of trades they have made. Stock market crashes occur when many owners of stocks seek to sell them at the same time with few willing buyers. The value of a stock is how much you can sell it for on the market. In normal conditions, there are about as many buyers as sellers, and the price moves small amounts up and down over time. Owners of shares know about how much their stock is worth in case they need to sell it to raise money. But the price depends on supply and demand, and if many buy stocks in the anticipation their prices will rise, stocks can become overvalued. When some begin selling off their stocks, others may believe that they must sell now or face large losses when the price goes down. This can produce panic selling and a large drop in the value of stocks. No one, even those who want to own and hold the stock for a long time, want to buy in such a panic. They can buy the stock more cheaply if they wait. The lack of buyers drives the price lower. Stock market crashes happen when panic selling occurs across many stocks in a market.

Mobile international capital also creates the possibility of financial crises driven by changes in exchange rates. The exchange rate is important for foreign investors. It determines how much their foreign investment are worth in the currency of their home country. If the exchange rate drops greatly, a foreign investment which is profitable in the local currency may not be in the currency of the investor's home country. The Asian Financial Crisis is an example of such a crisis of exchange rates.

The Asian Financial Crisis

In 1997, a series of currency collapses spread across East Asia, from Thailand, to the Phillipines, South Korea, Malaysia, and Indonesia. The exchange rate of each currency with respect to the dollar dropped dramatically in a short period of time. During the crisis, it was feared that the drops would extend to the currencies of other developing states, particularly China and Brazil. These countries had three similar characteristic: overvalued exchange rates, large amounts of external borrowing, and weak banking systems. The overvalued exchange rates led to speculation against the currencies, with the speculators betting on depreciation. When their currencies dropped relative to the major international currencies, such as the dollar, yen, and Swiss franc, the lenders to those countries called in their loans in an effort to get their money out of the country before the local currency dropped lower. Calling in these loans led to the collapse of businesses and local banks. The IMF provided loans to these countries to help them defend the value of their currencies. Austerity programs were connected to these loans which many believe made the crisis worse by cutting government spending as their economies shrank. The currencies of these countries fell at least 30% and some much more. Production in their economies also declined as business went bust. The GDP of Indonesia fell by more than 10% in a year. The crisis led to the fall of the leader of Indonesia, Suharto, who had ruled the country for 30 years. After this sharp downturn, the economies of these countries began growing briskly again.

[Picture of IMF Director Camdessus hovering over Suharto]

The crisis moved from country to country, aided in part by mobile capital. These countries were open to foreign capital and had overvalued currencies with fixed exchange rates. They maintained high interest rates before the crisis which attracted foreign investors. Borrowing from foreign sources of capital was common in part because their economies were growing rapidly. Speculators were able to target the overvalued currencies in sequence, increasing the pressure to devalue on each country in turn. The proceeds from one speculative attack on a currency helped to finance the next. In response to the crisis, some Asian countries, notably Malaysia, turned to capital controls to prevent another crisis by limiting foreign capital in their economies. The central banks of many Asian countries have accumulated large reserves of foreign currency, particularly U.S. dollars. They can defend the value of their currencies without the aid of the IMF now, a sign of how unpopular the IMF programs were in those countries during the crisis.

Why is mobility in finance more dangerous than trade, which is mobility in goods? Financial flows are much larger than the value of goods traded. In countries that are open to trade, the total value of imports and exports is less than the value of all goods produced in the country, with a few notable exceptions such as Hong Kong. In countries which are open to mobile capital, financial flows are much larger than the total value of the economy. In some developing countries, the net flow is several times larger than the total value of the economy. The large size of international financial flows poses two problems. First, speculation in a currency or the debt of a country can overwhelm the fundamental of its economy. Normally, large financial flows do not pose a problem because what comes into a country is about the same as what goes out. When investors decide that a country's currency is unsound or that they may not be able to get their money out if they wait, capital flight can have a big effect on the economy of the country. Second, small errors of judgment by investors can have large effects. When international investment is large compared to a country's economy, small changes in investment coming in or going out can have a large effect by reducing investment in the economy. Economic growth could slow rapidly because outside investors judge their investment to be at risk. Some would say that government policy should aim at reassuring investors in such situations, but that may not be easy.

The recent period of open capital movements poses another puzzle. Recall that mobile capital should seek the best return, presumably when it is scarce compared to the world overall. Investment should flow into developing countries because capital adds the most value to production. Openness should lead to capital moving from the countries where it is plentiful, the developed countries, to those where it is scarce, the developing countries. This is one of the gains of mobile capital. Except the aggregate flow of capital is not toward developing countries. Many developing countries have net capital outflows, more money leaves the country than enters it. Local capital in many cases moves to developed countries when it is free to move. Wealthy individuals in developing countries then prefer to shift some of their wealth into developed countries because they think it is safer there. They know they can get to their money in a pinch. Return is not the only concern of investors; they also worry about the safety of their investments.

Capital mobility has not proven to be an unalloyed boon. It has raised investment across borders and into developing countries. It has played an important role in the growth of the world economy over the last few decades. But it may have raised the risk of international financial crises at the same time. Capital also has not always gone where it will produce the greatest return. Some countries have returned to capital controls to limit these effects of mobile capital. Others remain open to the relatively free movement of capital.

Capital controls also eliminate the trilemma posed by the choice between fixed and floating exchange rates. The trilemma says that a country cannot have all three of: a fixed exchange rate, monetary policy autonomy, and mobile capital. In an era of mobile capital, the trilemma creates a choice between fixed rates and relying only on fiscal policy to manage the economy and floating rates which also makes monetary policy an effective tool to manage the economy. Many countries try to maintain a fixed exchange rate to encourage trade. The countries involved in the Asian financial crisis kept the values of their currencies high, which made them vulnerable to speculation. Other countries defend the value of their currency to keep it fixed in order to fight a history of inflation. The other choice is allowing the currency to float. Its value can then rise and fall with the economic conditions of the country. A floating rate allows the interest rate in the country to differ from that available on international markets; the difference will be reflected in a change in the exchange rate. But a floating rate creates exchange rate risk, which can hurt those involved in trade. The choice posed by the trilemma is not easy for many national leaders.

Capital controls solve the choice by eliminating it. When finance cannot flow freely into and out of a country, the government can change the local interest rate while maintaining a fixed exchange rate. Capital controls also limit the vulnerability of a national economy to international crises. China, for example, has always had capital controls which restrict investment in the country and the ability of investors to get their money out. It successfully rode out the Asian financial crisis in 1997 and seems to have suffered little from the recent crisis. Capital controls come with the price that they discourage outside investment in the country. The Chinese government worries little about whether its capital controls restrict outside investment. Investors consider the Chinese market so lucrative that they are willing to invest even given the restrictions placed by the Chinese government. This attraction has been called the "Two Billion Shoes" issue; with over a billion Chinese, that is at least two billion shoes to sell. The Chinese domestic market is so large that investors are willing to put up with stringent conditions to invest there.

The recent era of mobile capital and floating exchange rates has made monetary and exchange rate policies political. These financial policies were often thought to be technical matters only of interest to economists. No longer. People and firms in countries now care about the monetary and exchange rate policies of their government. These concerns create political pressures for the government to influence the interest rate and alter the exchange rate. Beginning in the Bush Administration, U.S. government officials have encouraged China to allow the value of its currency to rise against the dollar. Many economists believe that China has kept its value low to keep Chinese exports affordable to consumers in the U.S. and Europe. A rise in the value of the yuan would make those exports more expensive and imports into China cheaper. The Chinese government has allowed the value of the yuan to rise slightly against the dollar but not as much as some would like. Governments who allow their currency to float lose this control. The value of the U.S. dollar slid through most of this decade. It grew much stronger in 2008 as investors bought U.S. Treasury Bills during the financial crisis. They believed that T-Bills were one investment where their money was safe. As the crisis subsided from the peak of fear, investors bought back other riskier investments, and the value of the dollar has fallen again. Some economic observers argue that the dollar should fall further to help reduce imports into the U.S. and increase exports. These calls are an example of how political these policies are now.

EMU

European monetary union, not a flightless bird, is the process of creating a single currency for all of the countries of the European Union. Think of its as a parallel to the U.S. dollar where all 50 states use the same money. In 1998, many but not all members of the EU linked the values of their currencies to fixed rates to one another. In 2002, the new currency, the Euro, was introduced to replace the prior national currencies, such as the German Mark, the French France, the Italian Lira, and others. The Euro was worth less than one U.S. dollar when it was introduced into circulation, but its value has risen as the dollar has fallen. Most members of the EU use the Euro now as their currency. Some countries, notably Great Britain, chose to retain their own currency rather than join the Euro. Countries that have recently joined the EU must wait until their national finances are in order before they can join the Euro.

What are the advantages of the Euro? First, it encourages trade within the Euro zone. Firms no longer face exchange rate risk when they trade across national borders within the zone. Both their costs and their receipts are in Euros. EMU has also put many currency exchange bureaus in Europe out of business by eliminating the need to exchange money when you travel inside the Euro zone. A common currency also makes it easier for consumers to compare prices across national borders. Some differences in prices still exist across borders in the Euro zone, but those differences are less. Second, the common currency brings fiscal discipline to those member states that have had historical difficulties limiting government deficits. To enter the Euro, a country needs to reduce its government budget deficit to 3% or less of its GDP and its total public debt below 60% of GDP. Some countries in the Euro zone, notably Italy and Belgium, had historic problems with high government deficits. The requirements for entering the Euro helped those governments control their budget deficits. Third, EMU also created the European Central Bank (ECB) to set monetary policy for the Euro zone. This provided a common monetary policy, one directed at controlling inflation and supporting the value of the Euro. This discipline had been lacking in some countries. Fourth and finally, the Euro advances the program of European unification in the EU. A common currency is a powerful symbol of one Europe coming together under common governing institutions. A European government does not exist yet, but the Euro pushes that project along.

What are the disadvantages of the Euro? They are the flipsides of the advantages. First, a common currency eliminates exchange rates as a tool of economic adjustment within the Euro zone. When a country's economy slumps, a decline in the exchange rate helps it by making its imports more expensive and its exports cheaper in other countries. The exchange rate within the Euro zone cannot change among its members. Spain, for instance, has had both a boom earlier in this decade and a bust during the current economic crisis. Before the Euro, the peseta would have increased in value during the boom and fallen during the bust, moderating both. But that option was not available. Second, the stability pact that limits government deficits also limits the abilities of national governments to respond to changing economic conditions. If they run a deficit over 3% of GDP, they face additional fines. The political importance of some EU members raises the issue that they might be allowed to violate the stability pact, and so undermine the currency. France and Germany both broke the 3% limit earlier this decade but did not have to pay for their violations. Third, some Europeans are opposed to the idea of European unification and see the Euro as a symbol of that process out of control. Britain has not joined the Euro, choosing to keep the pound instead. Many in Britain are skeptical of further European integration and so oppose it. They see the British pound as the symbol of their sovereign independence. Some on the continent also cast a skeptical eye on further European integration.

Monetary union, such as the Euro, requires several conditions to work well. First, common economic shocks help. When the economies of the different regions of the monetary union grow and fall together, there is little need to use changes in exchange rates to offset any differences. Second, mobile labor also helps. Workers who are free to move in search of jobs help to even out differences in economic performance across regions within the union. Third, it helps to have preferences between inflation and unemployment be similar across the union. Central banks and government often choose to make either fighting inflation or raising employment their primary concern at the expense of the other. Each priority leads to different monetary and fiscal policies. If all governments within the union agree on these priorities, it is easier to set a common policy. When they disagree, it may be hard to do so.

Are these conditions present within the Euro zone? As mentioned earlier in the example of Spain, the economies of Euro zone do not grow and shrink together although they tend to move together. Labor is generally not mobile within the Euro zone. Most Europeans live only in their native country for their entire lives, indeed often living in the same city where they were born. They still think of themselves as Frenchmen, Belgians, or even Catalans first rather than Europeans. This is not true of the managerial class which are truly European. They speak multiple languages and often live in multiple European countries as a consequence of their jobs. But these Europeans are a thin layer on top of most who live in the national countries of Europe. There may also be important differences in views about monetary and fiscal policy across governments in the Euro zone. Germany has historically put fighting inflation first, while governments like France and Italy favor using government policy to raise employment. These differences were one reason behind the stability pact, to force the latter government to follow policies that would not cause inflation within the zone generally. To date, the Euro has held up well in the face of these stresses; will it continue to do so?

Is There a "Race to the Bottom"?

The "race to the bottom" argues that mobile capital will force governments to reduce their protection of the environment, loosen labor laws, and cut taxes on capital in order to attract footloose capital. Those governments that resist will find foreign investment drying up, which will hurt their economies. As each competes with one another for capital, these governments will drive their rules and regulations to the lowest possible standard all in pursuit of the almighty buck. If true, it would be a grim picture.

But is the "race" happening? If so, we should see the size of governments, as measured by their spending, shrink. After all, business interested only in profit do not need government programs. This, however, has not happened over the last two decades. The level of government spending as a share of GDP has not declined in developed countries, if anything, it has risen. Second, perfectly mobile capital should create a global interest rate. Money should pour into places where it can make a little more, driving down the rate of return and hence the interest rate. But that has not happened either; there are still important differences in national interest rates, even accounting for exchange rates. Government still possesses some ability to influence their economies through monetary policy. The race should drive most investment to developing countries because the rates of return should be highest there, with the weakest laws and regulations and the greatest pool of cheap, unskilled labor. But most FDI goes from one developed country to another, not to the developing world. If the "race to the bottom" is occurring, it is hard to see the evidence.

Embedded liberalism is one reason why developed countries do not join the "race". These countries benefit from their openness to trade, but that openness hurts some of their citizens. These governments use social programs in part to compensate those who are hurt by trade. The compensation seeks to convince those who lose their jobs to trade not to organize against it. The demands of openness create political incentives to stay out of the "race" for developed countries.

Even capital itself may not be interested in the "race". Firms continue to invest in areas with strong labor laws and environmental protection and which tax capital noticeably. They do so because those places are attractive for investment for other reasons. Costs are only part of any investment decision and often not a large part. Those laws in part help create places which skilled workers find attractive to live in. Firms often need such workers and so invest in places that have opted out of the "race". This is not to say that the competitive pressures of the "race" do not exist for governments, only that firms care about many other things as well when they invest. The pressure on governments then is not as great as the proponents of the "race" think.

Chapter Summary

The global economy has become more integrated over the last few decades. Trade is a larger portion of world product, and financial flows have increased dramatically. People move more freely than before. This openness is not novel to our time. The period before World War I also saw high levels of trade and cross-border investment. This period also carries the warning that globalization is not an irreversible process. It declined during the 1920s and 1930s to the detriment of the world economy. In our time, globalization has not had the effects many claim for it because it simply has not gone as far as some think. The world is not yet one seamless market; we do not live in "McWorld" yet, to borrow the term of one commentator. Still, openness in trade and investment has changed how governments respond to the global economy. What they can accomplish and how they pursue their objectives have changed with globalization.

Review Questions

1. Does skilled or unskilled labor in a developing country benefit as the country opens up to trade? How might the type of labor which suffers as trade opens compensate for their loss?

2. Explain the difference between foreign direct investment and portfolio capital. Which form of finance poses a greater risk of capital flight in a financial crisis?

3. Give one advantage and one disadvantage to the creation of the Euro for those countries that are in the Euro zone.

4. What is the "race to the bottom" that some claim that globalization causes? Name two state policies that are believed to be compromised by that race. Name one piece of evidence that suggests that this is not occurring.

Chapter 27
Cooperation on International Environmental Issues

The state of cooperation on international environmental issues is erratic. For some issues, it is good. Air pollution poses an international issue because it blows with the wind from the country where it is produced into the air of other countries. Motor vehicles, factories, and power plants all emit a variety of gases which pollute the air. The Convention on Long-Range Transboundary Air Pollution (CLRTAP) was negotiated to address this issue. The Convention and its Eight Protocols seek to regulate air pollution in member states, collect and disseminate information on the issue, and spread technology to clean up air pollution among the member states. Its members include the U.S., Canada, and European countries. A variety of organizations deal with fishing and whaling on international waters. Ships from all countries can fish in international waters. They have a shared interest in preserving the stocks of fish so that all can continue to fish from them. Organizations, such as the Northwest Atlantic Fisheries Organization (NAFO), collect information on the number of fish caught and assign quotas to each nation for each type of fish. These organizations have helped to preserve some stocks of fish, although others have declined dramatically under their watch. The Convention on International Trade in Endangered Species of Wild Fauna and Flora (CITES) does what its name says. It aims at protecting endangered species by preventing international trade in products from those animals and plants. Rhinoceros horn, for example, is highly sought in Yemen and Oman to be carved into handles for knives and for use in Asian medicines. The horns command a high price in these countries, leading poachers to kill rhinos just for their horns. The member states of CITES meet regularly to revise the list of protected species. Each member state must pass laws to outlaw trade in products from these species. CITES has succeeded in protecting endangered species. Some animal populations have grown enough that they are no longer considered endangered, and so no longer protected. Some criticize CITES for not going far enough to protect endangered species. It does not address the protection of habitat.

Cooperation on other environmental issues has not been strong. International efforts to limit global warming began with the UN Framework Convention on Climate Change (FCCC) in 1992. It committed nations to publish information on their emissions of greenhouse gases believed to be responsible for global warming and required voluntary reductions in those emissions, which is the same as not requiring anything a state did not wish to do. The Kyoto Protocol of 1997 added binding targets for industrialized countries with cuts below their emissions in 1990. The United States, the largest emitter of greenhouse gases until recently, has not ratified Kyoto, meaning it is not bound by those limits. Kyoto does not limit emissions from the developing world, which have increased greatly. Subsequent attempts to negotiate a stronger treaty than Kyoto have failed at The Hague in 2000 and Bali in 2007. On other examples of the failure of international economic cooperation, fishing is unlimited on large swathes of the open ocean. There are other environmental issues, some of which may not be understood yet, where there is no international cooperation. Why has cooperation on environmental issues been mixed?

Why Protection of the Environment is Difficult

Environmental degradation occurs as the by-product of economic activity. The resulting pollution must either be cleaned up or the activities that degrade the environment limited so that nature can restore itself. Such steps are costly either to limit damage from production or to clean it up afterwards. One of the central questions of environmental policy is "who pays?" This question alone often explains why protecting the environment is difficult.

Public Goods

Protection of the environment is generally a *public good*. We encountered public goods earlier when discussing things national leaders can provide to hold the loyalty of their supporters. The benefits of a public good are general to all. No one can be excluded from enjoying the benefits of a public good. Reducing air pollution is an example of this property. If we clean up the air over a city, you cannot stop someone from gaining the benefit of the cleaner air. This is not to say that everyone values that public good the same. An asthmatic values clean air more than one who does not suffer from that condition. If a public good is provided, everyone in a society benefits from it.

The cost of producing a public good, however, is specific to individuals. That personal cost to help produce a public good exceeds that individual's contribution to the public good. Cars are an important source of air pollution in many cities. The smog in Los Angeles was for a long time primarily from automobile emissions. Reducing that pollution requires car owners to install equipment that reduces emissions of the gases that cause smog. That equipment can cost several hundred dollars per car. But the effect of one dirty car on the air quality in a city is negligible. While everyone might want to breather cleaner air, no one is willing to pay the cost of cleaning up their own car. This leads to continued air pollution, a failure to provide the public good of clean air.

These two properties together, the inability to exclude someone from enjoying a public good and the small effect of anyone's contribution to a public good, explain why public goods are not provided. No one is willing to make the effort on their own to contribute toward its production. If everyone else contributes, then anyone who does not saves their personal cost of production. If no one else contributes, the efforts of one person alone will not produce the public good for him or her. The strategic logic is similar to that of the Prisoners' Dilemma, where not contributing parallels defection. No matter what others do, you can better off not contributing to the public good.

Fisheries provide another example. The public good here is the preservation of the stock of fish. Fish populations can collapse from over fishing, so there are not enough adult fish to have fry to replenish the stock. The North Atlantic used to be famous for its immense stock of cod. In the 1500s, fishers reported being able to catch cod in the Grand Banks off eastern Canada simply by dipping baskets over the sides of their ships and pulling them back full of cod. Cod became very popular to eat, so popular that fishers from Europe and North America caught so many cod that their numbers dropped dramatically. Restricting the catch allows the young to grow to maturity and the stock recover over time. Here each fisher must limit their own catch. This is costly to them because they could make more money if they catch and sell more fish. At the same time, one fishing vessel will not deplete the stock of fish on its own. But without such regulation of how many fish are caught in total, all fishers lose if the stock collapses, as do those who eat fish.

Four Ways to Provide Public Goods

Public goods are unlikely to be provided by voluntary contributions. The cost of contributing exceeds the benefit of that contribution. This makes the provision of public goods a social dilemma for domestic and international politics. All are worse off than if the public good could be provided. Three types of solutions are possible to the dilemma in domestic politics. Because the problem of the provision of public goods is general, the examples here are drawn from domestic politics.

First, a central authority could coerce everyone to contribute. In domestic politics, governments tax people to produce public goods. We encountered this solution earlier in the chapter on selectorate theory. Political leaders use their power to extract resources from society to provide public goods for the populace. Governments can also force people to contribute to public goods through law. Smog in the Los Angeles Basin was reduced noticeably after the State of California required all new cars sold to have equipment to reduce their emissions. It also required regular inspections to verify the equipment was working and that a car did not emit noxious gases beyond the legal limit. The state would not renew the license of cars that failed to pass the test, making them illegal to drive. As the fleet of cars driven in the Los Angeles area was replaced with newer, cleaner cars, the quality of the air improved. Now cars are no longer the major source of air pollution in the basin. As selectorate theory says, leaders may try to provide private benefits under the guise of providing public goods. This issue is important in domestic politics, less so in international politics.

Second, contributors could be given other benefits on top of the public good, where non-contributors do not get the extra benefits. Such benefits are called *selective benefits*. Public radio and television is a public good in the United States. These services are available freely on the airwaves, and anyone with a television or radio can watch or listen to these stations. They collect donations from listeners and viewers to cover their expenses. Because the stations are available to all freely, they are public goods. An individual's contribution has little effect on the financial viability of a station, but if few contribute, the station might be unable to pay its bills. Public stations provide gifts to donors–tote bags and coffee mugs with their logo, books, recordings, through member-only events with broadcasting personalities. These gifts are selective benefits to reward contributors and so encourage contributions now and in the future. In contrast, Great Britain finances the British Broadcasting Corporation (BBC) through license fees on televisions, an example of government coercion. Public stations claim publicly that only about one out of ten listeners and viewers contribute to the financial support of a station. The selective benefits encourage contributions, but they are not large enough to get all who use the stations to contribute.

Third, a single actor could pay the entire cost of the public good. Normally, each individual contribution has little effect on how much of the public good is provided. In some cases, though, an individual has the ability to pay the entire cost of a public good on their own. If that individual values the public good enough, he or she will provide it at their own expense. Everyone else gets the public good for free. The 19th Century industrialist Andrew Carnegie built and stocked thousands of libraries in the U.S., Great Britain, Canada, and other British territories. Carnegie had made a fortune in the steel industry and turned to philanthropy in his old age. The communities did have to agree to provide land and pay the operating costs of the library, so they were not completely free. But Carnegie's donations did build libraries in many communities that would not have one otherwise.

International politics poses particular problems for each of these ways to provide public goods. There is no world government to coerce contributions or provide selective benefits. One state might be large enough to provide some public goods. The U.S. Navy has dominated the oceans since the end of the World War II. It has enforced freedom of navigation on international waters against piracy and other threats. This protection is a public good for other countries. Of course, the U.S. has benefitted in other ways from its dominance of the seas through its ability to project power quickly anywhere in the world. International environmental issues, however, are unlikely to be solved by a single state.

The number of states is small, around two hundred. The Los Angeles Basin had millions of cars whose emissions needed to be reduced to clean the air by comparison. This small number makes it possible for states to coordinate on the provision of public goods. Only 88 states are members of the International Convention for the Regulation of Whaling. These states cover most nations which have caught whales in the past as well as other maritime nations. They can agree to monitor one another to ensure that all contribute to the public good. If they can also enforce that agreement on one another, they may be able to produce a public good. Coordinated provision has the same logic of enforcement we studied in the chapter on enforcing international cooperation. The small group is key, and there are examples of villages providing public goods through monitoring one another and enforcing contributions through social enforcement.

Provision by a small group of actors is the fourth way to provide a public good.

Bargaining over Public Goods

Cooperation to produce a public good requires deciding how to produce it as well as being able to enforce that agreement afterwards. Actors may disagree how much of the good to provide or even whether it should be provided. In the case of air pollution in the LA basin, people place different values on clean air. Asthmatics care more about it than those without a respiratory aliment. National defense is a public good, and the central question there was "how much is enough?" States may disagree about which species are endangered and so deserve protection.

Even if states agree about the level of an international public good to be produced, they have conflicting interests over how much each should pay. When a public good is produced by a small group of actors, they do not have to negotiate equal contributions from all. Some may have to pay more than others. Any negotiation over the division of the cost poses a problem of distribution. Everyone would like to pay less and see others pay more. Provision by a single actor poses the problem that it would often like to have others contribute something.

Some actors may also argue that the public good is not necessary. They believe that it is not worth the cost of provision. Japan argues that several species of whales are plentiful and so can be whaled without endangering the species. Other countries which are members of the International Convention for the Regulation of Whaling believe that all whaling must be stopped to protect whale populations. The cost for a state of this convention is stopping whaling, with some exceptions allowed for aboriginal populations that hunt whales for their livelihood. The first issue to negotiate is whether the public good even needs to be provided.

International agreements to protect the environment need to last for long periods of time. Controlling air pollution requires continued limits on emissions even after air quality rises. The long period of any agreement makes any distributional problem more difficult to solve. This is the "pizza problem" we discussed earlier in the chapter on how to cooperate. When you have to live with the consequences of an agreement for decades afterwards, you are careful to get an agreement you can live with. Renegotiation of an agreement can address some of this concern.

The above issues–how much of the good should be provided, who pays, and is it even worth providing–are all distributional issues. States disagree about which solution is best. Environmental issues also pose informational problems; what is the value of each possible solution? This uncertainty makes negotiations on the distributional issues more difficult.

Environmental issues pose issues of scientific uncertainty. We may not know how bad the problem is. One hundred years ago there was no international action on environmental issues because no one understood what problems pollution could pose. It took decades from the time when scientists first proposed the possibility of global warming before many states agreed that the issue should be addressed internationally. Fish stocks have to be estimated from samples before the number of fish that can be caught can be set. Scientific uncertainty about environmental problems leads some actors to conclude that there is not a problem that needs to be addressed. Even when most actors agree there is a problem, they may disagree about how bad it is because of the lack of complete common knowledge of it.

Even when the scientific dimensions of an environmental problem are understood by all, the economic costs and benefits of dealing with it may remain unclear. Cleaning and protecting the environment imposes costs on some. Production processes may need to be changed, raising the cost of production. Putting scrubbers on power plants which burn coal reduce air pollution from them but raise the cost of electricity to those who use the power produced. Resources may be devoted to cleanup efforts, taking them away from other uses through taxes. These costs are worthwhile when the benefits of cleaning up are larger. Often the benefits of action to improve the environment are unclear and uneven across actors. Politicians care about the economic costs and benefits because they ultimately answer to the people who pay those costs and enjoy the benefits. When politicians are unsure whether their people will on net benefit or lose from environmental action, they may be reluctant to act.

Both scientific and economic uncertainty make international environmental agreements more difficult to reach. Solving distributional problems, such as "who pays," is harder when it is unclear what will be gained and at what cost. Those who bear the greatest cost can argue that the benefit is not large enough to justify the cost they will have to bear. Actors might agree to lesser measures because they do not agree on the size of the problem.

International institutions that deal with environmental issues often focus on creating a common understanding of the problem first. International scientific commissions are created which conduct research generally into the problem. Their results are independent of the nationality of the scientists involved in the research. The hope is to detach the scientific understanding of the problem from the political questions of how to address it. These scientific organizations conduct research with multinational teams, hold international conferences, and publish their results generally as well as in scientific journals. This strategy for dealing with environmental issues separates the informational issues of what the problem is from the distributional problem of how to deal with it.

Externalities

Public goods affect many actors and often require the action of many to produce them for all. Externalities lie at the other end of the spectrum of the number of actors involved. One benefits from actions that hurt another in an *externality*. The first actor takes those actions to gain the benefit for itself. The costs to the second are external to the decision of the first, leading to the term externality. Cross-border air pollution is a classic environmental externality in world politics. Coal-burning power plants are major emitters of the gases–sulphur dioxide and nitrous dioxide–that lead to acid rain downwind from the plant. Internationally, power plants in the Midwest of the United States contribute to acid rain in Eastern Canada, as well as New England, because the predominant wind in North American blows from the west. Consumers in the Midwest and the power companies that supply them benefit from the electricity produced by these power plants, while those downwind in Canada suffer the consequence. In 1991, the U.S. and Canada concluded the Air Quality Agreement to address the issue by reducing emissions of these gases.

Externalities lead to bargaining. The party hurt by the externality would like the other to stop its activity, while the party that benefits from it would like the harmed party to pay for the cleanup. Negotiations over which party pays pose a distributional issue. Each wants the other to pay. Distributional bargaining is difficult because one party will lose from the deal or the absence of one. Legal rules, such as "the polluter pays," simplify such negotiations if not eliminate the need for them. The adoption of such rules is political precisely because those rules determine who pays.

Externalities also pose the problem of convincing the party doing the damage that the damage is real and that the benefit of cleaning it up exceeds the cost. Most nations that once caught whales follow the moratorium of the International Whaling Commission on commercial whaling. The moratorium allows some whales to be caught for scientific research. Japan and Norway continue to catch and kill whales. Japan uses the quota on scientific research to justify the whales it hunts. Norway filed a reservation on the treaty, allowing it to continue to whale certain species. Japan claims that whaling of the more numerous species can be conducted without threatening their viability as a species. In short, Japan does not believe that the gain from banning whaling exceeds the loss of the value of the whales caught. The issue of whether it is worth stopping an activity is an informational issue because the parties may disagree about both the cost and the benefit of the activity which produces the externality. Actors that do not wish to stop their activities, such as Japan with whaling, may not believe others' claims of damage.

Unlike public goods, enforcement is not as large a problem for externalities. With a small number of parties, each can monitor whether the other is living up to its end of the bargain. Legal enforcement can make defection from an agreement more costly to a party than compliance. Alternatively, a transfer payment, such as when the damaged party pays for the cleanup, can be withheld if the damage is not remedied.

International environmental issues pose distributional, informational, and enforcement problems. Environmental protection can be either a public good or an externality, with the difference lying in the number of actors involved. Public goods could be produced by many actors working together if they can monitor and enforce an agreement to do so. Externalities require negotiations between the emitter of the pollution and those who suffer from it to determine who will pay for the cleanup.

Deliberate Oil Pollution of the Ocean

Enforcement of environmental agreements is often problematic. Oil pollution of the oceans poses the problem that they are many ships moving cargo and the oceans are very large. Although oil spills from tankers that run aground or break up attract attention when they occur, regular emissions of oil residues from tankers posed a larger problem of pollution. Oil tankers carry much of the world's crude oil from where the oil is pumped out of the ground to refineries where it is processed into all the products extracted from oil such as gasoline and aviation fuel. Tankers fill their hulls with oil to maximize the amount of oil they can carry. Ships carry ballast, extra weight in the bottom of the hull to make the ship stable, most commonly by pumping ocean water into ballast tanks in the ship. Originally, oil tankers filled their hulls with crude oil, which then mixed with the ballast. After delivering their cargo, they would wash out the oil storage, mix the resulting mess with the ballast water, and dump it all in the ocean on their return voyage. States move to regulate these practices because they were a major source of oil pollution of the oceans over time.

Three different measures to limit waste discharges of oil were adopted. First, load-on-top required tankers to retain the messy mixture of ballast and waste oil, allow them to separate during the return voyage (crude oil floats on water), and then load their next cargo of oil on top of the oil that separated out from the ballast water. Strict rules were adopted on emissions of oil when ballast was flushed. These rules did not stop tankers from flushing waste oil into the ocean. There are many tanker voyages every year, and the ocean is vast. It is impossible to follow each tanker and verify that it never flushed out waste oil. A crew could simply sail out of port after delivering its cargo of crude oil and flush the waste out once it was 50 miles offshore. Tankers owned and operated by oil companies did use load-on-top procedures because they increase the amount of oil delivered over a number of voyages. Many tankers, however, are independent contractors who are paid only for the oil loaded on them rather than the amount they deliver on that given voyage. They did not make extra money for the higher recovery of oil over many deliveries using load-on-top. These operators had no economic incentive to use load-on-top and so often violated the rules on emissions.

The second measure was washing the oil tanks with crude oil instead of water after delivery. This measure reduced the amount of oil mixed into ballast water and so lowers emissions. It requires additional equipment to wash the tanks with crude oil, an added expense for ship owners. It does raise the amount of oil delivered by increasing the amount of oil pumped out and not left in the tanks. The added payment provides an economic incentive for ship owners to pay the cost to install the necessary equipment for crude oil washing.

The third measure separated the ballast tanks from the tanks containing the crude oil. Segregated ballast tanks reduce the contact between ballast water and the cargo of crude. The ballast water contains less oil when it is flushed out after a delivery. The tanks are expensive to add when a tanker is built or to retrofit to one in service already. In 1973, states agreed that all tankers built in 1980 or later would have to have segregated ballast tanks. These rules were effective. Despite the added cost of construction, segregated ballast tanks quickly became the standard for new oil tankers in the 1980s. Owners of existing tankers retrofitted many of them to meet this new standard despite the expense and the lack of a formal rule requiring them to do so.

The second and third measures–crude oil washing and segregated ballast tanks–succeeded when the first–load-on-top–failed because of the ability to enforce each measure. Ship captains were required to report violations of load-on-top if they flushed out too much oil with their ballast. Not surprisingly, few did. State authorities lacked the ability to verify compliance with load-on-top and its limits of the amount of oil dumped with ballast at sea. They could attempt to verify violations when tankers were in port, but strong enforcement might encourage shippers to shift to other ports with looser enforcement. Crude oil washing and segregated ballast tanks required construction work on the ships, a fact which could be verified by all interested parties. Governments could now ban tankers which did not meet these measures, as the U.S. threatened to do several times in the 1970s. Port authorities could detain ships which lacked documentation of the needed equipment for crude oil washing and segregated ballast tanks. Indirect enforcement was also important. Insurance companies could also verify which ships had the required equipment. They began to charge higher insurance rates–a major cost in international shipping–for tankers which did not meet the standards. The risk that a ship not in compliance could be detained in port justified the higher insurance rates. Because ships cannot do business without such insurance, owners of tankers installed the needed equipment to avoid higher insurance rates or possible denial of insurance. Finally, the transparency of whether ships had the necessary equipment made it easy for ship owners to determine that their competitors were also in compliance. That way no one ship owner was at a disadvantage compared to its competitors. The indirect cost together with the threat of detention was enough to convince ship owners to comply with the two measures that reduced oil pollution.

Fisheries

Over fishing can reduce a stock of a fish to the point where the catch drops dramatically. Over the last few decades, the technology of fishing has improved immensely. Large factory ships can stay at sea for months, ranging widely to catch and process fish of many species. A series of different fish species have become popular in the market, only to be over fished leading to a decline in the catch and an increase in their price. The maintenance of a fish stock requires estimating the populations, studying the biology of each species to determine how many fish of what age are needed to replenish the stock, and then limiting the catch to ensure that sufficient adult fish remain to repopulate the next generations. Each of these steps poses problems of information, distribution, and enforcement.

Fish have the annoying habit of swimming between international and national waters. Most countries with oceanfront claim a 200-mile economic zone into the ocean where they try to control fishing and other economic activities, such as drilling for oil offshore. Valuable fish stocks often extend from national into international waters. International cooperation on limiting catches may be necessary to protect those stocks of fish from over fishing in international waters. Maintenance of the stock is a public good because all lose if the stock of fish drops to a level where few fish are caught by anyone. The informational problem centers on what this level is. How large a catch can be sustained without damaging the stock of fish?

Limiting the catch of fish means that some fishers will not be able to catch as many fish as they would like. They will make less money. Consumers of the fish will not be able buy as many fish, and they will pay a higher price after the catch is limited. Allocation of the shares of the allowable catch is a distributional problem. Each nation fishing the waters in question would like as large a portion of the catch as possible. Those that receive smaller shares that they want may argue that more fish can be caught safely. This is an example of how a distributional problem can affect an informational problem. Restrictions on fishing also pose a problem for national budgets. Fishing villages are commonly remote and poor compared to more developed parts of these countries. In Canada, for example, Newfoundland has many fishing villages which can only be reached by boat. Many governments of advanced industrial states support communities reliant on fishing with subsidies to sustain their people. Many have also subsidized purchases of fishing boats and improvements in their ability to catch fish to help economic development in these areas. If the allowable catch is cut, fishing communities will suffer, and their governments pay more in subsidies to support them. Cuts to how many fish a nation's fishing fleet can catch creates a distributional problem across governments as well as among fishers. Additionally, national fishing fleets vary in their range and how they catch fish. Some national fishing fleets, such as those of Spain, Japan, and South Korea, are capable of ranging thousands of miles from their home ports in search of fish. Others are limited to nearby waters. Limiting the total catch is less of a problem for those ships with long ranges. They can simply sail to other fishing grounds, while those with shorter ranges cannot. The difference in range also affects how important the maintenance of the stock is for fishers and their governments. Ships with a shorter range have more at stake in preserving fish stocks close to their home ports.

Enforcing an agreement to limit the catch requires knowing how many fish have been caught. Each individual fishing vessel has an incentive to catch as many fish as it can. Spot inspections are conducted sometimes in national waters to determine what and how many fish a ship has taken. Self-reporting is more common. Fishing vessels report their catch to national authorities, who in turn report the total weight of fish caught to an international body. These reports not only help enforcement of any agreement to limit the total catch, they also provide a view into the current stock of fish in the ocean. If the stock crashes, fishers will catch fewer and smaller fish. A smaller catch is the strongest evidence of a problem of a falling stock.

Institutions to control over fishing separate the informational and distributional problems. International organizations, like NAFO, have scientific agencies which study fish stocks in the fisheries they have control over. They estimate how many fish there are and how many can be caught in a given fishing season. The allowable catch is then divided among the states fishing in those waters through set shares which do not change from year to year. These shares are set through a negotiation based in part on historical catches of each national fleet from that fishery. The set formula for dividing the catch solves the distributional problem at the cost of not dividing the political cost of the limits on the catch fairly. Limiting the catch imposes greater hardship on some fishers than others. Those with a long range can shift their efforts to other parts of the sea. A negotiation over which fishers suffer the most from a limit is difficult to conclude. All feel their own pain and thinks others should bear the costs of the limits. Fixed rules to divide the catch avoid such difficult negotiations.

The Politics of Global Warming

There is broad agreement among scientists that the climate of the Earth is warming and that human activities contribute to the warming. They point to the emission of greenhouse gases, primarily carbon dioxide but also methane and others, which increase the ability of the earth's atmosphere to retain heat from the sun. Burning of fossil fuels–coal, oil, and natural gas–and deforestation are primary sources of these emissions. Some skeptics remain among those scientists who study the issue. Those scientists who believe the climate is warming cannot provide precise estimates of how much nor how quickly the climate will warm. Nor can they tell us the local effects of global warming. The effects could be disastrous or benign, or anything in between.

The political question is "what should be done about it?" The economic and political effects of global warming, just like its local effects, are unclear. Most projections reported in the press focus on how global warming will harm people. Destructive storms might become more common, some areas may become deserts, while polar areas and mountain glaciers might suffer substantial loss of ice. Some may benefit from global warming as cooler areas acquire a warmer climate or if rainfall increases in dry areas. Global warming poses a distributional problem then where the winners and losers are not clear at this time.

Some losers from global warming are clear, and they often are the advocates of strong action now in the debate about what to do. The Maldive Islands in the Indian Ocean have repeated urged that measures be adopted to limit warming. The highest point in the Maldive Islands is 8 feet above sea level. Global warming should lead to a rise in the sea level, both from melting ice and from expansion of the water in the ocean as it warms. If the ocean rises eight or more feet, there are no more Maldive Islands. The Netherlands has also advocated strong measures against global warming. Much of the country has been reclaimed from the North Sea over the centuries and lies below sea level. Only elaborate flood control systems keep these areas dry. Other countries came to a realization that they could be hurt by global warming later than others. Switzerland is not threatened by the rise of the oceans, but skiing is very important to the Swiss. Their government's position on global warming changed as the perception among the Swiss public grew that skiing could be threatened over time. For others, it is unclear whether they will gain or lose from global warming. The northern Great Plains in North America–the Dakotas in the United States and the prairie provinces in Canada–could gain from a warmer climate with more rain or lose if they receive less rain on average.

This unpredictability of the effects of global warming makes a political solution difficult to craft. Measures should compensate the losers from the benefits received by areas that gain. It is hard to design such measures when you cannot tell who will be winners and who will be losers. This is a distributional problem of "who pays who" compounded by the informational problem posed by the uncertainty about the precise effects of global warming.

The economic costs of addressing global warming are also unclear. Some experts believe that there are measures that could be taken now at little cost that would have a significant impact on the increases in warming. Others place the cost of effective measures in the neighborhood of 2-3% of global production. This may sound small, but global economic growth has averaged in the same neighborhood over the last sixty years, the period of greatest economic growth in history. Even these levels of measures would allow for some warming of the climate over the next one hundred years. The science on global warming cannot make exact predictions about what temperatures will occur for different levels of greenhouse gases. This makes the economic decision more difficult. We do not know how much we have to pay to limit warming to a certain level.

The question of "who pays this cost?" also looms. Developed and developing countries are divided on this question. Leaders of developing countries argue that the developed world has caused this problem through their use of fossil fuels when they industrialized. They think the developed world should bear most of the cost of limiting global warming. Some developed countries accept that they must take the first steps on their own. Others, particularly the United States over time, argue that any limits they adopt on the emission of greenhouse gases will be swamped by the rise in emissions as developing countries industrialize. China has recently surpassed the U.S. as the country which emits the most greenhouse gases. The U.S. has argued that all countries must work to limit their emissions in the future. Some in the developing countries see that argument as preventing them from achieving the same standard of living that the developed world enjoys now. One way to address this divide would be for the developed world to pay for measures that limit emissions or mitigate causes of global warming in the developing world. Carbon-offset projects where the sponsor pays for activities that reduce emissions by the same amount as the sponsor emits in another activity are one example of such measures. Another is the purchase and preservation of forests in the developing world, as deforestation adds to global warming.

Any deal to address global warming is a deal that must last decades. This long period makes negotiating measures to address global warming more difficult. The consequences of an unfavorable deal are much larger than they would be if the bargain only held for a year or two. The Kyoto Protocol addresses this issue by expiring in 2012. By design, it lasted a short time to make it easier for states to agree and then see what the economic consequences would be. The drawback to having short-term deals is that new deals must be negotiated frequently. Given the difficulty resolving the distributional issues in each negotiation, there is a real possibility of having no deal for some years in the future. The decades-long nature of global warming also gives political leaders the option of setting deep cutbacks in emissions in the distant future. The leaders of the G-8 countries–the U.S., Canada, Japan, Russia, Germany, France, Great Britain, Italy–endorsed the idea of cutting world greenhouse gas emissions in half by 2050. As an aspirational goal, this is attractive, but the responsibility for those cuts will fall on their countries long after these leaders have left office. Indeed, most of them will be dead before any action must be taken to meet these goals. These measures please the concerned public while avoiding actions which might prove politically costly to those leaders.

The long-period of a deal should make it easier to enforce any deal by increasing the shadow of the future. Much longer, and so larger, punishments are possible. But enforcement of deals to limit greenhouse gas emissions face other problems. First, reciprocity makes little sense to enforce a deal. Does it make any sense for other countries to increase their own emissions if another fails to live up to its commitment to cut its own? Wrecking the climate for everyone is a punishment that lacks credibility. Second, the global nature of the problem makes it difficult to target violators specifically. Reciprocal punishments are most effective when they hurt just the violators and are enforced shortly after a violation.

More generally, violations may be difficult to deter if state leaders can reopen negotiations to change the terms of the deal. It is tempting to change the rules to keep a country in a deal rather than allow it to break out of the system completely. That way the appearance that all continue to honor and respect the deal to limit global warming is maintained. But that appearance comes at the cost of reducing the ability of the system to limit global warming. Why should a leader take costly measures if he or she can change the deal to avoid those costs? Some have proposed using other issues to enforce an agreement to limit greenhouse gases. Trade sanctions could be used against countries which do not limit their emissions. Others think it is a bad idea to use trade policy to enforce agreements to limit global warming. Enforcement is a serious problem for any attempt to limit global warming.

The history of international negotiations to address global warming reflects these problems of information, distribution, and enforcement. The UN Framework Convention on Climate Change was adopted at the Earth Summit in Rio de Janeiro, Brazil in 1992. It recognized the problem and called for further negotiations on the issue. It also required states to report information on their greenhouse gas emissions but did not require any binding action to limit them. The Kyoto Protocol signed in 1997 did call for developed countries to cut their emissions slightly from 1990 levels. It did not require any action by developing countries. The United States did not ratify Kyoto Protocol, in part because it required no action by developing countries. It is scheduled to expire in 2012, and attempts to negotiate a treaty to follow it have failed to date, both in Amsterdam in 2000, Montreal in 2005, and Bali in 2007. Another round of negotiations will be finished with an international conference in Copenhagen in December 2009.

The cuts in emissions in the Kyoto Protocol correspond closely to which countries ratified the treaty. The Maldives Islands was the fourth country to ratify the treaty on December 30, 1998. Most developing countries have ratified the treaty, and it imposes no obligations on them. The developed countries, referred to as Annex 1 countries in the treaty, are obligated to reduce their emissions below their level in 1990. Many Eastern European countries were already in compliance with this requirement at the time of the negotiation of the treaty. Under Communism, heavy industry and power plants there used large amounts of coal. After the Cold War ended, many of these industries went out of production because their goods could not compete with those produced in the West. The use of coal declined in these countries, meaning their level of greenhouse gas emissions by 1995 were much lower than they were in 1990. Many Western European governments were close to the levels Kyoto prescribed for them, making ratification costless. The emissions of other countries rose during the 1990s, meaning that Kyoto would require them to cut their emissions. Japan, Canada, and Australia all fall into this situation. Ratification by Japan and Russia moved the treaty into force in 2005, as its provisions require Annex 1 parties with 55% of world emissions to ratify the treaty for it to come into force. Although Russia's emissions of greenhouse gases had declined substantially since 1990, it is also a major oil producer and was reluctant to ratify the treaty. Australia did not ratify the Kyoto Protocol until 2007. Kyoto requires substantial cuts by the United States, which has not and will not ratify the treaty. The U.S. economy boomed during the 1990s, and a large wave of immigration increased the population. The two factors lead to a large increase in the emission of greenhouse gases by the U.S. The Clinton Administration never sent the treaty to the Senate for a vote on ratification, even though Vice President Al Gore signed the treaty as the U.S. representative at the Kyoto conference. President Bush announced that the U.S. would never ratify Kyoto shortly after taking office. Although the Obama Administration favors the Kyoto Protocol, there is little point in ratifying a treaty in 2009 which will expire in 2012. The demands of the treaty closely correspond to whether states ratified it.

[Figure showing levels of emissions and treaty levels]

Chapter Summary

International cooperation on the environment has been difficult because environmental protection often poses the problems of public goods and externalities. Because no one can be excluded from a public good and the cost to each of producing exceeds the personal benefit from that contribution, actors will not contribute to public goods on their own. When the number of actors is small, they may be able to create a system of monitoring and enforcement to ensure that all contribute to a public good. There is still the distributional problem of "how much of the public good should be produced" and "who pays how much". Externalities pose the distributional problem of "who pays". The science of environmental issues is not fully understood. This uncertainty leads to an informational problem. Finally, enforcement of environmental agreements can be difficult. The combination of these problems of cooperation lead to an erratic record of protection of the environment at the international level.

Review Questions

1.   Define the terms "public good" and "externality". How do they pose different problems for international cooperation on the environment?

2.   Give two of the three problems that make it difficult for states to cooperate on a common policy to address global warming. Explain specifically how those problems occur in the issue of global warming.

Chapter 28
International Law and Norms:
Humanitarian Law and Human Rights

International law on human rights is a novel feature of the post-World War II system. Millions of civilians were killed during the Second World War, in atrocities from the Rape of Nanking by the Japanese in 1937 to the six million victims of the industrial mass murder of the Nazis known as the Holocaust. Further, the conduct of the war led to the deaths of millions through those unable to escape as combat raged in the villages, towns, and cities where they lived, to the killing of civilians in anti-partisan sweeps to aerial bombings by the United States and Great Britain that culminated in the atomic bombings of Hiroshima and Nagasaki. The war was fought under law which sought to prescribe what militaries could do and what not in the interest of preserving human life and limiting the destruction of war. Some of these treaties were broadly followed, while others were pieces of paper that provided no protection to those exposed to the hurricane of modern total war.

Revulsion at the conduct of the Nazi and Japanese armies led to international trials for war crimes by their leaders. The victorious allies of the United Nations conducted these trials at Nuremberg for the Nazi leaders and Tokyo for the Japanese leaders. Many but not all of these leaders were executed or imprisoned for the atrocities they had overseen during the war. These trials created the category of "crimes against humanity" to capture the slaughters of civilians conducted by the Nazis. Others were tried for war crimes defined by the existing treaties on conduct during wartime. Other trials convicted lower-level officers and soldiers who committed violations against enemy soldiers and civilians during the war. While these trials were not the first in history, they were a milestone in the concept of holding state leaders responsible for what they did during wartime.

States negotiated an explosion of treaties to address these horrors in the aftermath of the war. The Universal Declaration of Human Rights, concluded in 1948, defines what human rights are universal. These include The Genocide Convention, also of 1948, defined genocide as a crime against humanity in response primarily to the Holocaust. Both of these treaties sought to create universal definitions of the responsibilities that states had to their citizens and residents. The laws of war were revised substantially as a result of the wartime experience. The Geneva Conventions of 1949 expanded the protections of prisoners of war and wounded enemy soldiers, limited conduct of war on the high seas, and expanded protection of civilians. Although the earlier Hague and Geneva conventions provided some protection on these issues, state leaders sought to strengthen them by specifying their obligations in greater detail. Cultural property and sites received legal protection in the following decade in response to Nazi looting of art during their occupation of other European countries and the destruction of irreplaceable cultural sites during the war.

Activity advancing human rights and humanitarian conduct during war languished in the following decades of the Cold War. Human rights was used by both superpowers to criticize one another's policies. Concern in advancing human rights gained during the 1970s. Non-governmental organizations, such as Amnesty International, focused attention on governments that abused their citizens. These NGOs began to push governments to expand treaty law on human rights to new areas. The number of human rights treaties expanded greatly. The large multilateral conferences that completed these treaties attracted large numbers of NGO representatives in addition to state representatives. The number of human rights NGOs also expanded to include many small groups organized in one state as well as large transnational organizations.

[Graph showing growth of number of human rights treaties over time]
[Graph showing growth in human rights NGOs]

The end of the Cold War led to greater attention to human rights in world politics, in part through the triumph of the Western view of human rights. The wars that followed the breakup of Yugoslavia from 1991 to 1995 saw atrocities of the types and scope that Europe had not experienced since World War II. The overthrow of the Rwandan government led to the new government killing hundreds of thousands of Rwandans, perhaps as high as 800,000, within four months. The killing stopped only when a rebel group drove that government from power and into exile in eastern Congo. The international outrage at these atrocities led the UN Security Council to create international tribunals to try those responsible for these criminal acts. These tribunals continue to operate today, more than 15 years after the crimes. The Rome Statute in 1998 created the International Criminal Court out of the desire to address genocide and war crimes through international trials. The Court was established in 2004 when the minimum number of states–60–accepted the court through the ratification of the Rome Statute.

Despite these developments, questions remain about whether human rights law makes a difference. International conventions against genocide did not stop the killings in Rwanda or the Yugoslav wars, not to mention other horrors. Many governments do not respect the rights of their citizens, instead imprisoning those who speak openly against their government. Some governments use torture routinely to put down dissent and criticism. Criminal trials are a sham before sentence is proclaimed on the accused. During wartime, governments kill their own citizens, often in the effort to suppress rebel movements. Civilians continue to be most of the casualties of these wars. The civil wars in Congo which followed after the overthrow of the dictator Mobutu have killed millions in the country, mainly civilians at the mercy of the armed bands fighting these wars. In some cases, other countries have intervened for humanitarian purposes, to stop the killing, protect civilians, and distribute aid to the victims of these conflicts. The United States and other countries sent troops under the authority of the UN to Somalia in December of 1992 in the face of civil conflict and massive famine. This intervention led to fighting between UN troops and local armed bands. A raid to seize Farrah Addid, the leader of one of these groups, led to the events depicted in the movie "Black Hawk Down," and the withdrawal of U.S. troops after the loss of 18 Army Rangers killed during the raid. Humanitarian intervention has been tried in other cases, such as Bosnia and Darfur, with mixed success at best. Has the explosion in human rights and humanitarian law made a difference?

Norms versus Law

To answer this question, we need to understand how international law could shape world politics. Its effects are different and more subtle than those of domestic law. A simple equation of the two misleads rather than clarifies. To do so, we need to think carefully about norms, law, and the difference between the two.

A norm states proper conduct for actors. The norm in human rights is the idea that governments should protect the rights of their citizens and residents. Many norms exist in world politics. National self-determination is the idea that national groups should be able to determine what state represents them. The creation of the nation-state led to demands for new states to represent national groups without a state. These demands contributed to the unification of Germany and Italy in the 1860s. They also led to some national groups to demand to secede from their state and either join another or create a new state. The norm of national self-determination led to conflict in some cases. The most recent example of national self-determination is the creation of Kosovo as an independent state in 2008. Not all states accept the creation of Kosovo as a sovereign nation-state. Non-discrimination is a key element of the international system of trade under the GATT and WTO. It states that all members must treat one another equally in their trade policies.

To carefully define the term, a *norm* is a shared principle about which actions are appropriate and which inappropriate for different social roles. Each part of the definition is important. Norms are normative; they specify what conduct is proper and which improper. Actors are allowed to do what is proper under the norm but are not supposed to do what is improper. These ideas of correct conduct must be shared across actors. Others also hold the norms and so can judge what an actor does. The norm may not be universal as some actors might reject it. Finally, norms are attached to social roles. We all fill many different social roles in life. States, for example, have different social roles in domestic and international politics. These different roles have different norms. A democratic government is supposed to observe human right domestically and protect the lives of its citizens. The same government is allowed to kill enemy soldiers during wartime. What conduct is appropriate changes with the role of the government. The connection between norms and social roles means that what actors are supposed to do can vary with the role it has in a situation.

Law specifies norms in detail. An example from domestic law may help with this distinction. Almost all human societies have norms against killing other people. But the law on murder differs from that general principle. Laws on homicide recognize a right of self-defense, that killing someone else may be justified if they are attacking you. The law also distinguished different types of homicide based on the circumstances. In U.S. law, first degree murder, when someone kills someone else with forethought and malice, is worse than negligent homicide, when someone dies because the accused was careless in a dangerous situation. The law specifies the penalty associated with the different circumstances of the killing, even if the application of the law to a case may be difficult. This detail is why the statements of laws are often long and complicated. Legal language exists for lawyers to state precisely what they mean to one another, even if that language is baffling to those without legal training.

International law is the codification of norms into formal treaties that define appropriate behavior and the consequences of inappropriate behavior as fully as possible. The difference between the norms of the trade system and WTO law are an example. The trade system has a number of norms. Non-discrimination is one, reduction of trade barriers is another. The treaties that created the WTO specify in detail what these principles mean in practice. What policies constitute illegal barriers to trade? The treaties seek to explain the principles by which states could judge which policies are acceptable and which unacceptable. The treaties also provide mechanisms to resolves disputes between members using those principles. Not all norms get turned into law. There is no clear international law on national self-determination, for example, no rules to specify which groups constitute nationalities and then hold the right to determine which state should govern them. Law also helps reconcile norms that contradict one another in practice, another way which actors holding the same norms might disagree about what behavior they direct in a given situation.

How Could International Law Shape International Politics?

International law lacks a central authority for its administration and enforcement. In domestic politics, the government creates institutions, such as courts and the police, for these purposes. But there is not a world government for international law. This absence does not mean that international law is worthless or empty. International law matters to the extent that actors can enforce it on one another. It could be that states follow international law because they agree with its principles and seek to comply with its prescriptions. Many areas of international law are self-enforcing in this sense. Their provisions help actors coordinate their actions. Some international standards work this way. The Vienna Convention provides rules for the negotiation of treaties and diplomatic practices. These rules capture the process of negotiation and ratification which had been developed over the centuries of international diplomacy. They are flexible enough that states can do what they like within the rules, giving states little reason to break them.

Reciprocity is another common form of enforcement of international law we have already discussed in general and in specific areas like trade. More generally, states follow international law because breaking it has consequences. "Rogue" states acquired that status because they broke international law frequently or flagrantly. After the Iranian Revolution in 1979, a mob of Iranian students seized the U.S. Embassy in Tehran in protest that the U.S. allowed the ex-Shah to enter the U.S. for medical treatment. The government of Ayatollah Khomeini backed up the seizure of the embassy. The embassy staff was held as hostages for 444 days before being released. This violation of diplomatic immunity–the law that embassies are sovereign territory of the nation being represented and the legal immunity of diplomats–led to a breakdown in relations between the U.S. and Iran that persists to this day. The U.S. no longer has an embassy in Teheran, and all embassy business, such as the issuing of visas to Iranians, is conducted through the good auspices of the Swiss.

States also follow international law because they support its aims. The treaties that embody international law exist because states negotiated them to realize the aims of those treaties. A broad consensus among states about the norms specified in a treaty is necessary before negotiation. Once a treaty has been negotiated, states can choose to accept it through ratification. Different states use various procedures for ratifying treaties. Some have their government declare that they have ratified, some require their legislature pass a law, and the United States requires that two-thirds of the Senate vote to ratify. Generally, states that do not ratify a treaty are not bound by it. Further, states can file reservations when they ratify a treaty. These statements identity parts of the treaty which the state does not accept. These procedures ensure that only states that accept a law are bound by it.

The procedure of ratification does not mean that law only obligates states to do what they would do without a treaty. International law helps states realize aims they might not in absence of a treaty. It clarifies their expectations of one another and makes it easier for them to anticipate how one another will act. Both of these can aid cooperation among states.

The Laws of War

The laws of war seek to limit the violence of war. They are an example of how international law codifies norms. Many societies had conventions about what was allowable and what not during wartime, but these limits were typically not written down in treaties. The modern history of the laws of war traces to the middle of the 19th century. Henry Dunant was appalled by the suffering of the casualties at the battle of Solferino during the War of Italian Unification in 1859. When he returned to Geneva, he convened meetings that led to the establishment of the Red Cross to relieve the suffering of those affected by war. During the American Civil War, President Lincoln commissioned Francis Lieber, a law professor at Columbia University, to draw up rules for the proper treatment of prisoners of war. Others took up the concern with limiting violence during war. The Hague Conventions of 1899 and 1907 provided rules that cover most aspects of the laws of war, including banning the dropping of bombs from observation balloons. Some of these rules were followed during World War I, others were broken, sometimes in spirit even if the offending party could claim it followed the letter of the law. The interwar period saw a burst of negotiations to revise the laws in new treaties. The Geneva Protocol of 1925 forbid the use of chemical weapons. The 1929 Geneva Convention strengthened rules to protect prisoners of war. Other attempts, such as limits on the use of submarines and bombing from airplanes, failed to reach agreement on a treaty. Again, some of the rules were observed during World War II while others failed dramatically. As mentioned earlier, the aftermath of World War led to another round of treaty negotiation to revise and improve the laws of war, culminating in the Geneva Conventions of 1949. Treaties in the last twenty years have strengthened limits on the production of chemical weapons and the use of land mines.

The laws of war cover many different issues in limiting violence. Prisoners of war (POWs) may be held until the end of the war in detention camps under humane conditions. The treaties on POWs also say who is entitled to POW status, how they signal their desire to surrender, and state the obligation to take prisoners. Soldiers have rights and responsibilities under these treaties, such as the famous requirement that captured soldiers are only obligated to tell their captors their name, rank, and serial number. They do this so the captor nation can report that the soldier in question is now a POW to his home nation. Chemical weapons cover lethal gases that have been used on the battlefield. During World War I, the Germans first used chlorine gas at the Second Battle of Ypres in 1915. After then, most of the countries at war used a variety of chemicals to kill or incapacitate enemy soldiers. These chemicals were either released on the battlefield or delivered in artillery shells. Treaties attempt to stop the use and production of chemical weapons. Biological weapons, the use of germs to infect soldiers of the other side, have also been banned. Other treaties limit the conduct of war at sea. Ships are not allowed to attack civilian shipping without warning in order to give the crew time to evacuate the ship before it is sunk. Warships are obligated to pick up shipwrecked enemy sailors even during battle. Submarines of many nations violated both of these provisions during the world wars. Treatment of civilians is a major issue. They are not supposed to be targets during wartime. Irregular resistance to military occupation complicates the protection of civilians because the occupying army has the right to defend itself against attack. But who do you attack when the enemy does not wear uniforms and blends into the civilian population? The 1949 Geneva Convention creates detailed rules regulating military occupation that say how a military occupation should be carried out to protect the rights of the civilian population. This brief survey does not cover the full range of issues in the laws of war but does provide you with an idea of the type and range of protections and responsibilities in those laws.

States comply with the laws of war because they have consequences. The laws of war matter when the parties are already at war with one another. Any threat to go to war over a violation is meaningless. But they can respond reciprocally to violations by each other. Further, violations of the laws of war have other consequences. For example, U.S. Army officers cite three different reasons why they try to follow the prescription for the proper treatment of prisoners in the Geneva Convention. First, they do not want to provide an excuse for the enemy to mistreat U.S. soldiers they take prisoner. Second, they want to encourage enemy soldiers to surrender to make their job on the battlefield easier. Third, they believe that the U.S. Army should follow the rules, that it is the right thing to do. When the Bush Administration allowed mistreatment of detainees held in military prisons in Iraq and Afghanistan, others reacted strongly when the news broke. Many U.S. citizens were appalled by what was done in their name. Other countries condemned what had been done. The enemies of the U.S. used these incidents to justify their own outrages. There were consequences for these acts.

The laws of war pose an additional problem for compliance. States could enforce some international law through the threat of war. Respect for the territory of other states can be enforced militarily, for example. But the states in question are already at war with one another when the laws of war are invoked. They have no recourse to a stronger response. Instead, they must rely on the willingness of one another to abide by the rules or their reciprocal responses to violations.

The laws of war reflect tension between two norms. The first is the protection of people and property during wartime. States negotiated the laws of war in an effort to reduce the destruction of war. Noncombatants are protected from attack. Non-military targets are not supposed to be damaged. The rules also try to create ways to distinguish protected places and people from combatants. Hospitals and medical personnel display the red cross to identify themselves as protected. Soldiers are supposed to wear a uniform or a distinctive badge and carry their arms openly to identify themselves to the enemy. After all, soldiers are allowed to kill enemy soldiers without warning on the battlefield. The second norm underlying the laws of war is against perfidy. Perfidy uses the protections of the laws of war to gain an unfair advantage. During the Gulf War in 1991, Iraq's air force was bombed on the ground to destroy the planes. To protect them, Iraq moved the planes next to archeological sites in the country. The coalition air forces were unwilling to attack these planes out of the fear that a bomb might miss and harm the protected site. Other forms of perfidy include wearing enemy uniforms to fool them and using protected sites as firing positions. The two norms of protection and perfidy are in tension. Acts of perfidy undermine the protections of the law as they may induce the other side to violate those protections.

Record of the Laws of War

The record of the laws of war during the 20th century is mixed. During World War II, some treaties were generally respected, such as the ban on the use of chemical weapons. Italy used poison gas during its invasion and conquest of Ethiopia in 1935, and Japan used chemical weapons against China early in their long war that began in 1937. But the other major powers did not, even though all of them produced and stockpiled significant amounts of poisonous gases. Treatment of prisoners of war varied greatly. Great Britain, the Commonwealth countries, and the United States treated prisoners well once they reached collection points behind the lines and then the camps where they were held for the remainder of the war. Nazi Germany generally reciprocated, treating U.S. and those who fought in the British army acceptably. On the other hand, Nazi Germany treated Soviet soldiers it took prisoner terribly. Camps did not provide basic shelter or sanitation in some cases, and the food was inadequate to maintain health, particularly during the early months of the Nazi invasion of the Soviet Union. Nazi treatment of Soviet prisoners improved in 1942, but only because the Nazi leadership realized that Soviet PoWs could then be used as slave labor. Japan treated U.S. and Commonwealth soldiers it took prisoner poorly. Many died from the brutal conditions and poor diet; others were executed as punishments. In the latter two cases, the conventions also broke down on the battlefield. Soviet soldiers learned that surrendering to the Nazis gave them little chance of surviving the war, so they fought to the death often and rarely took prisoners themselves. Once the Soviet Union began capturing large number of German soldiers, they were marched off to prison camps comparable to the Gulag prison camps used for political prisoners. Conduct on the battlefield also broke down during the War in the Pacific. Japanese soldiers used ruses which were perfidy, such as wounded Japanese soldiers attacking U.S. medical personnel trying to aid them. This led U.S. soldiers and marines to shoot or bayonet every Japanese body when occupying a battlefield. Better to make sure they were dead. The U.S. captured very few Japanese soldiers during World War II, although their treatment once in a prison camp was generally good. There was no treaty regulating aerial bombing despite efforts to negotiate one during the 1930s. The U.S. and Britain conducted campaigns of aerial bombing against German and Japanese cities which killed hundreds of thousands of civilians in both countries. These bombings were justified as attacking arms factories and transportation networks. But high-altitude bombing was very inaccurate in those days; bombers could consistently hit large cities but not specific buildings within those cities.

Other wars show this mixed pattern of compliance with the laws of war. Neither Iraq nor Iran observed the existing treaty law during their eight-year war in the 1980s. Both used chemical weapons on other (although Iraq did so more often), both fired ballistic missiles into the others' cities, and both attacked oil tankers and installations in the Persian Gulf to try and cut off the other's oil revenue. The U.S. generally treated prisoners properly during the Korean and Vietnam Wars, while conducting aerial bombing campaigns in both wars. North Vietnam, North Korea, and China did not treat U.S. soldiers taken prisoner well. There are many other examples of both violations of and compliance with the laws of war during the 20th century. These days the belief that states and their militaries should follow such rules is widely accepted. However, what states have done in the past does not fully meet these expectations of restraint during wartime.

How Could the Laws of War Work?

States might be able to enforce the laws of war if they were willing to respond in kind, that is, use reciprocity for enforcement. States do tend to meet violations with violations of their own. The cases where some treaties are broken occur on issues where the nation suffering the violations cannot respond in kind. Ethiopia and China had no chemical weapons and no ability to produce them. Italy and Japan could use gas against them without fear of retaliation. The U.S. has never suffered from aerial bombardment of its homeland, while engaging in such campaigns in almost every war it fought during the 20th century. Retaliation comes in kind, and in these cases, the other side could not retaliate in the same way as these violations.

Retaliation can also occur on the battlefield between the soldiers of the two sides. Soldiers on the battlefield hear rumors of mistreatment by the enemy. They may respond in kind for revenge or to protect themselves. U.S. soldiers and marines learned that Japanese soldiers often practiced perfidy, such as playing dead, or did not observe protections for medical personnel. In response, U.S. personnel did not take prisoners, and some U.S. army doctors armed themselves, which is a violation of their protected status. Violations by one side lead to retaliation by the other even if the state suffering the violations does not want to retaliate. The U.S. found that Japanese prisoners were valuable sources of military intelligence and tried to encourage the taking of prisoners. These prisoners were treated well once they reached collection points and camps behind U.S. lines. But few Japanese were taken prisoner. Retaliation can arise from the soldiers of an army even when their leaders would like to follow the rules.

The threat of retaliation deters initial violations only when both sides can anticipate that one another will respond to violations in kind. Treaty ratification helps both sides know that one another accepts the treaty and would like to follow it if possible. Joint ratification–when both sides have ratified the relevant treaty–creates a shared expectation of good conduct during war. When one side has not ratified the relevant treaty, it signals that it is unlikely to follow the rules. Japan had neither signed nor ratified the 1929 Geneva Convention on PoWs before World War II. After Pearl Harbor, its treatment of PoWs was bad as soon as they took prisoners. The Soviet Union had not ratified the PoW Convention either. Nazi Germany used that lack of ratification as a justification of their own policy of killing Commissars–Soviet political officers attached to military units–outright and failing to provide proper camps for regular soldiers they took prisoner. Some issues lack treaties which have been ratified by the states at war. Treaties limiting aerial bombing were negotiated during the 1930s, but no state signed or ratified them. The lack of law on aerial bombing allowed states to create their own rules for what types of bombing were acceptable during war. Ratification is how states signal that they intend to abide by a treaty.

In some cases, states will try to observe the limits imposed by a treaty even when the other side has not accepted that standard through ratification. Democracies are more likely to act with such unilateral restraint. They take their legal obligations more seriously than autocracies do. Democracies are law-bound states in the sense that their governments hold authority over their citizens through law and their leaders are not above the law. Autocrats use law as a tool to control their citizens and stop threats to their leadership, to the extent that they observe law. The unilateral restraint of democracies sometimes encourages violations by the other side by removing the threat of retaliation. Democracies sometimes observe treaties they have ratified because they are legal commitments. Autocracies, on the other hand, only fear the threat of retaliation.

Training of soldiers also matter for compliance with the laws of war. Violations and retaliation often happens on the battlefield beyond the command of a country's military and political leaders. The laws of war create rights and responsibilities for individual soldiers in addition to those they create for states. Militaries train their soldiers on these issues before sending them into combat. Some of this training focuses on the question of how to take prisoners and what a soldier's rights are when taken prisoner. The training on the laws of war is cursory in some armies. This can have unexpected consequences. Japan did not instruct its soldiers during World War II in their rights as PoWs. Instead, it taught its soldiers to never surrender and that those who did would suffer a fate worse than death; they would no longer exist in the eyes of Japan and their families. This is a major reason why few Japanese soldiers surrendered willingly on the battlefield. It also meant that those soldiers taken prisoner did not know that they had the right not to speak to their captor, that they only needed to give their name, rank, and serial numbers. Their willingness to talk to their captors made them valuable sources of military intelligence to the U.S. Training for ordinary soldiers is an important part of how the laws of war work on the battlefield.

Noise–difficulty in determining whether the other side is deliberately breaking the rules–complicates the enforcement of the laws of war. Compliance on some issues occurs behind enemy lines, making it difficult for one side to observe the conduct of the other. PoWs camps lie in enemy territory, for example. The captor state can censor mail from PoWs which describes improper treatment in camps. The International Committee of the Red Cross (ICRC), based in Geneva, plays an important role in policing camps. They inspect camps and report violations to the captor nation, but not the nation of the soldiers held prisoner. States at war would not give them access if their reports were public. Their power to inspect camps helps solve the noise problem because countries engaged in extensive violations do not give the ICRC access to their camps. Japan denied the ICRC the right to inspect its PoW camps during World War II, which the U.S. took as the first clear evidence that treatment of their men held prisoner did not meet the standards of the 1929 Geneva Convention. Soldiers wear uniforms to aid the other side in distinguishing them from civilians. Then the enemy can try to avoid targeting civilians. Often civilians are killed in combat, but the problem becomes worse when one side cannot tell who are civilians and who are enemy combatants.

The agency problem–the ability of a country to control its own soldiers–also creates noise. The violations you see on the battlefield may be deliberate state policy or they may result from undisciplined soldiers. Even the best disciplined armies commit some crimes on the battlefield. That is one reason why armies have systems of military justice, to discipline their own soldiers who commit crimes. Compliance with the laws of war is better on issues where the agency problem is less. The ban on the use of chemical weapons has been rarely broken in part because the use of chemical weapons is clearly a policy decision. There is no chance that soldiers can use chemical weapons acting on their own. The use of chemical weapons becomes public eventually, with consequences for the state using them. There was widespread revulsion when Italy used poison gas during its conquest of Ethiopia in 1935. Iran eventually retaliated against Iraq's extensive use of chemical weapons during their war with its own use. On other issues, such as treatment of civilians, it is harder to tell if the other side is deliberately violating the rules. That makes it hard to know whether to retaliate.

Which Standard?

The laws of war are universal and general. They are meant to hold for all wars between states, all states are supposed to ratify the treaties and follow them, and the standard does not differ across wars. States disagree about which standard should hold. They may have different ideas of how violence should be limited during wartime. Germany entered World War I believing that civilians in an occupied country had to follow the occupying military authorities no matter what. Other countries thought that civilians under occupation have the right to resist occupation. After the experience of the two World Wars, the 1949 Geneva Conventions limited how armies could treat civilians under their control through military occupation. A single standard allows states to screen one another through ratification. Those states that do not ratify the treaty do not accept that treaty and are unlikely to follow it during wartime. Their failure to ratify informs other states of their intention not to abide by the treaty. If states negotiated different standards of conduct for a war once it broke out, they would lose this ability to screen their opponents before the war began. A universal standard set before the outbreak of war could be enforceable even if one state preferred a different standard. The threat of retaliation might be great enough for it to follow the rules. In these two ways, a universal standard is better than ad hoc deals for the limitation of violence during war.

Those standards, however, may be arbitrary rather than being the standard generally viewed as the best. The laws of war arose from a historical process of negotiations from existing ideas about what acts were atrocities during war. They did not start with a blank slate and seek to find the best standard. Instead, the original rules were adopted and then revised when problems arose. One example is how much food must a captor nation provide the PoWs it holds. Great

Britain and its allies imposed a blockade on Germany that reduced food supplies. Many German civilians died during the war from the low diet enforced through rationing and high prices. Germany limited the PoWs it held to a similar diet as its civilians received which led to many deaths, which hoarding scarce food like meat for its own soldiers at the front. This standard was changed in the 1929 Geneva Convention to require captor nations to feed PoWs as well as their own soldiers. This, too, was founded to be inadequate when U.S. and Commonwealth soldiers could not survive on the same diet as Japanese soldiers. The 1949 Geneva Convention required captor nations to feed PoWs at a level that would maintain their health. The current status of the laws of war reflects the concerns of states historically and NGOs more recently.

Human Rights Law

International law on human rights establishes general principles for how states should treat their citizens. There are tens of these treaties on issues from fundamental human rights to guarantees of rights to education for women. Not all governments respect all those rights. Some states have not ratified all the treaties. The United States has often been reluctant to ratify even some of the core treaties. The Convention on the Prevention and Punishment of the Crime of Genocide was negotiated in 1948 and entered into force in 1951 when 20 states had ratified it. The U.S. did not ratify the Genocide Convention until 1986. Other governments violate their citizens' human rights even though they have ratified the relevant treaties.

Universal human rights conflict with the norms of state sovereignty. Some states believe that their internal autonomy trumps claims of universal rights which limit how they conduct their internal affairs. China and other Asian states like Singapore argue that social order is also an important value which often conflicts with human rights. These states believe that rules to preserve order domestically are worth some infringements of individual rights. Concepts of where sovereignty of the state resides also pose some problems for universal concepts of human rights. Human rights groups criticize the U.S. for its use of the death penalty as a criminal punishment. The sovereign power of the U.S. government resides in the American people, who generally support the use of the death penalty for certain cases. Do the universal standards of human rights law trump the power of the American people to rule themselves through their democratic institutions? The assertion of universal human rights means that sovereign states are limited in what they can do, no matter the source of their sovereign power.

States facing civil war have often killed substantial numbers of their own civilians who they suspected of supporting the rebels. They also often punish rebels they capture as criminals rather than giving them rights as PoWs. Rebel groups in turn often argue that they are at war, and so bound by the laws of war. This parallel asserts legal equality between rebel groups and their government, an equality which the government rarely grants. Some rebel groups then attempt to fight within the laws of war, while others have committed some of the worst atrocities of recent times. Civil war often leads to major violations of human rights by both government forces and rebel fighters. Terrorism is the most extreme version of political violence unbound by legal restraint.

The Enforcement of Human Rights Law

The major human rights treaties contain no provisions for their enforcement. The Universal Declaration of Human Rights, for example, asserts what the fundamental human rights are in 30 articles. These treaties aspire to what human rights should be, not how they can be realized.

Human rights law could be enforced in several ways outside the treaties. These mechanisms would have to be employed on their own as they are not in the treaties themselves. Nations which accept and abide by human rights law could agree to isolate those states that do not from the community of states. This form of enforcement is called *"in-group" versus "out-group"*. Those inside the group of states which follow law do not deal with those outside the law. The toughest form of enforcement would be trade restrictions with states in the out-group. As the most economically developed states also follow human rights law, limiting trade would cut states that do not out of much of the global economy. A more common form of such enforcement is public criticism from the "in-group". They point out when other states fail to respect the human rights of their citizens and call on them to do so. States that favor human rights could also recognize those citizens in other countries who attempt to call their government to account for its failure to observe human rights. The award of the Nobel Peace Prize is the most public version of such recognition, although it is not awarded by a government. There are limits to "in-group" versus "out-group" enforcement as well. States may be unwilling to cut their economic or political ties with states that do not protect human rights of their citizens. Other countries that do not fully accept human rights may step in and increase trade when the states who observe human rights restrict it with a country. Sudan has come under pressure for the killings of civilians in Darfur. China has increased its trade steadily as Western governments have increased their criticism of Sudan. Quiet diplomacy may be more effective than public pressure in getting a government to change its policies. South Korea and Taiwan were both autocracies that violated the human rights of their citizens for decades leading into the 1980s. Many in the United States publicly criticized the policies of these U.S. allies for their failures to observe human rights. The Reagan Administration used private diplomacy rather that public condemnation to convince both governments to open up their systems to democratic competition and begin protecting human rights. Both countries are now stable and vibrant democracies.

Others have argued for military intervention in the worst cases of human rights abuses. If the government in question will not stop the killing, then others have the obligation to do so, according to this view. The UN has intervened with military troops in many conflicts at many levels of presence. In some cases, it just sends lightly-armed peacekeepers, while in others it sends substantial military forces that engage in combat with local armed groups. The record of these UN interventions and other humanitarian military interventions is mixed. The UN mission to Rwanda did little to stop the genocide there, in part because they were vastly outnumbered by the killers. In other cases, like East Timor, peacekeepers have reduced violence and killings. Oddly, the most successful humanitarian military intervention may be the most notorious, Somalia. The "Black Hawk Down" battle led to the withdrawal of U.S. troops from the peacekeeping mission, followed by the remaining UN peacekeepers in 1995. The losses in Somalia was one reason why the Clinton Administration was reluctant to send more U.S. troops to Rwanda as the conflict built and then genocide began. The Somalia mission is often seen as a failure, but it probably saved the lives of hundreds of thousands of Somalis by ensuring the distribution of food aid during the winter of 1992-1993 before the UN peacekeepers began fighting the local armed groups.

The difficulties of enforcing human rights has led to a movement to create international courts to do so. The Nuremberg and Tokyo war crimes trials after World War II were the first example of such international trials. The International Tribunals formed in response to the atrocities in the former Yugoslav republics have tried accused criminals from all sides of these wars. The ICC seeks to establish a regular international court. All of these courts move toward the creation of international responsibility and enforcement for war crimes and crimes against humanity. Effective international punishment could deter national leaders from committing crimes. The Rome Statute creating the ICC also seeks to encourage member states to strengthen their own domestic enforcement of human rights and law of war. The ICC defers to domestic courts if they agree to prosecute suspects. Countries may be reluctant to do so because prominent military or political leaders are often suspects. The tribunal for former Yugoslavia has been unpopular among Serbs because many of them believe that the tribunal singles out Serbs over the other ethnic groups for prosecution. The ICC raises other issues as well. The United States has not ratified the Rome Statute and so is not a member of the court. The concern is that the ICC will seek to try U.S. military and civilian leaders when crimes are committed when they use force internationally. The military dominance of the U.S. means that its forces are critical to many peacekeeping operations and operate in many countries around the world, often with the forces of other governments. The Bush Administration signed many bilateral agreements with other countries, where the other countries pledged not to send U.S. personnel accused of crimes to the ICC for trial.

The creation of an international court raises the question of to whom is the court is responsible. The UN Security Council created the tribunals for the former Yugoslavia and Rwanda, and those courts are ultimately responsible to the Council. Prosecutions for crimes against humanity and war crimes are political because they cast the defendants as criminals. The Nuremberg and Tokyo trials were public demonstrations that the Nazi and Japanese leaders were criminals, that they had operated outside the lines of acceptable conduct for national leaders.

U.S. leaders are concerned that they might be subject to politically motivated prosecutions if the ICC answers to no outside authority. U.S. negotiators sought to have the UN Security Council to authorize all prosecutions. The U.S. could use its veto then to block an individual prosecution, but this provision was not included in the Rome Statute. As the ICC tries its initial cases, the development of the court will be closely watched.

These developments overlook the most important form of enforcement, the domestic politics of ratifying countries. Human rights law sets standards that states then aspire to uphold. States choose which standards they wish to observe. New democracies use human rights treaties to determine what rights they will seek to protect. Set standards solve the problem of negotiating what human rights should be for states negotiating a constitution for their new democracy. Existing democracies use reservations to limit the applicability of treaties in their country. Democracies are more likely to comply with human rights treaties after they ratify them compared to autocracies. Autocracies sometimes ratify human rights treaties, which they then ignore within their countries. These ratifications are sometimes cynical attempts to appease international public opinion. In other cases, they qualify their ratification with reservations that mean they are not obligated to protect any rights. Human rights law is a product of democracy, and it is no surprise that democracies are more likely to follow it than autocracies.

Human rights law has also contributed to the creation and growth of NGOs dedicated to the protection of human rights. Some of these NGOs are transnational, such as Human Rights Watch and Amnesty International, while others are based in one country and address their own government. Dissident groups grew in Eastern Europe after the Helsinki Accords of 1975. This agreement sought to improve relations between the Communist eastern bloc and the western bloc led by the U.S. Existing borders were guaranteed, the west accepts the sovereignty of the Communist states, and the east accepted respect for human rights. This public act served as a rallying point in Communist countries to form groups dedicated to monitoring whether those governments lived up to their obligations under the Accords. These groups lacked the power to compel Communist governments to respect human rights, but they formed the core of the movements that led to the downfall of Communism at the end of the Cold War. The transnational NGOs publish reports on human rights violations around the world. The U.S. State Department also publishes annual reports on human rights in other countries. These reports help concerned parties monitor compliance with human rights. Human rights law serves as the rallying point to create the institutions needed to help monitor compliance with this law.

Chapter Summary

Norms play important roles in world politics. Ideas of acceptable conduct shape state action, although they are not always in full compliance with such standards. Definitions of acceptable conduct in international law allow states to determine when others have violated those standards. Law and norms help states anticipate one another's actions and form proper responses to those actions. Legalization of world politics has made state action more ordered and predictable. States often follow international law because they negotiated those treaties to address issues of common concern. Reciprocity can be an effective tool for the enforcement of international law in some cases.

There are important limits on what can be accomplished through international norms and laws. States violate norms and do not always follow international law. Sometimes, they disagree about how international law should be applied to specific cases. The laws of war have limited some forms of violence during war, yet atrocities still happen during wartime. The effects of human rights law are less than the sweep of the values it advances. International law is an important but fragile tool in world politics.

Review Questions

1. Define an international norm. How does international law differ from a norm on the same topic; in what two ways does a law elaborate a norm?

2. Give examples of both success and failures of the laws of war in the 20th century.

3. Provide three reasons why a treaty on the laws of war might be more effective than a norm to limit the destruction and violence of war in preventing atrocities.

4. How might human rights law assist in the spread of human rights over time?

Chapter 29
Sovereignty:
Why a System of Sovereign States?

We live in a world dominated by sovereign states. Almost every habited place on Earth is part of a sovereign state. The state system regulates international relations. States are legal equals where none has the authority to command others. States possess internal and external autonomy. Internal autonomy is the power of a state to control affairs within its territory through its monopoly on the legitimate use of force. External autonomy is the power each state has to set its relations with other states. States are territorial. Their control is marked out and limited by their borders, which specify what territory the state control and where that control ends. These claims are not to say that sovereignty is absolute or that states do as they wish without regard to internal and external pressures. Norms and standards of behavior matter even when they are violated some of the time.

The world does not have to be organized through sovereignty. There have been other systems for how polities–political units like states–are defined and how they relate to one another. The sovereign state system began with the advent of modern states in Europe around about 1500. Diplomacy as an institution of how state representatives act and how their host states treat them arose in northern Italy at this time. The modern state defined by borders and controlling the legitimate use of force within those borders began with the centralization of England, France, and Spain. Before this time, the nature of political units was different as was the conventions they held for their relations and legitimate powers. Areas outside Europe retained older ways for polities to define themselves and relate to one another. The first question this chapter answers is why the sovereign state system prevailed over the alternatives. Why has the state system expanded out of Europe to encompass and structure all of world politics?

Sovereignty has not been a static concept. It has changed over time. The concerns of Europe in the 1500s and 1600s centered on religion, control of territory, and the consolidation of control where a King claimed possession. Now the state focuses on the economic welfare of its citizens, their rights as a nation, and the protection of their human rights (subject to disagreement about what those rights are). These changes have occurred over centuries and coincide with changes in the domestic institutions for the governance of the state. The second question this chapter answers is how the concept of sovereignty has changed and why, even as it has expanded to cover the world.

The answers to these two questions require understanding the historical process that led to the dominance and evolution of sovereignty. They require understanding what political factors shape the evolution of international conventions. They also require understanding the range of alternatives to sovereignty.

Systems Across History

The sovereign state system is not the only way that relations across polities have been organized in history. Before 1500 and often afterwards, empires were a primary form of how polities related to one another. Inequality among units is the defining property of empires in comparison to the sovereign state system. The center of the empire, known as the metropole, had the military power to dominate the outlying areas, known as the periphery. The metropole also holds the authority to control the periphery even if it chooses to allow local rulers to run portions of it. For example, Rome and its military power dominated the Roman Empire. Some portions of the empire were run as provinces under the rule of a Roman governor, while others were run by local rulers. These local rulers retain control of some of their internal affairs, including taxation and the grand lifestyle maintained by ruler compared to their subjects. These local rulers had no control over their foreign policy. They could not go to war on their own nor refuse to join if Rome requested their assistance. Such arrangements are not unique to Rome; the British Empire ruled portions of India through the Princely States. Rulers, commonly princes using the appropriate Indian title, hence the name, were the local authority within these states, but they could not act against what the British wanted. This imperial arrangement saves the metropole the trouble of running these territories while retaining control over them. The local ruler benefits by having the imperial power protect his position while retaining some control over his own territory. Empires often have ill-defined borders. Their frontiers are often "borderlands" where they use military power to limit threats from outside without controlling those areas. China historically faces this situation with the nomads in the Mongolian desert and steppes to their north. China could launch military expeditions against the nomads in response to raids, but it could never control them. The exact line of control was rarely clear. The Great Wall of China was built in the 1400s in part to create a clear line between the Chinese empire and the nomad beyond in addition to keeping the nomads out.

The feudal system of Medieval Europe had overlapping sources of authority. Nobles who controlled territories owed allegiance to their overlord, commonly a king. They had soldiers of their own personal retinue, and the king could call on the nobles to provide him with military aid for a set period. The nobles, however, often fought one another and sometimes even against their own king. The king then lacked a monopoly on the legitimate use of force within his realm. "Realm" rather than "territory" is the proper term because the king did not control or possess all the lands under his rule. The nobles did. Individuals could hold multiple titles and positions, producing conflicts in authority and loyalty. The King of England was both a rival of the King of France and one of his vassals, as he was also either the Duke of Normandy or of Aquitaine, regions of France. Kings eventually moved away from the feudal system and began hiring professional soldiers to raise an army. This was expensive, but the troops were more reliable than feudal levies. Kings and the Pope also competed for authority at the highest level. The

Pope claimed authority over all of Christianity as the vicar of Christ. The Holy Roman Emperor and kings resisted the authority of the Pope even to rule the Church within their realms. Because churches generated wealth, control of the bishops and archbishops who led the Church within areas was important for kings as well as the Pope. They fought over these appointments with both sides prevailing at different times. The Church slowly gained power over time as Popes centralized authority in the Church in their own hands. Church law was also supposed to limit when and how wars could be fought, although little restricted the military classes in their pursuit of glory and gain through arms. In contrast to the sovereign state system, rulers in medieval Europe possessed neither internal nor external autonomy.

Even during the period of the sovereign state system, there have been exceptions to sovereignty. Protectorates–arrangements where a powerful country protects a weaker one in exchange for control over some of its policies–were one way that modern empires extended their control across the globe. The European empires established protectorates with local leaders to control trade with those territories. The mandate system established by the League of Nations after World War I was a protectorate under other names. The colonial empires of the states that lost the war, Germany and the Ottoman Empires, were broken up. Mandates–control leading to the establishment of an independent state–were created in Middle East and some parts of Africa and Oceania. The states of the modern Middle East were mandates broken out of the Ottoman Empire. The local ruler in a protectorate lacks internal and external autonomy. The protecting power controls its foreign policy and has the right to intervene domestically in its affairs. Suzerainty is another form of such control. The Sultan of the Ottoman Empire was the suzerain of Christian territories which he controlled in Europe. These territories had local leaders who had some local authority but owed tribute to the Sultan. Christian boys who were trained to become Janissaries–crack troops in the Sultan's army–were one form of tribute in addition to money. Protectorates in all their different forms have been the prominent exception to state sovereignty.

Challenges to Sovereignty Now

State sovereignty faces several challenges now. There are non-state polities that act like states. Taiwan meets three of the four parts of the definition of a state, lacking recognition from other states. The Palestinian Authority does not control a defined territory and so does not have borders. Al Qaeda claims that it uses force legitimately even though it is not a state. As in earlier times, these exceptions to sovereignty do not render it null as a set of norms. They do pose challenges for the concept of sovereignty.

Some worry whether globalization leads to "the end of sovereignty." Increasing economic interdependence means that governments are losing control of their domestic economies. The trilemma limits the choices of national leaders, so they cannot have capital openness, a fixed exchange rate, and an effective monetary policy at the same time. National leaders also have to coordinate their economic policies with their trading partners, limiting their ability to pursue policies contrary to other countries. Security policies have to be multinational to succeed. The free movement of people erodes the importance of national borders and loyalties. Multinational corporations operate in many countries at once, producing products on one continent to sell on another. Their executives often work in different countries during their careers, moving from one to another every few years. This constant movement between countries breaks down their loyalty to the home country in favor of their loyalty to their company. The growth of transnational NGOs aids the idea of a "global citizen," who places the concerns of the world above those of his or her nation. Are nation-states becoming irrelevant historical oddities?

The European Union poses another challenge to the sovereign state system. It acts like a state in many ways. It negotiates international agreements with its trading partners. It has the authority to command its member states to change national policies that conflict with its directives. It has the organs of a government, concentrated primarily in Brussels, but also in other cities in western Europe. The EU is a supranational government. It, however, is not yet a "United States of Europe". Member governments still play the key roles in the EU, meaning that its decisions resemble negotiations among the member states rather than acts of a government with an independent base of power. Some member states, notably Great Britain, remain outside key parts of the EU project, such as the common currency of the Euro. The EU has also contributed to the breakdown of European states towards smaller political units. The EU provides economic benefits to poorer regions within member states. It sends subsidies, for example, to southern Italy but not northern Italy. Political movements for regional separatism have grown up in many member states, including Italy, Spain, and Belgium. Some people feel greater attachment to their region with a common language than they do to their national government or the EU. The EU then produces these twin forces of centralization and dissolution at the same time.

These developments challenge sovereignty. None of them means that the sovereign state system is disappearing in favor of some alternative way of arranging political power and relations among polities. Sovereignty has changed in the past without losing its essential character.

Change in Sovereignty Over Time

The sovereign state system emerged out of a mixture of different types of political units in early modern Europe. There were the nascent states forming as medieval kingdoms consolidated their power within their realms. England was the most consolidated of these nascent states. Spain was formed out of the union of Aragon and Castile. The French kings began the long and slow process of eliminating rival sources of power within their wide and diverse country. These nascent states claimed large areas but lacked close control over those areas and the resources produced by them. Their kings commonly relied on the revenues from their own personal holdings as well as taxes on the movement of goods within their realm for their court revenue. The kings answered to a nobility which also claimed personal domains and often had their own private military retinues. The city-states of northern Italy–Venice, Genoa, Milan, and Florence to name a few–were the second form of political unit. They were smaller in area than the nascent states but commanded great wealth in part through their dominance of trade entering Europe from Asia. Some of the city-states were republics which selected leaders who ruled for a limited duration. Others were controlled by families which inherited the ruler's position. Political intrigue was common in the city-states no matter how they were governed. There were also city-states scattered around northern Europe. They were centers of trade in a wide range of goods. The Holy Roman Emperor ruled Germany and northern Italy including the city-states, but his position carried less authority than that of the kings of the nascent states. Additionally, the Emperor was elected by a small set of German princes rather than inheriting the position. The Hanseatic League–a group of cities involved in trade in norther Europe–was the third different form of government in early modern Europe. Its member cities stretched across the North Sea and the Baltic Sea, connecting trade from Britain to what is now Russia. The League had formal meetings of representatives from its members who set common commercial policies to aid the movement of trade. This assembly also conducted foreign policy in that it could declare war on outside powers and raise military forces from its members. Eventually, the nascent states prevailed over the city-states and the city-league as forms of political organization.

[Map of the Hanseatic League: http://www.klitzfamily.com/files/hanseatic_league.jpg]

The concept of sovereignty is commonly dated to the Peace of Westphalia in 1648. The pair of treaties that formed the peace ended the Thirty Years War. The long series of war known by this name devastated Germany where most of the fighting took place. Much of the fighting, but not all, concerned religion, whether Catholic rulers could use military power to impose their religion on Protestant regions of Germany. Most of the treaties of Münster and Osnabrück (named after the two cities in northern Germany where they were negotiated) concern the distribution of territory among the warring parties. The treaties also acknowledged the idea of mutual territorial recognition among states which forms the basis of the sovereign state system. States are delimited by borders, and they recognize one another as legal equals with none possessing the authority to command another. The treaties also recognized the right of each ruler to determine the religion within his own domain. Neither of these ideas were new. The Peace of Augsburg in 1555 sought to end the first round of religious wars between Catholic and Protestant rulers in Germany with the same idea. Rulers had been operating as if they accepted mutual territorial recognition even before Westphalia. But Westphalia stated these ideas in writing, and they stuck afterwards.

The conventional dating of sovereignty to the Peace of Westphalia obscures both the continuity and the changes in sovereignty over time. It is not an unchanged law first imagined in 1648. Different issues have shaped what sovereignty entails for states and their leaders. The Protestant Reformation made religion a central issue in European politics. The Catholic Church claimed overarching authority over all of Christendom, an authority rejected by Protestants and the rulers who adopted the new sects of Protestantism. Wars both international and internal were fought in the name of religion during this time. Charles V, the ruler of the United Hapsburg realms of Spain and Austria, sought to use his military power to crush the Protestants in Germany. He failed, his efforts ended in the Peace of Augsburg, and he withdrew to a monastery outside Madrid for the remainder of his days. Civil wars between Catholic and Huguenot factions wracked France during the second half of the 1500s. Religion also played a large role in the Dutch Revolt against Spain, a conflict known as the Eighty-Years War before Spain accepted the independence of the Netherlands in the Peace of Westphalia.

After Westphalia, religion receded as a source of conflict in European politics. The contest over territory took its place. Mutual territorial recognition did not mean that all states accepted all frontiers as they were. States fought to expand their territory over the next 150 years. France under Louis XIV grew to be the most powerful state in Europe and expanded eastward toward what he thought were France's "natural frontiers". This expansion triggered counter-coalitions led by England, Austria, and the Dutch Republic. Eventually, they stopped France in the War of Spanish Succession. States began to fight over colonial empires in the Americas and India as well as over territory in Europe.

The French Revolution changes the issues facing sovereignty again by adding nationalism to the mix. The fusing of the nation with the state increased the power of France immensely. Its government could call on its people to sacrifice for the nation as they never would for their king. France began to expand again, and Napoleon accelerated that expansion into domination of Europe once he seized power in France. The other European states also had to appeal to their nations to create the military power needed to destroy Napoleon's domination. Once let loose, the ideas of nationalism and that the state was the tool to realize national ambitions could not be contained. Germans and Italians wondered why their nations should be denied a state, creating the movements that led to the unifications of Germany and Italy. State leaders now commanded greater resources at the price of having to answer to nationalist pressure groups. Nationalism also led to the issue of national self-determination. Groups that considered themselves nations but lacked a state of their own agitated for identification and independence. These pressures were greatest in multinational states such as Austria-Hungary. Nationalism also created conflicts among states when a national group was spread across the borders of two or more states. Nationalism contributed to the conflicts of interest that led to the World Wars.

Economic well-being and human rights rose as issues of international importance after World War II. The UN Charter sought to stop territorial gain as a legitimate idea in world politics by allowing the use of force only in self-defense. Nationalism still mattered, but most nations in Europe had their own states. Decolonization created new states in Africa and Asia, some of which had tenuous senses of nationhood among their people. People in the industrialized world saw the states as partly responsible for managing the national economy in the wake of the economic turmoil of the 1920s and 1930s. International institutions such as the World Bank, the IMF, and GATT were created to aid international economic cooperation. Human rights treaties sought to create universal standards to which all states were supposed to adhere. Transnational movements to implement human rights in states which did not observe them grew in the 1970s and on. The issues facing sovereignty have changed over the centuries, and the concept of sovereignty has changed in response.

Systemic Evolution

What process drives these changes? States are not a given form of organization. There are other ways that polities could recognize and deal with one another. The sovereign state system has evolved over the 500 years since its advent. The norms of the system have changed to control religious and then territorial conflict among states. No single actor controls or directs these changes; they result from the accumulation of decisions of many actors over time. The system evolves through a continual process of living with the current rules and pushing the boundaries of those rules.

Evolution selects those properties that do the best job of replicating themselves in the current environment. In biology, natural selection chooses the species and traits which are best capable of propagating themselves into future generations. Social evolution selects norms and forms of organization that are best capable to reproducing themselves over time. Change occurs when new forms supplant older ones by replicating themselves more effectively in their shared environment. Evolutionary change does not mean that social systems are getting "better" over time, only that the newer forms replicate better than the older forms. Stable forms could emerge if no other form of organization can replace them.

What are the dynamics of replication for the international system? Who makes the choices that produce changes in the international system? States as forms of organization do not act, but their leaders do act on their behalf. States are the vehicles of their leaders' ambitions. Leaders have an interest in shaping the organization of the polities they lead and how they relate to other polities. They do not have complete freedom to do so because they answer to their support coalition domestically and face pressures from other polities internationally. Instead, changes in domestic institutions emerge through negotiation between leaders and their followers, revolutions, and adaptation to the international environment. Changes in international institutions arise from negotiations among state leaders, competitive pressures within the system, and the rise of new actors. Both processes of change depend on and affect one another. The form of polities and their international relations depend in part on their leaders' interest in maintaining power in the face of domestic and external threats.

What arrangements favor leaders' interests in holding power? Internally, small winning coalitions increase leader tenure, but leaders generally cannot install such systems if they answer to a large winning coalition. Put in simple terms, established democracies are stable, and their leaders lack the power to change them to suit their own desires. Some leaders benefit from democratization under the right circumstances. Other pressure to expand a state's winning coalition comes from international competition. Increases in the size of the winning coalition have increased the military capabilities of some states. Others may have to adopt those innovations to keep up if they are in military competition with them. Externally, leaders share interests in limiting interstate competition when it threatens their hold on power. They adopt conventions to limit competition under some circumstances. These conventions do not prevent conflict; they only limit it.

The Historical Evolution of the Sovereign State System

States as a form of organization prevailed over city-states and the Hanseatic League in the first stage of evolution of the sovereign state system. Their competitive advantage lay in their greater size compared to the city-states and their centralized power compared to the Hanseatic League. The nascent states grew more powerful as they removed internal barriers to trade and their national economies grew. The city-states were small in comparison and could not keep up economically or militarily. Exploration opened up new trade routes and the New World, both of which hurt the trade that provided the wealth of the Italian city-states. The Hanseatic League found it difficult to act through its consensual institutions as some members refused to join wars where they were at greater risk. The 1500s also saw the spread of the norms of diplomacy from northern Italy around Europe. Diplomats received protected status which made it easier for them to operate. Secrecy of correspondence between diplomats and their rulers was also recognized. This secrecy allows confidential correspondence between a ruler and his diplomats when they were serving in another country, although it also allowed diplomats to spy on those countries. These conventions led to the establishment of permanent diplomatic missions which allowed for regular contact between state leaders.

Religious wars wracked Europe in the period from 1530 to 1648. The universal claims of the Catholic Church led some Catholic leaders to wage war to force Protestants to return to the Church. The Church was often an important and powerful group in Catholic countries. Other leaders adopted Protestantism to seize Church property and hold the loyalty of their population that converted to Protestantism. The Peace of Augsburg in 1555 sought to remove religion from international politics by allowing each leader to determine the religion of his domain. The Thirty Years War demonstrated that neither side would be able to impose its religion across Europe. France entered the war against Austria, Spain, and their Catholic allies, which broke the alignment along religious lines. The Peace of Westphalia finally set the principle of religious tolerance among states, which successfully reduced religion as a reason to wage war internationally. Religion did not totally disappear from European politics as it remained an issue of conflict inside countries with religious minorities. Domestically, this period saw the advent of greater state power in the beginnings of the absolute monarchy. Leaders began to consolidate their power within the realms by eliminating other sources of power in the nobility. Sometimes the consolidation was military and led to civil wars. In other times, the increasing wealth of kings allowed them to buy the loyalty of the nobility. The wars of this period were costly because raising and maintaining troops in the field all required money to hire recruits. Some states like France increased in power as they proved better able to finance these burdens. Others like Spain faltered because the financial cost of the competition was too much for them. Globally, some European states acquired empires and dominated trade between other continents and Europe. Spain destroyed the Aztec and Inca empires and extended its control over much of the Caribbean and Central and South America. Portugal established forts and bases for trading in India and what is now Indonesia. The Dutch seized much of this trade away from the Portuguese during their revolt against Spain which ended in their independence. England and France began to colonize North America. The slave trade from Africa to the Americas began in these years and was dominated by Europeans.

The removal of religion as a motivation for war did not end conflict in Europe. Kings now fought to gain territory or stop others from doing so. Absolute monarchs like Louis XIV of France created standing armies to wage these wars. They centralized power in the state apparatus, which could then extract more taxes from a growing population and economy. More territory meant more revenue. Kings used this revenue to build palaces and sponsor lavish courts as well as build professional armies. Absolute monarchs answered only to a small support coalition drawn from the nobility, which owed their privileged position to that monarch. International politics centered on the control of territory as a source of revenue. Norms of territorial compensation for rulers who lost territory in the resulting wars were observed in some cases. The use of violence in war was restrained in response to the destruction of the Thirty Years War, although these restraints were not always observed. Although states fought frequent and costly wars during this period, they did not fight them to the elimination of other states or the overthrown of other kings. This was the norm of non-intervention, that states did not intervene in one another's internal affairs.

The French Revolution ended the world of the absolute monarch. The mobilization of the nation through conscription greatly increased the power of France and allowed it to fight all of the other powers of Europe for over 20 years. The French revolutionary armies removed leaders and installed republics in their place. Napoleon later redrew the map of Europe, particularly in Germany and Italy, to cement his military domination of Europe. The other powers had to mobilize their own nations to create the military power necessary to break Napoleon's grip. These mobilizations led to constitutional monarchy, where the power of the monarch is limited by law. Constitutional monarchy also led to the inclusion of wealthy merchants in politics, in part to draw their wealth in support of the system. The Napoleonic Wars ended only with the complete defeat and exile of Napoleon, a war fought to remove his threat to the system permanently. The French Revolution added the issues of nationalism and liberal revolution to international politics. The system created at the Congress of Vienna in 1815 sought to control both forces through agreement among the monarchs of Europe. This system also limited territorial rivalry out of the fear that major war would lead to revolution and the downfall of kings. The growth of nationalism also made territorial aggrandizement more difficult as local populations would not give their loyalty to the governments of other nations.

Nationalism and liberalism led to the wars of German and Italian Unification as well as the spread of constitutional monarchy and limited government. Monarchs still headed most European states in 1900, but their powers were greatly limited compared to prior to the French Revolution. They also answered to larger support coalitions based across much of society, even when many citizens still lacked the vote. The United States and Great Britain became democracies, albeit with limited suffrage, with France following after its defeat in the Franco-Prussian War in 1871. The First World War accelerated these trends. The working class and women received the vote in most democracies, expanding the size of the winning coalition greatly. The destruction of the German, Austro-Hungarian, and Russian Empires brought in new, often unstable, political systems in place of autocratic rule. The leaders of both democracies and single-party autocracies answered to larger support coalitions than monarchs before the war. After World War II, most western European states became stable democracies. This growth in the size of the winning coalition had two effects on the sovereign state system. It led to the growth of the norm of territorial integrity, the idea that state borders can be changed only by peaceful agreement and not by military conquest. Nationalism also aided the growth of territorial integrity by raising the cost of conquering territory inhabited by those of other nations. The UN Charter limited the legitimate use of military force to self-defense, although it did not specify when self-defense was justified. The growth of the size of the winning coalition across many states also led to the demise of the norm of non-intervention with wars now fought to overthrown enemy leaders.

The European powers extended their control over much of the globe in the period of empire building in the 19th century. In addition to their superior military technology, sovereignty also gave the Europeans an advantage. They did not treat polities outside the European state system under the same limited rules they used for one another within that system. They used their military power to impose their ability to interfere in the internal politics of African and Asian polities and to control their foreign policies through protectorates. Eventually, this control was consolidated in the European colonial empires. Asians and Africans were not treated as legal equals to Europeans. Legal if not practical equality would come only with the establishment of sovereign African and Asian states through decolonization.

The expansion of the winning coalition through democracy and universal adult suffrage led leaders to make economic welfare a central concern of national policy. Leaders who answer to a large winning coalition provide public goods, and broad-based economic growth is one such good. Additionally, the costs of economic adjustment could not all be pushed onto the working class once they had the vote. The concern with economic performance contributed to the creation of international economic institutions, such as the IMF and GATT, at the end and after World War II. These institutions helped to support an open world economy which fostered growth through trade. The desire to improve economic performance also began the process of European integration. European leaders saw the EU as a way to further the growth of their national economies. Increasing globalization brought economic prosperity to regions that had not known it before, such as East Asia, as well as creating broad-based wealth in the industrialized countries. Those increasing international economic ties also limited state control over the domestic economy, changing again what sovereignty meant for state leaders.

The Legitimate Use of Force

The sovereign state system limits the legitimate use of force to states, as police power within their borders and through military power beyond them. The legitimate use of force and how it is controlled has changed along with sovereignty. Historically, the use of force has been limited by the weakness of the state, by its need to create the capabilities to use force. States in early modern Europe raised armies by hiring captains who recruited and equipped the soldiers. Recruits were drawn from any country. Mercenaries–soldiers hired as bands–formed an important part of most armies. The Swiss Guard of the Pope is the legacy of Swiss mercenaries that formed the backbone of the French army in the 1500s. States also employed privateers, essentially legal pirates. Privateers would be given letters of marque which allowed them to attack merchant ships of the enemy and keep a portion of whatever they took, splitting the proceeds with their ruler. In both cases, captains were hired to create military forces which often had more loyalty to their captain than to the ruler who commissioned them. Monarchs turned against the use of mercenaries and privateers as they developed standing armies. Privateers often continued their career of piracy after a war was over. The shared interest in ending piracy led states to stop commissioning privateers. States continued to use mercenaries for longer, although often recruiting them as individuals into their national armies. The French Foreign Legion and the Gurkha soldiers of the British army are examples of this practice. But the period from 1650 to 1850 saw the demise of these two ways of raising military power in favor of national armies and navies.

Norms constrain the legitimate use of force. The norms for the appropriate use of force have changed over time. Using force to seize territory used to permissible, while it is now seen as illegitimate. How force is used is now limited by the laws of war. Acts that once common and seen as acceptable, such as slaughtering the inhabitants of a town after it fell to a siege, are war crimes now. As war has become more destructive, the limits of the laws of war help to legitimate the use of force. Legitimacy arises from following commonly accepted rules. States that operate within the rules are more likely to receive support from others who accept those rules, while those that violate the rules openly provoke opposition, even if it is only verbal. Public opposition and outcry responds to violations of the laws of war now in a world with instantaneous, round-the-clock news. Such opposition may not deter violations, but it does express moral outrage at violation of the rules.

The open use of force by states also adds to its legitimacy. Open use of force makes it easier to trace responsibility. Others, including the party suffering a violation, know who to hold responsible. Open use of force makes reciprocal enforcement possible. Although states sometimes use force surreptitiously, legitimate uses of force are done openly.

Terrorism poses a challenge to the monopoly on the legitimate use of force by states. They use violence surreptitiously, not revealing their presence until they attack. Their attacks deliberately target people and sites protected under the laws of war. Unlike criminals who also attack surreptitiously, terrorists seek to kill as many as they can. Finally, terrorist groups claim that their actions are justified by their political causes, that their use of deadly force is legitimate. The challenge of terrorism to the monopoly on the legitimate use of force held by states is both a security issue and a challenge to the fundamental norms of sovereignty. Answering that challenge may lead to another evolution in the sovereign state system.

Chapter Summary

Sovereign states dominate world politics. They compose the system, limited by border and constituted with the powers of internal and external autonomy. The sovereign state system has grown to encompass the globe. It has been a very successful set of principles in the sense that it has replicated itself everywhere people live. Sovereignty is not a set, unchanging system of principles, however. Other systems for the constitution of polities and their relations have existed in history. The norms of the sovereign state system have evolved over time in response to changes in the system. The internal nature of states and their external relations affect one another in this process of evolution. One driving motivation for selection and replication of these principles is political leaders' interest in retaining power in the face of external and internal challenges and opportunities.

Review Questions

1. Sovereignty is the principle underlying how polities relate to one another in the modern state system. Give two other ways in which polities have related to one another internationally in history.

2. Give two of the four issues central to the organization of the sovereign state system since 1500. For instance, what was the central issue of contention in Europe before the Peace of Westphalia, and what is the central issue facing state leaders now? How have the principles or institutions of the sovereign state system changed in response to the two issues you have identified? Be specific.

Chapter 30
Conclusion

We have learned many things about world politics and why events happen in it. This concluding chapter takes a step back to examine the large themes of world politics and how we understand them. I discuss three large themes of this book: what we can learn by treating states as actors with national interests, how bargaining is the essence of world politics, and the dependence of domestic and international politics on one another in world politics.

States as Actors

Although states are not actors in the literal sense, there is much we can learn about world politics by treating them as such. State-level analysis focuses on the strategic environment states face and how it shapes their policies and actions. State capabilities, preferences and perceptions limit the choices states and their leaders have and influence which options look most attractive. Weaker states, for example, must choose their actions carefully to avoid antagonizing stronger states. State-level explanations focus either on how pairs of countries interact or on how many do so within the system.

The two causes of war that arise from bargaining are examples of state-level explanations. War can occur when two states fail to resolve an issue between them through negotiation. One side uses force in the hope of coercing the other side to give it what it wants. The other side bears some responsibility for the war in that it did not make sufficient concessions earlier. Bargaining could fail for two reasons. Signaling failures explain why the second state did not take the demands of the first state seriously enough or did not convince the first that it would fight rather than give in. Both sides seek the best possible deal and, as a result, exaggerate their own bargaining position and discount that of the other side. Commitment problems cause at least one side to doubt that a peaceful settlement is preferable to fighting, even though it prefers that settlement if enforced to war. It doubts that the other side will carry out its side of the bargain. If the other side reneges on the hypothetical settlement in the future, it will be in a worse position than if it fought to begin with. Both of these problems of bargaining are state-level explanations as they rely only on state preferences, perceptions, and choices. Audience costs, which are often tied to domestic politics, are one way to solve signaling problems, but there are others as well.

The tradeoff between arms and allies in security policy is another state-level argument. States can use these two tools to increase their security, but each has different effects. Alliances provide an immediate increase in military capabilities from your ally, but allies do not always fulfill their pledges of military assistance. Arming takes time to build weapons and to recruit and train troops, but they will fight to defend their country. Although states use both tools of security policy when faced by a new threat, the relative value of each influences the mixture of the two used by a state.

There were also state-level arguments for non-security issues. The problems of cooperation operate among states. The two stages of bargaining followed by enforcement reflect state-to-state negotiations on how to cooperate and then whether the agreement is enforced. Variation in whether and how states cooperated can be explained by the characteristics of different issues at the state level. Public goods problems and externalities are common on environmental issues and explain why cooperation has been inconsistent across the range of international environmental issues. Reciprocal enforcement of trade agreements can be explained by the prisoners' dilemma structure of optimal tariffs. The conflict between information and distribution in bargaining over how to cooperate also exists among states. Some issues, like trade, focus more on distributional issues, ensuring that all think the deal is fair, compared to other issues, such as environmental ones, where the parties address the information problem first in the hope of finding a solution that will widely be seen as best.

State-level explanations then allow us to understand much of world politics. They do not allow us to understand everything that goes on. Additionally, an understanding of the interaction of domestic politics with international politics leads to new question and richer explanations.

World Politics as Bargaining

Bargaining is the essence of world politics. States resolve their differences through negotiation. Actors within states bargain with one another and their government to get the foreign policies they want. Actors have both some interests in common and some that conflict. Bargaining allows them to resolve their differences so they can realize their common interests. On security issues, for instance, the parties share an interest in resolving their differences without fighting. On political economy issues, they may share the need to coordinate their economic policies to enhance the economic welfare of both societies. Bargaining theory then is essential to understanding world politics.

Bargaining theory begins with each actor's reservation point or level–the settlement it views as equal to a failure to reach an agreement. In conflict, a state's reservation level gives it the same value as it believes it can gain through fighting. A zone of agreement exists when there are ranges of settlements between the parties' reservation points–settlements which both prefer to no settlement. Actors negotiate to agree on a specific settlement within this range. Each typically does not know the reservation point of the other, making actors' reservation points their private information. In conflict, for instance, neither side knows how willing the other is to go to war. In trade negotiations, neither side knows exactly what concessions the other is willing to make. Bargaining can help reveal that private information and allow the parties to come to an agreement. Their divergent interests–the points where they disagree–make this process more difficult. Each commonly has an incentive to misrepresent their position in the effort to secure a deal which is more favorable to its own interests. This incentive leads actors to exaggerate their negotiating positions and discount those positions of the other side. In some cases, the parties cannot resolve their differences and they fail to reach an agreement even though they have some interests in common. These signaling explanations are one way that bargaining could fail.

Bargaining could also fail if a party fears that the other side will not live up to the deal. Agreements to cooperate rely on measures that monitor the parties' compliance and use some form of enforcement against those parties who fail to follow an agreement. Commitment issues lie at the heart of protracted conflicts. Often when the parties do not negotiate in earnest, there is a commitment problem.

International institutions aid states in negotiations. They can define the alternative to an agreement clearly and publicly. The WTO dispute resolution procedure helps states anticipate what will happen if they fail to negotiate a settlement to their disagreement over trade policy. Voting rules in the UN Security Council affect what actions it will endorse. Other states are less likely to support international interventions which are not endorsed by a Security Council resolution, such as the U.S. invasion of Iraq in 2003. Other institutions collect and disseminate information to states to aid them in how they cooperate. International scientific bodies seek to create a common understanding of environmental issues and how they should be addressed. States can ignore their recommendations, but the international nature of these bodies increases their influence on the negotiations. Institutions, however, do not solve all the problems of negotiations.

The Interaction of Domestic and International Politics

World politics concerns cross-border issues. Those issues have implications for domestic as well as international politics. The effects flow in both directions. Domestic politics shapes how national leaders respond to the international challenges their countries face, and international forces change domestic politics. Domestic and international politics impinge on one another in a globalized world.

Domestic politics affects how leaders respond to international affairs. This is not to say that they take actions simply to increase their hold on power, such as by provoking an international enemy. Rather, supporters and opponents of the leader respond to the successes and failure of his or her policy. The domestic political consequences of foreign policy enter into leaders' judgments of what international risks to take and which to avoid. Failures are punished, and successes rewarded. But those punishments and rewards also depend on domestic institutions. Leaders answer to their supporters ultimately and so adopt policies that are likely to hold their support. Those who answer to a small winning coalition worry less about conducting a successful policy and more on how to provide the private benefits that keep those supporters content. Those who answer to a large winning coalition have to pursue the general interests of their broad base of supporters. The war aims of leaders based on their domestic institutions is one example of how domestic politics affects international policy. Interest groups within a country lobby for international economic policies that favor their economic interests. State policy on international economic issues advances the agenda of some but not all domestic interest groups within the international environment. Domestic politics shapes what risks they are willing to take and what goals they pursue in their foreign policies. Leaders do address the international environment as well. It provides both opportunities and risks for them. Foreign policy is a balance between international calculations of power and interest and domestic considerations of support and holding power.

International politics also changes domestic politics and forces national leaders to make painful choices. The consequences of war have large effects on national leaders and their hold on power. Even if the enemy cannot depose them, often their own supporters do so. The tides of the international economy buffet national leaders through the pressure they put on their national economies. The Great Depression posed great challenges to national leaders in the countries tied into the world economy. Many reacted by trying to protect their supporters from the worst consequences of the depression and so made the economic collapse worse for all. The norms of sovereignty enable increases in national power through increasing the winning coalition within a country. These changes force leaders to expand their own winning coalitions even though they do not wish to. International competition and cooperation impel changes in domestic politics.

World politics forces leaders to "Think locally, act globally." They must be concerned about their position in domestic politics, in part because their supporters care about international politics. At the same time, they can try to change that international environment through their foreign policy. Of course, stronger states have greater leeway to do so, but even weak states possess some ability to lean against the wind of international politics.

Glossary of Terms

Actor: basic unit of analysis in world politics; an actor possesses the ability to determine what it does. Actors have preferences over outcomes, capabilities to realize its preferred outcomes, and perceptions about other actors, their preferences and capabilities.

Alliance (as a strategy to increase security): a formal military agreement between two states to coordinate their actions in the event of war. An alliance can increase the security of both allies by providing them with support from the other if war comes.

Alliances, types of:

> Multilateral vs. bilateral: Bilateral alliances are between two states; multilateral alliances between more than two.

> Offensive vs. Defense Pact: A defense pact commits the allies to come to one another's defense in the event of war; an offensive alliances has the parties work together to change the status quo.

> Symmetric vs. Asymmetric: a symmetric alliance is where both parties gain security (both have to be strong enough to defend each other), and an asymmetric alliance is where one party gains security and one gains something else (unequal strength where one partner protects the other in exchange for other concessions).

Arming (as a strategy to increase security): when a state increases the strength of its military by recruiting more soldiers or acquiring new and better equipment. Can increase the security of a state in the short run.

Arms race: the competitive increase in military power by both countries in a rivalry over a period of time. Arms races are an example of the security dilemma

Balance of power theory: focuses on how states come together against threats to dominate the system

Balance of power: A system where states coalesce against any state that seeks to dominate the system, which maintains the continued existence of all states

Balancing behavior: actions that states take to maintain a balance of power, which could be arming or forming alliances in response to a threat to the system

Bilateral: between two states. Compare to multilateral

Bright lines (used in reciprocal enforcement and international law): a clear standard of what acts are violations, so that all parties know when an agreement has been breached and reciprocal enforcement is appropriate.

Bureaucratic politics: explanation of how governments make foreign policy with an emphasis on how the U.S. government does so. Composed of two parts: organizational process and governmental politics.

Capital mobility: when a country allows investment to flow freely into and out of the country

Challenger (in power transition theory): state that catches up to the dominant state and then exceeds it in power at the transition point. It can seek to overturn the international system ordered by the old dominant state.

Civil war: war fought within a country over the legitimacy of its government. Two types of civil wars: those over control of the central government and wars of secession

Commitment device: alters the consequences of backing down and carrying out a threat or promise for the party making the threat or promise in order to make it want to carry out a costly threat or promise if it has to. Can raise effectiveness if it convinces the target that the other party will carry out its threat or promise.

Commitment problem : when one or both parties believe the other will undermine a settlement in the future, putting the former in a worse position. Commitment problems can lead actors to prefer war to peace.

Comparative advantage (the logic of): When different countries can produce various goods at different cost ratios. Each state produces goods where it has a comparative advantage and then trades, which raises the national income of all states.

Conflict of interest: where two actors disagree about how an issue should be resolved, so that satisfying one means the other will not be fully satisfied with the outcome.

Conscription: when a state obliging its young men (occasionally young women) to serve in the military for a set period of years. Called the draft in the U.S.

Contingent compliance: States raise resources from its potential power through taxes and conscription. Both are more effective when the citizens of the country voluntary comply with these demands from the state. Such voluntary compliance is more likely when citizens support the aims of the state in a war, making that compliance contingent on the war aims.

Cooperation (as in international cooperation): situations where states share some common interests but also disagree about how exactly to pursue those interests and need to work together to realize their shared interest. States would be better off if they could agree and implement a coordinated solution to the problem.

Corporate actor: actors that consist of more than one person that work together toward a common purpose, such as states, business firms, political parties, and government agencies.

Costly signal: Signals that separate resolute types from irresolute types because irresolute types are unwilling to pay the cost to send the signal that resolute types send.

Counterinsurgency: Strategy used to fight insurgency by protecting the population and separating them from insurgents. Then provide public goods to the population to increase legitimacy of the government.

Counterterror measure: steps taken by government against terrorist who target them and their people

> active vs. passive: Passive-make it difficult for terroists to carry out attacks; Active-take steps to neutralize terrorists before they can attack

> observable vs. unobservable: reflects how easily citizens can observe whether their government is taking steps to protect them from terror attacks. Examples: Observable-scanning at airports, armed guards, publicized counterstrikes. Unobservable-infiltrate terrorist groups, interdict financing and arms, intelligence work generally.

Credibility of a threat or promise: how likely the target thinks that the actor making the threat or promise will carry it out. Before the threat or promise is resolved, credibility is a matter of degree—how likely does the target think that the threat or promise will be a carried out. (contrast with effectiveness)

Democratic peace: the pair of regularities that democracies almost never fight each other but they fight in general almost as often as other states do.

Devaluation (of a fixed exchange rate): when a country deliberately reduces the value of its currency, typically to reduce the price of its exports and increase the price of imports into the country as a way to revive its economy.

Development (as in economic development): improvement in the economic sophistication of a country's economy and the standard of living of the people in the country

Dissatisfied (in power transition theory): states that reject the international order created by the dominant state

Distribution (problem of international cooperation): Actors disagree about which solution or way to cooperate is the best.

Dominant state (in power transition theory): the most powerful state that orders the international system into a hierarchy under its leadership

Drivers of economic growth:

Specialization: When people take on jobs that focus them on one particular type of economic activity instead of producing everything they need themselves. The more people specialize the more they can focus on what they do and do it more productively.

Exchange: people can take the product they specialize in and find ways to exchange their product for products they do not produce.

Accumulation: people can produce things that go above and beyond their immediate needs which can then be invested to produce more in the future.

Effectiveness of a threat or promise: whether the target of a threat or promise does as demanded. Before the threat or promise is resolved, effectiveness is a matter of degree—how likely is it that the target does as demanded. (contrast with credibility)

Empire: a system of governance where one country, the metropole, rules over colonies in other parts of the world, most often through military superiority. The colonies (or provinces) are under the authority of the metropole.

"The end of sovereignty": the argument that increased economic and social globalization is limiting national sovereignty

Enforcement (as problem of international cooperation): once states agree about how to cooperate, they must make certain that all follow through on the agreement. Enforcement is one way to ensure compliance by punishing those who violate an agreement.

Escalation: steps taken by a country to raise the level of tension during an international crisis. These steps can include threats, measures to strengthen threats already made, and efforts to prepare for war, such as a military build-up near the area of the dispute.

Exchange rate (of two currencies): the relative prices of currencies. They affect the prices of imports and exports. Rising currency make imports cheaper and exports more expensive.

Exports: goods produced in one country and sold in another

Externality (negative): an activity which benefits one party but imposes costs on another who does not benefit from it.

Factors (of economic production): Basic elements of any production process that can be owned by people.

Land: all naturally occurring resources whose supply is inherently fixed; the value of land, both for what it can produce, such as agriculture or minerals that can be extracted, and its location

Labor: the effort that people use in production. Workers own their own labor.

Capital: goods not used up in the production that increase the productivity of labor. Can be physical capital, like factories and machinery; human capital, like education and skills learned on the job; or financial capital that helps to purchase the other forms.

Factor mobility: factors (land, labor and capital) are mobile when owners of each can shift them easily and with no loss in the value they produce across sectors.

Fait accompli: a negotiating tactic where an actor seizes what it wants and forces the other actor to choose between accepting that outcome or going to war to reverse it

Fiscal policy (as tool to remedy an economic downturn): increase deficit of the government to put money into circulation, either through increased spending or tax cuts

Fixed exchange rate: when a country's exchange rate is fixed relative to another currency, typically the U.S. dollar. Its central bank must exchange currencies at those rates.

Floating exchange rate: when a country's exchange rate is determined by market forces

Force (way to make threat or promise more effective)- allows party making threat or promise to secure unilaterally the outcome it wants.

Foreign aid: economic aid provided by developed states to developing ones

GNP per capita: Gross Domestic Product (a measure of all goods and services produced in a country) divided by population; often used as measure of economic development.

Governmental politics: Policy is the outcome of a political struggle inside the Executive Branch including the top political appointees of the U.S. government.

Human rights: the idea that all people are entitled to certain rights. Codified in international treaties since the end of World War II.

IGO: InterGovernmental Organization, an international organization whose members are states who organize to solve a common problem. Examples: UN, IMF, and NATO.

Imports: goods produced in other countries and then sold in this country

Incentive to misrepresent: Because reservation points are private information, parties in crisis bargaining want to hide their true value for war to make their threats to use force more effective and so gain more on the issues in conflict.

Inflation: when the value of a country's currency declines over time, so prices rise

Information (as problem of international cooperation): Actors are uncertain about the exact value of each solution and so are uncertain about which solution is best for them.

"In-group" versus "out-group" enforcement: a system of enforcement where those who follow the rules are the "in-group" who then punish violators by cutting them out of the system, making the latter the "out-group". Some advocate the use of this system to enforce human rights treaties.

Institution: "rules of the game;" examples: formal decision rules in international organization and domestic politics and rules of appropriate conduct when others will respond to inappropriate conduct. They help actors form expectation about what others will do and allow actors to reveal their intentions. Examples of political institutions in world politics: the voting rules in IGOs, U.S. Constitution in U.S. domestic politics, rules of non-discrimination in international trade

Insurgency (guerrilla warfare): war fought small unit operating covertly and living off population. Common in civil wars.

International humanitarian law (also known as laws of war): treaties that seek to regulate conduct during war-Examples: the Hague and Geneva Conventions

Issues (of world politics): security, political economy, and transnational challenges (see each)

Legal definition of a state: 1. Has a defined territory 2. has a permanent population resident on that territory 3. Its government has effective control over the territory and population 4. has the ability to enter into relations with other states (diplomatic recognition).

Legitimacy: the degree to which an institution are accepted as binding, correct and proper by actors. Actors believe they must comply with legitimate institutions.

Limited war: a war where the existence of the state is not at risk, and so the state is fighting for limited aims. Ex: Vietnam. Compare with total war

"Lock in" (during an international crisis): when costly signals and escalation lead a party to prefer going to war to backing down; war will occur if the other side does not back down.

Loss-of-strength gradient: Militaries fight at less than full strength when they fight far away from home because food, people and munitions have to be shipped and this is costly, so cuts are made regarding what gets to go. The further away the war is, the less powerful the military will be there.

Mandate: protectorate set up by the League of Nations after World War I or the UN after World War II where a major power controls a country formed from the breakup of an empire with the intention of eventual independence.

Monetary policy (as tool to remedy an economic downturn) : policies by a country;s central bank of government to increase the supply of money in the economy, typically by cutting interest rates

Monitoring (of international cooperation): the problem of determining whether other states are complying with an agreement. Needed to make reciprocity work as enforcement.

Multilateral: between more than two states, such as an agreement. Compare to bilateral

Mundell-Fleming Trilemma-governments cannot have all three of: 1. Fixed Exchange Rate 2. Monetary policy autonomy 3. Capital Mobility. In a world of mobile capital, it forces countries to choose between having a fixed exchange rate and using fiscal policy to stimulate the economy or having a floating rate and using monetary policy.

"Naming and shaming": the strategy of publicizing violations of treaties in order to bring international shame on violators. Sometimes advocated as way to enforce human rights treaties.

Nation: is a set of people holding a common national identity often expressed through a common language, unified history, sports, national holidays, national symbols and flags, songs, pledges, and other signs of patriotism.

National self-determination: the idea that national groups should be able to determine which state represents and governs them; often used as argument to create new states for those nations.

Nation-state: fuses a national identity to the state and makes it more powerful both domestically and internationally, where the state serves the interests of the nation and the nation gives loyalty to the state.

NGO: NonGovernmental Oorganization that address international issues but have members than are not states. Examples: Greenpeace, the Int'l Committee of the Red Cross, Care, and Doctors without Borders.

Noise (as an issue that makes reciprocal enforcement of international cooperation more difficult): the inability to observe fully whether other parties are complying with a cooperative agreement because other things interfere with their compliance, such as violations by individuals or other forces that reduce compliance outside the control of any actor.

Nondiscrimination (in trade): all members must treat one another equally in their trade policies. They cannot favor one over another.

Non-Tariff Barrier (NTB): Any policy other than a tariff that advantages domestically produced goods over imports in the home market. Examples: quotas, product quality laws, health, safety and environmental regulations can be NTBs, but are not necessarily.

Norm: shared principles about which action are appropriate and which inappropriate for different social roles.

Normative theory seeks to understand what should be done; it concerns ideology, values, and political philosophy (contrast with positive theory)

Organization process: How organizations operate influences the information and options that top political leaders have in the government. Organizations have limited power and responsibilities and parochial views.

Peacekeeping: International forces moved into a war-torn country to help keep the peace afterwards. They monitor violations, enforce settlement, monitor decommissioning and provide capabilities to weak governments.

Perception: an actor's degree of belief about something about which it is uncertain. Perceptions express how likely an actors thinks something will happen. Credibility is the target's perception that the actor making a threat or promise will carry it out. Also see type.

Persuasion (way to make threat or promise more effective)—seeks to raise the credibility of a threat or promise to the target in order to increase effectiveness.

Political capacity: a state's ability to extract resources from society in order to mobilize military capabilities from its potential power.

Political economy issue: issues that concern the politics of international economics and other crossborder movements of goods, services, capital, and people, such as trade, development, and money

Pooling (of types): when different types of an actor take the same action so that other actors cannot discern its type from that action. Also see separation.

Positive theory seeks to explain why events happen using facts about the situation (contrast with normative theory)

Potential power: States derive their military capabilities come from the people of its country and what they produce. Potential power assess how large and sophisticated this pool is.

Power transition theory: focuses on how long-term shifts in power driven by industrialization shape struggles for dominance in world politics.

Power transition (in power transition theory): the moment when the challenger surpasses the dominant state in power

Private benefits: a policy of a government that benefits only the members of support coalition. Compare to public goods

Private information: Information that known only one actor. Reservation points are private information in a negotiation. Other actors have perceptions about an actor's private information.

Problems of international cooperation:

Distribution: Actors disagree about which solution or way to cooperate is the best.

Information: Actors are uncertain about the exact value of each solution and so are uncertain about which solution is best for them.

Enforcement: once states agree about how to cooperate, they must make certain that all follow through on the agreement. Enforcement is one way to ensure compliance by punishing those who violate an agreement.

Productivity (of economic factors): how efficiently factors of production are used to make final products. Greater productivity means that more can be produced from the same inputs of land, labor, and capital.

Promise: situation when actor A (promisor) indicates to actor B (target) that A will do something that B likes if B does what A wants. Also see rewards, punishment, force, and persuasion as ways to make promises more effective.

Protectorate: international governance arrangement where a powerful country protects a weaker one in exchange for control over some of its policies, most often including its foreign policy.

Protracted conflict: A conflict that remains unresolved over a period of time because the parties cannot agree on a final settlement of the issues in conflict.

Punishment (way to make threat or promise more effective): raises the cost of conflict, encouraging B to do as A wishes out of the desire to avoid punishment.

Public good: a policy of a government that benefits everyone in society. Public goods are non-excludable and jointly produced. Compare to private benefits

Reassurance: a policy used to defuse an international rivalry by trying to persuade the other side of its peaceful intentions, unlikely to succeed because the other side will worry the reassuring party is trying to get it to lower its guard.

Reciprocal trade sanction: when countries respond to another country's barriers to their exports by placing trade barriers of their own against the goods they import from the offending country.

Reciprocity: responding to others as they have acted towards you. It provides a way to enforce international agreements.

Reservation point (or reservation level): The outcome of an issue that an actor sees as the same as going to war, meaning it is the settlement it sees as equivalent to going to war. A party's reservation point is its private information.

Rewards (way to make threat or promise more effective): increases the target's value for doing what is demanded in a threat or promise in an effort to make it more effective.

Rivalry: An international rivalry occurs when two states view one another as major security threats.

Economic Sanction (economic sanctions): A policy by the sanctioning state that limits international trade with the target of the sanctions.

Satisfied coalition (in power transition theory): all the states that accept the international order set by the dominant state

Sector (of a country's economy, as opposed to factors): An area of production in an economy, often composed of all producers of those goods. Examples: cars, electronics, types of agriculture

Security (of a state): a state's ability to deter and defeat, if necessary, threats of violence from other states

Security dilemma: when steps each side takes to increase its security makes the other side less secure. If the other side responds to increase its own security, both can be worse off.

Security issue: issues where the threat of force or the use of force and violence exists as a way to impose an outcome, such as war, crises, alliances, and arming

Security threat (to a state): when a state perceives another as posing a long-term threat to it. To be a security threat, a state must have military power to make a threat effective and a conflict of interest combined with hostile intentions to provide a reason to make a threat. Example: U.S. and the Soviet Union during the Cold War

Selection effect : when only particular parties are willing to take some action. Example: economic sanctions are only executed against states that will not comply because states that will comply do so before the sanctions are imposed.

Selectorate (characteristic of a political system): the people in a polity that are politically relevant, and so can be members of a support coalition

Separation (of types): when different types of an actor take different actions which allows others to determine the type of the first actor. Also see pooling.

Shadow of the future: the degree to which an actor cares about the future relative to the present

Sovereignty: the idea that every state has control over its own foreign policy and domestic politics and no other state has authority over it

Internal autonomy: the idea that sovereign states have full control over their domestic affairs and a monopoly on the legitimate use of force

External autonomy: the idea that sovereign states can determine their own foreign policy

Spoiler (of a peace settlement in a civil war): groups that seek to undermine peace agreement and renew fighting

Standard operating procedure (SOP): a predetermined response or solution to a problem that a bureaucracy is likely to face

State: the basic political unit of modern world politics; it encompasses the territory and people it controls and the government that rules both. See legal definition of.

Status quo: the current resolution of international issues

Strategy of opposition: strategies available to those who oppose a government or wish to see it change: 1. Non-Violent activities: protest political organization. 2. Irregular or guerrilla warfare. 3. Terrorism.

Support coalition (of a leader): the people who currently support the leader in power

Suzerainty: a system of imperial control where territories had local leaders who had some local authority and power but owed obligations to the metropole of the empire.

Tariff: taxes on imports, typically paid when the goods enter the country

Terrorism: violence by a non-state actor directed at non-military personnel for political purposes.

Threat: situation when actor A (threatener) indicates to actor B (target) that A will do something that B does not like if B does not do what A wants. Also see rewards, punishment, force, and persuasion as ways to make threats more effective.

Tied aid: Foreign aid where the donor requires the recipient to use the aid to buy goods and services only from firms from the donor country

Time inconsistency: commitment problem caused when a party incentives shift over time, making unwilling to follow through on a deal that it entered into intending to comply.

Total war: war where the continued existence of the state is at risk. Ex: World War II Compare to limited war

Transnational challenge: other international issues outside of security and political economy where countries have to cooperate to address, such as transnational environmental issues and human rights

Type: When an actor is uncertain about something, it thinks that each different possibility is a type, only one of which is true. If an actor knows which is true while other actors do not, that private information is its type. Example: an irresolute type of an actor making a threat will not carry it out, but a resolute type of that actor will, and the target does not know which type it is facing.

Ultimatum: threat to go to war if the target of threat does not do what the state making the threat demands

UN: The United Nations

War of secession: Civil war where the rebels seek to detach part of the country and make it independent. Example: U.S. Civil War.

Winning coalition (characteristic of a political system): how large the support coalition must be for a leader to retain power

WTO: World Trade Organization, IGO based in Geneva which runs the rules for international trade

WTO dispute resolution procedure: Process under WTO law where one country can argue that a policy of one of its trading partners is an illegal barrier to trade and should be removed. The formal process is run by the WTO like a civil law suit. If successful, the target side must remove the policy that is a barrier to trade or suffer reciprocal trade sanctions from the complainant.

Zone of agreement: All outcomes between the two sides's reservation points. The set of all settlements that both sides see as preferable to war.

INDEX

Note: Figures are indicated by an italic 'f'; tables are indicated by an italic 't'.

constitutional monarchy, 462–463
constructivism, 14–16
containers, 373
contingent of German troops, 269
Convention on International Trade in Endangered Species of Wild Fauna and Flora (CITES), 423
Convention on Long-Range Transboundary Air Pollution (CLRTAP), 423
Convention on the Prevention and Punishment of the Crime of Genocide, 449
cooperation, 333–334
cooperation, international environmental issues, 423–437
cooperative agreements, 337–338
coordination games, informational problem, 358*f*
corporate actors, 11–12, 26, 27
corporations, 11, 22
corruption, 294
costly signals, 155–158
cost of defense, 212–214
costs of adjustment, 333, 397
costs of war, 111, 152*f*, 242
counterinsurgency, 307–308
counterterrorism, 174, 188
counterterrorist, 326
credibility, 4
credibility, increasing, 63
credibility of promise, 80, 91
credibility of threat, 58*f*, 59
credible commitments, 86, 89, 202–204
credible commitments creation, 311–312
credible threats, 62, 64, 68, 70, 73
Crimean War, 98, 234
"crimes against humanity," 438
criminal trials, 439
crisis, organizational issues, 184–185
cross-border air pollution, 428
cross-border financial, 371
crude oil, 332
Cuban Missile Crisis, 66, 156, 157, 164, 181–184, 195, 245, 298
currency collapse, 416
currency crisis, 395
currency speculation, 395–398
currency value, 393
Current Military Forces of Major Powers, comparison, 106–107, 107*t*

D

decisions, 45
decisions in world politics, 39
decision to make threat, 60–61, 61*f*
decolonization, 460

decommissioning, 327
defense burden, 213
defense of state, 193
defense pacts, 200, 206
deficit spending, 397
defined territory, 22
demands, in dispute, 154, 154*f*
demilitarized zones (DMZs), 85, 206
democracies, 82, 101, 447
democracies and war, 277
democracy, 275–292
democracy, Czechoslovakia, 277
democracy, Japan, 277
democratic government, 280, 441
democratic leaders, 276
democratic peace, 275–292
democratic politicians, 47, 252
democratic system, Great Britain, 275
democratic transitions, Spain and Portugal, 277
Department of Defense (DoD), 174–176
Department of Homeland Security (DHS), 188
Department of State, 174
Department of the Treasury, 174
Departments of State and Defense, 176
deterrence of threats, 192, 194
devaluation, 391, 393, 403, 404
development, economic, 368
DHS. *see* Department of Homeland Security (DHS)
diplomacy, 293–302
diplomatic recognition, 22
Director of National Intelligence, 114, 179
disaster/famine relief, 293
discount factor, actors, 47
discount rate, 397–398
dispute, issue, 142–143, 146–148
dispute resolution procedure, 30, 341, 345, 363, 388, 412, 469
dissatisfied, power transition theory, 229, 232
distributional bargaining, 429
distributional problems, 355
distribution and information, 353, 365
distribution problem, 359
DMZs. *see* demilitarized zones (DMZs)
DoD. *see* Department of Defense (DoD)
domestic actors, 27
domestic and international politics interaction, 469–470
domestic consequences of international conflict, 241–256
domestic politics, 6–9, 13, 17, 27–28, 142, 179, 187, 205, 253, 255, 263–264, 381–383, 403, 425, 469–470
dominant state, power transition theory, 229–232, 237–238

Franco-Prussian War, 145, 261, 299, 463
free financial flows, 408
free-moving capital, 396
free trade, 332–333, 376, 408–411, 414
French and Dutch voters, 362
French army, invasion of Russia, 100
French empires, 34
French Foreign Legion, 464
French government, 141
French kings, 457
French military, 134–135
French Revolution, 100, 459, 462, 463
Freon, 127–128

G

game tree of promise, 75–76, 76*f*, 78*f*, 79*f*
game tree of threat, 53–58, 54*f*, 56*f*, 57*f*
GATT. *see* General Agreement on Tariffs and Trade (GATT)
GDP. *see* gross domestic product (GDP)
General Agreement on Tariffs and Trade (GATT), 362–363, 373, 379, 386, 405, 411–412, 412, 460, 464
General Assembly, 31–32
General Motors, 376, 393
Geneva Accords, 1954, 105
Geneva Conventions, 33, 438, 443, 446
Geneva Protocol, 443
genocide, 38
The Genocide Convention, 438
German military, 104, 168, 191, 199, 233
German PTT, 352, 360
Germany and allied responses, 136*f*
Germany's defeat of France, 103
global economy, 10, 333, 373, 384, 399, 407–408, 450
globalization, 10, 28, 407–422, 456, 464
global warming, 114, 116–118, 423
"the Gnomes of Zurich," 395
GNP. *see* gross national product (GNP)
"Gold Standard," 391, 402
Good Friday Agreement, 327–328
Google Earth, 114, 185
government action in crisis, 281*f*
Government Acts, reaction of the opposition, 283*f*
government politics, 175, 178–181
government responses, 325
Grand Banks off eastern Canada, 425
Great Britain, 98
Great Depression, 391, 404–405
The Great Patriotic War, 96
greenhouse gases, 423, 433–436
Green Line, Palestinians, 163, 171–172
Greenpeace, 16, 33

Gregorian calendar, 144
grievances, 321–322
gross domestic product (GDP), 213, 367–368, 404, 416, 419–421
gross national product (GNP), 107–108, 213, 294
Guerrilla movements, 319–320
Gulf states, 98–99
Gulf War, 95, 103, 165, 241, 254, 257, 261, 270, 284, 444
guns *vs.* butter tradeoff, 46
Gurkhas, 98, 464

H

Hague Conventions, 438, 443
Hanseatic League, 458, 461
hard currency, 396, 408
Helsinki Accords, 1975, 452
hierarchy of power, power transition, 230*f*
high discount factor, 47
high tech industries, 98
high-tech weapons, 97
highways, observation of, 336
historical evolution of sovereign state system, 461–464
Hitler, Adolf, 119–123, 288
Hitler's army, 96
Hitler's control in Europe in 1945, 224–225
Hitler's Germany, expansion of, 137
Hitler's rearmament program, 135
"hole in the ozone," 127
homicide, laws on, 441
human intelligence, 114
humanitarian law, 438–453
human rights, 6, 26, 354, 438–453
human rights law, 439, 449–450
human rights treaties, 439, 450
Human Rights Watch, 1, 27
Hussein, Saddam (President), 61, 142, 156, 241–243, 254–255, 255, 262, 263, 271
hybrid game, 358

I

IAEA. *see* International Atomic Energy Agency (IAEA)
ICBMs. *see* intercontinental ballistic missiles (ICBMs)
IFIs. *see* International Financial Institutions (IFIs)
ILO. *see* International Labor Organization (ILO)
IMF. *see* International Monetary Fund (IMF)
Imperial Japan, 202, 234, 290
imports, 19, 30, 43, 59, 67, 71, 84, 263, 297, 333, 345, 373, 393, 401
incentives, 165–166
incentives to misrepresent, 154–155
income tax, 94
Indian economy, 98

war in Afghanistan, 95, 142, 143, 151
War Memorial Arena or Stadium, 141
War of Italian Unification, 1859, 442
war of nerves, 158, 159
war of secession, 304
Warsaw Pact, 200, 215, 216, 279
warships, 443
war termination, 169–171
waste discharges, 430
weapons inspections, Iraq, 270
weapons programs, Iraq's, 257
weapons, sophistication of, 96, 111
weapons, state secrets, 126
Weimar Constitution, 133, 268
Weimar Germany, 166, 267, 276–277
Weimar Republic, 133
Weinberger Doctrine, 176
West Berlin, 83–84
Western view of human rights, 439
willingness to take risks, 46
winning coalition, selectorate, 246,
    249–251, 255
Winter War of 1939–1940, 120

win wars, 110
WMD programs, Iraq's, 261–262, 271
World Bank, 30, 32, 85–87, 460
World Bank loans, 293–294
World Health Organization (WHO), 32
world politics, 9
world politics, implications, 111, 129–133
World Trade Organization (WTO), 19, 30, 32, 67, 336,
    340–341, 344, 345, 362, 363, 373, 374, 378, 386,
    389, 411–413, 441
World War I, 261, 267, 268, 277, 308, 443
World War II, 93–97, 101, 143, 258–259, 262, 268–269,
    277, 308, 394, 439, 443–445, 447, 459, 463
World Wars, views of, 232–233
WTO dispute resolution procedure, 30, 341, 345, 388,
    412, 469

Y
Yalu river, 96
Yugoslav Federation, 291

Z
zone of agreement, 148–155, 151*f*, 152*f*, 162, 164